75
READINGS
PLUS

FIRST CANADIAN EDITION

Santi V. Buscemi
Middlesex County College
Charlotte Smith
Adirondack Community College
Robert Wiznura
Grant MacEwan College

Toronto Montréal Boston Burr Ridge, IL Dubuque, IA
Madison, WI New York San Francisco St. Louis Bangkok
Bogotá Caracas Kuala Lumpur Lisbon London Madrid Mexico City
Milan New Delhi Santiago Seoul Singapore Sydney Taipei

ABOUT THE AUTHORS

Santi Buscemi teaches reading and writing and chairs the English Department at Middlesex County College in Edison, New Jersey.

Charlotte Smith teaches English composition and technical writing at Adirondack Community College in Queensbury, New York.

Robert Wiznura teaches literature at Grant MacEwan College in Edmonton, Alberta, and at Athabasca University.

CONTENTS

CHAPTER 1
Narration

CHAPTER 2
Description

CHAPTER 3

Process Analysis   **100**

CHAPTER 4

Definition   **136**

CHAPTER 5

Division and Classification   **172**

CHAPTER 6

Comparison and Contrast   **214**

CHAPTER 7

Illustration   253

CHAPTER 8

Cause and Effect   302

CHAPTER 9

Analogy   345

CHAPTER 10
Argument and Persuasion   376

THEMATIC CONTENTS

Perspectives on Human Existence

Descriptions of Place

Description of Nature and Animals

Portraits

Growing Up, Growing Old

Power and Politics

Problems, Solutions, and Consequences

Culture and Identity

The Media and the Arts

Science and Technology

Health and Medicine

Use and Abuse of Language

PREFACE TO THE CANADIAN EDITION

When I was approached to do the Canadian edition of *75 Readings Plus*, I plunged into the project in a rather headstrong manner, with very certain ideas of which Canadian writers should be added to this anthology. That attitude has changed, as has my own respect for the many Canadians who have penned essays through the years, not all of whom could be represented here. This introduction is something of an explanation for what is included in, and excluded from, the volume. The exclusion of such fine writers as Paul Wilson, Louis Dudek, and Joseph Škvorecký is painful and a genuine loss for readers; however, there were other concerns influencing these selections.

What criteria was used in choosing Canadian items for this anthology? First, I tried to capture the tradition of the essay in Canada. Canada has a long and powerful tradition of essayists, and I feel that these many eloquent writers deserve to be celebrated and recognized.

One major problem that I encountered when exploring the tradition of the essay in Canada was that the list of writers created a false impression of the development of the country: the writers were usually of European extract, white, and male. The other significant contributors to our society—women, immigrants, and the Native population—have often been overlooked or obscured. In this regard, I feel that *75 Readings Plus* breaks new ground. In the anthology, you will find essays that present viewpoints that are definitely outside of the mainstream. Alongside more standard selections are essays that present an outlook on life that is quite distinct. Some of these essays have the potential to strike a powerful chord with students as they come to terms with their own identities.

As an anthologist, I expect honesty and clarity from writers. Clarity does not mean that the essays are all simple to read. Some of the writings are not easy to wade through and will even, as I tell my students, "make your brain hurt." For some selections, you will even need a good dictionary. No, clarity does not mean simple. By clarity, I mean a certain transparency of structure and directness of approach. I don't appreciate writers who avoid the point.

This collection is not meant to be a collection of easily digestible tidbits. Will students like all of the Canadian essays? I hope not. These essays should stump, provoke, stimulate, and, maybe, excite. I hope students will find voices in the text that resonate with their own experience. I also hope that their ability to interpret their experience will be broadened by this collection.

The task of putting together an anthology is broadening in and of itself. Not only do I have a greater sense of the breadth and depth of the Canadian essay, my life has been enriched by encountering the many Canadian writers I have had the privilege to read. Lee Maracle and Alexander Wolfe, for example, allowed me to realize in a personal way the profundity of the storytelling tradition in Native culture. I appreciate the way these writers bring forth the idea of presence and intimacy. My own sense of identity has been challenged and expanded, and my hope is that each reader will be touched and broadened by the selections in this reader.

Robert Wiznura

ACKNOWLEDGEMENTS

Canadian Edition

This anthology has benefited from the thoughtful and insightful comments of instructors from across Canada who suggested changes to the US edition of *75 Readings Plus*, and who reviewed the selections of Canadian essays included in this edition. These instructors include:

John Achorn, University of Toronto
Marian Allen, Grant MacEwan Community College
Ruth Allison, University of Victoria
Lesley Checkland, John Abbott College
Mary Gerritsma, Seneca College
Mary Gossage, Dawson College
Jon Paul Henry, Douglas College
Stefanie Ketley, Fanshawe College
Moira Langley, Kwantlen University College
Claire McKenzie, University of Victoria
Mike Matthews, Malaspina University College
Wendy Robbins, University of New Brunswick
Mark Simpson, University of Alberta
Wendy Strachan, Simon Fraser University
John Webb, Langara College

Robert Wiznura

U.S. Edition

Special thanks are due to the following colleagues who made suggestions for the fifth U.S. edition of *75 Readings Plus*:

Tammy DiBenedetto, Riverside Community College
Terry Telfer, Monroe Country Community College
Nancy Schneider, University of Maine at Augusta
Joe Safdie, Lake Washington Technical College
Fred Misurella, East Stroudsberg University
Sonja Lynch, Southside Virginia Community College

We are grateful for the comments and suggestions of all of our colleagues who have used *75 Readings* and *75 Readings Plus* over the last 10 years. We welcome their ongoing contributions as we continue to improve these texts and make them even more responsive to the needs of our students. We would also like to thank our friends at McGraw-Hill who encouraged us and helped us continue these projects.

Santi Buscemi
Charlotte Smith

ABOUT THIS BOOK

The Canadian edition of *75 Readings Plus* is based on *75 Readings*, the popular collection of essays for composition first published in 1987 and now in its eighth edition.

75 Readings Plus incorporates instructional materials into the text. Accompanying each selection are an author biography, a set of discussion questions on content and strategy, and at least two suggestions for sustained writing. In addition, to help instructors exploit the connection between reading, writing, and critical thinking, *75 Readings Plus* offers a set of prompts for short writing inspired by each essay selection. These prompts can also be used as journal assignments or as warm-up exercises for projects such as those described in Suggestions for Sustained Writing. In some cases, they can even be expanded into assignments for complete essays.

Supplements

Instructor's Manual
Containing further questions and writing assignments specific to each essay in *75 Readings Plus*, the Instructor's Manual is available both as a printed supplement, and downloadable electronically from the text website.

Text Website
For further information about selected authors and essays in *75 Readings Plus*, visit the text website at *http://www.mcgrawhill.ca/college/buscemi/*.

1

Narration

One of the things that defines us as human is the universal desire and ability to create narrative. "Tell me a story," the child implores; and we willingly oblige by reciting an old favourite passed down through the generations or by making up one of our own.

We are naturally curious creatures, wanting to know what happened, when, and to whom—even if none of it is true. Perhaps that is why we feel compelled to create mythologies on one hand and to report the news or write history on the other.

Some narratives contain long evocative descriptions of setting. Others present fascinating characters whose predicaments rivet our attention or whose lives mirror our own. Still others seem more like plays, heavy with dialogue by which writers allow their characters to reveal themselves. Whatever combination of techniques authors use, all stories—from the briefest anecdotes to the longest novels—have a plot. They recount events in a more-or-less chronological order. They reveal what happened, and, in most cases, allow readers or listeners to draw their own conclusions about the significance of those events.

This is perhaps the chief difference between what you will read in Chapter 1 and the essays in other parts of this text. While some types of writing are aimed at explaining or persuading, narration dramatizes important human concerns by presenting events that, when taken together, create a world the author wants the reader to share.

Moving from beginning to end by order of time, narration generally relies on a more natural pattern of organization than other types of writing, but it is no less sophisticated or powerful a tool for explaining complex ideas or for changing readers' opinions than, say, analogy, classification, or formal argument. All story tellers, no matter how entertaining their tales, have something to say about human beings and the world they inhabit. If you have already read selections from the chapters that follow, you know that writers often couple narration with other techniques to develop ideas and support opinions that otherwise might have remained abstract, unclear, or unconvincing. A good story may reveal more about a person or a place, than physical description, and it can sometimes help readers understand an important problem or issue beyond our most valiant attempts to explain it "logically."

The point is that writers of narrative are not compelled to underscore the connection between the events in a story and the point it makes. Readers can find their own "theses."

Many of the essays you will read in this chapter are autobiographical: Maya Angelou, Jane Urquhart, and Anurita Bains show how they confronted difficult situations and, in the process, gained significant insight into themselves, their families, and the human personality. Although very different in content and purpose, Naton Leslie's "Don't Get Comfortable" provides similar insight into the human character, not to mention into a few real characters! The writing of essays like theirs often results from a profound compulsion to find meaning in what once seemed devoid of it, a process that may define the act of narration itself.

The selections by George Orwell and Maxine Hong Kingston might be placed in another category. They point beyond themselves to social and political issues that are universal and perennial.

However the pieces in this chapter seem to be related—and you will surely find connections of your own to talk about—remember that each has been included because it has a poignant story to tell. Read each selection carefully, and learn what you can about the techniques of narration. Here's hoping that at least a few will inspire you to narrate a personal vision of the world that will enrich both you and your readers.

A Hanging

George Orwell

George Orwell is the pseudonym of Eric Blair (1903–1950). Born in India, where his father served in the British colonial government, Orwell was educated at Eton. As a young man, he served as a British policeman in Burma, the setting for this selection. Later, he was wounded while fighting for the loyalists in the Spanish Civil War, about which he wrote in Homage to Catalonia. *Orwell despised the "Big Brother" mentalities of both the fascists and the communists, who backed opposing sides in that war. However, he also condemned the crass bureaucracy of the democratic governments of his time. In short, Orwell became an enemy of politics and politicians in general. He is remembered for* Animal Farm *(1946) and* 1984 *(1949), classics of political satire, and for his many essays.*

It was in Burma, a sodden morning of the rains. A sickly light, like yellow tinfoil, was slanting over the high walls into the jail yard. We were waiting outside the condemned cells, a row of sheds fronted with double bars, like small animal cages. Each cell measured about ten feet by ten and was quite bare within except for a plank bed and a pot of drinking water. In some of them brown silent men were squatting at the inner bars, with their blankets draped round them. These were the condemned men, due to be hanged within the next week or two.

One prisoner had been brought out of his cell. He was a Hindu, a puny wisp of a man, with a shaven head and vague liquid eyes. He had a thick, sprouting moustache, absurdly too big for his body, rather like the moustache of a comic man in the films. Six tall Indian warders were guarding him and getting him ready for the gallows. Two of them stood by with rifles and fixed bayonets, while the others handcuffed him, passed a chain through his handcuffs and fixed it to their belts, and lashed his arms tight to his sides. They crowded very close about him, with their hands always on him in a careful, caressing grip, as though all the while feeling him to make sure he was there. It was like men handling a fish which is still alive and may jump back into the water. But he stood quite unresisting, yielding his arms limply to the ropes, as though he hardly noticed what was happening.

Eight o'clock struck and a bugle call, desolately thin in the wet air, floated from the distant barracks. The superintendent of the jail, who was standing apart from the rest of us, moodily prodding the gravel with his stick, raised his head at the sound. He was an army doctor, with a grey toothbrush moustache and a gruff voice. "For God's sake hurry up, Francis," he said irritably. "The man ought to have been dead by this time. Aren't you ready yet?"

Francis, the head jailer, a fat Dravidian in a white drill suit and gold spectacles, waved his black hand. "Yes sir, yes sir," he bubbled. "All iss satisfactorily prepared. The hangman iss waiting. We shall proceed."

"Well, quick march, then. The prisoners can't get their breakfast till this job's over."

We set out for the gallows. Two warders marched on either side of the prisoner, with their rifles at the slope; two others marched close against him, gripping him by arm and shoulder, as though at once pushing and supporting him. The rest of us, magistrates and the like, followed behind. Suddenly, when we had gone ten yards, the procession stopped short without any order or warning. A dreadful thing had happened—a dog, come goodness knows whence, had appeared in the yard. It came bounding among us with a loud volley of barks, and leapt round us wagging its whole body, wild with glee at finding so many human beings together. It was a large woolly dog, half Airedale, half pariah. For a moment it pranced round us, and then, before anyone could stop it, it had made a dash for the prisoner, and jumping up tried to lick his face. Everyone stood aghast, too taken aback even to grab at the dog.

"Who let that bloody brute in here?" said the superintendent angrily. "Catch 7 it, someone!"

A warder, detached from the escort, charged clumsily after the dog, but it 8 danced and gambolled just out of his reach, taking everything as part of the game. A young Eurasian jailer picked up a handful of gravel and tried to stone the dog away, but it dodged the stones and came after us again. Its yaps echoed from the jail walls. The prisoner, in the grasp of the two warders, looked on incuriously, as though this was another formality of the hanging. It was several minutes before someone managed to catch the dog. Then we put my handkerchief through its collar and moved off once more, with the dog still straining and whimpering.

It was about forty yards to the gallows. I watched the bare brown back of the 9 prisoner marching in front of me. He walked clumsily with his bound arms, but quite steadily, with that bobbing gait of the Indian who never straightens his knees. At each step his muscles slid neatly into place, the lock of hair on his scalp danced up and down, his feet printed themselves on the wet gravel. And once, in spite of the men who gripped him by each shoulder, he stepped slightly aside to avoid a puddle on the path.

It is curious, but till that moment I had never realised what it means to de- 10 stroy a healthy, conscious man. When I saw the prisoner step aside to avoid the puddle, I saw the mystery, the unspeakable wrongness, of cutting a life short when it is in full tide. This man was not dying, he was alive just as we were alive. All the organs of his body were working—bowels digesting food, skin renewing itself, nails growing, tissues forming—all toiling away in solemn foolery. His nails would still be growing when he stood on the drop, when he was falling through the air with a tenth of a second to live. His eyes saw the yellow gravel and the grey walls, and his brain still remembered, foresaw, reasoned—reasoned even about puddles. He and we were a party of men walking together, seeing, hearing, feeling, understanding the same world; and in two minutes, with a sudden snap, one of us would be gone—one mind less, one world less.

The gallows stood in a small yard, separate from the main grounds of the 11 prison, and overgrown with tall prickly weeds. It was a brick erection like three sides of a shed, with planking on top, and above that two beams and a crossbar with the rope dangling. The hangman, a grey-haired convict in the white uniform of the prison, was waiting beside his machine. He greeted us with a servile crouch as we entered. At a word from Francis the two warders, gripping the prisoner more closely than ever, half led, half pushed him to the gallows and helped him clumsily up the ladder. Then the hangman climbed up and fixed the rope round the prisoner's neck.

We stood waiting, five yards away. The warders had formed in a rough circle round the gallows. And then, when the noose was fixed, the prisoner began crying out on his god. It was a high, reiterated cry of "Ram! Ram! Ram! Ram!", not urgent and fearful like a prayer or a cry for help, but steady, rhythmical, almost like the tolling of a bell. The dog answered the sound with a whine. The hangman, still standing on the gallows, produced a small cotton bag like a flour bag and drew it down over the prisoner's face. But the sound, muffled by the cloth, still persisted, over and over again: "Ram! Ram! Ram! Ram! Ram!"   12

The hangman climbed down and stood ready, holding the lever. Minutes seemed to pass. The steady, muffled crying from the prisoner went on and on, "Ram! Ram! Ram!" never faltering for an instant. The superintendent, his head on his chest, was slowly poking the ground with his stick; perhaps he was counting the cries, allowing the prisoner a fixed number—fifty, perhaps, or a hundred. Everyone had changed colour. The Indians had gone grey like bad coffee, and one or two of the bayonets were wavering. We looked at the lashed, hooded man on the drop, and listened to his cries—each cry another second of life; the same thought was in all our minds: oh, kill him quickly, get it over, stop that abominable noise!   13

Suddenly the superintendent made up his mind. Throwing up his head he made a swift motion with his stick. "Chalo!" he shouted almost fiercely.   14

There was a clanking noise, and then dead silence. The prisoner had vanished, and the rope was twisting on itself. I let go of the dog, and it galloped immediately to the back of the gallows; but when it got there it stopped short, barked, and then retreated into a corner of the yard, where it stood among the weeds, looking timorously out at us. We went round the gallows to inspect the prisoner's body. He was dangling with his toes pointed straight downwards, very slowly revolving, as dead as a stone.   15

The superintendent reached out with his stick and poked the bare body; it oscillated slightly. "*He's* all right," said the superintendent. He backed out from under the gallows, and blew out a deep breath. The moody look had gone out of his face quite suddenly. He glanced at his wrist-watch. "Eight minutes past eight. Well, that's all for this morning, thank God."   16

The warders unfixed bayonets and marched away. The dog, sobered and conscious of having misbehaved itself, slipped after them. We walked out of the gallows yard, past the condemned cells with their waiting prisoners, into the big central yard of the prison. The convicts, under the command of warders armed with lathis, were already receiving their breakfast. They squatted in long rows, each man holding a tin pannikin, while two warders with buckets marched round ladling out rice; it seemed quite a homely, jolly scene, after the hanging. An enormous relief had come upon us now that the job was done. One felt an impulse to sing, to break into a run, to snigger. All at once everyone began chattering gaily.   17

The Eurasian boy walking beside me nodded towards the way we had come, 18
with a knowing smile: "Do you know, sir, our friend (he meant the dead man), when
he heard his appeal had been dismissed, he pissed on the floor of his cell. From
fright. Kindly take one of my cigarettes, sir. Do you not admire my new silver case,
sir? From the boxwallah, two rupees eight annas. Classy European style."

Several people laughed—at what, nobody seemed certain. 19

Francis was walking by the superintendent, talking garrulously: "Well, sir, 20
all has passed off with the utmost satisfactoriness. It wass all finished—flick! like
that. It iss not always so—oah, no! I have known cases where the doctor wass
obliged to go beneath the gallows and pull the prisoner's legs to ensure decease.
Most disagreeable!"

"Wriggling about, eh? That's bad," said the superintendent. 21

"Ach, sir, it iss worse when they become refractory! One man, I recall, clung 22
to the bars of hiss cage when we went to take him out. You will scarcely credit, sir,
that it took six warders to dislodge him, three pulling at each leg. We reasoned with
him. 'My dear fellow,' we said, 'think of all the pain and trouble you are causing
to us!' But no, he would not listen! Ach, he wass very troublesome!"

I found that I was laughing quite loudly. Everyone was laughing. Even the su- 23
perintendent grinned in a tolerant way. "You'd better all come out and have a drink,"
he said quite genially. "I've got a bottle of whisky in the car. We could do with it."

We went through the big double gates of the prison, into the road. "Pulling 24
at his legs!" exclaimed a Burmese magistrate suddenly, and burst into a loud
chuckling. We all began laughing again. At that moment Francis's anecdote
seemed extraordinarily funny. We all had a drink together, native and European
alike, quite amicably. The dead man was a hundred yards away.

1931

QUESTIONS FOR DISCUSSION

Content

a. Does this narrative essay have a "message," or do you think Orwell deliberately avoided one?
b. Orwell avoids saying anything directly about the English presence in Burma—he neither explains the presence nor states his opinion explicitly. Nevertheless, his opinion is voiced. What is his attitude toward his country's presence in Burma?
c. How would you characterize Orwell's description of the Burmese in this piece? Of the Hindu prisoners? How do these descriptions relate to his attitude toward the British?
d. What details of the hanging does Orwell treat as significant? What are his reasons for including these details? What effect do they have on you?

Strategy and Style

e. In which paragraphs does Orwell use descriptive details most effectively? What other paragraphs do you find effective? Why?

f. Orwell is careful to tell us the dimensions of the prisoners' cells, the time, the number of people, the distance to the gallows, the distance between the officials and the prisoner, etc. Why are these numerical references important?

g. "A Hanging" is a mature writer's recollection of an earlier time in his life. Does Orwell present himself sympathetically, or does he describe himself with a satiric edge? Point to details that support your answer.

h. How does the use of dialogue affect the tone of the essay? In what way would your reaction have been different if Orwell had not used dialogue?

SUGGESTIONS FOR SHORT WRITING

a. Write a letter to Orwell, telling him what you do not understand about his essay. As best you can, tell him why you do not understand it.

b. Ask a question (or questions) about this essay, and then try to answer the question(s) by piecing together phrases drawn from the essay itself. Then write your own answer, or write a response to Orwell's "answer."

SUGGESTIONS FOR SUSTAINED WRITING

a. In paragraph 10, Orwell writes of an epiphany of sorts: "It is curious, but till that moment I had never realised what it means to destroy a healthy, conscious man. When I saw the prisoner step aside to avoid the puddle, I saw the mystery, the unspeakable wrongness, of cutting a life short. . . ." Tell the story of a time when something happened during an ordinary day that suddenly and profoundly changed your thinking. What details of the day do you remember? Make those details seem as significant to your readers as they are to you.

b. Orwell communicates his feelings about capital punishment and other issues in this essay. Use narration to present an issue about which you feel strongly. Present your opinion(s) implicitly by drawing on Orwell's narrative techniques: the use of dialogue, the detailed descriptions of characters, the chronological sequence of events, and the inclusion of humour, to name a few. In short, imbed your opinion within the framework of a story.

c. Orwell learned much about himself from this wrenching experience. Narrate a traumatic experience in your life that revealed something important about yourself.

Returning to the Village

Jane Urquhart

Jane Urquhart is a major Canadian poet and novelist. Born in 1947 at Little Long Lac, Ontario, she went on to study at the University of Guelph. She has written three books of poetry and a number of novels, the first being Whirlpool. *Her 1997 novel* The Underpainter *won the Governor General's Award for fiction. Her writing often interweaves place, history, and mythology, and the role of the individual to mediate between them.*

I wanted to be in a place that was both familiar and foreign, a place distant from 1
the dailiness of life and yet filled with the warmth of domesticity, and I knew I
could only do this by returning to the village.

The village was across an ocean, deep in the green heart of a country whose 2
larger landscape I had come to understand by collecting a series of bright, startling images and whose language I knew only superficially. The village, however, I knew well.
I lived there seven years before with my husband and two-year-old daughter for one
serene year. I had walked its narrow streets and gazed down into the valley from its
gates. I had followed the paths that branched out from its walls towards an ancient cross,
a medieval forest, a wash house, an enclosed garden. I had bought bread each morning
at its single *alimentation* and lit candles in its dark, cold church. Because my husband
worked each day in a studio which was separate from the house and my daughter attended *École Maternelle,* I had been, during the daylight hours, always alone in my ex-
plorations. It was the place where the writer in me—such as she is—was born.

The following few years had been filled with excitement and activity: peo- 3
ple, parties, bouts of blurred travel. Now I wanted separation from the world, solitude, wanted to rediscover what it was that had set the words spinning in the first
place. I needed to begin another book, and for this reason I felt it was necessary
that I return to the village alone.

Because I chose late November to make this pilgrimage, it was already dark 4
when I arrived in the village on a Thursday afternoon. I collected the key and six
brown eggs from the farming family across the street, and opened the familiar oak
door. The interior of the house was just as I remembered it; the tiles in the kitchen,
the cream-coloured walls, the old stone sink, the crack in the bedroom ceiling. I lit
room after room expecting to be confronted with some evidence of change. There
was none. Spoons in drawers, goblets in cabinets, the grain on the oak stairs, the
pattern on the salon rug, mirrors and pictures on walls, the figures of birds worked
into lace curtains were just as they had been.

This was a privilege and I knew it; to bring one's own altered body and psy- 5
che into a space, architectural or natural, that has remained constant over the passage of almost a decade is not an experience easy to come by in the last quarter of
the twentieth century. I thought of Wordsworth's "Tintern Abbey," of Yeats'
"Coole Park and Ballylee"; poems of memory and reassessment that had needed

8

the reassurance of familiar visual stimuli to trigger them. I had had to travel thousands of miles to get to the remembered, abandoned place, but I was blessed in that I had access to the return. I counted my blessings as I faced the fireplace.

The idea of the fireplace as a theatre had been planted in my mind seven [6] years before by the owner of the house when he had left instructions regarding the fires which were to be lit there. "Use lots of paper, lots of kindling," he had written, "and place the logs slightly to stage right." So began my relationship with this small corner of the universe, a corner which would grow in importance when the winds of January rattled the shutters and removed loose tiles from rooftops. Never housing a predictable entertainment, often difficult to cause to perform, this hearth and its fire became, over the course of that distant year, my own territory. I cursed the fire and I coaxed it. Often it had sent me choking to the windows or scrambling through outbuildings searching for materials which would guarantee flame. It was seldom well behaved, its unfolding plot rarely uncomplicated until I had been at it for some time. It wasn't until the winter was almost over that I realized that I had been working at the fire in precisely the same way that I had been working on my writing, experiencing, each day, the frustration, the fascination.

I awakened on the first morning of my return, as I had awakened every morning [7] years before, to the sound of the family across the street beginning their day—the moan of a cow, the sound of a milk pail striking cobblestone—and to the bells of the monastery on one side of the village and the convent on the other. In the intervening years I had thought a great deal about the convent, which had remained a hidden and mysterious female alternative, its activities made known only by the songs I had heard when I passed by its walls, or by a glimpse of its garden through a locked iron gate. Now I was grateful for its regularity: the fact that I knew that its bells would ring at the time of the day when bells should ring, that rituals were being performed, rituals I had never witnessed, mere steps from my door. All around me, I realized, a symphony was celebrating the sanctity of industry, continuity, inevitability. A tractor was fired up in a stone barn; children departed, chattering, for school; a milk truck arrived, picked up the fruits of the farmer's daybreak labours, and pulled away again; and I, the only pulse in the house, placed my bare feet on a familiar floor. Then I wandered through the house, pushing back the shutters, while behind me a series of rooms opened itself to the light.

After breakfast I took my remembered spiral walk around the village: out- [8] side the walls, inside the walls, through narrow streets, down alleyways, ending at the church square in the village's heart. I had brought along a basket which I filled at the *alimentation*. The woman there remembered me, mostly because of the "petite fille" who had sometimes accompanied me in the past. "Elle est comme ça," I said, holding my hand in front of me at shoulder level. The woman raised her eyebrows in astonishment.

In the early afternoon, after I had washed my few lunch and breakfast dishes, [9] I entered the salon and began my daily struggle with the fire. Then I turned to the round walnut table, pulled out the green chair, sat down and opened my notebook. Behind me was a case filled with English books—a good thing because I knew I was not ready to write. I pulled the two large volumes of *Scott's Last Expedition* from the shelf and spent the remainder of the afternoon attempting to survive the sea voyage to Antarctica on the one hand, and on the other trying to encourage the reluctant fire. Blizzards swept pages, huge waves crashed over the icy decks of the *Terra Nova*, familiar fire tools clanked against marble, the wind banged in the chimney. Two decorative female faces looked solemnly up at me from the end of the andirons, twin girls I had become intimate with a decade before. A large log, eaten through the centre by fire, collapsed between them and was replaced by a chunk of softwood which burst almost immediately into flame. During the ocean storm, Scott was sick with anxiety concerning the fate of the animals on board. In the end he reported, sadly, that two ponies had been lost and one dog.

On the third day I decided to clean the house, which had been vacant for some 10 months and was, as a result, somewhat dusty. This was a great pleasure in that it allowed me to run my hands over the surfaces of desks and cupboards, bureaus and tables that I hadn't consciously thought about for a long time but which, nevertheless, had remained in my memory so that the act of cleaning them, now, became a sort of ceremonial reunion. I recognized wood grains—sometimes even the reflections of windowpanes in wood grains—that I had known well in the past. I reacquainted myself with several small pieces of statuary; sad, resigned gestures and vulnerable expressions. In the kitchen I was able to see again the way a damp cloth caused the old blue-and-red tiles to shine until an opaque tide rolled over them from the direction of the radiator. All of this calmed and comforted me.

In the afternoon, and at a respectable distance, I followed a party of dark- 11 robed, contemplative seminarians on their daily walk out the narrow road that led eventually to the Camp de Caesar. They could not possibly have been, but they looked the same as the clusters of their brothers I had seen bicycling down poplar-lined lanes into the valley or taking this exact walk seven years before. I turned around, however, and began the trek back, stooping down now and then to collect sticks for the fire. There were several wonderful views of the village from this road, particularly now that the low winter sunlight shone on its walls. At one point a path I remembered plunged into the now leafless forest, and I walked down it to the place I had called my secret thicket. Here, there was an ancient stone bench and a view of the valley, the monastery, and, on the next ridge of hills, the neighbouring village. I sat down, and, not for the first time since my arrival, I confronted my former, younger self: her fantasies, expectations, disappointments, and obsessions.

That evening, while the fire behaved admirably, I sat in the gentleman's 12 chair, stage right, and did not even look at the round walnut table where so much writing had taken place in the past. Things were not going well in *Scott's Last Expedition;* shrieking winds, frostbite, snow blindness. But none of this stopped Ponting from taking his glorious photographs or Scott himself from reporting both disasters and triumphs in his clear, eloquent prose. But after he had left Cape Evans, the tone of his writing changed, became more forced and practical. Poetic images disappeared and at times the sentences became harsh, almost brutal. The weather, it seemed, was always against him, and he wasn't progressing as quickly as he had hoped. Sometimes he and his men were trapped for days inside tents while something white and furious took hold of the rest of the world.

At Camp Shambles the rest of the beloved ponies had to be shot.   13

It was almost midnight. Before finishing this tragic history I wanted to clear   14
my head, so I left the house for the village streets. All lamps were extinguished, except mine; all shutters were closed, including mine. The streetlights, in the interests of economy, had always been and were still switched off at nine P.M. There was a partial moon, and this, plus a carpet of brilliant stars, was my only source of illumination. But unlike Scott and his party I was safe, surrounded by a culture and civilization that had been left to me like a gift by preceding generations. Some of the narrower streets were so dark that I couldn't see my own feet, but I realized by my sure-footedness how intimate I had become with their surfaces, their dimensions, their distances. There was frost in the air; I could see its minimal shine on rooftops. But there was no ice underfoot. When I entered the house again, all the furniture seemed to greet me. I cut myself a chunk of bread on the old board in the kitchen, adding another incision to the thousands etched there, some by my own previous, younger hand.

After great hardship Scott and his men eventually reached the Pole only to   15
discover that they had been pre-empted by Amundson and the Norwegians. Returning, they found the weather had worsened. Petty Officer Evans had died, and Oates, sensing that his weaknesses were slowing the party's progress, had staggered off into a blizzard in order to relieve the others of the burden he felt he was becoming. And Scott, himself, would never again walk into familiar rooms or gaze out windows at familiar landscapes. After penning his last few feeble words, he lay down in his tent and prepared to freeze to death.

The following morning I opened my eyes to shafts of strong sunlight, which   16
penetrated the shutters and made narrow golden bars on the floor beside the bed. I had slept through the convent bells and the morning activities of my neighbours. When I opened first the windows, then the shutters, I was amazed to see that while everything in the village was crisp, frosty, and clear under a cloudless sky, the whole valley surrounding it was filled with a thick fog. I imagined what the village would look like from a distance, perched like a heavenly city on a prairie of soft cloud. The rest of the world, I realized, had simply disappeared.

In the afternoon, after setting a log slightly to stage right, I opened my note-   17
book on the round walnut table and began to write.

1994

QUESTIONS FOR DISCUSSION

Content

a. Urquhart writes that she is looking for a place both "familiar and foreign." Go through each paragraph and try to determine from the opening sentence if the paragraph will focus on the familiar or the foreign.

b. Go through each paragraph and consider each as a whole. Has the emphasis been on the familiar or the foreign?

c. Find the references to the fireplace. What is the significance of the fireplace in the essay?

d. Find references to the walnut table. What does the table come to represent by the end of the essay?

e. What does Urquhart realize when she walks through the streets in the darkness of night?

f. Why does she keep returning to *Scott's Last Expedition*?

Strategy and Style

g. Certain objects are mentioned repeatedly in the essay. Why does Urquhart want us to notice these items? Does the repetition cause us to seek a deeper meaning?

h. What words does Urquhart use that are usually associated with religion (for example, "pilgrimage")? How do these associations reflect on Urquhart's purpose for returning to the village?

i. The essay is divided into three sections. The first section marks her return. What aspects of the village does Urquhart stress in this section?

j. What aspects of the village are stressed in the second section?

k. Why does she refer to "the first morning of my return," but later refers to "the third day" rather than "the second morning"? Why doesn't she refer to "the first morning" as "the second day"? Why the inconsistency?

l. How does Scott's journey contrast with Urquhart's journey?

m. What has changed over the course of the essay that Urquhart can write at the end of it?

SUGGESTIONS FOR SHORT WRITING

a. Describe a familiar place as if it were unfamiliar, as if you were a tourist.

b. Write a description of a place to which you have travelled and have not returned. Give as many details as possible.

c. Which is more inspiring to you: a small village or a large city? Why?

SUGGESTIONS FOR SUSTAINED WRITING

a. Recall the place you made an important decision. Write an essay discussing the process of the decision and connect the process with a description of the place where you made the decision.

b. Think of an important event in your life (funeral, wedding, graduation, baptism, and so on). Describe the connection between location and event. Are there objects that take on symbolic importance? How do they take on this importance?

Grandmother's Victory

Maya Angelou

Born Marguerita Johnson in 1928, Maya Angelou spent most of her childhood in Stamps, Arkansas, where her family owned the general store that is the setting for this selection. After a difficult youth, Angelou became a dancer, actress, and writer. She has performed all over the world, most notably in the U.S. State Department–sponsored production of Porgy and Bess, *in the television miniseries "Roots," and in a production of Jean Genet's* The Blacks. *She has also taught dance in Rome and Tel Aviv. Active in the civil rights movement, Angelou was appointed northern director for the Southern Christian Leadership Conference by Martin Luther King, Jr., in the 1960s. In 1970, she published the first volume of her autobiography,* I Know Why the Caged Bird Sings, *of which this selection is the fifth chapter. Three other volumes followed. Angelou has also written several books of poetry, including* And Still I Rise *(1978) and* I Shall Not Be Moved *(1990). Recent works include three autobiographies:* The Heart of a Woman *(1981),* Shaker, Why Don't You Sing? *(1983), and* All God's Children Need Traveling Shoes *(1986).*

1 "Thou shall not be dirty" and "Thou shall not be impudent" were the two commandments of Grandmother Henderson upon which hung our total salvation.

2 Each night in the bitterest winter we were forced to wash faces, arms, necks, legs, and feet before going to bed. She used to add, with a smirk that unprofane people can't control when venturing into profanity, "and wash as far as possible, then wash possible."

3 We would go to the well and wash in the ice-cold, clear water, grease our legs with the equally cold stiff Vaseline, then tiptoe into the house. We wiped the dust from our toes and settled down for schoolwork, cornbread, clabbered milk, prayers, and bed, always in that order. Momma was famous for pulling the quilts off after we had fallen asleep to examine our feet. If they weren't clean enough for her, she took the switch (she kept one behind the bedroom door for emergencies) and woke up the offender with a few aptly placed burning reminders.

4 The area around the well at night was dark and slick, and boys told about how snakes love water, so that anyone who had to draw water at night and then stand there alone and wash knew that moccasins and rattlers, puff adders, and boa constrictors were winding their way to the well and would arrive just as the person washing got soap in her eyes. But Momma convinced us that not only was cleanliness next to Godliness, dirtiness was the inventor of misery.

5 The impudent child was detested by God and a shame to its parents and could bring destruction to its house and line. All adults had to be addressed as Mister, Missus, Miss, Auntie, Cousin, Unk, Uncle, Buhbah, Sister, Brother, and a thousand other appellations indicating familial relationship and the lowliness of the addressor.

6 Everyone I knew respected these customary laws, except for the powhitetrash children.

7 Some families of powhitetrash lived on Momma's farm land behind the school. Sometimes a gaggle of them came to the Store, filling the whole room,

13

chasing out the air, and even changing the well-known scents. The children crawled over the shelves and into the potato and onion bins, twanging all the time in their sharp voices like cigar-box guitars. They took liberties in my Store that I would never dare. Since Momma told us that the less you say to white-folks (or even powhitetrash) the better, Bailey and I would stand, solemn, quiet, in the displaced air. But if one of the playful apparitions got close to us, I pinched it. Partly out of angry frustration and partly because I didn't believe in its flesh reality.

They called my uncle by his first name and ordered him around the Store. 8 He, to my crying shame, obeyed them in his limping dip-straight-dip fashion.

My grandmother, too, followed their orders, except that she didn't seem to 9 be servile because she anticipated their needs.

"Here's sugar, Miz Potter, and here's baking powder. You didn't buy soda 10 last month, you'll probably be needing some."

Momma always directed her statements to the adults, but sometimes, Oh 11 painful sometimes, the grimy, snotty-nosed girls would answer her.

"Naw, Annie . . ."—to Momma? Who owned the land they lived on? Who 12 forgot more than they would ever learn? If there was any justice in the world, God should strike them dumb at once!—"Just give us some extra sody crackers, and some more mackerel."

At least they never looked in her face, or I never caught them doing so. No- 13 body with a smidgen of training, not even the worst roustabout, would look right in a grown person's face. It meant the person was trying to take the words out be-fore they were formed. The dirty little children didn't do that, but they threw their orders around the Store like lashes from a cat-o'-nine-tails.

When I was around ten years old, those scruffy children caused me the most 14 painful and confusing experience I had ever had with my grandmother.

One summer morning, after I had swept the dirt yard of leaves, spearmint- 15 gum wrappers and Vienna-sausage labels, I raked the yellow-red dirt, and made half-moons carefully, so that the design stood out clearly and mask-like. I put the rake behind the Store and came through the back of the house to find Grandmother on the front porch in her big, wide white apron. The apron was so stiff by virtue of the starch that it could have stood alone. Momma was admiring the yard, so I joined her. It truly looked like a flat redhead that had been raked with a big-toothed comb. Momma didn't say anything but I knew she liked it. She looked over toward the school principal's house and to the right at Mr. McElroy's. She was hoping one of those community pillars would see the design before the day's business wiped it out. Then she looked upward to the school. My head had swung with hers, so at just about the same time we saw a troop of powhitetrash kids marching over the hill and down by the side of the school.

I looked to Momma for direction. She did an excellent job of sagging from 16 her waist down, but from the waist up she seemed to be pulling for the top of the oak tree across the road. Then she began to moan a hymn. Maybe not to moan, but the tune was so slow and the meter so strange that she could have been moaning.

She didn't look at me again. When the children reached halfway down the hill, halfway to the Store, she said without turning, "Sister, go on inside."

I wanted to beg her, "Momma, don't wait for them. Come on inside with me. 17 If they come in the Store, you go to the bedroom and let me wait on them. They only frighten me if you're around. Alone I know how to handle them." But of course I couldn't say anything, so I went in and stood behind the screen door.

Before the girls got to the porch I heard their laughter crackling and popping 18 like pine logs in a cooking stove. I suppose my lifelong paranoia was born in those cold, molasses-slow minutes. They came finally to stand on the ground in front of Momma. At first they pretended seriousness. Then one of them wrapped her right arm in the crook of her left, pushed out her mouth and started to hum. I realized that she was aping my grandmother. Another said, "Naw, Helen, you ain't standing like her. This here's it." Then she lifted her chest, folded her arms and mocked that strange carriage that was Annie Henderson. Another laughed, "Naw, you can't do it. Your mouth ain't pooched out enough. It's like this."

I thought about the rifle behind the door, but I knew I'd never be able to hold 19 it straight, and the .410, our sawed-off shotgun, which stayed loaded and was fired every New Year's night, was locked in the trunk and Uncle Willie had the key on his chain. Through the fly-specked screen door, I could see that the arms of Momma's apron jiggled from the vibrations of her humming. But her knees seemed to have locked as if they would never bend again.

She sang on. No louder than before, but no softer either. No slower or faster. 20

The dirt of the girls' cotton dresses continued on their legs, feet, arms, and 21 faces to make them all of a piece. Their greasy uncolored hair hung down, uncombed, with a grim finality. I knelt to see them better, to remember them for all time. The tears that had slipped down my dress left unsurprising dark spots, and made the front yard blurry and even more unreal. The world had taken a deep breath and was having doubts about continuing to revolve.

The girls had tired of mocking Momma and turned to other means of agita- 22 tion. One crossed her eyes, stuck her thumbs in both sides of her mouth and said, "Look here, Annie." Grandmother hummed on and the apron strings trembled. I wanted to throw a handful of black pepper in their faces, to throw lye on them, to scream that they were dirty, scummy peckerwoods, but I knew I was as clearly imprisoned behind the scene as the actors outside were confined to their roles.

One of the smaller girls did a kind of puppet dance while her fellow clowns 23 laughed at her. But the tall one, who was almost a woman, said something very quietly, which I couldn't hear. They all moved backward from the porch, still watching Momma. For an awful second I thought they were going to throw a rock at Momma, who seemed (except for the apron strings) to have turned into stone herself. But the big girl turned her back, bent down and put her hands flat on the ground—she didn't pick up anything. She simply shifted her weight and did a hand stand.

Her dirty bare feet and long legs went straight for the sky. Her dress fell 24 down around her shoulders, and she had on no drawers. The slick pubic hair made a brown triangle where her legs came together. She hung in the vacuum of that lifeless morning for only a few seconds, then wavered and tumbled. The other girls clapped her on the back and slapped their hands.

Momma changed her song to "Bread of Heaven, bread of Heaven, feed me   25 till I want no more."

I found that I was praying too. How long could Momma hold out? What new   26 indignity would they think of to subject her to? Would I be able to stay out of it? What would Momma really like me to do?

Then they were moving out of the yard, on their way to town. They bobbed   27 their heads and shook their slack behinds and turned, one at a time:

"Bye, Annie."   28

"Bye, Annie."   29

"Bye, Annie."   30

Momma never turned her head or unfolded her arms, but she stopped singing   31 and said, "'Bye, Miz Helen, 'bye, Miz Ruth, 'bye, Miz Eloise."

I burst. A firecracker July-the-Fourth burst. How could Momma call them   32 Miz? The mean nasty things. Why couldn't she have come inside the sweet, cool store when we saw them breasting the hill? What did she prove? And then if they were dirty, mean, and impudent, why did Momma have to call them Miz?

She stood another whole song through and then opened the screen door to   33 look down on me crying in rage. She looked until I looked up. Her face was a brown moon that shone on me. She was beautiful. Something had happened out there, which I couldn't completely understand, but I could see that she was happy. Then she bent down and touched me as mothers of the church "lay hands on the sick and afflicted" and I quieted.

"Go wash your face, Sister." And she went behind the candy counter and   34 hummed, "Glory, glory, hallelujah, when I lay my burden down."

I threw the well water on my face and used the weekday handkerchief to   35 blow my nose. Whatever the contest had been out front, I knew Momma had won.

I took the rake back to the front yard. The smudged footprints were easy to   36 erase. I worked for a long time on my new design and laid the rake behind the wash pot. When I came back in the Store, I took Momma's hand and we both walked outside to look at the pattern.

It was a large heart with lots of hearts growing smaller inside, and piercing   37 from the outside rim to the smallest heart was an arrow. Momma said, "Sister, that's right pretty." Then she turned back to the Store and resumed, "Glory, glory, hallelujah, when I lay my burden down."

1970

QUESTIONS FOR DISCUSSION

Content

a. Is this simply a story about bad-mannered children and racism? Or is Angelou's intent more complex?

b. Why does the speaker bother to tell us that she made careful patterns when she raked the yard? Why did Momma admire these designs?

c. Angelou describes a number of outdated social observances such as never looking "right in a grown person's face." What other examples can you find in this selection? Why does she make it a point to include them in this recollection of her childhood?

d. Grandmother Henderson addresses each of the white girls as "Miz." Does her doing so have anything to do with her strange victory over these brats?

e. What details does Angelou use to create this obviously unflattering picture of "powhitetrash children"?

f. What does Angelou mean when she describes her uncle's limping in "dip-straight-dip fashion"?

Strategy and Style

g. In light of what she says early in the narrative, is it important for her to quote all three of the girls as they leave the store (paragraphs 28 through 30)? In general, what effect does Angelou's extensive use of dialogue create?

h. This selection begins with two rather odd commandments, which both startle and amuse the reader. Why are they important to the rest of the essay?

i. Angelou's use of metaphor is brilliant. In paragraph 18, she tells us that her "paranoia was born in those cold, molasses-slow minutes." What other examples of figurative language can you find?

j. How would you describe the speaker's tone at the beginning of this essay? When, exactly, does this tone change?

SUGGESTIONS FOR SHORT WRITING

a. What is victory to Angelou's grandmother?

b. Write your own definition of *victory*. What does it mean to you personally?

SUGGESTIONS FOR SUSTAINED WRITING

a. What kind of person is Grandmother Henderson? Based upon the details Angelou provides, jot down a few notes that might help explain her character to other readers. Then, relying on your own experiences, narrate an incident from the life of a close family relative. Through the use of description, dialogue, and action, make sure to include the kind of details that will provide the reader with a fairly vivid picture of the person you are recalling. Address your essay to someone who has never met this person and/or knows very little about him or her.

b. Grandmother Henderson's triumph may well have resided in the fact that she had done a far better job of raising children than many of her "powhitetrash" neighbours. Analyze Angelou's essay in order to explain this and other sources of "Momma's" victory.

c. The term *powhitetrash* has many connotations, several of which are apparent in this narrative. Choose a label often used in conversation to describe a type of person or group of persons. Using events from your life as illustrations, explain the kind of person(s) the label describes. Examples might include a hero/heroine, a creep, a spoiled brat, a winner/loser, an egghead, a yuppie, a jock, a nerd, a giver/taker, a witch.

No Name Woman

Maxine Hong Kingston

Born in 1940 to recently arrived immigrants from China, Maxine Hong Kingston grew up having to negotiate between two very different cultures. Her gender in a culture that valued males over females created further difficulties. These two issues are the main themes that inform much of Hong Kingston's work, most notably The Woman Warrior: Memoirs of a Girlhood among Ghosts *(1975), a collection of autobiographical narrative essays through which she seeks to understand her female ancestors and the ways they helped to form her own identity. "No Name Woman" is from this collection. The most well known of her other books are* China Men *(1980), a collection of character sketches from real and legendary sources; and* Tripmaster Monkey: His Fake Book *(1989), a novel. She has received over twenty awards, fellowships, and honorary degrees, including a National Book Critics Circle Award for* The Woman Warrior, *an American Book Award for* China Men, *and a PEN West Award in Fiction for* Tripmaster Monkey.

"You must not tell anyone," my mother said, "what I am about to tell you. In China your father had a sister who killed herself. She jumped into the family well. We say that your father has all brothers because it is as if she had never been born.

"In 1924 just a few days after our village celebrated seventeen hurry-up weddings—to make sure that every young man who went 'out on the road' would responsibly come home—your father and his brothers and your grandfather and his brothers and your aunt's new husband sailed for America, the Gold Mountain. It was your grandfather's last trip. Those lucky enough to get contracts waved goodbye from the decks. They fed and guarded the stowaways and helped them off in Cuba, New York, Bali, Hawaii. 'We'll meet in California next year,' they said. All of them sent money home.

"I remember looking at your aunt one day when she and I were dressing; I had not noticed before that she had such a protruding melon of a stomach. But I did not think, 'She's pregnant,' until she began to look like other pregnant women, her shirt pulling and the white tops of her black pants showing. She could not have been pregnant, you see, because her husband had been gone for years. No one said anything. We did not discuss it. In early summer she was ready to have the child, long after the time when it could have been possible.

"The village had also been counting. On the night the baby was to be born the villagers raided our house. Some were crying. Like a great saw, teeth strung with lights, files of people walked zigzag across our land, tearing the rice. Their lanterns doubled in the disturbed black water, which drained away through the broken bunds. As the villagers closed in, we could see that some of them, probably men and women we knew well, wore white masks. The people with long hair hung it over their faces. Women with short hair made it stand up on end. Some had tied white bands around their foreheads, arms, and legs.

"At first they threw mud and rocks at the house. Then they threw eggs and began slaughtering our stock. We could hear the animals scream their deaths—the

19

roosters, the pigs, a last great roar from the ox. Familiar wild heads flared in our night windows; the villagers encircled us. Some of the faces stopped to peer at us, their eyes rushing like searchlights. The hands flattened against the panes, framed heads, and left red prints.

"The villagers broke in the front and the back doors at the same time, even 6 though we had not locked the doors against them. Their knives dripped with the blood of our animals. They smeared blood on the doors and walls. One woman swung a chicken, whose throat she had slit, splattering blood in red arcs about her. We stood together in the middle of our house, in the family hall with the pictures and tables of the ancestors around us, and looked straight ahead.

"At that time the house had only two wings. When the men came back, we 7 would build two more to enclose our courtyard and a third one to begin a second courtyard. The villagers pushed through both wings, even your grandparents' rooms, to find your aunt's, which was also mine until the men returned. From this room a new wing for one of the younger families would grow. They ripped up her clothes and shoes and broke her combs, grinding them underfoot. They tore her work from the loom. They scattered the cooking fire and rolled the new weaving in it. We could hear them in the kitchen breaking our bowls and banging the pots. They overturned the great waist-high earthenware jugs; duck eggs, pickled fruits, vegetables burst out and mixed in acrid torrents. The old woman from the next field swept a broom through the air and loosed the spirits-of-the-broom over our heads. 'Pig.' 'Ghost.' 'Pig,' they sobbed and scolded while they ruined our house.

"When they left, they took sugar and oranges to bless themselves. They cut 8 pieces from the dead animals. Some of them took bowls that were not broken and clothes that were not torn. Afterward we swept up the rice and sewed it back up into sacks. But the smells from the spilled preserves lasted. Your aunt gave birth in the pigsty that night. The next morning when I went for the water, I found her and the baby plugging up the family well.

"Don't let your father know that I told you. He denies her. Now that you have 9 started to menstruate, what happened to her could happen to you. Don't humiliate us. You wouldn't like to be forgotten as if you had never been born. The villagers are watchful."

Whenever she had to warn us about life, my mother told stories that ran like 10 this one, a story to grow up on. She tested our strength to establish realities. Those in the emigrant generations who could not reassert brute survival died young and far from home. Those of us in the first American generations have had to figure out how the invisible world the emigrants built around our childhoods fits in solid America.

The emigrants confused the gods by diverting their curses, misleading them 11 with crooked streets and false names. They must try to confuse their offspring as well, who, I suppose, threaten them in similar ways—always trying to get things straight, always trying to name the unspeakable. The Chinese I know hide their names; sojourners take new names when their lives change and guard their real names with silence.

Chinese-Americans, when you try to understand what things in you are Chi- 12
nese, how do you separate what is peculiar to childhood, to poverty, insanities, one
family, your mother who marked your growing with stories, from what is Chinese?
What is Chinese tradition and what is the movies?

If I want to learn what clothes my aunt wore, whether flashy or ordinary, I 13
would have to begin, "Remember Father's drowned-in-the-well sister?" I cannot
ask that. My mother has told me once and for all the useful parts. She will add
nothing unless powered by Necessity, a riverbank that guides her life. She plants
vegetable gardens rather than lawns; she carries the odd-shaped tomatoes home
from the fields and eats food left for the gods.

Whenever we did frivolous things, we used up energy; we flew high kites. 14
We children came up off the ground over the melting cones our parents brought
home from work and the American movie on New Year's Day—*Oh, You Beautiful
Doll* with Betty Grable one year, and *She Wore a Yellow Ribbon* with John Wayne
another year. After the one carnival ride each, we paid in guilt; our tired father
counted his change on the dark walk home.

Adultery is extravagance. Could people who hatch their own chicks and eat 15
the embryos and the heads for delicacies and boil the feet in vinegar for party food,
leaving only the gravel, eating even the gizzard lining—could such people engender a prodigal aunt? To be a woman, to have a daughter in starvation time was a
waste enough. My aunt could not have been the lone romantic who gave up everything for sex. Women in the old China did not choose. Some man had commanded
her to lie with him and be his secret evil. I wonder whether he masked himself
when he joined the raid on her family.

Perhaps she had encountered him in the fields or on the mountain where the 16
daughters-in-law collected fuel. Or perhaps he first noticed her in the marketplace.
He was not a stranger because the village housed no strangers. She had to have
dealings with him other than sex. Perhaps he worked an adjoining field, or he sold
her the cloth for the dress she sewed and wore. His demand must have surprised,
then terrified her. She obeyed him; she always did as she was told.

When the family found a young man in the next village to be her husband, 17
she had stood tractably beside the best rooster, his proxy, and promised before they
met that she would be his forever. She was lucky that he was her age and she would
be the first wife, an advantage secure now. The night she first saw him, he had sex
with her. Then he left for America. She had almost forgotten what he looked like.
When she tried to envision him, she only saw the black and white face in the group
photograph the men had had taken before leaving.

The other man was not, after all, much different from her husband. They 18
both gave orders: she followed. "If you tell your family, I'll beat you. I'll kill you.
Be here again next week." No one talked sex, ever. And she might have separated
the rapes from the rest of living if only she did not have to buy her oil from him or
gather wood in the same forest. I want her fear to have lasted just as long as rape
lasted so that the fear could have been contained. No drawn-out fear. But women
at sex hazarded birth and hence lifetimes. The fear did not stop but permeated

everywhere. She told the man, "I think I'm pregnant." He organized the raid against her.

On nights when my mother and father talked about their life back home, 19
sometimes they mentioned an "outcast table" whose business they still seemed to be settling, their voices tight. In a commensal tradition, where food is precious, the powerful older people made wrongdoers eat alone. Instead of letting them start separate new lives like the Japanese, who could become samurais and geishas, the Chinese family, faces averted but eyes glowering sideways, hung on to the offenders and fed them leftovers. My aunt must have lived in the same house as my parents and eaten at an outcast table. My mother spoke about the raid as if she had seen it, when she and my aunt, a daughter-in-law to a different household, should not have been living together at all. Daughters-in-law lived with their husbands' parents, not their own; a synonym for marriage in Chinese is "taking a daughter-in-law." Her husband's parents could have sold her, mortgaged her, stoned her. But they had sent her back to her own mother and father, a mysterious act hinting at disgraces not told me. Perhaps they had thrown her out to deflect the avengers.

She was the only daughter; her four brothers went with her father, husband, 20
and uncles "out on the road" and for some years became western men. When the goods were divided among the family, three of the brothers took land, and the youngest, my father, chose an education. After my grandparents gave their daughter away to her husband's family, they had dispensed all the adventure and all the property. They expected her alone to keep the traditional ways, which her brothers, now among the barbarians, could fumble without detection. The heavy, deep-rooted women were to maintain the past against the flood, safe for returning. But the rare urge west had fixed upon our family, and so my aunt crossed boundaries not delineated in space.

The work of preservation demands that the feelings playing about in one's 21
guts not be turned into action. Just watch their passing like cherry blossoms. But perhaps my aunt, my forerunner, caught in a slow life, let dreams grow and fade and after some months or years went toward what persisted. Fear at the enormities of the forbidden kept her desires delicate, wire and bone. She looked at a man because she liked the way the hair was tucked behind his ears, or she liked the question-mark line of a long torso curving at the shoulder and straight at the hip. For warm eyes or a soft voice or a slow walk—that's all—a few hairs, a line, a brightness, a sound, a pace, she gave up family. She offered us up for a charm that vanished with tiredness, a pigtail that didn't toss when the wind died. Why, the wrong lighting could erase the dearest thing about him.

It could very well have been, however, that my aunt did not take subtle en- 22
joyment of her friend, but, a wild woman, kept rollicking company. Imagining her free with sex doesn't fit, though. I don't know any women like that, or men either. Unless I see her life branching into mine, she gives me no ancestral help.

To sustain her being in love, she often worked at herself in the mirror, guess- 23
ing at the colors and shapes that would interest him, changing them frequently in order to hit on the right combination. She wanted him to look back.

On a farm near the sea, a woman who tended her appearance reaped a rep- 24 utation for eccentricity. All the married women blunt-cut their hair in flaps about their ears or pulled it back in tight buns. No nonsense. Neither style blew easily into heart-catching tangles. And at their weddings they displayed themselves in their long hair for the last time. "It brushed the backs of my knees," my mother tells me. "It was braided, and even so, it brushed the backs of my knees."

At the mirror my aunt combed individuality into her bob. A bun could have 25 been contrived to escape into black streamers blowing in the wind or in quiet wisps about her face, but only the older women in our picture album wear buns. She brushed her hair back from her forehead, tucking the flaps behind her ears. She looped a piece of thread, knotted into a circle between her index fingers and thumbs, and ran the double strand across her forehead. When she closed her fingers as if she were making a pair of shadow geese bite, the string twisted together catching the little hairs. Then she pulled the thread away from her skin, ripping the hairs out neatly, her eyes watering from the needles of pain. Opening her fingers, she cleaned the thread, then rolled it along her hairline and the tops of her eyebrows. My mother did the same to me and my sisters and herself. I used to believe that the expression "caught by the short hairs" meant a captive held with a depilatory string. It especially hurt at the temples, but my mother said we were lucky we didn't have to have our feet bound when we were seven. Sisters used to sit on their beds and cry together, she said, as their mothers or their slaves removed the bandages for a few minutes each night and let the blood gush back into their veins. I hope that the man my aunt loved appreciated a smooth brow, that he wasn't just a tits-and-ass man.

Once my aunt found a freckle on her chin, at a spot that the almanac said 26 predestined her for unhappiness. She dug it out with a hot needle and washed the wound with peroxide.

More attention to her looks than these pullings of hairs and pickings at spots 27 would have caused gossip among the villagers. They owned work clothes and good clothes, and they wore good clothes for feasting the new seasons. But since a woman combing her hair hexes beginnings, my aunt rarely found an occasion to look her best. Women looked like great sea snails—the corded wood, babies, and laundry they carried were the whorls on their backs. The Chinese did not admire a bent back; goddesses and warriors stood straight. Still there must have been a marvelous freeing of beauty when a worker laid down her burden and stretched and arched.

Such commonplace loveliness, however, was not enough for my aunt. She 28 dreamed of a lover for the fifteen days of New Year's, the time for families to exchange visits, money, and food. She plied her secret comb. And sure enough she cursed the year, the family, the village, and herself.

Even as her hair lured her imminent lover, many other men looked at her. 29 Uncles, cousins, nephews, brothers would have looked, too, had they been home between journeys. Perhaps they had already been restraining their curiosity, and they left, fearful that their glances, like a field of nesting birds, might be startled and caught. Poverty hurt, and that was their first reason for leaving. But another, final reason for leaving the crowded house was the never-said.

She may have been unusually beloved, the precious only daughter, spoiled 30 and mirror gazing because of the affection the family lavished on her. When her husband left, they welcomed the chance to take her back from the in-laws; she could live like the little daughter for just a while longer. There are stories that my grandfather was different from other people, "crazy ever since the little Jap bayoneted him in the head." He used to put his naked penis on the dinner table, laughing. And one day he brought home a baby girl, wrapped up inside his brown western-style greatcoat. He had traded one of his sons, probably my father, the youngest, for her. My grandmother made him trade back. When he finally got a daughter of his own, he doted on her. They must have all loved her, except perhaps my father, the only brother who never went back to China, having once been traded for a girl.

Brothers and sisters, newly men and women, had to efface their sexual color 31 and present plain miens. Disturbing hair and eyes, a smile like no other, threatened the ideal of five generations living under one roof. To focus blurs, people shouted face to face and yelled from room to room. The immigrants I know have loud voices, unmodulated to American tones even after years away from the village where they called their friendships out across the fields. I have not been able to stop my mother's screams in public libraries or over telephones. Walking erect (knees straight, toes pointed forward, not pigeon-toed, which is Chinese-feminine) and speaking in an inaudible voice, I have tried to turn myself American-feminine. Chinese communication was loud, public. Only sick people had to whisper. But at the dinner table, where the family members came nearest one another, no one could talk, not the outcasts nor any eaters. Every word that falls from the mouth is a coin lost. Silently they gave and accepted food with both hands. A preoccupied child who took his bowl with one hand got a sideways glare. A complete moment of total attention is due everyone alike. Children and lovers have no singularity here, but my aunt used a secret voice, a separate attentiveness.

She kept the man's name to herself throughout her labor and dying; she did 32 not accuse him that he be punished with her. To save her inseminator's name she gave silent birth.

He may have been somebody in her own household, but intercourse with a 33 man outside the family would have been no less abhorrent. All the village were kinsmen, and the titles shouted in loud country voices never let kinship be forgotten. Any man within visiting distance would have been neutralized as a lover—"brother," "younger brother," "older brother"—one hundred and fifteen relationship titles. Parents researched birth charts probably not so much to assure good fortune as to circumvent incest in a population that has but one hundred surnames. Everybody has eight million relatives. How useless then sexual mannerisms, how dangerous.

As if it came from an atavism deeper than fear, I used to add "brother" silently 34 to boys' names. It hexed the boys, who would or would not ask me to dance, and made them less scary and as familiar and deserving of benevolence as girls.

But, of course, I hexed myself also—no dates. I should have stood up, both 35
arms waving, and shouted out across libraries, "Hey, you! Love me back." I had no
idea, though, how to make attraction selective, how to control its direction and magnitude. If I made myself American-pretty so that the five or six Chinese boys in the
class fell in love with me, everyone else—the Caucasian, Negro, and Japanese
boys—would too. Sisterliness, dignified and honorable, made much more sense.

Attraction eludes control so stubbornly that whole societies designed to or- 36
ganize relationships among people cannot keep order, not even when they bind
people to one another from childhood and raise them together. Among the very
poor and the wealthy, brothers married their adopted sisters, like doves. Our family allowed some romance, paying adult brides' prices and providing dowries so
that their sons and daughters could marry strangers. Marriage promises to turn
strangers into friendly relatives—a nation of siblings.

In the village structure, spirits shimmered among the live creatures, bal- 37
anced and held in equilibrium by time and land. But one human being flaring up
into violence could open up a black hole, a maelstrom that pulled in the sky. The
frightened villagers, who depended on one another to maintain the real, went to
my aunt to show her a personal, physical representation of the break she had made
in the "roundness." Misallying couples snapped off the future, which was to be
embodied in true offspring. The villagers punished her for acting as if she could
have a private life, secret and apart from them.

If my aunt had betrayed the family at a time of large grain yields and peace, 38
when many boys were born, and wings were being built on many houses, perhaps she
might have escaped such severe punishment. But the men—hungry, greedy, tired of
planting in dry soil—had been forced to leave the village in order to send food-money
home. There were ghost plagues, bandit plagues, wars with the Japanese, floods. My
Chinese brother and sister had died of an unknown sickness. Adultery, perhaps only
a mistake during good times, became a crime when the village needed food.

The round moon cakes and round doorways, the round tables of graduated 39
sizes that fit one roundness inside another, round windows and rice bowls—these
talismans had lost their power to warn this family of the law: A family must be
whole, faithfully keeping the descent line by having sons to feed the old and the
dead, who in turn look after the family. The villagers came to show my aunt and
her lover-in-hiding a broken house. The villagers were speeding up the circling of
events because she was too shortsighted to see that her infidelity had already
harmed the village, that waves of consequences would return unpredictably, sometimes in disguise, as now, to hurt her. This roundness had to be made coin-sized so
that she would see its circumference: Punish her at the birth of her baby. Awaken
her to the inexorable. People who refused fatalism because they could invent small
resources insisted on culpability. Deny accidents and wrest fault from the stars.

After the villagers left, their lanterns now scattering in various directions to- 40
ward home, the family broke their silence and cursed her. "Aiaa, we're going to
die. Death is coming. Death is coming. Look what you've done. You've killed us.
Ghost! Dead ghost! Ghost! You've never been born." She ran out into the fields,

far enough from the house so that she could no longer hear their voices, and pressed herself against the earth, her own land no more. When she felt the birth coming, she thought that she had been hurt. Her body seized together. "They've hurt me too much," she thought. "This is gall, and it will kill me." With forehead and knees against the earth, her body convulsed and then relaxed. She turned on her back, lay on the ground. The black well of sky and stars went out and out and out forever; her body and her complexity seemed to disappear. She was one of the stars, a bright dot in blackness, without home, without a companion, in eternal cold and silence. An agoraphobia rose in her, speeding higher and higher, bigger and bigger; she would not be able to contain it; there would be no end to fear.

Flayed, unprotected against space, she felt pain return, focusing her body. 41 This pain chilled her—a cold, steady kind of surface pain. Inside, spasmodically, the other pain, the pain of the child, heated her. For hours she lay on the ground, alternately body and space. Sometimes a vision of normal comfort obliterated reality: She saw the family in the evening gambling at the dinner table, the young people massaging their elders' backs. She saw them congratulating one another, high joy on the mornings the rice shoots came up. When these pictures burst, the stars drew yet further apart. Black space opened.

She got to her feet to fight better and remembered that old-fashioned women 42 gave birth in their pigsties to fool the jealous, pain-dealing gods, who do not snatch piglets. Before the next spasms could stop her, she ran to the pigsty, each step a rushing out into emptiness. She climbed over the fence and knelt in the dirt. It was good to have a fence enclosing her, a tribal person alone.

Laboring, this woman who had carried her child as a foreign growth that 43 sickened her every day, expelled it at last. She reached down to touch the hot, wet, moving mass, surely smaller than anything human, and could feel that it was human after all—fingers, toes, nails, nose. She pulled it up on to her belly, and it lay curled there, butt in the air, feet precisely tucked one under the other. She opened her loose shirt and buttoned the child inside. After resting, it squirmed and thrashed and she pushed it up to her breast. It turned its head this way and that until it found her nipple. There, it made little snuffling noises. She clenched her teeth at its preciousness, lovely as a young calf, a piglet, a little dog.

She may have gone to the pigsty as a last act of responsibility: she would 44 protect this child as she had protected its father. It would look after her soul, leaving supplies on her grave. But how would this tiny child without family find her grave when there would be no marker for her anywhere, neither in the earth nor the family hall? No one would give her a family hall name. She had taken the child with her into the wastes. At its birth the two of them had felt the same raw pain of separation, a wound that only the family pressing tight could close. A child with no descent line would not soften her life but only trail after her, ghostlike, begging her to give it purpose. At dawn the villagers on their way to the fields would stand around the fence and look.

Full of milk, the little ghost slept. When it awoke, she hardened her breasts 45 against the milk that crying loosens. Toward morning she picked up the baby and walked to the well.

Carrying the baby to the well shows loving. Otherwise abandon it. Turn its 46 face into the mud. Mothers who love their children take them along. It was probably a girl; there is some hope of forgiveness for boys.

"Don't tell anyone you had an aunt. Your father does not want to hear her 47 name. She has never been born." I have believed that sex was unspeakable and words so strong and fathers so frail that "aunt" would do my father mysterious harm. I have thought that my family, having settled among immigrants who had also been their neighbors in the ancestral land, needed to clean their name, and a wrong word would incite the kinspeople even here. But there is more to this silence: They want me to participate in her punishment. And I have.

In the twenty years since I heard this story I have not asked for details nor 48 said my aunt's name; I do not know it. People who can comfort the dead can also chase after them to hurt them further—a reverse ancestor worship. The real punishment was not the raid swiftly inflicted by the villagers, but the family's deliberately forgetting her. Her betrayal so maddened them, they saw to it that she would suffer forever, even after death. Always hungry, always needing, she would have to beg food from other ghosts, snatch and steal it from those whose living descendants give them gifts. She would have to fight the ghosts massed at crossroads for the buns a few thoughtful citizens leave to decoy her away from village and home so that the ancestral spirits could feast unharassed. At peace, they could act like gods, not ghosts, their descent lines providing them with paper suits and dresses, spirit money, paper houses, paper automobiles, chicken, meat, and rice into eternity—essences delivered up in smoke and flames, steam and incense rising from each rice bowl. In an attempt to make the Chinese care for people outside the family, Chairman Mao encourages us now to give our paper replicas to the spirits of outstanding soldiers and workers, no matter whose ancestors they may be. My aunt remains forever hungry. Goods are not distributed evenly among the dead.

My aunt haunts me—her ghost drawn to me because now, after fifty years 49 of neglect, I alone devote pages of paper to her, though not origamied into houses and clothes. I do not think she always means me well. I am telling on her, and she was a spite suicide, drowning herself in the drinking water. The Chinese are always very frightened of the drowned one, whose weeping ghost, wet hair hanging and skin bloated, waits silently by the water to pull down a substitute.

1975

QUESTIONS FOR DISCUSSION

Content

a. Is Hong Kingston's family ashamed of No Name Woman because she committed suicide or because she became pregnant by a man who was not her husband? Is the distinction important?

b. Why doesn't the author ever learn her aunt's name?

c. In what way does the story of No Name Woman cast light on Kingston's claim that her mother is guided "by Necessity" (paragraph 13)?

d. Why does Hong Kingston refer to her aunt as "prodigal" (paragraph 15)? What meanings does she associate with this term?

e. Does she see an affinity between herself and her aunt not shared by other members of the family? In what ways is this a defence of No Name Woman? Of all Chinese women? Of all women?

f. "The villagers punished [No Name Woman] for acting as if she could have a private life, secret and apart from them" (paragraph 37). How does this statement shed light upon the culture Hong Kingston is describing?

g. What motives does she ascribe to No Name Woman? To the man who raped her? To the villagers? To her family?

Strategy and Style

h. The author uses her mother's voice to relate the story of the villagers' attack. Would she have done better to tell this story from her own point of view?

i. Why does she address Chinese-Americans directly in paragraph 12? Is she writing to a limited audience?

j. What does she mean when, at the end of paragraph 20, she says, "the rare urge west had fixed upon our family, and so my aunt crossed boundaries not delineated in space"?

k. Why does she spend so much time describing the setting of her story?

l. Comment upon the author's use of verbs in the passage that recalls the attack of the townspeople. What effect does her choice of verbs create?

m. Among other things, "No Name Woman" is an indictment of sexism, intolerance, and violence against women. Is Hong Kingston's tone appropriate? Should she have made her criticism fiercer and more apparent? Should she have focused on this issue alone?

n. How would you describe the function of the writer in this selection? Is she simply a reporter, or does she have other functions? What might they be?

o. The author says she has participated in her aunt's punishment. What does she mean? Why might she have written this essay?

SUGGESTIONS FOR SHORT WRITING

a. Spend a few minutes explaining how people of the town in which you grew up might react to learning that one of their neighbours had become pregnant while her husband was away. Would attention focus on the woman, on her husband, or on the "other" man? Would the woman be condemned by some people no matter what the circumstances?

b. Review or reread "No Name Woman." As you do this, record your reactions to the sexism, violence, and intolerance in the culture Hong Kingston is describing. Can you find examples of such phenomena in your own environment?

c. Sketch out a few details that might serve as the outline to a story about a traumatic event in the history of your family. Choose an event that you experienced firsthand or that you learned about from a parent or other relative.

SUGGESTIONS FOR SUSTAINED WRITING

a. You can probably recall an interesting story about an ancestor or a living relative. Write this story down just as you heard it. Then, rewrite the story from at least two other perspectives: from the ancestor's or relative's perspective, from the perspective of another person involved in the story, and/or from the perspective you might use if you were to pass on the story to your children. How does the story change from one point of view to another? What elements are based on fact in each? What elements are based on speculation? Which version, in your opinion, is the most "truthful"?

b. Hong Kingston tells her versions of what might have happened to her aunt in order to lend substance to her memory of this woman and implicitly to explain the cruelty toward women that can be imbedded in a culture. Collect several personal memories that might illustrate some unfairness or injustice to you (as representative of a larger group) or to a subgroup within your culture. Then turn these memories into a coherent narrative essay. Though you need not make your work as detailed or complex as Hong Kingston's, try to interweave these memories closely so as to create a clear and coherent discussion of the injustice you wish to illustrate.

The Republic of Tricksterism

Paul Seesequasis

Born in Melfort, Saskatchewan, in 1958, Paul Seesequasis enjoys Plains Cree, Dakota, Ukrainian, and German ancestry. He believes this hybrid existence creates, "new imaginings of self." His writing is frequently concerned with transformation and borders. For him, the only two constants in life are love and change.

We were urban mixed-bloods. Shopping malls and beer parlours were our sacred grounds, reaching adolescence in the '70s, the Sex Pistols and the Clash provided the tribal drums. Fallen between the seams and exiled from the reserves we were the prisoners of bureaucratic apartheid, of red tape and parliamentary decrees. 1

Our tribal links were obscure, our colonial banishment confirmed by the Indian Act. White bureaucrats and tribal politicians alike were our oppressors. 'We are heading toward self-government,' proclaimed Tobe, the Grand Chief of the Fermentation of Saskatchewan Indian Nations (FSIN) as he shook the hand of then Saskatchewan Premier Allan Blakeney. 2

In his hands Tobe, the Grand Chief, held a paper promising tens-of-millions of dollars, but that money and power were destined only for a select few. The Grand Chief's vision was obscured by power and long-legged blondes. He denounced Indian women who had married white men, while at the same time blonde secretaries and assistants crossed their legs in his plush office at the FSIN. 3

Mary Seesequasis, aka Ogresko, was born on Beardy's reserve on January 20, 1934. The first child of Sam Seesequasis, of Beardy's reserve, and Mary Rose Nahtowenhow, of the Sturgeon Lake band. Sam, my *nimosom,* danced through life with gentleness and humour and became a leader in the community. Mary Rose, my *nohkom,* was large and became a bear when she laughed. She hunted rabbits, decapitated chickens, and farted in the direction of bureaucrats and posers. 4

They made love, had nine children, and seven lived to adulthood. 5

The grand-chief-to-be and his family lived downwind from my grandmother's farts. He was born the same day as my mother but their lives were destined to take far different paths. Tobe was born mixed-blood, his father Cree, his mother white. But the irony and humour of being mixed-race was lost on Tobe. He would grow up as mixed-race pure-blood, purer than thou and given to exaggerating the quantity of his half cup of tribal blood. Tobe lived in denial of his white parentage. 6

Being the same age, Tobe and my mother played together as children, they fell asleep infused with dreams of *Wesakaychuk* and *Pakakos,* they hid under the covers from the wetigoes and the hairy hearts. 7

But The Indian Act enabled Tobe to imagine himself the pure-blood. With Indian father and white mother he was allowed to stay on the reserve. In 1950 my mother met and fell in love with a white man, Dennis Ogresko, and because she was in love with a white man and she was *hisqueau,* a woman, she had to leave the reserve. 8

30

The hairy hearts ran amuck in 1950s Saskatchewan. Cannibal spirits plagued the 9
small towns and hid in the grain elevators. It was open season on squaws, wagon-
burners, and breeds. By courageously proclaiming brown-white love my parents
challenged the humourless segregational values of the time.

Unable to hide on the reserve they weathered taunts and jeers with laugh- 10
ter. That love could exist between races offended all the pure-bred breeders; and
in making love Dennis and Mary parented two cross-breed mutts, my brother
and I.

We experienced childhood between the seams, spending summers on the re- 11
serve, winters in the city. We played without leashes, without pedigree we learned
to live with our genetic-mixture coats and our lack of papers. We lived in a
no-man's land between Indian and white. At school we quickly learned to stick together to avoid the beatings of the pure bred-breeders. We found delight in the re-
pulsion others felt for us. We pissed on the city trees, marked our traditional urban
territories, and barked ferociously at the white poodles.

It was the 1960s and my mother, now a registered nurse, worked in the 12
Community Clinic in Prince Albert where she healed the urban orphans and
mixed-bloods who were now entering the cities in increasing numbers.

Tobe, the mixed-blood/full-blood too had grown up. He became a tribal 13
politician, a Chief of the reserve and a wearer of suits and ties. His hair was short
and his speeches were long. He spoke of self-government and economic development but his mind was on attending conferences and getting laid in hotels.

With enthusiasm he joined Wild Jean's Indian Affairs Bandwagon and Wild 14
West Show and with conferences here and there and blondes to his left and right,
it was the modern-day chief's delight. Tobe sold his Pontiac—*the Poor Old
Nechee'd Thought It Was A Cadillac*—and actually bought a real Cadillac, and a
blonde chauffeur. But while Tobe played the colonial game a revolution was brewing in Prince Albert.

Uncle Morris was a *rigoureau*; a mixed-blood shape-shifter. He often came to visit 15
our home on the east side, the poor side, of the city. My uncle was a co-founder of
the Metis Association of Alberta in the 1930s, and an urban activist who cut
through the lies of white bureaucrats and tribal politicians alike. His mission was
to liberate the urban reserves from the cannibal spirits and the hairy hearts. He told
my mother of his vision and Mary laughed and agreed to help him. Uncle Morris
wanted to take over the Prince Albert Friendship Centre and remove the metal detectors from the door. Those detectors beeped a warning anytime someone without a status card tried to walk in.

Malcolm spoke passionately about uniting all urban skins, mixed or full. 16
'Burn your status cards!' he proclaimed, 'and throw away your colonial pedigree
papers. Don't let the white man define us. Let's define ourselves.'

Uncle Morris knew how to respond to taunts and jeers with trickery. When 17
he laughed he became a bear and his joyous chuckles reverberated from deep

within. My mother would prepare dinner and then we would sit, expectedly, waiting to hear of his latest exploits.

As a *rigoureau* Morris was hated by the hairy hearts and the cannibal spir- 18
its. They envied his power, his ability to turn into a dog, a bear, or almost any kind of rodent he chose. I remember once his turning into a red squirrel, jumping from his chair and scurrying around the kitchen floor while my parents cried with laughter and said 'Enough! Enough!'

From Morris I learned to see the evil spirits around me. I saw them in the 19
frowns and looks of scorn us mixed-bloods received on the streets. I felt the disapproving glares of the police, farmers, tribal politicians and store owners. They were everywhere in the city and their numbers were increasing.

The cannibal spirits and the hairy hearts ruled the cities and reserves. They fed on 20
both Indians and whites. 'There just aren't enough of us *rigoureau*'s left to stop them,' uncle once told me. 'These evil spirits,' he explained, 'feed on souls that are empty, rub against their bodies and penetrate the skin. Sometimes a person can repel them if they are strong enough or if they can call on a *rigoureau* to drive the spirit away. But most people succumb and the cannibal spirits continue in their goal to create a world of hate. A world in which they can proliferate.'

Morris would often go to the clinic where my mother worked to watch and 21
to offer humour to those who were forgetting how to laugh. He played the compassionate trickster, upsetting the plans of the cannibal spirits, and frustrating the violent emotions of the hairy hearts. Many a body was purged of poison.

Then, one day, Uncle Morris went missing. Search parties were organized and 22
the mixed-bloods and urban orphans looked everywhere but it was the squirrels, the rodent friend of the *rigoureau,* who led us to him. He had been dumped into a grain chute and his body was badly beaten. We lowered ropes and a canvas stretcher. My mother was among those selected to gently retrieve his body from that dark cavern.

While the crows cawed mournfully and the stray dogs howled their lament, 23
our procession carried Morris back to our house. He was laid in the guest room and a group of women healers worked with him. They washed his bruised body, set his broken bones, removed all the grains that had been shoved down his throat and nostrils, and, after a few days, his heart began to beat again.

Time passed and Morris cracked a smile and we rejoiced, knowing he would 24
live. 'My spirit has tasted life again though parts of my body probably never will,' he confessed. True he was now paralysed from the waist down. We pooled our meagre resources and had made for him a cedar wood wheelchair with wheels of rounded stone. Being confined to a wheelchair didn't slow Morris down. Rather he called for a gathering of mixed-bloods and urban orphans.

I remember that day. We met at an old skating rink. Long benches had been set up 25
for the occasion. The building was packed. Uncle Morris's life history was in that building and each person had a story to tell. Some kindness, some help from trouble, some funny story. There were trappers from the north, none more than three

feet tall, with bristled faces and wooden pipes. I remember how they stamped their fur-covered feet in applause when Morris was wheeled into the arena. There were *kokums,* grandmothers, with shawls wrapped tightly around their heads and their aged but strong fingers beading leather. There were young street girls who took the day off from work. I recall the smell of perfume, their make-up, and the candy they gave to the children who ran up and down the aisles. And there were nurses, construction workers, loggers, teachers, drunks, and others and they had all come to hear my uncle.

'The main cannibal spirit has arrived in town,' Morris roared in his bear 26 voice. There was silence in the hall. 'He has come for me. I have frightened him and he seeks to destroy me with violence.'

'Shame!' cried the audience.   27

'He has come in the guise of an Indian. A Chief. A person you know well. 28 He is Chief Tobe, the plains warrior wearer of chokers and ties, the politician without humour. The one whose ideas are short and his speeches are long.'

The crowd laughed.   29

'You remember Tobe. He speaks of purity and his heart is cold. He has 30 chased the mixed-bloods from the reserves and he has created a world of urban orphans. I shall trick him with humour. With your help we will create a story. A myth. That is something that cannot be destroyed by violence. It will annoy him immensely because we will create a world he cannot shatter with hate, for it exists here,' Morris said, pointing to his head.

Uncle told of his plan to establish the Republic of Tricksterism, a place 31 where humour rules and hatred is banished, where love's freedom to go anywhere is proclaimed. 'Our headquarters will be the Indian Friendship Centre which, as you know, has been controlled by the hairy hearts. We don't seek permanence for our republic but a moment of time that lasts forever.'

We cheered and with Morris's wheelchair at the head, we marched down- 32 town on our mission of liberation. We marched into the Friendship Centre as the hairy hearts, panic-stricken, climbed out the back windows. They left in a rush, not having the time to shred their Indian Affairs hit list of their sacred status card membership rolls. We took their defining documents, turned them upside-down, and wallpapered the building. The children, myself included, were given crayons and told to draw freely. We created a world of merging colours, a world without paint-by-numbers.

The Republic of Tricksterism was proclaimed. All skins are equal was the 33 first constitutional decree and a pair of red drawers became the new flag. Skins from the street came in to help the social workers heal themselves and tribal lawyers were deprogrammed.

Chief Tobe was soon in a fury. He roared with anger and dark clouds pelted the 34 city with hail. He smashed his fists on the ground and the streets cracked and the sewers overflowed. He called loudly and the poisoned souls congregated outside the offices of the Prince Albert Regional Tribal Council to hear his message of

hate. The Tribal Council was in an uproar, they passed resolutions and sent ulti-
matums to the Republic of Tricksterism demanding they abdicate power. 'We are
the Chiefs!' they proclaimed. 'The big white men in Ottawa say so.' 'Ah—go on,'
replied the Republic of Tricksterism. When even memos from the Minister of
Indian Affairs failed to dislodge the trickster-upstarts, Tobe went into action.

A hundred tribal goons were summoned. They were armed with baseball 35
bats, dog repellent and mace. 'We shall disperse these mixed-bloods. These de-
filers of our traditions. These people without status!' The goons chanted their approval in unison. The Tribal Council Chiefs smiled, patted their beer bellies, and
licked their fat lips in anticipation.

The assault came at dawn. Calling in the mounties, who in honour of the 36
chiefs donned full regalia and did a musical ride, Tobe, the goons and the mounties marched in a column toward the Friendship Centre. But the urban animals, the
squirrels, raccoons and foxes, ran out ahead of the approaching army and barked
out a warning to the citizens of the Republic of Tricksterism.

'We must avert bloodshed,' Morris observed to the citizens. 'Violence is the 37
tool of fools. It is with humour and irreverence that us urban animals must survive.
Let them have their building back, let them issue their proclamations with dead
trees, let them have their dubious titles like national chief, let them become the media stars. We'll find our humour back on the streets.'

And so it came to be that Tobe and his goons recaptured the Prince Albert 38
Friendship Centre without bloodshed. 'These mixed-bloods are cowards,' Tobe
proclaimed, in disappointment.

Uncle Morris was captured by the tribal goons and brought before the Prince 39
Albert Regional Tribal Council. 'He must be punished as an example,' proclaimed Tobe. 'He has committed blasphemy and challenged our noble and sacred institutions.'

'Spare him!' yelled the urban orphans and mixed-bloods but, as always, the 40
chiefs were deaf to the sounds of the streets. On a Sunday, surrounded by a procession of goons, Morris was forced to wheel his chair to the highest hill in Prince
Albert.

There he was nailed to a metal medicine wheel, his arms and legs spread in 41
the four directions. Morris died soon after and his body was taken by the goons
and buried in an unmarked grave. The mixed-bloods and urban orphans mourned.
Crows flew high and cawed his name to the clouds. A wake was held and for four
days the memory fires burned from street corner garbage cans. On the fifth day the
crows told the people that my uncle had been resurrected but that he had come
back as a termite.

The urban people rejoiced and Morris, in his new life form, moved into the 42
regional Indian Affairs building and gnawed at the bureaucrats' desks until they
dissolved into sawdust. Meanwhile Tobe, sporting the retaking of the Friendship
Centre as another dishonourable feather in his war bonnet, ran for national leader
of the FSIN and won the big chief position at that fermenting organization.

'Who better to speak the politicians' garble? Who better to hide the truth be- 43
tween platitudes of self-government and economic development than Tobe?' proclaimed the FSIN in their press release announcing his victory.

Then, one day, despite the opposition of the FSIN, C-31 became law. At the stroke 44
of a bureaucratic pen, status was restored to those long denied, a government decree pronouncing the end of a hundred years' damage. 'Hallelujah, we're Indians,'
responded the mixed-bloods. Our hearts soared like drunken eagles. We donned
our chicken feather headdresses, our squirrel tail bustles, and fancy-danced
around the Midtown Plaza.

My mother, a full-blood Cree woman, could only laugh at the gesture. Mean- 45
while in the FSIN offices Tobe, the mixed-blood/pure-blood, and his Indiancrats,
were having a bad day. They grumbled, drank double shots of rye, and hit their
blonde secretaries.

But C-31 was only a temporary irritation for Tobe. His vision remained fo- 46
cused on careerism and playing the colonial card game. He wore blinkers whenever he entered the city to avoid seeing the urban orphans. He talked about first
nations as if the cities did not exist. He became bloated with his power and gained
weight by the hour. As the Honourable Heap Big Chief he increased his salary and
his belly respectively. Mary Seesequasis moved to Saskatoon and worked at the
20th Street Community Clinic where she administered to the mixed bloods: the
whores, dykes, queers, street people, everyone. My uncle's words, 'We are not victims. We are survivors,' was the motto she lived by. Tobe also was a survivor but
in a more dangerous game. My mother saw the Indian Act as a bad joke. Tobe embraced it as a career. His sense of humour was lost in the shuffle of colonial cards
and his heart was hardened by the cannibal spirits.

Meanwhile Uncle Morris, having completed his job in Prince Albert, found 47
his way into a chief's pocket and made it to Ottawa. Rumour has it that even today he has led an army of termites into a certain national chief's organization
where he is currently munching away at the legs of that chief's chair.

1997

QUESTIONS FOR DISCUSSION

Content

  a. What does the opening handshake between Chief Tobe and then-Saskatchewan
      premier Allan Blakeney indicate to the reader?
  b. Why does Seesequasis give us the geneology of both his mother and Chief Tobe?
  c. What does he mean by "hairy hearts" and "cannibal spirits"?
  d. What is a "rigoureau"?
  e. What is the "Republic of Tricksterism"? Where does it exist?
  f. What is C-31?

Strategy and Style

   g. How does Seesequasis make Tobe appear hypocritical?

   h. What is the effect of the phrase "His hair was short and his speeches were long"?

   i. Why does Seesequasis keep drawing our attention to the clinics in which his mother worked?

   j. Why does he state that Mary Rose "farted in the direction of bureaucrats and posers"?

   k. Seesequasis tells his story in an unconventional fashion. What makes it unconventional?

   l. How are anger and humour intertwined in the essay?

SUGGESTIONS FOR SHORT WRITING

   a. Many immigrants lose their language after the first generation. Does that mean they are no longer part of that culture?

   b. How do you define your own ancestry? Why do you identify yourself in this way?

   c. How do you know if someone is a hypocrite or a poser? How do you know if someone is genuine or authentic?

SUGGESTIONS FOR SUSTAINED WRITING

   a. Use humour to retell an incident that actually makes you very angry. How can you turn anger into laughter?

   b. Which is ultimately more powerful: ideas or weapons? Support your argument with pertinent examples.

   c. Read up on the history of satire. Discuss the importance or relevance of satire in a society.

Riding the Hyphen

Anurita Bains

Anurita Bains, as her essay states, came to Canada at the age of four where she spent many years trying to conform to "Canadian" standards in "one of the WASPiest towns in Canada." She currently is a freelance writer whose work appears in This Magazine, Now Magazine, The Toronto Star, *and the* Sikh Press.

After I secured a summer job a few years ago, my boss invited me and the other 1 employees out to lunch. It was June, so I showed up in shorts and a T-shirt. The lunch was basically a getting-to-know-you event and I didn't think much about it afterwards, that is, until a friend of mine who had also been there told me about a discussion she had later with my boss.

"Do you think Anne would be more comfortable doing tours in her tradi- 2 tional dress?" my boss asked. "Because, if she wants, she can do them in a salvaar chemise."

Her remarks, while infuriating and upsetting, aren't really that surprising. I 3 have become accustomed to being defined by stereotypes by those who purport to know me or something about me. Although there is no doubt that my boss had seen me—during the interview and at the casual lunch—her comments clearly illustrated she hadn't really seen me at all.

Though I eventually became angry, my initial reaction was defensive. Did I 4 look and act like someone who would wear a salvaar chemise? Hadn't she seen that I was wearing shorts and Doc Martens? Hadn't she noticed that my short haircut—usually one of the first signs of a non-practising Sikh, or at least of a rebellious one—was more than a fashion statement? Did I look that Indian?

How could such simple remarks rouse such complex feelings in me? I have 5 yet to reconcile my South Asian culture and history with my "Canadian" upbringing. But how could my boss know that her attempt at liberal sensitivity would provoke a crisis in me? I guess it's no surprise: I have gone through my whole life trying to prove how "Canadian" I am.

I am four years old and I sleep through most of the seemingly endless flight 6 to Canada. As soon as we arrive, my father and brother get their hair cut short—and so does my mother. The turbans are buried deep in the closet. We are abiding by the cardinal rule: look, be, act Canadian.

"Learn English," I am told, so I learn as quickly as I can because all I can re- 7 member is my torturously strict convent nursery school in India, where bad girls were dragged by their braids and bad boys got the ruler. I am so preoccupied with learning English that I forget Punjabi—something I later regret.

I am enrolled in school and registered as Anne, an anglicised version of my 8 name. This, I am told, will save me from embarrassment in the classroom when my name is called during attendance-taking.

My parents work and go to school, so I spend a lot of time at home alone. I 9
pass the time by watching television and napping, and while an hour seems to last
a lifetime, I teach myself how to answer the phone, take messages and make crafts.
I later realise my independent nature developed because of all the time I stayed at
home by myself.

I am mastering this "Canadian" thing: any hint of an accent is gone, I have 10
a "normal-sounding" name and kids to play with. I fit in. Unless someone explicitly asks, "Where are you from?" I can conceal that I am not Canadian, but a
Canadian citizen from India, and aside from the odd "paki" or "chocolate milk"
slur, I fare pretty well on the playground.

A year after a summer vacation in India, an Air India flight goes down over 11
the Atlantic. "Did we know anyone on it?" I ask my parents. Of course we did.
Everyone knew someone, I am told.

High school. We are now living in one of the richest towns in Canada, although 12
my family is not rich. The town is also one of the WASPiest towns in Canada. In
a high school of over 1,200 students, my brother, sister and I are three out of a
handful of Indian kids.

We are over-achievers and over-involved. Race doesn't seem to be an issue. 13
How can it be when many of the parents of our White friends are more proud of
us than they their own children? My Indianness is virtually invisible.

Every once in a while my sister and I plead with my mother to let us wear 14
"Canadian" clothes (whatever that means) when we go to Indian community functions. On the odd occasion when we lose that battle, we implore my father not to
take the car out of the garage before we get in, lest the neighbours spot us dressed
up in our elaborate outfits.

Every few months my parents tell us that only Punjabi will be spoken at 15
home. My brother and I repeat meaningless phrases in Punjabi. My parents' valiant
attempt doesn't last a day and even they revert to English as quickly as we do.

I go on my second summer vacation to India and impress my relatives with 16
my extensive knowledge of apartheid and South Africa. My aunt tells me that India
has its own form of apartheid. I do not understand what she means.

Fast forward to university. It's like waking from a long, deep and blissful sleep. 17

I get my nose pierced and everything seems to change. A simple nose pin has 18
made it easier for others to pin down who they think I am or should be. On campus—aside from the occasional "That's gross!" or "Did it hurt?"—I am hoisted to
cool, hip, activist status. (And to think all it took was a little body mutilation.)

I am no longer invisible but instead over-exposed. How many quotas, sur- 19
vey and committee requirements will I fill? How many liberal consciences will my
presence ease?

I feel constantly bombarded by surveys in the media (the *Globe and Mail* is 20
particularly prompt at reporting such "news") saying the majority of Canadians
want immigrants to assimilate. I'm an immigrant. What am I supposed to do?

Assimilate more? "They don't mean you," someone tells me. "You're not an immigrant. You're Canadian."

It's not enough any more for me to say that I am Canadian. No innate sense 21 of pride overwhelms me with that statement—no chills down my spine, no special history or traditions that cross my mind. If I tell someone over the phone, "I am Canadian," what image is conjured up? On its own, it's an empty identity.

It is a relief when I meet and become friends with a woman who also feels 22 lost, confused and isolated. It is as if a burden has been lifted. There is no need to explain the "background" when we exchange stories. I feel as if I have known her my entire life.

We tell each other stories about being in class and having certain expecta- 23 tions placed on us because our Indian identity is the first and only thing people see.

I am supposed to have a deeper understanding of Anita Desai and Salman 24 Rushdie novels because the novels take place where I was born. But the truth is, I relate more to Hanif Kureishi's short stories and to movies made by second-generation South-Asian Canadians, where characters are pinned in a space between their parents' traditions and their immediate environment, than I do to tales of colonialism and imperialism. It is in the former works that the predicament of floating in an undefined space is discussed with the seriousness and complexity it deserves. Having my experience reflected in a book or on the screen gives me courage and confidence, it is comforting, it legitimises an experience that is usually difficult to articulate, and it substantiates what most people refuse to admit exists.

What others don't realise is that mine is an identity and a culture in the mak- 25 ing. It's recognizing that both where I come from and where I am form my identity, and it's about being neither invisible nor over-exposed. It's about understanding that identity needn't have to be about fitting into someone else's mould or definition. If I can't be a part of the South-Asian community in Canada because they think I'm "too Canadian," and I don't quite fit into the mainstream Canadian culture, then I must seek and cultivate a community with others who realise that their identity won't be compromised for the sake of those who find it necessary to label and define us as something we are not.

As hyphenated Canadians we are somewhere in the middle, riding the hy- 26 phen, and we must create our own cultures, our own identities and tell our histories and stories with our own voices.

I feel sick when I think of the lengths I and many others have gone to, to as- 27 similate, to fit in, but I guess it's no surprise because no one wants to stand out. But there was no real reason, no justification. It was just something you did—no questions asked.

1997

QUESTIONS FOR DISCUSSION

Content

a. Why is Bains upset by her boss's "cultural sensitivity"?
b. Why does Bains mention the Air India disaster?
c. Why does Bains not understand her aunt when her aunt tells her that "India has its own form of apartheid"?
d. What does Bains mean when she says that being Canadian is "an empty identity"?
e. What does the title mean, "Riding the Hyphen"?

Strategy and Style

f. Why does Bains open with the anecdote? What is the effect of this anecdote on you as a reader?
g. How do we feel when we read that Bains forgets Punjabi and adopts an anglicized version of her own name?
h. How does Bains show her resistance to Indian culture in the section about her high school years?
i. Why does Bains describe university as "waking from a long, deep and blissful sleep"?
j. Does Bains want to stand out or fit in?

SUGGESTIONS FOR SHORT WRITING

a. Write about your own efforts to conform or resist conformity.
b. Do you identify yourself with a cultural or ethnic group? Discuss your relationship with this identity.
c. Most English-speaking Canadians have some relationship with a language other than English. If you still speak or read this language, discuss its importance to you. If you do not, discuss your feelings about the loss of this aspect of your heritage.

SUGGESTIONS FOR SUSTAINED WRITING

a. Examine the history of multiculturalism as a policy. Does the policy encourage the notion of "riding the hyphen"? Does the policy allow for being "Canadian"?
b. This essay comes from an anthology titled . . . *but where are you really from?* Have you heard this question asked of someone or has it been addressed to you? Discuss the meaning of this question. What do people communicate when they ask it? Why is this question important? What does this question tell us about our society? Try to use actual, not hypothetical, examples to illustrate your point.

Don't Get Comfortable

Naton Leslie

Naton Leslie (b. 1956) teaches at Siena College in Loudonville, New York. He has published essays and poetry in the North American Review, *the* Ohio Review, *and the* Kansas Quarterly, *among other periodicals in the United States. "Don't Get Comfortable" is from his collection entitled* Places Cursed by John Brown and Other Essays on History.

This story is about a railroad detective named Charley Best. Best worked in the 1920s on the narrow-gauge lines between Pittsburgh and the lumber and mining hill towns of northwestern Pennsylvania. My father tells this story and said his father told it to him, having known Best or known others who knew him. Or maybe my grandfather rode those rails to work in the camps; I know he worked for the railroad, lighting kerosene lamps on the bridge over the Allegheny River and during winter breaking ice from cables that hoisted lanterns high above the girders. 1

My father tells that story too, how when he was five years old his father would take him out at night when he made his rounds on the bridge over the Allegheny in Mahoning, Pennsylvania. His father would climb over the side, hanging on to the slick catwalk while he broke cables free after an ice storm. The night would be filled with frigid gusts, and the wind was particularly strong that high above the river. On the swaying iron bridge my grandfather ordered my father to "take a holt" of the side railing. He was never frightened during these trips because his father was so strong, sure-footed, and careful. It must have been like watching an athlete, my grandfather climbing catlike over the rail, hitting the ice-bound cables with steady blows from the ball-peen. He was a compact man, and every movement, every swing of the hammer, seemed to come from the center of his body. 2

This was 1934, and my grandfather was lucky to have this bit of a job, this small paycheck, in the mountains of Pennsylvania where no farm made it, where the mines had begun to play out. So, though the job was dangerous and hard, he did it, and because I remember my grandfather as a meticulous man, I'm sure he did it well. Why he took my father along is less clear, though my grandmother may have asked him to get him out of her hair for a while, not realizing the danger, or perhaps my grandfather assumed his son would have to do the job someday. He'd been taught how to plant, to shoe horses, to make medicines, and to build outbuildings by his own father on the homestead farm. Perhaps my grandfather was teaching his son about the railroad. 3

Once, as my father tells it, a train crossed the bridge while they were on it. It was a bitterly cold, moonless night, and the lanterns seemed to light only the barest arc of the old iron bridge. My grandfather was hanging from a side rail, breaking ice and edging a cable through the pulley, when the headlamp of the train broke the darkness. He hollered to my father to hop over the side of the bridge and hold on, to "get a purchase and don't let go no matter what." Then, as the train caused the bridge to quake and sway, my father felt his father's arm around him 4

41

and his own weight release from his arms as his father held them both by one arm, sixty feet above the icy Allegheny. "Imagine," my father says when he tells the story, "a five-year-old boy and I wasn't even scared," though I wonder if he says that in tribute to his naive courage or in acknowledgment of trusting his father so utterly that fear never occurred to him.

I don't know where my grandfather heard of Charley Best. The area was 5 sparsely populated; it had been homesteaded in the mid-nineteenth century and remained wholly wilderness until the first oil well in the nation, the Drake Well, was drilled in Titusville. Those who worked in the lumber and mining camps, and later in oil fields and railroad yards, were all like Charley Best and my grandfather, raised on hardscrabble farms in the Allegheny Mountains, farms now part of the Allegheny National Forest, a mixed old-growth-second-growth wilderness replacing their hard-won clearings and plantings. They were coarse, often violent people for whom fighting was merely another kind of work. For Charley Best, his work became violence. Best had a fierce reputation, and my father, who used to see him at Walker's store in Mahoning, said he looked the part. The railroad detective bought cigars at Walker's, and even there he carried a sidearm, what my father thought was an enormous Colt. He was a big man, and my father also remembers his wide hat, the high leather boots with the pant cuffs tucked inside, and the huge chain stretched across his chest, Prince Albert style, upon which hung a nickel-plated railroad watch my father thought was as big as an alarm clock. Mostly, though, he remembers that handgun and a handlebar mustache Best had cultivated to curl around his wide face. My father poses as Best as he tells the story, striding the catwalks and tops of railcars, wind whipping his mustache back like flames. But it's the same picture he paints of his grandfather, Doc, one of the original homesteaders in Forest County. We have a photograph of him, published in a volume of local history, his reportedly immense size diminished by a team of oxen behind him, that same mustache flaring like horns.

My father heard a story about Doc at the funeral of one of his uncles, and in 6 it his mustache and oxen are part of the scenery. Doc Leslie had taken cattle into Brookville, Pennsylvania, to sell. Later, while he was having a drink at the Sigel Hotel, one of the men from town said, "Aren't you scared traveling all the way back to Blue Jay Ridge with that much money on you, Doc?"

My father doesn't say what Doc said back—some grunt or mumble through 7 his mustache—but later, on Blood Road in his oxcart, Doc was jumped by three men wearing bandannas, like the outlaws they had read about in dime novels.

It was only a joke. These were friends of Doc's, out only to put a scare in 8 him, but when one of them said "Stick 'em up," Doc replied, "Stick 'em up, hell. There'll be feet up and shit flying," as he leaped from the cart, scattering the men with his bullwhip. When my father tells it, he pantomimes rolling up one sleeve to signify the fight, his eyes fierce and fixed. The story is frozen at that point: Doc poised for action, the flight of the men inevitable.

Part of Charley Best's story is arrested as well. Best patrolled the tops of 9 railcars as they sped across the hills toward the coal fields. My father said those who hopped trains rode Charley's line only twice: the first time you were warned, and if you took Detective Best's warning with humility, you got where you wanted to go. But Best remembered, and the second time he caught you riding free, you were off.

"Off?" I once asked, interrupting my father for once as he told the story. His 10 irritation was clear.

"Yeah, *off*," he said, his arms poised in the act of grabbing someone by the 11 scruff of the neck and back of the trousers. I remembered a postcard drawn by Wobbly leader Joe Hill, a comic portrait of himself being booted from a train, and had less admiration for Best and more sympathy for the hoboes who just wanted a ride and ended up flying.

I could see them soaring, sprawling like skydivers over the empty air of the 12 railroad cut, over the sixty-foot drop from the bridge in Mahoning. I've always been hesitant about heights—not actually frightened, only concerned and reluctant about climbing, a controllable vertigo. Not that I have suffered many spectacular falls. Once I fell off, or more accurately, ran off, the top of an extension ladder when a wasp landed on my nose. I simply turned around, stepped off the top of the ladder, and began to run, heading straight down to a gravel parking lot of the car dealership where I was working. I was pretty skinned up, landing on my forearms to protect my face from the gravel, and my coworker, a young biker named Rocky, said, "Man, did you crash 'n' burn!" Perhaps I got this timidity from my mother, who also shied from heights. I remember my father, mother, older sister, and myself climbing a fire tower in the Allegheny Mountains. My mother and I made it about halfway up when the open sides and the lack of a railing sent me back down. My father and sister made it to the top, and I watched from the ground as they laughed and climbed impossibly higher.

My sister trusted my wild and unpredictable father and would follow him, 13 while my trust in him had limits. Probably he had learned not to fear heights from his father on that railroad bridge; he even took a job as a tree-topper for a lumber company and later as a lineman for the power company. When he was sixteen he got a job as a ground hand, or "ground squirrel," as they called the young boys who dragged limbs by the butt to the burn pile. He grew to love the work, part of the postwar rural electrification program, and when not piling brush he watched the men high in trees worrying off limbs with bow saws.

Finally he got his own climbing gear: long hooks like bayonets that 14 strapped to his high-topped boots and a wide leather belt to wrap around tree trunks. He got so good he'd climb a tree, and eventually a utility pole, with only his hooks and hands on the trunk, using the belt only when he reached the top. He said he loved heights; on top of a tree on a mountain he said he could see all of Forest County, see deer move in herds and bears trailing cubs on the ridge miles away. Working for the power company, my father climbed poles on wide rights of way cut across the mountains, high power lines carrying thousands of volts from transformer substations to light lamps in a farmhouse on remote Blue Jay Ridge.

But he fell. Twice. The first time, he says, they were putting up new lines on 15
poles in residential Brookville. Poles were originally treated with creosote to prevent decay, a dark, oil-based coating that smelled vaguely of kerosene and urine,
now outlawed in favor of a pressure treatment with brine. These were old poles,
put up at the turn of the century during the first wave of utility construction, and
that morning my father climbed the first one. He says he had just hooked on his
belt and was looking up at the late autumn sky, a mix of clouds and high blue. He
thought, "Those clouds sure are moving fast," and then he realized it was he who
was moving, not the clouds, as the pole was falling, breaking off at the rotten base.
He tells how he managed to take off his belt and scamper to the other side, riding
the pole to the ground as it bent, then snapped.

The other time he fell was more dangerous, and more miraculous. He was at 16
the top of a forty-five-foot pole, and according to the newspaper article from the
Oil City Derrick his belt snapped and he pitched backward. My father says that after he felt the belt give he reached for the crossarm. His fingertips barely reached
the class insulators on his right, but he was unable to grasp them or the wooden
beam, and he fell. He flipped backward twice in the air, landed on his feet,
bounced, and fell on his side. He stood up, apparently unhurt, but when he tried to
unbuckle his tool harness he found the fingers on his left hand would not work; he
had broken his wrist in two places. Later he would develop severe back problems
and would suffer years of pain, caused I'm sure by that jarring fall, though he never
seemed to connect the two.

He doesn't tell either of those stories often. You don't tell stories that could 17
have ended so finally. I heard him once admit to waking up in the middle of the night,
years later, a dream of fingertips grazing the crossarm tearing him into sweaty wake-
fulness. And these stories are among the few illustrating a point or a moral. My father would sometimes say, after telling one of these stories, that there's only one
thing you need to know to do "high work": "Don't get comfortable." What he means
goes beyond the commonplace "Keep your wits about you." It's the lesson I forgot
when I ran off the top of that ladder—whenever doing anything high up, do it with
the knowledge of where you are. I use this advice whenever I work on ladders or
roofs—whenever I am moving about and stop thinking about being up high, I force
myself to remember, I stop and say aloud, "Don't get comfortable."

Charley Best would not have told his own story either. Perhaps that's why 18
others told the story for him. My father claims he grew mean and that his father did
not like Best, not because he threw men off trains but because he shot a twelve-year-
old boy in the back for stealing coal from the railyard at night. The boy, a homeless
child the railroad workers called Hard Rock Pete, hung around the railyards, and
the gandy dancers and switch operators often shared their lunches with him, casually adopting him. My grandfather said he was shy and weak, and they all assumed
he slept in abandoned works shacks or boxcars in the yard. Best, my grandfather
claimed, saw the boy at night, stooping over and pulling lumps of coal into a shirt
hooped to make a sack. Best claimed at the investigation that he couldn't tell it was

Hard Rock Pete—the boy was tall and wore bulky clothes that late fall evening, hiding his frail frame. When he stood up and lit a cigarette, Best saw him, and when the detective's menacing voiced called out, the boy ran. That's when Charley Best shot him with the big Colt.

But that's not the story of Charley Best my father often tells; that's another   19
story, or actually part of the longer version of the story, because it shows how mean Best got afterward, how what happened changed him. I remember once my father was telling the story at my grandmother Harnish's house, a gathering of men in his mother-in-law's parlor listening, among them Sam, her second husband, who in the last year had been forced to sit on the couch with an oxygen tank beside him, alternately reaching for the hose and mask to give him the oxygen black lung denied him and bending over, panting with effort, to spit tobacco juice into a plastic bucket.

My father began telling the story sitting down, but was standing by the time   20
he began describing Best, the Harnish men listening closely though they had heard the story before, while I sat watching the story being retold as I leaned forward in the straight-backed chair moved into the room and parked near the television. I had recently turned thirteen and was splitting my time between the room where adult men sat, talking slowly, and the cousins outside exploring the forty-acre farm I had already mapped over the years of visits. Sam's son Warren had finally finished a long-winded story that made my father edgy and restless, and how he had managed to get to the story of Charley Best I'm not sure, but the story was well under way.

Best had been assigned jurisdiction, lacking any other police, over several min-   21
ing camps in northwestern Pennsylvania, and was sent to arrest a miner in Chickasaw, near the New York border, who was accused of stealing. My father added that he probably only had stolen coal from the railyard, as everyone did in the 1930s. Warren interrupted briefly to tell how he and his brothers stole coal from the Clarion yards, but my father skillfully steered the conversation back to Best.

"Chickasaw was a rough mining camp, just up the river from Mahoning, and   22
Charley Best was sent there, where there was no other law, to arrest that miner," he began again, and everyone leaned comfortably back into the story, glad Warren had been stopped. He explained how Best arrived in town, Colt revolver displayed prominently, cigar under his ample mustache, and how he walked over to the tavern, a slapped-up, long and low shed affair, where he assumed he would find the thief. The men inside sat on rough stools, and the ceiling of plank was held up with twelve-inch rough-cut beams. "One of them eyes Best, and Best figured that was him and that he'd have to slug it out with the miner to take him." My father's eyes grew narrow and menacing.

I'd heard this story many times and knew the men in the room had heard it   23
too; they were sitting through the telling as though it were a ritual, a stage in their conversation they always reached, and passed. But then an unexpected reaction from Sam drew their attention from my father, who was perched on his knees at the end of the story. Sam did not speak much in those last years because speech was breath, and each breath was bought with larger portions of his strength. Yet

there in the room filled with his sons and the husbands of his daughters, he pushed out a hurried "Yes," and quickly drawing on the oxygen as the heads of the men turned to him, added, "I drove those miners to Chickasaw every day in an old buck-board—they were usually drunk. A rough, wild bunch," he said, spitting a brown stream and reaching for the hose again. "Yes, that's how it happened."

My father never worked in the mines, so was spared the black lung from 24 which Sam and so many others suffered, but he often spoke of the mines as though he had worked there, as he had lived among the miners, played with their children, fought with their sons, and eventually drunk and laughed with them after work on the power lines. In his father's day the miners began forming unions, and these hardened men formed even harder coal-black clumps of strikers. One of them, Piercy MacIntyre, was an organizer and therefore was even rougher than most. The bosses in Chickasaw claimed he had been sent in from the outside, an agitator, but some of the men said he came from around Blue Jay Ridge, from a hill farm so far back "the owls carried knapsacks."

My father had met Piercy MacIntyre, but he knew his son Jackie better. The 25 miners said Piercy had been a boxer in France during World War I, and whether true or not, he did teach his son Jackie how to box. He'd take the boy, eight or nine years old, down to Walker's store, and men would clear a makeshift ring in the cor-ner, moving stock to form a rough square. Walker would then hold the bets as Jackie's opponent, usually an older boy of twelve or so, was announced. My fa-ther claims Jackie beat all comers, and my father, younger by two or three years, always rooted for him as fervently as he did for Joe Louis when his father would struggle to pick up Louis's fights through the static on KDKA radio. He tells how Louis knocked out Max Schmeling, the Nazi superman, so quickly that once they got the station in, all they heard was the count to ten.

Twenty-five years later, after my father had moved one hundred miles away to 26 work in the mills of Ohio, he ran into Jackie MacIntyre at Republic Steel. He spoke to him, and though Jackie, now John, didn't remember him as one of his youngest fans among the dozens or more who had watched him fight as a kid, my father said they talked briefly of people they knew, even about Charley Best. My father said he was puzzled to see how the guys in the mill picked on him, and MacIntyre didn't seem to care. My father thought, "You guys don't know who you're dealing with."

Although my father had moved to the edge of the industrial Midwest, the 27 mountains and forests remained home to him, and we went back every weekend to visit. And he hunted in Pennsylvania, not along the industrial riverbanks of Ohio. My father liked only two sports, boxing and hunting, and he tried to teach me both. I never caught on to boxing, partly because my father couldn't coach me while we sparred without beginning to fight in earnest, burying me in a flurry of open-palmed combinations and jabs. I liked the fluidity of the movements, the backpedaling, the duck-and-jab; however, I was not destined to be a boxer. I have a glass jaw, a nerve positioned in my face that makes a knockout a matter of one punch. My father found this fatal flaw one day while we sparred in the living room. One quick jab to my left jaw and I felt nothing—I saw pinpoints of light and awoke to my father shaking his head and saying, "The kid's got a glass jaw." As a boxer I was finished.

But hunting was another matter. Early on, my father declared I was a natu- 28
ral good shot, that I had a "good eye" that made up, I suppose, for my bad jaw. I cold pick off pennies at twenty-five yards with a .22 caliber rifle, and after I got a shotgun, a 16-gauge, my father spent one long afternoon throwing clay pigeons, which I shot out of the air. He threw more than seventy, and I missed two. I enjoyed target shooting not only because I was good at it but because I did it without thinking. I simply knew when I was on target and then pulled the trigger. I guess it was instinct or something reflexive.

Yet, by age eighteen, I had pretty much lost interest in hunting. Animals 29
made poor targets; they were hard to find, but when found, too big and easy. For a target shooter, walking all day for one shot at an easy target was not much of a thrill. I still went hunting with my father when in my teens, but I had no real enthusiasm for the sport, as he did. I tried to find it; I remember not eating one day, thinking that it would make me a keener hunter, but it only made me a hungry one. What I liked was the evening, getting comfortable down at Archie's camp, near his stone fireplace, listening to hunting stories.

The last time I went hunting with my father I was eighteen. I hadn't been 30
deer hunting that last fall because the season fell during final exam week at college, and it was with some relief that I realized this would happen every year. However, I went hunting for turkey that spring. I think I liked turkey hunting most because the hunt occurred in midautumn and midspring, the two most beautiful times of the year to be in the forest. You also could go deeper into the woods because, unlike a deer, once a turkey was shot it was not hard to pull it out of the woods. Dragging a hundred pounds of deer carcass over several miles of rough terrain quickly dampened the thrill of the hunt.

It was a cold April in the mountains that year; patches of snow still clung to 31
rocks and roots in the forest, and springs remained frozen, even in the bright sunshine. My father led the way through the woods we hunted north of Brookville, stepping around the icy stones and fallen limbs with sure-footed grace and speed. Every hour or so we would stop and cradle our shotguns, and my father would bring out the wooden turkey call, a cedar box with a top that wagged loosely when shaken, chalk between box and lid giving off a decent gobble.

The turkey call was a new addition to our hunting gear. My father had never 32
gone in for gimmicks as a hunter, although he thought my aunt Clair's trick of rubbing apple cores on her boots to attract deer might account for her yearly success. However, in the over twenty-five years he had been hunting, he had never bagged a wild turkey. He was well known among the locals for regularly bringing out a deer. He'd have a deer within the first couple of hours of the opening day of the season and could be found down at Archie's camp or at the Sigel Hotel by early afternoon, telling how the deer, never a trophy buck but respectable, would have risen from his bed twenty-five yards from my father's stand at first light. But turkeys had

always eluded him, so he bought the call and had been practicing for months, brief chirps and throaty gobbles rising from our basement ever since September.

That day we had walked farther into the woods than usual, so far that we found ourselves on Windfall Ridge, or so it was called on my father's topo map. The ridge was steep and treeless, and the North Fork Creek ran noisily below. My father had noticed a stand of beech, and knowing turkey like beechnuts, we had stopped to look for signs. Sure enough, my father found a large patch where turkey had been scratching the winter-decayed leaves, a large flock probably discovered and broken up by other hunters earlier in the morning. The turkeys would still be in the area, scattered over Windfall, calling out to regroup. We stood and listened, but all I heard was the icy North Fork and a high wind in the trees. 33

So my father decided to try calling them in, making first a few hesitant chirps, then a long and short gobble that he'd heard was the turkey equivalent of "I'm over here." 34

And a turkey answered. The bird sounded like it was on the edge of the ridge, about fifty yards in front of us, but neither of us could see it. We walked cautiously toward the sound, my heart pounding for my father, hoping he'd at long last get a shot at the turkey. As we reached the ridge we split, my father wandering to the right of a tall pine growing in the fragile earth of the rim of the ridge, I to the left. The turkey flew out of the tree in a great bluster of wings. It flew left and was clearly my shot. 35

I snapped up my shotgun and found him quickly, flying high but in range. Then I thought about it. I wished the bird had flown right, to give my father the shot, wished it was not flying over the icy-filmed North Fork into which I would surely have to wade, waist high, to retrieve the bird. And I knew I did not want to kill the turkey; I had no need of it. 36

So I shot behind it, the bird's wings flapping comically faster after the sound echoed over the ridge. The turkey flew higher, out of range of another shot from me or my father, not landing until it reached the next ridge. I turned to look at my father, who said, "How'd you miss him?" 37

"Jerked the trigger, I think," I said, still looking over at the ridge where the bird had disappeared. "Or choked; I don't know," I added. 38

"Hell, a good shot like you must have hit him," he said. "Maybe he went down with a few shot in him." 39

"Nah, he was too high up, out of range," I answered, not wanting to have to wade the creek anyway and hike the next ridge looking for the bird. 40

But we did cross the creek, over the back of a windfallen tree, and after searching for the bird for a while decided we had had our shot for the day and gave up. It was midafternoon, and it was a long way back, and I, having slipped into the North Fork on the return crossing, wearily tramped behind my father, one boot sloshing with creek water. 41

By the time we arrived at the Sigel Hotel my father was convinced I had hit the gobbler but that, as he said, "death is invisible, while life can be seen." A slain 42 animal is still, and the natural camouflage is perfect. He believed we didn't find a dead turkey because it blended in with the rocks and undergrowth.

At the Sigel Hotel we sat at the long bar, adding our hunting outfits of red wool caps and canvas game vests to those of other hunters gathered there. My father began telling the story of our hunt to the man at his right elbow, and eventually to two or three down the counter. "The boy here got a shot, and I know he hit him—you should have seen the feathers fly! This kid is a great wingshot," he continued, telling of my slaughter of clay pigeons.

The other men answered his story with others, and through that, through the progress of stories to the next, he began telling the story of Charley Best. "He walked into this bar, a smoky place with a low ceiling supported by big, twelve-inch rough-cut post," he said, his hands surrounding one in the air, "rough like everything else in those camps."

Best looked around the smoky room, and when he spotted the man eyeing him he said, "You'd better finish that drink, because you're coming with me. You're under arrest."

The man sat with his stool tipped backward against a post, and when Best approached he said, "Well, I guess you're going to have to pull that big revolver, because I'm not going anywhere." Best was standing over him, and my father was on his feet in the Sigel Hotel, doing his best to look down at me as Best must have glared at the miner.

Then my father said, "The guy suddenly pulls a knife, cuts Best across the gut, and slips behind the thick post." My father's knees buckle.

Best was not used to working in the camps, so he was out of his element and forgot to watch himself. He was too comfortable, my father would say, and should have reminded himself that Chickasaw was a rough mining camp and that the man he sought could be armed and was drunk, that he was not simply approaching a frightened hobo on top of a rushing train. At this point my father's voice became a little squeezed, imitating the pain of the knife wound, but he continued, "He cut Best clear across the stomach, and his guts bulged and began to spill. With his left arm Best reached down and pulled his own guts back in, and with the right drew his gun and shot the miner." My father was fully on his knees now, his arm and hand holding in intestines, his other arm raising a Colt revolver.

"He hit him in the mouth. Killed him deader than hell."

This is where the story of Charley Best generally ends, though sometimes my father tells how they took him by train to a hospital in Brookville, how he got mean after that. But with my father on his knees, clutching his stomach in agony, this is when Charley Best appeared, or should have. He could have been a little fellow, age having shrunken him, a glass of clay-colored liquor in front of him at the bar, his mustache trimmed to a salt-and-pepper line under his nose. He'd sit near the opposite end of the counter, listening to but not telling his own story.

Best wouldn't wear hunting clothes. He'd stand up and, pulling out his flannel shirttails, say, "That's just the way it happened." Then he'd raise his shirt quickly, and we'd see the brutish pucker circling his waist. When Best sat back down he would drain the liquor in front of him, no one noticing that his left arm rested across his lap and against his body, holding the organs in, still trying to get comfortable with the wound.

1996

QUESTIONS FOR DISCUSSION

Content

a. In paragraph 3, the author tells us that in 1934 his grandfather was lucky to have a job. What circumstances or period is he referring to?

b. What does Charley Best's story have in common with other stories in this essay?

c. In what way was Charley Best similar to the author's grandfather and great-grandfather and their contemporaries? Begin your answer with reference to paragraph 5.

d. The narrator tells us a great deal about his father, grandfather, and great-grandfather. Explain what he also reveals about his own character.

e. Discuss the relationship that the narrator had with his father.

f. The thesis of this essay is expressed concisely in its three-word title. Citing details from the text, expand on that statement by explaining Leslie's point and purpose in this essay.

Strategy and Style

g. Why does the author tell about his and his father's falling from heights? How do these stories help the reader understand Charley Best? How do they help develop the essay's thesis?

h. The introduction and conclusion of this essay seem to reflect some uncertainty. Explain how and why the author expresses that uncertainty.

i. "Don't Get Comfortable" uses an introduction different from those found in other selections of this type. The essay begins by mentioning Charley Best, then quickly moves to stories about the author's father and grandfather before returning to Best in paragraph 5. What is it about the first four paragraphs that holds our attention?

j. Unlike other narratives in this chapter, "Don't Get Comfortable" does not follow a conventional plot line (events proceeding from beginning to end without interruption). The story of Charley Best is interrupted several times with other interesting tales, which apparently have nothing to do with it. Take a few minutes to outline the plot of this story; then, explain why the author has inserted these tales.

k. Where does the author use humour? What function does it serve in this essay?
l. In what way is the structure of this essay (not its contents) reflective of its title and thesis?
m. What does the author's tone reveal about the audience for this essay?

SUGGESTIONS FOR SHORT WRITING

a. Read Samuel Metcalfe's "Wooding" in Chapter 2. Compare the way these two writers reveal their narratives. Discuss whether they are aiming at similar purposes.
b. Read Lee Maracle's "Survival Work" in Chapter 6. In what ways is this essay similar to and different from "Don't Get Comfortable"?

SUGGESTIONS FOR SUSTAINED WRITING

a. Using your own experiences and/or the experiences of people you know well, write an essay that develops the same thesis as Leslie's "Don't Get Comfortable." You might choose a number of short tales or anecdotes to illustrate your thesis, or you might tell one longer story in full. Either way, make sure that all of the details that you include relate directly to your thesis. Finally, state the thesis in an introduction that, like Leslie's, captures and holds the reader's attention.
b. Narrate an exciting or frightening experience like one of the ones Leslie tells in his essay. This story need not be taken from personal experience; incidents from the history of your family or your community might work just as well. However you choose to approach this assignment, make your story exciting and colourful. Try using the kind of language and detail Leslie uses to re-create the incident in which his father and grandfather nearly fell off a railroad bridge or the one in which Charley Best was knifed by a miner.
c. Read your responses to the Suggestions for Short Writing. Extend one of them into a fully developed essay.

2

Description

Description makes for diversity. The people, places, and things described in the eight selections that follow vary as widely as the distinctive styles and perspectives of their authors. Nonetheless, each essay is a portrait sketched in details that are at once concrete, specific, and vivid.

Good description is never hurried; it is crafted with carefully chosen details that *show* the reader something. Take "Where the World Began," for example. Not content to tell us that watching the hometown fire company answer an alarm was "exciting, colourful, and noisy," Margaret Laurence savours the moment and helps us do the same:

> . . . the wooden tower's bronze bell would clonk and toll like a
> thousand speeded funerals in a time of plague, and in a few minutes
> the team of giant black horses would cannon forth, pulling the fire
> wagons like some scarlet chariot of the Goths, while the firemen
> clung with one hand, adjusting their helmets as they went.

Appealing to the senses—in this case sight and sound—is fundamental to the process of describing. Some writers rely almost solely upon vision and hearing as sources of descriptive detail, but the authors in this chapter teach us that we can use the other senses as well—taste, smell, and touch—to guide readers through our private worlds. Indeed, Simeti's "Easter in Sicily" invites us to a banquet for all the senses. As a result, we come away with a genuine taste of the place.

The above excerpt from "Where the World Began" also shows that writers of description exploit techniques often associated with narration, especially the use of verbs that are informative and evocative. More important, Laurence's use of figurative language—her comparison of the alarm to the sounds of bells at a "thousand speeded funerals," for example—reminds us that invoking facts and images from the knowledge we share with readers is a good way to show them something new. Flashes of brilliance appear throughout the chapter. Virginia Woolf's reference to the "narrow and intricate corridors" of her brain, for example, testifies to the power and clarity with which she invests her writing.

While relying heavily on physical description, none of the essays collected here is a purely sensate record of its subject. More often than not, describing is a means to an end. It is hard to read a narrative, for example, without stumbling over details that reveal setting and character. Even writers of scientific prose use information that appeals to the senses as a way to discuss the lives of plants and animals or to explore the workings of machines and processes.

Whether they are describing people, places, or things, the authors in this chapter use description to reveal the character or capture the essence of their subjects, though their purpose may not be immediately apparent. Consider Doris Lessing, who transcends physical appearance to expose the psychology of her father by allowing him to speak to us directly and by recalling his memories, his dreams, and his failures. Fascinating anecdotes and dialogue also enrich Laurence's portrait of home, allowing us to understand the place that nurtured the author and helped form her character. And Mary Taylor Simeti's vivid evocation of Easter festivals in Sicily reveals her ability to manipulate narrative and descriptive details brilliantly as she explores the unique character of her adopted homeland.

Like other writers in this chapter, Joan Didion and Hugh MacLennan remind us that discussing the people who inhabit a place is a way to reveal its soul. Finally, in recalling the death of a moth Virginia Woolf engages a seemingly banal subject not simply to describe an exterior reality but to tell us about herself, the real subject of her essay. Of course, something of this can also be said of MacLennan and Laurence.

As always, you are invited to make your own comparisons and to draw conclusions as you see fit. What makes the selections in this chapter so enjoyable is that each reveals the strong and distinctive voice of its author. Enjoy the artists behind the subjects they describe. They will teach you that your personal commitment to a subject—the "wonder" with which it fills you, Woolf might say—is worth sharing with others.

Where the World Began

Margaret Laurence

Born in Manitoba, Margaret (Wemyss) Laurence (1926–1987) was one of Canada's foremost novelists, essayists, and writers of short fiction and of children's books. She based much of her work on her travels in Africa and on her life in the small Canadian prairie town in which she was born. The former yielded A Tree for Poverty *(1954), a translation of Somali poems and stories she gathered during two years in the harsh Haud desert;* This Side Jordan *(1960), a novel;* The Tomorrow Tamer and Other Stories *(1963); and* The Prophet's Camel Bell *(1963), a travel memoir. Neepawa, the hometown that she renamed Manawaka in her fiction, figures in* The Stone Angel *(1964);* A Jest of God *(1966), republished as* Rachel, Rachel; Fire Dwellers *(1969); and* A Bird in the House *(1970). It is on the Manawaka books that Laurence's fame chiefly rests. However, she is also noted for her essays, a collection of which she published as* Heart of a Stranger *(1976). In a* Book Forum, *John Caldwell cited "the search for the lost Eden, for Jerusalem the Golden, for the promised land of one's own freedom" as an important ingredient in her work. For Laurence, that little prairie town "Where the World Began" might very well have contained the "promised land."*

A strange place it was, that place where the world began. A place of incredible 1
happenings, splendors, and revelations, despairs like multitudinous pits of isolated hells. A place of shadow-spookiness, inhabited by the unknowable dead. A place of jubilation and of mourning, horrible and beautiful.

It was, in fact, a small prairie town. 2

Because that settlement and that land were my first and for many years my 3
only real knowledge of this planet, in some profound way they remain my world, my way of viewing. My eyes were formed there. Towns like ours, set in a sea of land, have been described thousands of times as dull, bleak, flat, uninteresting. I have had it said to me that the railway trip across Canada is spectacular, except for the prairies, when it would be desirable to go to sleep for several days, until the ordeal is over. I am always unable to argue this point effectively. All I can say is— well, you really have to live there to know that country. The town of my childhood could be called bizarre, agonizingly repressive or cruel at times, and the land in which it grew could be called harsh in the violence of its seasonal changes. But never merely flat or uninteresting. Never dull.

In winter, we used to hitch rides on the back of the milk sleigh, our moc- 4
casins squeaking and slithering on the hard rutted snow of the roads, our hands in ice-bubbled mitts hanging onto the box edge of the sleigh for dear life, while Bert grinned at us through his great frosted mustache and shouted the horse into speed, daring us to stay put. Those mornings, rising, there would be the perpetual fascination of the frost feathers on windows, the ferns and flowers and eerie faces traced there during the night by unseen artists of the wind. Evenings, coming back from skating, the sky would be black but not dark, for you could see a cold glitter of stars from one side of the earth's rim to the other. And then the

54

sometime astonishment when you saw the Northern Lights flaring across the sky, like the scrawled signature of God. After a blizzard, when the snowplow hadn't yet got through, school would be closed for the day, the assumption being that the town's young could not possibly flounder through five feet of snow in the pursuit of education. We would then gaily don snowshoes and flounder for miles out into the white dazzling deserts, in pursuit of a different kind of knowing. If you came back too close to night, through the woods at the foot of the town hill, the thin black branches of poplar and chokecherry now meringued with frost, sometimes you heard coyotes. Or maybe the banshee wolf-voices were really only inside your head.

Summers were scorching, and when no rain came and the wheat became   5 bleached and dried before it headed, the faces of farmers and townsfolk would not smile much, and you took for granted, because it never seemed to have been any different, the frequent knocking at the back door and the young men standing there, mumbling or thrusting defiantly their requests for a drink of water and a sandwich if you could spare it. They were riding the freights, and you never knew where they had come from, or where they might end up, if anywhere. The Drought and Depression were like evil deities which had been there always. You understood and did not understand.

Yet the outside world had its continuing marvels. The poplar bluffs and the   6 small river were filled and surrounded with a zillion different grasses, stones, and weed flowers. The meadowlark sang undaunted from the twanging telephone wires along the gravel highway. Once we found an old flat-bottomed scow, and launched her, poling along the shallow brown waters, mending her with wodges of hastily chewed Spearmint, grounding her among the tangles of yellow marsh marigolds that grew succulently along the banks of the shrunken river, while the sun made our skins smell dusty-warm.

My best friend lived in an apartment above some stores on Main Street (its   7 real name was Mountain Avenue, goodness knows why), an elegant apartment with royal-blue velvet curtains. The back roof, scarcely sloping at all, was corrugated tin, of a furnace-like warmth on a July afternoon, and we would sit there drinking lemonade and looking across the back lane at the Fire Hall. Sometimes our vigil would be rewarded. Oh joy! Somebody's house burning down! We had an almost-perfect callousness in some ways. Then the wooden tower's bronze bell would clonk and toll like a thousand speeded funerals in a time of plague, and in a few minutes the team of giant black horses would cannon forth, pulling the fire wagon like some scarlet chariot of the Goths, while the firemen clung with one hand, adjusting their helmets as they went.

The oddities of the place were endless. An elderly lady used to serve, as her   8 afternoon tea offering to other ladies, soda biscuits spread with peanut butter and topped with a whole marshmallow. Some considered this slightly eccentric, when compared with chopped egg sandwiches, and admittedly talked about her behind her back, but no one ever refused these delicacies or indicated to her that they thought she had slipped a cog. Another lady dyed her hair a bright and cherry orange, by strangers often mistaken at twenty paces for a feather hat. My own beloved stepmother wore a silver fox neckpiece, a whole pelt, *with the embalmed (?) head still on.* My Ontario Irish grandfather said, "sparrow grass," a more interesting term than asparagus. The town dump was known as "the nuisance grounds," a phrase fraught with weird connotations, as though the effluvia of our lives was beneath contempt but at the same time was subtly threatening to the determined and sometimes hysterical propriety of our ways.

Some oddities were, as idiom had it, "funny ha ha"; others were "funny peculiar." Some were not so very funny at all. An old man lived, deranged, in a shack in the valley. Perhaps he wasn't even all that old, but to us he seemed a wild Methuselah figure, shambling among the underbrush and the tall couchgrass, muttering indecipherable curses or blessings, a prophet who had forgotten his prophecies. Everyone in town knew him, but no one knew him. He lived among us as though only occasionally and momentarily visible. The kids called him Andy Gump, and feared him. Some sought to prove their bravery by tormenting him. They were the medieval bear baiters, and he the lumbering bewildered bear, half blind, only rarely turning to snarl. Everything is to be found in a town like mine. Belsen, writ small but with the same ink. 9

All of us cast stones in one shape or another. In grade school, among the vulnerable and violet girls we were, the feared and despised were those few older girls from what was charmingly termed "the wrong side of the tracks." Tough in talk and tougher in muscle, they were said to be whores already. And may have been, that being about the only profession readily available to them. 10

The dead lived in that place, too. Not only the grandparents who had, in local parlance, "passed on" and who gloomed, bearded or bonneted, from the sepia photographs in old albums, but also the uncles, forever eighteen or nineteen, whose names were carved on the granite family stones in the cemetery, but whose bones lay in France. My own young mother lay in that graveyard, beside other dead of our kin, and when I was ten, my father, too, only forty, left the living town for the dead dwelling on the hill. 11

When I was eighteen, I couldn't wait to get out of that town, away from the prairies. I did not know then that I would carry the land and town all my life within my skull, that they would form the mainspring and source of the writing I was to do, wherever and however far away I might live. 12

This was my territory in the time of my youth, and in a sense my life since then has been an attempt to look at it, to come to terms with it. Stultifying to the mind it certainly could be, and sometimes was, but not to the imagination. It was many things, but it was never dull. 13

The same, I now see, could be said for Canada in general. Why on earth did generations of Canadians pretend to believe this country dull? We knew perfectly well it wasn't. Yet for so long we did not proclaim what we knew. If our upsurge of so-called nationalism seems odd or irrelevant to outsiders, and even to some of our own people (*what's all the fuss about?*), they might try to understand that for many years we valued ourselves insufficiently, living as we did under the huge 14 shadows of those two dominating figures, Uncle Sam and Britannia. We have only just begun to value ourselves, our land, our abilities. We have only just begun to recognize our legends and to give shape to our myths.

There are, God knows, enough aspects to deplore about this country. When 15 I see the killing of our lakes and rivers with industrial wastes, I feel rage and despair. When I see our industries and natural resources increasingly taken over by America, I feel an overwhelming discouragement, especially as I cannot simply say "damn Yankees." It should never be forgotten that it is we ourselves who have sold such a large amount of our birthright for a mess of plastic Progress. When I saw the War Measures Act being invoked in 1970, I lost forever the vestigial remains of the naïve wish-belief that repression could not happen here, or would not. And yet, of course, I had known all along in the deepest and often hidden caves of the heart that anything can happen anywhere, for the seeds of both man's freedom and his captivity are found everywhere, even in the microcosm of a prairie town. But in raging against our injustices, our stupidities, I do so *as family,* as I did, and still do in writing, about those aspects of my town which I hated and which are always in some ways aspects of myself.

The land still draws me more than other lands. I have lived in Africa and in 16 England, but splendid as both can be, they do not have the power to move me in the same way as, for example, that part of southern Ontario where I spent four months last summer in a cedar cabin beside a river. "Scratch a Canadian, and you find a phony pioneer," I used to say to myself in warning. But all the same it is true, I think, that we are not yet totally alienated from physical earth, and let us only pray we do not become so. I once thought that my lifelong fear and mistrust of cities made me a kind of old-fashioned freak; now I see it differently.

The cabin has a long window across its front western wall, and sitting at 17 the oak table there in the mornings, I used to look out at the river and at the tall trees beyond, green-gold in the early light. The river was bronze; the sun caught it strangely, reflecting upon its surface the near-shore sand ripples underneath. Suddenly, the crescenting of a fish, gone before the eye could clearly give image to it. The old man next door said these leaping fish were carp. Himself, he preferred muskie, for he was a real fisherman and the muskie gave him a fight. The wind most often blew from the south, and the river flowed toward the south, so when the water was windriffled, and the current was strong, the river seemed to be flowing both ways. I liked this, and interpreted it as an omen, a natural symbol.

A few years ago, when I was back in Winnipeg, I gave a talk at my old col- 18 lege. It was open to the public, and afterward a very old man came up to me and asked me if my maiden name had been Wemyss. I said yes, thinking he might have known my father or my grandfather. But no. "When I was a young lad," he said, "I once worked for your great-grandfather, Robert Wemyss, when he had the sheep ranch at Raeburn." I think that was a moment when I realized all over again something of great importance to me. My long-ago families came from Scotland and Ireland, but in a sense that no longer mattered so much. My true roots were here.

I am not very patriotic, in the usual meaning of that word. I cannot say "My   19
country right or wrong" in any political, social, or literary context. But one thing
is inalterable, for better or worse, for life.

This is where my world began. A world which includes the ancestors—both   20
my own and other people's ancestors who become mine. A world which formed
me, and continues to do so, even while I found it in some of its aspects, and continue to do so. A world which gave me my own lifework to do, because it was here
that I learned the sight of my own particular eyes.

1976

QUESTIONS FOR DISCUSSION

Content

a. Do you find Laurence's title intriguing? What exactly does she mean by it?
   Think about various Biblical allusions that John Caldwell, in the biography,
   makes in his remarks about Laurence.

b. The author's purpose goes beyond simply describing a prairie town. What is that
   purpose, and how does her use of descriptive details help her accomplish it?

c. How would you describe the audience to whom Laurence is writing?

d. What important distinction does Laurence draw in paragraph 3? Why is this
   distinction important? In what other parts of the essay does she allude to it?

e. In what way does her recollection of the "almost-perfect callousness" (paragraph 7) she possessed as a girl help develop the thesis? Why does she devote
   two entire paragraphs to "the oddities of the place" (paragraphs 8 and 9)?

f. What are the "Drought and Depression" mentioned in paragraph 5? In what
   ways does the author's mention of these "evil deities" help her recapture her
   childhood?

g. Who were "the young men . . . thrusting defiantly their requests for a drink of
   water and a sandwich" (paragraph 5)? What do they add to Laurence's description of her home?

h. In which of the world wars did the "uncles . . . whose bones lay in France" die
   (paragraph 11)? What are some of the context clues that help us determine the
   answer?

i. What is the one insidious notion about both Canada and her birthplace that
   Laurence wishes to dispel?

j. What does she mean by "plastic Progress" (paragraph 15)?

k. Paragraphs 16 and 17 explain Laurence's belief that she and other Canadians
   are "not yet totally alienated from physical earth. . . ." Why is it important for
   her to tell us this? What is the "omen" she describes in paragraph 17?

Strategy and Style

l. To a great degree this selection is really two essays. Where does one end and the other begin? In what way is the little town in which Laurence grew up a "microcosm" of the whole of Canada?

m. Like all good descriptive pieces, this selection uses details "to show" rather than "to tell." Nowhere is that statement more applicable than in paragraph 4. Explain why this paragraph is so effective in helping Laurence counter the charge that her prairie town was "dull."

n. Comment upon the author's choice of verbs in paragraph 4. In what other paragraphs of the essay is her language nearly as vivid and exciting?

o. Laurence's use of metaphors, similes, and other kinds of figurative language is superb. In paragraph 7, she compares a fire truck to "some scarlet chariot of the Goths." In paragraph 11, she uses an oxymoron (a rhetorical figure that contains contradictory elements) to tell us that the "dead lived in that place, too." What other examples of figurative language do you find?

p. Near the end of the essay, Laurence becomes almost rhapsodic in explaining how growing up as a Canadian influenced her writing. In what way does her chance meeting with one of her great-grandfather's farm workers help her create an appropriate conclusion for this essay?

q. What is the author's attitude toward herself, both as the adult who wrote this essay and as the child who is one of its subjects?

SUGGESTIONS FOR SHORT WRITING

a. Choose a passage (a sentence or a paragraph) and relate that passage to your own life.

b. Describe one of the "oddities of the place" (paragraph 8) of your hometown.

SUGGESTIONS FOR SUSTAINED WRITING

a. Describe your hometown or community. In what ways has it helped shape you as an individual and helped determine what you want out of life?

b. In what ways is your hometown a "microcosm" of your country? As Laurence has done, compare both positive and negative aspects.

c. Describe the small town (or big city, for that matter) in which you were raised in such a way as to prove that living there was anything but dull.

d. Everyone's community has its oddities. Describe some of the people, places, laws, rituals, etc., of your hometown that you find odd.

The Metropolitan Cathedral in San Salvador

Joan Didion

Born in Sacramento, California, Didion (b. 1934) served as associate feature editor for Vogue, *as a regular columnist for* The Saturday Evening Post, *and as a contributing editor to the* National Review. *Her essays are subtle portraits of the American experience. Her major works include novels:* Play It As It Lays *(1971),* A Book of Common Prayer *(1977), and* Democracy *(1984); collections of essays:* Slouching Toward Bethlehem *(1968) and* The White Album *(1979); and nonfiction:* Salvador *(1983) and* Miami *(1987). She is also coauthor of several screenplays, including* The Panic in Needle Park *(1971),* A Star Is Born *(1976), and* True Confessions *(1981). This excerpt is from* Salvador, *a book about her experiences in El Salvador.*

During the week before I flew down to El Salvador a Salvadoran woman who   1
works for my husband and me in Los Angeles gave me repeated instructions
about what we must and must not do. We must not go out at night. We must stay
off the street whenever possible. We must never ride in buses or taxis, never leave
the capital, never imagine that our passports would protect us. We must not even
consider the hotel a safe place: people were killed in hotels. She spoke with considerable vehemence, because two of her brothers had been killed in Salvador in
August of 1981, in their beds. The throats of both brothers had been slashed. Her
father had been cut but stayed alive. Her mother had been beaten. Twelve of her
other relatives, aunts and uncles and cousins, had been taken from their houses
one night the same August, and their bodies had been found some time later, in a
ditch. I assured her that we would remember, we would be careful, we would in
fact be so careful that we would probably (trying for a light touch) spend all our
time in church.

She became still more agitated, and I realized that I had spoken as a   2
norteamericana: Churches had not been to this woman the neutral ground they
had been to me. I must remember: Archbishop Romero killed saying mass in
the chapel of the Divine Providence Hospital in San Salvador. I must remember: More than thirty people killed at Archbishop Romero's funeral in the Metropolitan Cathedral in San Salvador. I must remember: More than twenty people killed before that on the steps of the Metropolitan Cathedral. CBS had
filmed it. It had been on television, the bodies jerking, those still alive crawling
over the dead as they tried to get out of range. I must understand: The Church
was dangerous.

I told her that I understood, that I knew all that, and I did, abstractly,   3
but the specific meaning of the Church she knew eluded me until I was actually there, at the Metropolitan Cathedral in San Salvador, one afternoon
when rain sluiced down its corrugated plastic windows and puddled around
the supports of the Sony and Philips billboards near the steps. The effect of

the Metropolitan Cathedral is immediate, and entirely literary. This is the cathedral that the late Archbishop Oscar Arnulfo Romero refused to finish, on the premise that the work of the Church took precedence over its display, and the high walls of raw concrete bristle with structural rods, rusting now, staining the concrete, sticking out at wrenched and violent angles. The wiring is exposed. Fluorescent tubes hang askew. The great high altar is backed by warped plyboard. The cross on the altar is of bare incandescent bulbs, but the bulbs, that afternoon, were unlit: there was in fact no light at all on the main altar, no light on the cross, no light on the globe of the world that showed the northern American continent in gray and the southern in white; no light on the dove above the globe, *Salvador del Mundo*. In this vast brutalist space that was the cathedral, the unlit altar seemed to offer a single ineluctable message: At this time and in this place the light of the world could be construed as out, off, extinguished.

In many ways the Metropolitan Cathedral is an authentic piece of politi- 4
cal art, a statement for El Salvador as *Guernica* was for Spain. It is quite devoid of sentimental relief. There are no decorative or architectural references to familiar parables, in fact no stories at all, not even the Stations of the Cross. On the afternoon I was there the flowers laid on the altar were dead. There were no traces of normal parish activity. The doors were open to the barricaded main steps, and down the steps there was a spill of red paint, lest anyone forget the blood shed there. Here and there on the cheap linoleum inside the cathedral there was what seemed to be actual blood, dried in spots, the kind of spots dropped by a slow hemorrhage, or by a woman who does not know or does not care that she is menstruating.

There were several women in the cathedral during the hour or so I spent 5
there, a young woman with a baby, an older woman in house slippers, a few others, all in black. One of the women walked the aisles as if by compulsion, up and down, across and back, crooning loudly as she walked. Another knelt without moving at the tomb of Archbishop Romero in the right transept. "Loor a Monsenor Romero," the crude needlepoint tapestry by the tomb read, "Praise to Monsignor Romero from the Mothers of the Imprisoned, the Disappeared, and the Murdered," the *Comité de Madres y Familiares de Presos, Desaparecidos, y Asesinados Politicos de El Salvador.*

The tomb itself was covered with offerings and petitions, notes decorated 6
with motifs cut from greeting cards and cartoons. I recall one with figures cut from a Bugs Bunny strip, and another with a pencil drawing of a baby in a crib. The baby in this drawing seemed to be receiving medication or fluid or blood intravenously, through the IV line shown on its wrist. I studied the notes for a while and then went back and looked again at the unlit altar, and at the red paint on the main steps, from which it was possible to see the guardsmen on the balcony of the National Palace hunching back to avoid the rain. Many Salvadorans are offended by the Metropolitan Cathedral, which is as it should be, because

the place remains perhaps the only unambiguous political statement in El Salvador, a metaphorical bomb in the ultimate power station.

1983

QUESTIONS FOR DISCUSSION

Content

a. Is Didion simply describing the Metropolitan Cathedral, or is she using her description as a metaphor for something else? If so, what is the metaphor?
b. Why does she describe the interior of the cathedral in such detail?
c. What senses does Didion appeal to in this description?
d. What does she tell us about the people who worship at the cathedral? How do references to people enrich her description of this place?
e. The author says that the churches in El Salvador are not "neutral ground" (paragraph 2). What does she mean? Does Didion give us an indication about why the Church is involved in Salvadoran politics?
f. What is the "specific meaning of the Church" (paragraph 3) that Didion says eluded her until she came to El Salvador?

Strategy and Style

g. Why does Didion begin by recalling the advice of the Salvadoran woman who works for her?
h. Is your overall reaction to the cathedral generally positive or negative? What details in the essay account for your reaction?
i. Is Didion justified in saying in paragraph 6 that "many Salvadorans are offended by the Metropolitan Cathedral, which is as it should be . . ."? Why would Salvadorans be offended by the cathedral?
j. Is she justified in saying that it is the "only unambiguous political statement in El Salvador . . ."? What is this statement saying?
k. How objective is Didion? Is she praising, criticizing, or trying to be neutral?
l. How would you describe her tone, and what elements in this essay reveal that tone?

SUGGESTIONS FOR SHORT WRITING

a. Try describing a place that is very familiar to you as if you had never seen it before. You might want to find a place in which you can sit, observe, and write unnoticed. First, sit for a while and try to see the place as a stranger would; then, write your description of it.

b. Try rewriting paragraph 4, excising all political language. What do you end up with? What words did you consider to be political?

SUGGESTIONS FOR SUSTAINED WRITING

a. Think of a building that you believe symbolizes a political or social situation. What physical details of this building mirror aspects of the situation? Write a description of the building in which you make the connection clear.

b. Describe the government of Canada, of another country, of your province, or of your hometown through the use of an extended metaphor developed through description. Like Didion, use carefully chosen descriptive details to show how a building or a place mirrors major aspects of that government.

c. Recall a time when you were an outsider—for example, when you travelled to a foreign country or moved to a new community. What were your thoughts about and reactions to this new place? Do you think your outsider status allowed you to see the situation more clearly than the "natives" did? Try describing this situation so that these "natives" might see their culture in a new way.

Wooding

Samuel Metcalfe

Samuel Metcalfe was born in Hebron, Labrador, in 1939. He was educated by Moravian missionaries and later attended Memorial University. He was the first mayor of Nain, Labrador. He writes, reads, and speaks both English and Inuktitut. The following essay first appeared in the journal Inuktitut *in 1984.*

After mother died, things were pretty quiet and lonely around the house. There 1 were three of us children in the family, born about a year apart; I was between two sisters. We lived in the village of Hebron on the Labrador coast, where there were about one hundred people. Dad worked for the HBC during the week while a babysitter took care of us. On weekends, dad had to go seal hunting or cut firewood, especially in the winter, by dog team. The wood was so scarce and hard to get that we used seal fat with it to try and make it last longer.

When my mother was still living, I remember we all went with dad to cut 2 trees for firewood for two or three weeks when he took his holidays in the winter. On a fine day we would take all day just to get to a place where there were trees, about thirty or forty miles from the village. On these wood cutting trips we would put up the tent, and after settling in dad would be out all day cutting wood while mom kept busy looking after us, or cooking and singing songs, or telling us stories. When we played outside, she would be sewing clothes or making sealskin boots, mitts and parkas for all of us. Sometimes she'd go out fishing on the lake through the ice or go hunting for ptarmigan. It seemed we always had lots to eat and never went hungry, and we always had the best and warmest clothes.

It was peaceful at camp and all was so still you could hear the silence. There 3 was a mixture of sounds such as the rustling of leaves blowing in the wind, the fire crackling in the tent stove, birds singing songs to each other, wolves howling, soft footsteps in the cold snow and chop-chop in the distance from dad's axe. We'd even hear the ice cracking at night from our tent. It was so quiet the place was always noisy. The sound travelled a long way without being interrupted.

When mom went out on the lake to cut a fishing hole with her ice chisel you 4 could see her lift the chisel and strike the ice again before you heard the sound. It never made a rough or a sharp bang like it would if you were close to it; it sounded more like a muffled twang. When the sound reached you it kept on going until you couldn't hear it anymore, or it came back to you in an even more muffled tone when it echoed back from a distant cliff. We would often go out on the lake when the night was clear and cold just to listen to the sound travel through the ice when we struck it with a stick. The ice made different sounds which travelled at different speeds according to its thickness.

Sometimes I would go with dad when he went cutting trees. I used to be very 5 proud and felt much older than my age (I was about five or six) because mom would pack a lunch bag for me which I would carry in my own little sealskin knapsack she made for me, and I would use a small pair of snowshoes made just for me by dad.

We would be gone all day from the tent, cutting trees and piling them up on the lake, taking a rest, shooting ptarmigan when we came upon them, chipping gum off the trees and eating when we got hungry. Late in the evening, we would start walking back to the tent. I would carry the gun and two or three partridges on my back. Sometimes dad would let me take the lead and he would follow close behind me. It seemed that during these brief walks he always took time to talk to me. While he was chopping trees down he'd hardly look at me, let alone have time to talk. He used to point out some prominent landmarks ahead of us and told me to head straight for a certain mark. When we got there we would stop and he'd ask me to turn around and study the place where we had come from. He always told me that it was not good enough just knowing where you were going. You had to know where you were coming from, which was why it was important to get a good idea of the lay of the land behind you. That way you'd never get lost because you could always go back somewhere and find out where you are. I think that's one of the reasons why I get lost in a city very easily; there is no time to stop to look back. You can only see straight ahead of you; there are too many buildings blocking your view. You can relax, take your time, find peace and comfort in the wide open spaces.

There were times when we'd stop and put on a fire to boil water for a cup of 6 hot tea. Of course I'd be a good boy and try to help dad in starting the fire. But he'd always tell me to start my own little fire. He wouldn't just sit down and instruct me how to do it. He would ask me to do as he did, step by step. When we got back to the camp and the village, I'd be very proud in telling everybody that I did all these things all by myself without any help.

There are many things that my father, grandfather and uncle taught me that I 7 can never forget because of their approach and manner—the very way they presented themselves. For instance, I still feel incomplete or not fully dressed unless I have a good quality penknife in my pocket. Grandfather, uncle and I were on a caribou hunting trip one time and my grandfather was wrestling with a crippled caribou. The caribou was shot in the leg and grandfather didn't want to waste another bullet to kill it. He asked me for my pocket knife which I had forgotten at home. So he got my uncle's knife and killed the caribou just by piercing the soft spot on its head. My grandfather didn't speak to me very much during the rest of the trip. I just let it go by without much concern.

We got home a few days later and after we had put everything away he said 8 to me, 'Come out to the porch with me and make sure you have your pocket knife.' When we got out he asked for my knife, opened it and pierced it into the frozen caribou, gave it a twist and pulled it back out, minus the blade. He threw away the rest of the knife and went back into the house grumbling away to himself, but I felt as though he was talking directly to me. 'I asked for a pocket knife and all I get is a piece of tin. And what a way to go hunting with no knife in your pocket! You might as well wear pocketless pants or have no pants on at all.' How I felt is hard to describe but it's something I'll never forget and will always appreciate. It has come in handy many, many times since.

1984

QUESTIONS FOR DISCUSSION

Content

a. How did the death of the mother affect the family?
b. Is this essay a description of a way of life, of the writer's relationship with his elders, or of a happy time of his life?
c. What must one always remember when travelling through the woods?
d. What is the relationship between clothing and a pocket knife?
e. What is Metcalfe's overall point? Why is it important or interesting to know about "wooding"?

Strategy and Style

f. When Metcalfe describes "wooding" when his mother was alive, are the images positive or negative?
g. What is the organizing principle of Metcalfe's description? How does he utilize this organizing principle?
h. Metcalfe writes, "you could hear the silence." How does he develop this statement? What phenomenon does he describe?
i. Why does Metcalfe make the reference about getting lost in the city?
j. Metcalfe says that "the very way they presented themselves" brought home the force of the lesson. How does he demonstrate this statement?

SUGGESTIONS FOR SHORT WRITING

a. Write about someone you watched when you were a child. Describe the person's movements with as much detail as possible.
b. Write about someone who taught you how to do something. How did he or she teach you?
c. Try to write about the same scene through the eyes of the father or grandfather.

SUGGESTIONS FOR SUSTAINED WRITING

a. For the Inuit, the family unit is quite important, especially the role the elders play. What role do elders play in children's education where you live? Should they have more of a role or less of a role?
b. Note the way the father and grandfather teach the child in the essay. Should our education system integrate the Inuit approach? What are the values of such an approach to education?
c. What effect does TV have on our conception of the family?

The Death of the Moth

Virginia Woolf

The daughter of the British essayist and scholar Leslie Stephen, Virginia Woolf (1882–1941) was at the centre of the Bloomsbury Group, a circle that included Lytton Strachey and John Maynard Keynes as well as several other important intellectuals, poets, and artists. With her husband, Leonard, Woolf founded the Hogarth Press and published the work of brilliant young writers such as T. S. Eliot and E. M. Forster. Her fiction is important because of her experimentation with the stream-of-consciousness technique and her ability to expose the psychology of her characters in a way that is at once subtle and vivid. Among her most memorable novels are Mrs. Dalloway *(1925),* To the Lighthouse *(1927),* Orlando *(1928), and* The Waves *(1931). Her nonfiction works include* A Room of One's Own *(1929) and* The Death of the Moth *(1942).*

Moths that fly by day are not properly to be called moths; they do not excite that pleasant sense of dark autumn nights and ivy-blossom which the commonest yellow-underwing asleep in the shadow of the curtain never fails to rouse in us. They are hybrid creatures, neither gay like butterflies nor sombre like their own species. Nevertheless the present specimen, with his narrow hay-coloured wings, fringed with a tassel of the same colour, seemed to be content with life. It was a pleasant morning, mid-September, mild, benignant, yet with a keener breath than that of the summer months. The plough was already scoring the field opposite the window, and where the share had been, the earth was pressed flat and gleamed with moisture. Such vigour came rolling in from the fields and the down beyond that it was difficult to keep the eyes strictly turned upon the book. The rooks too were keeping one of their annual festivities; soaring round the tree tops until it looked as if a vast net with thousands of black knots in it had been cast up into the air; which, after a few moments sank slowly down upon the trees until every twig seemed to have a knot at the end of it. Then, suddenly, the net would be thrown into the air again in a wider circle this time, with the utmost clamour and vociferation, as though to be thrown into the air and settle slowly down upon the tree tops were a tremendously exciting experience. 1

The same energy which inspired the rooks, the ploughmen, the horses, and even, it seemed, the lean bare-backed downs, sent the moth fluttering from side to side of his square of the windowpane. One could not help watching him. One was, indeed, conscious of a queer feeling of pity for him. The possibilities of pleasure seemed that morning so enormous and so various that to have only a moth's part in life, and a day moth's at that, appeared a hard fate, and his zest in enjoying his meagre opportunities to the full, pathetic. He flew vigorously to one corner of his compartment, and, after waiting there a second, flew across to the other. What remained for him but to fly to a third corner and then to a fourth? That was all he could do, in spite of the size of the downs, the width of the sky, the far-off smoke of houses, and the romantic voice, now and then, of a steamer out at sea. What he could do he did. Watching him, it seemed as if a fibre, very thin but pure, of the enormous energy of the world had been thrust into his frail and diminutive body. 2

As often as he crossed the pane, I could fancy that a thread of vital light became visible. He was little or nothing but life.

Yet, because he was so small, and so simple a form of the energy that was 3 rolling in at the open window and driving its way through so many narrow and intricate corridors in my own brain and in those of other human beings, there was something marvellous as well as pathetic about him. It was as if someone had taken a tiny bead of pure life and decking it as lightly as possible with down and feathers, had set it dancing and zig-zagging to show us the true nature of life. Thus displayed one could not get over the strangeness of it. One is apt to forget all about life, seeing it humped and bossed and garnished and cumbered so that it has to move with the greatest circumspection and dignity. Again, the thought of all that life might have been had he been born in any other shape caused one to view his simple activities with a kind of pity.

After a time, tired by his dancing apparently, he settled on the window ledge in 4 the sun, and, the queer spectacle being at an end, I forgot about him. Then, looking up, my eye was caught by him. He was trying to resume his dancing, but seemed either so stiff or so awkward that he could only flutter to the bottom of the windowpane; and when he tried to fly across it he failed. Being intent on other matters I watched these futile attempts for a time without thinking, unconsciously waiting for him to resume his flight, as one waits for a machine, that has stopped momentarily, to start again without considering the reason of its failure. After perhaps a seventh attempt he slipped from the wooden ledge and fell, fluttering his wings, on to his back on the window sill. The helplessness of his attitude roused me. It flashed upon me that he was in difficulties; he could no longer raise himself; his legs struggled vainly. But, as I stretched out a pencil, meaning to help him to right himself, it came over me that the failure and awkwardness were the approach of death. I laid the pencil down again.

The legs agitated themselves once more. I looked as if for the enemy against 5 which he struggled. I looked out of doors. What had happened there? Presumably it was midday, and work in the fields had stopped. Stillness and quiet had replaced the previous animation. The birds had taken themselves off to feed in the brooks. The horses stood still. Yet the power was there all the same, massed outside, indifferent, impersonal, not attending to anything in particular. Somehow it was opposed to the little hay-coloured moth. It was useless to try to do anything. One could only watch the extraordinary efforts made by those tiny legs against an oncoming doom which could, had it chosen, have submerged an entire city, not merely a city, but masses of human beings; nothing, I knew, had any chance against death. Nevertheless after a pause of exhaustion the legs fluttered again. It was superb this last protest, and so frantic that he succeeded at last in righting himself. One's sympathies, of course, were all on the side of life. Also, when there was nobody to care or to know, this gigantic effort on the part of an insignificant little moth, against a power of such magnitude, to retain what no one else valued or desired to keep, moved one strangely. Again, somehow, one saw life, a pure bead. I lifted the pencil again, useless though I knew it to be. But even as I did so, the unmistakable tokens of death showed themselves. The body relaxed, and instantly grew stiff. The struggle was over. The insignificant little creature now knew death. As I looked at the dead moth, this minute wayside triumph of so great a force over so mean an antagonist filled me with wonder. Just as life had been strange a few minutes before, so death was now as strange. The moth having righted himself now lay most decently and uncomplainingly composed. O yes, he seemed to say, death is stronger than I am.

1942

QUESTIONS FOR DISCUSSION

Content

a. Woolf's essay is obviously a serious discussion of the inevitability of death. Why does she rely on the death of so inconsequential a creature to convey her impressions? Why did she not describe the death of a human being instead?

b. To what is Woolf referring in paragraph 2 when she says, "The same energy which inspired the rooks, the ploughmen, the horses . . . sent the moth fluttering . . ."?

c. In the same paragraph, Woolf indicates that the moth was "little or nothing but life." Yet, by paragraph 5, the insect has died. Did the same power that gave him life strike him down?

d. What connection does Woolf draw between the moth and the world of living things outside her window? Why is it appropriate that the moth die at midday?

Strategy and Style

e. Throughout the first three paragraphs, Woolf refers to herself in the third person ("one"). In paragraphs 4 and 5, however, she uses the more familiar first-person pronoun ("I"). Does this change indicate a change in tone?

f. What other differences do you notice between the first three paragraphs and the last two in regard to both content and rhetorical strategy?

g. At the end of paragraph 1, Woolf uses an extended metaphor. What other interesting uses of figurative language can you identify?

SUGGESTIONS FOR SHORT WRITING

a. Choose a window or some equally limited area at home and describe the "world" of that area.

b. Study Woolf's opening paragraph, looking at the way she structures each sentence, the way she uses punctuation, the subject matter of each sentence. Then, with some animal other than a moth, write an opening paragraph of your own in Woolf's style.

SUGGESTIONS FOR SUSTAINED WRITING

a. Woolf's perspective on the death of the moth is, for the most part, subjective. As such, it is a perfect example of the extent to which our personal vision of the world can colour our perceptions of natural objects and events. Spend some time observing the night sky, a field of corn in autumn, a newborn calf, the backyard outside your bedroom window, a potted geranium, or some other natural subject. Write two short essays about it. In the first, be objective. Describe things accurately and scientifically. Use factual details only, and make reference to exact sizes, shapes, and colours. In the second, flex the muscles of your imagination by writing a subjective description. Let your emotions colour your perceptions. If possible, use metaphors and other figures of speech to convey your personal impressions of the subject.

b. Woolf proves that even a creature as insignificant as a moth is an appropriate subject for an essay that explores significant human questions. Go out and watch the activity in an anthill for ten or fifteen minutes, observe what a bird must go through to keep her chicks alive, or recall the birth of a puppy or kitten. What lessons can the natural world teach us about how to live our lives?

The Last Grass Dance

Alexander Wolfe

Alexander Wolfe was born in 1927 on the Sakimay Reserve in Saskatchewan. His early education was in a residential school run by the United Church of Canada. In 1950, his family moved to the Turtle Mountains of North Dakota and Wolfe went on to earn a teacher's aide certificate in preschool education. He believes that today's native storytellers must have a deep commitment to oral tradition but must use the written tradition to support it. With modern distractions, the time needed to listen to the ancient stories often does not exist. The storyteller must restore the art and principles of storytelling, but must also preserve the stories themselves.

Told by Standing Through the Earth

Grandfather Standing Through the Earth was an elder who was knowledgeable 1
about many things, both social and spiritual, and their application to the traditional and cultural ways of our people. Many times during his life I found him to be strange. Maybe this was because he was of one era and I was of another.

Whenever I would ask Grandfather a question that was of a humorous nature, 2
his response was immediate. Sometimes he would ask Grandmother to provide an answer. Whenever I asked questions that dealt with the facts of life, Grandfather was quick to respond, 'A'how, Medimoya (all right, old lady), our grandson wants to know, tell him what he wants to know.' Usually this amused him and he laughed.

Then there were times I would ask a certain kind of question and receive no 3
immediate response. Instead he would remain motionless, and after a period of silence, he would say, 'There is a period in the life of every person in which there is foolishness. When this period passes some people will grow up, remembering and using what they were told. For this we have a saying. "When you have had enough foolishness, then you become knowledgeable and know your mistakes." There are others who never go beyond this first stage; they remain foolish for the rest of their lives. To those people we say, "Your foolishness will accompany you to your old age."'

When I received this kind of response I was forced to practise patience and 4
wait for a later time to ask my question. Very early in life I learned not to ask questions about spiritual things—particularly those things directly related to Grandfather or any other older person. These things, I was told, were very personal and were to be held in utmost respect. They were only alluded to in story form. Ceremonies and rituals were never described in detail. To ask old people questions about their spiritual attributes was unthinkable.

When I first asked Grandfather about the grass dance I already knew some 5
things about it. From the stories told by Grandfather Earth Elder I knew where it had come from, and how it had come. On occasions when I asked my mother about it she only told me who performed the dance, not how or why the dance was

performed. To these questions, she always replied, 'Ask your grandfather, he was part of it.'

Once she made a comment that revealed her recollection of that period, 'The 6 *dancer who wore the eagle belts in the grass dance looked beautiful. They were good dancers, very quick and beautiful to watch.'*

My desire to know about the grass dance was to be satisfied one day.

It was a day in early summer. In the morning I helped Grandfather hitch his ponies 7 to the wagon. After this was done I was told to help load the wagon with the berry-picking pails, some water containers, and a box of food. I was told that my mother and grandmother were going to pick saskatoon berries and Grandfather was going to chop willow pickets for fence posts. I was to help him. I was to be the pack horse who pulled the pickets out of the bush as they were cut, a job I wasn't really looking forward to. After hours of going from this bush to that bush, and finding only a few pickets, we came upon the Goose Lake from a northerly direction. We were on an abandoned trail along what was once the northwestern shoreline of Goose Lake. Suddenly Grandfather pulled his ponies to a stop and said, *'Medimoyea* (old lady), remember a long time ago when the shoreline was here and there were many kinds of summer fowl on the lake? At times there were so many geese they looked like snow upon the water.'

After the old people reminisced for several minutes about the old days we 8 continued along what used to be the lake shore. A short time later we came upon a small clearing between two fairly large patches of trees and bushes. This was the place where the old log hall had stood by the shores of Goose Lake. The old hall was now gone.

As we approached the site I began to remember something about this place. 9 The winter before I went to boarding school we came here once to watch a dance which I knew was the grass dance. We lived about three quarters of a mile north of here, and the whole family piled into the sleigh to make this trip. That evening and night were very cold. I knew it was very cold because from the time we left our house till we got here I was completely covered in blankets. I could not see anything. All I could hear was the sound of sleigh runners as they slid along the snow, and the sound of harness tugs as the horse pulled the sleigh.

When we arrived and went into the hall, we saw many people with children 10 and many old people. Grandfather was there, so was Grandmother. My mother told me to sit in one place and to be quiet during the entire time we would be there. I cannot remember any of the other children making noise or running about either.

As we waited quietly for what was about to take place, I saw Grandfather 11 dressed in a white traditional costume sitting by the door. To his left, and coming from the far opposite side of the hall, was the sound of bells and the aroma of burning sweet grass. A drum was placed in the centre of the hall. All was quiet. Then one of our grandfathers, whom I knew quite well, said a prayer. His name, the name I always called him, was *Wahpossway* (Old Man Bunnie).

I remembered seeing men seated on the floor around the drum. These were 12 the singers. To one side of the singers stood another of the grandfathers, a brother to Grandfather Standing Through the Earth. His name was North Wind. This grandfather never danced. All he did was stand by the drum throughout the entire dance. The singing began and the dancers began their dance. During parts of the dance they danced slowly and at other times very fast. They let out shouts as they danced round and round the drum. On the ladies' side of the hall some elderly women stood dancing in one place. All at once there was a great shout. The dancers stopped dancing and the singers stopped singing.

There was something going on behind the drum and dancers that I could not 13 see. Then the singing began again. This time some other men danced, just plain men. They carried ladles which they waved as they shouted.

The best part came after the dance was finished. Food was served, along with 14 apples and bags of candy. My mother told me not to eat right away, first we had to listen. I remembered listening to another grandfather speak for a long time. He talked about us children and other children. This grandfather talked for such a long time, I couldn't hold out, I just had to dig into the candy. I'm sure I was not the only child to do this. I didn't remember what happened after that. I do know that a social dance followed—a round dance. I awoke the next morning back at our house. I knew that it had not been a dream because I still had some candy and apples.

As we neared the site where the old log hall had stood, Grandfather pulled 15 his ponies to a turn and made for the edge of the bush.

There in the shade of the trees and bushes Grandfather stopped and said, 'We 16 will stop here and eat.' Pointing to the bush along the lake bed, he said, 'The saskatoons used to be good here.'

We all got off the wagon and I helped Grandfather unhitch his ponies. In a 17 short time a fire was built, the tea made, and we all sat down to eat. As we ate I thought again about the old log hall, about the time we came here during that one winter. In my mind I debated whether I should ask or not.

Finally I turned to my mother, 'Should I ask Grandfather about the old hall 18 and what happened when we came here that one winter?'

Without saying a word she took out her tobacco, placed a pipeful in my 19 hand, and said, 'Here. Ask him.'

As I was about to offer the tobacco to Grandfather my mother spoke to him. 20 'He wants to ask you about the old hall and about the last time there was a grass dance here.'

With a look on his face that suggested he was deep in thought, Grandfather 21 took the tobacco.

'*Noozis* (grandchild),' he said, 'you have given me much tobacco in the past. 22 I have told you stories. These stories I have told you were stories by the old men (elders) who lived here at Goose Lake since the reserve was here. Some of these stories were told when there was no reserve, no whiteman, so long ago we don't know when.

'This,' he said, pointing to the sky and around him, 'what you see around 23
you is a story. What the *Anishnaybay* does and how he lives is a story. You, in time
to come, will tell about me. Your children will tell about you—if you are foolish
or not foolish—whatever they say about you will be a story. When your grand-
children come you will look back. You will see and know many things. This will
be your story. What you ask I will tell you.

'Long ago when your grandmother and I were young, we came here to 24
Goose Lake. (Grandfather was originally from the Riding Mountain area in central Manitoba and Grandmother came from the Turtle Mountains in Dakota
Territory.) The people here at Goose Lake already had the grass dance. The elder
Sanquis, father of my son-in-law, *Macheeaniquot* (Floating Cloud), had the ceremony. Elder *Sanquis* lived west of here at the other lake and had a big house.
Round dances were held there and sometimes at mid-winter the grass dance was
held there. I am told he got the dance as a gift from the Assiniboine people. This
hall that was here was not the first. There was another across the lake to the east
side. It was not really a hall but a big house.

'To have a part in the ceremony of the grass dance is an honour. In this 25
dance there were four dancers, four singers, and four servers. There were speakers, a keeper of the drum, which at that time was *Mechee* (brother) *Keeway-
tinopeenace* (North Wind), and a keeper of the door. I was the last keeper of the
door. When everyone who was to take part in the dance was ready, my part was
to shut the door. I didn't let anyone in or out until the dance was over. When the
door was shut a pipe was given to a speaker. Before the Elder *Sanquis* passed on,
this was his part, as leader and headman of the Grass Dance Society. There had
been other speakers in the past, like the father of *Nokeequon* (Soft Feather), Jim
Bunnie. The speaker prayed to the Thunder Bird Eagle to bless the men who were
holding the eagle belts which they were going to wear. These belts were sacred
and used only for this dance. I have never been given the right to wear the eagle
belt, only the eagle feather hat that I still have today. He also prayed for the keeper
of the drum and the men seated around the drum. Four rainbows were painted on
the drum, one for each direction, and at each direction sat a singer. The keeper of
the drum stood at the east side of the drum. On the women's side stood four elderly women. They were noted in the community for their generosity and sharing
with others. For these women, too, the speaker prayed. And for the children, and
for all children yet to come. He prayed that each would be blessed with a head of
grey and a long life.

'When this was done the dancers put on their belts. The dance was ready to 26
begin. These belts came from an eagle that had been skinned, removing the head,
the legs, the wings, and some of the tail feathers, and leaving only the back. From
this section the belt was made and then decorated with ribbons of different colours.

'There were four main songs in this dance. The keeper of the drum kept track 27
of them by passing a certain number of sticks from one hand to the other. The last
two songs were sung twice. When the keeper of the drum held up four sticks in

each hand we knew that this was the last part of the ceremony. This song was very fast and the dancers had to be very quick. The song ended when the lead dancer, who carried a sharpened stick, pierced a portion of the contents of a kettle, and held it up for all to see. The kettle held a cooked young dog that had been raised and prepared for this purpose. The lead dancer then took an eagle feather and dipped the tip of it into the broth and dropped one drop onto the tongue of each of his fellow dancers. Another song was sung to which the four men danced. They were the servers; their work, then, was to serve the food to the people.

'When this song was ended all the members of the Grass Dance Society **28** were served the contents of the kettle. When the meal was ended the chief of the band, or some other headman, recounted why this ceremony was held—it meant that one half of the winter was now past. The hardships of the second half would soon be over. With the coming of spring it would be as morning after a dark night. We would be glad when the grandfathers*, among whom would be Thunder Bird Eagle, would come to give rain and life to all things, and we, too, the *Anishnaybay* would have life.'

When Grandfather had finished his story, he added the comment, 'Because **29** of the changing times and forces outside our community, the Indians of tomorrow will never see, only hear of, the sacred ceremony and ritual called the grass dance.'

1988

QUESTIONS FOR DISCUSSION

Content

a. Why does Wolfe give an extended introduction of his Grandfather? What does this introduction tell us about the grandfather?
b. Why is it important to give the child's perspective of the events?
c. What is the importance of story, according to the grandfather?
d. Outline the structure of the dance. What is the organizing principle?
e. How does the grandfather's final comment tie into his opening comments about stories and storytelling?

Strategy and Style

f. Why does Wolfe give the translated name for Standing Through the Earth and the native name for *Wahpossway*?
g. Why are the candy and apples important? What do they provide the narrator?
h. Of what importance is the tobacco? What does it represent?
i. When the grandfather tells the story, the narrator disappears, why?
j. What details does the grandfather focus on?
k. The subtitle of the essay states, "Told by Standing Through the Earth." Is this entirely accurate?

*Grandfathers, as used here, denotes Thunderbirds, the rolling thunder of the early spring, among whom, it was said, was the Eagle Thunder Bird.

SUGGESTIONS FOR SHORT WRITING

a. Try to remember and relate a story passed down from your grandparents, parents, or guardians to you.
b. Write about a time when a specific place helped you recall an event.
c. Write about a significant event that involved a ceremony such as a wedding, a funeral, or a graduation. What details do you recall?

SUGGESTIONS FOR SUSTAINED WRITING

a. The grandfather says, "What the *Anishnaybay* does and how he lives is a story." In your life, what have been the attitudes toward the word "story"? Discuss what makes a good "story" and what a "story" is.
b. For many cultures, the notion of history is foreign. What is the function of history? Is history important? Why or why not?
c. People like Marshall McLuhan have discussed a forgetfulness of history in our society. What is the effect or danger of such a forgetfulness?

Portrait of a City

Hugh MacLennan

For many readers, Hugh MacLennan (1907–1990) was the quintessential Canadian writer. Well educated (Rhodes Scholar at Oxford, PhD in Classics from Princeton), he was determined to be a novelist. After a number of unsuccessful attempts, his memories of the Halifax Explosion in WWI became the backbone of Barometer Rising. *In his lifetime, he won the Governor General's Award more than any other writer: three times for fiction and twice for nonfiction. In both his fiction and nonfiction, description and place are particularly important. The following essay on MacLennan's childhood hometown captures both the insight and flavour of much of MacLennan's work.*

A few years ago, while travelling in the West, I happened to mention to a train-companion that I considered Halifax one of the few authentically beautiful cities in Canada. He smiled, like a polite man showing the required appreciation of a feeble joke. Then, seeing that I was serious, he burst out: "My God, have you ever been there?" 1

"Have you?" I asked. 2

"I was stationed in Halifax for two hundred and forty-seven days and if—" 3

To set down the rest of what the man said would be redundant, for you have heard it all before. He repeated most of the usual charges levelled against Halifax by inland Canadians during the war—the fleecing of service men by lodging-house keepers, the liquor law, the drabness, the lack of amusements for seamen exhausted by weeks of convoy duty in the North Atlantic. It never occurred to him that the same charges would have held good against any other Canadian town of similar size, if any other Canadian town had been saddled with a similar wartime job. Least of all did he realize that the war had nothing important to do with the feeling of frustrated anger which Halifax has always occasioned in the majority of inland Canadians. Long before 1939 Halifax was uniquely unpopular, and the reason for this unpopularity is an interesting sidelight on our national character. 4

Canadians of the interior generally take one look at Halifax and conclude that by all rules of comparison familiar to them, their own cities are vastly superior. Being a sensitive people, who wince with anger and guilt when they themselves are censured, they begin by criticizing Halifax gently. Haligonians don't listen. The inland voices rise higher as it becomes more necessary that Haligonians should admit a self-evident inferiority and search out ways of self-improvement. Haligonians don't even pay them the compliment of getting angry. Finally, the horrible truth reveals itself. Not only do Haligonians not give the smallest damn what hinterlanders think about Halifax; they don't care what hinterlanders think about anything on earth. 5

No, Halifax is not unpopular on account of her rôle in the war. She is unpopular in exactly the same way that an incorrigible boy is unpopular with his 6 schoolteachers. But there is more than this moral insensitivity to be set in the scales against the city. There is also a wealth of factual detail.

If you like Winnipeg, with its well-lit streets open to the cleansing winds, 7 how can you endure Halifax, where flickering arc lamps loom through the fog in streets as narrow as those of Dickensian London?

If you admire London (Ontario), a city so clean, progressive and business- 8 like that Americans feel it would be a credit to Ohio, how can you admire Halifax, which for years has been dirty, reactionary and mockingly indifferent to the entire North American ideal of progress?

If you admit the superiority of Toronto, where serious drinking has been con- 9 fined until recently to well-kept homes and hotel bedrooms, where love-making in private is modified by the discipline of the people and in public is impossible, what good word can you find for Halifax, where, in certain areas, bottles are tilted on street corners at high noon, and on warm evenings the park and the slopes of the Citadel are murmurous with sailors and the girls they have picked up on the lower streets?

Or perhaps you come from Montreal, our one city famous for tolerance. 10 What then can you make of the attitude of the better families of Halifax, who are as strict as people in Ontario, and have been convinced for years that Halifax *as a whole* leads a sober, upright and godly life?

There is only one conclusion to be drawn from such a variety of pictures. 11 Whether you love Halifax or not you must admit that she has character. She is distinct.

Whenever I hear Halifax condemned, I remember the great definition of 12 Lord Bacon. "There is no excellent beauty that hath not some strangeness in the proportions." All the proportions of Halifax are strange. She sits there on her iron-stone, generally in the wet, with all her faults exposed. Her face is towards Europe; her back (which is the city dump) greets strangers from the continent. The smells of tar, fish-meal, bilge, ozone, salt water, spruce forests and her own slums are rich in her nostrils. She is like an old trollop, lying in wait for weary seamen, if that is how you choose to regard her. She is like an old lady living in genteel poverty amid the disorder of her own past, if you think of her more gently. But, because all her imperfections are inherent in her nature, inherent even in her function, Halifax comes close to satisfying Lord Bacon's definition. She possesses the same kind of beauty Rembrandt discovered in the battered faces of the old men and women he loved best to paint.

But these are generalizations. What I should like to do is to tell you why this 13 city seems uniquely fascinating to me, who grew up there and still love her well.

There is no city in Canada, there is none in North America, which so amaz- 14 ingly concentrates life, in all its aspects, in a space so small. In most cities on our continent, the poor are separated from the well-to-do by railway tracks or by miles of streets. In the older parts of Halifax, the slums are back to back with the homes of the best families. You may dine in a house filled with antiques, rich in books, with old paintings on the walls. But a walk of a few minutes will take you to a boarding-house for seamen where you will encounter characters who could have walked out of a Conrad novel, and see rooms where, in living memory, drugs were put into the rum, and bos'ns and hard-case mates lurked in the back room with blackjacks in their pockets.

A boy growing up in Halifax may see life small, but he will see it as clearly 15 as if he were watching through the large end of the telescope. It is so compressed and vivid that he can see, grasp, smell, feel and understand the whole interdependent organism.

When I was in fifth grade, the boy one seat ahead of me smelled constantly 16 of dried sweat and fish. He was six years older than anyone else in the class because it had always taken him two and a half years to complete a single grade. At night he was too worn out from chores to do his home work, and frequently he disappeared for months at a time to go to sea. His hands were huge and horny, his fingers were permanently bent at the second joint from pulling on an oar since he had been old enough to sit upright on a thwart. He had a squint in one eye, his hair stuck out stiff over his forehead and he had lost his two upper front teeth. He was cheerful, friendly and gentle, and it never occurred to him to take advantage of his manifest superiority to the rest of us.

The boy opposite him spoke in what would sound to inland ears like an 17 English accent. He wore the type of tweed britches, tight at the knees, then popular on golf links. His family lived in a fine house with gardens and walls about three sides of it, a pile of cannon balls by the front door and a small eighteenth-century muzzle loader pointing outward from the bottom step.

In front of this boy was a girl whose father was a lawyer, then a minister's 18 son, then the daughter of a policeman. But alone at a corner desk was a boy who smelled so formidable that the teacher had been careful to seat him to leeward of the entire class. This boy had no father at all, and he was so tough and truculent that he ruled over us like a prince, receiving as his daily tribute the soggy apple cores of half the class.

Besides this concentration of life, which was a product of the city itself, the 19 history of the era found in Halifax a vivid and sometimes terrible focus.

At least once a day, during that year, we would bolt from our seats to look 20 out at the passing troops. The road was unpaved then, and the soldiers would trudge past on their route marches with the dust puffing up to their knees in the hot weather, and in winter with rime on their collars and the steam of their breath hanging over them like a cloud. We would watch them and wonder which ones would be killed. If they passed at recess-time, the boys would run along their flanks searching for familiar faces. "Look, there's Daddy! He's a captain!" And another boy might shout, "That's nothing, my father's a private!" There might easily be a fight over this.

One cold, clear December morning, while the boys were playing on the 21 packed ashes about the school, and the first fight of the day was brewing, there was a roar past all hearing, and we saw the windows of the school burst inward and the trees toss, and a teacher stagger out the front door with blood streaming from her face. During the following hours as the sky darkened first with smoke, then with clouds, and finally with the snow of a driving blizzard, we saw the north end of the city in flames and the dead and wounded streaming south in slovens, ash and garbage carts, wagons, cars, baby carriages, trucks, ambulances, in anything that would roll.

Later each of us had his own stories of the great explosion. The father of one boy knew a man who was blown from the fo'c'sle head of a ship in the harbour to the slope of Fort Needham, three-quarters of a mile away; the man struck the ground on the exact angle of his flight, skidded to a stop and walked away naked. Another boy went home to find that his house had disappeared. Three days later his father found him and told him that his mother and five brothers and sisters were all dead. While the boy wept, his father comforted him by saying, "Never mind, I'll get you a new mother and start in all over again. Inside six years we'll have a family again." 22

The last year of the war saw the schools working in double shifts. So vivid was the sense of destiny in Halifax in those days that, even as schoolboys, we were aware of it. To this day I can't watch water running down ice-rutted streets in the spring without feeling a recurrence of the mood of despair which struck Halifax on March 22, 1918, when the first reports of Ludendorff's great offensive reached home. The snow was melting, a grey mist hung over us as it hung over the trenches in France, half of Halifax was in ruins, all of us had seen dead bodies, and now it seemed that the war was going to be lost. 23

But the war ended soon afterwards, the customary riot occurred in Halifax, and a year or two later our days in grammar school ended, too. Some boys went to work, others of us passed on to the old Academy on the crest of Sackville Street. 24

Immediately the atmosphere in which we moved became subtly different. In the lower grades life had seemed raw and exciting. Now we became conscious that it is out of dangers that civilizations arise, and that we lived in a province with a great tradition of culture and adventure. The embodiment of that tradition, as I knew it, was the senior master in the Academy, the finest teacher I have ever known. No portrait I could draw of Halifax would be complete without him. Even the setting in which he worked was appropriately symbolic. 25

His classroom was on the top floor of the Academy, with one set of windows facing east to the inner harbour, another set looking south to the open sea. While we worked at set exercises, he used to stand in the windowbay with his fingers on a globe, his head domed like that of a Roman senator of the great period, his blue eyes looking out over the roofs to the lighthouse and the blink of the horizon. Latin was the subject he nominally taught, and we learned a lot of it from him. But what he really taught us was respect for life—not life as it might be, not life as it ought to be, but life as it is. 26

This man was sixty years old when I first saw him, and he had just left the army after four and a quarter years of war, more than two of which he had spent in the front line with a regiment which must have contained at least seventy of the boys he himself had once taught. In the summers he worked on a farm and read the classics by night. He must have known half the male population of Nova Scotia, he liked nearly all of them and the only things for which he never forgave 27 his province were the attempts it made to copy the rest of the continent in standardizing education, as well as the asinine liquor law imposed by the shameless self-righteousness of a few dry counties. He was the only teacher I have ever met with no desire to change or reform people. Though he drove us hard, he relished enormously the more colourful characters among us, including one boy with a villainous face who chewed tobacco and later did well in the smuggling trade. He nourished two and a half generations of Haligonians, and even after his eightieth year, Halifax remained to him the same exciting, beautiful city it had been when he was a boy, when the docks were a forest of sailing ships and the streets were filled with men who had seen Joe Howe plain.

But Halifax, as we grew older, inevitably began to appear small. We wanted 28 to turn the telescope around and look through the small end. We watched the ships sailing out over the horizon and some of us wished we were with them. As we neared the end of our high school days we realized that the city had subtly prepared us for the one solution Nova Scotia has discovered to balance her economic plight since the disappearance of wooden ships. Many of us knew we would have to emigrate whether we wanted to or not. Today at least half the boys I then knew well are scattered over the continent. Some are in England, one is even in Australia. We may still be parts of Halifax in our memories, but we are no longer Haligonians, and we know it.

The true Haligonians are the ones who were born in this outpost and have 29 stayed behind to keep it up. Although the rest of Canada has not appreciated their efforts, there are many Canadian cities that could learn a lot from them. In spite of the fact that Halifax, before the Second World War, never had a permanent population in excess of seventy thousand, she has never acquired the atmosphere of a small town. The technique by which this catastrophe has been averted may be a deplorable one, but at least it has worked.

A small town has been defined as a community of indeterminate size, dom- 30 inated by women. Small town men may speak their minds at their lodge meetings, but the words they utter there have small weight compared to those spoken in the sewing circles. A small town needs few laws to tame the instincts of the male animal. The tongues of the women do it instead.

In Halifax, no situation even vaguely resembling this definition has ever ex- 31 isted. Not only do the women have no control over the actual running of the city, they don't even control its manners and habits. Their ignorance of much that goes on in the self-confident male world surrounding them is regarded by their men as a salutary therapeutic for the social peace of mind. From the founding of the city as a naval and military colony, the men of Halifax have held together in a solid club against the great enemy of masculine equanimity—loose information about their habits, occupations, friends and amusements among the women they love. Elderly Halifax men have told me astonishing things about other elderly Halifax men. But they would no more dream of telling these same stories to their wives than they would consider informing their wives of the exact size of their personal incomes.

Of course there are defects in this male domination which even a man must 32
recognize. It is responsible for the city's eternal look of distinguished shabbiness;
men don't care for appearances as much as women do. And it is certainly the reason why the only entertainments for which Halifax has ever been famous seem
barbarous to compatriots of the interior.

In Admiralty House or Government House, Halifax can stage a ball more 33
stately than can be seen in any other Canadian city. Yet these are not the entertainments that her older men still mention with wistful eyes. In the old days there
were banquets from which officers, immaculate in mess jackets, were seen crawling on their hands and knees up the slope of Sackville Street to the fort on the top
of the Citadel.

They tell me that Halifax has changed, and perhaps she has. Most certainly 34
I will be told that I have libelled her, and perhaps I have done that, too. As a matter of statistical fact, the majority of middle-class citizens in Halifax really do lead
the sober life they profess to lead. People are beginning to paint their houses, the
women dress much better than they once did, and perhaps they are now on the
verge of coming into their own. Halifax is even willing to admit that she is
Canadian. The day seems past when a customs inspector on the dock can speak
the words I heard in 1930: "Nova Scotians in Aisle A, aliens and Canadians in
Aisle B." Perhaps the R.C.N.V.R. sailors who tore the city apart on VE-Day have
taught Halifax that she is a part of Canada in spite of Confederation.

On a fine evening last August, after an absence of many years, I walked 35
through the south end from the gates of the park to the slope of the Citadel. The
odour of lime trees was sweet along the sidewalks, the trees were stately, everyone I passed looked quiet, comely and respectable. Traffic was far heavier than I
had remembered it, and on a corner near where I once lived stood a large, three-
storey modern garage. But when I crossed Sackville Street I knew suddenly and
irrevocably that the changes were superficial.

A man was reclining on the grass on the slope of the hill. He was wearing 36
a rough cloth cap with a broken peak, his face was lined and pock-marked, he
wore no collar or tie and his shirt was secured at the neck by a large gilt stud. As
I passed him, he leered at me, grinned, leaned on his elbow to scratch his back-
side, then took from the pocket of a soiled jacket a flask-shaped bottle which he
tilted to his mouth.

I reached the top of the Citadel and looked out over the roofs to the sea. The 37
western horizon was rose and saffron as it always is at this hour of a fine summer
evening. As the first faint evening mists rose, the harbour bells began to sound in
the distance. Darkness increased, and the harsh angles of individual buildings
faded out. The city revealed herself as a unit in all her noble contours, compact
about the shield-like slope of the Citadel. I understood that she would care little
for my opinion of her, but at that moment I knew she was still beautiful.

1970

QUESTIONS FOR DISCUSSION

Content

a. What, for MacLennan, is the source of Halifax's beauty?

b. How does Halifax compare to other cities of Canada? What conclusion does MacLennan draw from these comparisons?

c. Is MacLennan writing about the physical look of the city? What kind of a portrait is he writing?

d. What points does the description of children in the classroom make?

e. What is the Halifax Explosion? Does MacLennan take the time to explain the event? What is his concern in the explosion?

f. Why is the Senior Master in the Academy essential to any portrait of the city? How does he embody what Halifax means for MacLennan?

g. What is a small town, according to MacLennan?

h. Has Halifax changed? How does MacLennan know?

Strategy and Style

i. What organizing principle does MacLennan use to structure his description or portrait?

j. Does MacLennan give many physical details of the city?

k. Why does MacLennan compare and contrast Halifax with other cities of Canada?

l. Note how often MacLennan refers to smell. Why is smell so important to understanding Halifax?

m. How many references to alcohol does MacLennan make over the course of the essay? How do these references tie into the portrait?

n. The essay physically begins in the West and ends in Halifax at the top of the Citadel. Why does MacLennan approach the city from the outside in?

SUGGESTIONS FOR SHORT WRITING

a. Describe the children you remember in your Grade 5 class. How did they dress, look, smell? What was distinguishing about each child?

b. Write a portrait of your neighbourhood strictly in terms of its people.

SUGGESTIONS FOR SUSTAINED WRITING

a. Think of an event that caused your city/town to appear on the national news. Describe your own response and memories of the event and how the event shaped the character of the place.

b. Create a portrait of your own city/town. Find an organizing principle, a defining characteristic, and then find examples of people, buildings, and events that demonstrate that characteristic.

c. MacLennan uses an unconventional definition of beauty: "strangeness in the proportions." What is our current definition of beauty? You may wish to consider advertisements, TV, or movies. How does this definition apply to beautiful places?

My Father

Doris Lessing

Doris Lessing (b. 1919) was born in Persia, the daughter of English parents who had moved there hoping to make a good living in banking. When that venture did not turn out as her father had hoped, the family moved to Rhodesia where they settled as farmers. In 1949, Doris Lessing moved to London, where her first novel, The Grass Is Singing *(1950), won her instant fame. Soon after, she won the Somerset Maugham Award for Five* Short Novels *(1954).* The Golden Notebook *(1962), a complex autobiographical novel that weaves an exploration of the psychology of women with Lessing's views of social history, is her best-known work. An experimenter with form and subject, she covers a wide range of themes and motifs in her novels. In* Briefing for a Descent into Hell *(1971) and* Memoirs of a Survivor *(1974), for example, she deals with psychological disturbances, engages in dreamlike fantasy, and portrays a pessimistic view of history. In 1979, she began a series of "space fiction" novels beginning with the novel* Shikasta. *Recent nonfiction includes* Prisons We Choose to Live Inside *(1986) and* The Wind Blows Away Our Worlds *(1987).*

We use our parents like recurring dreams, to be entered into when needed; they are always there for love or for hate; but it occurs to me that I was not always there for my father. I've written about him before, but novels, stories, don't have to be "true." Writing this article is difficult because it has to be "true." I knew him when his best years were over. 1

There are photographs of him. The largest is of an officer in the 1914–18 war. A new uniform—buttoned, badged, strapped, tabbed—confines a handsome, dark young man who holds himself stiffly to confront what he certainly thought of as his duty. His eyes are steady, serious, and responsible, and show no signs of what he became later. A photograph at sixteen is of a dark, introspective youth with the same intent eyes. But it is his mouth you notice—a heavily-jutting upper lip contradicts the rest of a regular face. His moustache was to hide it: "Had to do something—a damned fleshy mouth. Always made me uncomfortable, that mouth of mine." 2

Earlier a baby (eyes already alert) appears in a lace waterfall that cascades from the pillowy bosom of a fat, plain woman to her feet. It is the face of a head cook. "Lord, but my mother was a practical female—almost as bad as you!" as he used to say, or throw at my mother in moments of exasperation. Beside her stands, or droops, arms dangling, his father, the source of the dark, arresting eyes, but otherwise masked by a long beard. 3

The birth certificate says: Born 3rd August, 1886, Walton Villa, Creffield Road, S. Mary at the Wall, R.S.D. Name, Alfred Cook. Name and surname of Father: Alfred Cook Tayler. Name and maiden name of Mother: Caroline May Batley. Rank or Profession: Bank Clerk. Colchester, Essex. 4

They were very poor. Clothes and boots were a problem. They "made their own amusements." Books were mostly the Bible and *The Pilgrim's Progress.* Every Saturday night they bathed in a hipbath in front of the kitchen fire. No servants. 5

Church three times on Sundays. "Lord, when I think of those Sundays! I dreaded them all week, like a nightmare coming at you full tilt and no escape." But he rabbited with ferrets along the lanes and fields, bird-nested, stole fruit, picked nuts and mushrooms, paid visits to the blacksmith and the mill and rode a farmer's carthorse.

They ate economically, but when he got diabetes in his forties and subsisted   6
on lean meat and lettuce leaves, he remembered suet puddings, treacle puddings, raisin and currant puddings, steak and kidney puddings, bread and butter puddings, "batter cooked in the gravy with the meat," potato cake, plum cake, butter cake, porridge with treacle, fruit tarts and pies, brawn, pig's trotters and pig's cheek and homesmoked ham and sausages. And "lashings of fresh butter and cream and eggs." He wondered if this diet had produced the diabetes, but said it was worth it.

There was an elder brother described by my father as: "Too damned clever   7
by half. One of those quick, clever brains. Now I've always had a slow brain, but I get there in the end, damn it!"

The brothers went to a local school and the elder did well, but my father was   8
beaten for being slow. They both became bank clerks in, I think, the Westminster Bank, and one must have found it congenial, for he became a manager, the "rich brother," who had cars and even a yacht. But my father did not like it, though he was conscientious. For instance, he changed his writing, letter by letter, because a senior criticised it. I never saw his unregenerate hand, but the one he created was elegant, spiky, careful. Did this mean he created a new personality for himself, hiding one he did not like, as he hid his "damned fleshy mouth"? I don't know.

Nor do I know when he left home to live in Luton, or why. He found family   9
life too narrow? A safe guess—he found everything too narrow. His mother was too down-to-earth? He had to get away from his clever elder brother?

Being a young man in Luton was the best part of his life. It ended in 1914,   10
so he had a decade of happiness. His reminiscences of it were all of pleasure, the delight of physical movement, of dancing in particular. All his girls were "a beautiful dancer, light as a feather." He played billiards and ping-pong (both for his country); he swam, boated, played cricket and football, went to picnics and horse races, sang at musical evenings. One family of a mother and two daughters treated him "like a son only better. I didn't know whether I was in love with the mother or the daughters, but oh I did love going there; we had such good times." He was engaged to one daughter, then, for a time, to the other. An engagement was broken off because she was rude to a waiter. "I could not marry a woman who allowed herself to insult someone who was defenseless." He used to say to my wryly smiling mother: "Just as well I didn't marry either of *them;* they would never have stuck it out the way you have, old girl."

Just before he died he told me he had dreamed he was standing in a kitchen   11
on a very high mountain holding X in his arms. "Ah, yes, that's what I've missed in my life. Now don't you let yourself be cheated out of life by the old dears. They take all the colour out of everything if you let them."

But in that decade—"I'd walk 10, 15 miles to a dance two or three times a   12
week and think nothing of it. Then I'd dance every dance and walk home again

over the fields. Sometimes it was moonlight, but I liked the snow best all crisp and fresh. I loved walking back and getting into my digs just as the sun was rising. My little dog was so happy to see me, and I'd feed her, and make myself porridge and tea, then I'd wash and shave and go off to work."

The boy who was beaten at school, who went too much to church, who car- 13 ried the fear of poverty all his life, but who nevertheless was filled with the memories of country pleasures; the young bank clerk who worked such long hours for so little money, but who danced, sang, played, flirted—this naturally vigorous, sensuous being was killed in 1914, 1915, 1916. I think the best of my father died in that war, that his spirit was crippled by it. The people I've met, particularly the women, who knew him young, speak of his high spirits, his energy, his enjoyment of life. Also of his kindness, his compassion and—a word that keeps recurring— his wisdom. "Even when he was just a boy he understood things that you'd think even an old man would find it easy to condemn." I do not think these people would have easily recognised the ill, irritable, abstracted, hypochondriac man I knew.

He "joined up" as an ordinary soldier out of a characteristically quirky scru- 14 ple: it wasn't right to enjoy officers' privileges when the Tommies had such a bad time. But he could not stick the communal latrines, the obligatory drinking, the collective visits to brothels, the jokes about girls. So next time he was offered a commission he took it.

His childhood and young man's memories, kept fluid, were added to, grew, as 15 living memories do. But his war memories were congealed in stories that he told again and again, with the same words and gestures, in stereotyped phrases. They were anonymous, general, as if they had come out of a communal war memoir. He met a German in no-man's-land, but both slowly lowered their rifles and smiled and walked away. The Tommies were the salt of the earth, the British fighting men the best in the world. He had never known such comradeship. A certain brutal officer was shot in a sortie by his men, but the other officers, recognising rough justice, said nothing. He had known men intimately who saw the Angels at Mons. He wished he could force all the generals on both sides into the trenches for just one day, to see what the common soldiers endured—*that* would have ended the war at once.

There was an undercurrent of memories, dreams, and emotions much 16 deeper, more personal. This dark region in him, fate-ruled, where nothing was true but horror, was expressed inarticulately, in brief, bitter exclamations or phrases of rage, incredulity, betrayal. The men who went to fight in that war believed it when they said it was to end war. My father believed it. And he was never able to reconcile his belief in his country with his anger at the cynicism of its leaders. And the anger, the sense of betrayal, strengthened as he grew old and ill.

But in 1914 he was naïve, the German atrocities in Belgium inflamed him, 17 and he enlisted out of idealism, although he knew he would have a hard time. He knew because a fortuneteller told him. (He could be described as uncritically superstitious or as psychically gifted.) He would be in great danger twice, yet not die—he was being protected by a famous soldier who was his ancestor. "And sure enough, later I heard from the Little Aunties that the church records showed we were descended the backstairs way from the Duke of Wellington, or was it Marl-borough? Damn it, I forget. But one of them would be beside me all through the war, she said." (He was romantic, not only about this solicitous ghost, but also about being a descendant of the Huguenots, on the strength of the "e" in Tayler; and about "the wild blood" in his veins from a great uncle who, sent unjustly to prison for smuggling, came out of a ten-year sentence and earned it, very efficiently, along the coasts of Cornwall until he died.)

The luckiest thing that ever happened to my father, he said, was getting his **18** leg shattered by shrapnel ten days before Passchendaele. His whole company was killed. He knew he was going to be wounded because of the fortuneteller, who had said he would know. "I did not understand what she meant, but both times in the trenches, first when my appendix burst and I nearly died, and then just before Passchendaele, I felt for some days as if a thick, black velvet pall was settled over me. I can't tell you what it was like. Oh, it was awful, and the second time it was so bad I wrote to the old people and told them I was going to be killed."

His leg was cut off at mid-thigh, he was shell-shocked, he was very ill for **19** many months, with a prolonged depression afterwards. "You should always remember that sometimes people are all seething underneath. You don't know what terrible things people have to fight against. You should look at a person's eyes, that's how you tell. . . . When I was like that, after I lost my leg, I went to a nice doctor man and said I was going mad, but he said, don't worry, everyone locks up things like that. You don't know—horrible, horrible, awful things. I was afraid of myself, of what I used to dream. I wasn't myself at all."

In the Royal Free Hospital was my mother, Sister McVeagh. He married his **20** nurse which, as they both said often enough (though in different tones of voice), was just as well. That was 1919. He could not face being a bank clerk in England, he said, not after the trenches. Besides, England was too narrow and conventional. Besides, the civilians did not know what the soldiers had suffered, they didn't want to know, and now it wasn't done even to remember "The Great Unmentionable." He went off to the Imperial Bank of Persia, in which country I was born.

The house was beautiful, with great stone-floored high-ceilinged rooms **21** whose windows showed ranges of snow-streaked mountains. The gardens were full of roses, jasmine, pomegranates, walnuts. Kermanshah he spoke of with liking, but soon they went to Teheran, populous with "Embassy people," and my gregarious mother created a lively social life about which he was irritable even in recollection.

Irritableness—that note was first struck here, about Persia. He did not like, **22** he said, "the graft and the corruption." But here it is time to try and describe something difficult—how a man's good qualities can also be his bad ones, or if not bad, a danger to him.

My father was honourable—he always knew exactly what that word meant. **23** He had integrity. His "one does not do that sort of thing," his "no, it is *not* right," sounded throughout my childhood and were final for all of us. I am sure it was true he wanted to leave Persia because of "the corruption." But it was also because he was already unconsciously longing for something freer, because as a bank official he could not let go into the dream-logged personality that was waiting for him. And later in Rhodesia, too, what was best in him was also what prevented him from shaking away the shadows: it was always in the name of honesty or decency that he refused to take this step or that out of the slow decay of the family's fortunes.

In 1925 there was leave from Persia. That year in London there was an Empire Exhibition, and on the Southern Rhodesian stand some very fine maize cobs and a poster saying that fortunes could be made on maize at 25/-a bag. So on an impulse, turning his back forever on England, washing his hands of the corruption of the East, my father collected all his capital, £800, I think, while my mother packed curtains from Liberty's, clothes from Harrods, visiting cards, a piano, Persian rugs, a governess and two small children. **24**

Soon, there was my father in a cigar-shaped house of thatch and mud on the top of a kopje that overlooked in all directions a great system of mountains, rivers, valleys, while overhead the sky arched from horizon to empty horizon. This was a couple of hundred miles south from the Zambesi, a hundred or so west from Mozambique, in the district of Banket, so called because certain of its reefs were of the same formation as those called *banket* on the Rand. Lomagundi—gold country, tobacco country, maize country—wild, almost empty. (The Africans had been turned off it into reserves.) Our neighbours were four, five, seven miles off. In front of the house . . . no neighbours, nothing; no farms, just wild bush with two rivers but no fences to the mountains seven miles away. And beyond these mountains and bush again to the Portuguese border, over which "our boys" used to escape when wanted by the police for pass or other offences. **25**

And then? There was bad luck. For instance, the price of maize dropped from 25/- to 9/-a bag. The seasons were bad, prices bad, crops failed. This was the sort of thing that made it impossible for him ever to "get off the farm," which, he agreed with my mother, was what he most wanted to do. **26**

It was an absurd country, he said. A man could "own" a farm for years that was totally mortgaged to the Government and run from the Land Bank, meanwhile employing half-a-hundred Africans at 12/-a month and none of them knew how to do a day's work. Why, two farm labourers from Europe could do in a day what twenty of these ignorant black savages would take a week to do. (Yet he was proud that he had a name as a just employer, that he gave "a square deal.") Things got worse. A fortuneteller had told him that her heart ached when she saw the misery ahead for my father: this was the misery. **27**

But it was my mother who suffered. After a period of neurotic illness, which was a protest against her situation, she became brave and resourceful. But she never saw that her husband was not living in a real world, that he had made a captive of her common sense. We were always about to "get off the farm." A miracle would do it—a sweepstake, a goldmine, a legacy. And then? What a question! We would go to England where life would be normal with people coming in for musical evenings and nice supper parties at the Trocadero after a show. Poor woman, for the twenty years we were on the farm, she waited for when life would begin **28**

for her and for her children, for she never understood that what was a calamity for
her was for them a blessing.

Meanwhile my father sank towards his death (at 61). Everything changed in 29
him. He had been a dandy and fastidious, now he hated to change out of shabby
khaki. He had been sociable, now he was misanthropic. His body's disorders—
soon diabetes and all kinds of stomach ailments—dominated him. He was brave
about his wooden leg, and even went down mine shafts and climbed trees with it,
but he walked clumsily and it irked him badly. He greyed fast, and slept more in
the day, but would be awake half the night pondering about. . . .

It could be gold divining. For ten years he experimented on private theories 30
to do with the attractions and repulsions of metals. His whole soul went into it but
his theories were wrong or he was *unlucky*—after all, if he had found a mine he
would have had to leave the farm. It could be the relation between the minerals of
the earth and of the moon; his decision to make infusions of all the plants on the
farm and drink them himself in the interests of science; the criminal folly of the
British Government in not realizing that the Germans and the Russians were conspiring as Anti-Christ to . . . the inevitability of war because no one would listen
to Churchill, but it would be all right because God (by then he was a British Is-
raelite) had destined Britain to rule the world; a prophecy said 10 million dead
would surround Jerusalem—how would the corpses be cleared away?; people who
wished to abolish flogging should be flogged; the natives understood nothing but
a good beating; hanging must not be abolished because the Old Testament said "an
eye for an eye and a tooth for a tooth. . . ."

Yet, as this side of him darkened, so that it seemed all his thoughts were of 31
violence, illness, war, still no one dared to make an unkind comment in his presence or to gossip. Criticism of people, particularly of women, made him more and
more uncomfortable till at last he burst out with: "It's all very well, but no one has
the right to say that about another person."

In Africa, when the sun goes down, the stars spring up, all of them in their 32
expected places, glittering and moving. In the rainy season, the sky flashed and
thundered. In the dry season, the great dark hollow of night was lit by veld fires:
the mountains burned through September and October in chains of red fire. Every
night my father took out his chair to watch the sky and the mountains, smoking,
silent, a thin shabby fly-away figure under the stars. "Makes you think—there are
so many worlds up there, wouldn't really matter if we did blow ourselves up—
plenty more where we came from."

The Second World War, so long foreseen by him, was a bad time. His son 33
was in the Navy and in danger, and his daughter a sorrow to him. He became very
ill. More and more often it was necessary to drive him into Salisbury with him in
a coma, or in danger of one, on the back seat. My mother moved him into a pretty
little suburban house in town near the hospitals, where he took to his bed and a
couple of years later died. For the most part he was unconscious under drugs.
When awake he talked obsessively (a tongue licking a nagging sore place) about
"the old war." Or he remembered his youth. "I've been dreaming—Lord, to see

those horses come lickety-split down the course with their necks stretched out and the sun on their coats and everyone shouting. . . . I've been dreaming how I walked along the river in the mist as the sun was rising. . . . Lord, lord, lord, what a time that was, what good times we all had then, before the old war."

1956

QUESTIONS FOR DISCUSSION

Content

a. What was Lessing's motivation for writing this article? Does she ever reveal her motives?

b. What role does physical description play in this brilliant psychological portrait? To what extent does Lessing combine description with techniques normally associated with narration?

c. Does the overall image Lessing builds of her father satisfy you? Is the behaviour of her father accounted for in her description of specific, perhaps isolated, events?

d. What image does Lessing build of her father by contrasting his youth with his old age? By contrasting remembrances of the past with the present?

e. Does Lessing ever reveal who or what is the main cause of her father's deterioration? What do you think is the main cause?

f. How does World War I change Lessing's father? Why were the changes significant? What are Lessing's feelings about them?

g. Besides showing that her father relied on reminiscences to justify current situations, Lessing shows that he dreamt of future successes as a way to justify current hardships (paragraphs 26 through 28). What do reminiscing and dreaming reveal about the author's father? What do they reveal about the author?

Strategy and Style

h. In the first paragraph, Lessing says that this essay "has to be 'true.' " Why does she tell us this, and how does her insistence that the essay be true affect its content and tone?

i. Why does Lessing put quotation marks around "true"? How do you define this word? How closely does this essay conform to your definition? Must an essay be factual in order to be true?

j. Lessing uses details of her father's youth to counterbalance those about his old age, yet she must rely on his own reminiscences for information about his youth. In what ways might these reminiscences affect the essay's truthfulness?

k. Lessing distinguishes between types of memories: reminiscences (paragraph 10), living memories (paragraph 15), congealed war stories (paragraph 15), undercurrent of personal memories (paragraph 16), hallucinatory dreaming (paragraph 33). Why does she make these distinctions?

l. How objective is Lessing in recalling her father? Are there any phrases or passages that reveal positive or negative feelings about him?

SUGGESTIONS FOR SHORT WRITING

a. Annotate this essay, writing down, as well as you can remember, what you were thinking as you read. Write your comments in the margins or jot them down in your notebook.

b. Then, choose one of your annotations and write a short explanation to yourself about why you wrote that annotation.

SUGGESTIONS FOR SUSTAINED WRITING

a. Write a history of your father or mother in which you rely on photographs and reminiscences to build a "truthful" image of him or her. Keep in mind your motivation for doing this history.

b. What might a history of yourself, written by your parents, be like? How objective and/or truthful would it be? Write a history of yourself from either parent's point of view.

c. Read other essays in this anthology that use memory and personal reminiscence as a framework (for example, "No Name Woman," "Wooding," "Grandmother's Victory"). Write a reflective essay on the significance of memory as a means to create meaning and order out of past events.

Easter in Sicily*

Mary Taylor Simeti

Born and raised in New York City, Mary Taylor Simeti (b. 1941) celebrated her graduation from Radcliffe College in 1962 with a trip to Sicily. There she worked as a volunteer at a centre for community development started by Danilo Dolci, the social reformer whose writings on social, cultural, and economic life in Sicily had caught Simeti's attention while in college. After completing graduate work, she returned to Sicily, married a young agronomist ("Tonino"), and settled there. "Easter in Sicily" first appeared in On Persephone's Island: A Sicilian Journal *(1986). Set against the story of Persephone, the Greek vegetation myth about the changing of the seasons, Simeti's journal is both a meditation and an evocative exploration of Sicilian folklore, history, religion, and natural environment. It explains why Simeti decided to settle on this "island of dazzling sun and bright colors." Among her other works are* Pomp and Sustenance: Twenty-Five Centuries of Sicilian Food *(1991) and* A Taste of Ancient Rome *(1992).*

Beyond the vague intention of ending up at Prizzi to see the devils dance on Easter 1 afternoon, we have no set itinerary for the rest of the day and decide to drive east along the southern coast, turning or stopping at whim. And whim soon declares itself: only a short distance from Castelvetrano there are road signs indicating the turnoff for Selinunte, and it seems sinful not to make a stop when we have all the time in the world.

Selinunte is to me the least accessible of the Greek sites I have seen in Sicily. 2 The bare bones of a city sacked by man and toppled by earthquake lie in careless heaps on low cliffs overlooking the sea, building blocks abandoned by some infant Titan who has centuries since outgrown them. They are illegible in their very size, with the tourists clambering over the enormous fluted drums of fallen columns like tiny, multicolored ants. Today it is very crowded; parking is difficult and the air rings with a many-tongued babble and with the nagging claxons of the tourist buses gathering their various broods. We mingle with the crowds, wander through the eastern temples, and stroll along the road that leads down into the river valley and up to the acropolis on the opposite cliff until the heat and the confusion persuade us to turn back.

Selinunte was a revelation the first time I came, exactly twenty years ago yes- 3 terday. Apart from Tonino and me there were no more than a dozen people here, and even these disappeared, swallowed up by the vast sweep of sea and plain and the immoderate proportions of the ruins. We sat for hours on some stones and stared out across sea and centuries, the sea of flowers in the foreground no less brilliant than the Mediterranean that sparkled in the distance. The *selinon*, the wild celery that gave the ancient city its name, was submerged by the red of the sulla, the yellow of mayflowers and mustard, the blue of bugloss and borage, bobbing and trembling under the insistent and noisy prodding of thousands of bees. It was my first immersion in the Sicilian spring, in its colors and its perfumes and its heat, a baptism that caught and held me convert. Today the flowers are still as beautiful, the

*Editors' title.

93

sun perhaps even hotter, but the crowd and the confusion drown out the bees, and the ruins are silent, unable despite their size to cope with this Lilliputian invasion.

We continue eastward and then turn north on the road for Caltabellotta, which 4 winds up over the ridge of low mountains that separates the southern coastal plain east of Selinunte from the rolling hills of the interior. These mountains are quite barren, with patches of vineyard or wheat exploiting the rare flat spaces, an occasional olive or almond tree clinging to the steep and rocky slopes, and, as closer inspection reveals, a sparse carpeting of the crouching, grasping plants of arid soil and high altitudes: Purple squill, delicate white clusters of star-of-Bethlehem, the single tiny yellow-and-brown orchids of the lutea family, and the many-flowered stalks of the *orchis italica,* bristling with minute pink tentacles.

The village of Caltabellotta lies at the summit of the highest mountain in this 5 southern ridge, topped only by two great spurs of rock that thrust up behind it like giant tusks. The streets are narrow and zigzag steeply up the hillside; a policeman directing all five cars' worth of traffic instructs us to park the car and continue on foot if we want to see the procession. Of course we do, so we quickly park and follow the main street up to a point where it splits, one fork leading farther up a very steep slope, the other curving down to the right into a tiny piazza. The "procession" is here—townspeople and bandsmen, their instruments tucked forgotten under their elbows, have gathered in a circle to cheer and applaud a dancing saint, a life-size plaster statue of the Archangel Michael, the town's patron. Michael, dressed in the armor of a Roman legionary, is leaning against a column that has been completely wrapped in purple phlox, with a young laurel tree tied next to it so that the purple flowers glow against the dark leaves. As in Tràpani and Castelvetrano, the flower-decked platform that bears the statue is mounted on two poles—in this case very long, thick wooden beams that of themselves must weigh an enormous amount—and requires some thirty hefty young men to carry it. But "carry" is not the right word: they rock and jostle and bounce the statue in the most extraordinary manner, accompanied and encouraged by a crescendo of cheering and clapping from the crowd that presses in around them. Sweat pouring off their faces, the young men push and pull still harder on their poles, and the Archangel rocks and sways and reels in a frenzied dance, until his porters can bear it no longer, the movement subsides into a faint bobbing, and the statue itself seems to pant as the men fight to catch their breath, still holding all the weight on their shoulders.

Bottles of water and beer are passed around, the band recovers its role and 6 starts to play again, and considerable maneuvering is necessary to effect the passage of the statue around the curve and into the main street, where it pauses at the foot of the rise, gathering strength. Meanwhile another statue arrives, a little winged cherub about two feet high, with platform, poles, and porters in proportion: a handful of boys about twelve years old bounce the baby statue about in great excitement, egged on by an amused crowd.

The music dies out, and, at a sign from one of the porters, the drummer 7 sounds a roll. On the final snap of the drumsticks the men charge up the street, running and stumbling with their heavy burden up a slope so steep that the statue seems almost horizontal. The cheers of the onlookers assist them over the top and around the corner, quickly followed by the angel, who bobs gaily and effortlessly up the rise in the wake of his big brother.

We too turn and climb. We have lost the statues, but echoes of their progress **8** parallel to ours reach us at the street corners. A final hike up a street so sheer that the sidewalk is a flight of stairs brings us out onto the Piano della Matrice, the open square of the mother church, unexpectedly spectacular. In front of us a wide checkerboard of cobble and grass slopes gently up to the steps of the Matrice, built by Count Roger after he took Caltabellotta from the Saracens in 1090. The weathered gray stone of the Norman church blends into the sharp-toothed rock that rises abruptly behind it. On the left-hand side of the square stands the chapel of San Michele, its Gothic portal garlanded in laurel branches, and next to it a gate and a stairway carved into the live rock lead off toward the second, bigger pinnacle, ringed by the trees of the town park where the ruins of the Norman castle lie.

Commotion rising from below tells us that Saint Michael is about to make his **9** final assault on the mountain. The last steep rise is rendered more problematical by telephone wires and shop signs, and considerable measuring accompanied by animated discussion is necessary before a strategy can be agreed upon. At last somebody climbs out on a balcony and unties a laundry line, final directions are shouted out, and the group braces itself. Up they come, the initial momentum waning as they scramble up the cobbled street, their boots slipping and straining to find a grip on the polished stones. A final push and they burst into the square, where they bring up sharply, the statue swaying back and forth, evidently in some confusion as to where to go next.

One of the townsmen who has followed the progress of the statue explains **10** to us that the municipal *pro loco* committee has decided that Caltabellotta should cash in on the "Easter in Sicily" tourist boom and has organized a new procession for the afternoon, a version of the Castelvetrano Aurora, but the details have not been thought out all that well, and no one knows whether Michael should spend his lunch hour in the Matrice or in the chapel of San Michele, where the garlands declare a readiness to receive him sooner or later.

After a few false starts and some rather languishing discussion, Michael is car- **11** ried up the steps and into the dark interior of the Matrice. We start to follow it, but a priest, heretofore absent from the scene, closes the door firmly in our faces. Lunchtime. The Matrice is closed, the chapel is closed, the gate to the castle is closed. The best we can do is climb up some stone steps that lead around behind the Matrice, to discover that the rock is sheltering a miniature Alpine meadow, shaded by pine trees whose sun-warmed resin fills the air and dotted with tiny daisies, the kind whose white petals have had their tips dipped in red. I remember the flowers from a French children's book I had when I was little, and it is surprising yet suitable to find their smiling faces here in the shadow of the Norman walls. The view from the meadow is spectacular: We can look north toward the mountains of Palermo across the whole of Sicily, the hills and valleys flattened from this height into a gentle pool of green, flecked with the white foam of the blossoming fruit trees.

The priest had something, however. Our stomachs call us to more prosaic **12** questions. We discover that Caltabellotta offers a choice of two restaurants, one in the town itself and one just outside, around the back of the peak that rises above the castle ruins. Walking down toward the car we pass the first, which is occupied by a baptismal party and has no free tables. A winding road takes us out of town, past vegetable plots and tiny vineyards, to a huge baroque monastery, this too flanked by a cliff and by a charming restaurant with a trellised terrace. The proprietor is polite and extremely apologetic: A wedding reception is in progress, and there isn't a free chair in the place. Tonino, undaunted or perhaps desperate, asks if they couldn't fix us a little antipasto to go. After a brief wait the obliging host produces three foil-covered plates, a bottle of mineral water, and a round kilo loaf of fragrant, crusty bread. We drive back along the road a little way to a curve that offers space to park and some rocks to sit on. Our plates turn out to hold spicy olives, some slices of *prosciutto crudo* and of a peppery local salame, and two kinds of pecorino cheese, one fresh and mild, the other aged and sharper. With a bag of oranges from the car, the sun warm on our backs, the mountains rolling down at our feet to the southern coast and the sea beyond, where the heat haze clouds the horizon and hides Africa from view, we have as fine an Easter dinner as I have ever eaten.

The drive north to Prizzi, a rapid descent switchbacking down the north side 13 of the mountain to the green valleys we had seen from above, takes us along luxuriant riverbeds, over hills of green wheat, past isolated pear and apple trees in bloom. The hedgerows are overflowing with flowers, unable to contain such a riot of color, such an exuberance of form and texture. It is difficult to believe that in the space of a few months the velvet softness of the wheat fields, shifting from emerald to chartreuse with the wind, will give way to bristling, colorless stubble; these are the hills that the Lampedusa family cross in the Visconti film of *The Leopard,* in blinding light and smothering dust, their carriages creaking to the shrill song of the locusts.

But the extravagant hand of spring is less and less successful in concealing 14 the poverty of the agriculture the farther north we go. Our destination, the village of Prizzi, is quite high, slapped down on a hill of rock soil and stunted vegetation with none of the cozy shifting and filling with which most Sicilian towns have accommodated themselves to the bones of that island. The outskirts of the town are ringed with the usual half-finished houses, fruit of the emigrants' remittances, but once past them the streets are small and close and we are hard put to find a parking space and then to fight our way through the crowds that are thronging toward the center of town, the ranks of the Prizzitani being very much swollen by both foreign and Sicilian tourists. Tonino greets several of his students from the university, then most unexpectedly a hand claps down on my shoulder. It is Nicolò, a man who served on the school board with me. He is a native of Prizzi, a linesman for the telephone company, and after a period of technical schooling in Milan now lives in Palermo, where, fortified by his northern experience, he has become very active in the local section of the Communist party, in the neighborhood council, the trade union, and the school board. He proved a most unusual and valuable addition to the school board, able and willing to work on two levels in a way that is rare among Sicilians, ready to debate the ideological or educational implications of a policy decision and at the same time to fix a light plug or repair a busted slide projector himself rather than trusting to the lengthy meanderings of the school bureaucracy. But today he is here in Prizzi to be with his family and to see the devils dance.

We are lucky to run into him. We have arrived too late for the distribution of 15
the *cannateddi*, Prizzi's special Easter cakes, but Nicolò carries us off to the Cir-
colo della Caccia, the Hunters' Club, which the Chamber of Commerce has been
using as its headquarters for the occasion, and there he sets various cousins scurrying around to unearth some last undistributed *cannateddi* for us, oval cakes of
biscuit dough braided about an egg.

    Cannateddi in hand, we follow Nicolò out again and push our way along the 16
main street, which dips sharply down, then rises again in the distance. Nicolò
guides us to the lowest point in the street, where he tells us to stay put, this being
a grandstand seat for watching the triumph of Good over Evil. The street is filled
with people, strolling, talking, and shouting across from one crowded balcony to
another. Here at the bottom we can look up in either direction at a sea of faces. A
small and hornèd vortex is descending upon us from the eastern end: the devils are
coming, accompanied by the clanking of their chains and the squealing and shouting of a swarm of little boys. There are three masked figures, two devils escorting
Death. Death is dressed in yellow, a big, loose-fitting yellow jump suit and a yellow mask of soldered tin covering his whole head in the shape of a skull, in which
have been cut eyeholes, a black dent for the nose, and a mouth grinning around a
few long and crooked teeth. Under his arm is a crossbow with which he menaces
the crowd. The devils have rust-colored jump suits, ample enough to accommodate a variety of figures over the years, and their masks are large, flat tin ovals,
painted brown, with curved horns, long noses, and tongues sticking out from leering mouths. The backs of their heads and shoulders are covered by heavy, long-
haired goat pelts, black for one, white for the other, a touch of the genuine that is
somehow much more menacing than the masks themselves. The multicolored
stripes of Adidas sneakers show underneath the baggy trouser legs.

    Comfortable shoes are a must for the devils, whose loping, lolloping dance be- 17
trays considerable weariness. Well it may, says Nicolò: they have been dancing ever
since the hour of the Crucifixion on Friday, chasing about the town making mischief
and teasing all they encounter. Nicolò was a devil one year and assures us that the costumes are unbearably hot and heavy, especially on a sunny day like today—the only
thing that keeps you going is the wine. Anyone whom Death manages to hit with his
crossbow is obliged to stand the devils a round at the nearest tavern, and if Death is a
good shot, they all have quite a bit under their jump suits by the end of the day.

    There is movement up at either end of the street, and for the second time to- 18
day we are shoved back against the buildings by white-gloved policemen. The
street is long and I can barely make out the Madonna to the east, Christ to the west,
and just hear the loudest notes of the band. Down the hill come the forces of Good,
two angels in armor, with cardboard wings, red capes, ropes of beads and gilt chains
across their breasts, swords in hand, and strange flat-topped helmets that Francesco
is quick to notice have been cut out from Alemagna panettone boxes. The devils at
first have the best of these bizarre apparitions; a brief skirmish leads to a hasty retreat, and then a counterattack. Back and forth they run and clash and feint as the
statues continue their slow but steady descent. The battlefield shrinks as the statues
draw nearer, the dance and the swordwork grow more and more frenzied as the dev-

ils find themselves hemmed in between the advancing figures, until a last and desperate leap marks the meeting between the risen Christ and the rejoicing Madonna, and Death and the devils fall to earth, vanquished and immobile.

This scene will be repeated four more times this evening, the last time in the 19 dark in the big piazza in front of the Matrice, at the top of the hill. Nicolò urges us to stay, but it is a long way back to Bosco and it is already half past five, so we say good-bye. Drunk with all that we have seen, my cheeks burning from the sun and wind, and my eyes watering, I can hardly take in the landscape we drive through, nor do I notice where we are when Tonino turns his attention from the road to give me a reproachful glance.

"When I was a boy, I spent all my time *avoiding* processions!" 20

1986

QUESTIONS FOR DISCUSSION

Content

a. Simeti finds examples of both Gothic and Norman architectural styles in Caltabellota. Use an encyclopedia or unabridged dictionary to learn more about these styles. You might also want to consult an encyclopedia to learn a little about the history and geography of Sicily.
b. Is Simeti describing religious rituals, or is her focus on the people and places that give those rituals their special characters? Can you think of another reason she might have written this essay?
c. Why aren't Simeti and her husband, Tonino, upset about not being able to follow the statue of St. Michael into the Matrice? What does this tell you about the writer and her attitude about what she is witnessing?
d. At the essay's conclusion, we learn that the author and her husband are "Drunk with all that [they] have seen." What is Simeti driving at? If you could write a thesis statement for this essay, what would it be?

Strategy and Style

e. This essay is about the most important feast in the Christian calendar. Why, then, does the author begin with a visit to the ruins of Selinunte, a pre-Christian Greek settlement?
f. Paragraphs 4 and 5 reveal Simeti's ability to focus closely on a subject and describe it in fine detail. Where else in the essay is her ability to do this evident?
g. "Easter in Sicily" is heavy with narrative detail, yet its primary purpose is to describe, not to narrate. What defines this essay as descriptive?
h. This is a three-part essay, organized around places Simeti visits: Selinunte, Caltabellota, and Prizzi. Nonetheless, it remains unified and flows smoothly. What do the three parts of this essay have in common? What is the "glue" that holds them together?

i. What in Simeti's style tells us that this essay is aimed at readers who may not know much about Sicilian culture?

j. How would you define Simeti's tone—her attitude toward her subject? In what way is it appropriate to an essay that describes religious rituals?

k. What is the author's attitude toward the people who take part in the processions she observes?

l. This essay incorporates details from all of the senses. Identify places in the text that appeal to each of the five senses.

SUGGESTIONS FOR SHORT WRITING

a. Using a list, an outline, or freewriting, write down what you consider the most important features or aspects of a religious or civic ceremony with which you are very familiar or in which you have participated.

b. This essay displays Simeti's ability to paint lavish word pictures. Take paragraphs 12 and 18, for example. Write a paragraph that focuses on a street scene or landscape. Describe your subject by filling your paragraph with visual details (colour, size, shape, etc.) about the people, animals, vegetation, and objects you see. However, try to use information from the other senses as well.

SUGGESTIONS FOR SUSTAINED WRITING

a. Write a letter to a friend or classmate who is planning a first visit to a city or area that you have been to and remember well. Make your letter a kind of travel guide that will describe buildings, monuments, shops, markets, museums, historic homes, natural phenomena, or other points of interest. Like Simeti, also prepare your reader for the people and attractions he or she might encounter. Whether the place you write about is in your own country or in another country, focus on a limited area. For example, writing about three or four neighbourhoods in San Francisco is preferable to recalling your two-week trip to northern California.

b. Simeti uses description to explain ritual, specifically how she and others celebrated a religious holiday. Take your lead from "Easter in Sicily" by describing the rituals associated with a holiday, religious or not, that you know well. Focus on the visual, but whenever possible, rely on your other senses for information. For example, Simeti uses both visual and auditory details in paragraph 16. In paragraph 12, she appeals to several senses. If you responded to the first of the Suggestions for Short Writing above, you may have already gathered material to use in your essay.

3

Process Analysis

Often thought of as a way to develop scientific papers, process analysis can be used with a variety of topics and in combination with many of the other methods of development illustrated in this text. It is the type of writing used to convey instructions—how to change a tire, take someone's temperature, cook a carp, or paint a fresco! Process analysis can also explain how something happens or happened—the birth of a planet or the way you convinced your boss to give you a raise.

Like narratives, essays on such topics generally follow chronological order, with each step in the process likened to events in a well-developed plot. Much is made of transitional words and phrases to keep the reader on the right track. "First," Euell Gibbons tells us, "instead of merely scaling the fish [my brother] skinned them." And like any good storyteller, the writer of process analysis usually begins at the beginning and follows through to the end, sometimes listing steps by number but always providing sufficient detail to help the reader picture the activity accurately and concretely.

Sometimes writers of process analysis infuse their work with vivid, if not unnerving, description like the kind we find in Jessica Mitford's "Behind the Formaldehyde Curtain." More often than not, however, process papers also explain the relationship of causes and effects, as in Alexander Petrunkevitch's "The Spider and the Wasp."

Nonetheless, the purpose of process analysis is instructive in the most practical sense: Narration and description may show *what* happens, causal analysis may explain *why* it happens, but process analysis always focuses on *how* it happens. The most important aspect of any process essay, therefore, is clarity. Readers will not follow unless your explanations are complete, your language is familiar, and your organization is simple. Take your lead from Joe Fiorito, who gives important advice and information about cooking in easy-to-follow steps. And

100

whenever you give instructions, pay your readers the courtesy of preparing them for the task by mentioning required tools, materials, and expectations, as does Adam Goodheart in "How to Paint a Fresco."

Of course, explaining a process does not give you licence to produce prose that is dull. Sue Hubbell's "Honey Harvest" offers comic relief while explaining a process that is potentially painful and dangerous.

Like selections in other parts of this text, those that appear here represent a variety of subjects, approaches, and styles. But there is a common denominator. As you might expect, the selections that follow are models of clarity, but their authors never seem cold and detached, even when explaining what might first seem recondite or abstract. The committed, sometimes impassioned, voice of the writer always comes through. That is probably why we read these sometimes "technical" pieces with alacrity. Each selection has something important to teach us, but the lesson has relatively little to do with the process its author describes. What we learn here is a need to respect the reader, to understand our attitude toward the subject, and to believe that what we have to say is important.

The Spider and the Wasp

Alexander Petrunkevitch

*Alexander Petrunkevitch (1875–1964) arrived in the United States around the turn of
the last century after having studied in Russia, his native country, and in Germany. A
world-famous zoologist, Petrunkevitch taught at several American universities including
Harvard and Yale. As an expert on spiders, he published what is now a standard
reference in the field:* Index Catalogue of Spiders of North, Central and South America.
*Like Claudia Glenn Dowling, Petrunkevitch writes scientific prose that, while accurate
and well documented, is colourful, exciting, and accessible to readers with little
scientific training. "The Spider and the Wasp" first appeared in* Scientific American
in 1952.

To hold its own in the struggle for existence, every species of animal must have a 1
regular source of food, and if it happens to live on other animals, its survival may
be very delicately balanced. The hunter cannot exist without the hunted; if the latter should perish from the earth, the former would, too. When the hunted also prey
on some of the hunters, the matter may become complicated.

  This is nowhere better illustrated than in the insect world. Think of the com- 2
plexity of a situation such as the following: There is a certain wasp, *Pimpla in-
quisitor,* whose larvae feed on the larvae of the tussock moth. *Pimpla* larvae in turn
serve as food for the larvae of a second wasp, and the latter in their turn nourish
still a third wasp. What subtle balance between fertility and mortality must exist
in the case of each of these four species to prevent the extinction of all of them!
An excess of mortality over fertility in a single member of the group would ultimately wipe out all four.

  This is not a unique case. The two great orders of insects, Hymenoptera and 3
Diptera, are full of such examples of interrelationship. And the spiders (which are
not insects but members of a separate order of arthropods) also are killers and victims of insects.

  In the feeding and safeguarding of their progeny the insects and spiders ex- 4
hibit some interesting analogies to reasoning and some crass examples of blind instinct. The case I propose to describe here is that of the tarantula spiders and their
arch-enemy, the digger wasps of the genus Pepsis. It is a classic example of what
looks like intelligence pitted against instinct—a strange situation in which the victim, though fully able to defend itself, submits unwittingly to its destruction.

  A fertilized female tarantula lays from 200 to 400 eggs at a time; thus it is 5
possible for a single tarantula to produce several thousand young. She takes no
care of them beyond weaving a cocoon of silk to enclose the eggs. After they hatch,
the young walk away, find convenient places in which to dig their burrows and
spend the rest of their lives in solitude. Tarantulas feed mostly on insects and mil-

lipedes. Once their appetite is appeased, they digest the food for several days before eating again. Their sight is poor, being limited to sensing a change in the intensity of light and to the perception of moving objects. They apparently have little or no sense of hearing, for a hungry tarantula will pay no attention to a loudly chirping cricket placed in its cage unless the insect happens to touch one of its legs.

But all spiders, and especially hairy ones, have an extremely delicate sense 6 of touch. Laboratory experiments prove that tarantulas can distinguish three types of touch: pressure against the body wall, stroking of the body hair, and riffling of certain very fine hairs on the legs called trichobothria. Pressure against the body, by a finger or the end of a pencil, causes the tarantula to move off slowly for a short distance. The touch excites no defensive response unless the approach is from above where the spider can see the motion, in which case it rises on its hind legs, lifts its front legs, opens its fangs and holds this threatening posture as long as the object continues to move. When the motion stops, the spider drops back to the ground, remains quiet for a few seconds and then moves slowly away.

The entire body of a tarantula, especially its legs, is thickly clothed with hair. 7 Some of it is short and woolly, some long and stiff. Touching this body hair produces one of two distinct reactions. When the spider is hungry, it responds with an immediate and swift attack. At the touch of a cricket's antennae the tarantula seizes the insect so swiftly that a motion picture taken at the rate of 64 frames per second shows only the result and not the process of capture. But when the spider is not hungry, the stimulation of its hairs merely causes it to shake the touched limb. An insect can walk under its hairy belly unharmed.

The trichobothria, very fine hairs growing from disklike membranes on the 8 legs, were once thought to be the spider's hearing organs, but we now know that they have nothing to do with sound. They are sensitive only to air movement. A light breeze makes them vibrate slowly without disturbing the common hair. When one blows gently on the trichobothria, the tarantula reacts with a quick jerk of its four front legs. If the front and hind legs are stimulated at the same time, the spider makes a sudden jump. This reaction is quite independent of the state of its appetite.

These three tactile responses—to pressure on the body wall, to moving of 9 the common hair and to flexing of the trichobothria—are so different from one another that there is no possibility of confusing them. They serve the tarantula adequately for most of its needs and enable it to avoid most annoyances and dangers. But they fail the spider completely when it meets its deadly enemy, the digger wasp Pepsis.

These solitary wasps are beautiful and formidable creatures. Most species 10 are either a deep shiny blue all over, or deep blue with rusty wings. The largest have a wing span of about four inches. They live on nectar. When excited, they give off a pungent odor—a warning that they are ready to attack. The sting is much worse than that of a bee or common wasp, and the pain and swelling last longer. In the adult stage the wasp lives only a few months. The female produces but a few eggs, one at a time at intervals of two or three days. For each egg the mother must provide one adult tarantula, alive but paralyzed. The tarantula must

be of the correct species to nourish the larva. The mother wasp attaches the egg
to the paralyzed spider's abdomen. Upon hatching from the egg, the larva is many
hundreds of times smaller than its living but helpless victim. It eats no other food
and drinks no water. By the time it has finished its single gargantuan meal and becomes ready for wasphood, nothing remains of the tarantula but its indigestible
chitinous skeleton.

The mother wasp goes tarantula-hunting when the egg in her ovary is almost   11
ready to be laid. Flying low over the ground late on a sunny afternoon, the wasp
looks for its victim or for the mouth of a tarantula burrow, a round hole edged by
a bit of silk. The sex of the spider makes no difference, but the mother is highly
discriminating as to species. Each species of Pepsis requires a certain species of
tarantula, and the wasp will not attack the wrong species. In a cage with a tarantula which is not its normal prey the wasp avoids the spider, and is usually killed
by it in the night.

Yet when a wasp finds the correct species, it is the other way about. To iden-   12
tify the species the wasp apparently must explore the spider with her antennae. The
tarantula shows an amazing tolerance to this exploration. The wasp crawls under
it and walks over it without evoking any hostile response. The molestation is so
great and so persistent that the tarantula often rises on all eight legs, as if it were
on stilts. It may stand this way for several minutes. Meanwhile the wasp, having
satisfied itself that the victim is of the right species, moves off a few inches to dig
the spider's grave. Working vigorously with legs and jaws, it excavates a hole 8 to
10 inches deep with a diameter slightly larger than the spider's girth. Now and
again the wasp pops out of the hole to make sure that the spider is still there.

When the grave is finished, the wasp returns to the tarantula to complete   13
her ghastly enterprise. First she feels it all over once more with her antennae.
Then her behavior becomes more aggressive. She bends her abdomen, protruding her sting, and searches for the soft membrane at the point where the spider's
leg joins its body—the only spot where she can penetrate the horny skeleton.
From time to time, as the exasperated spider slowly shifts ground, the wasp turns
on her back and slides along with the aid of her wings, trying to get under the
tarantula for a shot at the vital spot. During all this maneuvering, which can last
for several minutes, the tarantula makes no move to save itself. Finally the wasp
corners it against some obstruction and grasps one of its legs in her powerful
jaws. Now at last the harassed spider tries a desperate but vain defense. The two
contestants roll over and over on the ground. It is a terrifying sight and the outcome is always the same. The wasp finally manages to thrust her sting into the
soft spot and holds it there for a few seconds while she pumps in the poison. Almost immediately the tarantula falls paralyzed on its back. Its legs stop twitch-
ing; its heart stops beating, yet it is not dead, as is shown by the fact that if taken
from the wasp it can be restored to some sensitivity by being kept in a moist
chamber for several months.

After paralyzing the tarantula, the wasp cleans herself by dragging her body   14
along the ground and rubbing her feet, sucks the drop of blood oozing from the

wound in the spider's abdomen, then grabs a leg of the flabby, helpless animal in her jaws and drags it down to the bottom of the grave. She stays there for many minutes, sometimes for several hours, and what she does all that time in the dark we do not know. Eventually she lays her egg and attaches it to the side of the spider's abdomen with a sticky secretion. Then she emerges, fills the grave with soil carried bit by bit in her jaws, and finally tramples the ground all around to hide any trace of the grave from prowlers. Then she flies away, leaving her descendant safely started in life.

In all this the behavior of the wasp evidently is qualitatively different from 15 that of the spider. The wasp acts like an intelligent animal. This is not to say that instinct plays no part or that she reasons as man does. But her actions are to the point; they are not automatic and can be modified to fit the situation. We do not know for certain how she identifies the tarantula—probably it is by some olfactory or chemo-tactile sense—but she does it purposefully and does not blindly tackle a wrong species.

On the other hand, the tarantula's behavior shows only confusion. Evidently 16 the wasp's pawing gives it no pleasure, for it tries to move away. That the wasp is not simulating sexual stimulation is certain, because male and female tarantulas react in the same way to its advances. That the spider is not anesthetized by some odorless secretion is easily shown by blowing lightly at the tarantula and making it jump suddenly. What, then, makes the tarantula behave as stupidly as it does?

No clear, simple answer is available. Possibly the stimulation by the wasp's 17 antennae is masked by a heavier pressure on the spider's body, so that it reacts as when prodded by a pencil. But the explanation may be much more complex. Initiative in attack is not in the nature of tarantulas; most species fight only when cornered so that escape is impossible. Their inherited patterns of behavior apparently prompt them to avoid problems rather than attack them. For example, spiders always weave their webs in three dimensions, and when a spider finds that there is insufficient space to attach certain threads in the third dimension, it leaves the place and seeks another, instead of finishing the web in a single plane. This urge to escape seems to arise under all circumstances, in all phases of life and to take the place of reasoning. For a spider to change the pattern of its web is as impossible as for an inexperienced man to build a bridge across a chasm obstructing his way.

In a way the instinctive urge to escape is not only easier but often more ef- 18 ficient than reasoning. The tarantula does exactly what is most efficient in all cases except in an encounter with a ruthless and determined attacker dependent for the existence of her own species on killing as many tarantulas as she can lay eggs. Perhaps in this case the spider follows its usual pattern of trying to escape, instead of seizing and killing the wasp, because it is not aware of its danger. In any case, the survival of the tarantula species as a whole is protected by the fact that the spider is much more fertile than the wasp.

1952

QUESTIONS FOR DISCUSSION

Content

a. In paragraph 1, Petrunkevitch claims that, for some species, "survival may be very delicately balanced." How does this statement relate to the rest of the essay?

b. How does the word "complicated" (paragraph 1) prepare the reader for what is to follow?

c. Based on your reading of this essay, in what way(s) is process analysis similar to narration?

d. Petrunkevitch makes it a point to describe a number of significant differences between the spider and the wasp. Identify a few of these. Why are they significant?

e. As you probably inferred from the two questions before this one, a variety of techniques, including narration and contrast, can be used to explain a process. What function does description play in this essay?

f. What, according to Petrunkevitch, may account for the tarantula's unwitting acceptance of its own destruction?

Strategy and Style

g. Outline Petrunkevitch's major points in an attempt to trace the organization of the essay.

h. Given the fact that this selection was first published in *Scientific American,* it is probably safe to assume that Petrunkevitch was writing for a highly educated reader but one who may not have had formal training in zoology. Comment upon his use of technical language. Why does the author stop to define unfamiliar words?

i. Petrunkevitch's tone is typically scientific—detached and objective—through most of this selection. At times, however, his language seems highly emotional and charged with excitement. Analyze his choice of words in these instances. What are the connotations of words such as *desperate* and *ghostly?* What images does Petrunkevitch evoke with phrases such as "she pumps in the poison" (paragraph 13)?

SUGGESTIONS FOR SHORT WRITING

a. Summarize the battle between the spider and the wasp in one short paragraph.

b. Closely observe a pet, if you have one, or an animal in a park or zoo for fifteen or twenty minutes, and describe its behaviour.

SUGGESTIONS FOR SUSTAINED WRITING

a. Write an explanation (process analysis) about the way in which an animal undertakes a task necessary to its survival or the survival of its species. Topics to choose from might include how a beaver constructs a dam, how ants build colonies, how deer forage for food, or how birds care for their young. In addition to observing animals firsthand, you might also want to research this topic in your college library.

b. In many ways, "The Spider and the Wasp" is a study in contrasts. Choose two animals or types of animals that, while apparently similar, exhibit distinctive differences in "personality" or behaviour. For instance, compare two house pets, two kinds of saltwater fish you have caught, a hawk and a crow, or two common insects.

c. As the author points out, nature can be cruel and terrifying. Write a description of a natural process that you find frightening, painful, or unpleasant. Be as specific as you can in conveying an objective picture of the process but, like Petrunkevitch, do not hesitate to allow your emotions to influence your writing.

How to Cook a Carp

Euell Gibbons

Euell Gibbons (1911–1975) was born and raised in Clarkesville, Texas, but left home when he was 15. He worked in Texas and New Mexico as a harvest hand, a cowboy, a carpenter, and a trapper before joining the army in 1934. After his discharge in 1936, he moved to Washington where he continued working odd jobs. He joined the Communist party but resigned when the Soviet Union attacked Finland in 1939. During World War II, he worked for the U.S. Navy as a civilian boat builder. After the war, he moved to Hawaii and turned beachcomber, living in a thatched hut for two years and subsisting entirely on wild food. He entered the University of Hawaii as a freshman at the age of 36. Shortly thereafter, he began a career of teaching, writing, and lecturing about wild foods. His books on foraging for wild foods combine detailed how-to instructions and recipes with delightfully entertaining narrative. Among his best-known works are Stalking the Wild Asparagus *(1962), from which "How to Cook a Carp" is taken;* Stalking the Blue-Eyed Scallop *(1964);* Stalking the Healthful Herbs *(1966); and* Euell Gibbons's Beachcomber's Handbook *(1967).*

When I was a lad of about eighteen, my brother and I were working on a cattle 1
ranch in New Mexico that bordered on the Rio Grande. Most Americans think of
the Rio Grande as a warm southern stream, but it rises among the high mountains
of Colorado, and in the spring it is fed by melting snows. At this time of the year,
the water that rushed by the ranch was turbulent, icy-cold and so silt-laden as to
be semisolid. "A little too thick to drink, and a little too thin to plow" was a common description of the waters of the Rio Grande.

A few species of fish inhabited this muddy water. Unfortunately, the most 2
common was great eight- to ten-pound carp, a fish that is considered very poor eating in this country, although the Germans and Asiatics have domesticated this fish,
and have developed some varieties that are highly esteemed for the table.

On the ranch where we worked, there was a drainage ditch that ran through the 3
lower pasture and emptied its clear waters into the muddy Rio Grande. The carp
swimming up the river would strike this clear warmer water and decide they preferred
it to the cold mud they had been inhabiting. One spring day, a cowhand who had been
riding that way reported that Clear Ditch was becoming crowded with huge carp.

On Sunday we decided to go fishing. Four of us armed ourselves with pitch- 4
forks, saddled our horses and set out. Near the mouth of the ditch, the water was
running about two feet deep and twelve to sixteen feet wide. There is a saying in
that part of the country that you can't get a cowboy to do anything unless it can be
done from the back of a horse, so we forced our mounts into the ditch and started
wading them upstream, four abreast, herding the carp before us.

By the time we had ridden a mile upstream, the water was less than a foot 5
deep and so crystal clear that we could see our herd of several hundred carp still
fleeing from the splashing, wading horses. As the water continued to shallow, our
fish began to get panicky. A few of the boldest ones attempted to dart back past us
and were impaled on pitchforks. We could see that the whole herd was getting rest-

108

less and was about to stampede back downstream, so we piled off our horses into the shallow water to meet the charge. The water boiled about us as the huge fish swirled past us and we speared madly in every direction with our pitchforks, throwing each fish we managed to hit over the ditch bank. This was real fishing— cowhand style. The last of the fish herd was by us in a few minutes and it was all over, but we had caught a tremendous quantity of fish.

Back at the ranch house, after we had displayed our trophies, we began won- 6 dering what we were going to do with so many fish. This started a series of typical cowboy tall tales on "how to cook a carp." The best of these yarns was told by a grizzled old *vaquero*, who claimed he had made his great discovery when he ran out of food while camping on a tributary of the Rio Grande. He said that he had found the finest way to cook a carp was to plaster the whole fish with a thick coating of fresh cow manure and bury it in the hot ashes of a campfire. In an hour or two, he said, the casing of cow manure had become black and very hard. He then related how he had removed the fish from the fire, broken the hard shell with the butt of his Winchester and peeled it off. He said that as the manure came off the scales and skin adhered to it, leaving the baked fish, white and clean. He then ended by saying, "Of course, the carp still wasn't fit to eat, but the manure in which it was cooked tasted pretty good."

There were also some serious suggestions and experiments. The chief ob- 7 jection to the carp is that its flesh is full of many forked bones. One man said that he had enjoyed carp sliced very thin and fried so crisp that one could eat it, bones and all. He demonstrated, and you really could eat it without the bones bothering you, but it was still far from being an epicurean dish. One cowboy described the flavor as "a perfect blend of Rio Grande mud and rancid hog lard."

Another man said that he had eaten carp that had been cooked in a pressure 8 cooker until the bones softened and became indistinguishable from the flesh. A pressure cooker is almost a necessity at that altitude, so we had one at the ranch house. We tried this method, and the result was barely edible. It tasted like the poorest possible grade of canned salmon flavored with a bit of mud. It was, however, highly appreciated by the dogs and cats on the ranch, and solved the problem of what to do with the bulk of the fish we had caught.

It was my brother who finally devised a method of cooking carp that not only 9 made it fit for human consumption, but actually delicious. First, instead of merely scaling the fish, he skinned them. Then, taking a large pinch, where the meat was thickest, he worked his fingers and thumb into the flesh until he struck the median bones, then he worked his thumb and fingers together and tore off a handful of meat. Using this tearing method, he could get two or three goodsized chunks of flesh from each side of the fish. He then heated a pot of bland vegetable shortening, rubbed the pieces of fish with salt and dropped them into the hot fat. He used no flour, meal, crumbs or seasoning other than salt. They cooked to a golden brown in a few minutes, and everyone pronounced them "mighty fine eating." The muddy flavor seemed to have been eliminated by removing the skin and the large bones. The forked bones were still there, but they had not been multiplied by cutting across them, and one only had to remove several bones still intact with the fork from each piece of fish.

For the remainder of that spring, every few days one or another of the cow- 10
boys would take a pitchfork and ride over to Clear Ditch and spear a mess of carp.
On these evenings, my brother replaced the regular *cocinero* and we enjoyed some
delicious fried carp.

The flavor of carp varies with the water from which it is caught. Many years 11
after the above incidents I attended a fish fry at my brother's house. The main
course was all of his own catching, and consisted of bass, catfish and carp, all from
Elephant Butte Lake farther down the Rio Grande. All the fish were prepared exactly alike, except that the carp was pulled apart as described above, while the bass
and catfish, being all twelve inches or less in length, were merely cleaned and fried
whole. None of his guests knew one fish from another, yet all of them preferred
the carp to the other kinds. These experiences have convinced me that the carp is
really a fine food fish when properly prepared.

Carp can, of course, be caught in many ways besides spearing them with 12
pitchforks from the back of a horse. In my adopted home state, Pennsylvania, they
are classed as "trash fish" and one is allowed to take them almost any way. They
will sometimes bite on worms, but they are vegetarians by preference and are more
easily taken on dough balls. Some states allow the use of gill nets, and other states,
because they would like to reduce the population of this unpopular fish, will issue
special permits for the use of nets to catch carp.

A good forager will take advantage of the lax regulations on carp fishing 13
while they last. When all fishermen realize that the carp is really a good food fish
when prepared in the right way, maybe this outsized denizen of our rivers and lakes
will no longer be considered a pest and will take his rightful place among our valued food and game fishes.

1962

QUESTIONS FOR DISCUSSION

Content

a. What do you think is Gibbons's goal in writing this essay? How successful is
    he in reaching this goal?
b. How would you describe Gibbons's ideal reader? If you were that reader, what
    use would this essay be to you?
c. Is there an argument implied in this essay? If so, how would you phrase the ar-
    gument? What would the counterargument be?
d. Carp is common throughout North America. Besides the obvious reason that
    the essay is based on personal experience, why would Gibbons set his narrative
    in the ranch country along the Rio Grande and not some other locale? How
    would the essay be different if it were set in, for example, Gibbons's "adopted
    home state, Pennsylvania"?

Strategy and Style

e. Though Gibbons titles his essay "How to Cook a Carp," he does not actually describe the process until paragraph 9. What does he do first, and what are his reasons for providing this long introduction?

f. Gibbons was an expert on foraging for and cooking wild plants and game, and this essay appears in one of his popular books about foraging. Why, then, does he describe so many failed attempts at cooking carp? Do these accounts add to or detract from his authority as an expert?

g. How do anecdotes such as the account of catching carp with pitchforks or the tale of the "old *vaquero*" (paragraphs 5 and 6) affect the essay? What purpose do they serve other than entertaining the reader?

h. What metaphors does Gibbons use to describe carp and the process of catching them? What effect do these metaphors have on the essay? On you?

SUGGESTIONS FOR SHORT WRITING

a. Have some fun and write a recipe for an inedible, or seemingly inedible, product. Include directions on how to capture or collect it, how to prepare it, and how to serve it.

b. Write an anecdote of a time when you tried an unusual food.

SUGGESTIONS FOR SUSTAINED WRITING

a. Write a narrative essay that explains how you accomplished a common but important task. Limit your essay to a simple process that can be explained fully in three or four typewritten pages. For example, explain how you learned to hang wallpaper, cook a Thanksgiving turkey, load software into a home computer, do laundry, set up an aquarium, change the oil in a car, or plant a vegetable patch. Put your comments in the form of a letter to a friend or classmate who has asked for instructions about a process you know well. Assume that your reader knows little about the process.

b. Recall (or create) a personal experience in which you learned by trial and error how to do something well. Write a descriptive account of this series of processes.

c. Write an essay in which you convince your readers to change their minds about some process they now consider uninteresting, difficult, or unimportant. Make them see that washing the dog, studying for final exams, or going on a special diet, for instance, might be fun, easy, or beneficial if they only understood the process as well as you do. Include an account of the process.

d. Conduct interviews and collect anecdotes and tall tales that relate to a process. Include them in an essay in which you explain, record, or satirize the process.

Behind the Formaldehyde Curtain

Jessica Mitford

Born in Great Britain to parents who were members of the nobility, Jessica Mitford (b. 1917) immigrated to the United States in 1939. In 1960, she published the first volume of her autobiography, Daughters and Rebels, *in which she described what it is like to grow up in an aristocratic English household and to receive one's education at home. The title of this book was to prove prophetic, for much of Mitford's later work is social criticism. For instance,* The American Way of Death *(1963), from which this selection is taken, is an indictment of morticians and their profession as well as of American funeral customs in general. In* Kind and Unusual Punishment: The Prison Business *(1973), Mitford exposes the scandal of the U.S. corrections system. In 1977, Mitford published the second part of her autobiography,* A Fine Old Madness. *Since then, she has published* Faces of Philip: A Memoir of Philip Toynbee *(1984) and* Grace Had an English Heart: The Story of Grace Darling *(1988).*

The drama begins to unfold with the arrival of the corpse at the mortuary. 1

Alas, poor Yorick! How surprised he would be to see how his counterpart of 2
today is whisked off to a funeral parlor and is in short order sprayed, sliced,
pierced, pickled, trussed, trimmed, creamed, waxed, painted, rouged and neatly
dressed—transformed from a common corpse into a Beautiful Memory Picture.
This process is known in the trade as embalming and restorative art, and is so uni-
versally employed in the United States and Canada that the funeral director does
it routinely, without consulting corpse or kin. He regards as eccentric those few
who are hardy enough to suggest that it might be dispensed with. Yet no law requires embalming, no religious doctrine commends it, nor is it dictated by con-
siderations of health, sanitation, or even of personal daintiness. In no part of the
world but in Northern America is it widely used. The purpose of embalming is to
make the corpse presentable for viewing in a suitably costly container; and here
too the funeral director routinely, without first consulting the family, prepares the
body for public display.

Is all this legal? The processes to which a dead body may be subjected are 3
after all to some extent circumscribed by law. In most states, for instance, the signature of next of kin must be obtained before an autopsy may be performed, before the deceased may be cremated, before the body may be turned over to a medical school for research purposes; or such provision must be made in the
decedent's will. In the case of embalming, no such permission is required nor is it
ever sought. A textbook, *The Principles and Practices of Embalming,* comments
on this: "There is some question regarding the legality of much that is done within
the preparation room." The author points out that it would be most unusual for a
responsible member of a bereaved family to instruct the mortician, in so many
words, to *"embalm"* the body of a deceased relative. The very term "embalming"
is so seldom used that the mortician must rely upon custom in the matter. The author concludes that unless the family specifies otherwise, the act of entrusting the

112

body to the care of a funeral establishment carries with it an implied permission to go ahead and embalm.

Embalming is indeed a most extraordinary procedure, and one must wonder 4 at the docility of Americans who each year pay hundreds of millions of dollars for its perpetuation, blissfully ignorant of what it is all about, what is done, how it is done. Not one in ten thousand has any idea of what actually takes place. Books on the subject are extremely hard to come by. They are not to be found in most libraries or bookshops.

In an era when huge television audiences watch surgical operations in the 5 comfort of their living rooms, when, thanks to the animated cartoon, the geography of the digestive system has become familiar territory even to the nursery school set, in a land where the satisfaction of curiosity about almost all matters is a national pastime, the secrecy surrounding embalming can, surely, hardly be attributed to the inherent gruesomeness of the subject. Custom in this regard has within this century suffered a complete reversal. In the early days of American embalming, when it was performed in the home of the deceased, it was almost mandatory for some relative to stay by the embalmer's side and witness the procedure. Today, family members who might wish to be in attendance would certainly be dissuaded by the funeral director. All others, except apprentices, are excluded by law from the preparation room.

A close look at what does actually take place may explain in large measure 6 the undertaker's intractable reticence concerning a procedure that has become his major *raison d'être*. It is possible he fears that public information about embalming might lead patrons to wonder if they really want this service? If the funeral men are loath to discuss the subject outside the trade, the reader may, understandably, be equally loath to go on reading at this point. For those who have the stomach for it, let us part the formaldehyde curtain. . . .

The body is first laid out in the undertaker's morgue—or rather, Mr. Jones 7 is reposing in the preparation room—to be readied to bid the world farewell.

The preparation room in any of the better funeral establishments has the tiled 8 and sterile look of a surgery, and indeed the embalmer-restorative artist who does his chores there is beginning to adopt the term "dermasurgeon" (appropriately corrupted by some mortician-writers as "demi-surgeon") to describe his calling. His equipment, consisting of scalpels, scissors, augers, forceps, clamps, needles, pumps, tubes, bowls, and basins, is crudely imitative of the surgeon's, as is his technique, acquired in a nine- or twelve-month post-highschool course in an embalming school. He is supplied by an advanced chemical industry with a bewildering array of fluids, sprays, pastes, oils, powders, creams, to fix or soften tissue, shrink or distend it as needed, dry it here, restore the moisture there. There are cosmetics, waxes and paints to fill and cover features, even plaster of Paris to replace entire limbs. There are ingenious aids to prop and stabilize the cadaver: A Vari-Pose Head Rest, the Edwards Arm and Hand Positioner, the Repose Block (to support the shoulders during the embalming), and the Throop Foot Positioner, which resembles an old-fashioned stock.

Mr. John H. Eckels, president of the Eckels College of Mortuary Science, 9
thus describes the first part of the embalming procedure: "In the hands of a skilled
practitioner, this work may be done in a comparatively short time and without mu-
tilating the body other than by slight incision—so slight that it scarcely would
cause serious inconvenience if made upon a living person. It is necessary to remove the blood, and doing this not only helps in the disinfecting, but removes the
principal cause of disfigurements due to discoloration."

Another textbook discusses the all-important time element: "The earlier this 10
is done, the better, for every hour that elapses between death and embalming will
add to the problems and complications encountered. . . ." Just how soon should one
get going on the embalming? The author tells us, "On the basis of such scanty information made available to this profession through its rudimentary and haphazard system of technical research, we must conclude that the best results are to be
obtained if the subject is embalmed before life is completely extinct—that is, before cellular death has occurred. In the average case, this would mean within an
hour after somatic death." For those who feel that there is something a little rudimentary, not to say haphazard, about this advice, a comforting thought is offered
by another writer. Speaking of fears entertained in early days of premature burial,
he points out, "One of the effects of embalming by chemical injection, however,
has been to dispel fears of live burial." How true; once the blood is removed,
chances of live burial are indeed remote.

To return to Mr. Jones, the blood is drained out through the veins and re- 11
placed by embalming fluid pumped in through the arteries. As noted in *The Principles and Practices of Embalming,* "every operator has a favorite injection and
drainage point—a fact which becomes a handicap only if he fails or refuses to for-
sake his favorites when conditions demand it." Typical favorites are the carotid artery, femoral artery, jugular vein, subclavian vein. There are various choices of embalming fluid. If Flextone is used, it will produce a "mild, flexible rigidity. The
skin retains a velvety softness, the tissues are rubbery and pliable. Ideal for women
and children." It may be blended with B. and G. Products Company's Lyf-Lyk tint,
which is guaranteed to reproduce "nature's own skin texture . . . the velvety appearance of living tissue." Suntone comes in three separate tints: Suntan; Special
Cosmetic Tint, a pink shade "especially indicated for female subjects"; and Regular Cosmetic Tint, moderately pink.

About three to six gallons of a dyed and perfumed solution of formaldehyde, 12
glycerin, borax, phenol, alcohol and water is soon circulating through Mr. Jones,
whose mouth has been sewn together with a "needle directed upward between the
upper lip and gum and brought out through the left nostril," with the corners raised
slightly "for a more pleasant expression." If he should be bucktoothed, his teeth
are cleaned with Bon Ami and coated with colorless nail polish. His eyes, meanwhile, are closed with flesh-tinted eye caps and eye cement.

The next step is to have at Mr. Jones with a thing called a trocar. This is a 13
long, hollow needle attached to a tube. It is jabbed into the abdomen, poked around
the entrails and chest cavity, the contents of which are pumped out and replaced

with "cavity fluid." This done, and the hole in the abdomen sewn up, Mr. Jones's face is heavily creamed (to protect the skin from burns which may be caused by leakage of the chemicals), and he is covered with a sheet and left unmolested for a while. But not for long—there is more, much more, in store for him. He has been embalmed, but not yet restored, and the best time to start the restorative work is eight to ten hours after embalming, when the tissues have become firm and dry.

The object of all this attention to the corpse, it must be remembered, is to make it presentable for viewing in an attitude of healthy repose. "Our customs require the presentation of our dead in the semblance of normality . . . unmarred by the ravages of illness, disease or mutilation," says Mr. J. Sheridan Mayer in his *Restorative Art.* This is rather a large order since few people die in the full bloom of health, unravaged by illness and unmarked by some disfigurement. The funeral industry is equal to the challenge: "In some cases the gruesome appearance of a mutilated or disease-ridden subject may be quite discouraging. The task of restoration may seem impossible and shake the confidence of the embalmer. This is the time for intestinal fortitude and determination. Once the formative work is begun and affected tissues are cleaned or removed, all doubts of success vanish. It is surprising and gratifying to discover the results which may be obtained." 14

The embalmer, having allowed an appropriate interval to elapse, returns to the attack, but now he brings into play the skill and equipment of sculptor and cosmetician. Is a hand missing? Casting one in plaster of Paris is a simple matter. "For replacement purposes, only a cast of the back of the hand is necessary; this is within the ability of the average operator and is quite adequate." If a lip or two, a nose or an ear should be missing, the embalmer has at hand a variety of restorative waxes with which to model replacements. Pores and skin texture are simulated by stippling with a little brush, and over this cosmetics are laid on. Head off? Decapitation cases are rather routinely handled. Ragged edges are trimmed, and head joined to torso with a series of splints, wires and sutures. It is a good idea to have a little something at the neck—a scarf or a high collar—when time for viewing comes. Swollen mouth? Cut out tissue as needed from inside the lips. If too much is removed, the surface contour can easily be restored by padding with cotton. Swollen necks and cheeks are reduced by removing tissue through vertical incisions made down each side of the neck. "When the deceased is casketed, the pillow will hide the suture incisions . . . as an extra precaution against leakage, the suture may be painted with liquid sealer." 15

The opposite condition is more likely to present itself—that of emaciation. His hypodermic syringe now loaded with massage cream, the embalmer seeks out and fills the hollowed and sunken areas by injection. In this procedure the backs of the hands and fingers and the under-chin area should not be neglected. 16

Positioning the lips is a problem that recurrently challenges the ingenuity of the embalmer. Closed too tightly, they tend to give a stern, even disapproving expression. Ideally, embalmers feel, the lips should give the impression of being ever so slightly parted, the upper lip protruding slightly for a more youthful appearance. This takes some engineering, however, as the lips tend to drift apart. Lip drift 17 can sometimes be remedied by pushing one or two straight pins through the inner margin of the lower lip and then inserting them between the two front upper teeth. If Mr. Jones happens to have no teeth, the pins can just as easily be anchored in his Armstrong Face Former and Denture Replacer. Another method to maintain lip closure is to dislocate the lower jaw, which is then held in its new position by a wire run through holes which have been drilled through the upper and lower jaws at the midline. As the French are fond of saying, *il faut souffrir pour être belle.*

If Mr. Jones has died of jaundice, the embalming fluid will very likely turn   **18** him green. Does this deter the embalmer? Not if he has intestinal fortitude. Masking pastes and cosmetics are heavily laid on, burial garments and casket interiors are color-correlated with particular care, and Jones is displayed beneath rose-colored lights. Friends will say "How *well* he looks." Death by carbon monoxide, on the other hand, can be rather a good thing from the embalmer's viewpoint: "One advantage is the fact that this type of discoloration is an exaggerated form of a natural pink coloration." This is nice because the healthy glow is already present and needs but little attention.

The patching and filling completed, Mr. Jones is now shaved, washed and   **19** dressed. Cream-based cosmetic, available in pink, flesh, suntan, brunette and blond, is applied to his hands and face, his hair is shampooed and combed (and, in the case of Mrs. Jones, set), his hands manicured. For the horny-handed son of toil special care must be taken; cream should be applied to remove ingrained grime, and the nails cleaned. "If he were not in the habit of having them manicured in life, trimming and shaping is advised for better appearance—never questioned by kin."

Jones is now ready for casketing (this is the present participle of the verb "to   **20** casket"). In this operation his right shoulder should be depressed slightly "to turn the body a bit to the right and soften the appearance of lying flat on the back." Positioning the hands is a matter of importance, and special rubber positioning blocks may be used. The hands should be cupped slightly for a more life like, relaxed appearance. Proper placement of the body requires a delicate sense of balance. It should lie as high as possible in the casket, yet not so high that the lid, when lowered, will hit the nose. On the other hand, we are cautioned, placing the body too low "creates the impression that the body is in a box."

Jones is next wheeled into the appointed slumber room where a few last   **21** touches may be added—his favorite pipe placed in his hand or, if he was a great reader, a book propped into position. (In the case of little Master Jones a Teddy bear may be clutched.) Here he will hold open house for a few days, visiting hours 10 AM to 9 PM.

All now being in readiness, the funeral director calls a staff conference to   **22** make sure that each assistant knows his precise duties. Mr. Wilber Kriege writes: "This makes your staff feel that they are a part of the team, with a definite assignment that must be properly carried out if the whole plan is to succeed. You never heard of a football coach who failed to talk to his entire team before they go on the field. They have drilled on the plays they are to execute for hours and days, and yet the successful coach knows the importance of making even the bench-warming third-string substitute feel that he is important if the game is to be won." The winning of *this* game is predicated upon glass-smooth handling of the logistics. The funeral director has notified the pallbearers whose names were furnished by the family, has arranged for the presence of clergyman, organist, and soloist, has provided transportation for everybody, has organized and listed the flowers sent by friends. In *Psychology of Funeral Service* Mr. Edward A. Martin points out: "He may not always do as much as the family thinks he is doing, but it is his helpful guidance that they appreciate in knowing they are proceeding as they should. . . . The important thing is how well his services can be used to make the family believe they are giving unlimited expression to their own sentiment."

The religious service may be held in a church or in the chapel of the funeral 23 home; the funeral director vastly prefers the latter arrangement, for not only is it more convenient for him but it affords him the opportunity to show off his beautiful facilities to the gathered mourners. After the clergyman has had his say, the mourners queue up to file past the casket for a last look at the deceased. The family is *never* asked whether they want an open-casket ceremony; in the absence of their instruction to the contrary, this is taken for granted. Consequently well over 90 percent of all American funerals feature the open casket—a custom unknown in other parts of the world. Foreigners are astonished by it. An English woman living in San Francisco described her reaction in a letter to the writer:

> I myself have attended only one funeral here—that of an elderly
> fellow worker of mine. After the service I could not understand why
> everyone was walking towards the coffin (sorry, I mean casket), but
> thought I had better follow the crowd. It shook me rigid to get there
> and find the casket open and poor old Oscar lying there in his brown
> tweed suit, wearing a suntan makeup and just the wrong shade of
> lipstick. If I had not been extremely fond of the old boy, I have a
> horrible feeling that I might have giggled. Then and there I decided
> that I could never face another American funeral—even dead.

The casket (which has been resting throughout the service on a Classic 24 Beauty Ultra Metal Casket Bier) is now transferred by a hydraulically operated device called Porto-Lift to a balloon-tired, Glide Easy casket carriage which will wheel it to yet another conveyance, the Cadillac Funeral Coach. This may be lavender, cream, light green—anything but black. Interiors, of course, are color-correlated, "for the man who cannot stop short of perfection."

At graveside, the casket is lowered into the earth. This office, once the pre- 25 rogative of friends of the deceased, is now performed by a patented mechanical lowering device. A "Lifetime Green" artificial grass mat is at the ready to conceal the sere earth, and overhead, to conceal the sky, is a portable Steril Chapel Tent ("resists the intense heat and humidity of summer and the terrific storms of winter . . . available in Silver Grey, Rose or Evergreen"). Now is the time for the ritual scattering of earth over the coffin, as the solemn words "earth to earth, ashes to ashes, dust to dust" are pronounced by the officiating cleric. This can today be accomplished "with a

mere flick of the wrist with the Gordon Leak-Proof Earth Dispenser. No grasping of a handful of dirt, no soiled fingers. Simple, dignified, beautiful, reverent!
The modern way!" The Gordon Earth Dispenser (at $5) is of nickel-plated brass
construction. It is not only "attractive to the eye and long wearing"; it is also "one of
the 'tools' for building better public relations" if presented as "an appropriate non-
commercial gift" to the clergyman. It is shaped something like a saltshaker.

Untouched by human hand, the coffin and the earth are now united.   26

It is in the function of directing the participants through this maze of gad-   27
getry that the funeral director has assigned to himself his relatively new role of
"grief therapist." He has relieved the family of every detail, he has revamped the
corpse to look like a living doll, he has arranged for it to nap for a few days in a
slumber room, he has put on a well-oiled performance in which the concept of
death has played no part whatsoever—unless it was inconsiderately mentioned by
the clergyman who conducted the religious service. He has done everything in his
power to make the funeral a real pleasure for everybody concerned. He and his
team have given their all to score an upset victory over death.

1963

QUESTIONS FOR DISCUSSION

Content

a. What is Mitford's purpose? Do you agree that "public information about embalming might lead patrons to wonder if they really want this service" (paragraph 6)?

b. In what ways does this selection resemble a narrative? What aspects are
   arranged in chronological order? How does Mitford indicate the passage of
   time?

c. According to Mitford, why is it odd that embalming remains so secretive a business? What can we infer about the reasons for the persistence of embalming as
   a widespread practice only in this part of the world?

d. Do you know of any important differences between funeral practices in North
   America and those in other parts of the world? Why does Mitford bother to
   mention such differences at the start of this essay?

e. The beginning of paragraph 2 alludes to Shakespeare's *Hamlet.* Who was
   Yorick, and why has Mitford chosen to include him in her introduction?

f. Why does the author make it a point to mention the brand names of the supplies and equipment used by undertakers?

Strategy and Style

g. Mitford's use of detail seems to be accurate and thorough. Is it too thorough?
   Could she have achieved her purpose without being so detailed?

h. Mitford relies heavily on the use of quoted material from embalming text-books to develop her indictment of morticians. Explain how these citations help her achieve her purpose.

i. In paragraph 6, before parting "the formaldehyde curtain," Mitford warns us about what is to follow. Why?

j. What other interesting metaphors does Mitford use? Do they help "enliven" her prose?

k. What is ironic about her calling the embalming procedure the mortician's *raison d'être*? Identify other examples of irony in this selection.

l. Look up the roots of the term *dermasurgeon* in a good dictionary. What do their meanings suggest? Now look up *demi*. What does the corruption *demi-surgeon* (paragraph 8) tell you about Mitford's view of undertakers? What does Mitford mean by "grief therapist" (paragraph 27)? Why does she say that funeral directors have "assigned" themselves this role?

m. How would you describe Mitford's tone? Analyze at least one paragraph closely (paragraph 13, 14, or 15 would be a good choice). How does her use of language make her attitude about the subject clear?

n. When does irony turn to sarcasm? Reread paragraph 25. What makes Mitford's treatment of graveside ceremonies so caustic?

SUGGESTIONS FOR SHORT WRITING

a. Write a response entirely made up of exclamatory statements.

b. Address a response to Mitford. Tell her what you think of her essay, and why.

SUGGESTIONS FOR SUSTAINED WRITING

a. Do you agree with Mitford's assessment of the undertaker's profession? If not, write an essay in which you refute her by explaining the important role current funeral customs and practices play. Address your essay to Mitford directly, perhaps in the form of a letter.

b. Funeral customs differ from country to country and from culture to culture. Have you ever witnessed or read about funeral rites that are distinctive from those one might consider typically North American? If so, write an essay in which you explain how such rites are carried out.

c. Do you believe funeral customs should be changed? What aspect of the way in which people deal with the dead do you object to most? Write an essay in which you explain the basis for your objection and suggest alternatives to current practices.

d. Mitford focuses on only one method of laying the dead to rest; actually there are many alternatives. One is cremation; another is burial at sea. Explain the process involved in any funeral practice other than the one she discusses.

Breakfast in Bed

Joe Fiorito

Joe Fiorito was born in Thunder Bay, Ontario, in 1948. He now lives in Toronto and writes for the National Post. *Over the years, he has worked for CBC radio and, while living in Montreal, he wrote regular food columns for* Hour Magazine. *These columns were collected into the book* Comfort Me With Apples, *from which the following selection is taken. His most recent book,* The Closer We Are to Dying, *is a moving memoir of his family and the Thunder Bay of the 1950s.*

The Inuit greet face to face, but they don't rub noses, exactly, and you shouldn't 1 call it kissing. It is a form of greeting every bit as intimate as a kiss, but it goes deeper than that; it's a way for friends to take in each other's smell. It's how friends fill the empty places caused by absence.

Smell is fundamental to happiness. I know a man who travels with a piece 2 of his wife's clothing sealed in a plastic bag. When the separation is too much to bear, he opens the bag and breathes.

Traces of this signature mark our sheets and pillows; this is what makes 3 crawling into bed on a cold night such a comfort.

Smell is one of the many nameless things you miss when love goes wrong. That 4 smell will linger, it will haunt you and exhaust you long after your lover has gone.

Think I'm exaggerating? Wake early one Sunday and smell the person sleep- 5 ing next to you. Do it. Lean over. The side of the neck will do, just below the ear. Take a deep breath. The knowledge of this scent is lodged in the deepest part of your brain. Breathe deeply, if only to remind yourself of why you are where you are, doing what you're doing.

Now go to the kitchen. Throw two eggs into a bowl with a cup of milk and 6 a cup of flour. Add a quarter teaspoon of salt and a tablespoon of melted butter. Mix until smooth, but don't overdo it.

Pour the batter into buttered muffin tins, filling the cups no more than half 7 full. Put the tins in a cold oven. Turn on the heat to 450°F. After fifteen minutes, turn the oven down to 350°F. Wait fifteen minutes more.

This recipe comes from the *Fannie Farmer Baking Book* by Marion Cunning- 8 ham. It's an important book, with clear recipes and much new thinking. For example, prior to Marion, popovers were always started in a hot oven. This is a small thing, but one which changed my life.

While you're changing yours, make some coffee and squeeze a couple of 9 oranges. Do what you want with a pear or a pineapple. Get a tray ready to take back to bed.

Now open the oven. It will make you smile. They don't call these things 10 popovers for nothing. They look like little domes, golden brown and slightly crisp on the outside. The texture inside is as soft as your partner's neck. The smell is just as warm and every bit as earthy.

Take them out of the muffin tins and put them in a basket. They'll steam as   11
you break them open. Eat them with a little butter and the best jam or honey in the
cupboard. A soft camembert isn't out of place if you have it.

Breakfast together is the second- or third-most intimate thing you can share.   12
If someone new is sleeping over and you want to make an impression, make these.
If you're worried about what to talk about while you're eating, remember what
Oscar Wilde said. Only dull people are brilliant at breakfast.

If you haven't got a partner, make popovers anyway. It's easy enough to cut   13
this recipe in half. It's good practise. It's its own reward. The butter melts into the
jam and the sun pours onto your breakfast bed. And you have another way to fill
the emptiness caused by absence.

1993

QUESTIONS FOR DISCUSSION

Content

a. Why does Fiorito, who is supposed to be giving a recipe for popovers, open with
   how the Inuit smell each other?
b. Why does his friend carry a piece of his wife's clothing when he travels?
c. What is Fiorito's point about smell?
d. How does Fiorito introduce the actual recipe?
e. What is Fiorito's thesis in this essay and how does the recipe fit into that thesis?

Strategy and Style

f. Why does Fiorito talk so much about "absence" and "empty places"?
g. Fiorito frequently uses the imperative—"Do it. Lean over" and "Breathe
   deeply." What is the effect of this use of the imperative?
h. Fiorito's sentences tend to be crisp and short. Do the sentences appear choppy
   and short or do they feel appropriate?
i. How does Fiorito move from point to point? How does he signal transitions?
j. What sense does Fiorito focus on and how does he use words to stimulate/
   simulate it?
k. How does Fiorito tie the end to the beginning of the essay?

SUGGESTIONS FOR SHORT WRITING

a. Write about your favourite food. Try to write about the process of preparing it.
b. Fiorito uses food to court. Discuss another courting ritual. Emphasize the
   process of the ritual.
c. Write about your ultimate restaurant experience (to date). Think particularly
   about the senses and how the process stimulated them.

SUGGESTIONS FOR SUSTAINED WRITING

a. Compare and contrast the attitudes towards food in Fiorito's essay with the attitude towards food in Lee Maracle's "Survival Work" in Chapter 6. What aspects of food does Fiorito emphasize? What aspects of food does Maracle emphasize?

b. Compare and contrast Fiorito's comments about the importance of smell to Marshall McLuhan's comments about our attitudes towards smell in "How Not to Offend" in Chapter 7.

c. What constitutes a "good smell" and what constitutes a "bad smell"? Interview a number of your peers and find out the criteria used to distinguish between smells. Discuss the significance of these criteria.

Leave Taking

Rita Moir

Rita Moir, born in 1952, resides at Winslaw, B.C. She works as a freelance journalist and has written for various media, regionally and nationally. She has also written dramatic works for the CBC and two memoirs: Buffalo Jump: A Woman's Travels *and* Survival Gear. *Moir is a member of a local burial society in the only Canadian province that still allows laypeople to prepare bodies for burial. The following essay describes her participation in these preparations and won a creative nonfiction prize when it was first published in the literary quarterly* Event.

We pulled down the stainless steel locker door and slid you out. The morgue was warm—a refrigeration breakdown, the nurse said, and it would get warmer as we worked. 1

I didn't know if I'd know you. I only knew you were Bert Carlson and you died in a motorcycle accident last Saturday in Silverton. Your friends asked our burial society to help prepare you for cremation. The society built the cemetery a few years ago, and some members learned how to do the simple things that help a dead person take leave. 2

I'd never done it before. I hoped I wouldn't be sick. I hoped I wouldn't be useless. 3

The hospital wrapping of plastic and linen had loosened around you. I saw your penis before I saw your face. It made you human, needing our help but not helpless. 4

The four of us, three women you didn't know, and your male friend, lifted you onto the metal table. We searched through a black plastic garbage bag lying with you. The belt buckle your girlfriend asked for lay at the bottom of the bag, broken. It was with another piece of metal, a piece of the car you collided with. 5

The section of bumper was silver and untarnished. Inside your helmet, the black foam was still wet. Your jeans and sheepskin jacket had blood on them, too. Nothing was awful. Nothing was horrifying. 6

My friends told me that the autopsy cut and stitching is disturbing. Especially in babies. It's a long cut from your navel to your breastbone, then a Y-shape to your shoulder blades. The coroner bastes you back up with a string heavier than that used on a turkey. They cut open your head, too, and the string hangs from your hair, waiting for the final trim. 7

You didn't look that damaged. Not like the pictures in the first aid book. Your deadness didn't alarm me. I'd been with death. It was animal death, but there's a connection. Even dead chickens have dignity. Not the kind of chickens bought frozen in the Safeway, but the ones I've had to kill myself. The bears our neighbor shot for fun, then gave us to butcher—they have power, too. My dog howled all night when I tried to boil a head to make bear-head cheese. I learned not to do things like that. There are some things that aren't done. Decent burials are important. Respect is important. Time is important. 8

123

When Amanda died in her crib, Penny held her for eight hours. A change came 9
over them both. They found peace together while they were leaving each other.

You needed to find your peace, too. It wasn't just for us, and for your family, 10
that we did this. You weren't three days dead. You weren't gone yet.

The Doukhobors who live in these valleys give the body three days to lie at 11
rest before burial. It goes back to the three days Christ had before rising. I know
you're not a Doukhobor, Bert, and no one ever accused me of being religious, but
here in this room it makes sense.

We struggled to put on your white cotton socks, tried to make your legs move 12
one more time. Were you one of the long-legged treeplanters who left us short-limbed
ones behind? Did you stride so fast a breeze cooled you in the hot spring sun? You
called out with joy when fireweed sweetened the air or nettle stung your fingertips,
leaving you shocked and laughing.

We couldn't get on your boots, even though we used pruning shears to cut 13
them up the back. Your feet weren't bending. We slipped your jeans on, rolling you
sideways, holding you in our arms, the four of us a team.

The hard part was your head. This most vulnerable place, this container with 14
all your thoughts. The head injury and the autopsy cut at the top—we didn't know
how to touch it. This was a test, but it wasn't grisly so far. We didn't want to be
afraid of you.

The nurse showed us how to move your head. Your man friend washed your 15
face. They brought us swabs, and I cleaned around your eyes and in your nostrils
and in your ears. Your friend cleaned your teeth. There was blood in these places.
You died from inside.

We wheeled you to the sink. I remembered last week at Margee's hair salon, 16
lying back as the warm water coursed over me, soothing, gentle. We couldn't wash
your hair, but we cleaned away the blood with damp cloths.

We snipped the string and I combed your hair. I'll have a hard time looking at 17
my lover for a while. The resemblance is only passing, the same receding hairline,
the same mustache.

Sometimes your eyes opened as we washed around them. I closed them. 18
I could see.

We didn't try to lift or bend you to put on your shirt. We used the coroner's 19
scissors from the white towel covered with the tools of his work, and snipped up the
back of your yellow T-shirt. The one that says Fleetwood, the name of your tree-
planting company. I thought of Fleetwood Mac, rock 'n' roll. The shirt stayed connected around your chest and we slipped it over your arms and tucked it round you.

Your flannel shirt was harder. We figured the only way was to cut it up the back, 20
right through the yoke and collar, slip on the two halves, and button up the front.

Your friend put on the baseball cap you always wore on the slopes. 21

Months ago Sally made the wood coffin that we kept in stock. Your friends 22
believed you would fit, but they were off by a few inches. You were six feet four.

Until then it had all been gentle. Now we had to use force. The four of us 23
looked at one another, drew our breath, and kept going.

We left you tucked in your coffin with your quilt and pillow, a sheet tucked 24
around your bent legs.

We washed up, then stood aside while your girlfriend came in with the nurse 25
to see you. We exchanged brief hugs. We didn't know her well, and she hadn't
cried yet.

She left the room and we screwed down the pine lid, 12 screws, lifted the 26
coffin and wheeled you out to the basement loading dock of the hospital where the
treeplanters' station wagon waited for you.

Your six men friends waiting below concentrated on the metal handles of the 27
coffin and didn't look up into our eyes. We passed you on. You were ready to take
your leave.

Your face came into my mind even when I left for a long time to go away to work. 28
You'd taken your leave, but now I needed to take mine, from you.

I phoned your girlfriend. I worried she would find my words too personal, 29
impertinent.

She did what I knew she'd do. She took out a snapshot. I braced myself. 30

There was still the chance that I would recognize you as someone I'd known. 31
But I didn't know you, was just glad to see how thick and dark your hair had been,
you leaning against the counter in your plaid shirt, tall man with big mustache and
cheeks whipped red and warm by the wind.

Your girlfriend completed the picture, helped me take my leave. 32

Last night I talked with a friend of mine. While I'd been away working, she 33
had helped prepare a man for burial. She'd never done it before either. She found
it moving, although she had not known the man in life. The same nurse said to her,
I like the way you people do this. This is so much better than the other way.

Her brother said to her, I hear you've been laying out stiffs in your spare time. 34

1989

QUESTIONS FOR DISCUSSION

Content

a. What worries does Moir have when she enters the morgue?
b. Why does Moir discuss boiling the head of the bear?
c. Who was Amanda and why is she mentioned?
d. What details does Moir focus on in the preparation of the body?
e. What is the problem with the coffin?
f. Why does she visit the girlfriend?

Strategy and Style

g. Why does Moir address the corpse? What is the effect on you as a reader?

h. What is the impact of Moir's description of the difficulty they had with the socks and boots?

i. What is the effect of Moir's connecting the word Fleetwood with the rock group Fleetwood Mac? Why does she mention this association?

j. Why does Moir contrast the nurse's comments with the brother's comments at the end of the essay?

SUGGESTIONS FOR SHORT WRITING

a. Discuss your own attitudes towards funerals, coffins, graveyards, and cremation.

b. How do you want your body disposed of after you die?

c. Who should be actively involved in funeral preparations?

SUGGESTIONS FOR SUSTAINED WRITING

a. British Columbia allows laypeople to prepare bodies for burial. Find out about the law in your area if you live somewhere other than B.C. Interview people about their attitudes about the law (even if you live in B.C. you can ask for people's comments). Write about the opinions of your own society towards this issue.

b. Visit a funeral home and interview people who work there on the importance of their work. Write about the attitudes towards death these answers exhibit.

c. Write a proposal for a law regarding the disposal of dead bodies.

Honey Harvest*

Sue Hubbell

Born in 1935 in Kalamazoo, Michigan, Hubbell attended Swarthmore College and the University of Michigan before getting a bachelor's degree from the University of Southern California in 1956 and a master's degree from Drexel Institute in 1963. She worked as a bookstore manager in New Jersey and as a school librarian in New Jersey and Rhode Island before boldly changing careers in 1973 to become a commercial beekeeper in the Ozark Mountains. In 1985 she added writing to beekeeping when she began writing A Country Year: Living the Questions *(1986), a collection of essays on life and nature. Since then she has published two books about insects,* A Book of Bees: . . . and How to Keep Them *(1988) and* Broadsides from the Other Orders: A Book of Bugs *(1993), which prompted a book reviewer to call her "one of the two or three best writers-about-bugs now living." She has also published collections of her essays,* On This Hilltop *(1991) and* Far Flung Hubbell *(1995), and contributes regularly to magazines such as the* New Yorker, Smithsonian, Time, *and* Newsweek. *She currently splits her time between her 18 million bees in Missouri and her husband in Washington, D.C. "Honey Harvest" (editor's title) is taken from* A Country Year.

I keep twenty hives of bees here in my home beeyard, but most of my hives are 1 scattered in outyards across the Ozarks, where I can find the thickest stands of wild blackberries and other good things for bees. I always have a waiting list of farmers who would like the bees on their land, for the clover in their pastures is more abundant when the bees are there to pollinate it.

One of the farmers, a third-generation Ozarker and a dairyman with a lively 2 interest in bees, came over today for a look at what my neighbors call my honey factory. My honey house contains a shiny array of stainless-steel tanks with clear plastic tubing connecting them, a power uncapper for slicing open honey comb, an extractor for spinning honey out of the comb, and a lot of machinery and equipment that whirs, thumps, hums, and looks very special. The dairyman, shrewd in mountain ways, looked it all over carefully and then observed, "Well . . . ll . . . ll, wouldn't say for sure now, but it looks like a still to me."

There have been droughty years and cold wet ones when flowers refused to 3 bloom and I would have been better off with a still back up here on my mountain top, but the weather this past year was perfect from a bee's standpoint, and this August I ran 33,000 pounds of honey through my factory. This was nearly twice the normal crop, and everything was overloaded, starting with me. Neither I nor my equipment is set up to handle this sort of harvest, even with extra help.

I always need to hire someone, a strong young man who is not afraid of be- 4 ing stung, to help me harvest the honey from the hives.

The honey I take is the surplus that the bees will not need for the winter; they 5 store it above their hives in wooden boxes called supers. To take it from them, I

*Editors' title.

127

stand behind each hive with a gasoline-powered machine called a bee-blower and blow the bees out of the supers with a jet of air. Meanwhile, the strong young man carries the supers, which weigh about sixty pounds each, and stacks them on pallets in the truck. There may be thirty to fifty supers in every outyard, and we have only about half an hour to get them off the hives, stacked and covered before the bees get really cross about what we are doing. The season to take the honey in this part of the country is summer's end, when the temperature is often above ninety-five degrees. The nature of the work and the temper of the bees require that we wear protective clothing while doing the job: a full set of coveralls, a zippered bee veil and leather gloves. Even a very strong young man works up a considerable sweat wrapped in a bee suit in hot weather hustling sixty-pound supers—being harassed by angry bees at the same time.

This year my helper has been Ky, my nephew, who wanted to learn some- 6
thing about bees and beekeeping. He is a sweet, gentle, cooperative giant of a young man who, because of a series of physical problems, lacks confidence in his own ability to get on in the world.

As soon as he arrived, I set about to desensitize him to bee stings. The first 7
day, I put a piece of ice on his arm to numb it; then, holding the bee carefully by her head, I placed her abdomen on the numbed spot and let her sting him there. A bee's stinger is barbed and stays in the flesh, pulling loose from her body as she struggles to free herself. Lacking her stinger, the bee will live only a short time. The bulbous poison sac at the top of the stinger continues to pulsate after the bee has left, its muscles pumping the venom and forcing the barbed stinger deeper into the flesh.

I wanted Ky to have only a partial dose of venom that first day, so after a 8
minute I scraped the stinger out with my fingernail and watched his reaction closely. A few people—about one percent of the population—are seriously sensitive to bee venom. Each sting they receive can cause a more severe reaction than the one before, reactions ranging from hives, difficulty in breathing and accelerated heartbeat, to choking, anaphylactic shock, and death. Ky had been stung a few times in his life and didn't think he was seriously allergic, but I wanted to make sure.

The spot where the stinger went in grew red and began to swell. This was a nor- 9
mal reaction, and so was the itchiness that Ky felt the next day. That time I let a bee sting him again, repeating the procedure, but leaving the stinger in his arm a full ten minutes, until the venom sac was emptied. Again the spot was red, swollen and itchy, but had disappeared the next day. Thereafter Ky decided that he didn't need the ice cube any more, and began holding the bee himself to administer his own stings. I kept him at one sting a day until he had no redness or swelling from the full sting, and then had him increase to two stings daily. Again the greater amount of venom caused redness and swelling, but soon his body could tolerate them without an allergic reaction. I gradually had him build up to ten full stings a day with no reaction.

To encourage Ky, I had told him that what he was doing might help protect 10
him from the arthritis that runs in our family. Beekeepers generally believe that getting stung by bees is a healthy thing, and that bee venom alleviates the symptoms

of arthritis. When I first began keeping bees, I supposed this to be just another one of the old wives' tales that make beekeeping such an entertaining occupation, but after my hands were stung the pain in my fingers disappeared and I too became a believer. Ky was polite, amused and skeptical of what I told him, but he welcomed my taking a few companionable stings on my knuckles along with him.

In desensitizing Ky to bee venom, I had simply been interested in building 11 up his tolerance to stings so that he could be an effective helper when we took the honey from the hives, for I knew that he would be stung frequently. But I discovered that there had been a secondary effect on Ky that was more important: He was enormously pleased with himself for having passed through what he evidently regarded as a rite of initiation. He was proud and delighted in telling other people about the whole process. He was now one tough guy.

I hoped he was prepared well enough for our first day of work. I have had 12 enough strong young men work for me to know what would happen the first day: He would be stung royally.

Some beekeepers insist that bees know their keeper—that they won't sting 13 that person, but *will* sting a stranger. This is nonsense, for summertime bees live only six weeks and I often open a particular hive less frequently than that, so I am usually a stranger to my bees; yet I am seldom stung. Others say that bees can sense fear or nervousness. I don't know if this is true or not, but I do know that bees' eyes are constructed in such a way that they can detect discontinuities and movement very well and stationary objects less well. This means that a person near their hives who moves with rapid, jerky motions attracts their attention and will more often be blamed by the bees when their hives are being meddled with than will the person whose motions are calm and easy. It has been my experience that the strong young man I hire for the honey harvest is always stung unmercifully for the first few days while he is new to the process and a bit tense. Then he learns to become easier with the bees and settles down to his job. As he gains confidence and assurance, the bees calm down too, and by the end of the harvest he usually is only stung a few times a day.

I knew that Ky very much wanted to do a good job with me that initial day 14 working in the outyards. I had explained the procedures we would follow in taking the honey from the hives, but of course they were new to him and he was anxious. The bees from the first hive I opened flung themselves on him. Most of the stingers could not penetrate his bee suit, but in the act of stinging a bee leaves a chemical trace that marks the person stung as an enemy, a chemical sign other bees can read easily. This sign was read by the bees in each new hive I opened, and soon Ky's bee suit began to look like a pincushion, bristling with stingers. In addition, the temperature was starting to climb and Ky was sweating. Honey oozing from combs broken between the supers was running down the front of his bee suit when he carried them to the truck. Honey and sweat made the suit cling to him, so that the stingers of angry bees could penetrate the suit and he could feel the prick of each one as it entered his skin. Hundreds of bees were assaulting him and finally drove him out of the beeyard, chasing him several hundred yards before they gave up the attack. There was little I could do to help him but try to complete the job quickly, so I took the supers off the next few hives myself, carried them to the truck and loaded them. Bravely, Ky returned to finish the last few hives. We tied down the load and drove away. His face was red with exertion when he unzipped his bee veil. He didn't have much to say as we drove to the next yard, but sat beside me gulping down ice water from the thermos bottle.

At the second yard the bees didn't bother Ky as we set up the equipment. I 15 hoped that much of the chemical marker the bees had left on him had evaporated, but as soon as I began to open the hives they were after him again. Soon a cloud of angry bees enveloped him, accompanying him to the truck and back. Because of the terrain, the truck had to be parked at an odd angle and Ky had to bend from the hips as he loaded it, stretching the fabric of the bee suit taut across the entire length of his back and rear, allowing the bees to sting through it easily. We couldn't talk over the noise of the beeblower's engine, but I was worried about how he was taking hundreds more stings. I was removing the bees from the supers as quickly as I could, but the yard was a good one and there were a lot of supers there.

In about an hour's time Ky carried and stacked what we later weighed in as a 16 load of 2500 pounds. The temperature must have been nearly a hundred degrees. After he had stacked the last super, I drove the truck away from the hives and we tied down the load. Ky's long hair was plastered to his face and I couldn't see the expression on it, but I knew he had been pushed to his limits and I was concerned about him. He tried to brush some of the stingers out of the seat of his bee suit before he sat down next to me in the truck in an uncommonly gingerly way. Unzipping his bee veil, he tossed it aside, pushed the hair back from his sweaty face, reached for the thermos bottle, gave me a sunny and triumphant grin and said, "If I ever get arthritis of the ass, I'll know all that stuff you've been telling me is a lot of baloney."

1983

QUESTIONS FOR DISCUSSION

Content

a. What about beekeeping does Hubbell find particularly appealing?
b. What are supers and what is their place in the process of collecting honey?
c. What is the process for being desensitized to bee venom, and how does it work?
d. How does harvesting honey benefit Hubbell's nephew, Ky?
e. What are some of the theories explaining why bees sting some people who work with them more than others?

Strategy and Style

f. What is the ideal audience for this essay? Who would most enjoy reading it? What in the essay indicates this audience?

g. Why does Hubbell describe the process of being stung by a bee in such detail (paragraph 7)? What purpose does this detailed and rather gruesome description serve?

h. How does this essay compare to one or two of the other selections in this chapter, in terms of style and organization? What do each of the writers do particularly well in describing processes?

i. In paragraphs 14, 15, and 16 Hubbell describes getting the honey from two out-yards. What descriptive words and phrases are especially effective?

j. Where does Hubbell use humour? How does humour help the story?

SUGGESTIONS FOR SHORT WRITING

a. List the steps in collecting honey.

b. Describe a "rite of initiation" (paragraph 11) of your own.

SUGGESTIONS FOR SUSTAINED WRITING

a. Describe the process of one of your hobbies or sports. Avoid writing this as a dull straightforward description; instead, write the process in story form, using lively examples and dialogue. If the hobby or sport is familiar to most readers, such as stamp collecting or basketball, find something about it that is new and surprising. If the hobby or sport is unfamiliar to your readers, such as palm reading or ice climbing, be sure to explain it as well as to tell a story about it.

b. Research a hobby, sport, or career that you might like to have. Describe how the hobby is done, the sport is played, or the career pursued.

How to Paint a Fresco

Adam Goodheart

An associate editor of Civilization, *the magazine of the Library of Congress, Adam Goodheart (b. 1970) writes a column called "Lost Arts," which contains essays on how to master arts that have passed into history. Among these interesting process essays are "How to Bleed a Patient," "How to Elect a Holy Roman Emperor," "How to Fight a Duel," "How to Hunt a Woolly Mammoth," "How to Mummify a Pharaoh," and "How to Paint a Fresco," which appeared in 1995. Goodheart, who was born in Philadelphia, attended Harvard University and has studied history and archaeology in Italy. His favourite Renaissance frescoes are those on the life of Pope Pius II by Pintoricchio. They can be found in Sienna's cathedral library.*

Although it must be painted in a very short time, a fresco will last a very long time— that is its great advantage. Many of the masterpieces of the golden age of fresco (from the 14th through the 18th centuries) are as brilliant now as when they were first painted. If you want to fresco a cathedral or palazzo today, you may have a few problems—papal and ducal commissions are scarcer than they once were, and the great Renaissance masters are no longer accepting applications for apprenticeships. Fortunately, a few of their trade secrets have come down to us through the ages. 1

EQUIPMENT

Lime 2
Sand
Water
A trowel
Paper
A needle
A small bag of charcoal dust
The bristles of a white hog
The hair of bears, sables and martens
The quills of vultures, geese, hens and doves
Ocher, burnt grapevines, lapis lazuli
Egg yolks
Goat's milk

   1. Preparing the wall. Cennino Cennini, a Tuscan master, advised pupils in 3
1437 to "begin by decking yourselves with this attire: Enthusiasm, Reverence, Obedience, and Constancy." You'd do better to deck yourself with some old clothes, though, since the first stage of the process is quite messy. Soak the wall thoroughly and coat it with coarse plaster, two parts sand to one part lime, leaving the surface uneven. (Andrea Pozzo, a 17th-century expert, recommended hiring a

professional mason to do this, since "the lime makes a foul odor, which is injurious to the head.")

2. *Tracing your design.* You should already have extensive drawings for 4 your fresco—these will be much sought by scholars and collectors in centuries to come. Make a full-size sketch, on sturdy paper, of a section of the fresco that you can paint in a day. Then go over the drawing with a needle, pricking holes along every line. Lay a coat of fine plaster on a section of the wall corresponding to the location, size, and shape of the sketch, and press the sketch against the plaster. Fill a loosely woven bag with charcoal dust and strike it lightly all over the surface of the paper. Now peel the sketch off. Your design will be outlined in black dots on the wet plaster, giving you a guide for the day's work.

3. *Painting.* Time is of the essence: You must paint the plaster while it is 5 wet, so that the pigments bind chemically with the lime. That gives you about six hours, although some painters had tricks to prolong drying. (Piero della Francesca packed the plaster with wet rags; problem was, this left indentations that are still visible after 500 years.) Use top-quality brushes. One 17th-century Flemish master recommended those made of "fish hair" (he probably meant seal fur), but most painters made brushes from bear, marten, or sable hairs inserted in hollow quills. Cennini suggested the bristles of a white hog for the coarser work. As for paints, every artist had his own favorite recipes, but all agreed that mineral pigments such as ocher or ground stone mixed with water were best. Avoid white lead. One 14th-century Umbrian used it to paint a nursing infant; the lime turned the white black and the milky babe into a "devilish changeling." A few pigments, such as dark blue azurite (often used for the Virgin Mary's mantle), must be mixed with egg yolk or goat's milk and added after the fresco is dry. Such colors will prove less durable.

Money is a consideration in choosing materials. When Michelangelo fres- 6 coed the Sistine ceiling, expenses came out of his fee, so he used cheap blue smalt for the sky. Twenty years later, when he did the *Last Judgment,* Michelangelo used semiprecious lapis lazuli for blue, since the pope was paying for the paint. (He made up for it by using burnt grapevines for black.)

4. *Casualties of style.* Realism, while a worthy goal, has its perils. Spinello 7 Aretino, a 14th-century Tuscan, is said to have painted a fresco that depicted Lucifer with such hideous accuracy that the Evil One himself came to the artist in a dream and demanded an explanation. Spinello went half-mad with fear and died shortly thereafter. On the other hand, a Florentine woodcut from 1500 depicts a painter who has portrayed the Virgin so skillfully that when he falls off the scaffold, she reaches out of the fresco and saves him.

WARNING

Frescoing ceilings can be rough on your back. While working on the Sistine 8 Chapel, Michelangelo wrote a poem complaining: "I've already grown a goiter at this drudgery . . . With my beard toward heaven . . . I am bent like a bow." Don't be discouraged, though. Bad posture is a small price to pay for immortality.

1995

QUESTIONS FOR DISCUSSION

Content

a. What are some of the problems painters of frescoes faced?
b. Why, according to Goodheart, would an artist want to attempt a fresco?
c. Why is time essential when painting a fresco?
d. What does the quotation from Cennini (paragraph 3) tell us about the art of fresco? What use, other than explanation, does Goodheart make of it?
e. Where is Tuscany? Where and what is the Sistine Chapel?

Style and Strategy

f. What is the effect of Goodheart's listing the equipment needed in a separate paragraph? Why didn't he simply mention tools and supplies in the course of explaining the process?
g. Explain the organizational logic behind this essay.
h. The author includes several examples (illustrations) in this essay. Where do they appear, and what is their function?
i. Where does Goodheart use comparison and contrast? To what end?
j. What kind of audience does this essay address? Explain your answer with reference to both style and content.
k. Identify important transitional devices—common to narrative and process analysis—in Goodheart's essay. Then, discuss other ways in which this essay resembles a narrative.

SUGGESTIONS FOR SHORT WRITING

a. Freewrite for ten minutes about a task you know a great deal about. For example, consider what it takes to write a college research paper, to paint the exterior of an old house, to set a large table for a holiday party, or to plan a wedding. Then, read your freewriting and list three or four of the major steps involved in the process. You might be able to use these steps as a rough outline for a full-length paper. Use the four steps in "How to Paint a Fresco" as your blueprint.
b. Notice that "How to Paint a Fresco" contains a warning at the end. From what you have learned about the art of fresco, what might you add to this warning?

SUGGESTIONS FOR SUSTAINED WRITING

a. Follow the outline you made above (in response to item *a* of Short Writing) and write a full-length process paper that explains how to complete a task with which you are familiar. Use the details you gathered during freewriting to get you started.

b. In your college library, research a "lost art" that interests you. Take notes from at least three sources. Then, write a process paper on this activity. For example, as Goodheart has, you might explain how to fight a duel or hunt a woolly mammoth. Then again, you can explain how to complete a cave painting, build a drawbridge, shoot a crossbow, weave a tapestry, smoke meat, make medicines from herbs, or build a Roman aqueduct. Make sure to give your sources credit by including internal citations as appropriate and a works-cited or references page.

4

Definition

Generally speaking, definitions fall into three broad categories: lexical, stipulative, and extended. The dictionary is of course the best place to begin familiarizing yourself with new concepts, but lexical definitions tend to be abstract, for they sometimes explain terms without reference to particular contexts. And stipulative definitions, while practical, are by their very nature limited to special purposes. Say you were writing a paper on the advantages and disadvantages of being a part-time student. You might *stipulate* that, for the purposes of your essay, "a part-timer is someone enrolled for less than two credits." Thus, while both lexical and stipulative definitions have their uses, extended definitions are the type used most often to explain complex topics like those discussed in this chapter.

The many practical uses to which extended definition can be applied make it a powerful tool for exposition. In the hands of writers like Claudia Glenn Dowling and Susan Sontag, it becomes a systematic way to grapple with social, moral, or even scientific questions. It can correct common, sometimes dangerous, misconceptions, as in Gloria Steinem's "Erotica and Pornography" or Jo Goodwin Parker's "What Is Poverty?" It can be used to expose abuses of language, as in the essay by John Leo, or to define "Authenticity" as Charles Taylor has shown. And it can even explain something as delicate as one's relationship to a religious text, as in Northrop Frye's "The Double Mirror."

Like process essays, extended definitions are developed by using a number of methods. Among the most common are analogy and comparison/contrast. Sontag discusses two notions of beauty in Catholic and Protestant countries, and Frye contrasts centripetal and centrifugal pull of words.

As a matter of fact, many techniques can be used to develop extended definitions. The examples and anecdotes (brief, illustrative stories) Jo Goodwin Parker uses to define poverty are powerful and incisive tools for correcting social myopia. Illustration, though used for a different purpose, also appears in Northrop Frye's "The Double Mirror."

136

Approaches to the process of defining, then, are as varied as the authors who use them. Sontag launches her discussion of beauty by tracing its etymology from the Greeks to the present. Leo analyzes the current uses of important words to show how badly those in positions of influence and power abuse the language. Sontag and Steinem rely on lexical and etymological information to introduce or clarify specific points in a larger context.

You can learn a great deal more about techniques for writing extended definitions by considering the Questions for Discussion and by addressing the Suggestions for Short Writing and for Sustained Writing that follow each selection in this chapter. Another good way to learn the skills of definition is to read each of the essays in this chapter twice. On your first pass, simply make sure you understand each selection thoroughly and accurately. The second time around, ask yourself how you might define the term being explained, whether you agree with the author's perception, or if you can add information to make the definition even more credible. The method described above might require more time than you had planned to spend on this chapter, but it is the kind of mental exercise that will strengthen your analytical muscles and help you use definition as a powerful tool whenever you need to explain complex ideas.

Beauty

Susan Sontag

Susan Sontag (b. 1933) took her BA at the University of Chicago and her MA at Radcliffe College. She also studied at Oxford University. She is an accomplished novelist, film director, and writer of screenplays. Through her essays, which have been published in magazines and journals across the United States, Sontag has established a reputation as a critic of modern culture. She will probably be best remembered, however, for her contribution to the theory of aesthetics. In her best-known work, Against Interpretation *(1966), Sontag enunciates a theory of art based upon a reliance on the senses and not the intellect. Her place of authority in the contemporary world of art criticism was confirmed when, in 1976, she published* On Photography. *Her novels include* The Benefactor *(1964) and* Death Kit *(1967). Sontag's nonfiction—*Trip to Hanoi *(1969),* Styles of Radical Will *(1969),* Vudu Urbano *(1985), and* AIDS and Its Metaphors *(1989)—demonstrate her ability to address current social and political realities with the same incisiveness that she approaches questions of art. In "Beauty," which she first published in* Vogue *in 1975, Sontag provides us with a feminist interpretation of the uses and misuses of that word throughout history.*

For the Greeks, beauty was a virtue: A kind of excellence. Persons then were as- 1
sumed to be what we now have to call—lamely, enviously—*whole* persons. If it did occur to the Greeks to distinguish between a person's "inside" and "outside," they still expected that inner beauty would be matched by beauty of the other kind. The well-born young Athenians who gathered around Socrates found it quite paradoxical that their hero was so intelligent, so brave, so honorable, so se-ductive—and so ugly. One of Socrates' main pedagogical acts was to be ugly—and teach those innocent, no doubt splendid-looking disciples of his how full of paradoxes life really was.

They may have resisted Socrates' lesson. We do not. Several thousand years 2
later, we are more wary of the enchantments of beauty. We not only split off—with the greatest facility—the "inside" (character, intellect) from the "outside" (looks); but we are actually surprised when someone who is beautiful is also intelligent, talented, good.

It was principally the influence of Christianity that deprived beauty of the 3
central place it had in classical ideals of human excellence. By limiting excellence (*virtus* in Latin) to *moral* virtue only, Christianity set beauty adrift—as an alien-ated, arbitrary, superficial enchantment. And beauty has continued to lose prestige. For close to two centuries it has become a convention to attribute beauty to only one of the two sexes: The sex which, however Fair, is always Second. Associating beauty with women has put beauty even further on the defensive, morally.

A beautiful woman, we say in English. But a handsome man. "Handsome" is 4
the masculine equivalent of—and refusal of—a compliment which has accumulated certain demeaning overtones, by being reserved for women only. That one can call a man "beautiful" in French and in Italian suggests that Catholic countries—unlike those countries shaped by the Protestant version of Christianity—still retain some

vestiges of the pagan admiration for beauty. But the difference, if one exists, is of degree only. In every modern country that is Christian or post-Christian, women *are* the beautiful sex—to the detriment of the notion of beauty as well as of women.

To be called beautiful is thought to name something essential to women's 5 character and concerns. (In contrast to men—whose essence is to be strong, or effective, or competent.) It does not take someone in the throes of advanced feminist awareness to perceive that the way women are taught to be involved with beauty encourages narcissism, reinforces dependence and immaturity. Everybody (women and men) knows that. For it is "everybody," a whole society, that has identified being feminine with caring about how one *looks*. (In contrast to being masculine—which is identified with caring about what one *is* and *does* and only secondarily, if at all, about how one looks.) Given these stereotypes, it is no wonder that beauty enjoys, at best, a rather mixed reputation.

It is not, of course, the desire to be beautiful that is wrong but the obligation to be—or to try. What is accepted by most women as a flattering idealiza- 6 tion of their sex is a way of making women feel inferior to what they actually are—or normally grow to be. For the ideal of beauty is administered as a form of self-oppression. Women are taught to see their bodies in *parts,* and to evaluate each part separately. Breasts, feet, hips, waistline, neck, eyes, nose, complexion, hair, and so on—each in turn is submitted to an anxious, fretful, often despairing scrutiny. Even if some pass muster, some will always be found wanting. Nothing less than perfection will do.

In men, good looks is a whole, something taken in at a glance. It does not 7 need to be confirmed by giving measurements of different regions of the body, nobody encourages a man to dissect his appearance, feature by feature. As for perfection, that is considered trivial—almost unmanly. Indeed, in the ideally good-looking man a small imperfection or blemish is considered positively desirable. According to one movie critic (a woman) who is a declared Robert Redford fan, it is having that cluster of skin-colored moles on one cheek that saves Redford from being merely a "pretty face." Think of the depreciation of women—as well as of beauty—that is implied in that judgment.

"The privileges of beauty are immense," said Cocteau. To be sure, beauty is 8 a form of power. And deservedly so. What is lamentable is that it is the only form of power that most women are encouraged to seek. This power is always conceived in relation to men; it is not the power to do but the power to attract. It is a power that negates itself. For this power is not one that can be chosen freely—at least, not by women—or renounced without social censure.

To preen, for a woman, can never be just a pleasure. It is also a duty. It is her 9 work. If a woman does real work—and even if she has clambered up to a leading position in politics, law, medicine, business, or whatever—she is always under pressure to confess that she still works at being attractive. But in so far as she is keeping up as one of the Fair Sex, she brings under suspicion her very capacity to be objective, professional, authoritative, thoughtful. Damned if they do—women are. And damned if they don't.

One could hardly ask for more important evidence of the dangers of consid- 10
ering persons as split between what is "inside" and what is "outside" than that in-
terminable half-comic half-tragic tale, the oppression of women. How easy it is to
start off by defining women as caretakers of their surfaces, and then to disparage
them (or find them adorable) for being "superficial." It is a crude trap, and it has
worked for too long. But to get out of the trap requires that women get some critical
distance from that excellence and privilege which is beauty, enough distance to see
how much beauty itself has been abridged in order to prop up the mythology of the
"feminine." There should be a way of saving beauty *from* women—and *for* them.

1975

QUESTIONS FOR DISCUSSION

Content

a. What is Sontag's thesis?
b. Sontag makes it a point to explain the differences between the connotations
    of the word *handsome* and those of *beautiful.* How does this contrast help her
    develop her thesis? In what other ways does she use contrast as a method of
    development?
c. Is Sontag's message aimed at a predominantly female audience? At a pre-
    dominantly male audience? At a mixed audience?
d. Consult appropriate sources in the reference section of your college library.
    Who are Socrates and Cocteau? Why does Sontag mention them (paragraphs
    1 and 8 respectively)?
e. What was it that caused beauty to "lose prestige" (paragraph 3)? How does our
    conception of beauty differ from the one the Greeks had?
f. What is Sontag referring to when she talks about countries that are "post-
    Christian" (paragraph 4)?
g. If beauty is "a form of power" (paragraph 8), what about it is "lamentable"?
h. What does Sontag mean when she claims that women are "Damned if they
    do. . . . And damned if they don't" (paragraph 9)?

Strategy and Style

i. Sontag launches the essay by spending considerable time discussing notions of
    beauty through history. Is such a long introduction justified? Why or why not?
j. Does the essay's conclusion echo its introduction? Explain.
k. In some instances, Sontag seems to be addressing the reader directly. Find a
    few such instances, and explain their effect on you.
l. Analyze the author's style. What is the effect of her insistence on varying sen-
    tence length and structure?
m. Overall, how would you describe Sontag's tone?

SUGGESTIONS FOR SHORT WRITING

a. Rewrite Sontag's essay as song lyrics. An easy way to do this is to use the melody of a well-known song for the structure of your lyrics. Try to remain true to what you believe to be Sontag's meaning.

b. Write a short definition of *ugliness*. Is it the antithesis of beauty, or do beauty and ugliness share some of the same characteristics?

SUGGESTIONS FOR SUSTAINED WRITING

a. In paragraph 5, the author claims that "the way women are taught to be involved with beauty encourages narcissism, reinforces dependence and immaturity." Think about some relevant television or magazine advertisements for beauty products. Is Sontag correct? Write an analytical essay in which you explain how such ads define *beauty*.

b. Is there such a thing as "inner beauty" as distinguished from one's physical appearance? Establish your own definition of *inner beauty*, but make sure to illustrate it with concrete details about a person or persons you know quite well.

c. Sontag seems to have concentrated on the negative effects of our preoccupation with physical beauty. Are there any positive effects? Write an essay from the other side of the issue.

What Is Poverty?

Jo Goodwin Parker

The author has requested that no biographical information be provided.

You ask me what is poverty? Listen to me. Here I am, dirty, smelly, and with no 1
"proper" underwear on and with the stench of my rotting teeth near you. I will tell
you. Listen to me. Listen without pity. I cannot use your pity. Listen with understanding. Put yourself in my dirty, worn out, ill-fitting shoes, and hear me.

Poverty is getting up every morning from a dirt- and illness-stained mattress. 2
The sheets have long since been used for diapers. Poverty is living in a smell that
never leaves. This is a smell of urine, sour milk, and spoiling food sometimes
joined with the strong smell of long-cooked onions. Onions are cheap. If you have
smelled this smell, you did not know how it came. It is the smell of the outdoor
privy. It is the smell of young children who cannot walk the long dark way in the
night. It is the smell of the mattresses where years of "accidents" have happened.
It is the smell of the milk which has gone sour because the refrigerator long has
not worked, and it costs money to get it fixed. It is the smell of rotting garbage. I
could bury it, but where is the shovel? Shovels cost money.

Poverty is being tired. I have always been tired. They told me at the hospi- 3
tal when the last baby came that I had chronic anemia caused from poor diet, a bad
case of worms, and that I needed a corrective operation. I listened politely—the
poor are always polite. The poor always listen. They don't say that there is no
money for iron pills, or better food, or worm medicine. The idea of an operation
is frightening and costs so much that, if I had dared, I would have laughed. Who
takes care of my children? Recovery from an operation takes a long time. I have
three children. When I left them with "Granny" the last time I had a job, I came
home to find the baby covered with fly specks, and a diaper that had not been
changed since I left. When the dried diaper came off, bits of my baby's flesh came
with it. My other child was playing with a sharp bit of broken glass, and my oldest was playing alone at the edge of a lake. I made twenty-two dollars a week, and
a good nursery school costs twenty dollars a week for three children. I quit my job.

Poverty is dirt. You can say in your clean clothes coming from your clean 4
house, "Anybody can be clean." Let me explain about housekeeping with no
money. For breakfast I give my children grits with no oleo or cornbread without
eggs and oleo. This does not use up many dishes. What dishes there are, I wash in
cold water and with no soap. Even the cheapest soap has to be saved for the baby's
diapers. Look at my hands, so cracked and red. Once I saved for two months to
buy a jar of Vaseline for my hands and the baby's diaper rash. When I had saved

enough, I went to buy it and the price had gone up two cents. The baby and I suffered on. I have to decide every day if I can bear to put my cracked sore hands into the cold water and strong soap. But you ask, why not hot water? Fuel costs money. If you have a wood fire it costs money. If you burn electricity, it costs money. Hot water is a luxury. I do not have luxuries. I know you will be surprised when I tell you how young I am. I look so much older. My back has been bent over the wash tubs every day for so long, I cannot remember when I ever did anything else. Every night I wash every stitch my school age child has on and just hope her clothes will be dry by morning.

Poverty is staying up all night on cold nights to watch the fire knowing one 5 spark on the newspaper covering the walls means your sleeping child dies in flames. In summer, poverty is watching gnats and flies devour your baby's tears when he cries. The screens are torn and you pay so little rent you know they will never be fixed. Poverty means insects in your food, in your nose, in your eyes, and crawling over you when you sleep. Poverty is hoping it never rains because diapers won't dry when it rains and soon you are using newspapers. Poverty is seeing your children forever with runny noses. Paper handkerchiefs cost money and all your rags you need for other things. Even more costly are antihistamines. Poverty is cooking without food and cleaning without soap.

Poverty is asking for help. Have you ever had to ask for help, knowing your 6 children will suffer unless you get it? Think about asking for a loan from a relative, if this is the only way you can imagine asking for help. I will tell you how it feels. You find out where the office is that you are supposed to visit. You circle that block four or five times. Thinking of your children, you go in. Everyone is very busy. Finally, someone comes out and you tell her that you need help. That never is the person you need to see. You go see another person, and after spilling the whole shame of your poverty all over the desk between you, you find that this isn't the right office after all—you must repeat the whole process, and it never is any easier at the next place.

You have asked for help, and after all it has a cost. You are again told to wait. 7 You are told why, but you don't really hear because of the red cloud of shame and the rising cloud of despair.

Poverty is remembering. It is remembering quitting school in junior high be- 8 cause "nice" children had been so cruel about my clothes and my smell. The attendance officer came. My mother told him I was pregnant. I wasn't, but she thought that I could get a job and help out. I had jobs off and on, but never long enough to learn anything. Mostly I remember being married. I was so young then. I am still young. For a time, we had all the things you have. There was a little house in another town, with hot water and everything. Then my husband lost his job. There was unemployment insurance for a while and what few jobs I could get. Soon, all our nice things were repossessed and we moved back here. I was pregnant then. This house didn't look so bad when we first moved in. Every week it gets worse. Nothing is ever fixed. We now had no money. There were a few odd jobs for my husband, but everything went for food then, as it does now. I don't know how we lived through three years and three babies, but we did. I'll tell you something, after the last baby I destroyed my marriage. It had been a good one, but could you keep on bringing children in this dirt? Did you ever think how much it costs for any kind of birth control? I knew my husband was leaving the day he left, but there were no goodbys between us. I hope he has been able to climb out of this mess somewhere. He never could hope with us to drag him down.

That's when I asked for help. When I got it, you know how much it was? It 9 was, and is, seventy-eight dollars a month for the four of us; that is all I ever can get. Now you know why there is no soap, no needles and thread, no hot water, no aspirin, no worm medicine, no hand cream, no shampoo. None of these things forever and ever and ever. So that you can see clearly, I pay twenty dollars a month rent, and most of the rest goes for food. For grits and cornmeal, and rice and milk and beans. I try my best to use only the minimum electricity. If I use more, there is that much less for food.

Poverty is looking into a black future. Your children won't play with my 10 boys. They will turn to other boys who steal to get what they want. I can already see them behind the bars of their prison instead of behind the bars of my poverty. Or they will turn to the freedom of alcohol or drugs, and find themselves enslaved. And my daughter? At best, there is for her a life like mine.

But you say to me, there are schools. Yes, there are schools. My children 11 have no extra books, no magazines, no extra pencils, or crayons, or paper and most important of all, they do not have health. They have worms, they have infections, they have pink-eye all summer. They do not sleep well on the floor, or with me in my one bed. They do not suffer from hunger, my seventy-eight dollars keeps us alive, but they do suffer from malnutrition. Oh yes, I do remember what I was taught about health in school. It doesn't do much good. In some places there is a surplus commodities program. Not here. The county said it cost too much. There is a school lunch program. But I have two children who will already be damaged by the time they get to school.

But, you say to me, there are health clinics. Yes, there are health clinics and 12 they are in the towns. I live out here eight miles from town. I can walk that far (even if it is sixteen miles both ways), but can my little children? My neighbor will take me when he goes; but he expects to get paid, *one way or another.* I bet you know my neighbor. He is that large man who spends his time at the gas station, the barbershop, and the corner store complaining about the government spending money on the immoral mothers of illegitimate children.

Poverty is an acid that drips on pride until all pride is worn away. Poverty is 13 a chisel that chips on honor until honor is worn away. Some of you say that you would do *something* in my situation, and maybe you would, for the first week or the first month, but for year after year after year?

Even the poor can dream. A dream of a time when there is money. Money 14 for the right kinds of food, for worm medicine, for iron pills, for toothbrushes, for hand cream, for a hammer and nails and a bit of screening, for a shovel, for a bit of paint, for some sheeting, for needles and thread. Money to pay *in money* for a trip to town. And, oh, money for hot water and money for soap. A dream of when asking for help does not eat away the last bit of pride. When the office you visit is as nice as the offices of other governmental agencies, when there are enough workers to help you quickly, when workers do not quit in defeat and despair. When you have to tell your story to only one person, and that person can send you for other help and you don't have to prove your poverty over and over and over again.

I have come out of my despair to tell you this. Remember I did not come 15 from another place or another time. Others like me are all around you. Look at us with an angry heart, anger that will help you help me. Anger that will let you tell of me. The poor are always silent. Can you be silent too?

1971

QUESTIONS FOR DISCUSSION

Content

a. How would you define the author's purpose? Besides paragraph 15, in what parts of the essay is that purpose most apparent?

b. Why does the speaker address her audience directly, especially in paragraphs 4 and 10? How would you describe that audience?

c. What is the speaker's attitude toward her estranged husband? Do you find it curious? What does it tell you about her? What does it tell you about Parker's purpose?

d. In paragraph 8, the speaker seems to describe a cycle of poverty into which the poor are born and in which they remain. Explain. In what other sections of the essay does she allude to this cycle?

e. How does she account for her inability to keep her family clean? Why is it futile for her to seek a job?

f. What is the distinction between "hunger" and "malnutrition" that she makes in paragraph 11? Why does she deny the usefulness of school lunch programs?

g. The speaker relates incidents in which she has had to endure both public and private humiliation in order to obtain help for her family. What is the source of such humiliation? How does Parker's inclusion of these incidents help her define *poverty*?

Strategy and Style

h. Often, the speaker makes sure to anticipate and to discuss opposing arguments. What is the effect of her doing so? How does this practice help illuminate her character?

i. Parker has organized the essay by having her speaker enunciate a series of characteristics that define *poverty*. What is the effect of her beginning several paragraphs with "Poverty is . . . "?

j. Comment upon the author's use of illustrations. To what physical senses does she appeal most often? What use does she make of metaphor?

k. Parker has created a "persona" or speaker who tells her story by using the first-person pronoun ("I"). How would you describe this "persona"?

l. What is the purpose of paragraph 15 besides concluding the essay? How would you describe the speaker's tone in this paragraph? Does it differ from the tone she uses in other parts of the essay?

SUGGESTIONS FOR SHORT WRITING

a. Write a dictionary definition of *poverty* without using a dictionary. Then look the word up and compare your definition with the dictionary's. How specific were you or the dictionary able to get?

b. Now write a definition by using examples drawn from life. In your opinion, which of the definitions is clearer?

SUGGESTIONS FOR SUSTAINED WRITING

a. Parker has done an excellent job of defining an abstract term by using concrete illustrations. Think about one abstract term that describes a human reality with which you are thoroughly familiar: power, personal ambition, grief, hunger, physical pain, pride, for example. Explain what that term means to you. Use your own personal experiences as illustrations.

b. The speaker tells us about material poverty. Are there other kinds of poverty that are less frequently talked about—intellectual, spiritual, or moral poverty, for instance? Try to define one of these less commonly discussed types of poverty by using concrete details and illustrations as Parker does in this selection.

c. Does Parker believe that many of her readers harbour unfair and unrealistic assumptions about the poor? If so, what are these assumptions? Do you agree that they are unfair and unrealistic? Use what you know about poverty and the poor to write an essay that addresses such assumptions.

The Double Mirror

Northrop Frye

Northrop Frye (1912–1991) was a literary scholar who profoundly shaped the way an entire generation approached literature. His book Fearful Symmetry *(1947), about the writings of poet William Blake, transformed the way Blake was understood. His search for a coherent method of literary study resulted in the* Anatomy of Criticism *(1957), a book of international importance. Throughout his work, Frye insisted that the study of literature is not secondary to such disciplines as psychology or philosophy, but that the study of literature sketches the borders of the human imagination. Underscoring all his writing is his warmth, his passion for literature, and his belief in a deeper level of existence.*

What I want mainly to talk about is my present preoccupation with the Bible, which 1 I am trying to study in relation to secular literature and criticism. This involves relating it to issues in critical theory, so far as I understand them. I get a strong impression that many contemporary critics are talking about the Bible even when they avoid mentioning it. Many critical issues originated in the hermeneutic study of the Bible; many critical theories are obscurely motivated by a God-is-dead syndrome that also arose from biblical criticism; many of the principles advanced by such theorists often seem to me more defensible when applied to the Bible than they are when applied elsewhere.

The traditional view of the Bible, as we all know, has been that it must be 2 regarded as "literally" true. This view of "literal" meaning assumes that the Bible is a transparent medium of words conveying a "true" picture of historical events and conceptual doctrines. It is a vehicle of "revelation," and revelation means that something objective, behind the words, is being conveyed directly to the reader. It is also an "inspired" book, and inspiration means that its authors were, so to speak, holy tape recorders, writing at the dictation of an external spiritual power.

This view is based on an assumption about verbal truth that needs examining. 3 Whenever we read anything our minds are moving in two directions at once. One direction is centripetal, where we establish a context out of the words read; the other is centrifugal, where we try to remember what the words mean in the world outside. Sometimes the external meanings take on a structure parallel to the verbal structure, and when this happens we call the verbal structure descriptive or non-literary. Here the question of truth arises: the structure is true if it is a satisfactory counterpart to the external structure it is parallel to. If there is no external counterpart, the structure is said to be literary or imaginative, existing for its own sake, and hence often considered a form of permissible lying. If the Bible is true, tradition says, it must be a nonliterary counterpart of something outside it. It is, as Derrida would say, an absence invoking a presence, the "word of God" as book pointing to the "word of God" as speaking presence in history. It is curious that although this view of biblical meaning was intended to exalt the Bible as a uniquely sacrosanct book, it in fact turned it into a servomechanism, its words conveying truths or events that by definition were more important than the words were. The written Bible, this view is really saying, is a concession to time: as Socrates says of writing in the *Phaedrus*, it is intended only to call to mind something that has passed away from presence. The real basis of the Bible, for all theologians down to Karl Barth at least, is the presence represented by the phrase "God speaks."

We have next to try to understand how this view arose. In a primitive society   4 (whatever we mean by primitive), there is a largely undifferentiated body of verbal material, held together by the sense of its importance to that society. This material tells the society what the society needs to know about its history, religion, class structure, and law. As society becomes more complex, these elements become more distinct and autonomous. Legend and saga develop into history; stories, sacred or secular, develop into literature; a mixture of practical knowledge and magic develops into science. Society struggles to contain these elements within its overriding concerns, and tries to impose on them a structure of authority that will keep them unified, as Christianity did in medieval times. About two generations ago there was a fashion for crying up the Middle Ages as a golden age in which all aspects of culture were unified by common sentiments and beliefs. Similar developments, with a similar appeal, are taking place today in Marxist countries.

However, artists, historians, scientists, theologians find increasingly that they   5 make discoveries within the growing structure of their discipline, and that they owe a loyalty to that structure as well as to the concerns of society. Thus astronomers had to advance a heliocentric view of the solar system even when social anxieties demanded a geocentric one; historians of Britain had to reject the Arthurian story although popular feeling clung to it. Social authority gives ground in some areas more willingly than others. The presence pointed to by the Bible was, in practice, identified with a theological interpretation which was the right interpretation, to be understood before the Bible itself could be understood. These interpretations took different linguistic forms before and after the Reformation, but were always primarily structures of authority, intended to impose a unity on believers that was really uniformity, in public expression at least.

Such interpretations grew up partly because the verbal texture of the Bible is   6 very different from that of descriptive writing, as a glance at it shows. A descriptive writer who aims at conveying some truth beyond his verbal structure avoids figures of speech, because all figuration emphasizes the centripetal aspect of words, and belongs either to the poetic or to the rhetorical categories. The Bible is full of explicit metaphors, hyperboles, popular etymologies, puns, in fact every figurative device possible, many of which are defined in dictionaries simply as errors of grammar or logic. But the vices of grammar and logic are often the virtues of poetry, and while no one would call the Bible a poetic structure, it has all the characteristics of poetry, which accounts for most of its very specific literary influence. Its narratives range from legend to partisan history, but historical fact as fact is nowhere marked off in it.

In short, the Bible is explicitly antireferential in structure, and deliberately   7 blocks off any world of presence behind itself. In Christianity, everything in the Old Testament is a "type" of which the "antitype" or existential reality is in the

New Testament. This turns the Bible into a double mirror reflecting only itself to itself. How do we know that the Gospel is true? Because it fulfills the prophecies of the Old Testament. But how do we know that the Old Testament prophecies are true? Because they are fulfilled by the Gospel. Is there any evidence for the existence of Jesus as a major historical figure outside the New Testament? None really, and the writers of the New Testament obviously preferred it that way. As long as we assume a historical presence behind the Bible to which it points, the phrase "word of God," as applied both to the Bible and the person of Christ, is only a dubious syllepsis. In proportion as the presence behind disappears, it becomes identified with the book, and the phrase begins to make sense. As we continue to study the significance of the fact that the Bible is a book, the sense of presence shifts from what is behind the book to what is in front of it.

As for "inspiration," if there is one thing that biblical scholarship has estab- 8 lished beyond reasonable doubt, it is that authorship, inspired or not, counts for very little in the Bible. The third Gospel is traditionally supposed to have Luke for its author, but the gospel itself is an edited and composite document, with nothing, beyond perhaps the first four verses, of which Luke is likely to be in any real sense the author. Editing and compiling are highly self-conscious activities, and the word *inspiration* cannot add much to a study of them. If the Bible is inspired in any sense, all the glossing and editing and splicing and conflating activities must be inspired too. There is no way of distinguishing the voice of God from the voice of the Deuteronomic redactor. This suggests a qualification of the view that biblical language is poetic, however, as the poetic and the inspired are often popularly supposed to be related.

Poetic language is closely associated with rhetorical language, as both make 9 extensive use of figures of speech. The Bible uses a language that is as poetic as it can be without actually becoming a poem. But it is not a poem; it is written in a mode of rhetoric, though it is rhetoric of a special kind, called by the theologian Bultmann, among others, *kerygma* or "proclamation." In a last effort to evoke the ghost of the referential, Bultmann says that to see this *kerygma* in the Gospels we must get rid of myth, which he regards as an obstacle to it. To a critic, however, myth means primarily *mythos* or narrative, more particularly the kind of self-contained narrative which is meant by the English word *story* in contrast to history. Such myth is the only possible vehicle of *kerygma,* and as every syllable of the Gospels is written in the language of myth, efforts to demythologize the Gospels would soon end by obliterating them.

The literal meaning of the Bible, then, if we are right, must be a mythical and 10 metaphorical meaning. It is only when we are reading as we read poetry that we can take the word *literal* seriously, accepting everything given us without question. There may be meanings beyond the literal, but that is where we start. In teaching the Bible I stress the unity and consistency of its narrative and imagery, and at some point a student will ask: "Why can't we have it both ways? Why not a body of narrative and imagery that is also a definitive replica of truths beyond itself?" The answer is that description is a subordinate function of words. Even one word is a sign and not a thing: two or three words begin to form grammatical fictions like those of subject and predicate. What words do with greatest power and accuracy is hang together. Of course there are verbal structures that are based on description and reference, but the Bible is too deeply rooted in the nature of words to be one of them. At a certain point of intensity a choice must be made between figurative and descriptive language, and the Bible's choice of the figurative is written on every page of it.

Questions of biblical criticism, we see, are models for many critical questions 11 about secular literature. When I began the study of literature as a student, it was generally assumed that the critic's duty was to work out an "interpretation" of the poem before him, and that when all the really expert critics compared their interpretations a consensus would emerge that would be, more or less, the right way to look at the poem. The fact that no such consensus ever emerged was a problem to faith, but nothing more. I now feel that the word *interpretation* is a red herring: to be given a poem and look round for an interpretation of it is like being given the kernel of a nut and looking round for a shell, which seems to me as perverse an approach to poems as it is to nuts. What I do think is that the text before us is something other than ourselves, that we have to struggle with it as Jacob did with the angel, but that there is nothing to come up from behind, like the Prussian army at Waterloo, to assist us. The otherness is the text itself. However, we are not quite as much on our own as Jacob was: there are other critics, and we do become increasingly aware that a text is the focus of a community.

This does not mean that all critics are going to agree any better than before, 12 but that in their disagreements an element that we may call the egocentric can get gradually diminished. It was Oscar Wilde who defined, in two almost unreasonably brilliant essays, the situation of criticism today. One was called "The Decay of Lying," which attacked the view that literature gains dignity and validity from its reference to something beyond itself. The word *lying* calls attention to the fact that literature turns its back on all such reference. The other was called "The Critic as Artist," which promoted the reader to a co-creator with the poet, completing the operation that the poet is compelled to leave half done. By a *critic* Wilde meant, I think, a serious and representative reader, who knows that his response is socially and culturally conditioned, but is nonetheless capable of weeding out of that response an egocentric element, such as: "I don't like the way this poem ends because if I were writing it I wouldn't end it that way." I have always connected this egocentric element with the conception of the critic as judge or evaluator. It is a commonplace now that observation is affected by the observer, even in the most quantitative sciences, and the necessity for observing the observer is now fairly acute in literary criticism. What I think happens is a struggle for identity in the course of which the false subject or ego and the false object or the referential signified get thrown out together.

In ordinary experience we think of ourselves as subjective, and of everything 13 else as objective. We also tend to think of the objective as the center of reality and the subjective as the center of illusion. But then we enter a theater and find that an illusion is presented to us on the stage objectively, as a sense datum. We could search the wings and dressing rooms forever without finding reality behind it: whatever is there that is not the play is in front of it, in the mood created in the audience. What reality there is seems to be emerging from the coinciding of two illusions. Thus in *The Tempest,* Prospero takes a group of people living in a reality so low as to be a form of illusion, soaks them in a different kind of illusion featuring hallucinations and elemental spirits, and sends them back home on a much higher level of reality.

We referred to Socrates' remark in the *Phaedrus* that the inventor of writing   14 was told by his critics that his was not an art of memory *(mneme)* but of reminding *(hypomnomena).* What his critics did not realize was that the act of recalling is a far more vivid and intense experience than memory itself. When Elizabethan critics used Horace's phrase about poetry as a "speaking picture," they implied that poetry gives us, not the familiar remembered thing, but the glittering intensity of the summoned-up hallucination. On this basis we can perhaps understand the long-standing association between written books and the art of magic, another theme of *The Tempest.* Without his books, says Caliban, Prospero would be as much of a sot as I am. Magic establishes a charmed circle where spirits can be invoked, held, and commanded by words, and in this unity of word and spirit we have perhaps the most genuine form of an altered state of consciousness. It has often been noted that the question of human freedom cannot be worked out on the basis of the relation of man and nature alone. As our view of the world becomes more objective, the question arises of what is not objective. For everything we see in ourselves is objective also. What is left can only be, as I think, our participation in a community of language, whether the language is that of words, mathematics, or one of the other arts. This is all that can really be distinguished from the objective world. As Nietzsche said, nature has no laws, only necessities; and just as we find our conception of necessity in the physical world, so we find in the languages of words and numbers and arts the charter of our freedom.

We notice that while the Bible ends with a vision of the end of time and of   15 history as we have known it, it is a remarkably open ending. It ends with an invitation to "come" or approach, under the image of drinking the water of life. The implication is that its reality starts in the reader's mind as soon as he finishes reading. Milton speaks of the Word of God in the heart, the possession of the Word by the reader, as having an authority higher than that of the Bible itself. Milton was not concerned about the chaos of "private judgment," the individual setting himself up as the measure of all things, because in his view the real reader was not the ego but the Holy Spirit, who would unite all readers without forcing them into uniformity.

Once again the biblical principle is an analogy to procedures in secular criticism.   16 If we say that authorship, inspiration, historical accuracy and the like are not important in the Bible, what is important? One thing that seems to me to be so is the conception of canon, the idea of a collection of books unified, not by consistency of argument or doctrine—there are no true rational arguments in the Bible—but of vision and imagery. There are no definable boundaries between canonical and uncanonical, but there are different areas or contexts, where some things are closer to us than others. Culture begins, we said, in a largely undifferentiated mixture of religious, historical, legal, and literary material which is important to the concerns of its society. It seems to be ending today in a vast chaos of *écriture* where there are no boundary lines between literature and anything else in words. Of course there are no boundary lines; but I think that when the present plague of darkness has lifted we shall start making discriminations again. We shall, I think, even reestablish the referential for the verbal structures that clearly require it, which would still exclude literature and the Bible. But our new discriminations will be contexts and not delimited areas. Such a word as *comedy* means something intelligible, and has conveyed an intelligible meaning for thousands of years. But there is no such "thing" as comedy: it cannot be defined as an essence which excludes other essences. We can express only its general range and ambience, and our feeling that sometimes we are inside it and at other times on its periphery or outside it.

Similarly, there is a canon in secular as in sacred literature, though there is no 17 way of establishing such a canon on a basis of value judgments. In those passages in the New Testament where the Bible has become self-conscious enough to comment on itself, we are told that the word of God is a two-edged sword, dividing things and not reconciling things. But this can hardly mean a dialectical instrument of the Hegelian kind, where every statement is a half-truth implying its own opposite. The real division is rather between the two worlds of spiritual life and spiritual death, and this division is made by a use of language that bypasses the argumentative and the aggressive. Much the same thing is true of secular literature. The word *classic* as applied to a work of literature means primarily a work that refuses to go away, that remains confronting us until we do something about it, which means also doing something about ourselves.

The main difference is one of initiative. The rhetoric of proclamation is a wel- 18 coming and approaching rhetoric, in contrast to rhetoric where the aim is victory in argument or drawing an audience together into a more exclusive unit. It speaks, according to Paul, the language of love, which he says is likely to last longer than most forms of communication. Wherever there is love there is sexual symbolism, and the rhetoric of the Bible, which seeks out its reader, is traditionally a male rhetoric, all its readers, whether men or women, being symbolically female. In secular literature, where the category is purely poetic, the sexual symbolism is reversed: there it is the poetic artifact that is symbolically female, the daughter of a Muse. These are metaphors, and of course any metaphor can be misleading or confusing. But metaphor was made for man and not man for metaphor; or, as my late and much beloved colleague Marshall McLuhan used to say, man's reach should exceed his grasp, or what's a metaphor?

1990

QUESTIONS FOR DISCUSSION

Content

a. According to Frye's introduction, he must use critical theory in order to understand the relationship between the Bible and secular literature. Why does Frye
feel it is important to know what we are doing as readers?
b. What does Frye mean by the centripetal and the centrifugal pull of words?
c. What is the difference between a "sacrosanct book" and a "servomechanism"?
d. How did the view arise that the Bible is a literal, not a literary, document,
according to Frye?
e. What is the role of social authority in the interpretation of the Bible?
f. How is the Bible different from descriptive writing?
g. What does Frye mean when he says, "the Bible is explicitly antireferential in
structure"? What examples does he give to illustrate his point?
h. How does Frye deal with the question of "inspiration"?
i. Why, according to Frye, must the "literal meaning of the Bible" be "a mythical
and metaphorical meaning"?
j. What is the connection between questions of biblical criticism and questions
of secular criticism?
k. Towards the end of the essay, Frye asks a question: "If we say that authorship,
inspiration, historical accuracy and the like are not important in the Bible, what
is important?" What is Frye's answer in both the Biblical and secular realm?
l. What is a "classic," according to Frye?

Strategy and Style

m. Frye opens his essay quite directly—"What I want mainly to talk about is. . . ."
Why do you think he is so direct in his approach?
n. Does Frye consistently define all the terms that he uses? If not, why not?
o. Frye says that he is discussing his own understanding of critical theory. From
the context of the entire essay (a centripetal reading), how would you define
the term "critical theory"?
p. What kind of vocabulary does Frye use? Does he demand much of us as readers?
Can we understand all the words from their context or must we use an external
reference (a dictionary)?
q. When talking about interpreting poetry, Frye uses an analogy of being given a nut
and searching for the shell. What is the effect of this analogy on you as a reader?
r. What does Frye reveal about himself when he writes about Wilde's essays: "two
almost unreasonably brilliant essays"? How does this statement shape your
conception of Frye?
s. Does Frye use topic sentences for his paragraphs?
t. Why is the Bible a "double mirror"? What is the effect of such an image on the
reader?

SUGGESTIONS FOR SHORT WRITING

a. Write about your attitudes towards the Bible. Is it a holy book for you? Are you familiar with it? Are you afraid of it? What about the Quran or the Gita or the Book of Mormon?

b. Frye has always believed that it is important to know what we are doing when we are reading. Do you agree?

c. If looking for the meaning of a poem is like looking for the shell after we have been given a nut, what are we supposed to do with poetry?

SUGGESTIONS FOR SUSTAINED WRITING

a. Find and read Plato's argument against poets in *The Republic*. Compare and contrast Plato's understanding of canonical texts with Frye.

b. Argue against Frye: literature and the Bible refer to the outside world and are only relevant to the degree to which they refer.

c. Create a canon of 10 movies that you feel are essential to one's education. Try to establish your criteria for inclusion or exclusion into your canon.

Erotica and Pornography

Gloria Steinem

Born in Toledo, Ohio, Gloria Steinem (b. 1934) took her BA at Smith College, then studied at the University of Delhi and the University of Calcutta in India. Early in her career, she was a television news writer for NBC's "That Was the Week That Was." She went on to write for a number of America's most important magazines including Vogue, Life, Cosmopolitan, *and* Glamour, *and she served as an editorial consultant to* Seventeen *and* Show. *One of the founders and leaders of the contemporary American feminist movement, Steinem went undercover for* Show *magazine in 1963 to write "I Was a Playboy Bunny," an article that brought her journalistic acclaim. However, she is best known for her work as cofounder of and contributing editor to* New York *magazine and* Ms. *magazine. Today, she is among the most influential women in American public life, and her work has brought her numerous awards and honours, including the United Nations Ceres Medal and the Front Page Award. Among her full-length works are* Outrageous Acts and Everyday Rebellions *(1983),* Marilyn: Norma Jean *(1986),* A Revolution from Within *(1993), and* Moving Beyond Words *(1994). "Erotica and Pornography" was first published in 1978 in* Ms.

1 Human beings are the only animals that experience the same sex drive at times when we can—and cannot—conceive.

2 Just as we developed uniquely human capacities for language, planning, memory, and invention along our evolutionary path, we also developed sexuality as a form of expression, a way of communicating that is separable from our need for sex as a way of perpetuating ourselves. For humans alone, sexuality can be and often is primarily a way of bonding, of giving and receiving pleasure, bridging differentness, discovering sameness, and communicating emotion.

3 We developed this and other human gifts through our ability to change our environment, adapt physically, and in the long run, to affect our own evolution. But as an emotional result of this spiraling path away from other animals, we seem to alternate between periods of exploring our unique abilities to change new boundaries and feelings of loneliness in the unknown that we ourselves have created; a fear that sometimes sends us back to the comfort of the animal world by encouraging us to exaggerate our sameness.

4 The separation of "play" from "work," for instance, is a problem only in the human world. So is the difference between art and nature, or an intellectual accomplishment and a physical one. As a result, we celebrate play, art, and invention as leaps into the unknown; but any imbalance can send us back to nostalgia for our primate past and the conviction that the basics of work, nature, and physical labor are somehow more worthwhile or even moral.

5 In the same way, we have explored our sexuality as separable from conception: A pleasurable, empathetic bridge to strangers of the same species. We have even invented contraception—a skill that has probably existed in some form since our ancestors figured out the process of birth—in order to extend this uniquely

155

human difference. Yet we also have times of atavistic suspicion that sex is not complete—or even legal or intended-by-god—if it cannot end in conception.

No wonder the concepts of "erotica" and "pornography" can be so crucially   6
different, and yet so confused. Both assume that sexuality can be separated from conception, and therefore can be used to carry a personal message. That's a major reason why, even in our current culture, both may be called equally "shocking" or legally "obscene," a word whose Latin derivative means "dirty, containing filth." This gross condemnation of all sexuality that isn't harnessed to childbirth and marriage has been increased by the current backlash against women's progress. Out of fear that the whole patriarchal structure might be upset if women really had the autonomous power to decide our reproductive futures (that is, if we controlled the most basic means of production), right-wing groups are not only denouncing prochoice abortion literature as "pornographic," but are trying to stop the sending of all contraceptive information through the mails by invoking obscenity laws. In fact, Phyllis Schlafly recently denounced the entire Women's Movement as "obscene."

Not surprisingly, this religious, visceral backlash has a secular, intellectual   7
counterpart that relies heavily on applying the "natural" behavior of the animal world to humans. That is questionable in itself, but these Lionel Tigerish studies make their political purpose even more clear in the particular animals they select and the habits they choose to emphasize. The message is that females should accept their "destiny" of being sexually dependent and devote themselves to bearing and rearing their young.

Defending against such reaction in turn leads to another temptation: To   8
merely reverse the terms, and declare that *all* nonprocreative sex is good. In fact, however, this human activity can be as constructive or destructive, moral or immoral, as any other. Sex as communication can send messages as different as life and death; even the origins of "erotica" and "pornography" reflect that fact. After all, "erotica" is rooted in *eros* or passionate love, and thus in the idea of positive choice, free will, the yearning for a particular person. (Interestingly, the definition of erotica leaves open the question of gender.) "Pornography" begins with a root meaning "prostitution" or "female captives," thus letting us know that the subject is not mutual love, or love at all, but domination and violence against women. (Though, of course, homosexual pornography may imitate this violence by putting a man in the "feminine" role of victim.) It ends with a root meaning "writing about" or "description of" which puts still more distance between subject and object, and replaces a spontaneous yearning for closeness with objectification and a voyeur.

The difference is clear in the words. It becomes even more so by example.   9

Look at any photo or film of people making love; really making love. The   10
images may be diverse, but there is usually a sensuality and touch and warmth, an acceptance of bodies and nerve endings. There is always a spontaneous sense of people who are there because they *want* to be, out of shared pleasure.

Now look at any depiction of sex in which there is clear force, or an un-   11
equal power that spells coercion. It may be very blatant, with weapons or torture or bondage, wounds and bruises, some clear humiliation, or an adult's sexual

power being used over a child. It may be much more subtle: A physical attitude of conqueror and victim, the use of race or class difference to imply the same thing, perhaps a very unequal nudity, with one person exposed and vulnerable while the other is clothed. In either case, there is no sense of equal choice or equal power.

The first is erotic: A mutually pleasurable, sexual expression between people who have enough power to be there by positive choice. It may or may not strike the sense-memory in the viewer, or be creative enough to make the unknown seem real; but it doesn't require us to identify with a conqueror or a victim. It is truly sensuous, and may give us a contagion of pleasure. 12

The second is pornographic: Its message is violence, dominance, and conquest. It is sex being used to reinforce some inequality, or to create one, or to tell us the lie that pain and humiliation (ours or someone else's) are really the same as pleasure. If we are to feel anything, we must identify with conqueror or victim. That means we can only experience pleasure through the adoption of some degree of sadism or masochism. It also means that we may feel diminished by the role of conqueror, or enraged, humiliated, and vengeful by sharing identity with the victim. 13

Perhaps one could simply say that erotica is about sexuality, but pornography is about power and sex-as-weapon—in the same way we have come to understand that rape is about violence, and not really about sexuality at all. 14

Yes, it's true that there are women who have been forced by violent families and dominating men to confuse love with pain; so much so that they have become masochists. (A fact that in no way excuses those who administer such pain.) But the truth is that, for most women—and for men with enough humanity to imagine themselves into the predicament of women—true pornography could serve as aversion therapy for sex. 15

Of course, there will always be personal differences about what is and is not erotic, and there may be cultural differences for a long time to come. Many women feel that sex makes them vulnerable and therefore may continue to need more sense of personal connection and safety before allowing any erotic feelings. We now find competence and expertise erotic in men, but that may pass as we develop those qualities in ourselves. Men, on the other hand, may continue to feel less vulnerable, and therefore more open to such potential danger as sex with strangers. As some men replace the need for submission from childlike women with the pleasure of cooperation from equals, they may find a partner's competence to be erotic, too. 16

Such group changes plus individual differences will continue to be reflected in sexual love between people of the same gender, as well as between women and men. The point is not to dictate sameness, but to discover ourselves and each other through sexuality that is an exploring, pleasurable, empathetic part of our lives; a human sexuality that is unchained both from unwanted pregnancies and from violence. 17

But that is a hope, not a reality. At the moment, fear of change is increasing both the indiscriminate repression of all nonprocreative sex in the religious 18 and "conservative" male world, and the pornographic vengeance against women's sexuality in the secular world of "liberal" and "radical" men. It's almost futuristic to debate what is and is not truly erotic, when many women are again being forced into compulsory motherhood, and the number of pornographic murders, tortures, and woman-hating images are on the increase in both popular culture and real life.

It's a familiar division: wife or whore, "good" woman who is constantly vul- 19 nerable to pregnancy or "bad" woman who is unprotected from violence. *Both* roles would be upset if we were to control our own sexuality. And that's exactly what we must do.

In spite of all our atavistic suspicions and training for the "natural" role of 20 motherhood, we took up the complicated battle for reproductive freedom. Our bodies had borne the health burden of endless births and poor abortions, and we had a greater motive for separating sexuality and conception.

Now we have to take up the equally complex burden of explaining that all 21 nonprocreative sex is *not* alike. We have a motive: Our right to a uniquely human sexuality, and sometimes even to survival. As it is, our bodies have too rarely been enough our own to develop erotica in our own lives, much less in art and literature. And our bodies have too often been the objects of pornography and the woman-hating, violent practice that it preaches. Consider also our spirits that break a little each time we see ourselves in chains or full labial display for the conquering male viewer, bruised or on our knees, screaming a real or pretended pain to delight the sadist, pretending to enjoy what we don't enjoy, to be blind to the images of our sisters that really haunt us—humiliated often enough ourselves by the truly obscene idea that sex and the domination of women must be combined.

Sexuality *is* human, free, separate—and so are we. 22

But until we untangle the lethal confusion of sex with violence, there will be 23 more pornography and less erotica. There will be little murders in our beds—and very little love.

1978

QUESTIONS FOR DISCUSSION

Content

a. What is the distinction between *erotica* and *pornography*?
b. What place does the notion of choice have in that distinction?
c. Why is Steinem's separating the notions of sexuality and conception important to this essay?
d. This selection was published in 1978. What does Steinem mean by "the current backlash against women's progress" (paragraph 6)?

e. Strong opinions are voiced in paragraphs 6 and 7. To what extent do you agree or disagree with them?

f. What, according to Steinem, is the danger in declaring "that *all* nonprocreative sex is good" (paragraph 8)?

g. In paragraph 13, we read that only by adopting "some degree of sadism or masochism" can we derive pleasure from pornography. Why is this notion central to Steinem's distinction between *erotica* and *pornography*?

h. What changes does Steinem predict in the attitudes of women and men toward sex? To what extent do you believe those changes have been realized since the publication of this essay?

i. Summarize Steinem's arguments in paragraphs 18 and 19. Then, explain to what extent you agree or disagree.

j. How do you interpret the phrase "little murders" (paragraph 23)?

Strategy and Style

k. Steinem sometimes uses etymology, the study of word origins. In what way does her explaining the origins of *erotica* and *pornography* help her differentiate them (paragraph 8)?

l. As you know, this essay first appeared in *Ms.*, a magazine whose readership consists largely of women. What in the essay's content also reveals that Steinem is addressing women?

m. Based on the language used in this piece, what else can you say about Steinem's audience?

n. Analyze the vocabulary in paragraphs 6 and 7. Regardless of the opinions stated, how would you characterize Steinem's tone in those paragraphs?

o. What use does the author make of illustration in this definition essay?

p. How does she use contrast and analysis?

q. Where do you find an example of descriptive writing?

r. In what way is Steinem's conclusion (paragraphs 21–23) a call to action?

SUGGESTIONS FOR SHORT WRITING

a. Paraphrase paragraphs 3 through 5. Then explain the function of these paragraphs in Steinem's essay. How do they relate to or help further her thesis?

b. Steinem's essay hinges on the distinction between two terms that are often confused. It is successful because the author is able to make that distinction clear. Choose two other terms that are often confused. Then list or explain differences between them. Here are topics like those you might choose to distinguish: sensuous/sensual, ideology/philosophy, art/craft, love/infatuation, discipline/denial, intelligence/cleverness, democracy/republicanism, knowledge/wisdom, leadership/intimidation, faith/orthodoxy, criticism/disapproval, naïveté/gullibility, stupidity/ignorance, tragic/disastrous.

SUGGESTIONS FOR SUSTAINED WRITING

a. If you responded to the second of the Suggestions for Short Writing above, use the details you have gathered in an essay that draws a distinction between two often confused concepts. Your goal will be to define each concept clearly and to allow your readers to distinguish one from the other easily. You may want to illustrate each concept by making reference to people or events that you have read about or learned about through personal experience.

b. Pretend that this is 1978 and that you have just read "Erotica and Pornography" in *Ms.* magazine. Write a letter to the editor of this periodical in which you defend or attack Steinem's thesis. Begin by identifying key points in her definition of *pornography*. Then, support or deny each of those points with facts and opinions of your own.

The Sources of Authenticity

Charles Taylor

Charles Taylor, philosopher and political theorist, was born in Montreal in 1931. An important philosopher internationally, his works include Explanations of Behaviour *and* Pattern in Politics. *The following essay was originally part of a longer lecture called* The Malaise of Modernity, *written for the Massey Lectures, recorded every year and broadcast on CBC radio. Taylor's lectures were published in book form in 1991 under two titles:* The Malaise of Modernity *and* The Ethics of Authenticity.

The ethic of authenticity is something relatively new and peculiar to modern culture. 1 Born at the end of the eighteenth century, it builds on earlier forms of individualism, such as the individualism of disengaged rationality, pioneered by Descartes, where the demand is that each person think self-responsibly for him- or herself, or the political individualism of Locke, which sought to make the person and his or her will prior to social obligation. But authenticity also has been in some respects in conflict with these earlier forms. It is a child of the Romantic period, which was critical of disengaged rationality and of an atomism that didn't recognize the ties of community.

One way of describing its development is to see its starting point in the 2 eighteenth-century notion that human beings are endowed with a moral sense, an intuitive feeling for what is right and wrong. The original point of this doctrine was to combat a rival view, that knowing right and wrong was a matter of calculating consequences, in particular those concerned with divine reward and punishment. The notion was that understanding right and wrong was not a matter of dry calculation, but was anchored in our feelings. Morality has, in a sense, a voice within.[1]

The notion of authenticity develops out of a displacement of the moral accent 3 in this idea. On the original view, the inner voice is important because it tells us what is the right thing to do. Being in touch with our moral feelings would matter here, as a means to the end of acting rightly. What I'm calling the displacement of the moral accent comes about when being in touch takes on independent and crucial moral significance. It comes to be something we have to attain to be true and full human beings.

To see what is new in this, we have to see the analogy to earlier moral views, 4 where being in touch with some source—God, say, or the Idea of the Good—was considered essential to full being. Only now the source we have to connect with is deep in us. This is part of the massive subjective turn of modern culture, a new form of inwardness, in which we come to think of ourselves as beings with inner depths. At first, this idea that the source is within doesn't exclude our being related to God or the Ideas; it can be considered our proper way to them. In a sense, it can be seen

[1]The development of this doctrine, at first in the work of Francis Hutcheson, drawing on the writings of the Earl of Shaftesbury, and its adversarial relation to Locke's theory, I have discussed at greater length in *Sources of the Self*, chapter 15.

just as a continuation and intensification of the development inaugurated by Saint Augustine, who saw the road to God as passing through our own reflexive awareness of ourselves.

The first variants of this new view were theistic, or at least pantheist. This is 5 illustrated by the most important philosophical writer who helped to bring about this change, Jean Jacques Rousseau. I think Rousseau is important not because he inaugurated the change; rather I would argue that his great popularity comes in part from his articulating something that was already happening in the culture. Rousseau frequently presents the issue of morality as that of our following a voice of nature within us. This voice is most often drowned out by the passions induced by our dependence on others, of which the key one is "amour propre" or pride. Our moral salvation comes from recovering authentic moral contact with ourselves. Rousseau even gives a name to the intimate contact with oneself, more fundamental than any moral view, that is a source of joy and contentment: "le sentiment de l'existence."[2]

Rousseau also articulated a closely related idea in a most influential way. This 6 is the notion of what I want to call self-determining freedom. It is the idea that I am free when I decide for myself what concerns me, rather than being shaped by external influences. It is a standard of freedom that obviously goes beyond what has been called negative liberty, where I am free to do what I want without interference by others because that is compatible with my being shaped and influenced by society and its laws of conformity. Self-determining freedom demands that I break the hold of all such external impositions, and decide for myself alone.

I mention this here not because it is essential to authenticity. Obviously the 7 two ideals are distinct. But they have developed together, sometimes in the works of the same authors, and their relations have been complex, sometimes at odds, sometimes closely bound together. As a result, they have often been confused, and this has been one of the sources of the deviant forms of authenticity, as I shall argue. I will return to this later.

Self-determining freedom has been an idea of immense power in our political 8 life. In Rousseau's work it takes political form, in the notion of a social contract state founded on a general will, which precisely because it is the form of our common freedom can brook no opposition in the name of freedom. This idea has been one of the intellectual sources of modern totalitarianism, starting, one might argue, with the Jacobins. And although Kant reinterpreted this notion of freedom in purely moral terms, as autonomy, it returns to the political sphere with a vengeance with Hegel and Marx.

---

[2]"Le sentiment de l'existence dépouillé de toute autre affection est par lui-même un sentiment précieux de contentement et de paix qui suffiroit seul pour rendre cette existence chère et douce à qui sauroit écarter de soi toutes les impressions sensuelles et terrestres qui viennent sans cesse nous en distraire et en troubler ici bas la douceur. Mais la pluspart des hommes agités de passions continuelles connoissent peu cet état et ne l'ayant goûté qu'imparfaitement durant peu d'instans n'en conservent qu'une idée obscure et confuse qui ne leur en fait pas sentir le charme." Rousseau, *Les Rêveries du Promeneur Solitaire*, Ve Promenade, in *Oeuvre Complètes*, vol. 1 (Paris: Gallimard, 1959), p. 1047.

But to return to the ideal of authenticity: it becomes crucially important because 9 of a development that occurs after Rousseau and that I associate with Herder— once again its major early articulator rather than its originator. Herder put forward the idea that each of us has an original way of being human. Each person has his or her own "measure" is his way of putting it.[3] This idea has entered very deep into modern consciousness. It is also new. Before the late eighteenth century no one thought that the differences between human beings had this kind of moral signif- icance. There is a certain way of being human that is *my* way. I am called upon to live my life in this way, and not in imitation of anyone else's. But this gives a new importance to being true to myself. If I am not, I miss the point of my life, I miss what being human is for *me*.

This is the powerful moral ideal that has come down to us. It accords crucial 10 moral importance to a kind of contact with myself, with my own inner nature, which it sees as in danger of being lost, partly through the pressures towards outward conformity, but also because in taking an instrumental stance to myself, I may have lost the capacity to listen to this inner voice. And then it greatly increases the importance of this self-contact by introducing the principle of originality: each of our voices has something of its own to say. Not only should I not fit my life to the demands of external conformity; I can't even find the model to live by outside myself. I can find it only within.

Being true to myself means being true to my own originality, and that is some- 11 thing only I can articulate and discover. In articulating it, I am also defining myself. I am realizing a potentiality that is properly my own. This is the background under- standing to the modern ideal of authenticity, and to the goals of self-fulfilment or self-realization in which it is usually couched. This is the background that gives moral force to the culture of authenticity, including its most degraded, absurd, or trivialized forms. It is what gives sense to the idea of "doing your own thing" or "finding your own fulfilment."

1991

QUESTIONS FOR DISCUSSION

Content

a. How do the positions of Descartes (disengaged rationality) and Locke (political individualism) differ?
b. How did earlier centuries view the idea of the "inner voice of morality"?
c. How do we achieve "moral salvation" according to Rousseau?
d. Define "self-determining freedom."

[3]"Jeder Mensch haat ein eigenes Mass, gleichsam eine eigne Stimmung aller seiner sinnlichen Gefühle zu einander." Herder, *Ideen*, vii. I., in *Herders Sämtliche Werke*, vol. XIII, ed. Bernard Suphan, 15 vols. (Berlin: Weidmann, 1877–1913), p. 291.

e. What idea does Herder contribute to the discussion?

f. What is the definition of "being true to myself"?

g. What is Taylor's thesis or point?

Strategy and Style

h. This essay was originally delivered as a lecture on radio. How does Taylor accommodate for the difference between an oral lecture and a read text? Does he?

i. Do Taylor's topic sentences accurately reflect the contents of his paragraphs?

j. Does Taylor assume knowledge about philosophy or does he adequately explain what the reader/listener needs to know?

k. How does Taylor use italics? What words does he privilege or emphasis? Why?

l. What sort of words or language does Taylor use? Did you need to consult a dictionary? You may wish to compare him with writers like Frye (in this chapter) and McLuhan (in Chapter 7) who are also academics.

SUGGESTIONS FOR SHORT WRITING

a. Write your own understanding of authenticity. What does it mean to be authentic?

b. What type of people are portrayed in the media (for example, *People* magazine) as "authentic"? What criteria is being used?

c. Taylor briefly discusses how we know what is right and wrong. Are things right or wrong simply because we say they are, or are there objective standards of what is right or wrong? If there are objective standards, how do we know what they are?

SUGGESTIONS FOR SUSTAINED WRITING

a. Define the word "cool." Trace the origins of the word and explain how the word has shifted its meaning through the years. Has it always been a desirable quality?

b. Watch a number of westerns or action films. How do these films define what it means to be an individual? What is the hero's relationship with society?

c. Discuss the nature of conformity, carefully defining the meaning of the term and giving examples of that meaning. Compare and contrast this conformity with the notion of individuality, again being careful to define and give examples of your definition of individuality. Which is more valued in our society? Support your contentions.

Fire in the Sky

Claudia Glenn Dowling

Two years after taking a degree in Chinese at Vassar College, Dowling began working for People *magazine, where she became a senior writer and editor of the movie column. She then became a staff writer for* Life, *covering a variety of subjects from the Gulf War to space exploration to treatments for breast cancer. Her thirteen years with* Life *have been exciting, taking her around the world and giving her the opportunity to race a Porsche through Mexico, visit with the Cofan Indians in the Amazon, and tour Kyrgyzstan with Al Gore. She even climbed part of the way up Mt. Everest with a British Special Forces team and got her passport taken away in China. Dowling is a fellow of the world-famous explorer's club and a winner of several awards for excellence in journalism. She is also the author of Warner Books' photo version of* The Bridges of Madison County. *"Fire in the Sky" was first published in* Life *in 1994.*

Nights are long and bitter in the polar winters, but the compensations can be spectacular: The skies blaze in a display of energy called the aurora borealis in the Arctic, aurora australis in the Antarctic. Ancient tribes who saw the lights believed they were caused by the bonfires of spirits; today we know that awe-inspiring physical forces create the heavenly arrays. And we're about to know more: A hardy breed of scientists—who don't mind odd hours or sub-zero temperatures—are investigating the powerful magnetic storms hidden within the aurora's glory. A few years ago some of these researchers put up a sign outside their University of Alaska lab near the tiny village of Poker Flats. It said it all: "Center for the Study of Something which, on the face of it, might seem trivial, but on closer examination takes on Global Significance." 1

Auroras are born on the sun, where thermonuclear storms tear apart hydrogen atoms, blasting protons and electrons toward earth at up to 1,000 miles per second. As this solar wind approaches earth's magnetic field, particles are drawn to the poles like iron filings to the ends of a bar magnet. When the particles collide with gases in the earth's atmosphere, they create electrical discharges that glow purple, green, red and white. The effect is similar to the collision of electrons and gases inside a color television tube. 2

The beauty of an auroral storm hides its violence—the release of millions of amperes of electricity, 20 times that found in a bolt of lightning. Surges within auroras, called substorms, tap energy trapped by the earth's magnetic field on the side of the planet away from the sun. One physicist poetically calls this energy pool earth's "electromagnetic soul." 3

A series of such storms knocked out power in all of Quebec as well as several U.S. states in 1989. Earlier this year surges damaged two communications satellites. NASA researchers theorize that the substorms, which produce nitrogen oxides, may also damage the ozone layer above the poles. No one knows what effect the electrical charge may have on human beings, although Japanese travel 4 agencies book tours to the Arctic specifically for couples who believe that their chances of conceiving a child are better under the aurora.

Lately, interest in mapping and predicting substorms has led to increased 5 government spending. (That may be why, not long ago, the sign at Poker Flats was changed to read: "This facility is uniquely dedicated to studies of the aurora borealis and other atmospheric research studies for the paying customer such as the National Aeronautics and Space Administration, the United States Air Force. . . .") Last month NASA launched a satellite—dubbed Wind—to monitor the solar wind as it howls toward earth. Another, called Polar, the size of a school bus, is planned to orbit closer to the planet, photographing auroras with sensitive cameras. Next year Russia will launch two similar probes. And in November a consortium of European nations will open a radar installation in Spitsbergen, Norway, with high-powered dishes that will collect information about the velocity, density and temperature of solar particles. A European satellite that is designed to circle the Arctic will collect similar data from above.

Still, a nonscientific observer need only be in the right place at the right time 6 to study this natural wonder. A jargon-filled recorded message from the National Oceanic and Atmospheric Administration in Boulder, Colo. (303-497-3235), tells aficionados when conditions are favorable for a good show. Although the aurora can be seen year-round—the atmosphere is always being bombarded by the solar wind—and is sometimes visible as far away as the equator, it occurs most often in the extreme north and south and is easiest to see on a clear, dark winter night. Photographer Norbert Rosing's favorite site is Churchill, Manitoba, where winter skies are cloudless 80 percent of the time. There, every February and March, he waits in the cold, warming his film with his car heater so it won't crack. "When you see the northern lights," he says, "you're in love."

1994

QUESTIONS FOR DISCUSSION

Content

a. How would you define the term *aurora?*
b. What are some of the effects scientists have attributed to auroral substorms?
c. What advice does Dowling give amateur astronomers who want to see the northern lights?
d. Besides definition, for what other purposes was this essay intended?

Strategy and Style

e. Analyze Dowling's introduction. What about that first paragraph makes the reader want to continue?

f. Besides the fact that this essay was first published in *Life* magazine, how can we tell that Dowling is addressing a general audience?

g. This essay makes excellent use of figurative language to explain natural phenomena. Identify at least two examples of such language.

SUGGESTIONS FOR SHORT WRITING

a. Dowling mentions both ancient and contemporary human reactions to the aurora. Do some library research on a natural phenomenon—such as an earthquake, a lightning storm, or a solar eclipse—and report on the folklore associated with it. Discuss one or two ways in which people have accounted for, explained, or reacted to this phenomenon.

b. Summarize the ideas in paragraph 3.

c. Dowling has conveyed the excitement and fascination that many professional and amateur stargazers experience when viewing the aurora. Think about a natural phenomenon that arouses your interest. Freewrite for about ten minutes to describe that phenomenon.

SUGGESTIONS FOR SUSTAINED WRITING

a. If you responded to item *a* in Suggestions for Short Writing, continue researching your topic and turn your short writing and other notes into a full-length essay that explains how people in the past accounted for, explained, or reacted to a particular natural phenomenon.

b. If you responded to item *c* in Suggestions for Short Writing, use your freewriting as the basis of a fully developed discussion of a natural occurrence that interests you. To gather even more information, try interviewing a professor who has knowledge of your subject, or continue doing library research on it.

Stop Murdering the Language

John Leo

John Leo writes "On Society," a weekly column for US News & World Report, *which also appears in 150 U.S. newspapers. Before joining* US News & World Report, *Leo wrote for* Time *magazine and for the* New York Times. *He has also been an associate editor at* Commonweal; *a writer for* Society *magazine; a columnist for the* Village Voice; *the editor of* The Catholic Messenger, *a weekly paper in Davenport, Iowa; and a deputy administrator for the City of New York's Environmental Protection Administration. He currently serves as an editorial advisor to the* Columbia Journalism Review. *Leo's* US News & World Report *columns have been collected in* Two Steps Ahead of the Thought Police *(1994); he has also published a humorous collection entitled* How the Russians Invented Baseball and Other Essays of Enlightenment *(1989). "Stop Murdering the Language" appeared in* US News & World Report *in 1993.*

If you doubt that word games are becoming crucial to our social and political 1 struggles, listen to Derek Humphry. A leading figure in the euthanasia movement, Humphry says his side lost at the polls in Washington State last fall largely because it lost the battle over language. The pro-euthanasia campaigners talked broadly about "aid in dying." But the media and public, Humphry says, "used the real words with relish"—suicide and euthanasia—and Initiative 119 went down.

In passing, Humphry pointed out the vagueness of "aid in dying." It can mean, 2 he says, "anything from a physician's lethal injection all the way to holding hands with a dying patient and saying, 'I love you.'" Anyone who stretches a phrase to cover both killing and moral support is a serious player in the language games.

This is, in fact, a big trend in the fast-growing field of language manipula- 3 tion. Specific terms give way to ever broader and gassier ones. "Blind" or "legally blind" was replaced by "visually impaired," which includes everyone who wears glasses. "Child abuse" now seems to cover almost anything a parent or a parental figure can do wrong. "Substance abusers" (formerly addicts and winos) now include any person who overuses or misuses anything at all. William Lutz, editor of the *Quarterly Review of Doublespeak,* says, "The whole world is composed of substance. . . . This doesn't promote clarity of discussion."

More often word stretching occurs for frankly polemic reasons. "Family has 4 been stretched to make nonfamilies eligible for various family benefits. Now the word is seriously used to refer to group renters, childless couples and even single people living alone. To circumvent zoning restrictions, two groups of recovering alcoholics in Cherry Hill, N.J., insisted they were families. A spokesman said, "Residents consider themselves a family, and no other family in the country has to announce itself or explain itself." As in "Alice in Wonderland," the word means what the speaker wants it to mean.

Another popular form of stretching is to associate some low-level complaint 5 with a higher-level one involving violence, thus presumably startling everyone into paying attention. A *Washington Post* columnist complained recently about "intellectual genocide" in D.C. public schools, meaning that students aren't taught well and aren't learning basic skills. Betty Friedan regularly complains about the media's "symbolic annihilation of women" (she means there still aren't enough news stories by and about women). A Manhattan man, dying of AIDS, said his death should be seen as "a form of political assassination" (he means Bush should have spent more on AIDS).

These stretching exercises are often more than publicity-grabbing hyper- 6 bole. Sometimes they are conscious attempts to ratchet up a minor offense into a major one. Ogling a woman, once considered harmless, or merely rude, is considered sexual harassment now and is often mentioned in the same breath as rape. Notice how the University of Minnesota's definition of sexual harassment blurs all lines between a glance, lack of sensitivity, serious harassment and rape: "Sexual harassment can be as blatant as rape or as subtle as a look. Harassment . . . often consists of callous insensitivity to the experience of women."

The verbal work of folding the entire category of harassment into the cate- 7 gory of rape goes on all the time. "Sexual harassment is a subtle rape," a psychologist named John Gottman told the *New York Times.* "Sexual harassment is a subset of rape with overtones of blackmail and extortion," columnist Carole Agus told her readers in *New York Newsday.*

Looser definitions keep blurring categories. The term "domestic violence," 8 for instance, once referred to physical assault in the home. Now it includes psychological abuse. Lenore Walker, a specialist in the field, defines wife battering to include bullying and manipulation ("making women do things they otherwise wouldn't . . . by eroding their self-esteem"). This mimics what happened when some definitions of date rape were expanded to include "psychological coercion," presumably including wheedling and pleading for sex.

A similar blurring occurs in the hate crime field. Often it's not very clear 9 whether we are talking about violence or nonviolence, crimes or noncriminal bias incidents, serious social offenses or minor and ambiguous run-ins. The National Institute Against Prejudice and Violence in Baltimore keeps feeding the media statistics on campus "ethnoviolence," but it defines violence to include slurs, graffiti and perceptions of slights (e.g., "I went to talk to someone who was black, and his friend stared at me the whole time as though she didn't want me there"). The effect of this tactic is to increase alarm about what's happening on campus and to raise doubts about the aims and methods of the statistics keepers.

The constant use of violent language for nonviolent incidents reflects the 10 current tensions among races and between sexes. But it probably also helps magnify those tensions by linking minor incidents to major assaults and putting everyone on full-time alert for offense. It's one price we're paying for these polemic word games.

1993

QUESTIONS FOR DISCUSSION

Content

a. What is Leo's thesis?
b. In what way does the statement by William Lutz support that thesis?
c. Definition can be used for a variety of purposes. To what end has Leo used it in this essay?
d. What, according to Leo, are some of the more common reasons that writers and speakers consciously manipulate language?

Strategy and Style

e. Does the reference to Derek Humphry in paragraphs 1 and 2 make for an appropriate introduction?
f. Where in this essay does Leo use illustration? Where does he use contrast?
g. The author's choice of words provides clues to his tone. How would you describe Leo's attitude toward his subject?
h. Why does Leo use so many direct quotations in this essay? Could he have paraphrased instead?
i. What is the effect of his referring to "Alice in Wonderland" in paragraph 4?
j. Where in this essay does Leo make an appeal to authority to support his thesis?

SUGGESTIONS FOR SHORT WRITING

a. Do you agree with Leo that "family" has been stretched to include groups that are not really families? Or do you believe that group renters, single people, and groups of recovering alcoholics, for example, might also be considered families? Freewrite for about 15 minutes to gather details about your personal definition of the term.
b. As Leo says, very specific terms often "give way to broader and gassier ones." Make a short list of such terms and their "gassier" alternatives.
c. Reread paragraphs 8 and 9. Respond to either of the two issues in these paragraphs by explaining why you agree or disagree with Leo's position.

SUGGESTIONS FOR SUSTAINED WRITING

a. Reread the University of Minnesota's definition of sexual harassment quoted in this essay. Is this close to your definition of the term? Would you advocate adopting such a policy at your school? Explain why or why not. If you are against adopting this kind of policy, use your essay as an opportunity to write your own definition of sexual harassment and to make a statement of policy that you would like adopted at your institution.

b. Though Leo makes several significant criticisms about the way in which some contemporary writers and speakers abuse language, one might argue that certain common terms can mean very different things to different people. Write an essay in which you compare your definition of an abstract term—such as *family, education, culture, wealth,* or *kindness*—with the definitions of this term held by two or three of your friends, classmates, or family members. Brainstorm with or interview these people to gather details for your essay. Make sure to take careful notes, and include direct quotations whenever possible.

5

Division and Classification

Division and classification are attempts to explain the nature and connections between bits of information that may, at first, seem unrelated and confusing. Writers often find it useful to identify like qualities or characteristics among various facts, ideas, people, or things so as to create related categories or classes by which the material can be divided logically and discussed systematically.

If you are a people watcher, you know that public places—a bus station, a sports stadium, or even a college library—offer a variety of subjects. Let's say that two days before a math midterm, you resolve to study hard in the library. As you walk into the main reading room, you hear the giggles of young lovers seated in a corner. A few yards beyond, you spot one of the college's maintenance workers who is spending her lunch hour noisily turning the pages of a large newspaper. To your right, you begin to eavesdrop on a few students discussing a fraternity party, and you realize that their chatter is annoying a woman trying to take notes for a term paper. In a less-crowded part of the room, two of your friends kill time by browsing through a few magazines they found lying about. After a while, you decide that the reading room offers too many distractions, so you find a corner in the basement where you can hide. It is no coincidence that other members of your math class had the same idea, so you sit down quietly and begin studying.

The decision to join your classmates and not stay in the reading room resulted from dividing the group of people you found at the library into three smaller categories: fun-seekers, browsers, and serious students! Your analysis may have been quick and informal, but it was effective. What's more, it revealed something important about the nature and function of classification: You began by observing similarities among various individuals; you created categories based on those similarities and placed each individual you observed into one of them; and you made a decision—to study in one place and not another—based upon what your classification revealed.

172

Classification is a versatile tool. It can be used to explain stages in human development as in Gail Sheehy's "Predictable Crises of Adulthood," to discuss current thinking about morality as in Meg Greenfield's "Why Nothing Is 'Wrong' Anymore," or to define one's ethnic and cultural identity as in Ayanna Black's "Inglish: Writing with an Accent." As Donald Hall shows in "Four Kinds of Reading," it can help us analyze and understand the processes and motivations behind the way we read, think, and comprehend. As a matter of fact, Ayanna Black and Susan Allen Toth show that classification makes an effective tool for self-analysis and for shedding light on aspects of our personalities and our lives that might parallel those of our readers.

The success of a classification paper depends upon how logically an author divides the material and how thoroughly and concretely he or she develops each category. Among the most effective methods to develop such an essay is illustration. Examples like those in Judith Viorst's "The Truth about Lying" are often essential to the writer's purpose. Without them, an essay might remain a list of ill-defined labels and abstractions. But good writers use a variety of techniques to keep readers interested. The essay by Toth contains anecdotes (narration) to support important points; Greenfield and Sheehy make excellent use of definition; and Foot and Stoffman rely on definition, contrast, and anecdote.

As you read the selections that follow, remember that almost any conglomeration of seemingly unrelated information can be classified to reveal patterns of meaning readers will find valuable and interesting. The perspectives from which you view a subject and the choices you make to impose order on the material should be determined only by your purpose. Read the Suggestions for Short Writing and for Sustained Writing after each selection. They describe activities that will help you use classification to accomplish a well-defined purpose. But even if you approach a writing assignment without a clear notion of purpose—something not uncommon even among experienced writers—you may still want to use classification in the early stages of your project to review the raw information you have collected, to group facts, ideas, and insights logically, and, ultimately, to improve your understanding both of the material and of your purpose.

Cinematypes

Susan Allen Toth

Born in Ames, Iowa, in 1940, Susan Allen Toth earned a PhD. at the University of Minnesota in 1969. She also holds a BA from Smith College (1961) and an MA from the University of California at Berkeley (1963). Since 1969, she has been on the faculty of Macalester College in St. Paul, Minnesota, where she teaches courses in the British and American novel, contemporary American literature, and creative writing. Toth's first book, Blooming: A Small-Town Girlhood *(1981), was named by the* New York Times *as one of the "notable books of the year."* Ivy Days: Making My Way Out East *was published in 1984, followed by* How to Prepare for Your High-School Reunion: And Other Mid-Life Musings *in 1988. Toth's stories, essays, and reviews have appeared in the* New York Times Book Review, Harper's, Ms., *and other publications. She has also written scholarly essays on late-nineteenth-century American local-colour literature. She is currently working on a fictional memoir about her grandmother. "Cinematypes" first appeared in* Harper's *in May 1980.*

1 Aaron takes me only to art films. That's what I call them, anyway: strange movies with vague poetic images I don't always understand, long dreamy movies about a distant Technicolor past, even longer black-and-white movies about the general meaninglessness of life. We do not go unless at least one reputable critic has found the cinematography superb. We went to *The Devil's Eye*, and Aaron turned to me in the middle and said, "My God, this is *funny*." I do not think he was pleased.

2 When Aaron and I go to the movies, we drive our cars separately and meet by the box office. Inside the theater he sits tentatively in his seat, ready to move if he can't see well, poised to leave if the film is disappointing. He leans away from me, careful not to touch the bare flesh of his arm against the bare flesh of mine. Sometimes he leans so far I am afraid he may be touching the woman on his other side. If the movie is very good, he leans forward, too, peering between the heads of the couple in front of us. The light from the screen bounces off his glasses; he gleams with intensity, sitting there on the edge of his seat, watching the screen. Once I tapped him on the arm so I could whisper a comment in his ear. He jumped.

3 After *Belle de Jour* Aaron said he wanted to ask me if he could stay overnight. "But I can't," he shook his head mournfully before I had a chance to answer, "because I know I never sleep well in strange beds." Then he apologized for asking. "It's just that after a film like that," he said, "I feel the need to assert myself."

4 Pete takes me only to movies that he thinks have redeeming social value. He doesn't call them "films." They tend to be about poverty, war, injustice, political corruption, struggling unions in the 1930s, and the military-industrial complex. Pete doesn't like propaganda movies, though, and he doesn't like to be too depressed, either. We stayed away from *The Sorrow and the Pity;* it would be, he said, just too much. Besides, he assured me, things are never that hopeless. So most of the movies we see are made in Hollywood. Because they are always topical, these movies offer what Pete calls "food for thought." When we saw *Coming*

174

Home, Pete's jaw set so firmly with the first half-hour that I knew we would end up at Poppin' Fresh Pies afterward.

When Pete and I go to the movies, we take turns driving so no one owes any- 5 one else anything. We leave the car far from the theater so we don't have to pay for a parking space. If it's raining or snowing, Pete offers to let me off at the door, but I can tell he'll feel better if I go with him while he finds a spot, so we share the walk too. Inside the theater Pete will hold my hand when I get scared if I ask him. He puts my hand firmly on his knee and covers it completely with his own hand. His knee never twitches. After a while, when the scary part is past, he loosens his hand slightly and I know that is a signal to take mine away. He sits companionably close, letting his jacket just touch my sweater, but he does not infringe. He thinks I ought to know he is there if I need him.

One night, after *The China Syndrome,* I asked Pete if he wouldn't like to stay 6 for a second drink, even though it was past midnight. He thought a while about that, considering my offer from all possible angles, but finally he said no. Rela- tionships today, he said, have a tendency to move too quickly.

Sam likes movies that are entertaining. By that he means movies that Will 7 Jones in the *Minneapolis Tribune* loved and either *Time* or *Newsweek* rather liked; also movies that do not have sappy love stories, are not musicals, do not have sub- titles, and will not force him to think. He does not go to movies to think. He liked *California Suite* and *The Seduction of Joe Tynan,* though the plots, he said, could have been zippier. He saw it all coming too far in advance, and that took the fun out. He doesn't like to know what is going to happen. "I just want my brain to be tickled," he says. It is very hard for me to pick out movies for Sam.

When Sam takes me to the movies, he pays for everything. He thinks that's 8 what a man ought to do. But I buy my own popcorn, because he doesn't approve of it; the grease might smear his flannel slacks. Inside the theater, Sam makes him- self comfortable. He takes off his jacket, puts one arm around me, and all during the movie he plays with my hand, stroking my palm, beating a small tattoo on my wrist. Although he watches the movie intently, his body operates on instinct. Once I inclined my head and kissed him lightly just behind his ear. He beat a faster tat- too on my wrist, quick and musical, but he didn't look away from the screen.

When Sam takes me home from the movies, he stands outside my door and 9 kisses me long and hard. He would like to come in, he says regretfully, but his steady girlfriend in Duluth wouldn't like it. When the *Tribune* gives a movie four stars, he has to save it to see with her. Otherwise her feelings might be hurt.

I go to some movies by myself. On rainy Sunday afternoons I often sneak 10 into a revival house or a college auditorium for old Technicolor musicals, *Kiss Me Kate, Seven Brides for Seven Brothers, Calamity Jane,* even, once, *The Sound of Music.* Wearing saggy jeans so I can prop my feet on the seat in front, I sit toward the rear where no one can see me. I eat large handfuls of popcorn with double but- ter. Once the movie starts, I feel completely at home. Howard Keel and I are old friends; I grin back at him on the screen. I know the sound tracks by heart. Some- times when I get really carried away I hum along with Kathryn Grayson, remembering how I once thought I would fill out a formal like that. I am rather glad now I never did. Skirts whirl, feet tap, acrobatic young men perform impossible feats, and then the camera dissolves into a dream sequence I know I can comfortably follow. It is not, thank God, Bergman.

If I can't find an old musical, I settle for Hepburn and Tracy, vintage Grant   11
or Gable, on adventurous days Claudette Colbert or James Stewart. Before I buy my ticket I make sure it will all end happily. If necessary, I ask the girl at the box office. I have never seen *Stella Dallas* or *Intermezzo*. Over the years I have developed other peccadilloes: I will, for example, see anything that is redeemed by Thelma Ritter. At the end of *Daddy Long Legs* I wait happily for the scene when Fred Clark, no longer angry, at last pours Thelma a convivial drink. They smile at each other, I smile at them, I feel they are smiling at me. In the movies I go to by myself, the men and women always like each other.

1980

QUESTIONS FOR DISCUSSION

Content

a. What does the last sentence in the essay reveal about Toth's experiences with movies and men? How does it reveal Toth's thesis? What is that thesis?

b. Why is it necessary to classify the activity of movie going? What benefits are gained from classifying this subject?

c. For whom is Toth writing? What might be their reasons for reading this essay?

d. Into what categories does Toth divide movies and men? Why does she choose these categories?

e. How does she distinguish between *film* and *movie*? Do her definitions of these terms match yours? What words does Toth use to reveal her opinion of them?

f. Into which category do you place yourself and your own boyfriend, girlfriend, or spouse? Do you find that you agree or disagree with Toth's opinions of movies and men?

g. Has Toth left any categories out? Has she overgeneralized with the categories she has chosen? If so, what might be her reasons for doing so?

Strategy and Style

h. Each category is structured in the same way: name of boyfriend, type of movie, titles of representative movies, mode of transportation to the movie, behaviour during the movie, etc. How do the components of one category relate to those of the others? What effect does this rigid structure have on the essay as a whole?

i. Why does Toth focus her description on her friends in the first three categories, leaving herself out until the fourth category?

j. The author does not use a standard introduction or conclusion. How effective is the essay without a standard beginning and ending? Does the abruptness increase or decrease the essay's effectiveness?

k. Why does Toth title her essay "Cinematypes"? Do you think these types refer to cinemas, movies, or moviegoers? What is the benefit of having an ambiguous title?

l. Describe Toth's tone. Is she being serious or humorous? What words, phrases, or sentences reveal her tone?

SUGGESTIONS FOR SHORT WRITING

a. Write the story of one of your own experiences with a date at a movie. Which cinematype did he or she resemble most closely?

b. Write personals ads for Toth, any of her cinematypes, and/or yourself, seeking to find the perfect movie date. You might find examples of such ads in the classified section of your newspaper.

SUGGESTIONS FOR SUSTAINED WRITING

a. Write an essay classifying a popular activity. Be sure that your reasons for classifying are clear to you and to your readers. Take into account the types of people and the types of behaviour associated with each category.

b. Write an essay in which you extend Toth's classification, discussing cinematypes that she did not include.

c. Write "Cinematypes" from a man's point of view. What aspects will remain the same? Which will differ?

Inglish: Writing with an Accent

Ayanna Black

Ayanna Black was born in Jamaica, moved to England, and finally came to Canada in 1964. She helped found the first magazine by women of colour, Tiger Lily, *and has served as president of Canadian Artists' Network—Black Artists in Action (CAN-BAIA). She has written a book called* No Contingencies *and has put together a number of important anthologies such as* Voices: Canadian Writers of African Descent.

Tahar Ben Jelloun writes, "the act of speaking is perhaps illusionary because it 1 occurs in the language of the Other . . ." For me, this word "Inglish" is far from being an illusion: it is a reality, it is our construct. We have spoken, and we have spoken within an important context! That's an important act. I cannot think of anyone who articulates it better than Jelloun when he says "What is most important . . . is not what the mother said, but the fact that she spoke."

As a writer of African descent, I asked myself, what does it mean: writing 2 with an accent? Is it writing out of an ancestral tradition that is central to speech? A synthesis of the oral, the literary and the visual? In Ghana, for example, symbols are painted on cloth, representing Ghanian proverbs, sayings and myths. Is this writing with an accent to be considered post-modern or post-colonial writing?

For the past five hundred years, books have been written to glorify European 3 culture and many of these are written from a patriarchal and imperialist perspective. That approach continues to flourish, particularly in institutions and among some writers and scholars. Euro-centrism persists in the "intellectualism" of even the more progressive thinkers. This is the kind of structural and institutional impediment that I must break down in order to create a space for my work. Historically, my ancestors did not sit and wait for institutions to bring about change. People of African descent have had to forge new pathways for themselves; before dub poetry became popular, it was not accepted in mainstream literary tradition but was viewed as a fringe phenomenon.

I have come to realise that I have to use the vernacular in the manner that I 4 see fit and that the English language falls into that terrain. The English language is not my enemy. I have the power to use it to my advantage, as did my ancestors, for survival and flexibility. I think that one of the strong points of the British is their understanding of the power of culture and language. In Paula Burnett's introduction to the *Penguin Book of Caribbean Verse*, she reminds us of those British characteristics when she writes "The British never made the mistake of underestimating the importance of language." Upon the arrival of slaves from Africa, they separated those who spoke the same language to prevent rebellion.

As an African-Canadian writer, I am drawing from a painful and complex 5 history of slavery and colonisation and the dispersal of Africans to various parts of what is termed the New World. But in spite of that exploitation and brutality, we have managed to overcome tremendous obstacles in order to create a synthesis of ancient African literary traditions and imperialist literary constructs. Thus, Jamaican Creole is a dynamic marriage of English and African languages. Louise Bennett's poetry is an excellent example of this. What follows is the last stanza from her poem, *Colonisation in Reverse*:

> Wat a devilment a Englan!
> Dem face war an brave de worse,
> But me wonderin how dem gwine stan
> Colonizin in reverse.

This poetry is relevant to those engaged in what Burnett describes as a 6 "search for forms of creative cohabitation" forms that allow for "the assertion of cultural self without the denial of that assertion to others, and the sharing of as much as can be shared."

Jamaican Creole was not taught nor was its use encouraged in my school 7 days. It was not spoken by me or my peers. Yet even though it was viewed as an inferior language, I was very interested in it and found my life illuminated when it was spoken, especially during the times I went to pantomime.

But I will admit that it wasn't until 1985 that I penned my first poem in 8 Jamaican Creole. It wasn't a very easy poem to write. Indeed, I was apprehensive. I wasn't sure that I could translate the music, the rhythm, with vigour and meaning and maintain the strong voice that I was hearing and feeling. Writing it opened an important path for me as a writer. I was no longer a silent listener, an observer, of that language. I was now an active speaker.

1993

QUESTIONS FOR DISCUSSION

Content

a. What is Black's point? Why does she distinguish Inglish from English?
b. What is Jamaican Creole?
c. How does the spelling of Jamaican Creole deviate from standard English? Is this the only difference?
d. Why was she hesitant to write in Jamaican Creole?
e. How did the British demonstrate an awareness of the importance of language?

Strategy and Style

f. Why does Black open the essay with a quote by Tahar Ben Jelloun, especially since she appears to reject it in the next sentence?
g. In the third paragraph, Black discusses Euro-centrism before finally establishing her point: "my ancestors did not sit and wait for institutions to bring about change." How does she support this contention?

h. In what sense can Black say, "The English language is not my enemy?" What does she mean by this statement?

i. After talking about Euro-centrism and the British, the essay shifts dramatically. How is the poem "Colonisation in Reverse" indicative of this shift?

j. In the end, Black embraces "Jamaican Creole" and states, "I was now an active speaker." How does this sentence relate to the opening quote by Tahar Ben Jelloun?

k. By *writing* a poem, Black claims she has become an active *speaker*. In contrasting types of English/Inglish, does she adequately distinguish between speaking and writing?

SUGGESTIONS FOR SHORT WRITING

a. Black states, "Jamaican Creole was not taught nor was its use encouraged in my school days." Should street languages be taught in the schools?

b. What does Black mean by becoming an active speaker? Do you think she would appreciate white Jamaicans writing in Jamaican Creole? Why or why not?

c. Jazz has been discussed as a hybrid form of black *and* white music; rock has been described as *white* rhythm and blues. With that said, does this mean there cannot be music such as Asian jazz or white reggae or black punk? Can people from outside a given culture learn "the cultural language"?

SUGGESTIONS FOR SUSTAINED WRITING

a. Examine a type of music (such as country or jazz) and identify an example of a subgenre within it (such as bluegrass or be-bop). Argue either that this deviation from the norm is legitimate (e.g., bluegrass is a type of country music, be-bop is a type of jazz) or that it constitutes something entirely different (e.g., bluegrass is not part of country music, be-bop is not jazz).

b. Black raises the issue of the legitimacy of Jamaican Creole as a language. Should there be an absolute standard in English? Who should set and regulate that standard? Or can there be many "Englishes"?

c. Writing in dialect is considered by many to be inappropriate, condescending, or mocking. Does writing in a dialect of a language perpetuate stereotypes about a culture or does it empower alternative uses of the language?

Predictable Crises of Adulthood

Gail Sheehy

Born in New York City and educated at the University of Vermont and Columbia University, Gail Sheehy (b. 1937) has been a contributing editor for New York Magazine *and has written for* Paris Match, *the* London Sunday Telegraph, *the* New York Times Magazine, Cosmopolitan, *and* Glamour. *Sheehy's first sustained work was* Lovesounds *(1970), a novel, which has been followed by several pieces of nonfiction, including* Hustling: Prostitution in Our Wide Open Society *(1973);* Character: America's Search for Leadership *(1988); and* Gorbachev: The Man Who Changed the World *(1990). In 1986, Sheehy published* Spirit of Survival, *the story of a Cambodian girl she found and later adopted as a result of a journalistic assignment on refugee children in Southeast Asia.* Passages *(1976), from which "Predictable Crises of Adulthood" is taken, discusses several natural crises through which everyone must pass and which, if understood and handled properly, can lay the foundation for a stable and fulfilling life.*

We are not unlike a particularly hardy crustacean. The lobster grows by developing and shedding a series of hard, protective shells. Each time it expands from within, the confining shell must be sloughed off. It is left exposed and vulnerable until, in time, a new covering grows to replace the old. 1

With each passage from one stage of human growth to the next we, too, must shed a protective structure. We are left exposed and vulnerable—but also yeasty and embryonic again, capable of stretching in ways we hadn't known before. These sheddings may take several years or more. Coming out of each passage, though, we enter a longer and more stable period in which we can expect relative tranquility and a sense of equilibrium regained. . . . 2

As we shall see, each person engages the steps of development in his or her own characteristic *step-style*. Some people never complete the whole sequence. And none of us "solves" with one step—by jumping out of the parental home into a job or marriage, for example—the problems in separating from the caregivers of childhood. Nor do we "achieve" autonomy once and for all by converting our dreams into concrete goals, even when we attain those goals. The central issues or tasks of one period are never fully completed, tied up, and cast aside. But when they lose their primacy and the current life structure has served its purpose, we are ready to move on to the next period. 3

Can one catch up? What might look to others like listlessness, contrariness, a maddening refusal to face up to an obvious task may be a person's own unique detour that will bring him out later on the other side. Developmental gains won can later be lost—and rewon. It's plausible, though it can't be proven, that the mastery of one set of tasks fortifies us for the next period and the next set of challenges. But it's important not to think too mechanistically. Machines work by units. The bureaucracy (supposedly) works step by step. Human beings, thank God, have an individual inner dynamic that can never be precisely coded. 4

Although I have indicated the ages when Americans are likely to go through each stage, and the differences between men and women where they are striking, 5 do not take the ages too seriously. The stages are the thing, and most particularly the sequence.

Here is the briefest outline of the developmental ladder.   6

PULLING UP ROOTS

Before 18, the motto is loud and clear: "I have to get away from my parents." But   7
the words are seldom connected to action. Generally still safely part of our families, even if away at school, we feel our autonomy to be subject to erosion from moment to moment.

After 18, we begin Pulling Up Roots in earnest. College, military service,   8
and short-term travels are all customary vehicles our society provides for the first round trips between family and a base of one's own. In the attempt to separate our view of the world from our family's view, despite vigorous protestations to the contrary—"I know exactly what I want!"—we cast about for any beliefs we can call our own. And in the process of testing those beliefs we are often drawn to fads, preferably those most mysterious and inaccessible to our parents.

Whatever tentative memberships we try out in the world, the fear haunts us   9
that we are really kids who cannot take care of ourselves. We cover that fear with acts of defiance and mimicked confidence. For allies to replace our parents, we turn to our contemporaries. They become conspirators. So long as their perspective meshes with our own, they are able to substitute for the sanctuary of the family. But that doesn't last very long. And the instant they diverge from the shaky ideals of "our group," they are seen as betrayers. Rebounds to the family are common between the ages of 18 and 22.

The tasks of this passage are to locate ourselves in a peer group role, a sex role,   10
an anticipated occupation, an ideology or world view. As a result, we gather the impetus to leave home physically and the identity to *begin* leaving home emotionally.

Even as one part of us seeks to be an individual, another part longs to restore   11
the safety and comfort of merging with another. Thus one of the most popular myths of this passage is: We can piggyback our development by attaching to a Stronger One. But people who marry during this time often prolong financial and emotional ties to the family and relatives that impede them from becoming self-sufficient.

A stormy passage through the Pulling Up Roots years will probably facili-   12
tate the normal progression of the adult life cycle. If one doesn't have an identity crisis at this point, it will erupt during a later transition, when the penalties may be harder to bear.

THE TRYING TWENTIES

The Trying Twenties confront us with the question of how to take hold in the adult   13
world. Our focus shifts from the interior turmoils of late adolescence—"Who am I?" "What is truth?"—and we become almost totally preoccupied with working

out the externals. "How do I put my aspirations into effect?" "What is the best way to start?" "Where do I go?" "Who can help me?" "How did *you* do it?"

In this period, which is longer and more stable compared with the passage that leads to it, the tasks are as enormous as they are exhilarating: To shape a Dream, that vision of ourselves which will generate energy, aliveness, and hope. To prepare for a lifework. To find a mentor if possible. And to form the capacity for intimacy without losing in the process whatever consistency of self we have thus far mustered. The first test structure must be erected around the life we choose to try.   14

Doing what we "should" is the most pervasive theme of the twenties. The "shoulds" are largely defined by family models, the press of the culture, or the prejudices of our peers. If the prevailing cultural instructions are that one should get married and settle down behind one's own door, a nuclear family is born. If instead the peers insist that one should do one's own thing, the 25-year-old is likely to harness himself onto a Harley-Davidson and burn up Route 66 in the commitment to have no commitments.   15

One of the terrifying aspects of the twenties is the inner conviction that the choices we make are irrevocable. It is largely a false fear. Change is quite possible, and some alteration of our original choices is probably inevitable.   16

Two impulses, as always, are at work. One is to build a firm, safe structure for the future by making strong commitments, to "be set." Yet people who slip into a ready-made form without much self-examination are likely to find themselves *locked* in.   17

The other urge is to explore and experiment, keeping any structure tentative and therefore easily reversible. Taken to the extreme, these are people who skip from one trial job and one limited personal encounter to another, spending their twenties in the *transient* state.   18

Although the choices of our twenties are not irrevocable, they do set in motion a Life Pattern. Some of us follow the lock-in pattern, others the transient pattern, the wunderkind pattern, the caregiver pattern, and there are a number of others. Such patterns strongly influence the particular questions raised for each person during each passage. . . .   19

Buoyed by powerful illusions and belief in the power of the will, we commonly insist in our twenties that what we have chosen to do is the one true course in life. Our backs go up at the merest hint that we are like our parents, that two decades of parental training might be reflected in our current actions and attitudes.   20

"Not me," is the motto, "I'm different."   21

CATCH-30

Impatient with devoting ourselves to the "shoulds," a new vitality springs from within as we approach 30. Men and women alike speak of feeling too narrow and restricted. They blame all sorts of things, but what the restrictions boil down to are the outgrowth of career and personal choices of the twenties. They may have been choices perfectly suited to that stage. But now the fit feels different. Some inner aspect that was left out   22 is striving to be taken into account. Important new choices must be made, and commitments altered or deepened. The work involves great change, turmoil, and often crisis—a simultaneous feeling of rock bottom and the urge to bust out.

One common response is the tearing up of the life we spent most of our 23 twenties putting together. It may mean striking out on a secondary road toward a new vision or converting a dream of "running for president" into a more realistic goal. The single person feels a push to find a partner. The woman who was previously content at home with children chafes to venture into the world. The childless couple reconsiders children. And almost everyone who is married, especially those married for seven years, feels a discontent.

If the discontent doesn't lead to a divorce, it will, or should, call for a seri- 24 ous review of the marriage and of each partner's aspirations in their Catch-30 condition. The gist of that condition was expressed by a 29-year-old associate with a Wall Street law firm:

"I'm considering leaving the firm. I've been there four years now; I'm getting 25 good feedback, but I have no clients of my own. I feel weak. If I wait much longer, it will be too late, too close to that fateful time of decision on whether or not to become a partner. I'm success-oriented. But the concept of being 55 years old and stuck in a monotonous job drives me wild. It drives me crazy now, just a little bit. I'd say that 85 percent of the time I thoroughly enjoy my work. But when I get a screwball case, I come away from court saying, 'What am I doing here?' It's a *visceral* reaction that I'm wasting my time. I'm trying to find some way to make a social contribution or a slot in city government. I keep saying, 'There's something more.' "

Besides the push to broaden himself professionally, there is a wish to expand 26 his personal life. He wants two or three more children. "The concept of a home has become very meaningful to me, a place to get away from troubles and relax. I love my son in a way I could not have anticipated. I never could live alone."

Consumed with the work of making his own critical lifesteering decisions, 27 he demonstrates the essential shift at this age: An absolute requirement to be more self-concerned. The self has new value now that his competency has been proved.

His wife is struggling with her own age-30 priorities. She wants to go to law 28 school, but he wants more children. If she is going to stay home, she wants him to make more time for the family instead of taking on even wider professional commitments. His view of the bind, of what he would most like from his wife, is this:

"I'd like not to be bothered. It sounds cruel, but I'd like not to have to worry 29 about what she's going to do next week. Which is why I've told her several times that I think she should do something. Go back to school and get a degree in social work or geography or whatever. Hopefully that would fulfill her, and then I wouldn't have to worry about her line of problems. I want her to be decisive about herself."

The trouble with his advice to his wife is that it comes out of concern with *his* 30 convenience, rather than with *her* development. She quickly picks up on this lack of goodwill: He is trying to dispose of her. At the same time, he refuses her the same latitude to be "selfish" in making an independent decision to broaden her horizons. Both perceive a lack of mutuality. And that is what Catch-30 is all about for the couple.

ROOTING AND EXTENDING

Life becomes less provisional, more rational and orderly in the early thirties. We   31
begin to settle down in the full sense. Most of us begin putting down roots and
sending out new shoots. People buy houses and become very earnest about climbing career ladders. Men in particular concern themselves with "making it." Satisfaction with marriage generally goes downhill in the thirties (for those who have
remained together) compared with the highly valued, vision-supporting marriage
of the twenties. This coincides with the couple's reduced social life outside the
family and the inturned focus on raising their children.

THE DEADLINE DECADE

In the middle of the thirties we come upon a crossroads. We have reached the   32
halfway mark. Yet even as we are reaching our prime, we begin to see there is a
place where it finishes. Time starts to squeeze.

The loss of youth, the faltering of physical powers we have always taken for   33
granted, the fading purpose of stereotyped roles by which we have thus far identified ourselves, the spiritual dilemma of having no absolute answers—any or all of
these shocks can give this passage the character of crisis. Such thoughts usher in
a decade between 35 and 45 that can be called the Deadline Decade. It is a time of
both danger and opportunity. All of us have the chance to rework the narrow identity by which we defined ourselves in the first half of life. And those of us who
make the most of the opportunity will have a full-out authenticity crisis.

To come through this authenticity crisis, we must reexamine our purposes   34
and reevaluate how to spend our resources from now on. "Why am I doing all this?
What do I really believe in?" No matter what we have been doing, there will be
parts of ourselves that have been suppressed and now need to find expression.
"Bad" feelings will demand acknowledgment along with the good.

It is frightening to step off onto the treacherous footbridge leading to the sec-   35
ond half of life. We can't take everything with us on this journey through uncertainty. Along the way, we discover that we are alone. We no longer have to ask permission because we are the providers of our own safety. We must learn to give
ourselves permission. We stumble upon feminine or masculine aspects of our na-
tures that up to this time have usually been masked. There is grieving to be done
because an old self is dying. By taking in our suppressed and even our unwanted
parts, we prepare at the gut level for the reintegration of an identity that is ours and
ours alone—not some artificial form put together to please the culture or our
mates. It is a dark passage at the beginning. But by disassembling ourselves, we
can glimpse the light and gather our parts into a renewal.

Women sense this inner crossroads earlier than men do. The time pinch of-   36
ten prompts a woman to stop and take an all-points survey at age 35. Whatever options she has already played out, she feels a "my last chance" urgency to review

those options she has set aside and those that aging and biology will close off in the now *foreseeable* future. For all her qualms and confusion about where to start looking for a new future, she usually enjoys an exhilaration of release. Assertiveness begins rising. There are so many firsts ahead.

Men, too, feel the time push in the mid-thirties. Most men respond by pressing down harder on the career accelerator. It's "my last chance" to pull away from the pack. It is no longer enough to be the loyal junior executive, the promising young novelist, the lawyer who does a little *pro bono* work on the side. He wants now to become part of top management, to be recognized as an established writer, or an active politician with his own legislative program. With some chagrin, he discovers that he has been too anxious to please and too vulnerable to criticism. He wants to put together his own ship.   37

During this period of intense concentration on external advancement, it is common for men to be unaware of the more difficult, gut issues that are propelling them forward. The survey that was neglected at 35 becomes a crucible at 40. Whatever rung of achievement he has reached, the man of 40 usually feels stale, restless, burdened, and unappreciated. He worries about his health. He wonders, "Is this all there is?" He may make a series of departures from well-established lifelong base lines, including marriage. More and more men are seeking second careers in midlife. Some become self-destructive. And many men in their forties experience a major shift of emphasis away from pouring all their energies into their own advancement. A more tender, feeling side comes into play. They become interested in developing an ethical self.   38

RENEWAL OR RESIGNATION

Somewhere in the mid-forties, equilibrium is regained. A new stability is achieved, which may be more or less satisfying.   39

If one has refused to budge through the midlife transition, the sense of staleness will calcify into resignation. One by one, the safety and supports will be withdrawn from the person who is standing still. Parents will become children; children will become strangers; a mate will grow away or go away; the career will become just a job—and each of these events will be felt as an abandonment. The crisis will probably emerge again around 50. And although its wallop will be greater, the jolt may be just what is needed to prod the resigned middle-ager toward seeking revitalization.   40

On the other hand . . .   41

If we have confronted ourselves in the middle passage and found a renewal of purpose around which we are eager to build a more authentic life structure, these may well be the best years. Personal happiness takes a sharp turn upward for partners who can now accept the fact: "I cannot expect *anyone* to fully understand me." Parents can be forgiven for the burdens of our childhood. Children can be let go without leaving us in collapsed silence. At 50, there is a new warmth and mellowing. Friends become   42 more important than ever, but so does privacy. Since it is so often proclaimed by peo-ple past midlife, the motto of this stage might be "No more bullshit."

1976

QUESTIONS FOR DISCUSSION

Content

a. The author explains that each of us has our own "step-style." What does she mean?

b. Do any people you know—your parents for example—fit neatly into Sheehy's ladder? Explain.

c. What qualifications does the author include in her introductory paragraphs to allow her to generalize?

d. Why should we not think "too mechanistically" (paragraph 4) when it comes to understanding how people move through life stages?

e. Why are "rebounds to the family" (paragraph 9) common between the ages of 18 and 22?

f. What, according to Sheehy, is the common response to approaching age 30?

g. How is establishing identity during the Deadline Decade different from estab-lishing it during earlier years? What does Sheehy mean by "disassembling our-selves" (paragraph 35)?

h. In what way might reaching age 50 bring renewal? In what way might it bring resignation?

Strategy and Style

i. Is the analogy in the introduction appropriate? Does it help prepare us for what is to follow?

j. Sheehy's approach is, for the most part, objective, even detached. At times, however, she does express her personal reaction to the material. Find places in which the author's personal voice can be heard.

k. Why are explanations of the steps on the developmental ladder written in fairly generalized terms? Would it have been possible to be more specific? What are some of the strategies Sheehy uses to make these explanations seem specific?

SUGGESTIONS FOR SHORT WRITING

a. Sheehy begins this passage with an analogy linking humans to lobsters. What other animals could you use in an analogy to describe human development? Make a list of two or three, and explain the analogy you see.

b. Briefly explain to what extent your chosen "course in life" is different from that of your parents or of other members of your family.

SUGGESTIONS FOR SUSTAINED WRITING

a. Where are you on Sheehy's developmental ladder? Write a narrative essay, using specific examples from your life, to discuss how your life fits Sheehy's categories, or how it does not fit. This essay can be extended to include other members of your family.

b. Do you know someone who has gone through the "middle passage" Sheehy discusses in paragraphs 39–42? Briefly tell the story of this passage, and explain whether this individual experienced a "renewal" or a "resignation."

c. For a researched essay, find other theories of adult development. Categorize each of them by applying age groups as Sheehy has done. Then, compare and contrast the theories, speculating on which most accurately describes adult development. Use your own experiences and your observations of your family and friends to form criteria for judging the theories.

Why Nothing Is "Wrong" Anymore

Meg Greenfield

Meg Greenfield (1930–1999) studied in Rome and as a Fulbright scholar at Cambridge University in England before she returned in 1957 to the United States to work for The Reporter, *first as a writer and later as an editor. When* The Reporter *ceased publication in 1968, she took a job with* The Washington Post *as an editorial writer. In 1978 she won a Pulitzer for editorial writing. Greenfield was* The Washington Post's *editorial page editor for 20 years and also wrote a regular column for* Newsweek, *in which "Why Nothing Is 'Wrong' Anymore" appeared on July 28, 1986.*

There has been an awful lot of talk about sin, crime, and plain old antisocial be- 1
havior this summer—drugs and pornography at home, terror and brutality abroad. Maybe it's just the heat; or maybe these categories of conduct (sin, crime, etc.) are really on the rise. What strikes me is our curiously deficient, not to say defective, way of talking about them. We don't seem to have a word anymore for "wrong" in the moral sense, as in, for example, "theft is wrong."

Let me quickly qualify. There is surely no shortage of people condemning 2 other people on such grounds, especially their political opponents or characters they just don't care for. Name-calling is still very much in vogue. But where the concept of wrong is really important—as a guide to one's own behavior or that of one's own side in some dispute—it is missing; and this is as true of those on the religious right who are going around pronouncing great masses of us sinners as it is of their principal antagonists, those on the secular left who can forgive or "understand" just about anything so long as it has not been perpetrated by a right-winger.

There is a fairly awesome literature that attempts to explain how we have 3 changed as a people with the advent of psychiatry, the weakening of religious institutions and so forth, but you don't need to address these matters to take note of a simple fact. As a guide and a standard to live by, you don't hear so much about "right and wrong" these days. The very notion is considered politically, not to say personally, embarrassing, since it has such a repressive, Neanderthal ring to it. So we have developed a broad range of alternatives to "right and wrong." I'll name a few.

Right and stupid: This is the one you use when your candidate gets caught 4 stealing, or, for that matter, when anyone on your side does something reprehensible. "It was really so dumb of him"—head must shake here—"I just can't understand it." Bad is dumb, breathtakingly dumb and therefore unfathomable; so, conveniently enough, the effort to fathom it might just as well be called off. This one had a big play during Watergate and has had mini-revivals ever since whenever congressmen and senators investigating administration crimes turn out to be guilty of something similar themselves.

Right and not necessarily unconstitutional: I don't know at quite what 5 point along the way we came to this one, the avoidance of admitting that something is wrong by pointing out that it is not specifically or even

189

inferentially prohibited by the Constitution or, for that matter, mentioned by name in the criminal code or the Ten Commandments. The various parties that prevail in civil-liberty and civil-rights disputes before the Supreme Court have gotten quite good at making this spurious connection: it is legally permissible, therefore it is morally acceptable, possibly even good. But both as individuals and as a society we do things every day that we know to be wrong even though they may not fall within the class of legally punishable acts or tickets to eternal damnation.

Right and sick: Crime or lesser wrongdoing defined as physical and/or psy-   6
chological disorder—this one has been around for ages now and as long ago as 1957 was made the butt of a great joke in the "Gee Officer Krupke!" song in "West Side Story." Still, I think no one could have foreseen the degree to which an originally reasonable and humane assumption (that some of what once was regarded as wrongdoing is committed by people acting out of ailment rather than moral choice) would be seized upon and exploited to exonerate every kind of misfeasance. This route is a particular favorite of caught-out officeholders who, when there is at last no other recourse, hold a press conference, announce that they are "sick" in some wise and throw themselves and their generally stunned families on our mercy. At which point it becomes gross to pick on them; instead we are exhorted to admire them for their "courage."

Right and only to be expected: You could call this the tit-for-tat school; it   7
is related to the argument that holds moral wrongdoing to be evidence of sickness, but it is much more pervasive and insidious these days. In fact it is probably the most popular dodge, being used to justify, or at least avoid owning up to, every kind of lapse: The other guy, or sometimes just plain circumstance, "asked for it." For instance, I think most of us could agree that setting fire to live people, no matter what their political offense, is—dare I say it?—wrong. Yet if it is done by those for whom we have sympathy in a conflict, there is a tendency to extenuate or disbelieve it, receiving it less as evidence of wrongdoing on our side than as evidence of the severity of the provocation or as enemy-supplied disinformation. Thus the hesitation of many in the antiapartheid movement to confront the brutality of so-called "necklacing," and thus the immediate leap of Sen. Jesse Helms to the defense of the Chilean government after the horrifying incineration of protesters there.

Right and complex: This one hardly takes a moment to describe; you know   8
it well. "Complex" is the new "controversial," a word used as "controversial" was for so long to flag trouble of some unspecified, dismaying sort that the speaker doesn't want to have to step up to. "Well, you know, it's very complex. . . ." I still can't get this one out of my own vocabulary.

In addition to these various sophistries, we also have created a rash of "ethics 9 committees" in our government, of course, whose function seems to be to dither around writing rules that allow people who have clearly done wrong—and should have known it and probably did—to get away because the rules don't cover their offense (see Right and not necessarily unconstitutional). But we don't need any more committees or artful dodges for that matter. As I listen to the moral arguments swirling about us this summer I become ever more persuaded that our real problem is this: the "still, small voice" of conscience has become far too small—and utterly still.

1986

QUESTIONS FOR DISCUSSION

Content

a. Summarize Greenfield's argument. Do you agree or disagree with it?
b. What is her purpose? Is it simply to explain a series of excuses people use to justify their irresponsibility?
c. What is the significance of her indicting both the "religious right" and the "secular left" (paragraph 2)? Is there evidence elsewhere in this essay that Greenfield's approach is balanced?
d. We don't hear so much about "right and wrong" anymore as "a guide and a standard to live by," claims Greenfield in paragraph 3. Why not? What purpose does the word *wrong* now serve?
e. Look up "sophistries" (paragraph 9). How are the categories Greenfield creates examples of sophistry?

Strategy and Style

f. How do the subheads lend clarity to this essay? Do they also help strengthen Greenfield's argument? Why or why not?
g. How would you describe Greenfield's intended audience?
h. What is the author's attitude toward her subject? Is her tone appropriate to an essay on contemporary moral attitudes?
i. Given Greenfield's purpose, is classification an appropriate method to organize her material? What other methods could she have used?
j. What use does she make of illustration?
k. Greenfield occasionally uses high-level vocabulary—"exonerate every kind of misfeasance," for example (paragraph 6). However, these words can usually be defined from their context. Using context clues, define *exonerate* and *misfeasance*; then, check your definitions in the dictionary. How would you define other unfamiliar words?

SUGGESTIONS FOR SHORT WRITING

a. Brainstorm with classmates to find other categories that might continue Greenfield's list. Title each category in your list "right and _____."

b. Identify and briefly discuss one or two acts you have observed, read about, or done yourself that might be classified as "right and stupid" or "right and sick" or that might fit one of Greenfield's other categories.

c. Discuss another term people avoid using because it seems unpleasant, embarrassing, or threatening. Begin by listing two or three popular alternatives. Then explain differences in meaning between the term you are discussing and its "more acceptable" synonyms. Some terms you might discuss are *selfish, egotistical, materialistic, promiscuous, irresponsible, greedy, ostentatious, self-centred, rude,* or *fanatical.*

SUGGESTIONS FOR SUSTAINED WRITING

a. Write a rebuttal to Greenfield's column. Point out to your readers why you think the author is being overly pessimistic about the current state of things. Make sure you take into account each of her points.

b. If you basically agree with Greenfield, apply her list, and any other categories you can add to it, to current events and/or to current political candidates. Find specific examples to illustrate each of her categories.

Four Kinds of Reading
Donald Hall

A prolific writer of prose and poetry, Donald Hall was born in New Haven, Connecticut, in 1928. He studied at Harvard, Stanford, and Oxford universities, and he has taught at both Stanford University and the University of Michigan. From 1953 to 1961, he was poetry editor for the Paris Review, *a prestigious literary journal. He has twice won National Book Awards, in 1968 and 1992. Hall's books of poetry include* Exiles and Marriages *(1955),* A Roof of Tiger Lilies *(1963),* The One Day *(1988), and* The Museum of Clear Ideas *(1993). Among his essay collections are* To Keep Moving *(1980),* Fathers Playing Catch with Sons: Essays on Sport *(1985), and* Here at Eagle Pond *(1989). Hall has also written biography, short fiction, and drama, as well as several volumes of children's literature. "Four Kinds of Reading" was first published in* The New York Times *in 1969.*

Everywhere one meets the idea that reading is an activity desirable in itself. It is 1 understandable that publishers and librarians—and even writers—should promote this assumption, but it is strange that the idea should have general currency. People surround the idea of reading with piety, and do not take into account the purpose of reading or the value of what is being read. Teachers and parents praise the child who reads, and praise themselves, whether the text be *The Reader's Digest* or *Moby Dick.* The advent of TV has increased the false values ascribed to reading, since TV provides a vulgar alternative. But this piety is silly; and most reading is no more cultural nor intellectual nor imaginative than shooting pool or watching *What's My Line.*

It is worth asking how the act of reading became something to value in it- 2 self, as opposed for instance to the act of conversation or the act of taking a walk. Mass literacy is a recent phenomenon, and I suggest that the aura which decorates reading is a relic of the importance of reading to our great-great-grandparents. Literacy used to be a mark of social distinction, separating a small portion of humanity from the rest. The farm laborer who was ambitious for his children did not daydream that they would become schoolteachers or doctors; he daydreamed that they would learn to read, and that a world would therefore open up to them in which they did not have to labor in the fields fourteen hours a day for six days a week in order to buy salt and cotton. On the next rank of society, ample time for reading meant that the reader was free from the necessity to spend most of his waking hours making a living. This sort of attitude shades into the contemporary man's boast of his wife's cultural activities. When he says that his wife is interested in books and music and pictures, he is not only enclosing the arts in a female world, he is saying that he is rich enough to provide her with the leisure to do nothing. Reading is an inactivity, and therefore a badge of social class. Of course, these reasons for the piety attached to reading are never acknowledged. They show themselves in the shape of our attitudes toward books; reading gives off an air of gentility.

It seems to me possible to name four kinds of reading, each with a charac- 3
teristic manner and purpose. The first is reading for information—reading to learn
about a trade, or politics, or how to accomplish something. We read a newspaper
this way, or most textbooks, or directions on how to assemble a bicycle. With most
of this material, the reader can learn to scan the page quickly, coming up with what
he needs and ignoring what is irrelevant to him, like the rhythm of the sentence, or
the play of metaphor. Courses in speed reading can help us read for this purpose,
training the eye to jump quickly across the page. If we read the *New York Times*
with the attention we should give a novel or a poem, we will have time for nothing else, and our mind will be cluttered with clichés and dead metaphor. Quick
eye-reading is a necessity to anyone who wants to keep up with what's happening,
or learn much of what has happened in the past. The amount of reflection, which
interrupts and slows down the reading, depends on the material.

But it is not the same activity as reading literature. There ought to be another 4
word. If we read a work of literature properly, we read slowly, and we *hear* all the
words. If our lips do not actually move, it's only laziness. The muscles in our throat
move, and come together when we see the word "squeeze." We hear the sounds so
accurately that if a syllable is missing in a line of poetry we hear the lack, though
we may not know what we are lacking. In prose we accept the rhythms, and hear
the adjacent sounds. We also register a track of feeling through the metaphors and
associations of words. Careless writing prevents this sort of attention, and becomes offensive. But the great writers reward it. Only by the full exercise of our
powers to receive language can we absorb their intelligence and their imagination.
This kind of reading goes through the ear—though the eye takes in the print, and
decodes it into sound—to the throat and the understanding, and it can never be
quick. It is slow and sensual, a deep pleasure that begins with touch and ends with
the sort of comprehension that we associate with dream.

Too many intellectuals read in order to reduce images to abstractions. One 5
reads philosophy slowly, as if it were literature, but much time must be spent with
the eyes turned away from the page, reflecting on the text. To read literature this
way is to turn it into something it is not—to concepts clothed in character, or philosophy sugar-coated. I think that most literary intellectuals read this way, including brighter professors of English, with the result that they miss literature completely, and concern themselves with a minor discipline called the history of ideas.
I remember a course in Chaucer at my university in which the final exam required
the identification of a hundred or more fragments of Chaucer, none as long as a
line. If you like poetry, and read Chaucer through a couple of times slowly, you
found yourself knowing them all. If you were a literary intellectual, well-informed
about the great chain of being, chances are you had a difficult time. To read literature is to be intimately involved with the words on the page, and never to think of
them as the embodiments of ideas which can be expressed in other terms. On the
other hand, intellectual writing—closer to mathematics on a continuum that has at
its opposite pole lyric poetry—requires intellectual reading, which is slow because
it is reflective and because the reader must pause to evaluate concepts.

But most of the reading which is praised for itself is neither literary nor in- 6
tellectual. It is narcotic. Novels, stories, and biographies—historical sagas,
monthly regurgitations of book clubs, four- and five-thousand word daydreams of
the magazines—these are the opium of the suburbs. The drug is not harmful except to the addict himself, and is no more injurious to him than Johnny Carson or
a bridge club, but it is nothing to be proud of. This reading is the automated daydream, the mild trip of the housewife and the tired businessman, interested not in
experience and feeling but in turning off the possibilities of experience and feeling. Great literature, if we read it well, opens us up to the world, and makes us
more sensitive to it, as if we acquired eyes that could see through walls and ears
that could hear the smallest sounds. But by narcotic reading, one can reduce great
literature to the level of *The Valley of the Dolls*. One can read *Anna Karenina* pas-
sively and inattentively, and float down the river of lethargy as if one were reading a confession magazine: "I Spurned My Husband for a Count."

I think that everyone reads for narcosis occasionally, and perhaps most con- 7
sistently in late adolescence, when great readers are born. I remember reading to
shut the world out, away at a school where I did not want to be; I invented a word
for my disease: "Bibliolepsy," on the analogy of narcolepsy. But after a while the
books became a window on the world, and not a screen against it. This change
doesn't always happen. I think that late adolescent narcotic reading accounts for
some of the badness of English departments. As a college student, the boy loves
reading and majors in English because he would be reading anyway. Deciding on
a career, he takes up English teaching for the same reason. Then in graduate school
he is trained to be a scholar, which is painful and irrelevant, and finds he must write
papers and publish them to be a Professor—and at about this time he no longer requires reading for narcosis, and he is left with nothing but a Ph.D. and the prospect
of fifty years of teaching literature; and he does not even like literature.

Narcotic reading survives the impact of television, because this type of read- 8
ing has even less reality than melodrama; that is, the reader is in control: Once the
characters reach into the reader's feelings, he is able to stop reading, or glance away,
or superimpose his own daydream. The trouble with television is that it embodies
its own daydream. Literature is often valued precisely because of its distance from
the tangible. Some readers prefer looking into the text of a play to seeing it performed. Reading a play, it is possible to stage it oneself by an imaginative act; but
it is also possible to remove it from real people. Here is Virginia Woolf, who was
lavish in her praise of the act of reading, talking about reading a play rather than seeing it: "Certainly there is a good deal to be said for reading *Twelfth Night* in the book
if the book can be read in a garden, with no sound but the thud of an apple falling
to the earth, or of the wind ruffling the branches of the trees." She sets her own stage;
the play is called *Virginia Woolf Reads Twelfth Night in a Garden*. Piety moves into
narcissism, and the high metaphors of Shakespeare's lines dwindle into the flowers
of an English garden; actors in ruffles wither, while the wind ruffles branches.

1968

QUESTIONS FOR DISCUSSION

Content

a. What are the four types of reading discussed in this selection?

b. What assumption does Hall tell us about in paragraph 1? To what end does he do this?

c. Explain "the aura which decorates reading," mentioned in paragraph 2.

d. What, according to Hall, accounts for the "piety" that we attach to reading?

e. What does Hall imply about the role of a reader in appreciating literature?

f. To what end does Hall recommend taking courses in speed reading (paragraph 3)?

g. In what ways are reading for information and reading literature dissimilar?

h. What distinction does the author make between literature and the history of ideas in paragraph 5?

i. What fault does Hall find in television?

j. Write one sentence of your own that might serve as this essay's thesis.

Strategy and Style

k. Is Hall's two-paragraph introduction appropriate to this essay? In what way?

l. What methods of development, other than classification, are used in this essay?

m. How does Hall support his argument that the fourth type of reading is "nothing to be proud of" (paragraph 6)?

n. Explain the order in which Hall chose to address the four types of reading. For example, why does he begin with informational reading and end with narcotic reading?

o. Describe the intended audience for this essay.

p. Hall's tone is formal, and his style is somewhat elevated. Could he have approached his subject using a lighter tone and more familiar language?

SUGGESTIONS FOR SHORT WRITING

a. "The trouble with television is that it embodies its own daydream," Hall claims in paragraph 8. What does he mean? Cite examples from your own television viewing that would support or oppose this notion.

b. Write a paragraph explaining Hall's belief that books should be "a window on the world, and not a screen against it" (paragraph 7). Do you agree with this statement? Why or why not? Under what circumstances, if any, might you find it appropriate to use reading as a screen?

c. Make an outline of the four types of reading Hall discusses. Then, list the titles of books, magazines, and other materials you have read under the appropriate category. What does your list tell you about your reading habits? Should you change them?

SUGGESTIONS FOR SUSTAINED WRITING

a. Write an essay that discusses at least four different reasons for pursuing a particular goal, activity, or pastime. For example, write about the different reasons for which you go to the movies, explain why people choose a particular college major, or discuss four different reasons that people have babies.

b. Interview a few friends and classmates on the subject of study habits. Then, write a paper in which you explain three or four good methods you might recommend to someone who is trying to become a successful student. If you want, include a discussion of study methods that you would not recommend in the last section of your paper.

c. Read what you wrote in response to items *a* or *b* in the Suggestions for Short Writing above. Expand that material into a full essay.

Boomers and Other Cohorts

David Foot and Daniel Stoffman

After completing an undergrad degree in Australia and his doctorate in economics at Harvard, David Foot became a popular professor of economics at the University of Toronto. He has published both academic and popular works on a wide variety of topics. Daniel Stoffman is an award-winning journalist who frequently writes on social issues for magazines such as Report on Business, Saturday Night, *and* Canadian Living. *Together, this scholar and journalist produced the best-selling book* Boom, Bust & Echo: How to Profit from the Coming Demographic Shift *(1996). The following essay is an excerpt from that book.*

Each of us is a member of a "cohort." The baby boom is a cohort that includes 1 everyone born during a 20-year span of sustained high numbers of births in Canada. It also includes those born elsewhere during those same years but now living in Canada. The other cohorts in Canada span shorter periods of time.

Most of us think of ourselves as individuals and underestimate how much we 2 have in common with fellow members of our cohort. And of course, each of us *is* an individual. The 70-year-old who continues a lifelong pursuit of rock climbing while most in her age group have switched to more sedate recreations is a unique individual. So is the 12-year-old who prefers opera to rock music. But the chances are good that the young opera lover will rent his first apartment, buy his first car, and get married at about the same age as his peers. The timing of those events in his life will be determined largely by demographics. Before we can understand what demographics have in store for him and for all of us, we need to know the various cohorts that make up the Canadian population. Let's take a look at them now.

PRE-WORLD WAR I (BORN 1914 AND EARLIER)

Forget about the outmoded notion of "senior citizens" as one unified group sharing 3 many characteristics in common. It's no longer true, if it ever was. An 85-year-old has no more in common with a 65-year-old than a 45-year-old has with a 25-year-old. They are different people, from different generations, with different interests, different financial circumstances, and different preoccupations and needs.

The most senior of seniors—the over-80-year-olds—constitute the one seg- 4 ment of the over-65 population that is currently growing rapidly because they were born in the first decade and a half of this century, when a high birth rate accompanied a booming Canadian economy. During this period, Canada also welcomed the largest concentrated influx of immigration in its history as part of a policy to settle the prairie provinces. Although the over-80s have a higher death rate than people in younger age groups, they are a growing cohort in the sense that those turning 80 during the 1990s are more numerous than their predecessors in the over-80 category. In 1996, 627,000 members of this cohort, born both in Canada and elsewhere, are living in Canada.

Because women, on average, live six years longer than men, most of this group is female. In their productive years, few women had independent careers outside the household and so they had little income of their own. They were married to men who didn't have transferable pensions. Not surprisingly, therefore, most of them are poor. Their greatest needs are appropriate housing and good health care. And their tragedy is that not enough of us are paying attention to them. As a society, we should be searching for innovative ways to combine housing with health care and related support services so that these women can conclude their lives in dignity and comfort. But the public sector is too preoccupied with deficit-cutting to think about imaginative solutions to social problems, and the senior seniors are too poor to interest the private sector.

The increase over the next decade in the number of elderly widows in our society is going to have a major impact on a younger group of people—people in their 50s and 60s who will be taking on the responsibility of caring for elderly, and increasingly ill, mothers. Traditionally, this is a task that falls to daughters more than to sons. Some women will be shouldering this new obligation on top of major responsibilities at work.

Imagine a vice-president of a large corporation in Toronto, preparing for a crucial meeting. She's an ambitious and talented woman who doesn't plan on making vice-president her final stop on the corporate ladder. She has her eye on the CEO's job, and this meeting is an important step in that direction. Then she gets an urgent call from Saskatoon, saying her mother has just broken her hip. Forget the big meeting: Mom needs her now more than ever, and she's on the next plane to Saskatoon. For the next few years, a great deal of her time and energy will be devoted to her mother. Because of real-life scenarios like this, many women who have the ability to make it to the top in business and government are not going to get there.

WORLD WAR I (1915 TO 1919)

It's always an advantage to be part of a small cohort. That's why even a small difference in one's date of birth can make a big difference in life. If you were born in 1910, you were part of a big cohort. If you were born in 1917, you were part of a smaller group. That in itself was no guarantee of success, but it was an important advantage. It meant you were in a smaller class at school and therefore had more attention from the teacher. And when it was time to go out to work, there were fewer competitors for what jobs were available.

During World War I, many Canadian men went off to battle and, as a result, many Canadian women stopped having babies. That's why people born in the last half of the teens of this century have enjoyed the lifelong advantage of having little peer-group competition. On the other hand, they entered the workforce while Canada was still in the grip of the Great Depression and jobs were few. After that, their careers were disrupted by World War II. Even so, they were better off than those born a few years earlier, who were part of a larger group and had to establish careers during the Depression. In 1996, 589,000 members of this cohort live in Canada. In general, people born in the second part of the teens have done better than those born just before.

THE ROARING TWENTIES (1920 TO 1929)

When the boys came home from the war, they quickly made up for lost time, with 10 the result that lots of babies were produced during the 1920s. These offspring of the Roaring Twenties are young seniors in the mid-1990s and, despite the lifelong disadvantage of being part of a large cohort, they've had a pretty good run. Some of them went overseas to fight in World War II, which had the result of reducing competition for jobs for those who remained in Canada.

Moreover, because of the war effort the economy was growing, and so the 11 1920s kids had a better chance to get established than those born in the 1910s. The Roaring Twenties generation also helped to produce the baby boom that began in 1947. The boomers proceeded to drive up the price of the real estate and other assets that the kids of both the 1910s and 1920s owned. So, in general, these people have done well but, because they were members of a large flock, numbering almost 2 million in 1996, not as well as the favoured group that followed them.

THE DEPRESSION BABIES (1930 TO 1939)

In hard economic times, many Canadians couldn't afford children, and so fertility 12 declined. The lucky ones who were born then became the golden group of Canadian society. Although they had a tough start, they have subsequently lived a life of incredible good fortune. These are the people entering senior citizenship during the mid-1990s, and yet again their timing is flawless: they are going to have free banking, reduced theatre ticket prices, and all the other breaks our society gives to seniors, because it will be several years yet before the dispensers of these perks wake up and realize that today's youngest seniors are the cohort least in need of such advantages.

The Depression kids haven't always had it easy. The 1930s were a time of 13 hardship for everyone, including young children. They lived through World War II, hardly a carefree time to be alive. Because of their youth, they didn't have to serve in the war. But once the war ended, everything went their way. Entering the workforce during the postwar reconstruction of the 1950s, they never had to worry about finding a job. On the contrary, they had their choice of jobs. They never had to worry about being promoted; rather, they were promoted faster than they ever expected to be. Because they were doing so well, they went out and got more of everything, including kids. The Depression kids gave us the baby boom because they could afford a house full of children on only one salary.

Most of them had three or four children, and that was the best investment they 14 could have made. Their kids sent real estate prices into the stratosphere in the 1980s, and subsequently they boosted the value of their parents' stock market holdings. Recently, some Depression kids have been cashing in these assets, using the proceeds to bolster their retirement nest eggs as well as for travel.

In 1996, 2.5 million Depression kids are living in Canada and still doing 15 pretty well for themselves. They are holding down many of the senior jobs in this country—in government, in business, in major educational and other institutions. Some of them are smart and capable and some of them aren't. Few of them realize how much they owe their success to being part of a small cohort that has always been in the right place at the right time.

WORLD WAR II (1940 TO 1946)

For those who postponed having children because of the Depression, the biological 16 clock was running out by the end of the 1930s and the early years of the 1940s. Then the war kick-started the economy—and the fertility rate. Canada, away from the main arenas of war, was a pretty good place to be. Canadians had plenty of food and jobs were plentiful. And so maternity wards started to fill up again. These wartime babies, the pre-boomers, number 2.2 million in 1996. They aren't as prosperous as the 1930s generation before them because more of them were born during each year. (The total number of Depression kids is larger because their cohort spans ten years, compared with only seven for the children of World War II.) On the other hand, the war babies haven't had nearly as much peer-group competition as those born in the following decade; so by comparison with everyone except the Depression kids, they've done extremely well.

Why did Canada experience a decline in births during World War I and an 17 increase in births during World War II? A larger percentage of Canadian men went overseas during World War I than in World War II, and many more lost their lives: 60,661 in World War I, compared with 42,042 in World War II. Moreover, in August 1918, almost as many Canadians were killed by a worldwide influenza epidemic as fell victim to enemy fire during the war. Both calamities reduced the numbers of Canadians in the child-producing age groups. Another reason for the difference was that while World War I followed a period of prosperity and high fertility, World War II followed the Depression. People had been postponing having families in the 1930s, and those in a position to start having children during World War II were eager to do so. Yet another reason was that Canada's economy got a bigger boost from World War II than from World War I. During World War II Canada became a major producer of ships, cargo carriers, aircraft, tanks, and other military vehicles. As a result, Canadian incomes rose, and rising incomes always mean increased demand for everything, including children.

THE BABY BOOM (1947 TO 1966)

Even people with no knowledge of demographics have heard of the group born 18
from 1947 to 1966. These are the baby-boomers. Some members of this particular
cohort seem to think they are pretty special. To hear them talk, you'd think they were
the most innovative and creative bunch of people Canada had ever seen, infusing
all of society with new ways of thinking and new ways of doing things. This is
nonsense. In fact, when they were 20, baby-boomers weren't much different from
the 20-year-olds who had preceded them. And now that many of them are in their
late 40s, they are behaving just as middle-aged people have always behaved.

The only thing special about the baby-boomers is that there are so many of 19
them. It seems hard to imagine now, but at the height of the boom, Canadian women
were averaging four offspring each. Canada produced more than 400,000 new
Canadians in each year of the baby boom, peaking at 479,000 in 1959. But examining Canadian births alone isn't sufficient to define the baby boom. The largest
single-year age group in Canada in the mid-1990s is those born in 1961, even though
3,600 fewer people were born here in that year than in 1959. That's because the
1961 group includes immigrants born in that year somewhere else. The most
important demographic fact about 35-year-olds is how many of them there are in
Canada in 1996, not how many people were born in Canada in 1961. The baby boom,
both those born in Canada and those born elsewhere, totals 9.8 million people in
1996, almost 33% of the Canadian population.

Canada's was the loudest baby boom in the industrialized world. In fact, only 20
three other Western countries—the United States, Australia, and New Zealand—
had baby booms. Part of the reason was that these four countries were immigrant
receivers, and immigrants tend to be in their 20s, the prime childbearing years. The
U.S. boom started earlier, in 1946, and it also ended earlier, in 1964. That's why
American periodicals in 1996 are full of articles about baby-boomers turning 50,
an event that will be delayed until 1997 in Canada.

At its peak in 1957, the U.S. boom hit 3.7 children per family, nearly half a 21
baby fewer than Canadian women were producing at the peak of the Canadian
boom. The Americans started their boom earlier because more of their war effort
was in the Pacific, and the Pacific war wound down sooner. The U.S. troops were
brought home in 1945 and kids started appearing in 1946. Canadian troops came
home later, so Canadian births did not leap upwards until 1947. As for the Australians,
they never got much higher than three babies per woman, but they compensated
by continuing their boom ten years longer than Canada did. That happened because
Australians were slower to adopt the birth-control pill and because Australian
women were slower than their North American counterparts to enter the workforce
in large numbers.

Because the Canadian baby boom was so big, Canadian boomers are a slightly 22
more important factor in Canadian life than American boomers are in American
life. Fully one-third of Canadians today are boomers, and for that reason alone,
when they get interested in a particular product or idea, we all have to sit up and take

notice. It's not that the product or idea is so great, it's just that everyone seems to be talking about it. The result is that phenomena such as the return to "family values" are often mistakenly identified as new social trends rather than the predictable demographic events they really are. (There is nothing new or remarkable about 35-year-olds raising families being interested in family values.)

Why did the baby boom happen? A likely explanation is that during those 20 [23] years, Canadians knew they could afford large families. The postwar economy was robust, the future seemed full of promise, and young couples wanted to share that bright future with a big family. A second reason was the high immigration levels that prevailed during the 1950s; immigrants tend to be people of childbearing age, and they made an important contribution to the boom. The combination of two ingredients—lots of people in their high fertility years and high incomes—is a surefire recipe for filling up maternity wards. But you need both: immigration levels were raised in the early years of the 1990s but the fertility rate didn't respond because incomes were falling, and Canadians, immigrants and non-immigrants alike, didn't think they could afford extra mouths to feed.

Why did the boom end? Towards the end of the 1960s, an increasing number [24] of women were pursuing higher education or entering the workforce. As a result, they were postponing childbirth and deciding to have fewer children. The introduction of the birth-control pill made this easier than ever to achieve. The more rapid acceptance of the pill in the United States may explain why the American boom ended before Canada's.

Like the seniors, the boomers break down into separate sub-groups. The [25] front-end boomer, pushing 50, with a bulging waistline and equally bulging Registered Retirement Savings Plan, doesn't share much in the way of cultural attitudes or life experiences with the Generation-Xer, in his early 30s, whose career hasn't yet got off the ground and who has trouble scraping up rent money every month. But as boomers, they have one very important thing in common: they are part of a huge cohort. For the front-end boomers, this was an advantage they could exploit. For the back-end boomers of Generation X, it is the cause of most of their problems.

It's important to grasp this point because the mass media have thoroughly [26] confused it. Newspaper articles often mix up Generation X with the baby-bust generation that followed it. Well into the 1990s, the media are still calling Gen-Xers "twenty-somethings" even though most of them have already celebrated their 30th birthdays. Some writers are so confused they seem to think Generation X is the children of the boomers. But it isn't. Most boomers weren't yet old enough to have children when Generation X came along. To clarify matters, we'll look at the characteristics of each subgroup of boomers in turn.

The front-end boomers have done pretty well for themselves. There are a lot [27] of them, so they had to compete for jobs when they entered the workforce over the 1960s. But the entry of vast numbers of younger baby-boomers into the marketplace through the 1970s and 1980s created wonderful opportunities for the front-enders already entrenched in business and government. New products, new services, new government programs, new universities—it was a period of seemingly endless expansion. The front-end boomers got there first, so they are the ones in good jobs now in both the public and private sectors. They understand the needs of the baby boom because they are the leading edge of it.

Those born towards the end of the 1950s also understand the baby boom but, 28 unlike the front-enders, they are less well positioned to profit from that knowledge. Generally, most members of this boomer subgroup have just managed to get a house. But that house is in the suburbs, and during the first part of the 1990s, its value crashed as the peak of the boom passed through its prime purchasing years. Most of these people are in a career, but that career seems to be going nowhere because the rungs ahead of them are clogged with older boomers who are still 15 to 20 years from retirement.

Things are tough for the late-1950s group, but not nearly as bad as for the 29 back end that arrived just after them. These are the 2.6 million people born from 1960 to 1966. They are the same age as the characters in Douglas Coupland's novel *Generation X*, which gave the early 1960s group its name. Many of them are still living at home with their parents because, faced with horrendous obstacles in the labour market, they haven't been able to get their careers on track. That is why, while front-end boomers were earning 30% more than their fathers by age 30, back-enders were making 10% less than their fathers at the same age.

Gen-Xers' life experience has led them to distrust any sort of large institu- 30 tion, whether in the public or private sector. It didn't take them long to learn that, in an overcrowded world, they had no choice but to "look out for number one." On their first day in kindergarten, the Gen-Xers discovered there weren't enough seats for them. In elementary school, many of them were squeezed into portables. They have been part of a crowd ever since. Whether it was trying to enrol in a ballet class, get into a summer camp, or find a part-time job, waiting lists have been a way of life for Generation X.

The millions of baby-boomers who preceded them drove up rents, drove up 31 house prices, and claimed all the best jobs and opportunities. As if that weren't enough, the Gen-Xers entered the labour market in the late 1970s and early 1980s, just when a brutal recession gripped the Canadian economy. In the best of circumstances, there would have been few jobs; in the recession there were virtually none. And when economic recovery finally began to create new demand for labour, the Gen-Xers were told they were too old for entry-level jobs and too short of experience for more senior ones. Is it any wonder we have 30-year-olds living at home in the mid-1990s?

One of the worst things the Gen-Xers have to cope with is their parents— 32 the Depression generation. These are the 55-to-60-year-olds sitting at the top of the corporate ladder, approaching the end of very successful careers, and unable to fathom why their 30-year-old offspring are living at home. Tension is tremendous in these families. Often the father is certain that his own success is based solely on his own merit while he sees his son's failure as a result of lack of drive and ambition.

THE BABY BUST (1967 TO 1979)

The commercial introduction of the birth-control pill in 1961 and the rising par- 33
ticipation of women in the labour market led to declining fertility over the 1960s.
The result was a decline in births and a smaller cohort, often called the baby bust.
In 1996, 5.4 million Canadians are in this cohort. The baby-busters have done
pretty well so far, especially the younger ones. They have been able to get into just
about any school or summer camp they wanted. They had no difficulty finding
babysitting, lawn-mowing, and other part-time jobs in high school, unlike their
older brothers and sisters, who had less opportunity to earn money while in high
school because they had so many competitors. During the 1990s, university entry
standards have been falling, making it easier for busters to get into the school of
their choice.

There is good reason for the twenty-something of the mid-1990s to be both 34
more realistic and more idealistic than the thirty-something of Generation X. In fact,
the baby-busters resemble the front-end boomers, who could espouse idealistic
causes during the 1960s safe in the knowledge that a good job and a prosperous
lifestyle would be there for the taking once they were ready for those bourgeois
things. But the backend boomers, as we have seen, had no choice but to look out
for their own best interests. They were less idealistic than their elders, not because
they were worse people but because they couldn't afford to be idealistic. In contrast,
the baby-busters have had a pretty good life so far, and when the world has treated
you well, you have the luxury of being able to pay attention to social issues, such
as peace, the environment, and AIDS, and therefore are more inclined to do so.

That's not to say there are no similarities between the Gen-Xers and the 35
baby-busters. Both groups started their working careers in tough economic times
when corporations were more interested in trimming payrolls than in hiring new
staff. As a result, the older baby-busters face the same problems and frustrations
that Generation X knows so well. But when the economy turns around, the 20-year-
old with minimal experience will have better prospects than the 30-year-old with
minimal experience. That's partly because employers usually prefer younger people
for entry-level positions, because they are cheaper and more adaptable; partly
because there are fewer busters than Gen-Xers; and partly because the busters
are better equipped than the Gen-Xers with the computer skills that today's job
market demands.

THE BABY-BOOM ECHO (1980 TO 1995)

These are the children of the boomers. The boomers were already having children 36
in the 1970s, but by 1980 enough of them were reproducing to produce a mini-boom
of their own. The boomers, however, never matched the reproductive prowess of
their parents. At its peak, in 1990, the echo produced 406,000 babies from a population of 27.7 million, compared with 479,000 from a population of only 17.5

million in 1959. This generation is most noticeable in Ontario and western Canada. Quebec and the Atlantic provinces (except for Halifax) haven't had much of a baby-boom echo because so many of their boomers moved to Ontario and the western provinces and had their children there. So the echo won't have as much impact on society in eastern Canada as it will in Ontario and the west.

As of 1996, there are 6.9 million members of the echo generation. The boomers   37 haven't finished having children, but over the remaining years of the decade the echo will dwindle to an end. This is predictable because most boomer women are past their prime childbearing years. Even if these women now decide they want big families, they won't be able to have them because they are too old.

What is the outlook for the echo kids? It won't be quite as smooth sailing as   38 the baby-busters have had, but it won't be as disastrous as for Generation X either. These echo kids are part of a large cohort and that's always bad news. They crowded nurseries in the 1980s, pushed elementary school enrolments up in the late 1980s, and are about to do the same for high school enrolments in the mid-1990s. Like the baby boom, the echo has a front end, born in the 1980s, that will have an easier ride than its back end, born in the first half of the 1990s. The latter group, Generation X-II, will experience the familiar disadvantages of arriving at the rear of a large cohort. Think of a cohort as a group of people all wanting to get into the same theatre to see the same show. There is no reserved seating. So who claims the best seats? The ones who get there first. The back end of the echo generation, Gen X-II, will have a life experience similar to that of its parents, the first Generation X. Just as the first Gen-Xers have done, Gen X-II will have to scramble.

However, Gen X-II should be better prepared than its parents were to cope   39 with high youth unemployment and other difficulties associated with a large cohort. That's because these kids have their Gen-X parents to teach them. By contrast, the original Generation X was the offspring of a small cohort that wasn't equipped to prepare them for the difficult world they encountered when they left home in the early 1980s.

THE FUTURE (1995 TO 2010)

These are the millennium kids, the generation that is following the baby-boom   40 echo. The women producing them are the baby-busters, a cohort 19% smaller in each year than the baby-boomers and 45% smaller in total. Because of immigration, the millennium kids won't necessarily be 45% fewer than the echo kids, but they will definitely be a smaller group. As a result, as this book goes to press, we see another small, and therefore favoured, cohort emerging from Canada's maternity wards.

1996

QUESTIONS FOR DISCUSSION

Content

a. What is the thesis of this excerpt?
b. Is it an advantage or a disadvantage to be part of a small group?
c. Why do the authors spend so much time discussing and clarifying what Gen-X means?
d. Why have the boomers had such an impact on society?
e. Which group has had the greatest economic success?

Strategy and Style

f. What is the basis for the divisions and the ordering of their presentation?
g. How does the essay indicate shifts in discussion?
h. What kind of words are used: everyday, academic, colloquial? (Compare with Northrop Frye in Chapter 4 or M. NourbeSe Philip in Chapter 6.)
i. Are there references to other works of literature? Why is this work mentioned?
j. What is the narrator's attitude towards the subject: Reverential? Serious? Humorous?
k. What are the effects that these groups cause? Is this relationship of causality assumed or demonstrated?
l. What is the effect of the analogy of the movie theatre?

SUGGESTIONS FOR SHORT WRITING

a. Find a way to divide your class into subgroups. You may choose to base it on clothing, hairstyle, music tastes, or any other thing.
b. Discuss how being in your demographic group has been an advantage or a disadvantage.
c. In your opinion, are any of the demographic groupings superior (morally or otherwise) to any other? Why or why not?

SUGGESTIONS FOR SUSTAINED WRITING

a. Part of the title of Foot and Stoffman's book is *How to Profit from the Coming Demographic Shift.* Argue for or against the use of demographics for profit (think of things like grey power insurance, special villages for people over 50, and so on).
b. Should credit card companies be entitled to information about age so they can determine our proper demographic (and credit rating)?
c. Go to a video store and examine how they classify movies. Select a number of films from a single category and find out the characteristics that define that category or subgenre.

The Truth about Lying

Judith Viorst

A contributing editor at Redbook *magazine, Judith Viorst (b. 1931) began her career as a poet in 1965 when she published* The Village Square. *This book of verse was followed by several other volumes of prose and poetry with intriguing titles. Among them are* It's Hard to Be Hip Over Thirty and Other Tragedies of Married Life *(1968),* People and Other Aggravations *(1971),* Yes, Married: A Saga of Love and Complaint *(1972), and* When Did I Stop Being Twenty and Other Injustices *(1987). Viorst has also published several works of children's fiction and nonfiction as well as a musical drama,* Birthday and Other Humiliations. *"The Truth about Lying" first appeared in* Redbook *in 1981.*

I've been wanting to write on a subject that intrigues and challenges me: the sub- 1
ject of lying. I've found it very difficult to do. Everyone I've talked to has a quite intense and personal but often rather intolerant point of view about what we can—and can never *never*—tell lies about. I've finally reached the conclusion that I can't present any ultimate conclusions, for too many people would promptly disagree. Instead, I'd like to present a series of moral puzzles, all concerned with lying. I'll tell you what I think about them. Do you agree?

SOCIAL LIES

Most of the people I've talked with say that they find social lying acceptable and 2
necessary. They think it's the civilized way for folks to behave. Without these little white lies, they say, our relationships would be short and brutish and nasty. It's arrogant, they say, to insist on being so incorruptible and so brave that you cause other people unnecessary embarrassment or pain by compulsively assailing them with your honesty. I basically agree. What about you?

Will you say to people, when it simply isn't true, "I like your new hairdo," 3
"You're looking much better," "It's so nice to see you," "I had a wonderful time"?

Will you praise hideous presents and homely kids? 4

Will you decline invitations with "We're busy that night—so sorry we can't 5
come," when the truth is you'd rather stay home than dine with the So-and-sos?

And even though, as I do, you may prefer the polite evasion of "You really 6
cooked up a storm" instead of "The soup"—which tastes like warmed-over coffee—"is wonderful," will you, if you must, proclaim it wonderful?

There's one man I know who absolutely refuses to tell social lies. "I can't 7
play that game," he says; "I'm simply not made that way." And his answer to the argument that saying nice things to someone doesn't cost anything is, "Yes, it does—it destroys your credibility." Now, he won't, unsolicited, offer his views on the painting you just bought, but you don't ask his frank opinion unless you want *frank*, and his silence at those moments when the rest of us liars are muttering, "Isn't it lovely?" is, for the most part, eloquent enough. My friend does not indulge

in what he calls "flattery, false praise and mellifluous comments." When others tell fibs he will not go along. He says that social lying is lying, that little white lies are still lies. And he feels that telling lies is morally wrong. What about you?

PEACE-KEEPING LIES

Many people tell peace-keeping lies; lies designed to avoid irritation or argument; 8 lies designed to shelter the liar from possible blame or pain; lies (or so it is rationalized) designed to keep trouble at bay without hurting anyone.

   I tell these lies at times, and yet I always feel they're wrong. I understand 9 why we tell them, but still they feel wrong. And whenever I lie so that someone won't disapprove of me or think less of me or holler at me, I feel I'm a bit of a coward, I feel I'm dodging responsibility, I feel . . . guilty. What about you?

   Do you, when you're late for a date because you overslept, say that you're 10 late because you got caught in a traffic jam?

   Do you, when you forget to call a friend, say that you called several times 11 but the line was busy?

   Do you, when you didn't remember that it was your father's birthday, say 12 that his present must be delayed in the mail?

   And when you're planning a weekend in New York City and you're not in 13 the mood to visit your mother, who lives there, do you conceal—with a lie, if you must—the fact that you'll be in New York? Or do you have the courage—or is it the cruelty?—to say, "I'll be in New York, but sorry—I don't plan on seeing you"?

   (Dave and his wife Elaine have two quite different points of view on this 14 very subject. He calls her a coward. She says she's being wise. He says she must assert her right to visit New York sometimes and not see her mother. To which she always patiently replies: "Why should we have useless fights? My mother's too old to change. We get along much better when I lie to her.")

   Finally, do you keep the peace by telling your husband lies on the subject of 15 money? Do you reduce what you really paid for your shoes? And in general do you find yourself ready, willing and able to lie to him when you make absurd mistakes or lose or break things?

   "I used to have a romantic idea that part of intimacy was confessing every 16 dumb thing that you did to your husband. But after a couple of years of that," says Laura, "have I changed my mind!"

   And having changed her mind, she finds herself telling peace-keeping lies. 17 And yes, I tell them too. What about you?

PROTECTIVE LIES

Protective lies are lies folks tell—often quite serious lies—because they're con- 18 vinced that the truth would be too damaging. They lie because they feel there are certain human values that supersede the wrong of having lied. They lie, not for personal gain, but because they believe it's for the good of the person they're lying to. They lie to those they love, to those who trust them most of all, on the grounds that breaking this trust is justified.

They may lie to their children on money or marital matters.   19

They may lie to the dying about the state of their health.   20

They may lie about adultery, and not—or so they insist—to save their own   21
hide, but to save the heart and the pride of the men they are married to.

They may lie to their closest friend because the truth about her talents or son   22
or psyche would be—or so they insist—utterly devastating.

I sometimes tell such lies, but I'm aware that it's quite presumptuous to   23
claim I know what's best for others to know. That's called playing God. That's called manipulation and control. And we never can be sure, once we start to juggle lies, just where they'll land, exactly where they'll roll.

And furthermore, we may find ourselves lying in order to back up the lies   24
that are backing up the lie we initially told.

And furthermore—let's be honest—if conditions were reversed, we cer-   25
tainly wouldn't want anyone lying to us.

Yet, having said all that, I still believe that there are times when protective   26
lies must nonetheless be told. What about you?

If your Dad had a very bad heart and you had to tell him some bad family   27
news, which would you choose: to tell him the truth or to lie?

If your former husband failed to send his monthly childsupport check and in   28
other ways behaved like a total rat, would you allow your children—who believed he was simply wonderful—to continue to believe that he was wonderful?

If your dearly beloved brother selected a wife whom you deeply disliked,   29
would you reveal your feelings or would you fake it?

And if you were asked, after making love, "And how was that for you?"   30
would you reply, if it wasn't too good, "Not too good"?

Now, some would call a sex lie unimportant, little more than social lying, a   31
simple act of courtesy that makes all human intercourse run smoothly. And some would say all sex lies are bad news and unacceptably protective. Because, says Ruth, "a man with an ego that fragile doesn't need your lies—he needs a psychiatrist." Still others feel that sex lies are indeed protective lies, more serious than simple social lying, and yet at times they tell them on the grounds that when it comes to matters sexual, everybody's ego is somewhat fragile.

"If most of the time things go well in sex," says Sue, "I think you're allowed   32
to dissemble when they don't. I can't believe it's good to say, 'Last night was four stars, darling, but tonight's performance rates only a half.' "

I'm inclined to agree with Sue. What about you?   33

TRUST-KEEPING LIES

Another group of lies are trust-keeping lies, lies that involve triangulation, with *A*   34
(that's you) telling lies to *B* on behalf of *C* (whose trust you'd promised to keep).

Most people concede that once you've agreed not to betray a friend's confidence, you can't betray it, even if you must lie. But I've talked with people who don't want you telling them anything that they might be called on to lie about.

"I don't tell lies for myself," says Fran, "and I don't want to have to tell them 35 for other people." Which means, she agrees, that if her best friend is having an affair, she absolutely doesn't want to know about it.

"Are you saying," her best friend asks, "that if I went off with a lover and I 36 asked you to tell my husband I'd been with you, that you wouldn't lie for me, that you'd betray me?"

Fran is very pained but very adamant. "I wouldn't want to betray you, so . . . 37 don't ask me."

Fran's best friend is shocked. What about you?   38

Do you believe you can have close friends if you're not prepared to receive 39 their deepest secrets?

Do you believe you must always lie for your friends?   40

Do you believe, if your friend tells a secret that turns out to be quite immoral 41 or illegal, that once you've promised to keep it, you must keep it?

And what if your friend were your boss—if you were perhaps one of the 42 President's men—would you betray or lie for him over, say, Watergate?

As you can see, these issues get terribly sticky.   43

It's my belief that once we've promised to keep a trust, we must tell lies to 44 keep it. I also believe that we can't tell Watergate lies. And if these two statements strike you as quite contradictory, you're right—they're quite contradictory. But for now they're the best I can do. What about you?

Some say that truth will out and thus you might as well tell the truth. Some 45 say you can't regain the trust that lies lose. Some say that even though the truth may never be revealed, our lies pervert and damage our relationships. Some say . . . well, here's what some of them have to say.

"I'm a coward," says Grace, "about telling close people important, difficult 46 truths. I find that I'm unable to carry it off. And so if something is bothering me, it keeps building up inside till I end up just not seeing them any more."

"I lie to my husband on sexual things, but I'm furious," says Joyce, "that he's 47 too insensitive to know I'm lying."

"I suffer most from the misconception that children can't take the truth," 48 says Emily. "But I'm starting to see that what's harder and more damaging for them is being told lies, is *not* being told the truth."

"I'm afraid," says Joan, "that we often wind up feeling a bit of contempt for 49 the people we lie to."

And then there are those who have no talent for lying.   50

"Over the years, I tried to lie," a friend of mine explained, "but I always got 51 found out and I always got punished. I guess I gave myself away because I feel guilty about any kind of lying. It looks as if I'm stuck with telling the truth."

For those of us, however, who are good at telling lies, for those of us who lie 52 and don't get caught, the question of whether or not to lie can be a hard and serious moral problem. I liked the remark of a friend of mine who said, "I'm willing to lie. But just as a last resort—the truth's always better."

"Because," he explained, "though others may completely accept the lie I'm 53 telling, I don't."

I tend to feel that way too. 54

What about you? 55

1981

QUESTIONS FOR DISCUSSION

Content

a. Is the essay's thesis explicit? What is it?
b. What arguments does the author offer to defend social lying? What arguments does she offer against social lying?
c. Why does Viorst believe that telling protective lies is a form of manipulation?
d. What else does she find objectionable or dangerous about protective lies?
e. Under what conditions does the author believe that telling protective lies is appropriate?
f. In what way is her position on trust-keeping lies contradictory? How does she respond to that contradiction?

Strategy and Style

g. What is the introduction to this essay designed to do? Does it succeed?
h. To what end does Viorst address the reader directly?
i. What is the effect of her asking "What about you?" at the end of each section?
j. Where and to what end does Viorst use contrast? How does her creating contrast relate to her thesis?
k. Viorst uses examples throughout this essay. What form do these examples take? Are they convincing?
l. Where in the essay does the author engage in definition?
m. Does Viorst's quoting her friends make an effective way to develop this essay? Why or why not?
n. What point does the author make in the conclusion? Does it bring closure to the essay, or is it simply another of the "moral puzzles" she mentions in her introduction?

SUGGESTIONS FOR SHORT WRITING

a. Can you think of another type of lie, one that Viorst does not discuss? Write a short paragraph that explains this category. Like Viorst, include examples and direct quotations from others to develop your point.

b. Respond to Viorst by explaining how you react to what she says about one of the four kinds of lies she discusses. In other words, respond to the question with which she closes each section of this essay: "What about you?"
c. List examples of representative social, peace-keeping, protective, and trust-keeping lies that you tell or are told by others.

SUGGESTIONS FOR SUSTAINED WRITING

a. Write a letter to Viorst explaining why you tell lies like those discussed in her essay or why you refuse to tell such lies.
b. Write a classification essay in which you develop three or four major categories relating to a type of human behaviour or activity about which you have mixed feelings. For example, you might discuss "the truth about dieting," "the truth about gambling," "the truth about exercising," "the truth about being assertive," or "the truth about gossiping."

6

Comparison and Contrast

The human tendency to measure one thing against another is so pervasive that it is only natural it to be used as a way to explore and explain complex ideas in writing. Comparison reveals similarities; contrast, differences. Both allow the writer to explain and explore new ideas by making reference to what the reader already knows. One way to begin describing a microwave oven to someone who has never seen one is to liken it to the oven in the conventional kitchen stove with which he or she is familiar. Both use energy to heat and cook food. Both are relatively easy to use, and both are no fun to clean! But there the similarities end. A microwave is quicker and more economical. And whoever heard of making popcorn in a conventional oven? Spend enough time explaining similarities and differences, and you are sure to give your reader at least rudimentary acquaintance with this appliance.

As with all writing, the key to composing effective comparison/contrast papers is to collect important information—and plenty of it—before you begin. Look at your subjects long and hard, take careful notes, and gather the kinds of details that will help you reveal differences and similarities of the most telling kind.

You can use a variety of techniques to develop a comparison or contrast. As suits his purpose, Mark Twain relies heavily on description in "Two Views of the Mississippi" while Lydia Minatoya includes both narrative and descriptive details to create a complex essay about the relationships among cultures. Narration also informs Lee Maracle's "Survival Work" and Mark Mathabane's discussion of superstition in South Africa and in the West.

One of the major advantages of using comparison/contrast to explain ideas is that it can lend itself quite naturally to two easy-to-arrange and easy-to-follow patterns of organization. In the point-by-point method, writers address a series of characteristics or features shared by the two subjects; they compare or contrast the two subjects on one point, then move on to the next point.

214

In the subject-by-subject method, one subject is thoroughly discussed before the writer moves on to the second. You can see good examples of the subject-by-subject method in the essays by Mark Twain and Suzanne Britt. For example, Twain first describes the beautiful and poetic Mississippi before going on to the dangerous Mississippi.

The selections in this chapter present a variety of subjects and purposes—from analyzing psychological motivations behind the way men and women communicate to assessing the virtues of toys. Carefully consider the Questions for Discussion and the Suggestions for Short Writing and for Sustained Writing following each essay. They will lead you to many more insights about using comparison/contrast as a way to explore new ideas and to make your writing more powerful no matter what your topic or purpose.

The Absence of Writing or How I Almost Became a Spy

M. NourbeSe Philip

M. NourbeSe Philip was born in 1947 in Tobago. She emigrated to Canada in 1968 after finishing her economics degree at the University of the West Indies, went on to finish an MA in political science, and eventually become a lawyer. In order to dedicate herself more fully to her writing, she gave up the practice of law in 1982. Her poetry, essays, and fiction have been published in a variety of literary journals, and her book of poetry She Tries Her Tongue, Her Silence Softly Breaks *won the Casa de las Americas prize for poetry. In 1990, she received a Guggenheim Award for her poetry and returned to Tobago to complete her novel* Looking for Livingstone: An Odyssey of Silence.

1   I wasn't hard-backed but I definitely wasn't no spring chicken when I started to write—as a way of living my life I mean, although like a lot of women I had been doing it on the quiet quiet filling up all kinds of notebooks with poems, thinkings—deep and not so deep—curses and blessings.

2   The last thing I expected to end up doing was writing, and when I upsed and left a safe and decent profession—second oldest in the world, they say—for writing, I was the most surprised person. Is in those growing up years as a child in Trinidad and Tobago that you will find the how, why and wherefore of this take-me-by-surprise change.

3   If someone had asked me when I was growing up to tell them what pictures came to mind when I heard the word "writer" I would have said nothing. What I wanted to be most of all was a spy, and after reading about spies in World War II, spying was much more real to me than writing. After all there was an Empire and we, its loyal subjects, had to defend it. Black and brown middle class people—my family, short on money but long on respectability, belonged to this class—wanted their children to get "good jobs" and, better yet, go into the professions. Massa day was done and dreams were running high high—my son the doctor! Education was open to everyone, girl and boy alike—my daughter the lawyer! And if your son or daughter didn't manage to get that far, there was always nursing, teaching or accounting. Failing that there was always the civil service.

4   Some people might say that this was normal since the writers we had heard about—all white—had usually starved and you couldn't say this about doctors or lawyers. Education was going to be the salvation of the black middle classes—so we believed—and a profession was the best proof that you had put servitude behind you, and were becoming more like the upper classes. Writing was no help in this at all.

5   In high school I was learning and learning about many things—English literature, French history, American history and finally in my fifth year, West Indian history—poor-ass cousin to English history and the name V.S. Naipaul was there somewhere. V.S. Naipaul, writer. It was a sister of his who taught me in high school who first mentioned him to us, her students. But V.S. Naipaul was Indian

216

and, in the context of Trinidad at that time, in the eyes of the blacks, this was a strike against him. V.S. Naipaul the writer we didn't understand or care to understand. Maybe, without knowing it, we were already understanding how he was going to use us in his writing life.

Books for so! I wasn't no stranger to them—they were all around since my 6 father was a headmaster and living in the city meant I could get to the library easily. Books for so! rows and rows of them at the library as greedy-belly I read my way through Dostoevsky, Moravia, Shakespeare, Dickens. Books for so! Other people were writing them. I was reading them.

I wasn't different from any of the twenty or so girls in my sixth-form class. None 7 of them were looking to writing as a career, or even thinking the thought as a possibility. Profession, vocation, career—we all knew those words; we, the black and brown middle classes, scholarship girls whom our teachers were exhorting to be the cream of society, the white salt of the earth. Profession, vocation, career—anything but writer.

Some people are born writing, some achieve writing and some have writing 8 thrust upon them. My belonging is to the last group, coming slowly to accept the blessing and yoke that is writing, and with so doing I have come upon an understanding of language—good-english-bad-english english, Queenglish and Kinglish— the anguish that is english in colonial societies. The remembering—the revolutionary language of "massa day done"—change fomenting not in the language of rulers, but in the language of the people.

Only when we understand language and its role in a colonial society can we 9 understand the role of writing and the writer in such a society; only then, perhaps, can we understand why writing was not and still, to a large degree, is not recognized as a career, profession, or way of be-ing in the Caribbean and even among Caribbean people resident in Canada.

What follows is my attempt to analyse and understand the role of language 10 and the word from the perspective of a writer resident in a society which is still very much colonial—Canada; a writer whose recent history is colonial and continues to cast very long shadows.

Fundamental to any art form is the image, whether it be the physical image 11 as created by the dancer and choreographer, the musical image of the composer and musician, the visual image of the plastic artist or the verbal image, often metaphorical, of the writer and poet. (For the purposes of this essay I will be confining myself for the most part to the concept of image as it relates to the writer.) While, however, it may be quite easy to see the role of image as it relates to the visual artist, it may be less easy to do so with respect to the writer. The word "image" is being used here to convey what can only be described as the irreducible essence—the i-mage—of creative writing; it can be likened to the DNA molecules at the heart of all life. The process of giving tangible form to this i-mage may be called i-maging, or the i-magination. Use of unconventional orthography, "i-mage" in this instance, does not only represent the increasingly conventional deconstruction of certain words, but draws on the Rastafarian practice of privileging the "I" in many words.[1]

[1]Readers interested in exploring Rastafarian language further are referred to the works of Jamaican writer Valma Pollard.

"I-mage" rather than "image" is, in fact, a closer approximation of the concept under discussion in this essay. In her attempt to translate the i-mage into meaning and non-meaning, the writer has access to a variety of verbal techniques and methods— comparison, simile, metaphor, metonymy, symbol, rhyme, allegory, fable, myth— all of which aid her in this process. Whatever the name given to the technique or form, the function remains the same—that of enabling the artist to translate the i-mage into meaningful language for her audience.

The power and threat of the artist, poet or writer lies in this ability to create   12
new i-mages, i-mages that speak to the essential being of the people among whom and for whom the artist creates. If allowed free expression, these i-mages succeed in altering the way a society perceives itself and, eventually, its collective consciousness. For this process to happen, however, a society needs the autonomous i-mage-maker for whom the i-mage and the language of any art form become what they should be—a well-balanced equation.

When, in the early 1900s, Picasso and his fellow artists entered their   13
so-called "primitive stage" they employed what had traditionally been an African aesthetic of art and sculpture and succeeded in permanently altering the sensibilities of the West toward this aesthetic. In the wake of European colonial penetration of Africa and Oceania the entire art world was, in fact, revolutionized and the modernist art movement was born. These changes did not necessarily increase the understanding or tolerance of the West for Africans and Africa, but people began to perceive differently.

I-mages that comprised the African aesthetic had previously been thought to   14
be primitive, naive, and ugly, and consequently had been dismissed not only by white Westerners, but by the Africans themselves living outside Africa—so far were Africans themselves removed from their power to create, control and even understand their own i-mages. The societies in which these New World Africans lived—North and South America, England, the Caribbean—lacked that needed matrix in which the autonomous i-mage-maker could flourish. The only exception to this is to be found in musical traditions, where despite the hostility of these predominantly white societies, the African i-mage-maker in musical art forms was successful in producing authentic art which has also permanently influenced Western music.

Caribbean society has been a colonial society for a much longer time than   15
not, and the role of the i-mage, i-mage-making, and i-mage control are significant. The societies that comprise the Caribbean identity may be identified by:

(a) a significant lack of autonomy in the creation and dissemination of i-mages;

(b) opposition by the ruling classes both at home and abroad to the creation of i-mages that challenge their i-mage making powers and the status quo;

(c) restricting of indigenously created i-mages to marginal groups, e.g. reggae and calypso.

While changes like independence have improved some of these circum-   16
stances both within the Caribbean and within Caribbean societies in the large metropolitan centres overseas, these factors continue to affect the artist and particu-

larly the writer. The tradition of writing for the Caribbean and Caribbean people is a brief one, and briefer still is the Afro-centric tradition in that writing.

It is, perhaps, ironic that New World Africans, descendants of cultures and soci- 17 eties where the word and the act of naming was the focal point and fulcrum of societal forces,[2] should find themselves in a situation where the word, their word and the power to name was denied them. Traditionally, for instance, in many West African societies, until named, a child did not even acquire a recognizable and discernible human identity. In the New World after the destruction of the native peoples, Africans would be renamed with the name of the stranger. If what the artist does is create in her own i-mage and *give name* to that i-mage, then what the African artist from the Caribbean and the New World must do is create in, while giving name to, her own i-mage—and in so doing eventually heal the word wounded by the dislocation and imbalance of the word /i-mage equation. This can only be done by consciously restructuring, reshaping and, if necessary, destroying the language. When that equation is balanced and unity of word and i-mage is once again present, then and only then will we have made the language our own.

In the accompanying journal I kept as I worked on *She Tries Her Tongue* I write 18 as follows:

> *I am laying claim to two heritages—one very accessible, the other hidden. The apparent accessibility of European culture is dangerous and misleading especially what has been allowed to surface and become de rigeur. To get anything of value out of it, one has to mine very, very deeply and only after that does one begin to see the connections and linkages with other cultures. The other wisdoms—African wisdom needs hunches, gut feelings and a lot of flying by the seat of the pants, free falls only to be caught at the last minute. It calls for a lot more hunting out of the facts before one can even get to the essence, because in almost exact reversal with European culture not much has been allowed to surface—am almost tempted to say that one can for that reason trust that information more.*

I must add now that lack of information bears directly on one's ability to 19 make i-mages.

The linguistic rape and subsequent forced marriage between African and 20 English tongues has resulted in a language capable of great rhythms and musicality; one that is and is not English, and one which is among the most vital in the English-speaking world today. The continuing challenge for me as a writer/poet is to find some deeper patterning—a deep structure, as Chomsky puts it—of my language, the Caribbean demotic. The challenge is to find the literary form of the

[2]Janheinz Jahn, *Muntu* (New York: Grove Press, 1961), p. 125.

demotic language. As James Baldwin has written, "Negro speech is not a question of dropping s's or n's or g's but a question of the beat."[3] At present the greatest strength of the Caribbean demotic lies in its oratorical energies which do not necessarily translate to the page easily. Just as the language that English people write is not necessarily or often that which is spoken by them, so too what is spoken in the streets of Trinidad, or by some Caribbean people in Toronto, is not always going to be the best way of expressing it on the page. To keep the deep structure, the movement, the kinetic energy, the tone and pitch, the slides and glissandos of the demotic within a tradition that is primarily page-bound—that is the challenge.

While I continue to write in my father tongue, I continue the quest I identified in   21
1983 to discover my mother tongue, trying to engender by some alchemical practice a metamorphosis within the language from father tongue to mother tongue. Will I recognize this tongue when I find it, or is it rather a matter of developing it rather than finding it? Whatever metaphorical i-mages one uses—discovery or development—the issue of recognition is an important one, since implied within the word itself is the meaning, the i-mage of knowing again. . . .

1989

QUESTIONS FOR DISCUSSION

Content

a. Identify some cultural and language issues that Philip introduces into her essay.
b. What cultures or what aspects of culture is Philip comparing and contrasting?
c. How does the notion of colonialism allow Philip to compare and contrast?
d. This selection was originally part of an introduction to a volume of Philip's poetry. Does seeing it as an introduction allow you to read the essay differently than the way we present it here, as an essay unto itself?
e. What kind of a reader does Philip address?
f. What do you think "massa day" is? Does the essay create enough of a context for you to understand this phrase or do you need to do research to understand what she is referring to?
g. Do you need background in the history of Trinidad and Tobago and colonialism in order to understand what Philip is writing about?
h. What does Philip mean by "good-english-bad-english english, Queenglish and Kinglish"?

---

[3]*Conversations with James Baldwin*, ed. Fred L. Standley and Louis H. Pratt (Jackson: University Press of Mississippi, 1989).

i.   Why does Philip write "image" as "i-mage"?

j.   What is Philip's overall point?

Strategy and Style

k.   In her essay, Philip quotes herself from a journal she kept while writing the collection. Why does she not simply integrate the passage into the essay? Why do we need to know that it comes from her journal?

l.   Why does Philip mention her childhood desire to be a spy? For such a short reference (it only appears in one paragraph), does it belong as part of the title?

m.   What is the tone of the opening of the essay ("I wasn't hard-backed but I definitely wasn't no spring chicken. . . .")? (Note how she uses a colloquialism, "hard-backed," a cliché, "spring chicken," and a double negative, "wasn't no"). Does she maintain this tone through the course of the essay?

n.   Why did Philip not consider writing a profession? How is this belief central to her comparison of cultures?

o.   Colonialism and its aftermath created a situation, according to Philip, where artists lost the autonomy to create "i-mages," where the ruling classes opposed new "i-mages" that threatened the status quo, where indigenously created "i-mages" were marginalized. What would be a healthy situation, according to Philip?

p.   What is the identifying quality of European culture according to Philip? Of African culture? Why must her writing reconcile or reunite these two polarities?

q.   With the discussion of "i-mage," does the essay adopt a different standard of language?

r.   Philip writes, "To keep the deep structure, the movement, the kinetic energy, the tone and pitch, the slides and glissandos of the demotic within a tradition that is primarily page-bound—that is the challenge." Does this sentence succeed in doing what Philip claims is her goal? Does it match the style of the opening of the essay? For what is Philip using prose?

s.   What does Philip mean by her distinction between father and mother tongue? Does it relate to her distinction between European and African cultures?

SUGGESTIONS FOR SHORT WRITING

a.   Write briefly on the distinction between American popular music and Canadian popular music. Does Canadian music respond to the "Father tongue" of American music?

b.   Does colonialism still exist? How and in what form? If not, why did it disappear?

c.   Compare and contrast a European film and an American film. What is the central difference?

d.   Whose comedians are funniest: Canada's, Britain's, or America's? Why?

SUGGESTIONS FOR SUSTAINED WRITING

a. Examine paintings of Canadian landscape from the 1900s and then by the Group of Seven. Compare and contrast the way the landscape is presented. Explain why the difference exists.

b. Find some recordings of indigenous music from the African coast and from the Caribbean. Compare and contrast the music.

c. Find out about Picasso's "primitive stage." Did the introduction of African art into European culture exploit African culture?

d. Does an artist like Paul Simon (*Graceland*, *Rhythm of the Saints*), who introduces lucrative North American audiences to world music, exploit/colonize these indigenous cultures or integrate them with a larger world?

Gals and Dolls: The Moral Value of "Bad" Toys
Marni Jackson

Marni Jackson was born in 1947 and lives in Toronto. She is well known for the bestselling book The Mother Zone: Love, Sex and Laundry in the Modern Family. *She is a regular contributor to the* Globe and Mail *and has written for* Saturday Night, The National Post, *and* Rolling Stone. *She has also written for the stage, served as a co-host for TVOntario's show* Imprint, *and taught writing at Ryerson School of Journalism. In all her writing, Jackson integrates her personal experience, her warmth, and her sense of humour.*

In the days before I actually had a child, child-rearing was a clearcut proposition: 1 simply Raise Them Right. Minimal TV, no hooker-type dolls or plastic Uzis, and a constant flow of high-fibre ideas from the morally evolved parent to the vulnerable, blank-slate child. I felt sorry for parents who didn't have the gumption to stick to this plan. Then I had a son, and the rest is—well, not so much history as culture.

Not since the days of Spock[1] have we had so much parental advice in the 2 air—how to raise kids, how to ruin them, how to "juggle work and family." This is why it's so refreshing to read someone like Alice Miller, the psychoanalyst-turned-writer whose books explore the childhood roots of violence and creativity. She doesn't have a theory about raising kids. In fact, she argues that *any* system of moral values imposed on children is potentially damaging, because too often the rules are there to serve the emotional needs of the parents, not the children. In the name of morality, we try to keep the unruly passions of children—not to mention memories of our own childhood—safe, tidy, and under control. Most pedagogy, good or bad, sends a hidden message to the child: "Your desires and feelings are not good enough. Feel this, think that, instead." If children require so much correction, then deep down—so they reason—they must be bad. Sooner or later the child who only hears this message learns to assemble an other-pleasing, false self around a core of inexplicable shame.

This doesn't mean that Miller thinks children ought to fingerpaint with their 3 food and otherwise disport themselves as gods. Post-Spockian permissiveness is just another form of pedagogy, really. But the experience of her own patients convinced her that it was the ones who were raised rigidly, with an overabundance of "good values," who were most likely to grow into benumbed adults, lost to themselves and predisposed to violence. The violence erupts in response to long-stifled childhood anger, which began as a perfectly human response to a voice that said "Don't be who you are, be good." The moral here—if we dare draw one—is that excessive handwringing about the values we are giving our kids may be as much about peer vanity as anything else. Values are not external; they are intrinsic to the sort of relationship we have with our children, arising out of the ordinary, humdrum

---

[1]**Dr. Spock:** Benjamin Spock (b. 1903) American pediatrician whose books on child-rearing influenced generations of parents.

way a family works and plays. The boy or girl who receives fair treatment, as opposed to "moral" correction, quickly develops an exquisite sense of justice—one that is more likely to shame the parent, rather than the other way round. (I'm moralizing here, of course.) Even young children bring a surprising amount of savvy and shit-detection to the moral bargaining table. To assume otherwise is to inflate our roles as parents into the architects and owners of our children's souls.

Now, Miller was talking about some fairly rigid, loveless households—   4
Hitler's[2] and Goebbels',[3] for instance. She wasn't necessarily addressing the problem of whether or not to buy your son a Nintendo, or to give your niece a Wet 'n' Wild Barbie. Nevertheless, I detect a lot of dubious pedagogy in our much-cogitated attitudes towards "good" and "bad" toys.

I know what happened with toy guns in our household. I went from a serene   5
pre-child conviction that guns would never cross our threshold to the ridiculous but amiable compromise my seven-year-old son and I have reached. Childish logic is impeccable. If you give him an innocent green water pistol for the bathtub, then why not the hideous toy M-16 in the backyard? If he can brandish a popsicle stick, why not a space laser? So he now owns a bow and arrow and a noncombat rawhide whip (history? art?), but he knows I have a "thing" about realistic guns, so he doesn't ask for them. He watches plenty of TV (all right, too much), but after flat-out indoctrination on my part—moral interference in the name of what I can or cannot stand to overhear—he now flips past the more violent kids' shows, of his own volition. Of course, our definitions of "violent" are continually being refined. But he's kind by nature, and always has been. I try not to improve on that too much.

There was a time, not so long ago, that Barbie dolls were considered the worst   6
sort of sex-stereotype propaganda. Barbie, with her foot permanently arched in the shape of a high heel, her long, scissoring legs, her high, hard, de-nippled breasts. It's true she's unswervingly represented a career gadfly, a weak-chinned Caucasian princess and a fashion flibbertigibbet—11 1/2 inches of beige plastic that has been accused of encouraging eating disorders, mindless consumerism and low self-esteem in little girls. Small wonder that to the Birkenstock generation,[4] Barbie was bad.

But little girls are not pushovers. They know what they like and they like   7
Barbie. Now 31 years old (but ever ageless and firm of chin), Barbie has triumphed over pedagogy, to the tune of over $500-million annually. Last year was the biggest year for Barbie sales in history. Some 98 percent of Canadian girls aged four to ten have a Barbie—or four—in their bedrooms. Like Coca-Cola, she has insinuated her hourglass, bottle-shaped self into 67 countries around the world. None of this will surprise parents with daughters, but it was news to me.

[2]**Hitler:** Adolf Hitler (1889–1945) Austrian-born demagogue who, as Führer, or leader, of the National Socialist Party, became Chancellor of Germany in 1933; Hitler was the architect of Germany's "Final Solution," a plan which led to the mass extermination of millions of people, mostly Jews, in death camps across eastern Europe during World War II.

[3]**Goebbels:** Josef Goebbels (1897–1945) Propaganda minister for the Nazi Party under Hitler.

[4]**"the Birkenstock generation":** a reference to the hippie counter-culture of the 1960s; many who participated in the social movement wore the famously comfortable Birkenstock sandals.

I went into several department stores to get a blast of Barbie, a feel for   8
Barbie, and there she was—row upon row of her and her almost identical pals, including li'l sister Skipper, brown-skinned Christie, freckle-faced sporty Midge,
Hispanic Nia, red-haired vixen Ashley. Her countless outfits run the gamut from
the tiny tubes of her pantyhose to wild salsa dresses, purses that turn into skirts and
skirts that turn into hair bows. Her eminently loseable accessories include teacups,
toe paint, Ferraris, guitars and running shoes.

After twenty years of feminism, you may ask, why don't little boys play with   9
Barbies? What *is* it about girls and dolls, anyway? Boys play with He-men and
Ninja turtle figures but the marriage between girls and their Barbies seems more
enduring. Girls' sense of pink and blueness also seems more acute, more pre-
cocious, although I base this only on the fact that I bought my son some plain but
purplish boots last year. They didn't bother him until he came home from school one
day and announced he couldn't wear them because they were "girls' boots." Who
had decreed this? "The girls in my room."

Are girls more proprietorial about identifiable girl things because they've   10
already detected an imbalance in the adult world, between boy toys (tanks and
guns) and female fun? Or is it something simpler—that at a certain age, children
want some kind of sex identity. Just because adults have bequeathed them a culture
that offers only testosterone-poisoned orange He-men and anorexic beige Barbies,
must we insist on snuffing out any sign of gender?

An eight-year-old girl in the neighborhood lugged over her five Barbies, in   11
two pink vehicles, for my inspection. While twirling and braiding the long blonde
tresses on one of them, she explained that although she doesn't want to *be* Barbie,
she really likes to play with her. "We make up stories that are like real life and then
we make the Barbies act them out," she said with admirable succinctness. "Her
body isn't very realistic," she admits, pointing the ballistic bosom of one towards
me. "In fact, the only realistic thing about it is her ears." If she were designing
them, she would go for more variation. "Like, it would be neat to have a tattooed
Barbie, or one with a bigger head. Her head is too small for her body." And Ken's
definitely in a rut. "I wouldn't mind a bald Ken, for example."

The sad truth is, Barbie has left the bland, rug-haired Ken behind in a span-   12
gled cloud of dust. Ken sales only amount to 35 percent of their combined total—and in fact, his shelf presence suggests more like a ratio of ten Barbies to
one Ken. Ken is looking more and more like a rented gigolo, or the guy who
takes Barbie's outfits to the cleaners and back. His accessories are laughable
(a slice of pizza, a kite, a basketball) and his weekend outfits are a bore (blue
pin-striped smock and navy pants). The only thing you can do with him, apart
from suicidal dives off the couch, is change his hair color from a terrible
fecal-mustard color to an obviously touched-up brown. While Barbie has a
choice of five stylish wedding gowns, Ken's lone wedding tuxedo is deplorable,
a nylon unitard with an ill-fitting white jacket and a shiny bow tie. His loafers
are interchangeable little boats. No wonder Barbie seems to prefer the company
of her on-the-go girlfriends.

When I saw Ken strapped stiffly into the passenger seat of Barbie's huge new 13
pink RV trailer, with plates that say "Barbie," I felt a stab of compassion for him.
As I was gazing at this harsh spectacle, a couple wandered down the aisle. "Oh
there's Ken," said the woman. "We were always so mean to Ken with our Barbies,
we used to do terrible things to him. I don't know why." Laughing, they moved
down the aisle to inspect a Baby Uh-Oh ("Give her a drink and uh-oh! . . . time to
change her diaper!").

However retrograde she appears to be, I sense Barbie is a survivor. Her mad- 14
deningly firm little bosom and fashion-victim personality, her fickle careers are all
voodoo tricks to ward off parental approval. If we had given Barbie a social conscience and sensible shoes, she might have moldered away at the bottom of the toy
bin. As it is, girls play with their uneducational Barbies as they always have, playing out the "mean babysitter" scenario, madly acting away, with no parent-pleasing
values to inhibit their stories. Therapists may envy the Barbie blankness—she too
can create a private, privileged space where any and every feeling is permitted. May
Barbie be "bad" as long as she reigns, for it is her lack of redeeming social value that
helps keep her true to the child's sense of play, instead of the parents' worst fears.

1991

QUESTIONS FOR DISCUSSION

Content

a. Why does Jackson like reading someone like Alice Miller?
b. Is the rejection of "*any* system of moral values" also a system?
c. Does Miller endorse absolute permissiveness and the rejection of all moral
   codes? What does she endorse?
d. What does Jackson say about "Childish logic"?
e. Why does Jackson spend more time dealing with Barbies than with toy guns?
f. Why is Barbie a "survivor"?
g. What is Jackson's understanding of children's play?
h. What is Jackson's thesis?

Strategy and Style

i. Why does Jackson open with her pre-parental opinions about child-raising?
j. Is the equation "If children require so much correction, then deep down—so
   they reason—they must be bad" sound reasoning?
k. Why does Jackson write, "The moral here—if we dare draw one"? Why does
   she hesitate to draw "a moral"?
l. What is the effect of bringing in names like "Hitler's and Goebbels'"?

m. How come Jackson is comfortable with "flat-out indoctrination on my part" when it comes to TV? Why does she openly admit her inconsistency on this front?

n. What does Jackson mean by "voodoo tricks"?

SUGGESTIONS FOR SHORT WRITING

a. Write about a "bad" toy that you secretly enjoyed.

b. Write about a guilty pleasure: a song you wouldn't want your friends to know you enjoy, a movie you would be embarrassed if your significant other knew you love, and so on.

c. How did you feel when your parents rejected certain toys or confiscated certain toys?

SUGGESTIONS FOR SUSTAINED WRITING

a. Explore the history of Barbie. Has Barbie changed over the years? How did these changes reflect what was going on in the society? (Remember, a reaction or a rejection is also reflection.)

b. Explore the historical connection between children's toys and TV. What is the relationship between the two? Use authentic examples to demonstrate your point.

c. In the seventeenth century, John Milton, defending freedom of the press, wrote, "Assuredly we bring not innocence into the world, we bring impurity much rather: that which purifies us is trial, and trial is by what is contrary." In her argument for morally "bad" toys, is not Jackson essentially endorsing the view that children are not innocent and that humanity is corrupt? Support your position from Jackson's text.

Two Views of the Mississippi

Mark Twain

Mark Twain (1835–1910) was, of course, the pen name of Samuel Langhorne Clemens, the Missourian who learned to pilot Mississippi riverboats and who grew to become one of America's leading humorists, social critics, and men of letters. Twain recorded his experiences in numerous newspaper features and columns and in several books, including Life on the Mississippi *(1883),* The Adventures of Tom Sawyer *(1876), and his masterpiece,* The Adventures of Huckleberry Finn *(1885). Indeed, for some literary historians, the true American novel has its beginnings in the work of Twain. In the selection that follows, Twain contrasts his views of the Mississippi first as a novice and then as an experienced river pilot.*

Now when I had mastered the language of this water, and had come to know every 1 trifling feature that bordered the great river as familiarly as I knew the letters of the alphabet, I had made a valuable acquisition. But I had lost something, too. I had lost something which could never be restored to me while I lived. All the grace, the beauty, the poetry, had gone out of the majestic river! I still keep in mind a certain wonderful sunset which I witnessed when steamboating was new to me. A broad expanse of the river was turned to blood; in the middle distance the red hue brightened into gold, through which a solitary log came floating black and conspicuous; in one place a long, slanting mark lay sparkling upon the water; in another the surface was broken by boiling, tumbling rings, that were as many-tinted as an opal; where the ruddy flush was faintest, was a smooth spot that was covered with graceful circles and radiating lines, ever so delicately traced; the shore on our left was densely wooded, and the somber shadow that fell from this forest was broken in one place by a long, ruffled trail that shone like silver; and high above the forest wall a clean-stemmed dead tree waved a single leafy bough that glowed like a flame in the unobstructed splendor that was flowing from the sun. There were graceful curves, reflected images, woody heights, soft distances; and over the whole scene, far and near, the dissolving lights drifted steadily, enriching it every passing moment with new marvels of coloring.

I stood like one bewitched. I drank it in, in a speechless rapture. The world 2 was new to me, and I had never seen anything like this at home. But as I have said, a day came when I began to cease from noting the glories and the charms which the moon and the sun and the twilight wrought upon the river's face; another day came when I ceased altogether to note them. Then, if that sunset scene had been repeated, I should have looked upon it without rapture, and should have commented upon it, inwardly, after this fashion: "This sun means that we are going to have wind tomorrow; that floating log means that the river is rising, small thanks to it; that slanting mark on the water refers to a bluff reef which is going to kill somebody's steamboat one of these nights, if it keeps on stretching out like that; those tumbling 'boils' show a dissolving bar and a changing channel there; the lines and circles in the slick water over yonder are a warning that that troublesome place is shoaling up dangerously; that silver streak in the shadow of the forest is the 'break' from a new snag, and he has located himself in the very best place he could have found to fish for steamboats; that tall dead tree, with a single living branch, is not going to last long, and then how is a body ever going to get through this blind place at night without the friendly old landmark?"

No, the romance and beauty were all gone from the river. All the value any 3 feature of it had for me now was the amount of usefulness it could furnish toward compassing the safe piloting of a steamboat. Since those days, I have pitied doctors from my heart. What does the lovely flush in a beauty's cheek mean to a doctor but a "break" that ripples above some deadly disease? Are not all her visible charms sown thick with what are to him the signs and symbols of hidden decay? Does he ever see her beauty at all, or doesn't he simply view her professionally, and comment upon her unwholesome condition all to himself? And doesn't he sometimes wonder whether he has gained most or lost most by learning his trade?

1883

QUESTIONS FOR DISCUSSION

Content

a. Why does Twain pity doctors?
b. What purpose does paragraph 3 serve? Why does Twain compare the work of a steamboat pilot to that of a doctor? In what way is the conduct of their work similar?
c. Twain fully describes his view of the river as a novice, then goes on to talk about his perception of it as a trained pilot. Does this pattern serve him better than discussing various aspects of the river point by point?
d. What details does Twain offer to prove that at one time in his life the river held grace, beauty, and poetry for him?

Strategy and Style

e. Twain's thesis, which appears in paragraph 1, is presented in an obvious and straightforward manner. How does it help determine the organization of the rest of the piece?
f. The first paragraph is filled with descriptive language that captures a subjective, almost rhapsodic, view of the river. How would you characterize the language found in paragraph 2?
g. What use does paragraph 2 make of the details Twain has already introduced in paragraph 1?

SUGGESTIONS FOR SHORT WRITING

a. Brainstorm a list of metaphors and similes that Twain might have used to describe the Mississippi River. For example, "the Mississippi River is a _____," or "the Mississippi River is like a _____."

b. Write the copy for a travel brochure for a steamboat holiday on the Mississippi.

SUGGESTIONS FOR SUSTAINED WRITING

a. Select a person or place you have known for a long time. Have your views on this individual or place changed significantly over the years? For better or worse? Explain.

b. As children, we become excited, enraptured, and even mystified by the rituals and customs associated with important religious or national holidays: Christmas, Yom Kippur, Thanksgiving, Halloween, the Fourth of July. Think about the holiday you found most exciting as a child. Has your view of it changed? Explain.

c. Twain's training as a pilot seems to have had a negative effect in that it took the romance out of his view of the river. However, learning more about a subject may enhance one's appreciation of it. Can you relate an instance from your own experience to illustrate this notion? For example, mastering the fundamentals of swimming may have given you the confidence you needed to try skin diving. Tuning your first engine may have motivated you to learn more about auto mechanics in general.

d. In a sense, Twain may be hinting at his disillusionment over his life as a pilot. Have you ever become disillusioned with a job? What were the causes of this disillusionment? Explain.

Survival Work

Lee Maracle

*Lee Maracle was born in 1950 in Vancouver. Maracle dropped out of school and joined the hippie subculture of the '60s before eventually attending Simon Fraser University. Maracle has written poetry (*Bent Box*), nonfiction (*I am woman: a native perspective on sociology and feminism*), novels (*Ravensong* and *Sundogs: A Novel*), and a collection of short stories (*Sojourner's Truth*). Her works frequently deal with issues of racism, sexism, and the domination of white culture.*

It's funny how there is such emphasis on women being in the kitchen. Some think 1
the negative. For me, it's so old, so understood, that it seems natural.

For us it was never an imprisonment—survival work—like chopping and 2
hauling wood must have been for the boys. But the kitchen was more than that for
me. It still is. I don't quite know how to describe my qualms about women who
don't like cooking, doing that kind of work. It isn't the cooking I love—only fools
enjoy washing dishes—though my mother swears she likes it. Solitary, she always
said. Alone time. It isn't the work. The kitchen is like the heart of the home. If the
body is ailing no one would suggest you cut out the heart, and yet, because there
is illness in our homes women want to cut the kitchen out of their lives.

The kitchen was where I really saw my mother, heard her thoughts and came 3
to understand her. Women can be alone in a crowd of people in the kitchen. It's
like that even now. My mom regrets the harshness of our childhood, and every now
and then I can see she wants to talk and we retreat to the kitchen. She washes
dishes and I rinse and put them away, slowly, while she hums out her sorrowful
memories, her children, working away, fending for themselves, me playing mom
to four little kids.

As a child, it never dawned on me that life was hard. There were no con- 4
veniences then, everything was done by hand from grinding corn meal to making
our own peanut butter—everything. Clothes were washed by hand and hung out
on the line or hung up inside the porch on one of those wooden foldouts. How
much each family would need, who had new children, whose kids were teenagers
and eating more, we planned our work according to how much food was needed
to bring us through another year. There was one occasion when no one had much
more than bannock and tea.

It was a rare day when there was no bannock and tea. I do recall the odd oc- 5
casion when the tea got used twice though. Generally, if we ran out of store tea lots
of kids were ready to pick wild tea—mint, comfrey, Labrador or the like.
Springtime rolled around and the dandelions were ready for picking, salmon berry
shoots, mint leaves and fiddleheads—that was salad. I still pick fiddleheads,
blanch them and melt them with butter—sautéed.

Everything was kind of slippery in our community then. I remember Dad 6
when he fell out of work—not fishing—he cooked, cleaned, or did whatever to

keep himself busy. If there was nothing to build, then there was something to clean. Even us kids. We had this old galvanized gray tub. Three times a week we all got cleaned up. The canning kettle would be on the stove, filled with water heating up to boil and the tub was half full of cold water. Mom would heave them around, or Dad, depending on who was there. One by one we jumped in and one of our parents, usually Mom, scrubbed us up. I don't suppose Mom thought it was such a gay time, but we loved it. We were all ticklish so it made it hard for her to wash our necks. We'd be jumping and dancing around, scrunching down our heads so she couldn't reach our necks, and giggling like crazy—that happened in the kitchen. When Dad was out of work, he was right there next to her, drying us up and laughing too.

I never actually taught my daughters to cook. We expect our children will remember what they need to know through watching or helping out. We never had anyone standing up there classroom-style and droning on about *it's time for cooking lessons*. My second daughter, not too long ago, was moaning one day that she didn't know how to cook. I told her, "My gawd, girl, you've been standing beside me in the kitchen, cutting up vegetables for years. Weren't you watching what I did with them? Didn't you see me stick them in a pot, not even once?" She laughed and said she was too busy listening to me talk to myself. She figured it out though, and now she is a pretty good cook—I am not sure if she just grew up or if being with her new man just naturally led her to domestic work. 7

There is an order to us working in the kitchen. When I was younger, before I had children and after I wasn't little anymore—between 10 and 20—I used to help out with the cooking wherever we were, tending the children or cleaning. No one told me I had to, but I think these things get passed on through watching others and kind of mastering who does what in the back of your mind—subconsciously. My kids don't have children and they are pretty big, so wherever we go they pitch in. If I am visiting someone my own age and we have teenage kids, they busy themselves serving us; if there are a lot of women, young and old, and no men, my husband and sons will start feeding us; sometimes if it's a more formal occasion and I want to show off, I cook. I expect my kids to help but not my company. Nothing is ever said, everything just kind of works itself out—like the same sense of order belongs to all of us. Some of our people are different, only women cook and in some of the younger families, the men share all the work. Now that my daughters are older they get to join the women more often. 8

In First Nations communities nothing seems to be preplanned or pre-determined. Everything depends on what you think/feel is expected of you. Planning is felt, order is sensed. You walk into the kitchen and look at your host and you know, she looks tired, or she looks like she wants to talk—with you—and you respond accordingly. Every home seems a bit different. That doesn't bother us because we can see the order of the home as soon as we walk in the door. In fact, we know that other Canadians don't know how to look and see the lay of the land. They'll come into your kitchen and ask if they can help. We never tire of laughing about that. 9

Nothing has changed for me except things are a little easier and a whole lot   10
less desperate. I still pick huckleberries with my brother, blackberries sometimes
with my kids, and put up fish and fruit. But now, if we run out, we can go to
Safeway or IGA. It is more for pleasure and just good eating than it used to be. I
don't think I will ever quit food gathering. When my brother and I go picking
huckleberries, we reminisce, laugh and just generally talk about how we feel about
life, family, folks. We even talk about the world, our philosophy and how the world
would be better off if people just did things our way, thought the way we do about
the world. What's the contemporary word for that—therapy—First Nations style.

There are foods out there in the bush that my body really needs, like fiddle-   11
heads, or certain medicines. You can buy fiddleheads, but those crazy people
charge a fortune for them. A little bitty jar costs a lot of money—and of course,
you can't buy any of the medicines we use. Besides, picking is social for us, like
visiting in the kitchen. I know two, three times a year I come up for gatherings with
writers in Penticton or Terrace, or to plan something. First thing the women do is
go out and pick berries if it's summer. Once I was late getting in. I didn't want to
wake Jeannette Armstrong up, so I stayed in the motel here and went straight to
the office in the morning. (I try not to be late for work.) I waited for the women. I
sat in that office for three hours before Delphine, Jeannette's sister, told me they
were all out picking berries. Well, I teased them when they got back after what
seemed like forever. I told them I was jealous. I think the meeting went better for
them having gone up the hill to gather food.

Once in Terrace, Ola and some white women organized a women's gather-   12
ing. In the morning before the workshops started one of the Native women said the
huckleberries were ripe. Pretty soon all the Native women were rummaging
around in the kitchen, looking for bowls or containers, and heading up the hill. We
talked and laughed, about some of the things our different Nations had in common,
culturally. It seems like every time we get together we tell about our ways and dig
around for things our different peoples have in common and we do it best when
we are working around the kitchen or out picking berries. I think we see things
more clearly when we are outside on a hill, plucking fat berries and swatting at
mosquitoes and thinking about eating or preparing food. There must be some connection between planning and eating. Anyways, turns out the white women were
angry about us later. Called us 'isolationist'. After the conference, a debate took
place by mail among them about the nature of our participation and whether or not
it was negative and divisive. They were upset about how we were able to hang out
together as though we had known each other a long time. No one told them to stay
in the lodge.

When I first moved to the city I left all those traditional foods behind. I got   13
sick and went back to the hills behind my home and memories came back. I had
such fun. I wondered why I had left it behind. Maybe you need to be hungry to appreciate your own foods and the food gathering process. The first time I realized
there wasn't enough money to carry us through the month, there I was gathering
dandelion leaves, camomile, comfrey and vetch peas and making salad—eating

grass, my kids said. They still tease me about that. They tell their friends when they were small and hungry I used to make them eat grass. My kids would say, "What are these?" and I'd say, "Never mind, just eat them, they're good for you." To tell the truth I don't remember the names for some of the things we still eat.

I only cooked for a living once. It was for a family of white people in South   14 Vancouver. I was 13 years old, though I don't think the woman realized I was that young. I had to babysit her three children all day—cook for them, etc.—and at night I cooked the main meal for the whole family. By the time we were five years old we knew how to watch people and see how they acted before we did anything dense. Well, I knew these white folk were different; not having been in any white people's homes, I wasn't sure just how to act, but I made out like I knew what I was doing anyway. Cooking for the kids wasn't too bad; they were fussy, saying they didn't like this or that, but I ignored them and fed them what their parents told me to. I didn't mind cooking for them, but I did not like cooking for their parents. I am not sure why. It wasn't that I had to work for someone else. I had done that in various farmers' fields. It wasn't that. All the cooking was done in the kitchen— alone. No one came by for dinner or even coffee. The eating was done in the dining room and the table was pre-set (by me). The meal was served by the father. A portion was handed out, pre-determined by the dad, and second helpings were unheard of. On top of all that, no one could leave until her plate was empty. The children were not allowed to talk. I presumed that meant me too. Once in a while the man and woman would argue. In front of us.

Maybe because I was a stranger—a stranger to their ways—we never got to   15 be friends. They were friendly enough, treating me like some long lost buddy or something, but I knew they were strangers in a way none of my own folks were. I was aware that I was not at home, nor in the home of anyone like me.

I had to decide on what to cook based on what I imagined their sense of eat-   16 ing to be—eating is so intimate and cultural. They didn't eat the same as we did. I didn't recognize half the stuff in the cupboards. What is Mr. Ragu anyway? There was a lot of instant this and instant that that I had no idea how to prepare.

She told me what the dinner menu was, pork chops on Monday, roast beef   17 on Tuesday, etc., and I was supposed to dream up some way of cooking it. Never in my life had we ever eaten that way. You gathered food all during the spring and summer, gathered whatever spices you could and tried like the devil to make it different and interesting each time you made it. No one had 'recipes' and I knew I couldn't read a cookbook to save my life. There I was standing in the middle of the kitchen, all the cupboards open, saying "Let's see what we got here, what am I supposed to do with all this stuff?" They ate a lot of pork, which I didn't like, and beef, my second least favourite food. When she said 'chops' I got a little confused. Chop was something you did with an axe to wood. Pork chops and applesauce (out of a store-bought jar, of course). My idea of fruit and meat is huckleberries and venison or salad and moose. I faked it. It took me half the day to make up some applesauce—later they showed me the canned goods. They never complained, but the formality of dinner was very uncomfortable for me. At home there are usually a dozen or so people sitting around yammering away, half the people not listening to the other half. It was like they, these white people, couldn't wait to finish their meal and get down to some serious TV watching. I think they don't like talking to each other much.

After dinner the woman would get on the phone and talk for ages to her 18 friends—electronic visiting, I called it when I told my sisters what it was like there. We had a lot of pretty good laughs about those people and their ways.

He was kind of mean to his kids too, though I don't think he thought himself 19 mean. The first day he asked me if all the children had eaten all of their breakfast and lunch. Theresa, the middle daughter, had not eaten her mush. Thinking he was just curious, I told him the truth. After dinner he goes into this strange ceremonial performance talking to his bird—a cockateel—and makes out like the bird tells him Theresa didn't eat her mush and then he punishes her—spanks her and sends her to bed. She hates the bird and tells the bird off before going to her room. I never told him the truth after that. What a ritual. Their sense of ceremony was weird.

That experience shaped me, somehow. Even though there are lots of things 20 I would rather do besides cooking, or eating for that matter, I could never 'hire' someone to do my cooking. But then, I have never been able to bring myself to a "beauty shop" so someone can fiddle with my hair. Grooming and survival work seem to be intimate, too personal to impose on someone else in your own home. It isn't like a restaurant. I think people who don't like doing their own cooking should go and eat at a restaurant. I have never felt resentful about spending so much time in the kitchen. We have a sense of pride about 'feeding the people' and our folks always treat the cooks good.

The kitchen is the heart of our homes. To have some stranger wander around 21 banging your pots and pans in front of your face would be like watching someone do your laundry or something. It wouldn't feel right.

I know a lot of young women feel differently, feel there shouldn't be so 22 much emphasis on women being the only ones who have to do the cooking and cleaning. Life is different now, it isn't like our men have to spend a lot of time building the family furniture and hauling firewood; and the jobs they do have don't seem as difficult as they used to be. Not even longshoremen work without machines. And women work. We all work all day; few of our families are structured so that the man works and the woman stays home. Young people are working out a new way of sharing, but I wouldn't like to lose the intimacy, the closeness of family and friends in our kitchens in the process.

Life has changed and we have to change with it. But I don't think that means 23 getting rid of the way we relate to each other, it just means coming to a new sense of cooperation. Now when I go home, we all seem to organize ourselves, cleaning up and cooking, and then we sit down and really enjoy the meal, report the day's news—gossip—and share a few laughs. No one thinks I am solely responsible for doing the physical labour of preparing the meal, but at the same time, I have not lost my voice in the family. My counsel, my advice has weight in my family. My family prefers it that way. I don't make any internal family decisions without consulting my family, but in the end, I plan with the full knowledge that my word has tremendous weight. I feel most comfortable, safe, in our environment the way it is. I think my daughters, young as they are, feel that way too. No one had to teach our fathers to share in the work: they knew that gathering wood used to be part of food preparation, and cooking is just another part of that process. Since it isn't necessary to gather wood anymore, young men will have to learn to cooperate in new ways. Just because my father gathered wood to help my mother cook, didn't mean he was her boss and she had no voice in the family; likewise, because a man helps with the cooking and cleaning ought not to erode the voice of women.

I don't think we are as hung up about the decision-making process and the 24 work process as a lot of white people. I mean everyone has to eat, so everyone gets busy. We also take each other's advice more seriously, respect each other's words. If someone wants to do something in a certain way, it is given careful consideration, particularly if that someone is the woman in whose home you are. We don't care whose name is on the mortgage documents, the home still belongs to the woman.

It is important that when we change, we change the things that aren't good 25 and keep the things that are. Our sense of cooperation, the sense that food is not personal property but a gift of creation that everyone is entitled to have. These things are important to our humanity. I would not like to visit my daughters by telephone and have to arrange an appointment to visit them and eat some of their food. That would upset me. It would destroy our families and erase our culture if the kitchen ceased to have its old meaning for us.

1992

QUESTIONS FOR DISCUSSION

Content

a. Maracle, after mentioning her mother, talks about her childhood. What kind of memories does she focus on?
b. How does Maracle teach her children?
c. How does Maracle develop and explain that "In First Nations communities nothing seems to be preplanned or pre-determined"?
d. How is berry picking therapeutic? What examples does she give to reinforce this idea?
e. How does Maracle show the difference between Native and white attitudes towards food and food gathering?
f. What cultural differences does Maracle discover when she cooks for the family in Vancouver?
g. What is the connection between voice and working in the kitchen?
h. How do men fit into the world of the kitchen?
i. What is Maracle's thesis or overall point?

Strategy and Style

j. What analogy does Maracle make between the kitchen and the body?

k. Why does she write that her father "fell out of work"?

l. Maracle begins a section about her childhood with her mother and ends the section with her father. How does this framing comment on gender in her family?

m. Why does Maracle tell the story of berry picking at the women's gathering?

n. How does Maracle use humour to show the clash of culture when she describes her experience cooking for the Vancouver family?

o. What is the effect of the story of the father who spanks his child for not eating? When she writes, "Their sense of ceremony was weird," do we agree?

SUGGESTIONS FOR SHORT WRITING

a. Write about your own attitudes towards working in the kitchen.

b. Write about the foods you like to cook. Why do you enjoy cooking them?

c. Maracle writes about gathering food. If you've ever picked wild berries or mushrooms or herbs or dandelions, describe the experience and why you did it. Is the experience of finding food different from growing or purchasing food?

SUGGESTIONS FOR SUSTAINED WRITING

a. Examine the machines that are in your kitchen. Discuss how each of them has altered our conception of the food we eat.

b. Which facilitates communication more: doing the dishes by hand or using a dishwasher and sitting down to tea/coffee? Why? Give real-life examples, not hypothetical examples.

c. The kitchen/hearth was once the most sacred part of any home. Is this still the case? Discuss which part of the home is the most significant today (you may even consider it to be the front lawn!). Support your position with examples. The real estate section of the newspaper may help you in this essay.

Neat People vs. Sloppy People

Suzanne Britt

Suzanne Britt teaches English at Meredith College in North Carolina. She writes a regular column for North Carolina Gardens and Homes *and for the* Dickens Dispatch, *a newsletter for fans of Charles Dickens. She has also published articles in the* New York Times, Newsweek, *and the* Boston Globe. *In addition to two composition textbooks, Britt has published two collections of essays,* Skinny People Are Dull and Crunchy Like Carrots *(1982) and* Show and Tell *(1983), from which the following selection is taken.*

I've finally figured out the difference between neat people and sloppy people. The distinction is, as always, moral. Neat people are lazier and meaner than sloppy people. 1

Sloppy people, you see, are not really sloppy. Their sloppiness is merely the unfortunate consequence of their extreme moral rectitude. Sloppy people carry in their mind's eye a heavenly vision, a precise plan, that is so stupendous, so perfect, it can't be achieved in this world or the next. 2

Sloppy people live in Never-Never Land. Someday is their métier. Someday they are planning to alphabetize all their books and set up home catalogs. Someday they will go through their wardrobes and mark certain items for tentative mending and certain items for passing on to relatives of similar shape and size. Someday sloppy people will make family scrapbooks into which they will put newspaper clippings, postcards, locks of hair, and the dried corsage from their senior prom. Someday they will file everything on the surface of their desks, including the cash receipts from coffee purchases at the snack shop. Someday they will sit down and read all the back issues of the *New Yorker*. 3

For all these noble reasons and more, sloppy people never get neat. They aim too high and wide. They save everything, planning someday to file, order, and straighten out the world. But while these ambitious plans take clearer and clearer shape in their heads, the books spill from the shelves onto the floor, the clothes pile up in the hamper and closet, the family mementos accumulate in every drawer, the surface of the desk is buried under mounds of paper and the unread magazines threaten to reach the ceiling. 4

Sloppy people can't bear to part with anything. They give loving attention to every detail. When sloppy people say they're going to tackle the surface of the desk, they really mean it. Not a paper will go unturned; not a rubber band will go unboxed. Four hours or two weeks into the excavation, the desk looks exactly the same, primarily because the sloppy person is meticulously creating new piles of papers with new headings and scrupulously stopping to read all the old book catalogs before he throws them away. A neat person would just bulldoze the desk. 5

Neat people are bums and clods at heart. They have cavalier attitudes toward possessions, including family heirlooms. Everything is just another dustcatcher to them. If anything collects dust, it's got to go and that's that. Neat people will toy with the idea of throwing the children out of the house just to cut down on the clutter. 6

239

Neat people don't care about process. They like results. What they want to 7
do is get the whole thing over with so they can sit down and watch the rasslin' on
TV. Neat people operate on two unvarying principles: Never handle any item
twice, and throw everything away.

The only thing messy in a neat person's house is the trash can. The minute 8
something comes to a neat person's hand, he will look at it, try to decide if it has
immediate use and, finding none, throw it in the trash.

Neat people are especially vicious with mail. They never go through their 9
mail unless they are standing directly over a trash can. If the trash can is beside the
mailbox, even better. All ads, catalogs, pleas for charitable contributions, church
bulletins and money-saving coupons go straight into the trash can without being
opened. All letters from home, postcards from Europe, bills and paychecks are
opened, immediately responded to, then dropped in the trash can. Neat people
keep their receipts only for tax purposes. That's it. No sentimental salvaging of
birthday cards or the last letter a dying relative ever wrote. Into the trash it goes.

Neat people place neatness above everything, even economics. They are in- 10
credibly wasteful. Neat people throw away several toys every time they walk
through the den. I knew a neat person once who threw away a perfectly good dish
drainer because it had mold on it. The drainer was too much trouble to wash. And
neat people sell their furniture when they move. They will sell a La-Z-Boy recliner
while you are reclining in it.

Neat people are no good to borrow from. Neat people buy everything in ex- 11
pensive little single portions. They get their flour and sugar in two-pound bags. They
wouldn't consider clipping a coupon, saving a leftover, reusing plastic nondairy
whipped cream containers or rinsing off tin foil and draping it over the unmoldy dish
drainer. You can never borrow a neat person's newspaper to see what's playing at the
movies. Neat people have the paper all wadded up and in the trash by 7:05 A.M.

Neat people cut a clean swath through the organic as well as the inorganic 12
world. People, animals, and things are all one to them. They are so insensitive. After they've finished with the pantry, the medicine cabinet, and the attic, they will
throw out the red geranium (too many leaves), sell the dog (too many fleas), and send
the children off to boarding school (too many scuffmarks on the hardwood floors).

1983

QUESTIONS FOR DISCUSSION

Content

a. What does Britt mean by the moral distinction between neat and sloppy people? How is this a *moral* distinction? Why, according to Britt's implication, are
neat people immoral?

b. Do you agree that "sloppiness is merely the unfortunate consequence of . . . extreme moral rectitude" (paragraph 2)? Where is this idea repeated?

c. What kind of neatness and sloppiness is the author actually talking about? She focuses on clutter, but does she imply other kinds of neatness and sloppiness?

d. Is Britt a neat or a sloppy person? How can you tell from the clues she gives in the essay?

e. On the surface, this essay might seem frivolous. Are there serious implications to it?

f. Does the author ever prove that neat people are lazy and mean and that sloppy people are less so?

Strategy and Style

g. Analyze the vocabulary Britt used to discuss sloppy people. How would you describe Britt's tone in this part of the essay? What tone does she use to discuss neat people?

h. Comment upon her use of generalizations. Why does she make statements like "Neat people place neatness above everything, even economics" (paragraph 10)?

i. Britt calls neat people "bums and clods at heart" (paragraph 6). Is she being harsh? If so, does her attitude destroy her credibility, or does it serve another purpose?

j. Where does Britt use irony especially well? How does the irony establish the tone of the piece?

SUGGESTIONS FOR SHORT WRITING

a. Define yourself as neat or sloppy. Write a short description of your bedroom, your closet, or the inside of your car; talk about your grooming habits and your clothing; or discuss the way you go about completing a common task like preparing a meal, painting a bedroom, or packing a suitcase.

b. Britt attributes various character traits to neat and sloppy people. In paragraph 7, for example, she says that "Neat people don't care about process." Challenge one such assertion by using personal experience as a source of information.

SUGGESTIONS FOR SUSTAINED WRITING

a. Turn the tables on Britt, and write an essay in which you argue that sloppy people are immoral, neat people moral. Begin by trying to answer each of Britt's assertions about neat people. Then explain what is immoral about sloppiness. You might find inspiration and information for this assignment in your responses to the second of the Suggestions for Short Writing.

b. Select two other oppositions into which people, animals, or objects can be divided, and write an essay in which you compare and contrast them. Depending upon your topic, consider using the subject-by-subject pattern, seen in Britt's essay, to organize your work.

At the Mercy of the Cure*

Mark Mathabane

Born in Alexandra township, South Africa, Mark Mathabane (b. 1960) came to the United States on a tennis scholarship and attended several American schools, including Dowling College, from which he took his bachelor's degree in 1983. By the age of 26, he had published the first volume of his autobiography, Kaffir Boy: The True Story of a Black Youth's Coming of Age in Apartheid South Africa *(1986). Mathabane describes his birthplace as a land of poverty and violence that can debilitate the strongest spirits.* Kaffir, *a term of extreme disparagement applied to black South Africans, prepares the reader for the physical and psychological degradation visited upon Mathabane's family, friends, and neighbours. Among the author's most vivid memories are the many times policemen raided his shantytown home to arrest his father. Mathabane's parents had emigrated "illegally" from one of the homelands, or tribal reserves, and his father lacked the proper documents to live under the same roof with his family. "At the Mercy of the Cure" is taken from the second volume of his autobiography,* Kaffir Boy in America *(1989). Mathabane is now a freelance lecturer and writer, living in North Carolina. His most recent book is* Out of the Madness: From the Projects to a Life of Hope *(1998), written with and about Jerrold Ladd.*

Upon returning to Dowling in the new year, 1982, I found a letter from home waiting for me with the miraculous news: My mother had finally been cured of her insanity. I was overwhelmed with joy. The contents of the letter related how Aunt Queen, the *isangoma,* had spent over a year treating my mother. She was said to have used *muti* (tribal medicine), consisting of special herbs, bark, and roots—and divination, a seeing into the past and future using bones. 1

Apparently my mother's kindness had done her in. While in South Africa she had, against my protestations and those of the family, taken in as boarders from the Giyani homeland in the Northern Transvaal a tall, raw-boned *nyanga* (medicine man) with bloodshot eyes, named Mathebula, and his family of five. They had nowhere else to go. The shack became home for about fifteen people; some slept under the tables, others curled up in corners and near the stove; there was no privacy. My mother had made it clear that their moving in with us was only a temporary measure, to provide them a roof over their heads while they hunted for their own shack. When months passed without the Mathebulas making any attempts at finding alternative housing, my mother had politely requested them to leave. This angered the wizard, a proud and chauvinistic man. Nonetheless he speedily constructed a shack in one of the rat-infested alleyways. But he never forgave my mother. 2

From strands of my mother's hair and pieces of her clothing, which he had gathered while he lived in our house, he allegedly concocted his voodoo and drove my mother mad. It took Aunt Queen almost a year to piece together what she 3

*Editors' title.

242

deemed a "dastardly plot." Daily, out in the yard, under the hot African sun, with my mother seated cross-legged across from her, my aunt shook bones and tossed them onto the ground. From interpreting their final positions she believed that she was able to name the sorcerer and the method he used to bewitch my mother. To a Western mind this of course sounds incredible and primitive. But witchcraft is a time-honored tradition among many African tribes, where convenient scapegoats are always blamed for events which, through limited knowledge and technology, seem inexplicable. Belief in witchcraft can be compared to a Westerner's belief in astrology holding answers to man's future and fate.

"Now you know the truth," Aunt Queen said to my mother at the end of her 4 confinement, when she was finally cured. The two spoke in Tsonga. "What do you want me to do?"

"Protect my family from further mischief."

"Is that all?"   5

"That's all."   6

                                                                                                              7

"Don't you want revenge? Are you simply going to let him go scot-free?"   8

"I'm not a witch. I'm a child of God. I harbor no malice toward him or his 9 family. I seek no revenge." My mother, despite her belief in witchcraft, still considered the Christian God to be all-powerful. This position of course had its contradictions, and since this episode occurred I have pointed them out to her from time to time. She has modified her beliefs and is now more under the sway of Christianity.

"But your ancestors must be satisfied," Aunt Queen said. "And what about 10 the pain he caused you? Do you know that he intended to kill you?"

"But Christ prevented that. He led me to you and gave you the power to 11 cure me."

"You know, Mudjaji [my mother's maiden name], you're so loving that it's 12 impossible for me to understand why anyone would want to harm you. The only thing left for me to do to complete your cure and prevent a relapse is to send the mischief back to its perpetrator." It was believed that no cure of witchcraft was complete until the black magic had reverted to the sorcerer.

"Please don't do anything that would harm him or his family," my mother 13 pleaded.

"The gods will decide," Aunt Queen said.   14

Two weeks after my mother returned to Alexandra, the sorcerer's favorite 15 son was stabbed to death during an argument in a *shebeen*. Hardly had he been buried when another of his sons was stabbed to death by *tsotsis* (gangsters) during a robbery and dumped in a ditch. My mother felt remorse over the deaths and grieved for the sorcerer's family. Aunt Queen told her that there was nothing she could have done to prevent their fate.

Here I was in America, in the heart of Western civilization itself, having to 16 grapple with the reality or unreality of witchcraft. I remember how my mother's incredible story tested my "civilized mentality," my Western education, my dependency on reason, my faith in science and philosophy. But in the end I realized that her insanity, of course, had rational causes, just as did Uncle Piet's gambling, matrimonial problems, my father's alcoholism, and the family's poverty—all of which they tended to blame on witchcraft. Either my mother's undiagnosed and untreated diabetes or the oppressive conditions under which she lived, or a combination of the two, had deranged her. Aunt Queen was the tribal equivalent of a shrink. Her "magical" treatments of diseases owed much to the power of suggestion and her keen knowledge of the medicinal effects of certain herbs, bark, leaves, and roots, from which, it has been discovered, a good deal of Western medicine has gained real remedies. As for the deaths of the Wizard's sons, this was, of course, pure coincidence, since Alexandra, especially the neighborhood in which my family lived, was an extremely violent place: On one weekend over a dozen murders were committed.

I realized all this from the knowledge I had gained since coming to America 17 and discovering that there was a branch of medicine of which I had been completely ignorant while I lived in South Africa: Psychoanalysis and psychiatry. The inhuman suffering experienced by blacks under apartheid had devastating effects on their mental and physical well-being. Given the primitive state of health care in the ghettos, endemic illiteracy, and the sway of tribal beliefs, my mother and most blacks were ignorant of causal relationships. They therefore blamed witchcraft for mental illnesses like schizophrenia and paranoia; diseases like malnutrition and tuberculosis; problems like unemployment, alcoholism, and gambling; and unlucky coincidences, such as being arrested during a pass raid while neighbors escaped, or being fired from a job. Their lack of access to qualified medical doctors, psychotherapists, and social workers forced them to rely on the dubious and often dangerous "cures" of *isangomas,* especially since such "cures" at least offered the victim much-needed psychological relief.

Superstition is present in Western societies as well, astrology being one ex- 18 ample. Some people also blame their misfortunes on the Devil. And many govern their lives through card-reading and palmistry, and rely on charlatans to cure them of cancer, AIDS, blindness, varicose veins, and other diseases. Until education dispelled my ignorance and fortified my reason I was to a degree superstitious and believed in witchcraft.

The psychological problems experienced by blacks in South African ghet- 19 tos are somewhat similar to those experienced by inmates of concentration camps during the Second World War. *From Death-Camp to Existentialism,* by Viktor E. Frankl, explains how psychotic behavior can become a "normal" way of life, a means of survival, for helpless people whose sense of identity and self-worth are under constant attack by an all-powerful oppressor. Jews in concentration camps were at the mercy of their Nazi guards, just as blacks in the ghettos of South Africa are at the mercy of apartheid's Gestapo-like police. Some victims of oppression even come to identify with their oppressors and persecute with relish their own kind. There are cases of Jews, known as Capos, who, in return for special privileges like food and cigarettes doled out by SS guards, treated other Jews sadistically and even herded them into crematoriums and gas chambers. In South Africa black policemen, in return for special privileges such as better housing, residential permits, and passbooks for relatives, shoot and kill unarmed black protesters, torture them in jail, uproot black communities under the homeland policy, and launch brutal raids into the ghettos to enforce Kafkaesque apartheid laws. Such are the evil consequences of unbearable pressures.

1989

QUESTIONS FOR DISCUSSION

Content

a. What is the author's purpose, and how do the comparisons he makes in this essay help him achieve that purpose?
b. Explain how the author's mother reconciled her belief in Christianity and her belief in witchcraft.
c. To what does the author attribute his mother's illness?
d. In what ways are the "cures" of the *isangomas* beneficial?

Strategy and Style

e. How does the frequent use of dialogue help make this complex essay clear?
f. Why does the author bother to tell us that superstition can also be found in the West? Why does he explain that Western medicine owes much to the "herbs, barks, leaves, and roots" Aunt Queen used as medicine (paragraph 16)?
g. Consider Mathabane's definition of terms. Is it important for us to be familiar with these terms? How do they help the author show similarities and differences between cultures?
h. Why did he introduce new ideas in the essay's conclusion? What light do they shed on what he said earlier?
i. This selection is an excerpt from a book. What expectations might the concluding paragraph establish about what will come next in that book?
j. In what ways is this piece typical of other comparison/contrast essays you have read? In what ways is it different? What other methods of development are used in this selection?

SUGGESTIONS FOR SHORT WRITING

a. Africa is not the only place where superstition maintains a strong hold. Mathabane mentions the popularity of astrology, card-reading, and palmistry in the West. List evidence you have observed that superstition has a place in Western society.
b. If you know someone who is suffering from a psychological disorder, drug or alcohol abuse, an addiction to gambling, or any other emotional problem, explain in logical terms the causes of his or her predicament.

SUGGESTIONS FOR SUSTAINED WRITING

a. Write a personal narrative about your mother or other member of the family who has been a powerful figure in the community. Show how that person has helped shape or guide the community. Like Mathabane, include dialogue and, if appropriate, make comparisons/contrasts with other people to reveal your subject's character.

b. Write an extended analytical response to Mathabane's essay. Begin by jotting down your thoughts about, and questions to, each paragraph; then, consider how these thoughts combine to form your overall opinion of, or reaction to, the piece. Finally, tell your readers how you have read and understood the essay, and point out to them what they may not have noticed in a casual reading.

Discordant Fruit

Lydia Minatoya

Lydia Minatoya (b. 1950) was born in Albany, New York. Her parents had emigrated to the United States from Japan, and had moved from the west coast to New York. Growing up so far away from relatives in California and Japan made Minatoya curious about her family and its history, so, after earning a PhD in psychology from the University of Maryland in 1981 and teaching briefly in Boston, she left to teach and travel in Japan, China, and Nepal. This trip prompted her to write Talking to High Monks in the Snow: An Asian-American Odyssey *(1992), which won the 1991 PEN/Jerard Fund Award. In this memoir, Minatoya focuses on her experiences growing up in a predominantly European-ancestry area and on her travels in Asia. "Discordant Fruit" is a chapter from this book; in it, Minatoya describes the awkward cultural tension she experiences during dinner with her upper-class relatives in Japan.*

Once, in a cross-cultural training manual, I came across a riddle. In Japan, a young 1 man and woman meet and fall in love. They decide they would like to marry. The young man goes to his mother and describes the situation. "I will visit the girl's family," says the mother. "I will seek their approval." After some time, a meeting between mothers is arranged. The boy's mother goes to the girl's ancestral house. The girl's mother has prepared tea. The women talk about the fine spring weather: Will this be a good year for cherry blossoms? The girl's mother serves a plate of fruit. Bananas are sliced and displayed in an exquisite design. Marriage never is mentioned. After the tea, the boy's mother goes home. "I am so sorry," she tells her son. "The other family has declined the match."

In the training manual, the following question was posed. How did the boy's 2 mother know the marriage was unacceptable? That is easy, I thought when I read it. To a Japanese, the answer is obvious. Bananas do not go well with tea.

All of my life, I have been fluent in communicating through discordant fruit. 3

"You're not serious about applying to be a foreign exchange student!" ex- 4 claims a high school teacher. "The point is to sponsor an *American* kid." On my application, I deliberately misspell the teacher's name. I cross it out with an unsightly splotch. "Take that you mean narrow man," I gloat in triumph.

"Your mother is so deferential, so *quiet*," says a boyfriend. "Women like that 5 drive me crazy." *His* mother is an attorney. That morning, I scorch his scrambled eggs. I hide the sports section of the Sunday news. "No insight, loudmouth fool," I mutter. Vengeance, I think, is mine.

The Japanese raise their daughters differently than their sons. *"Gambatte!"* 6 they exhort their sons. "Have courage, be like the carp, swim upstream!" *"Kiotsukete,"* they caution their daughters. "Be careful, be modest, keep safe."

In the old stories, men are warriors: Fierce and bold. But a lady never lunges 7 to slash the throat of an assailant. Instead, she writes a poem about harsh winter; how it can snap a slender stalk. Then she kills *herself* in protest. How the old stories galled me!

My mother was raised in a world such as this, in a house of tradition and 8 myth. And although she has traveled across continents, oceans, and time, although she considers herself a modern woman—a believer in the sunlight of science—it is a world that surrounds her still. Feudal Japan floats around my mother. Like an unwanted pool of ectoplasm, it quivers with supernatural might. It followed her into our American home and governed my girlhood life.

And so, I was shaped. In that feudal code, all females were silent and yield- 9 ing. Even their possessions were accorded more rights. For, if mistreated, belongings were granted an annual holiday when they could spring into life and complain.

And so, I was haunted. If I left my clothes on the floor, or my bicycle in the rain; if I yanked on my comb with roughness; if it splintered and lost its teeth (and 10 I did these things often and deliberately, trying to challenge their spell); then my misdeeds pursued me in dreams.

Emitting a hair-raising keening, my mittens would mourn for their mates. The floors I had scuffed, the doors I had slammed, herded me into the street. Bro- 11 ken dishes and dulled scissors joined them to form a large, shrill, and reproachful parade of dutiful ill-treated items. How I envied white children and the simple absolution of a spanking.

While other children were learning that in America you get what you ask for, I was being henpecked by inanimate objects. While other children were learning 12 to speak their minds, I was locked in a losing struggle for dominance with my clothing, my toys, and my tools.

The objects meant me no harm; they meant to humble and educate me. "Ownership," they told me "means obligation, caretaking, reciprocity." And al- 13 though I was a resistant student, in time I was trained. Well-maintained, my possessions live long, useful, and mercifully quiet lives of service.

The consequence, however, is that I cannot view my belongings as mere 14 conveniences. They cannot serve as simple timesavers. For me, acquisitiveness holds little allure. The indebtedness is much too great.

I am a woman who apologizes to her furniture. "Excuse me," I say when I 15 bump into a chair. My voice resonates with solicitude. In America, such behavior is viewed as slightly loony.

I am a woman caught between standards of East and West. "I disagree," I say to 16 elders, to the men in my life. My voice rises and cracks with shame. "Razor-tongue," relatives say with the pleasure of knowing. "No wonder she still is unmarried."

All these incongruities came flooding back while visiting my Japanese fam- 17 ily. The pull to be deferent. The push to be bold. The tension and richness between.

In the evening, after we left the patriarch's house, Sachikosan prepared a 18 feast. She kneeled before us, cooking a huge skillet of sukiyaki. She plucked plump morsels of tender beef from the pot and popped them onto my plate. Her teenaged daughters slipped shyly in and out of the room, bearing flasks of sake and platters of sushi.

Tadao-san, Yoshi, Mark, and I were seated at the table. Sachiko-san and the girls ate in the kitchen. "Where are the other women?" Mark asked Yoshi. "Yuri-chan is the guest," he replied. "She is being paid the house's high honor." 19

Loosened by the sake, chaffing from days of communicating only with me or through me, Mark bombarded Yoshi with questions. Did Yoshi like American rock and roll? Who were his favorite performers? 20

Uncomfortable with being the focus of attention, Yoshi attempted to generalize every query. "How familiar are Japanese youth with popular American music?" he translated for Tadao-san. 21

But Tadao-san was not fooled. Excluded in his own house, shunned in favor of his translator, Tadao-san grew increasingly irritable. 22

"How long has this one been riding autobikes?" he suddenly interjected. "Has he ever had an accident? Would he know how to make repairs should the autobike become disabled?" 23

At first, the American in me grinned. Clearly Tadao-san had grown weary of his subordinate role. He was asserting his authority. "How are you providing for Yuri-chan's safety?" his questions implied. "Do not forget you are welcome only in so far as you provide service to members of my house." 24

But quickly, the Japanese in me surfaced. The evening was not going smoothly and I was responsible. 25

"You're putting Yoshi on the spot!" I hissed into Mark's ear. "After all, he is not your host. Address your comments to the household head and try to act with more deference!" 26

"No kidding!" exclaimed Mark. He thought everything had been going along just fine. 27

I smiled apologetically at Yoshi and Tadao-san. My annoyance and bossy instructiveness had not gone unnoticed. I flushed mightily. I knew my behavior was most unseemly for a lady. 28

"So Tadao-san," said Mark heartily, "what do you think about all these protests of American military presence in Japan?" 29

Yoshi reeled in horror. How could he translate, with delicacy, such an openly confrontational question? 30

"Don't you think it's a little, uhmmm, *ungrateful?*" continued Mark. "After all, by picking up the bill for your country's defense, America has allowed Japan to become an economic competitor." 31

"How can you be so rude!" I croaked in anger. I staggered under the responsibility of having brought a boor into the ancestral house. 32

"Relax. You're overreacting," snapped Mark. "Besides, this is my conversation." Mark was growing tired of my conduct coaching. I could hardly blame him. Only a few days earlier, as we sat in a coffee shop and I instructed him on the proper method of ordering, I had overheard a comment. *"Rimokon,"* a woman had murmured to her companion. She had nodded in Mark's direction. *Rimokon* is a shortened form of *rimoto-kontororu.* It is the Japanese pronunciation of remote control: Slang for a henpecked man. 33

Tadao-san looked questioningly at Yoshi. What was the meaning of all this 34 clamor? Yoshi rushed to translate.

"This is a most difficult question," said Tadao-san after hearing an edited 35 translation.

I cringed. When a Japanese says a question is difficult he is requesting re- 36 lease from an uncomfortable situation.

"I work on a military base," said Mark, "and the sentiment is that Japan is 37 complaining about a free ride."

I wished we never had left the subject of rock and roll. I wished I were not 38 the honored guest. I wished I was with Sachiko-san, in the refuge of the kitchen.

Tadao-san and Yoshi caucused for a while. "Some Japanese believe that 39 America's motives are not fully benevolent," said Yoshi. His voice hesitated with the task of defusing the situation. "They say Americans do not fully view Asians as people. Japan and her people are expendable. Perhaps the point is not to defend Japan but rather to move the site of possible conflict. Asia may be a buffer zone. If war is based from Japan, South Korea, or the Philippines, the soil and civilians of these countries, not America, would be the first at risk."

"I don't know about that," muttered Mark.

"In each country, there are prejudices," said Tadao-san. "We Japanese are 40 prejudiced against the Koreans. I have read your history. Has there not been dis- 41 crimination against Japanese in America? Is there not discrimination today?"

"No," said Mark flatly.   42

"Of course there is!" I cried. We argued hotly for a minute. Then, remem- 43 bering that I was trying to act like a credit to my mother's upbringing, I demurred.

"Mark and I share slight disagreement about this point," I murmured with 44 sudden modesty.

Perhaps Mark was right. Perhaps I was overreacting. Perhaps among men, 45 even in Japan, verbal confrontations and positioning for power are acceptable so- cial forms. Perhaps when two samurai meet, they must engage in hostile sword play and find themselves well matched, before they can be friends.

The exchange of political opinions left me shaken, but Mark, Tadao-san, and 46 Yoshi seemed unscathed. They raised their cups and had a seemingly splendid time.

But then again, perhaps I was right. Before the evening ended, Tadao-san 47 slipped me an envelope. "In case you wish to leave the autobike, to continue, alone, by train," he said. Inside, was a staggering sum of money.

After midnight, Sachiko-san led me to her daughters' room. It was the room 48 of teenagers, a sweet jumble of stuffed animals and pinups of popular singers. Sev- eral pencil sketches were carefully mounted on one wall. Through a window, I saw the crescent moon.

"Come Yuri-chan." Sachiko-san led me to the sketches. "Come and see your 49 past."

The drawings were light, romantic renderings, of princesses all gowned and 50 gloved.

"Your mother lived here briefly, when she was a girl," Sachiko-san ex- 51
plained. "These are her drawings. My daughters found them in storage and thought
them pretty." She paused in reflection. "Your young mother's dreams have been
rescued and honored, mounted here on my little ones' wall."

Through the open window came the sound of a bamboo flute. Sachiko- 52
san looked at me with the warmth of a sister. She touched my hair gently and
smiled. "The hearts of young girls," she whispered to me, "their visions, forever, the same."

1992

QUESTIONS FOR DISCUSSION

Content

a. What does the title mean and why is it appropriate?

b. In paragraph 3 Minatoya says that she has "been fluent in communicating
   through discordant fruit." What are some of the examples she includes of this
   communication?

c. According to Minatoya, how are Japanese sons and daughters raised differently?

d. What are the main attributes of a typical American girl that Minatoya finds appealing? How are these traits seen as negative in traditional Japanese culture?

e. Why does Minatoya feel a sense of obligation to her possessions?

f. What is the "American in me" (paragraph 24) and the "Japanese in me" (paragraph 25)? How are they in conflict?

g. What is the relationship of language—word choice as well as gestures—to behaviour? How is some language appropriate and some language inappropriate,
   depending on the culture one is in?

h. Why is it difficult for Minatoya to assess whether the dinner party conversation was hostile or not?

Strategy and Style

i. Why is the comparison and contrast format effective for this essay? What exactly is being compared and contrasted?

j. How does the example about her possessions (paragraphs 9–14) help Minatoya make a point about Japanese women?

k. Where does Minatoya use humour and irony to make a point? Identify specific
   paragraphs. What are the points she makes with humour?

l. What storytelling technique does Minatoya use to make this unlike a "typical"
   essay?

m. What is the purpose of the last section (paragraphs 48–52)? How does it comment on the rest of the essay?

SUGGESTIONS FOR SHORT WRITING

a. Describe your relationship with your possessions. Do you feel responsible toward them? What do your possessions say about you?

b. Write the "script" of a conversation you had or heard in which people misunderstood each other. What were the reasons for the misunderstandings?

SUGGESTIONS FOR SUSTAINED WRITING

a. Compare and contrast two cultures with which you are familiar. If your family recently emigrated, your choice is easy, but you can also compare and contrast more subtly different cultures, such as comparing home to school, one block in your neighbourhood to another block, a rural area to an urban area, or one part of the country to another. Try some of the techniques that Minatoya uses, such as dialogue, personal examples, and humour to make your essay interesting.

b. Compare and contrast acceptable boys'/men's behaviour and girls'/women's behaviour as you have observed it in your family, neighbourhood, and school. Define what you see as the rules for acceptable behaviour for each sex. If you see any rules being challenged or changed, discuss these changes.

7

Illustration

Illustration is a natural habit of mind. How often have we offered a "for example" or "for instance" when, as we try to make a point, our listeners respond quizzically or simply shake their heads in disbelief? "What's so unhealthy about my diet?" demands a good friend whose eating habits you have just impugned. "For starters," you respond, "you are a French-fry fanatic, stuffing your face with the greasy, salt-laden sticks at nearly every meal. You eat so much red meat, butter, ice cream, and candy that the *New England Journal of Medicine* ought to report your intake of cholesterol, calories, and fat. And you probably don't even remember what fruits and vegetables look like."

The three examples that explain what you meant by *unhealthy* are products of a powerful and effective technique common to all types of expository or persuasive prose. Good writers are rarely content to tell their readers what they mean; they want to show it. One way to do this is to fill your work with relevant, well-developed illustrations—concrete representations of abstract ideas.

Effective illustrations make possible the explanation of ideas that might otherwise remain vague because they enable the reader to grasp particular realities behind the abstraction, to see specific and pertinent instances of the generality. "My Aunt Tillie is the most unselfish person in town," you may well exclaim. But consider how much more convincing your claim would become if you recalled the times she opened her home to folks who had no place to live, donated her savings to the hospital building fund, and took time off from work to help sick friends and relatives.

The clarity and strength illustration brings to your writing does not depend on the number of examples you include—although sheer volume can be convincing—but on the degree to which each example is clear, well developed, and appropriate to your thesis. Marshall McLuhan builds his entire essay around a single advertisement. The ad, however, is so startling that he can discuss it at length.

Depending on your purpose, you can choose from several kinds of examples to give your writing variety and power. Annie Dillard ranges widely and freely to gather illustrations from science, philosophy, and her own observations of nature as she considers the mystery that living things must die so that life can go on. Developments in the history of eating, each analyzed thoroughly, provide Peter Farb and George Armelagos with a trove of examples to show how the changes in table manners "reflect fundamental changes in human relationships." Edward T. Hall uses many brief scenarios of intercultural communication to make his point about the necessity of learning about other cultures. And Alice Bloom uses examples from her travels to make a point about American tourists and tourism.

Like most other methods of development, illustration is rarely used to the exclusion of other rhetorical techniques. In the selection by Robertson Davies, for instance, well-chosen examples develop categories (classification) through which the author sheds new and interesting light on the subject. Perhaps the richest variety of materials can be found in Jonathan Kozol's "Distancing the Homeless," where well-researched statistics, first-hand experience, and expert testimony make a compelling argument about the politics of homelessness.

Enjoy the selections in this chapter. They vary significantly in purpose, tone, and subject. Each is effective, however, because it explains an abstract idea in terms that will allow the reader to experience the concrete realities for which that abstraction stands. Each shows us ways to grapple with even the most unwieldy notions in language that is clear, powerful, and convincing.

How Not to Offend

Marshall McLuhan

Edmonton-born Marshall McLuhan (1911–1980) began his career as an English professor but soon came to be known internationally as a communications theorist. His ideas about the media made McLuhan a celebrity in the 1960s and '70s (he even makes a cameo appearance as himself in Woody Allen's Oscar-winning movie Annie Hall*). He gave us many of the terms and phrases that today are commonplace in understanding our media world: "global village," "hot and cool media," and "the medium is the message." The following early essay comes from a collection called* The Mechanical Bride, *written in 1951. In this collection of essays, McLuhan examines advertising as an art form that controls public consciousness.*

Closely related to the combination of moral fervor and know-how is the cult of 1 hygiene. If it is a duty to buy those appliances which free the body from toil and thus enable housewives not to hate their husbands, equally urgent is the duty to "be dainty and fresh." Under the scream caption we are told in tones of Kaltenborn unction:

> Too late, when love has gone, for a wife to plead that no one warned her of danger. Because a wise, considerate wife makes it her business to *find out* how to safeguard her daintiness in order to protect precious married love and happiness.

It would take much space just to list the current words and phrases related 2 to B.O. and to "leading the life of Life Buoy." Mouth washes, gargles, tooth pastes, hair removers, bubble baths, skin cleansers, and dirt chasers are backed by long-standing national advertising campaigns. "Even your best friends won't tell you." "Why be an Airedale?" and so on.

The present ad for Lysol, "a concentrated germ-killer," is typical of the shrill 3 melodramatic warnings that accompany these products and should be thought of in connection with the agonies of the daytime soap serials. The colored comics in the Sunday supplements frequently carry six or eight frame spot-dramas of the terrible penalties and dazzling rewards that life hands out to those who are neglectful or careful, as the case may be. In one of these, entitled "Georgie's Black Eye," a twelve-year-old boy is bragging to his mother how he got a shiner for defending her honor at school. Some of the fellows were sneering that her husband was running out on her. She didn't have what it takes to keep a man. Mom, mortified, gets busy with the tooth paste. Soon Dad is waltzing her around the living room and Georgie calls in the fellows to see for themselves. "Gosh," they say, "looks like he's going to haul off and kiss her."

Most of these ads feature ravishing chicks left in sordid isolation because 4 they "offend." Or a young couple on a bench sitting too far apart, the boy sulking. Overhead an old owl says, "Ooh, ooh, no woo." Or a handsome lad with dance card asks, "May I have the last waltz?" to an indignant girl who raps out, "You've *had* it!" Again, two girls are making up a party list and one says, with disgust on her face: "Invite *him*?—Over my dead body!" Of course, he was a swell kid, but: "Of late he had been pretty careless about a rather important thing, and the news got around fast. . . . While some cases of halitosis are of systemic origin, most cases, say a number of authorities . . ."

Another full-page spread shows a threesome in a panic: "Here comes Herb! 5 For Pete's sake duck!" After Herb goes back to his big car, they go on to say, "There ought to be a law."

Nair, a "cosmetic lotion to remove hair safely" pictures the sun leering at a 6 pair of legs: Have "Second Look" legs! . . . leaves legs smoother . . . more exciting.

> For Legs that Delight
> Use *Nair* Tonight

Pages could be filled with familiar items like "Kissing is fun when you use . . ." and "Keep daintier for dancing this way," and "Their lost harmony restored by . . ." and "Use *Fresh* and be lovelier to love."

It all adds up to this, that when the hideous specter of body odor looms, all 7 human ties are canceled. The offender, whether parent, spouse, or friend, puts himself outside the law. And when lovely woman stoops to B.O., she is a Medusa freezing every male within sniff. On the other hand, when scrubbed, deloused, germ-free, and depilatorized, when doused with synthetic odors and chemicals, then she is lovely to love. The question remains as to what is being loved, that gal or that soap? There is an age-old notion that healthy body odor is not only an aphrodisiac but a principal means of establishing human affinities.

Implied in the cult of hygiene is a disgust with the human organism which 8 is linked with our treating it as a chemical factory. D.H. Lawrence, rebelling against the puritan culture in which he was reared, insisted all his life that industrialization was linked to the puritan hatred of the body and detestation of bodily tasks. This, he claimed, not only was reflected in our hatred of housework and physical tasks but in our dislike of having servants smelling up our houses while helping with that work. So that the small, hygienic family unit of our cities and suburbs is, from this viewpoint, the realization of a Calvinist dream.

There is an old Huguenot hymn which goes: "Everybody stinks but Jesus." 9 And Kenneth Burke, in his *Ideas in History,* argues that the very synonym for scrupulous cleanliness, "a Dutch kitchen," means a Calvinist kitchen, and that the puritan world has merely substituted soap for the confessional. In the same way, Lewis Mumford in his *Culture of Cities* notes that: "Today, the degradation of inner life is symbolized by the fact that the only place sacred from interruption is the private toilet." Yet in the seventeenth century, when personal privacy was much valued, the highest classes of society openly performed acts of excretion at their *bidets* beside crowded dining tables. But today privacy stinks. The privacy that was once the refreshment of the mind and spirit is now associated only with those "shameful" and strenuous tasks by which the body is made fit for contact with other bodies. The modern nose, like the modern eye, has developed a sort of microscopic, intercellular intensity which makes our human contacts painful and revolting: "We might have had a wonderful life, but now she puts out both the cat and me." This is the world of Jonathan Swift, who foresaw and foresmelt these horrors. His Gulliver in the land of the giants records his disgust with the huge pores and monstrous smells of the Brobdingnagian beauties exactly in the spirit of current ad-agency rhetoric.

Clifton Webb as Lynn Belvedere recently enacted for the movies the role of 10
the impeccable gentleman. In creating this role he has at once embodied mechanical efficiency, moral disdain for ordinary humanity, and horror at human messiness
and dirt. He masters people and problems by sheer contempt. This witty role provides genuine insight into the cult of hygiene and the puritan mechanisms of modern applied science. Mr. Webb, as it were, satirically unrolls an entire landscape of
related activities and attitudes. In that landscape human reproduction would be ef-
fected, if at all, by artificial insemination. "Sex pleasure" would be entirely
auto-erotic. The feeding of babies would dispense with the foulness of the human
and animal secretion known as milk. The preparation and consumption of food
would be conducted in a clinic by white-coated officials. And excretion from the
cradle to the grave would be presided over by a special caste of robots, who would
care for the victims of such necessities in germ- and odor-proof laboratories.

Fear of the human touch and hatred of the human smell are perfectly 11
recorded by Mr. Webb in his role of Lynn Belvedere, the super baby trainer. They
are also a principal theme of Dr. Mead's *Male and Female,* where the reader will
discover her indignation that the child's earliest notions of virtue are associated
with punctual urination and excretion:

> The clean white-tiled restaurant and the clean white-tiled bathroom are both
> parts of the ritual, with the mother's voice standing by, saying: "If every rule
> of health is complied with, then you can enjoy life."

The bathroom has been elevated to the very stratosphere of industrial folklore, it
being the gleam, the larger hope, which we are appointed to follow. But in a world
accustomed to the dominant imagery of mechanical production and consumption,
what could be more natural than our coming to submit our bodies and fantasies to
the same processes? The anal-erotic obsession of such a world is inevitable. And
it is our cloacal obsession which produces the hysterical hygiene ads, the paradox
here being much like our death and mayhem obsession in the pulps on one hand,
and, on the other, our refusal to face death at all in the mortician parlor.

1951

QUESTIONS FOR DISCUSSION

Content

a. What is McLuhan's point about human body odour?
b. What examples does McLuhan use to demonstrate his point?
c. How does McLuhan support his argument that there is a basic "disgust with
the human organism"?
d. McLuhan quotes people from D.H. Lawrence to Kenneth Burke to Lewis
Mumford. Does he expect us to agree with him because these people appear to
agree with him (argument from authority)? Are these quotations effective? If
so, why? If not, why not?

e. McLuhan shifts from a discussion of Jonathan Swift, an eighteenth-century writer, to a Hollywood movie starring Clifton Webb. Are these shifts jarring? What is their effect on the reader?

f. The central ad discussed in the essay—Lysol as a douching solution for women—is rather shocking and extreme. Why does McLuhan use such an extreme example to build his essay around?

Strategy and Style

g. McLuhan uses a number of colloquial (and dated) terms such as "ravishing chicks." Why does he abandon a more formal academic tone?

h. McLuhan uses a rhetorical question—"The question remains as to what is being loved, that gal or that soap?" What answer is implied?

i. McLuhan makes the statement, "There is an age-old notion that healthy body odor is not only an aphrodisiac but a principal means of establishing human affinities." Why does he not bother to support this statement?

j. What is the effect of the term "anal-erotic obsession"?

k. In what sense has the bathroom been elevated "to the very stratosphere of industrial folklore"? How has McLuhan led up to this conclusion?

l. Does the essay maintain a consistent tone and use of language? Is the essay chatty, academic, or something akin to both?

SUGGESTIONS FOR SHORT WRITING

a. Describe your morning hygienic "routine." What parts can be omitted and what parts are essential?

b. Write about your feelings as you approach a job interview and realize that you forgot to use deodorant.

c. Write about any precautions you take to ensure that your breath, body, clothes, or home smells "fresh."

SUGGESTIONS FOR SUSTAINED WRITING

a. Examine the ads in a popular magazine or that appear on a single night of prime-time TV. Note the number that target anxiety about odour. Write about our current attitudes towards odour, using the examples to demonstrate your point.

b. Research the history of toothpaste or deodorant or bathing and soaps. Write an essay examining what the shift in concern and attitude indicates about our society.

c. Examine ads that appear on TV or in magazines. Try to determine the anxieties that they feed on. Write an essay about the anxieties that drive people's behaviour in our culture.

A Few Kind Words for Superstition

Robertson Davies

One of Canada's best-known satirists, novelists, and playwrights, Robertson Davies (1913–1995) was educated at Upper Canada College in Toronto, at Queen's University in Kingston, and at Oxford University in England. He began his career as a London actor and then worked as an editor for Saturday Night *in Toronto and for the* Examiner *in Peterborough, Ontario. He taught English at the University of Toronto and at Massey College, and served as Governor of the Stratford Shakespearean Festival in Stratford, Ontario. He was a fellow of the Royal Society of Canada and was a recipient of the Stephen Leacock Medal for Humour. He was also the first Canadian to become an honorary member of the American Academy and Institute of Arts and Letters. Davies published numerous plays and critical studies on drama and stagecraft and is known throughout Canada for the delightful satires he wrote under the pseudonym "Samuel Marchbanks." However, his reputation rests chiefly on his novels.* The Salterton Trilogy, *which includes* Tempest-Tost (1951), Leaven of Malice (1954), *and* A Mixture of Frailties (1958), *is a study of a fictional university town in Canada and of its middle-class inhabitants. The* Deptford Trilogy, *which is made up of* Fifth Business (1970), The Manticore (1972), *and* World of Wonders (1976), *affirms the important part that the irrational plays in an individual's search for spiritual identity. Other popular books by Davies are* What's Bred in the Bone (1985), The Papers of Samuel Marchbanks (1986), *and* The Lyre of Orpheus (1989).*

1 In grave discussions of "the renaissance of the irrational" in our time, superstition does not figure largely as a serious challenge to reason or science. Parapsychology, UFO's, miracle cures, transcendental meditation and all the paths to instant enlightenment are condemned, but superstition is merely deplored. Is it because it has an unacknowledged hold on so many of us?

2 Few people will admit to being superstitious; it implies naïveté or ignorance. But I live in the middle of a large university, and I see superstition in its four manifestations, alive and flourishing among people who are indisputably rational and learned.

3 You did not know that superstition takes four forms? Theologians assure us that it does. First is what they call Vain Observances, such as not walking under a ladder, and that kind of thing. Yet I saw a deeply learned professor of anthropology, who had spilled some salt, throwing a pinch of it over his left shoulder; when I asked him why, he replied, with a wink, that it was "to hit the Devil in the eye." I did not question him further about his belief in the Devil: but I noticed that he did not smile until I asked him what he was doing.

4 The second form is Divination, or consulting oracles. Another learned professor I know, who would scorn to settle a problem by tossing a coin (which is a humble appeal to Fate to declare itself), told me quite seriously that he had resolved a matter related to university affairs by consulting the I Ching. And why not? There are thousands of people on this continent who appeal to the I Ching, and their general level of education seems to absolve them of superstition. Almost, but not quite. The I Ching, to the embarrassment of rationalists, often gives excellent advice.

259

The third form is Idolatry, and universities can show plenty of that. If you 5
have ever supervised a large examination room, you know how many jujus, lucky
coins and other bringers of luck are placed on the desks of the candidates. Modest
idolatry, but what else can you call it?

The fourth form is Improper Worship of the True God. A while ago, I learned 6
that every day, for several days, a $2 bill (in Canada we have $2 bills, regarded by
some people as unlucky) had been tucked under a candlestick on the altar of a college chapel. Investigation revealed that an engineering student, worried about a
girl, thought that bribery of the Deity might help. When I talked with him, he did
not think he was pricing God cheap, because he could afford no more. A reasonable argument, but perhaps God was proud that week, for the scientific oracle went
against him.

Superstition seems to run, a submerged river of crude religion, below the 7
surface of human consciousness. It has done so for as long as we have any chronicle of human behavior, and although I cannot prove it, I doubt if it is more prevalent today than it has always been. Superstition, the theologians tell us, comes
from the Latin *supersisto,* meaning to stand in terror of the Deity. Most people
keep their terror within bounds, but they cannot root it out, nor do they seem to
want to do so.

The more the teaching of formal religion declines, or takes a sociological 8
form, the less God appears to great numbers of people as a God of Love, resum-
ing his older form of a watchful, minatory power, to be placated and cajoled. Superstition makes its appearance, apparently unbidden, very early in life, when children fear that stepping on cracks in the sidewalk will bring ill fortune. It may
persist even among the greatly learned and devout, as in the case of Dr. Samuel
Johnson, who felt it necessary to touch posts that he passed in the street. The psy-
choanalysts have their explanation, but calling a superstition a compulsion neuro-
sis does not banish it.

Many superstitions are so widespread and so old that they must have risen 9
from a depth of the human mind that is indifferent to race or creed. Orthodox Jews
place a charm on their door-posts; so do (or did) the Chinese. Some peoples of
Middle Europe believe that when a man sneezes, his soul, for that moment, is absent from his body, and they hasten to bless him, lest the soul be seized by the
Devil. How did the Melanesians come by the same idea? Superstition seems to
have a link with some body of belief that far antedates the religions we know—
religions which have no place for such comforting little ceremonies and charities.

People who like disagreeable historical comparisons recall that when 10
Rome was in decline, superstition proliferated wildly, and that something of the
same sort is happening in our Western world today. They point to the popularity of astrology, and it is true that sober newspapers that would scorn to deal in
love philters carry astrology columns and the fashion magazines count them
among their most popular features. But when has astrology not been popular?
No use saying science discredits it. When has the heart of man given a damn for
science?

Superstition in general is linked to man's yearning to know his fate, and to   11
have some hand in deciding it. When my mother was a child, she innocently joined
her Roman Catholic friends in killing spiders on July 11, until she learned that this
was done to ensure heavy rain the day following, the anniversary of the Battle of
Boyne, when the Orangemen would hold their parade. I knew an Italian, a good scientist, who watched every morning before leaving his house, so that the first person he met would not be a priest or a nun, as this would certainly bring bad luck.

I am not one to stand aloof from the rest of humanity in this matter, for when   12
I was a university student, a gypsy woman with a child in her arms used to appear
every year at examination time, and ask a shilling of anyone who touched the
Lucky Baby; that swarthy infant cost me four shillings altogether, and I never
failed an examination. Of course, I did it merely for the joke—or so I thought then.
Now, I am humbler.

1978

QUESTIONS FOR DISCUSSION

Content

a. What is Davies's thesis? Which paragraphs supply examples supporting this
   thesis?
b. Davies asserts in paragraph 11 that "superstition in general is linked to man's
   yearning to know his fate, and to have some hand in deciding it." Do you agree
   with this assertion? Is this a generalization?
c. What examples of superstitions does Davies include? What were his probable
   reasons for including them?
d. Are the examples of superstitions used as persuasive devices? If so, what are
   the readers being persuaded to do?
e. To what does the phrase " 'the renaissance of the irrational' " in the first sentence refer? What examples does Davies use? What examples can you add to
   the list?
f. What is Davies's answer to the last question in the first paragraph? How do you
   know? Why might Davies have used a question rather than a statement?
g. What are the four kinds of superstition? Do you agree with Davies that these
   types of superstition are still prevalent today?
h. Do you believe in any of the superstitions that Davies describes? Do you know
   of people who do? How do you account for belief in superstitions?
i. In the last paragraph Davies admits that what he did jokingly as a college student to ensure passing his examinations was actually done in earnest. Have you
   had any similar experiences?
j. According to Davies, what is the relationship between superstition and religion? Between superstition and science? Between superstition and history?

Strategy and Style

k. Why might Davies have first listed the four forms of superstition and then gone on to a discussion of superstition in general? How do the four forms of superstition establish expectations for the rest of the essay?

l. The author traces the word *superstition* to its Latin origin, "supersisto" (paragraph 7). Look up the origin of the words *divination, idolatry,* or any of the superstitions he lists. How do the origins of these words and superstitions help to illustrate his thesis?

m. What is Davies's attitude toward superstition? How is his attitude revealed through the tone of the piece?

SUGGESTIONS FOR SHORT WRITING

a. Describe the superstitions you or someone you know adhere to. Into which of Davies's categories do they fall?

b. Are the several questions Davies asks merely rhetorical? Try writing an answer to one or more of them.

SUGGESTIONS FOR SUSTAINED WRITING

a. Trace a popular superstition to its origins and write an essay explaining the relationship of the current superstition to its earlier forms. Try to account for the perseverance of the superstition.

b. Interview friends and fellow students, asking them what superstitions they have and how strongly they believe in them. Using these examples as the raw material for your essay, analyze these superstitions, putting forth your theory of why people believe in them.

c. Write a few unkind words for superstition. In what ways does belief in superstition harm society? Why should people try to divest themselves of superstitious beliefs?

Fecundity

Annie Dillard

Born in Pittsburgh in 1945, Annie Dillard made her mark early as a contributing editor to Harper's *magazine from 1973 to 1981. Before she was thirty, she had won a Pulitzer prize for* Pilgrim at Tinker Creek *(1974), a narrative about Virginia's Roanoke Valley, where she once lived. She has served on the U.S. Cultural Delegation to the People's Republic of China and on the National Commission of U.S.–China Relations. From these experiences came* Encounters with Chinese Writers *(1984). She has published two anthologies of narrative essays:* Holy the Firm *(1977) and* Teaching a Stone to Talk *(1982). She has also published poetry, including* Tickets for a Prayer Wheel *(1974). Dillard's most recent books are* An American Childhood *(1988),* The Writing Life *(1992),* The Living: A Novel *(1993), and* Mornings Like This *(1995). "Fecundity" is taken from* Pilgrim at Tinker Creek.

I have to look at the landscape of the blue-green world again. Just think: In all the clean beautiful reaches of the solar system, our planet alone is a blot; our planet alone has death. I have to acknowledge that the sea is a cup of death and the land is a stained altar stone. We the living are survivors huddled on flotsam, living on jetsam. We are escapees. We wake in terror, eat in hunger, sleep with a mouthful of blood. 1

Death: W. C. Fields called death "the Fellow in the Bright Nightgown." He shuffles around the house in all the corners I've forgotten, all the halls I dare not call to mind or visit for fear I'll glimpse the hem of his shabby, dazzling gown disappearing around a turn. This is the monster evolution loves. How could it be? 2

The faster death goes, the faster evolution goes. If an aphid lays a million eggs, several might survive. Now, my right hand, in all its human cunning, could not make one aphid in a thousand years. But these aphid eggs—which run less than a dime a dozen, which run absolutely free—can make aphids as effortlessly as the sea makes waves. Wonderful things, wasted. It's a wretched system. Arthur Stanley Eddington, the British physicist and astronomer who died in 1944, suggested that all of "Nature" could conceivably run on the same deranged scheme. "If indeed she has no greater aim than to provide a home for her greatest experiment, Man, it would be just like her methods to scatter a million stars whereof one might haply achieve her purpose." I doubt very much that this is the aim, but it seems clear on all fronts that this is the method. 3

Say you are the manager of the Southern Railroad. You figure that you need three engines for a stretch of track between Lynchburg and Danville. It's a mighty steep grade. So at fantastic effort and expense you have your shops make nine thousand engines. Each engine must be fashioned just so, every rivet and bolt secure, every wire twisted and wrapped, every needle on every indicator sensitive and accurate. 4

You send all nine thousand of them out on the runs. Although there are engineers at the throttles, no one is manning the switches. The engines crash, collide, 5 derail, jump, jam, burn . . . At the end of the massacre you have three engines, which is what the run could support in the first place. There are few enough of them that they can stay out of each others' paths.

You go to your board of directors and show them what you've done. And 6 what are they going to say? You know what they're going to say. They're going to say: It's a hell of a way to run a railroad.

Is it a better way to run a universe? 7

Evolution loves death more than it loves you or me. This is easy to write, 8 easy to read, and hard to believe. The words are simple, the concept clear—but you don't believe it, do you? Nor do I. How could I, when we're both so lovable? Are my values then so diametrically opposed to those that nature preserves? This is the key point.

Must I then part ways with the only world I know? I had thought to live by 9 the side of the creek in order to shape my life to its free flow. But I seem to have reached a point where I must draw the line. It looks as though the creek is not buoying me up but dragging me down. Look: Cock Robin may die the most grue-some of slow deaths, and nature is no less pleased; the sun comes up, the creek rolls on, the survivors still sing. I cannot feel that way about your death, nor you about mine, nor either of us about the robin's—nor even the barnacles'. We value the individual supremely, and nature values him not a whit. It looks for the mo-ment as though I might have to reject this creek life unless I want to be utterly bru-talized. Is human culture with its values my only real home after all? Can it pos-sibly be that I should move my anchor-hold to the side of a library? This direction of thought brings me abruptly to a fork in the road where I stand paralyzed, un-willing to go on, for both ways lead to madness.

Either this world, my mother, is a monster, or I myself am a freak. 10

Consider the former: The world is a monster. Any three-year-old can see 11 how unsatisfactory and clumsy is this whole business of reproducing and dying by the billions. We have not yet encountered any god who is as merciful as a man who flicks a beetle over on its feet. There is not a people in the world who behaves as badly as praying mantises. But wait, you say, there is no right and wrong in nature; right and wrong is a human concept. Precisely: We are moral creatures, then, in an amoral world. The universe that suckled us is a monster that does not care if we live or die—does not care if it itself grinds to a halt. It is fixed and blind, a robot programmed to kill. We are free and seeing; we can only try to outwit it at every turn to save our skins.

This view requires that a monstrous world running on chance and death, ca- 12 reening blindly from nowhere to nowhere, somehow produced wonderful us. I came from the world, I crawled out of a sea of amino acids, and now I must whirl around and shake my fist at that sea and cry Shame! If I value anything at all, then I must blindfold my eyes when I near the Swiss Alps. We must as a culture dis-semble our telescopes and settle down to back-slapping. We little blobs of soft tis-sue crawling around on this one planet's skin are right, and the whole universe is wrong.

Or consider the alternative. 13

Julian of Norwich, the great English anchorite and theologian, cited, in the 14
manner of the prophets, these words from God: "See, I am God: See, I am in all
things: See, I never lift my hands off my works, nor ever shall, without end . . .
How should anything be amiss?" But now not even the simplest and best of us sees
things the way Julian did. It seems to us that plenty is amiss. So much is amiss that
I must consider the second fork in the road, that creation itself is blamelessly,
benevolently askew by its very free nature, and that it is only human feeling that
is freakishly amiss. The frog that the giant water bug sucked had, presumably, a
rush of pure feeling for about a second, before its brain turned to broth. I, however,
have been sapped by various strong feelings about the incident almost daily for
several years.

Do the barnacle larvae care? Does the lacewing who eats her eggs care? If 15
they do not care, then why am I making all this fuss? If I am a freak, then why
don't I hush?

Our excessive emotions are so patently painful and harmful to us as a species 16
that I can hardly believe that they evolved. Other creatures manage to have effective matings and even stable societies without great emotions, and they have a
bonus in that they need not ever mourn. (But some higher animals have emotions
that we think are similar to ours: Dogs, elephants, otters, and the sea mammals
mourn their dead. Why do that to an otter? What creator could be so cruel, not to
kill otters, but to let them care?) It would seem that emotions are the curse, not
death—emotions that appear to have devolved upon a few freaks as a special curse
from Malevolence.

All right then. It is our emotions that are amiss. We are freaks, the world is 17
fine, and let us all go have lobotomies to restore us to a natural state. We can leave
the library then, go back to the creek lobotomized, and live on its banks as un-
troubled as any muskrat or reed. You first.

Of the two ridiculous alternatives, I rather favor the second. Although it is 18
true that we are moral creatures in an amoral world, the world's amorality does not
make it a monster. Rather, I am the freak. Perhaps I don't need a lobotomy, but I
could use some calming down, and the creek is just the place for it. I must go down
to the creek again. It is where I belong, although as I become closer to it, my fellows appear more and more freakish, and my home in the library more and more
limited. Imperceptibly at first, and now consciously, I shy away from the arts, from
the human emotional stew. I read what the men with telescopes and microscopes
have to say about the landscape. I read about the polar ice, and I drive myself
deeper and deeper into exile from my own kind. But, since I cannot avoid the library altogether—the human culture that taught me to speak in its tongue—I bring
human values to the creek, and so save myself from being brutalized.

What I have been after all along is not an explanation but a picture. This is 19
the way the world is, altar and cup, lit by the fire from a star that has only begun
to die. My rage and shock at the pain and death of individuals of my kind is the

old, old mystery, as old as man, but forever fresh, and completely unanswerable. My reservations about the fecundity and waste of life among other creatures is, however, mere squeamishness. After all, I'm the one having the nightmares. It is true that many of the creatures live and die abominably, but I am not called upon to pass judgment. Nor am I called upon to live in that same way, and those creatures who are are mercifully unconscious.

20   I don't want to cut this too short. Let me pull the camera back and look at that fork in the road from a distance, in the larger context of the speckled and twining world. It could be that the fork will disappear, or that I will see it to be but one of many interstices in a network, so that it is impossible to say which line is the main part and which is the fork.

21   The picture of fecundity and its excesses and of the pressures of growth and its accidents is of course no different from the picture I painted before of the world as an intricate texture of a bizarre variety of forms. Only now the shadows are deeper. Extravagance takes on a sinister, wastrel air, and exuberance blithers. When I added the dimension of time to the landscape of the world, I saw how freedom grew the beauties and horrors from the same live branch. This landscape is the same as that one, with a few more details added, and a different emphasis. I see squashes expanding with pressure and a hunk of wood rapt on the desert floor. The rye plant and the Bronx ailanthus are literally killing themselves to make seeds, and the animals to lay eggs. Instead of one goldfish swimming in its intricate bowl, I see tons and tons of goldfish laying and eating billions and billions of eggs. The point of all the eggs is of course to make goldfish one by one—nature lives the *idea* of the individual, if not the individual himself—and the point of a goldfish is pizzazz. This is familiar ground. I merely failed to mention that it is death that is spinning the globe.

22   It is harder to take, but surely it's been thought about. I cannot really get very exercised over the hideous appearance and habits of some deep-sea jellies and fishes, and I exercise easy. But about the topic of my own death I am decidedly touchy. Nevertheless, the two phenomena are two branches of the same creek, the creek that waters the world. Its source is freedom, and its network of branches is infinite. The graceful mockingbird that falls drinks there and sips in the same drop a beauty that waters its eyes and a death that fledges and flies. The petals of tulips are flaps of the same doomed water that swells and hatches in the ichneumon's gut.

23   That something is everywhere and always amiss is part of the very stuff of creation. It is as though each clay form had baked into it, fired into it, a blue streak of nonbeing, a shaded emptiness like a bubble that not only shapes its very structure but that also causes it to list and ultimately explode. We could have planned things more mercifully, perhaps, but our plan would never get off the drawing board until we agreed to the very compromising terms that are the only ones that being offers.

24   The world has signed a pact with the devil; it had to. It is a covenant to which every thing, even every hydrogen atom, is bound. The terms are clear: If you want to live, you have to die; you cannot have mountains and creeks without space, and

space is a beauty married to a blind man. The blind man is Freedom, or Time, and he does not go anywhere without his great dog Death. The world came into being with the signing of the contract. A scientist calls it the Second Law of Thermodynamics. A poet says, "The force that through the green fuse drives the flower/ Drives my green age." This is what we know. The rest is gravy.

1974

QUESTIONS FOR DISCUSSION

Content

a. What is Dillard's thesis? What is her purpose?

b. How does nature view the individual? How does this differ from the way human society views the individual?

c. What is Dillard getting at in the railroad analogy in paragraph 5?

d. Who is Cock Robin (paragraph 9), and why does Dillard mention this figure?

e. Explain how Julian of Norwich "sees things" (paragraph 14). To what end does the author quote this English theologian?

f. In what way, according to Dillard, is fecundity, a sign that there is something "amiss" in the world?

g. What does Dillard mean when she says, "The world has signed a pact with the devil; it had to" (paragraph 24)?

h. Why does the author's quoting W. C. Fields help her develop this essay?

i. In the end, this essay is about a very specific concern: Dillard's own mortality. Trace the development of this essay and explain how the author manages to arrive at that idea.

Strategy and Style

j. What illustrations does Dillard use to develop her essay? Why are they appropriate to her purpose?

k. What other methods of development does she use?

l. Why is Malevolence capitalized in paragraph 16?

m. Find evidence of humour in this selection.

n. What use does the author make of figurative language? Where does she use analogy?

o. Reread the essay's introduction. What about it is so compelling?

p. How would you describe the author's tone? What kind of audience is she writing to?

q. Analyze the style of any one of this essay's longer paragraphs, say 3, 9, 14, or 21. What kind of vocabulary and sentence structure does Dillard use? How does she manage to convey so much energy, excitement, and passion in a piece about so abstract a subject?

SUGGESTIONS FOR SHORT WRITING

a. This essay is filled with a number of provocative statements, such as "Evolution loves death more than it loves you or me" (paragraph 8) and "Either this world, my mother, is a monster, or I myself am a freak" (paragraph 10). Find one such statement that interests you, and interpret or explain it from your own point of view.

b. What do the creek and the library stand for? Write a paragraph or two to explain the analogy Dillard creates by contrasting these two places. Use details from the text to develop your explanation.

c. Write a paragraph in which you agree or disagree with Dillard's notion that nature does not value the individual (paragraph 9). Cite an example or examples to explain your answer.

SUGGESTIONS FOR SUSTAINED WRITING

a. Using Dillard's definition of *fecundity* as a starting point, explain your view of nature by using examples from your reading or experience. Is it a blind force that creates and destroys without plan or concern? Or is it more benevolent and purposeful?

b. Are right and wrong solely human concepts? Or are they present in nature as well? Defend your response by discussing examples of natural occurrences and animal behaviour that you have seen or read about.

c. Dillard seems to be trying to come to terms with her own mortality, something human beings have been trying to do for thousands of years. Discuss three or four examples of the ways in which people today deal with or come to terms with death. If you can, discuss at least one way in which we try to achieve immortality.

The Patterns of Eating

Peter Farb and George Armelagos

An anthropologist, naturalist, and acknowledged expert on the American Indian, Peter Farb (1929–1980) wrote numerous studies on the natural history of North America and of its original inhabitants. He also published several introductions to scientific subjects for young readers. Farb was educated at Vanderbilt and Columbia Universities. He worked as feature editor for Argosy *from 1950 to 1952 and as curator for the Riverside Museum in New York City from 1964 to 1971. He also held teaching positions at Yale University and at Calhoun College and served as a consultant to the Smithsonian Institution in Washington, D.C. From 1959 to 1963, Farb wrote a column for* Better Homes and Gardens *and has contributed numerous articles on science and nature to many other popular American magazines. Some of his best-known full-length works include* Living Earth *(1959),* The Forest *(1961),* Face of North America: The Natural History of a Continent *(1963), and* Man's Rise to Civilization as Shown by the Indians of North America from Primeval Times to the Coming of the Industrial State *(1968).*

George Armelagos (b. 1936) received his PhD in anthropology from the University of Colorado and is now professor of anthropology at the University of Massachusetts at Amherst. He has completed extensive research on the relationship between nutrition and human evolution.

Consuming Passions (1980), the book from which this selection was taken, is a fascinating and extremely well-documented look at the development of eating habits through the centuries. In it, Farb and Armelagos explain how the rituals we have come to associate with food preparation, table manners, and dietary practices in general have helped both reveal and define our cultural identity. "The interrelation of men and menus," wrote one Time *book reviewer, "has filled hundreds of texts. But none of them has digested so many facts so well."*

Among the important societal rules that represent one component of cuisine are 1 table manners. As a socially instilled form of conduct, they reveal the attitudes typical of a society. Changes in table manners through time, as they have been documented for western Europe, likewise reflect fundamental changes in human relationships. Medieval courtiers saw their table manners as distinguishing them from crude peasants; but by modern standards, the manners were not exactly refined. Feudal lords used their unwashed hands to scoop food from a common bowl and they passed around a single goblet from which all drank. A finger or two would be extended while eating, so as to be kept free of grease and thus available for the next course, or for dipping into spices and condiments—possibly accounting for today's "polite" custom of extending the finger while holding a spoon or small fork. Soups and sauces were commonly drunk by lifting the bowl to the mouth; several diners frequently ate from the same bread trencher. Even lords and nobles would toss gnawed bones back into the common dish, wolf down their food, spit onto the table (preferred conduct called for spitting under it), and blew their noses into the tablecloth.

By about the beginning of the sixteenth century, table manners began to   2
move in the direction of today's standards. The importance attached to them is indicated by the phenomenal success of a treatise, *On Civility in Children,* by the
philosopher Erasmus, which appeared in 1530; reprinted more than thirty times in
the next six years, it also appeared in numerous translations. Erasmus' idea of good
table manners was far from modern, but it did represent an advance. He believed,
for example, that an upper class diner was distinguished by putting only three fingers of one hand into the bowl, instead of the entire hand in the manner of the
lower class. Wait a few moments after being seated before you dip into it, he ad-
vises. Do not poke around in your dish, but take the first piece you touch. Do not
put chewed food from the mouth back on your plate; instead, throw it under the
table or behind your chair.

By the time of Erasmus, the changing table manners reveal a fundamental   3
shift in society. People no longer ate from the same dish or drank from the same
goblet, but were divided from one another by a new wall of constraint. Once the
spontaneous, direct, and informal manners of the Middle Ages had been repressed,
people began to feel shame. Defecation and urination were now regarded as private activities; handkerchiefs came into use for blowing the nose; nightclothes
were now worn, and bedrooms were set apart as private areas. Before the sixteenth
century, even nobles ate in their vast kitchens; only then did a special room designated for eating come into use away from the bloody sides of meat, the animals
about to be slaughtered, and the bustling servants. These new inhibitions became
the essence of "civilized" behavior, distinguishing adults from children, the upper
classes from the lower, and Europeans from the "savages" then being discovered
around the world. Restraint in eating habits became more marked in the centuries
that followed. By about 1800, napkins were in common use, and before long they
were placed on the thighs rather than wrapped around the neck; coffee and tea
were no longer slurped out of the saucer; bread was genteelly broken into small
pieces with the fingers rather than cut into large chunks with a knife.

Numerous paintings that depict meals—with subjects such as the Last Sup-   4
per, the wedding at Cana, or Herod's feast—show what dining tables looked like
before the seventeenth century. Forks were not depicted until about 1600 (when
Jacopo Bassano painted one in a Last Supper), and very few spoons were shown.
At least one knife is always depicted—an especially large one when it is the only
one available for all the guests—but small individual knives were often at each
place. Tin disks or oval pieces of wood had already replaced the bread trenchers.
This change in eating utensils typified the new table manners in Europe. (In many
other parts of the world, no utensils at all were used. In the Near East, for example, it was traditional to bring food to the mouth with the fingers of the right hand,
the left being unacceptable because it was reserved for wiping the buttocks.) Utensils were employed in part because of a change in the attitude toward meat. During the Middle Ages, whole sides of meat, or even an entire dead animal, had been
brought to the table and then carved in view of the diners. Beginning in the seventeenth century, at first in France but later elsewhere, the practice began to go out

of fashion. One reason was that the family was ceasing to be a production unit that did its own slaughtering; as that function was transferred to specialists outside the home, the family became essentially a consumption unit. In addition, the size of the family was decreasing, and consequently whole animals, or even large parts of them, were uneconomical. The cuisines of Europe reflected these social and economic changes. The animal origin of meat dishes was concealed by the arts of preparation. Meat itself became distasteful to look upon, and carving was moved out of sight to the kitchen. Comparable changes had already taken place in Chinese cuisine, with meat being cut up beforehand, unobserved by the diners. England was an exception to the change in Europe, and in its former colonies—the United States, Canada, Australia, and South Africa—the custom has persisted of bringing a joint of meat to the table to be carved.

Once carving was no longer considered a necessary skill among the well-bred, changes inevitably took place in the use of the knife, unquestionably the earliest utensil used for manipulating food. (In fact, the earliest English cookbooks were not so much guides to recipes as guides to carving meat.) The attitude of diners toward the knife, going back to the Middle Ages and the Renaissance, had always been ambivalent. The knife served as a utensil, but it offered a potential threat because it was also a weapon. Thus taboos were increasingly placed upon its use: It was to be held by the point with the blunt handle presented; it was not to be placed anywhere near the face; and most important, the uses to which it was put were sharply restricted. It was not to be used for cutting soft foods such as boiled eggs or fish, or round ones such as potatoes, or to be lifted from the table for courses that did not need it. In short, good table manners in Europe gradually removed the threatening aspect of the knife from social occasions. A similar change had taken place much earlier in China when the warrior was supplanted by the scholar as a cultural model. The knife was banished completely from the table in favor of chopsticks, which is why the Chinese came to regard Europeans as barbarians at their table who "eat with swords." 5

The fork in particular enabled Europeans to separate themselves from the eating process, even avoiding manual contact with their food. When the fork first appeared in Europe, toward the end of the Middle Ages, it was used solely as an instrument for lifting chunks from the common bowl. Beginning in the sixteenth century, the fork was increasingly used by members of the upper classes—first in Italy, then in France, and finally in Germany and England. By then, social relations in western Europe had so changed that a utensil was needed to spare diners from the "uncivilized" and distasteful necessity of picking up food and putting it into the mouth with the fingers. The addition of the fork to the table was once said to be for reasons of hygiene, but this cannot be true. By the sixteenth century people were no longer eating from a common bowl but from their own plates, and since they also washed their hands before meals, their fingers were now every bit as hygienic as a fork would have been. Nor can the reason for the adoption of the fork be connected with the wish not to soil the long ruff that was worn on the sleeve at the time, since the fork was also adopted in various countries where ruffs were not then in fashion. 6

Along with the appearance of the fork, all table utensils began to change and   7
proliferate from the sixteenth century onward. Soup was no longer eaten directly
from the dish, but each diner used an individual spoon for that purpose. When a
diner wanted a second helping from the serving dish, a ladle or a fresh spoon was
used. More and more special utensils were developed for each kind of food: Soup
spoons, oyster forks, salad forks, two-tined fondue forks, blunt butter knives, special utensils for various desserts and kinds of fruit, each one differently shaped, of
a different size, with differently numbered prongs and with blunt or serrated edges.
The present European pattern eventually emerged, in which each person is provided with a table setting of as many as a dozen utensils at a full-course meal. With
that, the separation of the human body from the taking of food became virtually
complete. Good table manners dictated that even the cobs of maize were to be held
by prongs inserted in each end, and the bones of lamb chops covered by ruffled
paper pantalettes. Only under special conditions—as when Western people consciously imitate an earlier stage in culture at a picnic, fish fry, cookout, or
campfire—do they still tear food apart with their fingers and their teeth, in a nostalgic reenactment of eating behaviors long vanished.

Today's neighborhood barbecue recreates a world of sharing and hospitality   8
that becomes rarer each year. We regard as a curiosity the behavior of hunters in
exotic regions. But every year millions of North Americans take to the woods and
lakes to kill a wide variety of animals—with a difference, of course: What hunters
do for survival we do for sport (and also for proof of masculinity, for male bonding, and for various psychological rewards). Like hunters, too, we stuff ourselves
almost whenever food is available. Nibbling on a roasted ear of maize gives us, in
addition to nutrients, the satisfaction of participating in culturally simpler ways. A
festive meal, however, is still thought of in Victorian terms, with the dominant
male officiating over the roast, the dominant female apportioning vegetables, the
extended family gathered around the table, with everything in its proper place—a
revered picture, as indeed it was so painted by Norman Rockwell, yet one that becomes less accurate with each year that passes.

1980

QUESTIONS FOR DISCUSSION

Content

a. What were the Last Supper, the wedding at Cana, and Herod's feast? How do
references to paintings of these events help illustrate important points about the
history of table manners?
b. Summarize the illustrations Farb and Armelagos use to distinguish manners in
the Renaissance from those of earlier eras. Does their treatment of the subject
need to be as graphic as it is?

c. What illustrations do Farb and Armelagos use to explain the Europeans' "ambivalent" attitude toward knives?

d. Who was Erasmus, and how did his ideas help advance table manners?

e. To what are Farb and Armelagos alluding when they tell us that the new table manners adopted by Europeans during the Renaissance distinguished them "from the 'savages' then being discovered around the world" (paragraph 3)? Why is the word *savages* in quotes?

f. This essay attempts to trace various developments that led to "the separation of the human body from the taking of food" (paragraph 7). How would you interpret this statement?

g. The authors claim that, early in the seventeenth century, the family "was ceasing to be a production unit" (paragraph 4). What did this development have to do with the profound changes in the way Europeans prepared and served meat?

h. Explain the Chinese's opinion of European eating habits. Why did the Chinese banish knives from their tables, and how did their doing so affect the development of their cuisine?

i. Why did forks come into use? What other "special utensils" and instruments have since become common in table settings?

j. What accounts for the fact that, in Canada, the United States, and other English-speaking countries, people still carve large cuts of meat at the table? Why do Farb and Armelagos consider this custom as well as the contemporary American cookout "a nostalgic reenactment of eating behaviors long vanished" (paragraph 7)?

k. How would you describe the work of Norman Rockwell, and why is one of his "revered pictures" mentioned in the conclusion?

Strategy and Style

l. How would you define the terms *Middle Ages* and *Renaissance?* Why does this essay begin with the former? Should the authors have begun with an earlier period of history?

m. What are the "Victorian terms" to which the authors allude in the concluding paragraph?

n. To what extent are Farb and Armelagos making fun of people's eating habits? Point out instances where the tone becomes humorous.

SUGGESTIONS FOR SHORT WRITING

a. Write about what you thought of eating etiquette before you read this essay. In what ways did the essay corroborate or challenge your thinking? Did it change your mind about what is proper etiquette?

b. Describe the eating habits of your family, your roommates, or the students at the campus cafeteria. At which stage of the evolution of eating patterns would you say they belong?

SUGGESTIONS FOR SUSTAINED WRITING

a. Describe and evaluate the table manners people use in your college's dining hall or cafeteria. Like Farb and Armelagos, use as many concrete illustrations as you can to make your writing vivid and convincing. You might want to submit this essay for publication in your college newspaper or literary magazine, so keep your audience in mind!

b. What makes a meal "festive"? Using illustration as your dominant method of development, discuss how this term might apply to your favourite holiday dinner. You need not focus on table manners exclusively. Describing place settings and table decorations or explaining the elaborate rituals that go into preparing traditional family dishes might also help illustrate your idea of "festive."

c. Describe one or more eating or cooking rituals from another culture that you find interesting. You might be able to gather many details about this topic from personal experience, from conversations with the foreign students you meet in your classes, or from chats with people who have immigrated to this country but still follow the traditional culinary practices of their homelands. Address this essay to someone who knows very little about the culture you're discussing, and be sure to include a sufficient number of examples and explanatory detail.

The Anthropology of Manners
Edward T. Hall

Edward T. Hall (b. 1914) is a well-known anthropologist and an expert on cultural differences in communication, manners, and perception of time. He studied at Pomona College; the University of Denver, where he received an AB; the University of Arizona, where he received an MA in 1938; and Columbia University, where he received a PhD in 1942. He did fieldwork from 1933 to 1942 with the Hopi and Navajo, some of which has reemerged in his most recent book, West of the Thirties *(1994). During World War II, Hall taught at the University of Denver and at Bennington College; after the war he worked on the atoll of Truk (Micronesia) helping the Truks and the U.S. Navy personnel understand each other's behaviour and cultures. On his return to the United States, Hall became the director of the Point Four program in the Foreign Service Institute, part of the U.S. State Department, from 1950 to 1955. There he designed training programs for workers assigned to posts in Latin America and the Middle East. He has had an active career, bridging both the academic and the commercial worlds. From 1955 to 1960, he was president of Overseas Training and Research, Inc., in Washington, D.C.; founded his own consulting firm in 1960; and he taught anthropology at the Illinois Institute of Technology from 1963 to 1967 and at Northwestern University from 1967 to 1977. Meanwhile, he was writing scholarly and popular books, only a few of which are* The Silent Language *(1959);* The Hidden Dimension *(1966);* Beyond Culture *(1976), from which "The Anthropology of Manners" is drawn; and* Dance of Life *(1983), which discusses time as a cultural concept.*

> The Goops they lick their fingers
>   and the Goops they lick their knives;
> They spill their broth on the table cloth—
>   Oh, they lead disgusting lives.
> The Goops they talk while eating,
>   and loud and fast they chew;
> And that is why I'm glad that I
>   am not a Goop—are you?

In Gelett Burgess' classic on the Goops we have an example of what anthropologists call "an enculturating device"—a means of conditioning the young to life in our society. Having been taught the lesson of the goops from childhood (with or without the aid of Mr. Burgess) Americans are shocked when they go abroad and discover whole groups of people behaving like goops—eating with their fingers, making noises and talking while eating. When this happens, we may (1) remark on the barbarousness or quaintness of the "natives" (a term cordially disliked all over the world) or (2) try to discover the nature and meaning of the differences in behavior. One rather quickly discovers that what is good manners in one context may be bad in the next. It is to this point that I would like to address myself.

The subject of manners is complex; if it were not, there would not be so 2 many injured feelings and so much misunderstanding in international circles everywhere. In any society the code of manners tends to sum up the culture—to be a frame of reference for all behavior. Emily Post goes so far as to say: "There is not a single thing that we do, or say, or choose, or use, or even think, that does not follow or break one of the exactions of taste, or tact, or ethics of good manners, or etiquette—call it what you will." Unfortunately many of the most important standards of acceptable behavior in different cultures are elusive: They are intangible, undefined and unwritten.

An Arab diplomat who recently arrived in the U.S. from the Middle East at- 3 tended a banquet which lasted several hours. When it was over, he met a fellow countryman outside and suggested they go get something to eat, as he was starving. His friend, who had been in this country for some time, laughed and said: "But, Habib, didn't you know that if you say, 'No, thank you,' they think you really don't want any?" In an Arab country etiquette dictates that the person being served must refuse the proffered dish several times, while his host urges him repeatedly to partake. The other side of the coin is that Americans in the Middle East, until they learn better, stagger away from banquets having eaten more than they want or is good for them.

When a public-health movie of a baby being bathed in a bathinette was 4 shown in India recently, the Indian women who saw it were visibly offended. They wondered how people could be so inhuman as to bathe a child in stagnant (not running) water. Americans in Iran soon learn not to indulge themselves in their penchant for chucking infants under the chin and remarking on the color of their eyes, for the mother has to pay to have the "evil eye" removed. We also learn that in the Middle East you don't hand people things with your left hand, because it is unclean. In India we learn not to touch another person, and in Southeast Asia we learn that the head is sacred.

In the interest of intercultural understanding various U.S. Government agen- 5 cies have hired anthropologists from time to time as technical experts. The State Department especially has pioneered in the attempt to bring science to bear on this difficult and complex problem. It began by offering at the Foreign Service Institute an intensive four-week course for Point 4 technicians. Later these facilities were expanded to include other foreign service personnel.

The anthropologist's job here is not merely to call attention to obvious 6 taboos or to coach people about types of thoughtless behavior that have very little to do with culture. One should not need an anthropologist to point out, for instance, that it is insulting to ask a foreigner: "How much is this in real money?" Where technical advice is most needed is in the interpretation of the unconscious aspects of a culture—the things people do automatically without being aware of the full implications of what they have done. For example, an ambassador who has been kept waiting for more than half an hour by a foreign visitor needs to understand that if his visitor "just mutters an apology" this is not necessarily an insult.

The time system in the foreign country may be composed of different basic units, so that the visitor is not as late as he may appear to us. You must know the time system of the country to know at what point apologies are really due.

Twenty years of experience in working with Americans in foreign lands convinces me that the real problem in preparing them to work overseas is not with taboos, which they catch on to rather quickly, but rather with whole congeries of habits and attitudes which anthropologists have only recently begun to describe systematically. 7

Can you remember tying your shoes this morning? Could you give the rules for when it is proper to call another person by his first name? Could you describe the gestures you make in conversation? These examples illustrate how much of our behavior is "out of awareness," and how easy it is to get into trouble in another culture. 8

Nobody is continually aware of the quality of his own voice, the subtleties of stress and intonation that color the meaning of his words or the posture and distance he assumes in talking to another person. Yet all these are taken as cues to the real nature of an utterance, regardless of what the words say. A simple illustration is the meaning in the tone of voice. In the U.S. we raise our voices not only when we are angry but also when we want to emphasize a point, when we are more than a certain distance from another person, when we are concluding a meeting and so on. But to the Chinese, for instance, overloudness of the voice is most characteristically associated with anger and loss of self-control. Whenever we become really interested in something, they are apt to have the feeling we are angry, in spite of many years' experience with us. Very likely most of their interviews with us, however cordial, seem to end on a sour note when we exclaim heartily: "WELL, I'M CERTAINLY GLAD YOU DROPPED IN, MR. WONG." 9

The Latin Americans, who as a rule take business seriously, do not understand our mixing business with informality and recreation. We like to put our feet up on the desk. If a stranger enters the office, we take our feet down. If it turns out that the stranger and we have a lot in common, up go the feet again—a cue to the other fellow that we feel at ease. If the office boy enters, the feet stay up; if the boss enters and our relationship with him is a little strained at the moment, they go down. To a Latin American this whole behavior is shocking. All he sees in it is insult or just plain rudeness. 10

Differences in attitudes toward space—what would be territoriality in lower forms of life—raise a number of other interesting points. U.S. women who go to live in Latin America all complain about the "waste" of space in the houses. On the other hand, U.S. visitors to the Middle East complain about crowding, in the houses and on the streetcars and buses. Everywhere we go space seems to be distorted. When we see a gardener in the mountains of Italy planting a single row on each of six separate terraces, we wonder why he spreads out his crop so that he has to spend half his time climbing up and down. We overlook the complex chain of communication that would be broken if he didn't cultivate alongside his brothers and his cousin and if he didn't pass his neighbors and talk to them as he moves from one terrace to the next. 11

A colleague of mine was caught in a snowstorm while traveling with com-   12
panions in the mountains of Lebanon. They stopped at the next house and asked
to be put up for the night. The house had only one room. Instead of distributing the
guests around the room, their host placed them next to the pallet where he slept
with his wife—so close that they almost touched the couple. To have done otherwise in that country would have been unnatural and unfriendly. In the U.S. we dis-
tribute ourselves more evenly than many other people. We have strong feelings
about touching and being crowded; in a streetcar, bus or elevator we draw ourselves in. Toward a person who relaxes and lets himself come into full contact with
others in a crowded place we usually feel reactions that could not be printed on
this page. It takes years for us to train our children not to crowd and lean on us. We
tell them to stand up, that it is rude to slouch, not to sit so close or not to "breathe
down our necks." After a while they get the point. By the time we Americans are
in our teens we can tell what relationship exists between a man and woman by how
they walk or sit together.

In Latin America, where touching is more common and the basic units of   13
space seem to be smaller, the wide automobiles made in the U.S. pose problems.
People don't know where to sit. North Americans are disturbed by how close the
Latin Americans stand when they converse. "Why do they have to get so close
when they talk to you?" "They're so pushy." "I don't know what it is, but it's something in the way they stand next to you." And so on. The Latin Americans, for their
part, complain that people in the U.S. are distant and cold—*retraídos* (withdraw-
ing and uncommunicative).

An analysis of the handling of space during conversations shows the fol-   14
lowing: A U.S. male brought up in the Northeast stands 18 to 20 inches away when
talking face to face to a man he does not know very well; talking to a woman under similar circumstances, he increases the distance about four inches. A distance
of only eight to 13 inches between males is considered either very aggressive or
indicative of a closeness of a type we do not ordinarily want to think about. Yet in
many parts of Latin America and the Middle East distances which are almost sexual in connotation are the only ones at which people can talk comfortably. In Cuba,
for instance, there is nothing suggestive in a man's talking to an educated woman
at a distance of 13 inches. If you are a Latin American, talking to a North American at the distance he insists on maintaining is like trying to talk across a room.

To get a more vivid idea of this problem of the comfortable distance, try   15
starting a conversation with a person eight or 10 feet away or one separated from
you by a wide obstruction in a store or other public place. Any normally encultur-
ated person can't help trying to close up the space, even to the extent of climbing
over benches or walking around tables to arrive within comfortable distance. U.S.
businessmen working in Latin America try to prevent people from getting uncomfortably close by barricading themselves behind desks, typewriters or the like, but
their Latin American office visitors will often climb up on desks or over chairs and
put up with loss of dignity in order to establish a spatial context in which interaction can take place for them.

The interesting thing is that neither party is specifically aware of what is 16 wrong when the distance is not right. They merely have vague feelings of discomfort or anxiety. As the Latin American approaches and the North American backs away, both parties take offense without knowing why. When a North American, having had the problem pointed out to him, permits the Latin American to get close enough, he will immediately notice that the latter seems much more at ease.

My own studies of space and time have engendered considerable coopera- 17 tion and interest on the part of friends and colleagues. One case recently reported to me had to do with a group of seven-year-olds in a crowded Sunday-school classroom. The children kept fighting. Without knowing quite what was involved, the teacher had them moved to a larger room. The fighting stopped. It is interesting to speculate as to what would have happened had the children been moved to a smaller room.

The embarrassment about intimacy in space applies also to the matter of ad- 18 dressing people by name. Finding the proper distance in the use of names is even more difficult than in space, because the rules for first-naming are unbelievably complex. As a rule we tend to stay on the "mister" level too long with Latins and some others, but very often we swing into first naming too quickly, which amounts to talking down to them. Whereas in the U.S. we use Mr. with the surname, in Latin America the first and last names are used together and señor (Sr.) is a title. Thus when one says, "My name is Sr. So-and-So," it is interpreted to mean, "I am the Honorable, his Excellency So-and-So." It is no wonder that when we stand away, barricade ourselves behind our desks (usually a reflection of status) and call ourselves mister, our friends to the south wonder about our so-called "good neighbor" policy and think of us as either high-hat or unbelievably rude. Fortunately most North Americans learn some of these things after living in Latin America for a while, but the aversion to being touched and to touching sometimes persists after 15 or more years of residence and even under such conditions as intermarriage.

The difference in sense of time is another thing of which we are not aware. 19 An Iranian, for instance, is not taught that it is rude to be late in the same way that we in the U.S. are. In a general way we are conscious of this, but we fail to realize that their time system is structured differently from ours. The different cultures simply place different values on the time units.

Thus let us take as a typical case of the North European time system (which 20 has regional variations) the situation in the urban eastern U.S. A middle-class businessman meeting another of equivalent rank will ordinarily be aware of being two minutes early or late. If he is three minutes late, it will be noted as significant but usually neither will say anything. If four minutes late, he will mutter something by way of apology; at five minutes he will utter a full sentence of apology. In other words, the major unit is a five-minute block. Fifteen minutes is the smallest significant period for all sorts of arrangements and it is used very commonly. A half hour of course is very significant, and if you spend three quarters of an hour or an hour, either the business you transact or the relationship must be important. Normally it is an insult to keep a public figure or a person of significantly higher status than yourself waiting even two or three minutes, though the person of higher position can keep you waiting or even break an appointment.

Now among urban Arabs in the Eastern Mediterranean, to take an illustra- 21 tive case of another time system, the unit that corresponds to our five-minute period is 15 minutes. Thus when an Arab arrives nearly 30 minutes after the set time, by his reckoning he isn't even "10 minutes" late yet (in our time units). Stated differently, the Arab's tardiness will not amount to one significant period (15 minutes in our system). An American normally will wait no longer than 30 minutes (two significant periods) for another person to turn up in the middle of the day. Thereby he often unwittingly insults people in the Middle East who want to be his friends.

How long is one expected to stay when making a duty call at a friend's house 22 in the U.S.? While there are regional variations, I have observed that the minimum is very close to 45 minutes, even in the face of pressing commitments elsewhere, such as a roast in the oven. We may think we can get away in 30 minutes by saying something about only stopping for "a minute," but usually we discover that we don't feel comfortable about leaving until 45 minutes have elapsed. I am referring to afternoon social calls; evening calls last much longer and operate according to a different system. In Arab countries an American paying a duty call at the house of a desert sheik causes consternation if he gets up to leave after half a day. There a duty call lasts three days—the first day to prepare the feast, the second for the feast itself and the third to taper off and say farewell. In the first half day the sheik has barely had time to slaughter the sheep for the feast. The guest's departure would leave the host frustrated.

There is a well-known story of a tribesman who came to Kabul, the capital 23 of Afghanistan, to meet his brother. Failing to find him, he asked the merchants in the market place to tell his brother where he could be found if the brother showed up. A year later the tribesman returned and looked again. It developed that he and his brother had agreed to meet in Kabul but had failed to specify what year! If the Afghan time system were structured similarly to our own, which it apparently is not, the brother would not offer a full sentence of apology until he was five years late.

Informal units of time such as "just a minute," "a while," "later," "a long 24 time," "a spell," "a long, long time," "years" and so on provide us with the culturological equivalent of Evil-Eye Fleegle's "double-whammy" (in *Li'l Abner*). Yet these expressions are not as imprecise as they seem. Any American who has worked in an office with someone else for six months can usually tell within five minutes when that person will be back if he says, "I'll be gone for a while." It is simply a matter of learning from experience the individual's system of time indicators. A reader who is interested in communications theory can fruitfully speculate for a while on the very wonderful way in which culture provides the means whereby the receiver puts back all the redundant material that was stripped from such a message. Spelled out, the message might go somewhat as follows: "I am going downtown to see So-and-So about the Such-and-Such contract, but I don't know what the traffic conditions will be like or how long it will take me to get a place to park nor do I know what shape So-and-So will be in today, but taking all this into account I think I will be out of the office about an hour but don't like to commit myself, so if anyone calls you can say I'm not sure how long I will be; in any event I expect to be back before 4 o'clock."

Few of us realize how much we rely on built-in patterns to interpret mes- 25 sages of this sort. An Iranian friend of mine who came to live in the U.S. was hurt and puzzled for the first few years. The new friends he met and liked would say on parting: "Well, I'll see you later." He mournfully complained: "I kept expecting to see them, but the 'later' never came." Strangely enough we ourselves are exasperated when a Mexican can't tell us precisely what he means when he uses the expression *mañana*.

The role of the anthropologist in preparing people for service overseas is to 26 open their eyes and sensitize them to the subtle qualities of behavior—tone of voice, gestures, space and time relationships—that so often build up feelings of frustration and hostility in other people with a different culture. Whether we are going to live in a particular foreign country or travel in many, we need a frame of reference that will enable us to observe and learn the significance of differences in manners. Progress is being made in this anthropological study, but it is also showing us how little is known about human behavior.

1955

QUESTIONS FOR DISCUSSION

Content

a. What are some of the differences between U.S. and Arab cultures, and between U.S. and Latin American cultures?

b. What is the difference between "taboos" and "habits and attitudes" (paragraph 7)? Why do habits and attitudes cause more problems for outsiders than taboos cause?

c. In paragraph 8 Hall mentions the "rules for when it is proper to call another person by his first name." What are some of the rules that Hall includes in this essay? What other rules can you add to the list?

d. What are some of the ways people of different cultures deal with space, both personal and architectural space?

e. What do anthropologists like Hall do? Why are their skills important?

Strategy and Style

f. Why is the Goop poem at the beginning of the essay so effective?

g. What is an "enculturating device" (paragraph 1)? Give some examples from the essay and from your own experience.

h. Go through the essay and mark or list the examples Hall uses. How many examples does he use for each point he makes?

i. Hall uses multiple examples to make his points, but he uses specific examples to represent a culture as a whole. In your opinion, are there any examples that might misrepresent the culture?

j. Hall writes quite informally. What might the essay sound like if he had written to an audience of scholars and other anthropologists? Why is the informal style more appropriate for general readers? What about Hall's style makes it informal?

SUGGESTIONS FOR SHORT WRITING

a. Reread paragraph 18. Describe the movement from formal to informal address as it occurs in the culture with which you are most familiar.

b. Write a humorous description, in the voice of an anthropologist if you would like, of one of your habits, explaining how that habit reflects your culture.

SUGGESTIONS FOR SUSTAINED WRITING

a. Observe and record behaviour in a study area, at a party, at a sports event, at a family gathering, etc. Try to find the rules that people are following but are not conscious of. Write an analytical essay in which you explain the rules, using specific examples from your observations. As a twist to this assignment, you could move from observer to participant, purposely break a rule, and record what happens. For example, in a nearly empty study area, break the rule of personal space by sitting next to a stranger to study.

b. List behaviours or other things from other cultures that puzzle you. Research—in the library but also by interviewing people from that culture—and write an essay explaining the culture to readers unfamiliar with the culture but who are planning to visit that country or countries. Make your goal similar to Hall's: "to open their eyes and sensitize them to the subtle qualities of behavior—tone of voice, gestures, space and time relationships" (paragraph 26).

c. What is "American culture"? Does the United States have a single, unchanging culture? Do you think the United States is a "melting pot" or a "patchwork" of distinctly different cultures? Write an opinion essay about these questions. If you think the United States is a melting pot, describe the American cultural traditions shared by everyone. If you think ethnic groups within the United States will always remain distinct and separate, explain, with examples, why this will be.

Distancing the Homeless

Jonathan Kozol

Teacher, author, and recipient of two National Book Awards, Jonathan Kozol (b. 1936) took his bachelor's degree at Harvard University and did graduate work at Magdalen College, Oxford. He writes extensively on the problems of homelessness, illiteracy, and poverty especially as they affect children. Kozol's best-known works, Death at an Early Age *(1967),* Illiterate America *(1985),* Rachel and Her Children: Homeless Families in America *(1988), and* Savage Inequalities: Children in American Schools *(1991) have helped arouse the conscience of a generation to problems that our presumably affluent society was supposed to have solved. This selection attacks many popular notions about homelessness and the homeless.*

It is commonly believed by many journalists and politicians that the homeless of America are, in large part, former patients of large mental hospitals who were de-institutionalized in the 1970s—the consequence, it is sometimes said, of mis-guided liberal opinion, which favored the treatment of such persons in commu-nity-based centers. It is argued that this policy, and the subsequent failure of society to build such centers or to provide them in sufficient number, is the pri-mary cause of homelessness in the United States.

Those who work among the homeless do not find that explanation satisfactory. While conceding that a certain number of the homeless are, or have been, mentally unwell, they believe that, in the case of most unsheltered people, the primary reason is economic rather than clinical. The cause of homelessness, they say with disarming logic, is the lack of homes and of income with which to rent or acquire them.

They point to the loss of traditional jobs in industry (2,000,000 every year since 1980) and to the fact that half of those who are laid off end up in work that pays a poverty-level wage. They point to the parallel growth of poverty in families with children, noting that children, who represent one quarter of our population, make up 40 percent of the poor; since 1968, the number of children in poverty has grown by 3,000,000, while welfare benefits to families with children have de-clined by 35 percent.

And they note, too, that these developments have coincided with a time in which the shortage of low-income housing has intensified as the gentrification of our major cities has accelerated. Half a million units of low-income housing have been lost each year to condominium conversion as well as to arson, demolition, or abandonment. Between 1978 and 1980, median rents climbed 30 percent for peo-ple in the lowest income sector, driving many of these families into the streets. Af-ter 1980, rents rose at even faster rates. In Boston, between 1982 and 1984, over 80 percent of the housing units renting below $300 disappeared, while the num-ber of units renting above $600 nearly tripled.

Hard numbers, in this instance, would appear to be of greater help than psy-chiatric labels in telling us why so many people become homeless. Eight million

American families now pay half or more of their income for rent or a mortgage. Six million more, unable to pay rent at all, live doubled up with others. At the same time, federal support for low-income housing dropped from $30 billion (1980) to $9 billion (1986). Under Presidents Ford and Carter, 500,000 subsidized private housing units were constructed. By President Reagan's second term, the number had dropped to 25,000. "We're getting out of the housing business, period," said a deputy assistant secretary of the Department of Housing and Urban Development in 1985.

One year later, the *Washington Post* reported that the number of homeless 6 families in Washington, D.C., had grown by 500 percent over the previous 12 months. In New York City, the waiting list for public housing now contains 200,000 names. The waiting is 18 years.

Why, in the face of these statistics, are we impelled to find a psychiatric ex- 7 planation for the growth of homelessness in the United States?

A misconception, once it is implanted in the popular imagination, is not easy 8 to uproot, particularly when it serves a useful social role. The notion that the homeless are largely psychotics who belong in institutions, rather than victims of displacement at the hands of enterprising realtors, spares us from the need to offer realistic solutions to the fact of deep and widening extremes of wealth and poverty in the United States. It also enables us to tell ourselves that the despair of homeless people bears no intimate connection to the privileged existence we enjoy— when, for example, we rent or purchase one of those restored town houses that once provided shelter for people now huddled in the street.

But there may be another reason to assign labels to the destitute. Terming 9 economic victims "psychotic" or "disordered" helps to place them at a distance. It says that they aren't quite like us—and, more important, that we could not be like them. The plight of homeless families is a nightmare. It may not seem natural to try to banish human beings from our midst, but it is natural to try to banish nightmares from our minds.

So the rituals of clinical contamination proceed uninterrupted by the eco- 10 nomic facts described above. Research that addresses homelessness as an *injustice* rather than as a medical *misfortune* does not win the funding of foundations. And the research which is funded, defining the narrowed borders of permissible debate, diverts our attention from the antecedent to the secondary cause of homelessness. Thus it is that perfectly ordinary women whom I know in New York City—people whose depression or anxiety is a realistic consequence of months and even years in crowded shelters or the streets—are interrogated by invasive research scholars in an effort to decode their poverty, to find clinical categories for their despair and terror, to identify the secret failing that lies hidden in their psyche.

Many pregnant women without homes are denied prenatal care because they 11 constantly travel from one shelter to another. Many are anemic. Many are denied essential dietary supplements by recent federal cuts. As a consequence, some of their children do not live to see their second year of life. Do these mothers sometimes show signs of stress? Do they appear disorganized, depressed, disordered? Frequently. They are immobilized by pain, traumatized by fear. So it is no surprise that when researchers enter the scene to ask them how they "feel," the resulting reports tell us that the homeless are emotionally unwell. The reports do not tell us we have *made* these people ill. They do not tell us that illness is a natural response to intolerable conditions. Nor do they tell us of the strength and the resilience that so many of these people still retain despite the miseries they must endure. They set these men and women apart in capsules labeled "personality disorder" or "psychotic," where they no longer threaten our complacence.

I visited Haiti not many years ago, when the Duvalier family was still in 12 power. If an American scholar were to have made a psychological study of the homeless families living in the streets of Port-au-Prince—sleeping amidst rotten garbage, bathing in open sewers—and if he were to return to the United States to tell us that the reasons for their destitution were "behavioral problems" or "a lack of mental health," we would be properly suspicious. Knowledgeable Haitians would not merely be suspicious. They would be enraged. Even to initiate such research when economic and political explanations present themselves so starkly would appear grotesque. It is no less so in the United States.

One of the more influential studies of this nature was carried out in 1985 by 13 Ellen Bassuk, a psychiatrist at Harvard University. Drawing upon interviews with eight homeless parents, Dr. Bassuk contends, according to the *Boston Globe*, that "90 percent [of these people] have problems other than housing and poverty that are so acute they would be unable to live successfully on their own." She also precludes the possibility that illness, where it does exist, may be provoked by destitution. "Our data," she writes, "suggest that mental illness tends to precede homelessness." She concedes that living in the streets can make a homeless person's mental illness worse; but she insists upon the fact of prior illness.

The executive director of the Massachusetts Commission on Children and 14 Youth believes that Dr. Bassuk's estimate is far too high. The staff of Massachusetts Human Services Secretary Phillip Johnston believes the appropriate number is closer to 10 percent.

In defending her research, Bassuk challenges such critics by claiming that 15 they do not have data to refute her. This may be true. Advocates for the homeless do not receive funds to defend the sanity of the people they represent. In placing the burden of proof upon them, Dr. Bassuk has created an extraordinary dialectic: How does one prove that people aren't unwell? What homeless mother would consent to enter a procedure that might "prove" her mental health? What overburdened shelter operator would divert scarce funds to such an exercise? It is an unnatural, offensive, and dehumanizing challenge.

Dr. Bassuk's work, however, isn't the issue I want to raise here; the issue is 16 the use or misuse of that work by critics of the poor. For example, in a widely syndicated essay published in 1986, the newspaper columnist Charles Krauthammer argued that the homeless are essentially a deranged segment of the population and that we must find the "political will" to isolate them from society. We must do this, he said, "whether they like it or not." Arguing even against the marginal benefits of homeless shelters, Krauthammer wrote: "There is a better alternative, however, though no one dares speak its name." Krauthammer dares: That better alternative, he said, is "asylum."

One of Mr. Krauthammer's colleagues at the *Washington Post,* the colum-   17
nist George Will, perceives the homeless as a threat to public cleanliness and argues that they ought to be consigned to places where we need not see them. "It is," he says, "simply a matter of public hygiene" to put them out of sight. Another journalist, Charles Murray, writing from the vantage point of a social Darwinist, recommends the restoration of the almshouses of the 1800s. "Granted Dickensian horror stories about almshouses," he begins, there were nonetheless "good almshouses"; he proposes "a good correctional 'halfway house' " as a proper shelter for a mother and child with no means of self-support.

In the face of such declarations, the voices of those who work with and know   18
the poor are harder to hear.

Manhattan Borough President David Dinkins made the following observa-   19
tion on the basis of a study commissioned in 1986: "No facts support the belief that addiction or behavioral problems occur with more frequency in the homeless family population than in a similar socioeconomic population. Homeless families are not demographically different from other public assistance families when they enter the shelter system . . . Family homelessness is typically a housing and income problem: The unavailability of affordable housing and the inadequacy of public assistance income."

In a "hypothetical world," write James Wright and Julie Lam of the Univer-   20
sity of Massachusetts, "where there were no alcoholics, no drug addicts, no mentally ill, no deinstitutionalization, . . . indeed, no personal social pathologies at all, there would still be a formidable homelessness problem, simply because at this stage in American history, there is not enough low-income housing" to accommodate the poor.

New York State's respected commissioner of social services, Cesar Perales,   21
makes the point in fewer words: "Homelessness is less and less a result of personal failure, and more and more is caused by larger forces. There is no longer affordable housing in New York City for people of poor and modest means."

Even the words of medical practitioners who care for homeless people have   22
been curiously ignored. A study published by the Massachusetts Medical Society, for instance, has noted that the most frequent illnesses among a sample of the homeless population, after alcohol and drug use, are trauma (31 percent), upper respiratory disorders (28 percent), limb disorders (19 percent), mental illness (16 percent), skin diseases (15 percent), hypertension (14 percent), and neurological illnesses (12 percent). (Excluded from this tabulation are lead poisoning, malnutrition, acute diarrhea, and other illnesses especially common among homeless infants and small children.) Why, we may ask, of all these calamities, does mental illness command so much political and press attention? The answer may be that

the label of mental illness places the destitute outside the sphere of ordinary life. It personalizes an anguish that is public in its genesis; it individualizes a misery that is both general in cause and general in application.

The rate of tuberculosis among the homeless is believed to be 10 times that 23 of the general population. Asthma, I have learned in countless interviews, is one of the most common causes of discomfort in the shelters. Compulsive smoking, exacerbated by the crowding and the tension, is more common in the shelters than in any place that I have visited except prison. Infected and untreated sores, scabies, diarrhea, poorly set limbs, protruding elbows, awkwardly distorted wrists, bleeding gums, impacted teeth, and other untreated dental problems are so common among children in the shelters that one rapidly forgets their presence. Hunger and emaciation are everywhere. Children as well as adults can bring to mind the photographs of people found in camps for refugees of war in 1945. But these miseries bear no stigma, and mental illness does. It conveys a stigma in the Soviet Union. It conveys a stigma in the United States. In both nations the label is used, whether as a matter of deliberate policy or not, to isolate and treat as special cases those who, by deed or word or sheer presence, represent a threat to national complacence. The two situations are obviously not identical, but they are enough alike to give Americans reason for concern.

Last summer, some 28,000 homeless people were afforded shelter by the city 24 of New York. Of this number, 12,000 were children and 6,000 were parents living together in families. The average child was six years old, the average parent 27. A typical homeless family included a mother with two or three children, but in about one-fifth of these families two parents were present. Roughly 10,000 single persons, then, made up the remainder of the population of the city's shelters.

These proportions vary somewhat from one area of the nation to another. In 25 all areas, however, families are the fastest-growing sector of the homeless population, and in the Northeast they are by far the largest sector already. In Massachusetts, three-fourths of the homeless now are families with children; in certain parts of Massachusetts—Attleboro and Northampton, for example—the proportion reaches 90 percent. Two-thirds of the homeless children studied recently in Boston were less than five years old.

Of an estimated two to three million homeless people nationwide, about 26 500,000 are dependent children, according to Robert Hayes, counsel to the National Coalition for the Homeless. Including their parents, at least 750,000 homeless people in America are family members.

What is to be made, then, of the supposition that the homeless are primarily 27 the former residents of mental hospitals, persons who were carelessly released during the 1970s? Many of them are, to be sure. Among the older men and women in the streets and shelters, as many as one-third (some believe as many as one-half) may be chronically disturbed, and a number of these people were deinstitutionalized during the 1970s. But in a city like New York, where nearly half the homeless are small children with an average age of six, to operate on the basis of such a supposition makes no sense. Their parents, with an average age of 27, are not likely to have been hospitalized in the 1970s, either.

Nor is it easy to assume, as was once the case, that single men—those who   28 come closer to fitting the stereotype of the homeless vagrant, the drifting alcoholic of an earlier age—are the former residents of mental hospitals. The age of homeless men has dropped in recent years; many of them are only 21 to 28 years old. Fifty percent of homeless men in New York City shelters in 1984 were there for the first time. Most had previously had homes and jobs. Many had never before needed public aid.

A frequently cited set of figures tells us that in 1955, the average daily cen-   29 sus of nonfederal psychiatric institutions was 677,000, and that by 1984, the number had dropped to 151,000. Subtract the second number from the first, conventional logic tells us, and we have an explanation for the homelessness of half a million people. A closer look at the same number offers us a different lesson.

The sharpest decline in the average daily census of these institutions oc-   30 curred prior to 1978, and the largest part of that decline, in fact, appeared at least a decade earlier. From 677,000 in 1955, the census dropped to 378,000 in 1972. The 1974 census was 307,000. In 1976 it was 230,000; in 1977 it was 211,000; and in 1978 it was 190,000. In no year since 1978 has the average daily census dropped by more than 9,000 persons, and in the six-year period from 1978 to 1984, the total decline was 39,000 persons. Compared with a decline of 300,000 from 1955 to 1972, and of nearly 200,000 more from 1972 to 1978, the number is small. But the years since 1980 are the period in which the present homeless crisis surfaced. Only since 1983 have homeless individuals overflowed the shelters.

If the large numbers of the homeless lived in hospitals before they reap-   31 peared in subway stations and in public shelters, we need to ask where they were and what they had been doing from 1972 to 1980. Were they living under bridges? Were they waiting out the decade in the basements of deserted buildings?

No. The bulk of those who had been psychiatric patients and were released   32 from hospitals during the 1960s and early 1970s had been living in the meantime in low-income housing, many in skid-row hotels or boarding houses. Such housing—commonly known as SRO (single-room occupancy) units—was drastically diminished by the gentrification of our cities that began in 1970. Almost 50 percent of SRO housing was replaced by luxury apartments or by office buildings between 1970 and 1980, and the remaining units have been disappearing at even faster rates. As recently as 1986, after New York City had issued a prohibition against conversion of such housing, a well-known developer hired a demolition team to destroy a building in Times Square that had previously been home to indigent people. The demolition took place in the middle of the night. In order to avoid imprisonment, the developer was allowed to make a philanthropic gift to homeless people as a token of atonement. This incident, bizarre as it appears, reminds us that the profit motive for displacement of the poor is very great in every major city. It also indicates a more realistic explanation for the growth of homelessness during the 1980s.

Even for those persons who are ill and were deinstitutionalized during the 33 decades before 1980, the precipitating cause of homelessness in 1987 is not illness but loss of housing. SRO housing, unattractive as it may have been, offered low-cost sanctuaries for the homeless, providing a degree of safety and mutual support for those who lived within them. They were a demeaning version of the community health centers that society had promised; they were the de facto "halfway houses" of the 1970s. For these people too, then—at most half of the homeless single persons in America—the cause of homelessness is lack of housing.

A writer in the *New York Times* describes a homeless woman standing on a 34 traffic island in Manhattan. "She was evicted from her small room in the hotel just across the street," and she is determined to get revenge. Until she does, "nothing will move her from that spot. . . . Her argumentativeness and her angry fixation on revenge, along with the apparent absence of hallucinations, mark her as a paranoid." Most physicians, I imagine, would be more reserved in passing judgment with so little evidence, but this author makes his diagnosis without hesitation. "The paranoids of the street," he says, "are among the most difficult to help."

Perhaps so. But does it depend on who is offering the help? Is anyone of- 35 fering to help this woman get back her home? Is it crazy to seek vengeance for being thrown into the street? The absence of anger, some psychiatrists believe, might indicate much greater illness.

The same observer sees additional symptoms of pathology ("negative symp- 36 toms," he calls them) in the fact that many homeless persons demonstrate a "gross deterioration in their personal hygiene" and grooming, leading to "indifference" and "apathy." Having just identified one woman as unhealthy because she is so far from being "indifferent" as to seek revenge, he now sees apathy as evidence of illness; so consistency is not what we are looking for in this account. But how much less indifferent might the homeless be if those who decide their fate were less indifferent themselves? How might their grooming and hygiene be improved if they were permitted access to a public toilet?

In New York City, as in many cities, homeless people are denied the right to 37 wash in public bathrooms, to store their few belongings in a public locker, or, in certain cases, to make use of public toilets altogether. Shaving, cleaning of clothes, and other forms of hygiene are prohibited in the men's room of Grand Central Station. The terminal's three hundred lockers, used in former times by homeless people to secure their goods, were removed in 1986 as "a threat to public safety," according to a study made by the New York City Council.

At 1:30 every morning, homeless people are ejected from the station. Many 38 once attempted to take refuge on the ramp that leads to Forty-Second Street because it was protected from the street by wooden doors and thus provided some degree of warmth. But the station management responded to this challenge in two ways. The ramp was mopped with a strong mixture of ammonia to produce a noxious smell, and when the people sleeping there brought cardboard boxes and newspapers to protect them from the fumes, the entrance doors were chained wide open. Temperatures dropped some nights to 10 degrees. Having driven these people to the streets, city officials subsequently determined that their willingness to risk exposure to cold weather could be taken as further evidence of mental illness.

At Pennsylvania Station in New York, homeless women are denied the use   39 of toilets. Amtrak police come by and herd them off each hour on the hour. In June 1985, Amtrak officials issued this directive to police: "It is the policy of Amtrak to not allow the homeless and undesirables to remain. . . . Officers are encouraged to eject all undesirables. . . . Now is the time to train and educate them that their presence will not be tolerated as cold weather sets in." In an internal memo, according to CBS, an Amtrak official asked flatly: "Can't we get rid of this trash?"

I have spent many nights in conversation with the women who are huddled   40 in the corridors and near the doorway of the public toilets in Penn Station. Many are young. Most are cogent. Few are dressed in the familiar rags suggested by the term *bag ladies.* Unable to bathe or use the toilets in the station, almost all are in conditions of intolerable physical distress. The sight of clusters of police officers, mostly male, guarding a toilet from use by homeless women speaks volumes about the public conscience of New York.

Where do these women defecate? How do they bathe? What will we do   41 when, in her physical distress, a woman finally disrobes in public and begins to urinate right on the floor? "Gross deterioration," someone will call it, evidence of mental illness. In the course of an impromptu survey in the streets last September, Mayor Koch observed a homeless woman who had soiled her own clothes. Not only was the woman crazy, said the mayor, but those who differed with him on his diagnosis must be crazy, too. "I am the number one social worker in this town—with sanity," said he.

It may be that this woman was psychotic, but the mayor's comment says a   42 great deal more about his sense of revulsion and the moral climate of a decade in which words like these may be applauded than about her mental state.

A young man who had lost his job, then his family, then his home, all in the   43 summer of 1986, spoke with me for several hours in Grand Central Station on the weekend following Thanksgiving. "A year ago," he said, "I never thought that somebody like me would end up in a shelter. Nothing you've ever undergone prepares you. You walk into the place [a shelter on the Bowery]—the smell of sweat and urine hits you like a wall. Unwashed bodies and the look of absolute despair on many, many faces there would make you think you were in Dante's Hell. . . . What you fear is that you will be here forever. You do not know if it is ever going to end. You think to yourself: It is a dream and I will awake. Sometimes I think: It's an experiment. They are watching you to find out how much you can take. . . . I was a pretty stable man. Now I tremble when I meet somebody in the ordinary world. I'm trembling right now. . . . For me, the loss of work and loss of wife had left me rocking. Then the welfare regulations hit me. I began to feel that I would be reduced to trash. . . . Half the people that I know are suffering from chest infections and sleep deprivation. The lack of sleep leaves you debilitated, shaky. You exaggerate your fears. If a psychiatrist came along he'd say that I was crazy. But

I was an ordinary man. There was nothing wrong with me. I lost my kids. I lost my home. Now would you say that I was crazy if I told you I was feeling sad?"

"If the plight of homeless adults is the shame of America," writes Fred **44** Hechinger in the *New York Times,* "the lives of homeless children are the nation's crime."

In November 1984, a fact already known to advocates for the homeless was **45** given brief attention by the press. Homeless families, the *New York Times* reported, "mostly mothers and young children, have been sleeping on chairs, counters, and floors of the city's emergency welfare offices." Reacting to such reports, the mayor declared: "The woman is sitting on a chair or on a floor. It is not because we didn't offer her a bed. We provide a shelter for every single person who knocks on our door." On the same day, however, the city reported that in the previous 11 weeks it had been unable to give shelter to 153 families, and in the subsequent year, 1985, the city later reported that about 2,000 children slept in welfare offices because of lack of shelter space.

Some 800 homeless infants in New York City, reported the National Coali- **46** tion for the Homeless, "routinely go without sufficient food, cribs, health care, and diapers." The lives of these children "are put at risk," while "high-risk pregnant women" are repeatedly forced to sleep in unsafe "barracks shelters" or welfare offices called Emergency Assistance Units (EAUs). "Coalition monitors, making sporadic random checks, found eight women in their *ninth* month of pregnancy sleeping in EAUs. . . . Two women denied shelter began having labor contractions at the EAU." In one instance, the Legal Aid Society was forced to go to court after a woman lost her child by miscarriage while lying on the floor of a communal bathroom in a shelter which the courts had already declared unfit to house pregnant women.

The coalition also reported numerous cases in which homeless mothers were **47** obliged to choose between purchasing food or diapers for their infants. Federal guidelines issued in 1986 deepened the nutrition crisis faced by mothers in the welfare shelters by counting the high rent paid to the owners of the buildings as a part of family income, rendering their residents ineligible for food stamps. Families I interviewed who had received as much as $150 in food stamps monthly in June 1986 were cut back to $33 before Christmas.

"Now you're hearing all kinds of horror stories," said President Reagan, **48** "about the people that are going to be thrown out in the snow to hunger and [to] die of cold and so forth. . . . We haven't cut a single budget." But in the four years leading up to 1985, according to the *New Republic,* Aid to Families with Dependent Children had been cut by $4.8 billion, child nutrition programs by $5.2 billion, food stamps by $6.8 billion. The federal government's authority to help low-income families with housing assistance was cut from $30 billion to $11 billion in Reagan's first term. In his fiscal 1986 budget, the president proposed to cut that by an additional 95 percent.

"If even one American child is forced to go to bed hungry at night," the pres- **49** ident said on another occasion, "that is a national tragedy. We are too generous a people to allow this." But in the years since the president spoke these words, thousands of poor children in New York alone have gone to bed too sick to sleep and far too weak to rise the next morning to attend a public school. Thousands more have been unable to attend school at all because their homeless status compels them to move repeatedly from one temporary shelter to another. Even in the affluent suburbs outside New York City, hundreds of homeless children are obliged to ride as far as 60 miles twice a day in order to obtain an education in the public schools to which they were originally assigned before their families were displaced. Many of these children get to school too late to eat their breakfast; others are denied lunch at school because of federal cuts in feeding programs.

Many homeless children die—and others suffer brain damage—as a direct 50 consequence of federal cutbacks in prenatal programs, maternal nutrition, and other feeding programs. The parents of one such child shared with me the story of the year in which their child was delivered, lived, and died. The child, weighing just over four pounds at birth, grew deaf and blind soon after, and for these reasons had to stay in the hospital for several months. When he was released on Christmas Eve of 1984, his mother and father had no home. He lived with his parents in the shelters, subways, streets, and welfare offices of New York City for four winter months, and was readmitted to the hospital in time to die in May 1985.

When we met and spoke the following year, the father told me that his wife 51 had contemplated and even attempted suicide after the child's death, while he had entertained the thought of blowing up the welfare offices of New York City. I would tell him that to do so would be illegal and unwise. I would never tell him it was crazy.

"No one will be turned away," says the mayor of New York City, as hundreds 52 of young mothers with their infants are turned from the doors of shelters season after season. That may sound to some like denial of reality. "Now you're hearing all these stories," says the president of the United States as he denies that anyone is cold or hungry or unhoused. On another occasion he says that the unsheltered "are homeless, you might say, by choice." That sounds every bit as self-deceiving.

The woman standing on the traffic island screaming for revenge until her 53 room has been restored to her sounds relatively healthy by comparison. If 3,000,000 homeless people did the same, and all at the same time, we might finally be forced to listen.

1988

QUESTIONS FOR DISCUSSION

Content

a. Why did Kozol write this essay? What is his thesis?
b. The author cites several examples of changes in U.S. public policy during the 1980s that significantly contributed to increases in homelessness. Identify two or three.

c. In several instances, he challenges our conventional perception of homelessness by picturing homeless people as sane while exposing public policy governing them as quite the opposite. Find and discuss such instances.

d. What is the author's response to those who argue that mental illness precedes and is a major cause of homelessness?

e. How does he answer Dr. Ellen Bassuk's claim that advocates for the homeless have been unable to provide data to prove that these people are not "unwell" (paragraph 15)?

f. Summarize the arguments of those who advocate isolating the homeless from the rest of society. How do you respond to such arguments?

g. What examples does Kozol include to illustrate inconsistency in public policy and attitudes toward the homeless?

h. What examples of public denial does the author cite?

i. Kozol has always been an advocate for children. In what way does this essay reflect that role?

Strategy and Style

j. What use does Kozol make of rhetorical questions? Where can such questions be found?

k. Why does he bother to compare homelessness in America with homelessness in Haiti?

l. What is similar about the way in which mental illness is viewed in the former Soviet Union and in the United States? Why does Kozol make this comparison?

m. Statistics can be powerful tools for illustration; they make abstract ideas clearer and more convincing. Where in this essay does Kozol use statistical or numerical data? Do you find such information convincing?

n. Why does the author bring up the case of the young man he quotes in paragraph 43? Why does he tell us about the woman who stands on a traffic island in Manhattan (paragraph 34)? Would his essay have been more effective had he explained the effects of homelessness on the population as a whole?

SUGGESTIONS FOR SHORT WRITING

a. How do you react when you come upon someone who is homeless? Do some freewriting that captures both your rational and your emotional response to what you see.

b. "A misconception, once it is implanted in the popular imagination, is not easy to uproot, particularly when it serves a useful social role," says Kozol in paragraph 8. Spend a few minutes explaining how this statement might apply to any social problem other than homelessness.

c. Isolate a section of this essay (two or three paragraphs) that argues a specific point about the nature of homelessness, about its causes or effects, or about public policy toward the homeless. Then, write a short statement in which you defend or attack the opinion expressed in those paragraphs.

SUGGESTIONS FOR SUSTAINED WRITING

a. If you responded to the first of the Suggestions for Short Writing above, review what you wrote. Next do some more freewriting about your overall impression of the problem of homelessness, its causes, and its effects. Use all of these notes to begin an essay that explains what, if anything, should be done about the problem.

b. If you live in a city with organizations that help the homeless, volunteer for at least a short time in a soup kitchen or shelter, or get involved in some other way with the organization. Then, write a narrative essay about your experiences, citing Kozol's article when appropriate. Your experiences could also form the basis for an argumentative essay.

c. Using Kozol's organization as a general model, research a critical current issue about which you feel strongly. Begin by becoming familiar with the general background and parameters of the issue, making a list of questions you (and perhaps your readers as well) have about it. Using your list as a guide, try to find facts and statistics that answer the questions. If possible, use the material you have so far to conduct interviews with local people involved in the issue. Then, write your findings as a report with an argumentative bent.

On a Greek Holiday

Alice Bloom

Alice Bloom is a critic and fiction writer, and teaches English at the University of Maine, Farmington. Her articles have appeared in the New England Review, Breadloaf Quarterly, *and* The Hudson Review, *from which the following piece was taken. The selection is an excerpt from a much longer essay with the same title.*

The only interesting question on a trip for me is—what sustains life elsewhere? 1
How deep does it go? Can one see it? This hope, this anticipation, is forcibly
blocked. Henry Miller, in 193—, stood in Epidaurus, alone, in a "weird solitude,"
and felt the "great heart of the world beat." We stand at Epidaurus with several
thousand others, some of whom are being called "my chickens" by their tour guide
who calls herself "your mother hen," whose counterpart, this time at Delphi, explains several times that what is being looked at is the "belly button of the world,
okay? The Greeks thought, this is the belly button of the world, okay?" "These
stones all look alike to me," someone grumbles. There is no help for it; we're there
with guidebooks ourselves; but this fact—tourism is big business—and others,
throw us back, unwilling, into contemplation of our own dull home-soul, our dull
bodily comforts, our own dull dwindling purse, our own dull resentments; because
the other—in this case, Greece—is either rapidly disappearing or else, self-
protective, is retreating so far it has disappeared. You can get there, but you can't
get at it.

For instance, a study of travel posters and brochures, which in the process 2
of setting dates and buying tickets always precedes a trip, shows us, by projection
into these pictured, toothy, tourist bodies, having some gorgeous piece of inges-
tion: The yellow beach, the mossy blue ruin, a dinner table laden with food and
red wine of the region, dancing, skiing, golfing, shopping, waving to roadside natives as our rented car sails by, as though we only go to play, as though all we do
here at home is work, as though, for two or four weeks abroad, we seek regression.

Also in the posters, but as part of the landscape, there are the natives— 3
whether Spanish, Greek, Irish, etc.—costumed as attractions, performing in
bouzouki or bag-pipe bands, or doing some picturesque and nonindustrial piece of
work such as fishing, weaving, selling colorful cheap goods in open-air markets,
herding sheep or goats. The journey promised by the posters and brochures is a
trip into everyone's imaginary past: One's own, drained of the normal childhood
content of fear, death, space, hurt, abandonment, perplexity, and so forth, now presented as the salesmen think we think it should have been: One in which we only
ate, slept, and played in the eternal sun under the doting care of benevolent elders.

And we are shown the benevolent elders, the imaginary natives who also, for 4
a handsome fee, exist now, in the present of the trip we are about to take. ("Take"
is probably a more telling verb here than we think.) They exist in a past where they
are pictured having grown cheerfully old and wise doing only harmless, enjoyable,

preindustrial, clean, self-employed, open-air work, in pink crinkled cheeks, merry eyes, and wonderful quaint clothes, with baskets, nets, toyshaped boats, flower boxes, cottages, sheep crooks, country roads, whitewashed walls, tea shop signs, and other paraphernalia of the pastoral wish. I have never seen a travel poster showing natives of the country enjoying their own food or beaches or ski-jumps or hotel balconies; nor have I ever seen a travel poster showing the natives working the nightshift in the Citroën factory, either.

The natives in the posters (are they Swiss, Mexican, Chilean, Turkish mod-   5 els?) are happy parent figures, or character dolls, and their faces, like the faces of the good parents we are supposed to have dreamed, show them pleased with their own lot, busy but not too busy with a job that they obviously like, content with each other, and warmly indulgent of our need to play, to be fed good, clean food on time, and to be tucked into a nice bed at the end of our little day. They are the childhood people that also existed in early grammar school readers, and nowhere else: Adults in your neighborhood, in the identifiable costumes of their humble tasks, transitional-object people, smiling milkman, friendly aproned store owner in his small friendly store, happy mailman happy to bring your happy mail, happy mommy, icons who make up a six-year-old's school-enforced dream town, who enjoy doing their nonindustrial, unmysterious tasks: Mail, milk, red apple, cooky, just for you, so you can learn to decipher: See, Jip, see.

A travel remark I have always savored came from someone surprised in love   6 for a place, just returned from a month in the Far East (no longer tagged "the mysterious," I've noticed), and who was explaining this trip at a party. She said, "I just loved Japan. It was so authentic and Oriental." Few people would go quite so naked as that, but the charm of her feelings seemed just right. Perhaps she had expected Tokyo to be more or less a larger version of the Japanese Shop in the Tokyo Airport. It is somewhat surprising that she found it to be anything much more.

One of the hushed-tone moral superiority stories, the aren't-we-advanced sto-   7 ries told by those lucky enough to travel in Soviet Russia, has to do with that government's iron management of the trip. There are people who can't be met, buildings that can't be entered, upper story windows that can't be photographed, streets that can't be strolled, districts that can't be crossed, cities in which it is impossible to spend the night, and so on. However, our notions of who we are and what comforts we demand and what conditions we'll endure, plus any country's understandably garbled versions of who we are, what we want, and what we'll pay for, are far more rigid than the strictures of any politburo because such strictures don't say "This is you, this is what you must want," but "This is what you can't, under any circumstances, do." That, though it inhibits movement, and no doubt in some cases prevents a gathering of or understanding of some crucial or desired bit of information, has at least the large virtue of defining the tourist as potentially dangerous. What we meet most of the time, here and abroad, is a definition of ourselves as harmless, spoiled babies, of low endurance and little information, minimal curiosity, frozen in infancy, frozen in longing, terrified for our next square meal and clean bed, and whose only potential danger is that we might refuse to be separated from our money.

Suppose, for a moment, that tourism—the largest "industry" in Greece (it employs, even more than shipping, the most people)—were also the largest industry in America. Not just in Manhattan or Washington, D.C., or Disneyland or Disney World or at the Grand Canyon or Niagara Falls, but in every motel, hotel, restaurant, in every McDonald's and Colonel Sanders and Howard Johnson's and Mom & Pop's, in every bar and neighborhood hangout, truck stop, gas station, pharmacy, department store, museum, church, historical site, battleground, in every taxi, bus, subway, train, plane, in every public building, in post offices and banks and public bathrooms, on every street in every city, town, village and hamlet from West Jonesport, Maine, to Centralia, Illinois, to Parachute, Colorado, and every stop in between and beyond, just as it is in Greece: Tourists.

Suppose that every other business establishment across the country therefore found it in their best interest to become a souvenir shop, selling cheap, mass-produced "gifts" for the tourists to take back home that, back home, would announce that they had visited America. What images would we mass produce for them? Millions of little bronzed Liberty Bells? Tepees? St. Louis Arches? Streetcars named "Desire"? Statues of Babe Ruth? of Liberty? of Daniel Boone? In Greece we saw miniature bottles of ouzo encased in tiny plastic replicas of the temple of Athena Nike. Could we do something so clever, and immediately recognizable, with miniatures of bourbon? Encase them in tiny plastic Washington Monuments? Lincoln Memorials? Would we feel misrepresented?

Third, suppose that a sizable portion of these tourists wanting gifts, toilets, rooms, baths, meals, dollars, film, drinks, stamps, directions, are Greek; or else, let us suppose that we assumed, that whether actually Greek or not, wherever they come from they speak Greek as a second language. Assume, therefore, that our map and traffic and road signs, postings of instruction and information, advertisements, timetables, directions—"stop," "go," "hot," "cold," "men," "women," "open," "closed," "yes," "no,"—to name a few rudiments of life, plus all the menus in all those sandwich counters, truck stops, fast-food outlets, lunch rooms, and so forth, had to be in Greek as well as in English. We have never been, so far, an occupied country, whether by forces enemy or not. Undoubtedly, if we were, as an ongoing fact of our "in-season" summer months, we Americans, having to offer our multitudinous wares in Greek, would come up with items as hilarious as those we collected from the English side of Greek menus: Baygon and egs. Xamberger steake. Veat. Orange juise. Rost beef. Shrimp carry. Potoes, Spaggeti. Morcoroni. And our favorite, Fried Smooth Hound. (This turned out to be a harmless local fish, much to the disappointment of our children, born surrealists.)

Suppose that we had to post Bar Harbor, Plum Island, Chincoteague, Key West, Bay St. Louis, Galveston, Big Sur and Seattle beaches with "No Nakedness Allowed" signs, but that the Greeks and other tourists, freed from the cocoons of air-conditioned tour buses, armed with sun-oil in every degree of protection, rushed beachwards past the signs and stripped to their altogether, anyway? Would our police sit quietly in the shade and drink with other men and turn, literally, their khaki-clad rumps to the beach, as did the Greek police?

And food. Suppose we had to contrive to feed them, these hungry hordes?   12
They will come here, as we go there, entrenched in their habits and encumbered
with fears of being cheated, fears of indigestion, of recurrent allergies, of breaking their diets, of catching American trots, of being poisoned by our water, fattened
by our grease and starch, put off by our feeding schedules, sickened by something
weird or local. Suppose we decided, out of some semiconscious, unorganized, but
national canniness, that what these tourists really want is our cobbled version of
their national foods. Whom will we please: The English who want their teas at
four, or the Italians who want supper at nine at night? Or both? And what will we
cook and serve, and how will we spell it?

Or suppose they want to eat "American" food. What tastes like us? What fla-   13
vors contain our typicality, our history, our heroes, our dirt, our speeches, our poets, our battles, our national shames? The hot dog? Corn on the cob? I have eaten,
barring picnics and occasional abstention, probably about 130 meals in Greece.
And Greek food, I feel somewhat qualified to say, contains their history, and tastes
of sorrow and triumph, of olive oil and blood, in about equal amounts. It is the
most astounding and the most boring food that I, an eater, have ever eaten.

Greek food is tragic. Why? Because each bite is a chomp into history, our   14
history. Why? Because this lunch—small fish, cheese, olives, wine, bread—
exactly this lunch, and tomorrow's lunch—fish, cheese, olives, wine, bread—has
been eaten since the time of the glory that will someday be called Greece, the glory
that existed for a moment, the glory that Greece was, and the glory that mankind—
for Greece is that, not Greek, but mankind—might yet be. Each bite is archaeo-
logical, into fine layers of millennia: Fish, oil, cheese, wine, bread—in the par-
taking we join, on the back of the tongue, Amazon forces and single crazy saints,
mythical men who married their mythical mothers, and men, and mothers, who today and tomorrow only dream of it.

One uses a big word like "timeless" with caution, if at all. But there is noth-   15
ing timely about two things in Greece; therefore it is not rhetorical to claim that,
in Greece, the quality of the heat of the sun on the skin and the quality of the food
in the mouth are perhaps as close as we can come to the taste of "timelessness."
Along with the oldest human question—how can we make God happy?—this sun
and this food are among the most ancient sensations recorded.

Under this summer sun every meal, beginning with breakfast, is eaten in 100   16
degrees of heat and hotter—115, 120—by afternoon. The meal, any one of them,
is composed of food that grows best in this climate and yet is entirely unsuited to
it as daily refreshment. No one could possibly, certainly not a tourist, need this oil-
soaked food for fuel in mid-July. It tastes and feels, though, like fuel: Heavy, shiny,
slow-moving food, purple, brown, red—tomatoes, eggplants, fish, lamb, olives,
black wine, blinding white cheese, much bread. We eat this three times a day; three
times a day the tourists eat it and the Greeks eat it. Everyone seems to look forward to the next meal, and all around our table, where we eat again with relish, are
others eating with relish, sometimes even with a look of reprieve and relief. And
there is no escape from it. Who would risk whatever "shrimp carry" might be?

There is no ordering something else—a salad of lettuce for a change, or a thin chicken sandwich. There is nothing but this food with its taste and texture of ancient days, of old crimes, forbidden loves, of something tinny and resigned, something of both gluttony and renunciation.

In addition to being a tragic cuisine, a sacramental cuisine, it is also practi- 17 cal, cheap, crude, and uninventive. The raw materials are without equal: Eggplants hang with the burnish of Dutch interiors; the fish still flap as they are headed oilwards; the lamb chop's mother befouls the yard next to your table; fruit so perfect, so total, that the scent of a single peach in a paper bag perfumes the whole room overnight and brings tears of love of God to the eyes. On a walk into the hills, meadows of thyme and mint and basil are idly crushed under heel. What happens to all this in the pot is a miracle of transformation, of negligence or brutality; or possibly, stubborn evidence of some otherwise lost political knowledge of what draws out the best, most noble, and most beautiful in the masses.

For the food is destroyed, each meal, in the process from vine or net or gar- 18 den to violent table. Its facts are these: It has always been eaten thus, with the exception of the late-coming tomato. It is—lamb, eggplant, olive, fish, white cheese —even now, perfectly indigenous. It is plain cooking. It is cooked for hours, all day; oil is poured on without restraint, discretion, or mercy. Every morsel is the same temperature and consistency by the time it reaches the palate. In a profound way, it is stupid food, overfeeding the flesh while tasting as though one should renounce the flesh forever.

We did not, to be fair, eat in a single Greek home. However, we were care- 19 ful to eat where the Greeks ate, and the Greeks eat out—in family groups, starched, ironed, slicked-down heads, whited summer shoes, strictly disciplined children; or in tense, dark groups of greedy, hasty men; which is how, as families or as men, the Greeks travel through the day. From the second-story, open-air, Greek-family-filled restaurant where we ate most of our meals while on the island, we could, if we had a table near the edge, throw our bread scraps, if we had any left over, straight down into the blue-green sea for the melon and dove-colored fish to mouth; and we could watch the evening sky turn from the day's bleached-out white to a pale English blue, then to lime-green streaked with apricot, and finally, with the fall of night, to a grape-purple that rose, in that instant, up from the sea.

1983

QUESTIONS FOR DISCUSSION

Content

a. Although this selection is taken from the middle of a longer essay, the introductory paragraph of this excerpt marks a new direction in the whole essay. As an introduction, what expectations does it set up? In other words, what does it tell you about what follows?

b. After reading the entire selection, go back to the three questions that begin the piece. What do these questions mean? How would Bloom answer them based on her experience in Greece?

c. Who is the "we" that Bloom keeps referring to? Look especially at paragraphs 7, 8, and 9. She is obviously speaking of Americans, but specifically what kinds of Americans?

d. In paragraphs 8 through 13 Bloom presents some hypothetical examples as a way to criticize something. What is it that she is criticizing?

e. At the end of paragraph 9 Bloom asks, "Would we feel misrepresented" if foreign tourists considered mass-produced souvenirs, such as bronzed Liberty Bells, tepees, or St. Louis Arches, as representative of the United States? Would an American feel misrepresented by such objects?

f. Bloom asserts that "Greek food is tragic" (paragraph 14) and also that Greek food is "sacramental" (paragraph 17). What does she mean? What adjectives would she, or you, use to describe American food?

g. Why is there so much attention on food? What has food got to do with travel and culture?

Strategy and Style

h. Bloom's tone in the first few paragraphs (2–7) could be described as snide and critical of the travel industry. Underline or point to phrases in these paragraphs that convey this tone.

i. Each of paragraphs 8 through 13 includes "suppose" in the first phrase. Why might Bloom have used so many hypothetical examples?

j. The vocabulary Bloom uses is fairly simple; however, her prose is difficult to read because of sentence structure and length. Find two or three sentences that tripped you up, and paraphrase them.

k. To whom does Bloom seem to be writing? Who are her ideal readers? How do you know? Point to phrases that seem directed to a particular kind of reader.

SUGGESTIONS FOR SHORT WRITING

a. Write a paraphrase or a summary of the opening paragraph of this difficult selection.

b. Notice the logical leap from paragraph 13 to 14, from a brief description of American and Greek food to the statement that "Greek food is tragic." What is the transition here? Write a short transitional paragraph that shows the logical connection between the two paragraphs. Concentrate on making the logic clear; do not worry about matching Bloom's style.

SUGGESTIONS FOR SUSTAINED WRITING

a. In paragraph 3 Bloom shows that the tourist industry sells actual trips by promising another, figurative, trip. She writes, "The journey promised by the posters and brochures is a trip into everyone's imaginary past: One's own, drained of the normal childhood content of fear, death, space, hurt, abandonment, perplexity, and so forth, now presented as the salesmen think we think it should have been: One in which we only ate, slept, and played in the eternal sun under the doting care of benevolent elders."

   Find posters or brochures in a local travel office, or ads for exotic travel in a magazine such as *Travel and Leisure* or *National Geographic Traveller.* Write an essay in which you analyze the posters, brochures, or ads, pointing out details of the images and the ad copy that promise something other than the actual, physical trip. Address the questions: What are the figurative journeys promised by these materials? What is the relationship between the figurative journey and the actual trip? In what ways do the images and words implicitly create the promise of another type of journey?

b. In paragraph 9 Bloom lists images that would make good mass-produced souvenirs. Think of the one image or object (from Bloom's list or one of your own) that would say "America" to foreign tourists. Describe the image/object, and explain your choice. What connections are there between the image or object and American culture? What makes this image or object essentially American?

c. Reread Bloom's essay, and write both a paraphrase of it and an extended response to it, pointing out how Bloom structures the essay, how she sequences her examples, and commenting on her choice of examples. Include your opinion of the effectiveness of her structure and content choices.

8

Cause and Effect

If you read Chapter 3, you know that explaining causes and effects is similar to analyzing a process. While the latter explains how something happens, however, the former seeks to reveal why it happens. Causal analysis is often used to explore questions in science, history, economics, and the social sciences. If you have taken courses in these subjects, you may have written papers or essay exams that discuss the major causes of World War I; explain changes in the U.S. banking system brought on by the Great Depression; or predict the environmental consequences of uncontrolled pollution.

Causal analysis is so natural an activity that it appears in the earliest of stages of mental awareness. It is a tool by which we reflect upon and learn from our past: The child who burns her hand knows why she should stay away from the stove. But it is also a common way to anticipate the future. Peering into metaphorical crystal balls, we create elaborate plans, theorize about the consequences of our actions, and make appropriate changes in the way we live. "If I graduate in four years and get a fellowship to law school," dreams the ambitious college freshman, "I might land a job with Biddle and Biddle and even run for city council by the time I'm thirty. But, first, I'd better improve my grades, which will mean studying harder and spending less time socializing."

The student's thinking illustrates an important point about the connection between causes and effects: It is often more complex than we imagine. For example, in "If Hitler Asked You to Electrocute a Stranger Would You? Probably," Philip Meyer cannot theorize about people's willingness to obey authorities until he thoroughly explains Stanley Milgram's experiment and discusses Milgram's conclusions.

Keep this example in mind as you begin to use causal analysis as a way to develop ideas. More often than not, each cause and effect you discuss will require a thorough explanation using details that are carefully chosen and appropriate to your purpose. Remember, too, that you can call on a variety of skills and techniques to help you develop your analysis. For example, Ellen Goodman joins illustration with cause and effect, a brilliant combination that reveals the irony behind why planners and nonplanners reap the same rewards.

An important question any time you use cause and effect is where to place your emphasis. Will you discuss what caused a particular phenomenon or will you focus on its effects? Shelby Steele discusses the relationship between "black power" and "white guilt" and the results these two forces have had on American attitudes and political policy. Cecil Foster, on the other hand, spends most of his time providing background to the events about which he writes. Of course, you may decide to strike a balance, as does George Woodcock when he discusses our servitude to time.

As with the other kinds of writing in this text, purpose determines content and strategy. You read earlier that causal analysis is used frequently to explain historical or scientific phenomena. Such writing is often objective and dispassionate, but causal analysis has many applications. Because it is an especially powerful tool for persuasion, you might even want to use it to express a strong voice over issues to which you are firmly committed. Take your lead from Woodcock, for example, who encourages his reader to "return again to a balanced view of life." Like Suzuki, warn your readers about an environmental danger. Express concern over the state of the family, as does Barbara Dafoe Whitehead in "Where Have All the Parents Gone?" You might even want to analyze your reactions to social, political, or other types of problems to see what they tell you about yourself.

Black and Blue

Cecil Foster

*Cecil Foster was born in Barbados in 1954 and, since immigrating to Canada in 1978,
has become an important journalistic voice in this country. He has written for the* Globe
and Mail, The Toronto Star, *and* The Financial Post. *He also edited* Contrast, *Canada's
first black-oriented newspaper. The following selection comes from his book* A Place
Called Heaven: The Meaning of Being Black in Canada *(1996).*

At its heart, the colour of Canadian justice is blue. At least that is the case in   1
Etobicoke Courtroom 208 Metropolitan Toronto on December 7, 1994. This is the
day the state begins bringing to justice one Clinton Junior Gayle for the murder of
a Toronto policeman, Todd Baylis, and the attempted murder of his partner, P.C.
Michael Leone. This is the trial that would be the catharsis for an entire nation, especially for those who feel this country is too soft when it comes to questions of
law and order, when it comes to dealing firmly with perennial whiners and misfits,
such as members of the black community.

In this case, colour means everything. Gayle is a black man accused of   2
killing a white policeman. After the shooting, the media and talk shows did not try
to disguise the racism in their commentary. Neither did anyone appear to pretend
that Gayle would, at the very least, be considered innocent until proven guilty in
the court. From the moment the story of the killing broke, media reports and
talk-show hosts dispensed with the routine use of the word "alleged" when describing a murderer named Gayle. Such a formality might have been misconstrued
as a weakness, a sop to the black community, an encouragement to others har-
bouring such bad intentions. In this case, the general population doesn't worry too
much about a miscarriage of justice or about ensuring that Gayle gets a fair trial.
Rather, it's about retribution. In this case, in the eyes of many, Clinton Junior
Gayle represents all black men in this country, and dealing with him appropriately
is the right way to send a stern message to all those whiners, to all those who do
not respect Canadian institutions, to all those living outside the Canadian mainstream who should be brought to heel.

Gayle's case had ramifications for many, including a nondescript immigra-   3
tion adjudicator, Ivan Rashid, who ordered Gayle released from jail while waiting
for deportation. Rashid, his identity made public before an almost incensed
Canadian citizenry, had to atone publicly for a "bad" decision.

Gayle was held up as this brutal and brutish thug who gunned down an offi-   4
cer of the law, robbing the community of a fine young man, and Baylis' girl-friend
of a future husband and father of her children. All of which was true. But the condemnation went further than just a battle of good and evil: race and skin colour made
a difference. Soon broad swipes were being taken at any breathing black person.

That Gayle is black and from the Caribbean, specifically Jamaica, gave   5
added colour to the incident and eventually made it an international issue. But the

harshest effects were felt on the streets of Toronto, especially in neighbourhoods with a strong black presence. In one fell swoop, Blacks were painted as gangsters, irresponsible louts who had little respect for life. Furthermore, here was an example of what happens when Canada throws open its doors to the dredges of the world, people with no respect for institutions, for law and order, the result of an immigration policy too lax and ill-suited for this country.

There were some factors that gave legitimacy for these virulent attacks on 6 Gayle—but not on all other Blacks. Gayle had been in trouble many times with the law, running up 13 convictions, including possession of firearms, and had been ordered deported to Jamaica. At the time he fired the bullets that killed Baylis and wounded Leone, Gayle was under a 10-year ban prohibiting him from possessing firearms. Along the way, his deportation papers got lost. Some critics jumped on this as an example of how the immigration process and the justice system had broken down, how the two federal departments were conspiring to let loose on society heinous criminals, most of them black, and notably, Jamaican or West Indian. The Metro Toronto Police Association, supposedly also representing the black members of the force, took the argument one step further. It followed up its virulent anti-Black rhetoric with action: a lawsuit for $100 million, in the names of the slain, against the federal government. Somebody has to pay for the killing of one of its members, and the police association was not willing to settle only for the price that society would demand of Gayle in a criminal trial.

For months preceding the shooting of Todd Baylis, there was much talk 7 about justice and Blacks in Canada. Several months earlier, the mainstream media had a special story to tell. It was about young black men in Nova Scotia who set up a white prostitution ring across the country. As the story was told, innocent young girls from Halifax were finding themselves in Montreal, Toronto, Vancouver and any big city or town in between, in the inescapable clutches of black pimps. This was not just another prostitute and pimp story. Nobody in the media worked to find out if any of these supposedly innocent white women were runaways, attracted to the big city, and finding themselves having to get by the same way many others have always had to survive in the streets of Los Angeles, New York or Toronto. Also noticeable was that nobody seemed too concerned about whether any of these innocent young women on the hustle were black. But the colour of the pimps was of the utmost importance. Here is how the issue was reported in *The Globe and Mail* on April 24th, 1993:

> When Joan is out on the baseball mound, the ball spinning toward her, she likes to imagine she's about to swing her bat at the head of a black pimp. She knows she shouldn't harbour such anger towards other people, but she just can't help it. Joan is mad as hell at the men she blames for destroying her daughter's life.
>
> Hillary, her eldest child, is one of hundreds of hookers who got their start in the Halifax area in recent years. Today many of these girls, most of them

over 13 but some as young as 10, populate big-city "strolls," the streets and byways walked by prostitutes across Canada and as far afield as New York, California and Europe.

Most of these young prostitutes, virtually all of them white, work for a loosely organized community of Nova Scotia Black men.

The writing could hardly be more graphic or coloured. With so much talk of 8 this white slave ring, life became a lot tougher for young black men in the Preston area of Halifax. The police came frequently knocking, often with the national media in tow. Some of the youths saw the inside of jails. Others just had to put up with police harassment. Some men from the Preston area were arrested across the country, charged and convicted. Of course, the convictions were duly recorded as if to ease the fears of the wider community that the black menace was finally under control.

The concern about Blacks and justice took on an even greater dimension 9 across the country in the summer of 1994. In Toronto, three black men entered an eating establishment named Just Desserts in a trendy part of the city. While robbing the restaurant and its patrons, a patron was killed by a shotgun blast. The city, and indeed parts of the country, reacted viscerally. The murdered woman, Georgina "Vivi" Leimonis, became a representative of all the ills black men can inflict on white women. Just as with the hype over the so-called white prostitution ring, the colour of the perpetrators seemed to be the most important aspect of this robbery and murder. The police also acted as though colour were the only thing that mattered; they issued out-of-focus photographs to the media with instructions that citizens call the police if they saw any of the men. The pictures were splashed on the television screens and on the front pages of newspapers, along with instructions for people to clip them out and keep the pictures handy in their car for easy reference. But the pictures were so murky, the only thing clear about the suspects was the colour of their skin. Immediately, every black man became a suspect. As was the case in Halifax, the mainstream dismissed this concern. Much emphasis was placed on the loss of innocence in the city. Who would not shed a tear for a young woman cut down in her prime, a woman who wore her intended wedding gown as a burial shroud?

Similar claims about the city being robbed of its innocence had been made 10 only two years earlier when a crowd of primarily black youth "rioted" on Yonge Street. This so-called riot coincided with the destruction and pillage in Los Angeles that came to be known as the Rodney King riots, the spark occurring when an all-white jury acquitted some Los Angeles police officers for brutally beating a black man. The fact that Rodney King's beating was captured on video was dismissed by the jury. Blacks across North America rose up against this affront, and the hard feelings boiled over in Toronto, too, where there had been many recent flashpoints over police shootings of Blacks. This would not be the first or last time that parallels would be drawn between the treatment of Blacks in Canada and the United States. As the Yonge Street disturbances proved—as did smaller but similar incidents in Halifax and other Canadian centres—few people in the black community see any differences in the way the police and justice systems treat Blacks on either side of the border.

Eventually, the ranting quietened down. Many people, in sombre reflection, 11 examined why society felt so threatened over this one killing at Just Desserts. It was pointed out that the only difference in this case was that three black men were accused of killing a white woman. After all, murders and heists at restaurants are quite routine in major Canadian cities. Most people argued that it was the "randomness" of the shooting that frightened them. "You mean to say that you can't even go into a restaurant to eat a piece of cake without getting shot?" some asked. But two points were undefeatable in this argument. For a long time, these types of killings had been happening in the black community. Many young men and women had been slaughtered at illegal house parties and after-hours clubs. Some of the killings hardly merited mention in the newspapers and certainly not an outpouring of sympathy. The national media paid no attention when anyone was brought to trial, or when the murdered persons were buried. It seemed that as long as Blacks were killing Blacks, the city was still safe. Also, there was no doubt the security of feeling that as long as Blacks killed Blacks in black areas, then the wider community didn't have to worry. If a white person walked through a predominantly black area of Toronto like Jane and Finch, Lawrence Heights or the Peanut in North York, then they deserved what they got.

People reacted to the Just Desserts killing as though it were anything but ran- 12 dom. They made it appear as though the entire city had become lawless—black youths with ski masks were running rampant throughout the city, and anyone, especially Whites, could be slaughtered. What they were, in fact, arguing is that because the killing had spilled over into a middle-class and largely white area, the mainstream was sitting up and taking notice. And they wanted this supposedly random violence stamped out.

Gayle's shooting of Constable Todd Baylis in the garage of an apartment 13 building in a mixed neighbourhood was another example of this violence, spilling over into other areas, affecting the wrong people. It would become the lightning rod for feelings in the mainstream.

The morning the news came that someone had shot a cop, I was in the news- 14 room of the CBC writing news scripts for *World Report,* the first major newscast heard right across the country every morning. As I read the news flashes on the wires, I knew this shooting was serious, and I hoped that I would not have to write that a *black* man had killed a policeman. (Many black people have admitted feeling the same way when they hear the first reports of a shooting, murder or robbery. How they hope a black person is not involved and how they release a collective sigh of relief when they find out the criminal is white. Talk about collective guilt; or is it collective responsibility? Either one, many Blacks respond this way to news because they know that if the criminal is black, innocent Blacks can expect to be scrutinized on the subway and on buses, in convenience stores, and at work and at play.)

At the time we began to write the scripts, we knew only that two cops and 15 the alleged gunman were in hospital. One of the policemen was in critical condition. A short while later, CBC police reporter Raj Ahluwalia arrived in the newsroom to prepare a report. He confirmed that the worst had happened, although the news was not official. "Looks like the cop is dead. They are holding off making the announcement until they have informed his family." The first edition of the newscast to the Maritimes told of the shooting and critical wounding of a cop in Toronto. Shortly thereafter, I would read the confirmation of the death on my computer screen, and would amend the newscast. Listeners in Manitoba, Alberta and British Columbia and in U.S. border states were to hear on their first major newscast about the murder of a cop on the beat. Eventually, the news of the shooting would be broadcast around the world on the various CBC national and international programs.

In the following week, listeners, including many in the Caribbean, would   16 hear similar reports on the discussion about the violence and lawlessness, of the failure of the judicial and immigration systems. And they would hear the explanation that all of these things were responsible for the death of one of Metro's finest at the hands of one of Canada's most undesirable. Most of the media unquestioningly bought into the statements of the Metro police, and their reports resorted to caricature, depicting Gayle as lawless, a drug dealer, fatherless, a street hustler and someone who should have been kicked out of the country long ago. *The Toronto Sun* took to running billboards across the city under the caption, "We'll be there." Underneath the statement was a picture of three men with the word DEPORTED stamped across their faces. Many in the black community felt that these billboards had a direct connection with the death of Toronto policeman Baylis. And it was hard not to make this connection after a series of articles and columns linked the crime with deportation.

"Almost every day now, we could present another case of someone who   17 should have been deported, and wasn't; or was deported, but came back; or was ordered deported, but was then released to disappear into the streets," wrote *Sun* columnist Christie Blatchford.

"This is how dreadfully routine such cases have become, this in the 20 days   18 since Clinton Junior Gayle, a Jamaican immigrant whose deportation order was never executed, was arrested in the slaying of Metro Toronto Police Const. Todd Baylis and the wounding of his partner, Const. Mike Leone."

"Today's poster boy fits all three categories, with the added little fillips that   19 a) he apparently enjoys posing with a gun in his hand and b) that on one of the last occasions his presence was officially noted, he was driving Clinton Gayle's car."

And to bring home her point, she later added: "If it is safe to say that the   20 Gayle case has opened eyes and lips both . . . and provided Canadians with a window into the shambles that is their federal immigration department, it is also a sure thing that this is just the tip of the proverbial iceberg."[1]

Who says hysteria doesn't sell?   21

The general outcry in reaction to this death would come from across the   22 country and would be heard across the nation. Police officers poured into Toronto

[1]*The Toronto Sun*, July 6, 1994.

from all corners of the world, including Jamaica, to form the largest contingent of foreign police officers to attend a funeral in Canada. (That some of the policemen came from Jamaica was important to the media because Gayle is Jamaican. But more important, Gayle's biological father is a superintendent in the Jamaica Police Force and on hearing of the shooting is reported to have roundly condemned his son. Apparently, that was the first time Gayle's father had heard of his whereabouts in years.) And the funeral was huge. Local television stations carried it live. The streets of north Metro Toronto were closed off for hours as police officers paraded and paid their last respects. Photojournalists snapped pictures as members of 12 Division of the Metro Toronto Police Force, colleagues of the slain officer, served as pallbearers. The coffin was draped in the Canadian flag. And once again, every Black in the city felt those eyes on us. We were all Clinton Gayles, cop killers and murderers.

Now, in this courtroom, society was seeking to start the long process of hand- 23
ing out justice for someone cut down in the line of duty, by someone who ought not to have been in the country. But does the fact that the man who shot Baylis grew up in Canada, learned to become a criminal in Canada and knew nobody in the country of his birth matter to this discussion? It certainly did enter the debate in the Caribbean, where the argument was intense and became an international issue. But Gayle was Jamaican and was being rejected physically and psychologically from the country in which he had lived almost continuously for 20 years.

This case of *Regina v. Clinton Junior Gayle* was to be a test of the will of 24
this country. Can a black person ever fully become a Canadian citizen? At what point do you stop being a Jamaican, Barbadian, Trinidadian, Ghanaian or Nigerian and become a full-fledged citizen of this country, to be accepted, faults and all, as a product of this society? This preliminary hearing was the start of the process of sending a clear, unmistakable message. Someone was going to sing the blues for this killing. Real Canadians were going to take back their country. And they were going to impose some common sense on how real Canadians run this country's judiciary, police and immigration systems.

1996

QUESTIONS FOR DISCUSSION

Content

a. Why is the essay titled "Black and Blue"?
b. Does Foster imply that Gayle is innocent? If not, what is his point?
c. What is the connection between black pimps and the Gayle case?
d. How does the media, according to Foster, report incidents where blacks kill other blacks?
e. Why does Foster discuss his own involvement in writing up the story for the CBC about the shooting?
f. What is Foster's thesis?

Strategy and Style

g. What is the emotional impact of words like "whiners and misfits"?

h. Why does Foster deliberately quote the *Globe and Mail*'s version of the story about the pimps? Why not the *Toronto Star*'s or the *Toronto Sun*'s?

i. Why does Foster keep mentioning the name of the restaurant, Just Desserts?

j. Why does Foster write, "Talk about collective guilt; or is it collective responsibility?"? What is the effect of hearing Foster's personal response to the story?

k. With the exception of a final comment, "Who says hysteria doesn't sell?" Foster quotes Christie Blatchford extensively and accurately. Why doesn't he comment and criticize more directly and extensively?

l. Foster opens the essay in the present tense. Why does he do this? What is the effect on the reader?

SUGGESTIONS FOR SHORT WRITING

a. Discuss your own relationship with the police and the law.

b. Have you experienced people being treated differently on the basis of colour, religion, sex, or any other external reason? Write about the incident and how you felt about it.

c. Is it pertinent to mention the ethnic heritage of a person in the news? If so, why? If not, why not? Are there any exceptions? At what point does it become relevant/irrelevant?

SUGGESTIONS FOR SUSTAINED WRITING

a. Research the media response to a criminal case that involved a member of a visible minority. Do not look at the case itself, but only examine the attitudes that underlie the reporting of the event and how those attitudes betrayed themselves.

b. Interview individuals from a visible minority in your community. How do these individuals feel the community perceives them as a group? Why do these individuals feel that way?

c. Present an argument for or against greater representation by minorities, even if it means preferential hiring, in the police force.

The Tyranny of the Clock

George Woodcock

George Woodcock (1912–1995) did not come to Canada until the age of 37. Politically an anarchist, Woodcock was friends with George Orwell and later wrote one of the best biographies of Orwell, The Crystal Spirit *(1966). In 1962, Woodcock wrote the book* Anarchism, *tracing the history of the anarchist movement. The book rejuvenated the movement and became its centrepiece. Woodcock primarily conceived of himself as a poet/essayist, and his writings are vast and too numerous to name. He wrote books on figures such as Gandhi, Thomas Merton, and Orwell; he wrote political works; he wrote literary criticism; and he wrote travel books. For Canadian literature, he is a particularly important figure in that he was one of the first to write critically on it and treat it as a worthy subject.*

In no characteristic is existing society in the west so sharply distinguished from the earlier societies, whether of Europe or the East, than in its conception of time. To the ancient Chinese or Greek, to the Arab herdsman or Mexican peon of today, time is represented by the cyclic processes of nature, the alternation of day and night, the passage from season to season. The nomads and farmers measured and still measure their day from sunrise to sunset, and their year in terms of seedtime and harvest, of the falling leaf and the ice thawing on the lakes and rivers. The farmer worked according to the elements, the craftsman for as long as he felt it necessary to perfect his product. Time was seen as a process of natural change, and men were not concerned in its exact measurement. For this reason civilizations highly developed in other respects had the most primitive means of measuring time: the hour glass with its trickling sand or dripping water, the sun dial, useless on a dull day, and the candle or lamp whose unburnt remnant of oil or wax indicated the hours. All these devices were approximate and inexact, and were often rendered unreliable by the weather or the personal laziness of the tender. Nowhere in the ancient or mediæval world were more than a tiny minority of men concerned with time in the terms of mathematical exactitude. 1

Modern, western man, however, lives in a world which runs according to the mechanical and mathematical symbols of clock time. The clock dictates his movements and inhibits his actions. The clock turns time from a process of nature into a commodity that can be measured and bought and sold like soap or sultanas. And because, without some means of exact time keeping, industrial capitalism could never have developed and could not continue to exploit the workers, the clock represents an element of mechanical tyranny in the lives of modern men more potent than any individual exploiter or than any other machine. It is therefore valuable to trace the historical process by which the clock influenced the social development of modern European civilization. 2

It is a frequent circumstance of history that a culture or civilization develops the device that will later be used for its destruction. The ancient Chinese, for example, invented gunpowder, which was developed by the military experts of the 3

311

West and eventually led to the Chinese civilization itself being destroyed by the high explosives of modern warfare. Similarly, the supreme achievement of the craftsmen of the mediæval cities of Europe was the invention of the clock which, with its revolutionary alteration of the concept of time, materially assisted the growth of the middle ages.

There is a tradition that the clock appeared in the eleventh century, as a device for ringing bells at regular intervals in the monasteries which, with the regimented life they imposed on their inmates, were the closest social approximation in the middle ages to the factory of today. The first authenticated clock, however, appeared in the thirteenth century, and it was not until the fourteenth century that clocks became common as ornaments of the public buildings in German cities.

These early clocks, operated by weights, were not particularly accurate, and it was not until the sixteenth century that any great reliability was attained. In England, for instance, the clock at Hampton Court, made in 1540, is said to have been the first accurate clock in the country. And even the accuracy of the sixteenth-century clocks is relative, for they were equipped only with hour hands. The idea of measuring time in minutes and seconds had been thought out by the early mathematicians as far back as the fourteenth century, but it was not until the invention of the pendulum in 1657 that sufficient accuracy was attained to permit the addition of a minute hand, and the second hand did not appear until the eighteenth century. These two centuries, it should be observed, were those in which capitalism grew to such an extent that it was able to take advantage of the techniques of the industrial revolution to establish its economic domination over society.

The clock, as Lewis Mumford has pointed out, is the key machine of the machine age, both for its influence on technics and for its influence on the habits of men. Technically, the clock was the first really automatic machine that attained any importance in the life of man. Previous to its invention, the common machines were of such a nature that their operation depended on some external and unreliable force, such as human or animal muscles, water or wind. It is true that the Greeks had invented a number of primitive automatic machines, but these were used, like Hero's steam engine, either for obtaining 'supernatural' effects in the temples or for amusing the tyrants of Levantine cities. But the clock was the first automatic machine that attained public importance and a social function. Clock-making became the industry from which men learnt the elements of machine-making and gained the technical skill that was to produce the complicated machinery of the Industrial Revolution.

Socially the clock had a more radical influence than any other machine, in that it was the means by which the regularization and regimentation of life necessary for an exploiting system of industry could best be assured. The clock provided a means by which time—a category so elusive that no philosophy has yet determined its nature—could be measured concretely in the more tangible terms of space provided by the circumference of a clock dial. Time as duration became disregarded, and men began to talk and think always of 'lengths' of time, just as if they were talking of lengths of calico. And time, being now measurable in mathematical symbols, was regarded as a commodity that could be bought and sold in the same way as any other commodity.

The new capitalists, in particular, became rabidly time-conscious. Time, **8** here symbolizing the labour of the workers, was regarded by them almost as if it were the chief raw material of industry. "Time is money" was one of the key slogans of capitalist ideology, and the timekeeper was the most significant of the new types of official introduced by the capitalist dispensation.

In the early factories the employers went so far as to manipulate their clocks **9** or sound their factory whistles at the wrong times in order to defraud the workers of a little of this valuable new commodity. Later such practices became less frequent, but the influence of the clock imposed a regularity on the lives of the majority of men that had previously been known only in the monasteries. Men actually became like clocks, acting with a repetitive regularity which had no resemblance to the rhythmic life of a natural being. They became, as the Victorian phrase put it, "as regular as clockwork." Only in the country districts where the natural lives of animals and plants and the elements still dominated existence, did any large proportion of the population fail to succumb to the deadly tick of monotony.

At first this new attitude to time, this new regularity of life, was imposed by **10** the clock-owning masters on the unwilling poor. The factory slave reacted in his spare time by living with a chaotic irregularity which characterized the gin-sodden slums of early nineteenth-century industrialism. Men fled to the timeless worlds of drink or Methodist inspiration. But gradually the idea of regularity spread downwards and among the workers. Nineteenth-century religion and morality played their part by proclaiming the sin of "wasting time." The introduction of mass-produced watches and clocks in the 1850's spread time-consciousness among those who had previously merely reacted to the stimulus of the knocker-up or the factory whistle. In the church and the school, in the office and the workshop, punctuality was held up as the greatest of the virtues.

Out of this slavish dependence on mechanical time which spread insidiously **11** into every class in the nineteenth century, there grew up the demoralizing regimentation which today still characterizes factory life. The man who fails to conform faces social disapproval and economic ruin—unless he drops out into a nonconformist way of life in which time ceases to be of prime importance. Hurried meals, the regular morning and evening scramble for trains or buses, the strain of having to work to time schedules, all contribute, by digestive and nervous disturbance, to ruin health and shorten life.

Nor does the financial imposition of regularity tend, in the long run, to **12** greater efficiency. Indeed, the quality of the product is usually much poorer, because the employer, regarding time as a commodity which he has to pay for, forces the operative to maintain such a speed that his work must necessarily be skimped. Quantity rather than quality becoming the criterion, the enjoyment is taken out of the work itself, and the worker in his turn becomes a 'clock-watcher', concerned only with when he will be able to escape to the scanty and monotonous leisure of industrial society, in which he 'kills time' by cramming in as much time-scheduled and mechanical enjoyment of cinema, radio and newspaper as his wage packet and his tiredness will allow. Only if he is willing to accept the hazards of living by his faith or his wits can the man without money avoid living as a slave to the clock.

The problem of the clock is, in general, similar to that of the machine. 13 Mechanized time is valuable as a means of coordinating activities in a highly developed society, just as the machine is valuable as a means of reducing unnecessary labour to a minimum. Both are valuable for the contribution they make to the smooth running of society, and should be used in so far as they assist men to co-operate efficiently and to eliminate monotonous toil and social confusion. But neither should be allowed to dominate men's lives as they do today.

Now the movement of the clock sets the tempo of men's lives—they become 14 the servants of the concept of time which they themselves have made, and are held in fear, like Frankenstein by his own monster. In a sane and free society such an arbitrary domination of man's functions by either clock or machine would obviously be out of the question. The domination of man by man-made machines is even more ridiculous than the domination of man by man. Mechanical time would be relegated to its true function of a means of reference and co-ordination, and men would return again to a balanced view of life no longer dominated by time-regulation and the worship of the clock. Complete liberty implies freedom from the tyranny of abstractions as well as from the rule of men.

1972

QUESTIONS FOR DISCUSSION

Content

a. What is Woodcock's thesis?
b. For whom is this essay written?
c. What examples does Woodcock give of a society that develops a device that later destroys it?
d. How does Woodcock support his contention that "the clock was the first really automatic machine that attained any importance in the life of man"?
e. How did people conceive of time as they forgot about "time as duration"?
f. Which group in society embraced and encouraged the new conception of time? Why?
g. According to Woodcock, does awareness of time create greater efficiency?
h. What is the problem of the clock?

Strategy and Style

i. In the opening paragraph, Woodcock discusses "the ancient Chinese or Greek, to the Arab herdsman or Mexican peon of today." What is the effect of this list on the reader?

j. In the opening paragraph, Woodcock contrasts "natural" with "mathematical exactitude." In the second paragraph, he uses phrases like "mechanical and mathematical symbols of clock time." What is the effect of the contrast between nature and math?

k. Examine Woodcock's language when discussing clocks: "dictates," "inhibits," "commodity," "demoralizing regimentation," and so on. How does this language affect you as a reader?

l. When Woodcock discusses the invention of gunpowder, is he making an analogy with the invention of the clock? What is his point?

m. Woodcock refers to people in the monasteries as "inmates." What is he implying?

n. Why does Woodcock mention the manipulation of clocks by employers? Is this information integral to what he is arguing?

o. What is the effect of contrasting "clock-owning masters" with "unwilling poor"?

p. Why does Woodcock refer to Frankenstein?

SUGGESTIONS FOR SHORT WRITING

a. If you use a daytimer, write about its importance or unimportance in your life.

b. Argue for or against the need for strict deadlines in schools, universities, or in society.

c. How do you feel when you are not wearing a watch? How do you feel if you are in a room (like a classroom) and there is no clock?

SUGGESTIONS FOR SUSTAINED WRITING

a. Take one piece of technology—lightbulbs, e-mail, telephones, cell-phones, beepers—and discuss its history and the effects it has created in society. How has the technology changed people and society as a whole?

b. Examine the way time is used in advertising and in the media. What relationship with time does the media encourage? How are we to respond to the clock according to the media?

c. Examine how artists portray and alter our conception of time in literature, movies, painting, or sculpture. Write an essay discussing different techniques, the effect on the audience, and if the technique alters our relationship with or understanding of time (in other words, is the technique consistent with society's view or is it counter-culture?).

Watching the Grasshopper Get the Goodies

Ellen Goodman

Ellen Goodman was born in Boston in 1941. She received her bachelor's degree from Radcliffe College and attended Harvard University on a Nieman Fellowship. Goodman began her journalistic career with Newsweek, *then moved to the* Detroit Free Press, *and is now writing for the* Boston Globe. *Her syndicated column, "At Large," appears in more than 200 newspapers across the United States. She has won several awards for her commentary, including a Pulitzer Prize in 1980. Many of her columns have been collected in* Close to Home *(1979);* At Large *(1981), in which "Watching the Grasshopper Get the Goodies" appears; and* Value Judgments *(1993).*

I don't usually play the great American game called Categories. There are already 1 too many ways to divide us into opposing teams, according to age, race, sex and favorite flavors. Every time we turn around, someone is telling us that the whole country is made up of those who drive pick-up trucks and those who do not, and then analyzing what this means in terms of the Middle East.

Still, it occurs to me that if we want to figure out why people are angry right 2 now, it's not a bad idea to see ourselves as a nation of planners and nonplanners. It's the planners these days who are feeling penalized, right down to their box score at the bank.

The part of us which is most visibly and vocally infuriated by inflation, for 3 example, isn't our liberal or conservative side but, rather, our planning side. Inflation devastates our attempts to control our futures—to budget and predict and expect. It particularly makes fools out of the people who saved then to buy now. To a certain extent, it rewards instant gratification and makes a joke out of our traditional notions of preparation.

It is no news bulletin that the people who dove over their heads into the real- 4 estate market a few years ago are now generally better off than those who dutifully decided to save up for a larger down payment. With that "larger down payment" they can now buy two double-thick rib lambchops and a partridge in a pear tree.

But inflation isn't the only thing that leaves the planners feeling betrayed. 5 There are other issues that find them actively pitched against the nonplanners.

We all know families who saved for a decade to send their kids to college. 6 A college diploma these days costs about the same amount as a Mercedes-Benz. Of course, the Mercedes lasts longer and has a higher trade-in value. But the most devoted parent can be infuriated to discover that a neighboring couple who spent its income instead of saving is now eligible for college financial aid, while they are not. To the profligate go the spoils.

This can happen anywhere on the economic spectrum. There is probably 7 only one mother in the annals of the New York welfare rolls to save up a few thousand dollars in hopes of getting off aid. But she would have been better off spending it. When she was discovered this year, the welfare department took the money back. She, too, was penalized for planning.

In these crimped times, the Planned Parents of the Purse are increasingly an- 8 noyed at other parents—whether they are unwed or on welfare or just prolific. For the first time in my own town, you can hear families with few children complaining out loud at the tax bill for the public schooling of families with many children.

One man I heard even suggesting charging tuition for the third child. He ad- 9 mitted, "It's not a very generous attitude, I know. But I'm not feeling very generous these days." He is suffering from planner's warts.

At the same time I've talked with friends whose parents prepared, often with 10 financial difficulty, for their "old age" and illness. They feel sad when this money goes down a nursing home drain, but furious when other people who didn't save get this same care for free.

Now we are all aware that if many people don't plan their economic lives, it 11 may be because they can't. It does no one any good to keep the cashless out of college, to stash the old and poor into elderly warehouses, to leave the "extra" children illiterate. We do want to help others, but we also want our own efforts to make a difference.

There is nothing that grates a planner more than seeing a nonplanner profit. 12 It's as if the ant had to watch the grasshopper get the goodies.

Our two notions about what's fair end up on opposite sides. It isn't fair if the 13 poor get treated badly, and it isn't fair if those who work and save, plan and postpone aren't given a better shake. We want the winners to be the deserving. Only there is no divining rod for the deserving.

The hard part is to create policies that are neither unkind nor insane. It is, af- 14 ter all, madness not to reward the kind of behavior we want to encourage. If we want the ranks of the planners to increase in this massive behavior-modification program called society, we have to give them the rewards, instead of the outrage.

1981

QUESTIONS FOR DISCUSSION

Content

a. What purpose might Goodman have had in starting her essay with a criticism of categorizing and then turning around and categorizing people into "planners and nonplanners"? Into which category does she implicitly place herself?
b. According to the author, what happens when you make long-range plans? Is she suggesting that people should never plan?
c. What might be her motives for writing this essay?
d. To whom is Goodman probably writing? How would you describe the ideal reader of this essay (age, occupation, level of education, opinions, etc.)?
e. What or whom does she specify as the cause of people's anger? Just what are people angry about?

f. To what does the title allude? Why is the title appropriate?

g. Do you think that Goodman paints an overly pessimistic picture of what happens as a result of planning?

h. What type of person is Goodman criticizing in the first paragraph? What harmful effects could "the great American game called Categories" have? Would this criticism also apply to those essays in Chapter 5?

Strategy and Style

i. What rhetorical devices does Goodman use to protect herself from counter-arguments?

j. What statements in this essay are sarcastic? What does this sarcasm reveal about Goodman? Does it help to place her in one of her two categories?

k. What action is Goodman proposing in the last paragraph? Is the tone of this paragraph different from the rest of the essay?

SUGGESTIONS FOR SHORT WRITING

a. Create another fable that would make the same point that Goodman makes in her essay. Write an outline for the fable or briefly describe the characters.

b. Are you a planner or a nonplanner? Write an anecdote that illustrates that you are one or the other.

SUGGESTIONS FOR SUSTAINED WRITING

a. In this essay, Goodman focuses on money as the cause of unhappiness among planners. Could there be other causes as well? Write an essay in which you show that other things may have caused this unhappiness.

b. Write an essay about a practice, law, or situation that you feel is unfair, not only to you but to a large segment of society. Show the harmful effects this has on people and suggest what might be done to correct the situation.

c. Find another fable with a real-life equivalent. Using this fable as a starting point, describe the real-life situation, explain what is wrong with the situation and what has caused it, and suggest ways to correct the problem.

White Guilt

Shelby Steele

Shelby Steele (b. 1946) is a social critic who teaches literature and writing at San Jose State University. As an undergraduate, he led a student civil rights group called SCOPE, which was philosophically linked to Martin Luther King, Jr.'s, Southern Christian Leadership Conference. Later, however, influenced by Malcolm X, he shifted his energies to the black power movement. While studying for his MA in sociology at Southern Illinois University, he taught African-American literature in an experimental program designed to provide college credit to blacks who could not afford tuition. His experiences as an activist and educator provide a foundation for his sometimes controversial writings. His best-known book is The Content of Our Character: A New Vision of Race in America *(1990), which won the National Book Critics Circle Award. He also helped to create "Seven Days in Bensonhurst," a film documentary about the racial unrest following the murder of a black teenager in a white New York City neighbourhood in 1989. In a 1990* New York Times *profile, Steele said, "Some people say I shine a harsh light on difficult problems. But I never shine a light on anything I haven't experienced or write about fear I don't see in myself first."*

I don't remember hearing the phrase "white guilt" very much before the mid1960s. 1 Growing up black in the 1950s, I never had the impression that whites were much disturbed by guilt when it came to blacks. When I would stray into the wrong restaurant in pursuit of a hamburger, it didn't occur to me that the waitress was unduly troubled by guilt when she asked me to leave. I can see now that possibly she was, but then all I saw was her irritability at having to carry out so unpleasant a task. If there was guilt, it was mine for having made an imposition of myself. I can remember feeling a certain sympathy for such people, as if I was victimizing them by drawing them out of an innocent anonymity into the unasked-for role of racial policemen. Occasionally they came right out and asked me to feel sorry for them. A caddymaster at a country club told my brother and me that he was doing us a favor by not letting us caddy at this white club and that we should try to understand his position, "put yourselves in my shoes." Our color had brought this man anguish and, if a part of that anguish was guilt, it was not as immediate to me as my own guilt. I smiled at the man to let him know he shouldn't feel bad and then began my long walk home. Certainly I also judge him a coward, but in that era his cowardice was something I had to absorb.

In the 1960s, particularly the black-is-beautiful late 1960s, this absorption 2 of another's cowardice was no longer necessary. The lines of moral power, like plates in the earth, had shifted. White guilt became so palpable you could see it on people. At the time what it looked like to my eyes was a remarkable loss of authority. And what whites lost in authority, blacks gained. You cannot feel guilty about anyone without giving away power to them. Suddenly, this huge vulnerability had opened up in whites and, as a black, you had the power to step right into it. In fact, black power all but demanded that you do so. What shocked me in the late 1960s, after the helplessness I had felt in the fifties, was that guilt had changed the nature of the white man's burden from the administration of inferiors to the up-lift of equals—from the obligations of dominance to the urgencies of repentance.

I think what made the difference between the fifties and sixties, at least as   3 far as white guilt was concerned, was that whites underwent an archetypal Fall. Because of the immense turmoil of the civil rights movement, and later the black-power movement, whites were confronted for more than a decade with their will-ingness to participate in, or comply with, the oppression of blacks, their indiffer-ence to human suffering and denigration, their capacity to abide evil for their own benefit and in the defiance of their own sacred principles. The 1964 Civil Rights Bill that bestowed equality under the law on blacks was also, in a certain sense, an admission of white guilt. Had white society not been wrong, there would have been no need for such a bill. In this bill the nation acknowledged its fallenness, its lack of racial innocence, and confronted the incriminating self-knowledge that it had rationalized for many years a flagrant injustice. Denial is a common way of handling guilt, but in the 1960s there was little will left for denial except in the most recalcitrant whites. With this defense lost there was really only one road back to innocence—through actions and policies that would bring redemption.

In the 1960s the need for white redemption from racial guilt became the   4 most powerful, yet unspoken, element in America's social-policy-making process, first giving rise to the Great Society and then to a series of programs, policies, and laws that sought to make black equality and restitution a national mission. Once America could no longer deny its guilt, it went after redemption, or at least the look of redemption, and did so with a vengeance. Yet today, some twenty years later, study after study tells us that by many measures the gap between blacks and whites is widening rather than narrowing. A University of Chicago study indicates that segregation is more entrenched in American cities today than ever imagined. A National Research Council study notes the "status of blacks relative to whites (in housing and education) has stagnated or regressed since the early seventies." A follow-up to the famous Kerner Commission Report warns that blacks are as much at risk today of becoming a "nation within a nation" as we were twenty years ago, when the original report was made.

I think the white need for redemption has contributed to this tragic situation   5 by shaping our policies regarding blacks in ways that may deliver the look of in-nocence to society and its institutions but that do very little actually to uplift blacks. The specific effect of this hidden need has been to bend social policy more toward reparation for black oppression than toward the much harder and more mundane work of black uplift and development. Rather than facilitate the devel-opment of blacks to achieve parity with whites, these programs and policies—affirmative action is a good example—have tended to give blacks special entitle-ments that in many cases are of no use because blacks lack the development that would put us in a position to take advantage of them. I think the reason there has been more entitlement than development is (along with black power) the unac-knowledged white need for redemption—not true redemption, which would have concentrated policy on black development, but the appearance of redemption, which requires only that society, in the name of development, seem to be paying back its former victims with preferences. One of the effects of entitlements, I believe, has been to encourage in blacks a dependency both on entitlements and on the white guilt that generates them. Even when it serves ideal justice, bounty from another man's guilt weakens. While this is not the only factor in black "stagnation" and "regression," I believe it is one very potent factor.

It is easy enough to say that white guilt too often has the effect of bending 6 social policies in the wrong direction. But what exactly is this guilt, and how does it work in American life?

I think white guilt, in its broad sense, springs from a knowledge of ill-gotten 7 advantage. More precisely, it comes from the juxtaposition of this knowledge with the inevitable gratitude one feels for being white rather than black in America. Given the moral instincts of human beings, it is all but impossible to enjoy an ill-gotten advantage, much less to feel at least secretly grateful for it, without consciously or unconsciously experiencing guilt. If, as Kierkegaard writes, "innocence is ignorance," then guilt must always involve knowledge. White Americans *know* that their historical advantage comes from the subjugation of an entire people. So, even for whites today for whom racism is anathema, there is no escape from the knowledge that makes for guilt. Racial guilt simply accompanies the condition of being white in America.

I do not believe that this guilt is a crushing anguish for most whites, but I do 8 believe it constitutes a continuing racial vulnerability—an openness to racial culpability—that is a thread in white life, sometimes felt, sometimes not, but ever present as a potential feeling. In the late 1960s almost any black could charge this vulnerability with enough current for a white person to feel it. I had a friend who had developed this activity into a sort of specialty. I don't think he meant to be mean, though certainly he was mean. I think he was, in that hyperbolic era, exhilarated by the discovery that his race, which had long been a liability, now gave him a certain edge—that white guilt was the true force behind black power. To feel this power he would sometimes set up what he called "race experiments." Once I watched him stop a white businessman in the men's room of a large hotel and convince him to increase his tip to the black attendant from one to twenty dollars.

My friend's tactic was very simple, even corny. Out of the attendant's 9 earshot he asked the man simply to look at the attendant, a frail, elderly, and very dark man in a starched white smock that made the skin on his neck and face look as leathery as a turtle's. He sat listlessly, pathetically, on a straight-backed chair next to a small table on which sat a stack of hand towels and a silver plate for tips. Since the attendant offered no service whatever beyond the handing out of towels, one could only conclude the hotel management offered his lowly presence as flattery to their patrons, as an opportunity for that easy noblesse oblige that could reassure even the harried and weary traveling salesman of his superior station. My friend was quick to make this point to the businessman and to say that no white man would do in this job. But when the businessman put the single back in his wallet and took out a five, my friend only sneered. Did he understand the tragedy of a life spent this way, of what it must be like to earn one's paltry living as a symbol of inferiority? And did he realize that his privilege as an affluent white businessman (ironically he had just spent the day trying to sell a printing press to the Black Muslims for their newspaper *Mohammed Speaks*) was connected to the deprivation of this man and others like him?

But then my friend made a mistake that ended the game. In the heat of argument, which until then had only been playfully challenging, he inadvertently mentioned his father. This stopped the victim cold and his eyes turned inward. "What about your father?" the businessman asked. My friend replied, "He had a hard life, that's all." "How did he have a hard life?" the businessman asked. Now my friend was on the defensive. I knew he did not get along with his father, a bitter man who worked nights in a factory and demanded that the house be dark and silent all day. My friend blamed his father's bitterness on racism, but I knew he had not meant to exploit his own pain in this silly "experiment." Things had gotten too close to home, but he didn't know how to get out of the situation without losing face. Now, caught in his own trap, he did what he least wanted to do. He gave forth the rage he truly felt to a white stranger in a public men's room. "My father never had a chance," he said with the kind of anger that could easily turn to tears. "He never had a freakin' chance. Your father had all the goddamn chances, and you know he did. You sell printing presses to black people and make thousands and your father probably lives down in Fat City, Florida, all because you're white." On and on he went in this vein, using—against all that was honorable in him—his own profound racial pain to extract a flash of guilt from a white man he didn't even know.

He got more than a flash. The businessman was touched. His eyes became mournful, and finally he simply said, "You're right. Your people got a raw deal." He took a twenty dollar bill from his wallet and walked over and dropped it in the old man's tip plate. When he was gone my friend and I could not look at the old man, nor could we look at each other.

It is obvious that this was a rather shameful encounter for all concerned— my friend and I, as his silent accomplice, trading on our racial pain, tampering with a stranger for no reason, and the stranger then buying his way out of the situation for twenty dollars, a sum that was generous by one count and cheap by another. It was not an encounter of people but of historical grudges and guilts. Yet, when I think about it now twenty years later, I see that it had all the elements of a paradigm that I believe has been very much at the heart of racial policy-making in America since the 1960s.

My friend did two things that made this businessman vulnerable to his guilt—that brought his guilt into the situation as a force. First he put this man in touch with his own knowledge of his ill-gotten advantage as a white. The effect of this was to disallow the man any pretense of racial innocence, to let him know that, even if he was not the sort of white who used the word *nigger* around the dinner table, he still had reason to feel racial guilt. But, as disarming as this might have been, it was too abstract to do much more than crack open this man's vulnerability, to expose him to the logic of white guilt. This was the five-dollar, intellectual sort of guilt. The twenty dollars required something more visceral. In achieving this, the second thing my friend did was something he had not intended to do, something that ultimately brought him as much shame as he was doling out: He made a display of his own racial pain and anger. (What brought him shame was not the pain and anger, but his trading on them for what turned out to be a mere twenty bucks.) The effect of this display was to reinforce the man's knowledge of ill-gotten advantage, to give credibility and solidity to it by putting a face on it. Here was human testimony, a young black beside himself at the thought of his father's racially constricted life. The pain of one man evidenced the knowledge of the other. When the businessman listened to my friend's pain, his racial guilt—normally only one source of guilt lying dormant among others—was called out like a neglected debt he would finally have to settle. An ill-gotten advantage is not hard to bear—it can be marked up to fate—until it touches the genuine human pain it has brought into the world. This is the pain that hardens guilty knowledge.

Such knowledge is a powerful influence when it becomes conscious. What 14 makes it so powerful is the element of fear that guilt always carries, the fear of what the guilty knowledge says about us. Guilt makes us afraid for ourselves, and thus generates as much self-preoccupation as concern for others. The nature of this preoccupation is always the redemption of innocence, the reestablishment of good feeling about oneself.

In this sense, the fear for the self that is buried in all guilt is a pressure to- 15 ward selfishness. It can lead us to put our own need for innocence above our concern for the problem that made us feel guilt in the first place. But this fear for the self does not only inspire selfishness; it also becomes a pressure to *escape* the guilt-inducing situation. When selfishness and escapism are at work, we are no longer interested in the source of our guilt and, therefore, no longer concerned with an authentic redemption from it. Then we only want the look of redemption, the gesture of concern that will give us the appearance of innocence and escape from the situation. Obviously the businessman did not put twenty dollars in the tip plate because he thought it would uplift black Americans. He did it selfishly for the appearance of concern and for the escape it afforded him.

This is not to say that guilt is never the right motive for doing good works 16 or showing concern, only that it is a very dangerous one because of its tendency to draw us into self-preoccupation and escapism. Guilt is a civilizing emotion when the fear for the self that it carries is contained—a containment that allows guilt to be more selfless and that makes genuine concern possible. I think this was the kind of guilt that, along with the other forces, made the 1964 Civil Rights Bill possible. But since then I believe too many of our social policies related to race have been shaped by the fearful underside of guilt.

Black power evoked white guilt and made it a force in American institutions, 17 very much in the same way as my friend brought it to life in the businessman. Few people volunteer for guilt. Usually others make us feel it. It was the expression of black anger and pain that hardened the guilty knowledge of white ill-gotten advantage. And black power—whether from militant fringe groups, the civil rights establishment, or big city political campaigns—knew exactly the kind of white guilt it was after. It wanted to trigger the kind of white guilt in which whites fear for their own decency and innocence; it wanted the guilt of white self-preoccupation and escapism. Always at the heart of black power, in whatever form, has been a profound anger at what was done to blacks and an equally profound feeling that there should be reparations. But a sober white guilt (in which fear for the self is still contained) seeks a strict fairness—the 1964 Civil Rights Bill that guaranteed equality under the law. It is of little value when one is after more than fairness. So black power made its mission to have whites fear for their innocence, to feel a visceral guilt from which they would have to seek a more profound redemption. In such redemption was the possibility of black reparation. Black power upped the ante on white guilt.

With black power, all of the elements of the hidden paradigm that shape   18
America's race-related social policy were in place. Knowledge of ill-gotten advantage could now be shown and deepened by black power into the sort of guilt from which institutions could only redeem themselves by offering more than fairness—by offering forms of reparation and compensation for past injustice. I believe this bent our policies toward racial entitlements at the expense of racial development. In 1964, one of the assurances Senator Hubert Humphrey and others had to give Congress to get the landmark Civil Rights Bill passed was that the bill would not in any way require employers to use racial preferences to rectify racial imbalances. But this was before the explosion of black power in the late 1960s, before the hidden paradigm was set in motion. After black power, racial preferences became the order of the day.

If this paradigm brought blacks entitlements, it also brought the continuation   19
of the most profound problem in American society, the invisibility of blacks as a people. The white guilt that this paradigm elicits is the kind of guilt that preoccupies whites with their own innocence and pressures them toward escapism—twenty dollars in the plate and out the door. With this guilt, as opposed to the contained guilt of genuine concern, whites tend to see only their own need for quick redemption. Blacks then become a means to this redemption and, as such, they must be seen as generally "less than" others. Their needs are "special," "unique," "different." They are seen exclusively along the dimension of their victimization, so that they become "different" people with whom whites can negotiate entitlements but never fully see as people like themselves. Guilt that preoccupies people with their own innocence blinds them to those who make them feel guilty. This, of course, is not racism, and yet it has the same effect as racism since it makes blacks something of a separate species for whom normal standards and values do not automatically apply.

Nowhere is this more evident today than in American universities. At some   20
of America's most elite universities administrators have granted concessions in response to black student demands (black power) that all but sanction racial separatism on campus—black "theme" dorms, black student unions, black yearbooks, homecoming dances, and so forth. I don't believe administrators sincerely believe

in these separatist concessions. Most of them are liberals who see racial separatism as wrong. But black student demands pull administrators into the paradigm of self-preoccupied white guilt, whereby they seek a quick redemption by offering special entitlements that go beyond fairness. As a result, black students become all but invisible to them. Though blacks have the lowest grade point average of any racial group in American universities, administrators never sit down with them and "demand" in kind that black students bring their grades up to par. The paradigm of white guilt makes the real problems of black students secondary to the need for white redemption. It also cuts administrators off from their own values, which would most certainly discourage racial separatism and encourage higher academic performance for black students. Lastly, it makes for escapist policies. There is no difference between giving black students a separate lounge and leaving twenty dollars in the tip plate on the way out the door.

1990

QUESTIONS FOR DISCUSSION

Content

a. In paragraph 2 Steele writes, "You cannot feel guilty about anyone without giving away power to them." What does he mean by this?

b. According to Steele, what has caused white guilt? Trace the causal links he describes.

c. At the end of paragraph 6, Steele asks, "But what exactly is this guilt, and how does it work in American life?" How does he answer his question?

d. What does he mean when he says that "white guilt was the true force behind black power" (paragraph 8)?

e. What happened in the men's room between Steele's friend and the white businessman (paragraphs 8–13)? What was Steele's friend's "racial experiment"? What went "wrong" and why?

f. Why does the businessman put the twenty dollars in the tip plate?

g. How does Steele define *guilt?* What is the difference between the general term *guilt* and the specific term *white guilt?*

h. According to Steele, what effects does white guilt have on society? What are both its positive and its negative effects?

i. What is the relationship between black power and white guilt?

j. According to Steele, what did the Civil Rights Act of 1964 cause?

Strategy and Style

k. Look up *visceral,* a key word in paragraphs 13 and 17. What does this word mean in the context of these paragraphs? What other words does Steele use in these paragraphs to help define the word? Why was being visceral a problem?

l. What is the effect on you of the example of the "racial experiment"? Is it more of a "visceral" effect or an intellectual effect? What effect might Steele have intended with this example?

m. Look up *paradigm* (paragraph 20). What does the word mean by itself? What does it mean in the phrase "paradigm of white guilt"?

n. How would you characterize the tone of this essay? Does Steele sound calm, angry, impassioned, etc.?

SUGGESTIONS FOR SHORT WRITING

a. Use the statement from the first of the Questions for Discussion and describe an event or two from your own life that illustrates it.

b. Summarize this essay in the form of a letter to your parents telling them about the reading you are doing for this class. Besides your summary, mention the one or two things that strike you as most important about the essay.

SUGGESTIONS FOR SUSTAINED WRITING

a. Do some research into a particular period or event mentioned by Steele—the black power movement of the late 1960s, or the 1964 Civil Rights Act, for examples. Do not merely summarize your research, but use it to come to an understanding of Steele's essay. You may wish to write the paper as a comparison of how you understood the essay on a first reading to how you understand it after your research.

b. By the end of the essay Steele begins to suggest ways to solve the problem of racial separatism; however, he does not elaborate on his suggestions. Write an essay in which you pick up on the points raised in paragraph 20, and present a detailed solution to the problem.

Where Have All the Parents Gone?

Barbara Dafoe Whitehead

Barbara Dafoe Whitehead (b. 1944) is a social historian who heads the Family in American Culture Project for the Institute of American Values. She has written many articles about family issues, including this essay, which originally appeared in New Perspectives Quarterly *in 1990.*

"Invest in kids," George Bush mused during his 1988 presidential campaign, "I like it." Apparently so do others. A growing number of corporate CEOs and educators, elected officials and child-welfare advocates have embraced the same language. "Invest in kids" is the bumper-sticker for an important new cause, aptly tagged the *kids as capital* argument. It runs as follows:

America's human capital comes in two forms: The active work force and the prospective work force. The bulk of tomorrow's workers are today's children, of course. So children make up much of the stockpile of America's potential human capital.

If we look at them as tomorrow's workers, we begin to appreciate our stake in today's children. They will determine when we can retire, how well we can live in retirement, how generous our health insurance will be, how strong our social safety net, how orderly our society. What's more, today's children will determine how successfully we compete in the global economy. They will be going head-to-head against Japanese, Korean, and West German children.

Unfortunately, American children aren't prepared to run the race, let alone win it. Many are illiterate, undernourished, impaired, unskilled, poor. Consider the children who started first grade in 1986: 14 percent were illegitimate; 15 percent were physically or emotionally handicapped; 15 percent spoke another language other than English; 28 percent were poor; and fully 40 percent could be expected to live in a single-parent home before they reached eighteen. Given falling birth rates, this future work force is small—all the more reason to worry about its poor quality. So "invest in kids" is not the cry of the soft-hearted altruist but the call of the hardheaded realist.

Kids as capital has caught on because it responds to a broad set of national concerns. Whether one is worried about the rise of the underclass, the decline of the family, our standing in the global economy, the nation's level of educational performance, or intergenerational conflict, kids as capital seems to offer an answer.

Further, *kids as capital* offers the rationale for a new coalition for child-welfare programs. The argument reaches beyond the community of traditional children's advocates and draws business into the child-saving fold. American corporations clearly have a stake in tomorrow's work force as they don't have in today's children. *Kids as capital* gives the toughminded, fifty-five-year-old CEO a reason to "care" about the eight-year-old, Hispanic school girl.

Nevertheless, the argument left unchallenged could easily become yet an- 7
other "feel-good" formula that doesn't work. Worse, it could end up betraying
those it seeks to save—the nation's children.

First, *kids as capital* departs from a classic American vision of the future. 8
Most often, our history has been popularly viewed as progressive, with each generation breaking with and improving on the past. As an immigrant nation, we have
always measured our progress through the progress of our children; they have been
the bearers of the dream.

Kids as capital turns this optimistic view on its head. It conjures up a picture 9
of a dark and disorderly future. Essentially, kids as capital is dystopic—closer to the
spirit of *Blade Runner* and *Black Rain* than *Wizard of Oz* or *It's a Wonderful Life.*
Children, in this view, do not bear the dream. They carry the seeds of our destruction. In short, *kids as capital* plays on our fears, rather than our hopes. It holds out
the vision of a troubled future in order to secure a safer and more orderly present.

There is something troubling, too, in such an instrumental view of children. 10
To define them narrowly as tomorrow's wonders is to strip them of their full status
as humans, as children: Kids can't be kids; they can only be embryonic workers. And
treating *kids as capital* makes it easier to measure them solely through IQ tests, class
standing, SAT scores, drop-out ratios, physical fitness tests. This leaves no place in
the society for the slow starter, the handicapped, the quirky, and the nonconforming.

Yet *kids as capital* has an even more serious flaw. It evades the central fact 11
of life for American children: They have parents.

As we all know, virtually every child in America grows up in a family with one 12
or more parents. Parents house children. Parents feed children. Parents clothe children. Parents nurture and protect children. Parents instruct children in everything
from using a fork to driving a car. To be sure, there have been vast changes in family
life, and, increasingly, parents must depend on teachers, doctors, day-care workers,
and technology to help care for and educate their children. Even so, these changes
haven't altered one fundamental fact: In American society, parents still bear the primary responsibility for the material and spiritual welfare of children. As our teachers
and counselors and politicians keep reminding us, everything begins at home. So, if
today's children are in trouble, it's because today's parents are in trouble.

As recently as a dozen years ago, it was the central argument of an ambi- 13
tious report by the Carnegie Council on Children. The Council put it plainly: "The
best way to help children tomorrow is to support parents today." Yet, that view has
been lost. The *kids as capital* argument suppresses the connection between parents
and children. It imagines that we can improve the standing of children without improving the standing of the parents. In the new rhetoric, it is hard even to find the
word "parent." Increasingly, kids are portrayed as standing alone out there somewhere, cosmically parent-free.

As a result, *kids as capital* ignores rather than addresses one of the most im- 14
portant changes in American life: The decline in the power and standing of the nation's parents.

Only a generation ago, parents stood at the center of society. First of all, 15
there were so many of them—fully half the nation's households in 1960 were par-

ent households with one or more children under eighteen. Moreover, parents looked alike—Dad worked and Mom stayed at home. And parents marched through the stages of childbearing and child rearing in virtual lockstep: Most couples who married in the 1940s and 1950s finished having their 3.2 children by the time they were in their late twenties.

Their demographic dominance meant two things: First, it made for broad 16 common ground in child rearing. Parents could do a great deal to support each other in raising the new generation. They could, and did, create a culture hospitable to children. Secondly, it made for political clout. When so many adults were parents and so many parents were part of an expanding consumer economy, private and public interests converged. The concerns of parents—housing, health, education—easily found their way into the national agenda. Locally, too, parents were dominant. In some postwar suburbs like Levittown, Pennsylvania, three-quarters of all residents were either parents or children under ten. Not surprisingly, there was little dissent when it came to building a new junior high or establishing a summer recreation program or installing a new playground. What's more, parents and kids drove the consumer economy. Every time they bought a pair of sneakers or a new bike, they were acting in the nation's best interest.

Behind this, of course, lurked a powerful pronatal ideology. Parenthood was 17 the definitive credential of adulthood. More than being married, more than getting a job, it was having a child that baptized you as an adult in postwar America. In survey after survey, postwar parents rated children above marriage itself as the greatest reward of private life. For a generation forced to make personal sacrifices during the Depression and the war, having children and pursuing a private life represented a new kind of freedom.

By the 1970s, parents no longer enjoyed so central a place in the society. To 18 baby boom children, postwar family life seemed suffocating and narrow. Women, in particular, wanted room to breathe. The rights movements of the sixties and seventies overturned the pronatal ideology, replacing it with an ideology of choice. Adults were free to choose among many options: Single, married, or divorced; career-primary or career-secondary; parent, stepparent, or child-free.

Thus, parenthood lost its singular status. It no longer served as the definitive 19 credential of maturity and adult achievement. In fact, as careers and personal fulfillment beckoned, parenthood seemed just the opposite: A serious limitation on personal growth and success. As Gloria Steinem put it, "I either gave birth to someone else or I gave birth to myself."

As the pronatal ideology vanished, so did the close connection between pri- 20 vate families and the public interest. Raising children was no longer viewed as a valuable contribution to the society, an activity that boosted the economy, built citizen participation, and increased the nation's confidence in the future. Instead, it became one option among many. No longer a moral imperative, child rearing was just another "lifestyle choice."

Viewed this way, raising children looked like an economic disaster. Starting 21 out, parents had to shell out $3,000 for basic prenatal care and maternity costs; $3,000–$5,000 per child for day care; and $2,500 for the basic baby basket of goods and services. Crib-to-college costs for middle-class Americans could run as high as $135,000 per child. And, increasingly, the period of economic dependency for children stretched well beyond age eighteen. College tuitions and start-up subsidies for the new college graduate became part of the economic burden of parenthood. In an ad campaign, Manufacturers Hanover Trust gave prospective parents fair warning: "If you want a bundle of joy; you'll need a bundle of money."

Hard-pressed younger Americans responded to these new realities in several 22 ways. Some simply chose not to have children. Others decided to have one or two, but only after they had a good job and solid prospects. Gradually, the number of parent households in the nation declined from one-half to one-third, and America faced a birth dearth.

For those who chose the parent option, there was only one way to face up to 23 the new economic pressures of child rearing: Work longer and harder outside the home. For all but the extremely well-off, a second income became essential. But in struggling to pay the bills, parents seemed to be short-changing their children in another way. They weren't taking their moral responsibilities seriously enough. They weren't spending enough time with their kids. They weren't reading to the children or playing with the kids or supervising homework. And, most important, they weren't teaching good values.

This emerging critique marked a dramatic change in the way society viewed 24 parents. In the postwar period, the stereotypical parent was self-sacrificing, responsible, caring, attentive—an impossible standard, to be sure, but one that lent enormous popular support and approval to adults engaged in the messy and difficult work of raising children. Cruel, abusive, self-absorbed parents might exist, but the popular culture failed to acknowledge them. It was not until parents began to lose their central place in the society that this flattering image faded. Then, quite rapidly, the dominant image of The Good Parent gave way to a new and equally powerful image—the image of The Bad Parent.

The shift occurred in two stages. The first-stage critique emerged in the sev- 25 enties and focused on an important new figure: The working mother. Working mothers were destroying their children and the family, conservative critics charged. They weren't feeding kids wholesome meals, they weren't taking the kids to church, they weren't serving as moral exemplars. Liberals sided with working mothers, but conceded that they were struggling with some new and difficult issues: Was day care as good as mother care? Was quality time good enough? Were the rewards of twelve-hour workdays great enough to make up for the loss of sleep and leisure-time? Where did the mother of a feverish child belong—at the crib or at her desk?

On the whole, the first-stage critique was a sympathetic critique. In its view, 26 parents might be affected by stress and guilt, but they weren't yet afflicted by serious pathology. After all, in the seventies, the nation's most suspect drug was laetrile, not crack or ice. Divorce was still viewed as a healthy alternative to an unhappy family life. But as the eighties began, a darker image of parents appeared. In the second-stage critique, . . . parents became toxic.

Day after day, throughout the eighties, Americans confronted an ugly new 27 reality. Parents were hurting and murdering their children. Day after day, the newspapers brought yet another story of a child abandoned or battered. Day after day, the local news told of a child sexually abused by a father or a stepfather or a mother's boyfriend. Week by week, the national media brought us into courtrooms where photographs of battered children were held up to the camera. The sheer volume of stories suggested an epidemic of historic proportion. In even the most staid publications, the news was sensational. The *New York Times* carried bizarre stories usually found only in tabloids: A father who tortured his children for years; a mother who left her baby in a suitcase in a building she then set on fire; parents who abandoned babies dead or alive, in toilets, dumpsters, and alleyways.

Drug use among parents was one clear cause of abuse. And, increasingly 28 child abuse and drug abuse were linked in the most direct way possible. Pregnant women were battering their children in the womb, delivering drugs through their umbilical cords. Nightly images of crack-addicted babies in neonatal units destroyed any lingering public sympathy for mothers of the underclass. And as the highly publicized Joel Steinberg case made clear, middle-class parents, too, took drugs and killed babies. Even those parents who occasionally indulged were causing their children harm. The Partnership for Drug-Free America ran ads asking: "With millions of parents doing drugs, is it any wonder their kids are too?"

More than drugs, it was divorce that lay at the heart of middle-class parental 29 failure. It wasn't the crackhouse but the courthouse that was the scene of their collapse. Parents engaged in bitter custody battles. Parents kidnapped their own children. Parents used children as weapons against each other or simply walked away from their responsibilities. In an important new study on the long-term effects of divorce, Judith Wallerstein challenged the earlier notion that divorce is healthy for kids. She studied middle-class families for fifteen years after divorce and came up with some startling findings: Almost half of the children in the study entered adulthood as worried, underachieving, self-deprecating, and sometimes angry young men and women; one in four experienced a severe and enduring drop in their standard of living; three in five felt rejected by at least one parent. Her study concluded: "Divorce is almost always more devastating for children than for their parents. . . . [W]hile divorce can rescue a parent from an intolerable situation, it can fail to rescue the children."

As a group, today's parents have been portrayed as selfish and uncaring: 30 Yuppie parents abandon the children to the au pair; working parents turn their kids over to the mall and the video arcade; single parents hang a key around their kids' necks and a list of emergency numbers on the refrigerator. Even in the healthiest families, parents fail to put their children first.

The indictment of parents is pervasive. In a survey by the Carnegie Founda- 31 tion, 90 percent of a national sample of public school teachers say a lack of parental support is a problem in their classrooms. Librarians gathered at a national convention to draft a new policy to deal with the problem of parents who send unattended children to the library after school. Daycare workers complain to Ann Landers that all too often parents hand over children with empty stomachs and full diapers. Everywhere, parents are flunking the most basic tests.

Declining demographically, hard-pressed economically, and disarrayed po- 32
litically, parents have become part of the problem. For proponents of the *kids as
capital* argument, the logic is clear: Why try to help parents—an increasingly marginal and unsympathetic bunch—when you can rescue their children?

To blame parents for larger social changes is nothing new. In the past, child- 33
saving movements have depended on building a public consensus that certain parents have failed. Child reformers in the Progressive Era, for example, were able to
expand the scope of public sector responsibility for the welfare of children by exploiting mainstream fears about immigrant parents and their child-rearing practices. But what is new is the sense that the majority of parents—up and down the
social ladder—are failing. Even middle-class parents, once solid, dependable
caretakers of the next generation, don't seem to be up to the job.

By leaving parents out of the picture, *kids as capital* conjures up the image 34
of our little workers struggling against the little workers of Germany and the little
workers of Japan. But this picture is obviously false. For the little workers of Germany and Japan have parents too. The difference is that their parents are strongly
valued and supported by the society for their contributions *as parents*. We won't
be facing up to reality until we are ready to pit our parents against their parents,
and thus our family policy against theirs.

1990

QUESTIONS FOR DISCUSSION

Content

a. What is the "kids as capital" argument (paragraphs 2–6)?
b. What is Dafoe Whitehead's initial response to this argument (paragraphs
   7–14)?
c. Though this essay is in part a cause/effect analysis, it is also an argument. What
   is Dafoe Whitehead arguing?
d. What is the main cause/effect relationship that this argument is based on?
e. Paraphrase and elaborate on paragraph 9. What is Dafoe Whitehead's point in
   this paragraph? Do you agree with her?
f. In paragraph 17, the author refers to a "pronatal ideology." What does she
   mean?
g. What are the stages in the shift from the rosy view of parenthood in the 1950s
   to the dark view of parenthood now? What has happened at each stage to further harm the image of parents?

Strategy and Style

h. Writers who use the cause/effect approach will often use particular words or
   phrases to signal the cause/effect relationships. Some of these words/phrases

that Dafoe Whitehead uses are "as a result," "thus," "behind this," "then," "gave way to," and "lay at the heart of." Find these and other clues in this essay, and explain what the cause/effect relationships are.

i. Dafoe Whitehead begins her essay with several paragraphs (2–6) that present the other side of the argument; she then presents her own argument (paragraphs 7–14). What might have been her reasons for giving the other side so much attention?

j. Paragraph 7 is a transition between the two arguments. How does it link the two arguments? What are the key words that link the "kids as capital" argument with Dafoe Whitehead's argument?

k. Look at the transition words and phrases that frequently begin paragraphs (for example, "unfortunately" in paragraph 4, "further" in paragraph 6, "nevertheless" in paragraph 7, and "as we all know" in paragraph 12). What job do these words/phrases perform?

SUGGESTIONS FOR SHORT WRITING

a. List the points of the "kids as capital" argument (paragraphs 2–6) that Dafoe Whitehead summarizes before she presents her own argument. Then list the points of her own argument (paragraphs 7–14). Write a brief comparison of the two arguments. Which seems stronger?

b. Look up the Joel Steinberg case (mentioned in paragraph 28) in the *New York Times Index* and/or on an electronic database such as InfoTrak. Find and summarize one or two articles about the case.

SUGGESTIONS FOR SUSTAINED WRITING

a. Write a counterargument to Dafoe Whitehead's argument. Before you begin drafting your paper, outline her essay so that you can clearly see its logic and the main points. Then brainstorm a list of points that you could make against her points. Also mark places in your argument where facts and statistics would strengthen it.

b. Conversely, agree with Dafoe Whitehead's argument, and write an essay that expands upon it. Look up in the library the surveys and studies she cites. Use at least one of these studies as the basis for your essay.

c. Dafoe Whitehead does not provide a plan for solving the problem she has described because her intention in this essay is merely to convince us of what the real problem is. She does, however, imply in her conclusion that we must find a way to value parents and to create stability in parenting. Write an essay in which you present a specific plan to achieve this.

If Hitler Asked You to Electrocute a Stranger, Would You? Probably

Philip Meyer

Philip Meyer (b. 1930) earned a BS in 1952 from Kansas State University, an MA in 1963 from the University of North Carolina, and did graduate work at Harvard University during 1966 and 1967. While attending college he worked as the assistant state editor of the Topeka Daily Capital *and as a reporter for the* Miami Herald. *From 1962 to 1978 he was the Washington, D.C., correspondent for Knight-Ridder Newspapers, and from 1978 to 1982 he was Knight-Ridder's director of news and circulation research in Miami. Since then he has taught journalism at the University of North Carolina at Chapel Hill. In 1968 he shared a Pulitzer Prize with the staff of the* Detroit Free Press *for covering the Detroit riots in 1967. He has written several books about journalism, including* Precision Journalism, *which was first published in 1973 and has reappeared in subsequent editions;* To Keep the Republic, *written in collaboration with David Olson in 1975; and* Editors, Publishers, and Newspaper Ethics *(1983); among other books. He also contributes regularly to* Public Opinion Quarterly *and* Esquire. *"If Hitler Asked You . . ." was first published in* Esquire *in 1970.*

In the beginning, Stanley Milgram was worried about the Nazi problem. He doesn't worry much about the Nazis anymore. He worries about you and me, and, perhaps, himself a little bit too. 1

Stanley Milgram is a social psychologist, and when he began his career at Yale University in 1960 he had a plan to prove, scientifically, that Germans are different. The Germans-are-different hypothesis has been used by historians, such as William L. Shirer, to explain the systematic destruction of the Jews by the Third Reich. 2

The appealing thing about this theory is that it makes those of us who are not Germans feel better about the whole business. Obviously, you and I are not Hitler, and it seems equally obvious that we would never do Hitler's dirty work for him. But now, because of Stanley Milgram, we are compelled to wonder. Milgram developed a laboratory experiment which provided a systematic way to measure obedience. His plan was to try it out in New Haven on Americans and then go to Germany and try it out on Germans. He was strongly motivated by scientific curiosity, but there was also some moral content in his decision to pursue this line of research, which was, in turn, colored by his own Jewish background. If he could show that Germans are more obedient than Americans, he could then vary the conditions of the experiment and try to find out just what it is that makes some people more obedient than others. With this understanding, the world might, conceivably, be just a little bit better. 3

But he never took his experiment to Germany. He never took it any farther than Bridgeport. The first finding, also the most unexpected and disturbing finding, was that we Americans are an obedient people: Not blindly obedient, and not 4 blissfully obedient, just obedient. "I found so much obedience," says Milgram softly, a little sadly, "I hardly saw the need for taking the experiment to Germany."

There is something of the theatre director in Milgram, and his technique, which 5 he learned from one of the old masters in experimental psychology, Solomon Asch, is to stage a play with every line rehearsed, every prop carefully selected, and everybody an actor except one person. That one person is the subject of the experiment. The subject, of course, does not know he is in a play. He thinks he is in real life.

The experiment worked like this: If you were an innocent subject in Milgram's 6 melodrama, you read an ad in the newspaper or received one in the mail asking for volunteers for an educational experiment. The job would take about an hour and pay $4.50. So you make an appointment and go to an old Romanesque stone structure on High Street with the imposing name of The Yale Interaction Laboratory. It looks something like a broadcasting studio. Inside, you meet a young, crew-cut man in a laboratory coat who says he is Jack Williams, the experimenter. There is another citizen, fiftyish, Irish face, an accountant, a little overweight, and very mild and harmless-looking. This other citizen seems nervous and plays with his hat while the two of you sit in chairs side by side and are told that the $4.50 checks are yours no matter what happens. Then you listen to Jack Williams explain the experiment.

It is about learning, says Jack Williams in a quiet, knowledgeable way. Science does not know much about the conditions under which people learn and this experiment is to find out about negative reinforcement. Negative reinforcement is getting punished when you do something wrong, as opposed to positive reinforcement which is getting rewarded when you do something right. The negative reinforcement in this case is electric shock.

Then Jack Williams takes two pieces of paper, puts them in a hat, and shakes 8 them up. One piece of paper is supposed to say, "Teacher" and the other, "Learner." Draw one and you will see which you will be. The mild-looking accountant draws one, holds it close to his vest like a poker player, looks at it, and says, "Learner." You look at yours. It says, "Teacher." You do not know that the drawing is rigged, and both slips say "Teacher." The experimenter beckons to the mild-mannered "learner."

"Want to step right in here and have a seat, please?" he says. "You can leave 9 your coat on the back of that chair . . . roll up your right sleeve, please. Now what I want to do is strap down your arms to avoid excessive movement on your part during the experiment. This electrode is connected to the shock generator in the next room.

"And this electrode paste," he says, squeezing some stuff out of a plastic bot- 10 tle and putting it on the man's arm, "is to provide a good contact and to avoid a blister or burn. Are there any questions now before we go into the next room?"

You don't have any, but the strapped-in "learner" does.   11

"I do think I should say this," says the learner. "About two years ago, I was 12 at the veterans' hospital . . . they detected a heart condition. Nothing serious, but as long as I'm having these shocks, how strong are they—how dangerous are they?"

Williams, the experimenter, shakes his head casually. "Oh, no," he says. "Al- 13
though they may be painful, they're not dangerous. Anything else?"

Nothing else. And so you play the game. The game is for you to read a se- 14
ries of word pairs: For example, blue-girl, nice-day, fat-neck. When you finish the
list, you read just the first word in each pair and then a multiple-choice list of four
other words, including the second word of the pair. The learner, from his remote,
strapped-in position, pushes one of four switches to indicate which of the four answers he thinks is the right one. If he gets it right, nothing happens and you go on
to the next one. If he gets it wrong, you push a switch that buzzes and gives him
an electric shock. And then you go to the next word. You start with 15 volts and
increase the number of volts by 15 for each wrong answer. The control board goes
from 15 volts on one end to 450 volts on the other. So that you know what you are
doing, you get a test shock yourself, at 45 volts. It hurts. To further keep you aware
of what you are doing to that man in there, the board has verbal descriptions of the
shock levels, ranging from "Slight Shock" at the left-hand side, through "Intense
Shock" in the middle, to "Danger: Severe Shock" toward the far right. Finally, at
the very end, under 435- and 450-volt switches, there are three ambiguous X's. If,
at any point, you hesitate, Mr. Williams calmly tells you to go on. If you still hesitate, he tells you again.

Except for some terrifying details, which will be explained in a moment, this 15
is the experiment. The object is to find the shock level at which you disobey the
experimenter and refuse to pull the switch.

When Stanley Milgram first wrote this script, he took it to fourteen Yale psy- 16
chology majors and asked them what they thought would happen. He put it this
way: Out of one hundred persons in the teacher's predicament, how would their
breakoff points be distributed along the 15-to-450-volt scale? They thought a few
would break off very early, most would quit someplace in the middle and a few
would go all the way to the end. The highest estimate of the number out of one
hundred who would go all the way to the end was three. Milgram then informally
polled some of his fellow scholars in the psychology department. They agreed that
very few would go to the end. Milgram thought so too.

"I'll tell you quite frankly," he says, "before I began this experiment, before 17
any shock generator was built, I thought that most people would break off at
'Strong Shock' or 'Very Strong Shock.' You would get only a very, very small proportion of people going out to the end of the shock generator, and they would constitute a pathological fringe."

In his pilot experiments, Milgram used Yale students as subjects. Each of 18
them pushed the shock switches, one by one, all the way to the end of the board.

So he rewrote the script to include some protests from the learner. At first, 19
they were mild, gentlemanly, Yalie protests, but, "it didn't seem to have as much effect as I thought it would or should," Milgram recalls. "So we had more violent
protestation on the part of the person getting the shock. All of the time, of course,
what we were trying to do was not to create a macabre situation, but simply to generate disobedience. And that was one of the first findings. This was not only a tech-

nical deficiency of the experiment, that we didn't get disobedience. It really was the first finding: That obedience would be much greater than we had assumed it would be and disobedience would be much more difficult than we had assumed."

As it turned out, the situation did become rather macabre. The only mean- 20 ingful way to generate disobedience was to have the victim protest with great anguish, noise, and vehemence. The protests were tape-recorded so that all the teachers ordinarily would hear the same sounds and nuances, and they started with a grunt at 75 volts, proceeded through a "Hey, that really hurts," at 125 volts, got desperate with, "I can't stand the pain, don't do that," at 180 volts, reached complaints of heart trouble at 195, an agonized scream at 285, a refusal to answer at 315, and only heart-rending, ominous silence after that.

Still, sixty-five percent of the subjects, twenty- to fifty-year-old American 21 males, everyday, ordinary people, like you and me, obediently kept pushing those levers in the belief that they were shocking the mild-mannered learner, whose name was Mr. Wallace, and who was chosen for the role because of his innocent appearance, all the way up to 450 volts.

Milgram was now getting enough disobedience so that he had something he 22 could measure. The next step was to vary the circumstances to see what would encourage or discourage obedience.

He put the learner in the same room with the teacher. He stopped strapping 23 the learner's hand down. He rewrote the script so that at 150 volts the learner took his hand off the shock plate and declared that he wanted out of the experiment. He rewrote the script some more so that the experimenter then told the teacher to grasp the learner's hand and physically force it down on the plate to give Mr. Wallace his unwanted electric shock.

"I had the feeling that very few people would go on at that point, if any," Mil- 24 gram says. "I thought that would be the limit of obedience that you would find in the laboratory."

It wasn't.
25

Although seven years have now gone by, Milgram still remembers the first 26 person to walk into the laboratory in the newly rewritten script. He was a construction worker, a very short man. "He was so small," says Milgram, "that when he sat on the chair in front of the shock generator, his feet didn't reach the floor. When the experimenter told him to push the victim's hand down and give the shock, he turned to the experimenter, and he turned to the victim, his elbow went up, he fell down on the hand of the victim, his feet kind of tugged to one side, and he said, 'Like this, boss?' ZZUMPH!"

The experiment was played out to its bitter end. Milgram tried it with forty 27 different subjects. And thirty percent of them obeyed the experimenter and kept on obeying.

"The protests of the victim were strong and vehement, he was screaming his 28 guts out, he refused to participate, and you had to physically struggle with him in order to get his hand down on the shock generator," Milgram remembers. But twelve out of forty did it.

Milgram took his experiment out of New Haven. Not to Germany, just 29
twenty miles down the road to Bridgeport. Maybe, he reasoned, the people obeyed
because of the prestigious setting of Yale University.

The new setting was a suite of three rooms in a run-down office building in 30
Bridgeport. The only identification was a sign with a fictitious name: "Research
Associates of Bridgeport." Questions about professional connections got only
vague answers about "research for industry."

Obedience was less in Bridgeport. Forty-eight percent of the subjects stayed 31
for the maximum shock, compared to sixty-five percent at Yale. But this was enough
to prove that far more than Yale's prestige was behind the obedient behavior.

For more than seven years now, Stanley Milgram has been trying to figure out 32
what makes ordinary American citizens so obedient. The most obvious answer—that
people are mean, nasty, brutish and sadistic—won't do. The subjects who gave the
shocks to Mr. Wallace to the end of the board did not enjoy it. They groaned, protested,
fidgeted, argued, and in some cases, were seized by fits of nervous, agitated giggling.

"They even try to get out of it," says Milgram, "but they are somehow engaged 33
in something from which they cannot liberate themselves. They are locked into a
structure, and they do not have the skills or inner resources to disengage themselves."

Milgram's theory assumes that people behave in two different operating 34
modes as different as ice and water. He does not rely on Freud or sex or toilet-
training hang-ups for this theory. All he says is that ordinarily we operate in a state
of autonomy, which means we pretty much have and assert control over what we
do. But in certain circumstances, we operate under what Milgram calls a state of
agency (after agent, n . . . one who acts for or in the place of another by authority
from him; a substitute; a deputy.—*Webster's Collegiate Dictionary*). A state of
agency, to Milgram, is nothing more than a frame of mind.

"There's nothing bad about it, there's nothing good about it," he says. "It's 35
a natural circumstance of living with other people. . . . I think of a state of agency
as a real transformation of a person; if a person has different properties when he's
in that state, just as water can turn to ice under certain conditions of temperature,
a person can move to the state of mind that I call agency . . . the critical thing is
that you see yourself as the instrument of the execution of another person's wishes.
You do not see yourself as acting on your own. And there's a real transformation,
a real change of properties of the person."

So, for most subjects in Milgram's laboratory experiments, the act of giving 36
Mr. Wallace his painful shock was necessary, even though unpleasant, and besides
they were doing it on behalf of somebody else and it was for science.

Stanley Milgram has his problems, too. He believes that in the laboratory sit- 37
uation, he would not have shocked Mr. Wallace. His professional critics reply that in
his real-life situation he has done the equivalent. He has placed innocent and naïve
subjects under great emotional strain and pressure in selfish obedience to his quest
for knowledge. When you raise this issue with Milgram, he has an answer ready.
There is, he explains patiently, a critical difference between his naïve subjects and

the man in the electric chair. The man in the electric chair (in the mind of the naïve subject) is helpless, strapped in. But the naïve subject is free to go at any time.

Immediately after he offers this distinction, Milgram anticipates the objection. 38

"It's quite true," he says, "that this is almost a philosophic position, because 39 we have learned that some people are psychologically incapable of disengaging themselves. But that doesn't relieve them of the moral responsibility."

The parallel is exquisite. "The tension problem was unexpected," says Mil- 40 gram in his defense. But he went on anyway. The naïve subjects didn't expect the screaming protests from the strapped-in learner. But they went on.

"I had to make a judgment," says Milgram. "I had to ask myself, was this 41 harming the person or not? My judgment is that it was not. Even in the extreme cases, I wouldn't say that permanent damage results."

Sound familiar? "The shocks may be painful," the experimenter kept saying, 42 "but they're not dangerous."

After the series of experiments was completed, Milgram sent a report of the 43 results to his subjects and a questionnaire, asking whether they were glad or sorry to have been in the experiment. Eighty-three and seven-tenths percent said they were glad and only 1.3 percent were sorry; 15 percent were neither sorry nor glad. However, Milgram could not be sure at the time of the experiment that only 1.3 percent would be sorry.

Kurt Vonnegut Jr. put one paragraph in the preface to *Mother Night,* in 1966, 44 which pretty much says it for the people with their fingers on the shock-generator switches, for you and me, and maybe even for Milgram. "If I'd been born in Germany," Vonnegut said, "I suppose I would have *been* a Nazi, bopping Jews and gypsies and Poles around, leaving boots sticking out of snowbanks, warming myself with my sweetly virtuous insides. So it goes."

Just so. One thing that happened to Milgram back in New Haven during the 45 days of the experiment was that he kept running into people he'd watched from behind the one-way glass. It gave him a funny feeling, seeing those people going about their everyday business in New Haven and knowing what they would do to Mr. Wallace if ordered to. Now that his research results are in and you've thought about it, you can get this funny feeling too. You don't need one-way glass. A glance in your own mirror may serve just as well.

1970

QUESTIONS FOR DISCUSSION

Content

a. Originally, what did Stanley Milgram intend his experiments to test? What unexpected turns did the experiment take?

b. Why did Milgram change the location and the details of the situation after the first experiment?

c. What are the probable reasons that the "teachers" in Milgram's experiments continued to administer shocks to the "learners"? List reasons Milgram gives plus any other reasons you think are likely.

d. What does Milgram conclude about people's willingness to obey?

e. In your opinion, what other changes to the experiment would have made the results different? What might have been these other results?

Strategy and Style

f. The use of "you," starting in paragraph 6, puts you directly into the action, into the role of the "teacher." What effect does this have on you? What is your reaction to the experimenter's requests?

g. What does the startling title and bluntly worded first paragraph make you think the article will be about? Are your expectations met? Are the title and opening effective?

h. What techniques does Meyer use to make this nonfiction article read like a fictional story?

i. Meyer wrote this article for *Esquire,* a magazine aimed primarily for college-educated, fashion-conscious men. How would the effect of the article change if it were written for radically different audiences, such as scholars, psychiatrists, or young children?

j. How does the reference to Kurt Vonnegut's novel, *Mother Night* (paragraph 44), interpret Milgram's experiment? What is Meyer's opinion, as expressed in paragraphs 44 and 45? Do you agree with his take on Milgram's findings?

SUGGESTIONS FOR SHORT WRITING

a. Describe what you would have done as a "teacher" in the experiment. Try to be as truthful as you can.

b. Do you think that Milgram's experiment was ethical? In other words, was it right of him to put his subjects in such a situation? Write a paragraph to explain your opinion about this.

SUGGESTIONS FOR SUSTAINED WRITING

a. Do you agree with Meyer's and Vonnegut's opinion that, if you had been born in Germany, you would have become a Nazi (paragraphs 44 and 45)? Write an argumentative essay in which you expand that basic opinion, explaining why you agree or disagree with their opinion and defending your answer against possible counterarguments.

b. Do you think that continual exposure to violence (on television, on the news, in movies) desensitizes viewers to violence, even makes viewers violent themselves? Write a cause/effect essay in which you argue that, yes, exposure to violence has a direct relationship to increased violent crimes or, no, exposure to violence does not lead to violent behaviour. You will need to do some research to support your opinion.

Repeating History at Our Peril

David Suzuki

David Suzuki was born in Vancouver in 1936. He studied genetics and taught zoology at the University of British Columbia before becoming something of a celebrity through his TV show The Nature of Things *and through his strong stands on the environment. Suzuki writes a regular column and has published a number of books. His writings tend to focus on our relationship with the natural world.*

More than 13,000 years ago when humans first set foot in the Americas, there were 1 no roads crisscrossing the landscape, no sprawling cities, no vast fields of food crops, no high-powered rifles or global positioning systems.

Instead, the visitors found a land of plenty—an incredible variety of unusual 2 species, from massive 100-kilogram birds to saber-toothed tigers twice the size of today's great cats, to giant mammoths and kangaroos. And in less than 1,200 years, more than half of them would be extinct.

Last week, two reports in the journal Science pointed the finger squarely on 3 human activities as the culprit in this mass extinction, and a similar one that occurred in Australia 35,000 years earlier. The reports both found that human hunting and related activities are the most likely cause of the extinctions. Those losses included 73 per cent of the plant-eating species in the Americas, and all of the Australian land mammals, reptiles and birds weighing over 100 kilograms.

This issue has been debated for years, as some scientists contend that a rel- 4 atively small human population armed with stone-age weapons could not have been responsible for such widespread species losses. Instead, they argue that changes in climate, or an emerging disease of some sort, were the likely culprits.

But the North American report's author, John Alroy of the University of 5 California, says that no matter how stupid and slow his models assumed the hunters were, they still ended up as the driving force behind the extinction of most species. He concludes, "Human population growth and hunting almost invariably leads to a major mass extinction."

If that was true 13,000 years ago, then it should come as no surprise that the 6 rate of extinction today is so high. According to the World Resources Institute, human activities are driving species to extinction 100 to 1,000 times faster than what would occur naturally. Worldwide, more than 5,000 known animal species are threatened. And in North America, one in every three known plant species is threatened.

Of course, the most cynical of people may ask, "So what? The two studies 7 show us that humans have continued to survive and thrive even after exterminating a huge number of important food species. We are the ultimate adapters."

That may be true. But what will it do to our quality of life? Healthy ecosys- 8 tems cleanse our water, refresh our air and provide us with a tremendous variety of important resources. Most people recognize this on some level. According to a recent poll, for example, environmental pollution and natural resource depletion topped Canadians' concerns as "very serious" global problems.

Yet such problems continue to be put on the political back burner. Our fed- 9 eral government, for example, contends that we can substantially increase our production of fossil fuels for sale to the US, and yet somehow still reduce our greenhouse gas emissions. It also insists that proposed federal legislation can protect endangered species without protecting their habitats. Such attitudes overlook the exquisite interconnectedness of everything on the planet and do not bode well for the future.

Studies have shown that a diversity of species can make ecosystems more 10 resilient against stresses like drought or disease. When an asteroid slammed into the earth 65 million years ago and triggered the great extinction that eliminated the dinosaurs, the "terrible lizards" may have already been in their twilight years. Some scientists say that changing weather patterns may have already taken their toll on dinosaur ecosystems, greatly reducing the diversity of life and leaving them vulnerable. The asteroid collision and the resulting rapid climate changes may have been the final nail in the dinosaur coffin.

Humans are a much more adaptable species. But our own survival is by no 11 means guaranteed. If we continue to ignore the warning signs and behave as ignorantly as we did when our population was small and our most formidable technology was a spear, the last great extinction may one day be our own.

2001

QUESTIONS FOR DISCUSSION

Content

a. What was North America like 13,000 years ago? Why does Suzuki describe it this way?
b. What is the conclusion of the paper published by John Alroy?
c. Does Suzuki outline the argument of Alroy?
d. What are we, as human beings, doing, according to the World Resources Institute?
e. How does Suzuki respond to the question "So what?"? Why should his reader be concerned?
f. What is the political attitude, according to Suzuki, to such issues? What does he imply it should be?

Strategy and Style

g. Why doesn't Suzuki present the reasoning behind Alroy's conclusions?
h. What is the World Resources Institute and why should you, as a reader, accept its position?

i. Suzuki emphasizes that these issues affect "our quality of life." If these issues didn't visibly affect our quality of life, does it follow that we could ignore these issues?
j. When Suzuki places self-interest first—"our quality of life"—what is he assuming about human beings?
k. Why does Suzuki talk about the dinosaurs, considering their extinction occurred millions and millions of years ago, before the context of his discussion and argument?
l. What is the emotional impact of the word "extinction"?

SUGGESTIONS FOR SHORT WRITING

a. Write about how you feel when you hear that a certain animal (like the elephant) faces extinction.
b. Write about how you feel when you hear that a certain plant or insect (like the mosquito) or disease (like smallpox) faces extinction.
c. Discuss your own relationship to the environment. What does nature mean to you?

SUGGESTIONS FOR SUSTAINED WRITING

a. Examine the issue of Genetically Modified Foods (GMOs). If GMOs alter the environment or the interaction between disease, plants, and animals, should we unleash them on the environment?
b. Research the issues surrounding DDT, which is still used around the world to control the spread of malaria. Should we stop using DDT because it negatively affects the environment, even if it will lead to countless deaths of human beings?
c. Immunization and the use of antibiotics have greatly altered our relationship with nature. If the use of these weapons against disease, which have obviously benefited humanity, results in the destruction of other aspects of nature, how can we argue for their continued use? Should we continue to see ourselves as a dominant species or should we be trying to balance our own desires against the planet's needs?

9

Analogy

Have you ever taken a test that requires you to evaluate relationships between pairs of items or ideas? A typical question might go something like this:

Truck is to driver as horse is to _____ .

When used to develop ideas in writing, analogies take the form of well-developed comparisons that reveal particular similarities between members of the same or different classes. Like other forms of comparison, analogy introduces new subjects or ideas by referencing and drawing parallels to information with which the reader is already familiar. Writers often use analogy to create unexpected and quite startling comparisons between items from very different classes. Consider Loren Eiseley's discussion of our earthly environment as a kind of cosmic prison and his startling revelation that our perspective on this planet may be as limited as that of a white blood cell travelling through the body of a cat. Nonetheless, the beauty of analogy is that it can be used effectively to shed new light even on items from the same class.

Analogies, then, bring to light important relationships that can help define a term, describe a person, place, or object, or even argue an important point. Scientific writers rely on analogy to make their descriptions of complex mechanisms or obscure phenomena both interesting and accessible to lay readers. Analogy can also be used to emphasize the significance of particular scientific phenomena or issues.

Philosophical concepts, by their very nature abstract, also benefit from explanation through analogy. Plato's "The Myth of the Cave" is a cornerstone in the history of ideas; Camus's recounting the Sisyphus myth illuminates his definition of the absurd and explains why fate is a "human matter." Analogy is indeed a versatile tool. Consider how Neil Bissoondath uses the commonplace, a cafeteria, to discuss the notion of multiculturalism. Consider too the personal portrait of a writer's anguish in Alice Walker's "Am I Blue?"

The Suggestions for Short Writing and Sustained Writing that follow each selection should help you create and develop interesting analogies of your own.

But the essays themselves are so provocative they might even help you come to grips with problems, issues, or concerns that play a significant role in your daily life. Can you compare your current social environment to a prison? Is taking fifteen credits and working twenty hours a week like trying to roll a boulder uphill? Does the way modern college students date resemble courtship rituals among "primitive" peoples (real or fictitious)? If questions like these pop into your mind as you read this chapter, write them down and show them to your instructor; they might make good topics for an essay. At the very least, they will help you begin using analogy as a tool for thinking and for writing.

The Myth of the Cave
Plato

The great Athenian philosopher of the fourth century BC, Plato was the student of Socrates, whom he made the principal speaker in his dialogues. "The Myth of the Cave" appears in book VII of The Republic. In it, Socrates addresses a series of questions to Glaucon in an attempt to explain that the world in which we live is a world of illusions and shadows—a mere reflection of the "real world" of the intellect. He explains that the "idea of the good" is the "universal author of all things beautiful and right, the parent of light . . . in this visible world, and the immediate source of reason and truth in the intellectual. . . ."

And now, I said, let me show in a figure how far our nature is enlightened or un- 1 enlightened:—Behold! human beings living in an underground den, which has a mouth open toward the light and reaching all along the den; here they have been from their childhood, and have their legs and necks chained so that they cannot move, and can only see before them, being prevented by the chains from turning round their heads. Above and behind them a fire is blazing at a distance, and be- tween the fire and the prisoners there is a raised way; and you will see, if you look, a low wall built along the way, like the screen which marionette players have in front of them, over which they show the puppets.

I see. 2

And do you see, I said, men passing along the wall carrying all sorts of ves- 3 sels, and statues and figures of animals made of wood and stone and various ma- terials, which appear over the wall? Some of them are talking, others silent.

You have shown me a strange image, and they are strange prisoners. 4

Like ourselves, I replied; and they see only their own shadows, or the shad- 5 ows of one another, which the fire throws on the opposite wall of the cave?

True, he said; how could they see anything but the shadows if they were 6 never allowed to move their heads?

And of the objects which are being carried in like manner they would only 7 see the shadows?

Yes, he said. 8

And if they were able to converse with one another, would they not suppose 9 that they were naming what was actually before them?

Very true. 10

And suppose further that the prison had an echo which came from the other 11 side, would they not be sure to fancy when one of the passers-by spoke that the voice which they heard came from the passing shadow?

No question, he replied. 12

To them, I said, the truth would be literally nothing but the shadows of the 13 images.

That is certain. 14

And now look again, and see what will naturally follow if the prisoners are 15
released and disabused of their error. At first, when any of them is liberated and
compelled suddenly to stand up and turn his neck round and walk and look toward the light, he will suffer sharp pains; the glare will distress him, and he will
be unable to see the realities of which in his former state he had seen the shadows; and then conceive some one saying to him, that what he saw before was an
illusion, but that now, when he is approaching nearer to being and his eye is
turned toward more real existence, he has a clearer vision—what will be his reply? And you may further imagine that his instructor is pointing to the objects as
they pass and requiring him to name them—will he not be perplexed? Will he not
fancy that the shadows which he formerly saw are truer than the objects which
are now shown to him?

Far truer.   16

And if he is compelled to look straight at the light, will he not have a pain in 17
his eyes which will make him turn away to take refuge in the objects of vision
which he can see, and which he will conceive to be in reality clearer than the things
which are now being shown to him?

True, he said.   18

And suppose once more, that he is reluctantly dragged up a steep and rugged 19
ascent, and held fast until he is forced into the presence of the sun himself, is he not
likely to be pained and irritated? When he approaches the light his eyes will be dazzled, and he will not be able to see anything at all of what are now called realities.

Not all in a moment, he said.   20

He will require to grow accustomed to the sight of the upper world. And first 21
he will see the shadows best, next the reflections of men and other objects in the
water, and then the objects themselves; then he will gaze upon the light of the
moon and the stars and the spangled heaven; and he will see the sky and the stars
by night better than the sun or the light of the sun by day?

Certainly.   22

Last of all he will be able to see the sun, and not mere reflections of him in 23
the water, but he will see him in his own proper place, and not in another; and he
will contemplate him as he is.

Certainly.   24

He will then proceed to argue that this is he who gives the season and the 25
years, and is the guardian of all that is in the visible world, and in a certain way
the cause of all things which he and his fellows have been accustomed to behold?

Clearly, he said, he would first see the sun and then reason about him.   26

And when he remembered his old habitation, and the wisdom of the den and 27
his fellow-prisoners, do you not suppose that he would felicitate himself on the
change, and pity them?

Certainly, he would.   28

And if they were in the habit of conferring honors among themselves on 29
those who were quickest to observe the passing shadows and to remark which of
them went before, and which followed after, and which were together; and who

were therefore best able to draw conclusions as to the future, do you think that he would care for such honors and glories, or envy the possessors of them? Would he not say with Homer,

> Better to be the poor servant of a poor master,

and to endure anything, rather than think as they do and live after their manner?

Yes, he said, I think that he would rather suffer anything than entertain these false notions and live in this miserable manner. 30

Imagine once more, I said, such a one coming suddenly out of the sun to be re- 31 placed in his old situation; would he not be certain to have his eyes full of darkness?

To be sure, he said. 32

And if there were a contest, and he had to compete in measuring the shad- 33 ows with the prisoners who had never moved out of the den, while his sight was still weak, and before his eyes had become steady (and the time which would be needed to acquire this new habit of sight might be very considerable), would he not be ridiculous? Men would say of him that up he went and down he came without his eyes; and that it was better not even to think of ascending and if any one tried to loose another and lead him up to the light, let them only catch the offender, and they would put him to death.

No question, he said. 34

This entire allegory, I said, you may now append, dear Glaucon, to the pre- 35 vious argument; the prison-house is the world of sight, the light of the fire is the sun, and you will not misapprehend me if you interpret the journey upwards to be the ascent of the soul into the intellectual world according to my poor belief, which, at your desire, I have expressed—whether rightly or wrongly God knows. But, whether true or false, my opinion is that in the world of knowledge the idea of good appears last of all, and is seen only with an effort; and, when seen, is also inferred to be the universal author of all things beautiful and right, parent of light and of the lord of light in this visible world, and the immediate source of reason and truth in the intellectual; and that this is the power upon which he who would act rationally either in public or private life must have his eye fixed.

I agree, he said, as far as I am able to understand you. 36

Moreover, I said, you must not wonder that those who attain to this beatific 37 vision are unwilling to descend to human affairs; for their souls are ever hastening into the upper world where they desire to dwell; which desire of theirs is very natural, if our allegory may be trusted.

Yes, very natural. 38

And is there anything surprising in one who passes from divine contempla- 39 tions to the evil state of man, misbehaving himself in a ridiculous manner; if, while his eyes are blinking and before he has become accustomed to the surrounding darkness, he is compelled to fight in courts of law, or in other places, about the images or the shadows of images of justice, and is endeavoring to meet the conceptions of those who have never yet seen absolute justice?

Anything but surprising, he replied. 40

Anyone who has common sense will remember that the bewilderments of 41
the eyes are of two kinds, and arise from two causes, either from coming out of the
light or from going into the light, which is true of the mind's eye, quite as much as
of the bodily eye; and he who remembers this when he sees any one whose vision
is perplexed and weak, will not be too ready to laugh; he will first ask whether that
soul of man has come out of the brighter life, and is unable to see because unac-
customed to the dark, or having turned from darkness to the day is dazzled by excess of light. And he will count the one happy in his condition and state of being,
and he will pity the other; or, if he have a mind to laugh at the soul which comes
from below into the light, there will be more reason in this than in the laugh which
greets him who returns from above out of the light into the den.

That, he said, is a very just distinction.   42

ca. 373 BC

QUESTIONS FOR DISCUSSION

Content

a. Why does Plato refer to "the world of sight" as a "prison-house"?
b. Does the fact that Plato has cast this extended analogy into a dialogue make it
   more effective than if he had written in conventional essay form?
c. What does the sun represent in Plato's analogy?
d. Consult an unabridged dictionary, encyclopedia, or reference book on ancient
   literature or civilization. Who was Homer? Why does Plato allude to him?
e. What is the "beatific" vision that Socrates describes to Glaucon? Why is it important that one "who would act rationally" experience this vision?
f. How does Plato account for the fact that honourable people, who are able to see
   the truth and to relate it to others, often experience scorn and ridicule?
g. What has Glaucon learned by the end of the dialogue?

Strategy and Style

h. How effective is the dialogue form used in this selection? What is the function
   of Glaucon's brief responses? Of Socrates' questions?
i. How do Socrates' questions help determine the organization?
j. What is Plato's role in this selection? Is he invisible, a mere transcriber of the
   dialogue, or is his voice heard in some way?

SUGGESTIONS FOR SHORT WRITING

a. Write a short dialogue between yourself and Plato or between yourself and one
   of the dwellers in the cave.

b. This is an especially difficult selection. Try to capture the essence of Plato's ideas in a summary of one or two paragraphs.

SUGGESTIONS FOR SUSTAINED WRITING

a. Describe the human condition using another analogy besides the cave.

b. Do you believe that we are prisoners of the material world as Plato suggests? If so, write an essay in which you illustrate how people let their appetites (for food, money, sex, material possessions, for example) determine the course of their lives.

c. Do you believe that whatever is spiritual in a person can prevail? Write an essay in which you illustrate (from your own experiences, from those of people you know well, or from those you have read about) that people will deny themselves physical or material gratification in order to preserve the ethical principles or moral codes they believe in.

d. Create your own analogy by talking about the place where you work, live, or attend school in terms more usually associated with a prison, playground, resort, etc. Or you may want to describe the personality of someone you know well and create an analogy between him/her and an animal, either wild or domesticated, with which your readers might be familiar. You may need to include more than one animal in the analogy.

The Myth of Sisyphus

Albert Camus

Born in what was the French colony of Algeria, Albert Camus (1913–1966) was educated at the University of Algeria. He began his career as an actor and playwright, but he soon gave up the theatre for journalism and began writing for Alger Republicain *and for* Paris-Soir *in France. During World War II, Camus was very active in the French resistance and contributed regularly to* Combat, *an important underground newspaper. He is remembered as a leading existentialist, a proponent of the modern philosophical movement (if it can be termed that), which defines the individual as utterly free and totally responsible for his own destiny. For many existentialists, God does not exist, and the world is devoid of meaning except for that which the individual is able to create for him/herself. Unlike the literature of many of his contemporaries, however, the works of Camus expose a view of life that, while hardly optimistic, encourages a belief in the inherent nobility and courage of the human character even in the face of a hostile universe. Though clearly evident in his famous novels,* The Stranger *(1942),* The Plague *(1947), and* The Rebel *(1951), nowhere is this belief expressed more eloquently than in "The Myth of Sisyphus."*

The gods had condemned Sisyphus to ceaselessly rolling a rock to the top of a 1 mountain, whence the stone would fall back of its own weight. They had thought with some reason that there is no more dreadful punishment than futile and hopeless labor.

If one believes Homer, Sisyphus was the wisest and most prudent of mor- 2 tals. According to another tradition, however, he was disposed to practice the profession of highwayman. I see no contradiction in this. Opinions differ as to the reasons why he became the futile laborer of the underworld. To begin with, he is accused of a certain levity in regard to the gods. He stole their secrets. Aegina, the daughter of Aesopus, was carried off by Jupiter. The father was shocked by that disappearance and complained to Sisyphus. He, who knew of the abduction, offered to tell about it on condition that Aesopus would give water to the citadel of Corinth. To the celestial thunderbolts he preferred the benediction of water. He was punished for this in the underworld. Homer tells us also that Sisyphus had put Death in chains. Pluto could not endure the sight of his deserted, silent empire. He dispatched the god of war, who liberated Death from the hands of her conqueror.

It is said also that Sisyphus, being near to death, rashly wanted to test his 3 wife's love. He ordered her to cast his unburied body into the middle of the public square. Sisyphus woke up in the underworld. And there, annoyed by an obedience so contrary to human love, he obtained from Pluto permission to return to earth in order to chastise his wife. But when he had seen again the face of this world, enjoyed water and sun, warm stones and the sea, he no longer wanted to go back to the infernal darkness. Recalls, signs of anger, warnings were of no avail. Many years more he lived facing the curve of the gulf, the sparkling sea, and the smiles of earth. A decree of the gods was necessary. Mercury came and seized the

352

impudent man by the collar and, snatching him from his joys, led him forcibly back to the underworld, where his rock was ready for him.

You have already grasped that Sisyphus is the absurd hero. He is, as much 4 through his passions as through his torture. His scorn of the gods, his hatred of death, and his passion for life won him that unspeakable penalty in which the whole being is exerted toward accomplishing nothing. This is the price that must be paid for the passions of this earth. Nothing is told us about Sisyphus in the underworld. Myths are made for the imagination to breathe life into them. As for this myth, one sees merely the whole effort of a body straining to raise the huge stone, to roll it and push it up a slope a hundred times over; one sees the face screwed up, the cheek tight against the stone, the shoulder bracing the clay-covered mass, the foot wedging it, the fresh start with arms outstretched, the wholly human security of two earth-clotted hands. At the very end of his long effort measured by skyless space and time without depth, the purpose is achieved. Then Sisyphus watches the stone rush down in a few moments toward that lower world whence he will have to push it up again toward the summit. He goes back down to the plain.

It is during that return, that pause, that Sisyphus interests me. A face that toils 5 so close to stones is already stone itself! I see that man going back down with a heavy yet measured step toward the torment of which he will never know the end. That hour like a breathing-space which returns as surely as his suffering, that is the hour of consciousness. At each of those moments when he leaves the heights and gradually sinks toward the lairs of the gods, he is superior to his fate. He is stronger than his rock.

If this myth is tragic, that is because its hero is conscious. Where would his 6 torture be, indeed, if at every step the hope of succeeding upheld him? The workman of today works every day in his life at the same tasks, and this fate is no less absurd. But it is tragic only at the rare moments when it becomes conscious. Sisyphus, proletarian of the gods, powerless and rebellious, knows the whole extent of his wretched condition: it is what he thinks of during his descent. The lucidity that was to constitute his torture at the same time crowns his victory. There is no fate that cannot be surmounted by scorn.

If the descent is thus sometimes performed in sorrow, it can also take place 7 in joy. This word is not too much. Again I fancy Sisyphus returning toward his rock, and the sorrow was in the beginning. When the images of earth cling too tightly to memory, when the call of happiness becomes too insistent, it happens that melancholy rises in man's heart: this is the rock's victory, this is the rock itself. The boundless grief is too heavy to bear. These are our nights of Gethsemane. But crushing truths perish from being acknowledged. Thus, Oedipus at the outset obeys fate without knowing it. But from the moment he knows, his tragedy begins. Yet at the same moment, blind and desperate, he realizes that the only bond linking him to the world is the cool hand of a girl. Then a tremendous remark rings out: "Despite so many ordeals, my advanced age and the nobility of my soul make me conclude that all is well." Sophocles' Oedipus, like Dostoevsky's Kirilov, thus gives the recipe for the absurd victory. Ancient wisdom confirms modern heroism.

One does not discover the absurd without being tempted to write a manual of 8
happiness. "What! by such narrow ways—?" There is but one world, however. Happiness and the absurd are two sons of the same earth. They are inseparable. It would be a mistake to say that happiness necessarily springs from the absurd discovery. It happens as well that the feeling of the absurd springs from happiness. "I conclude that all is well," says Oedipus, and that remark is sacred. It echoes in the wild and limited universe of man. It teaches that all is not, has not been, exhausted. It drives out of this world a god who had come into it with dissatisfaction and a preference for futile sufferings. It makes of fate a human matter, which must be settled among men.

All Sisyphus' silent joy is contained therein. His fate belongs to him. His 9
rock is his thing. Likewise, the absurd man, when he contemplates his torment, silences all the idols. In the universe suddenly restored to its silence, the myriad wondering little voices of the earth rise up. Unconscious, secret calls, invitations from all the faces, they are the necessary reverse and price of victory. There is no sun without shadow, and it is essential to know the night. The absurd man says yes and his effort will henceforth be unceasing. If there is a personal fate, there is no higher destiny, or at least there is but one which he concludes is inevitable and despicable. For the rest, he knows himself to be the master of his days. At that subtle moment when man glances backward over his life, Sisyphus returning toward his rock, in that slight pivoting he contemplates that series of unrelated actions which becomes his fate, created by him, combined under his memory's eye and soon sealed by his death. Thus, convinced of the wholly human origin of all that is human, a blind man eager to see who knows that the night has no end, he is still on the go. The rock is still rolling.

I leave Sisyphus at the foot of the mountain! One always finds one's burden 10
again. But Sisyphus teaches the higher fidelity that negates the gods and raises rocks. He too concludes that all is well. This universe henceforth without a master seems to him neither sterile nor futile. Each atom of that stone, each mineral flake of that night-filled mountain, in itself forms a world. The struggle itself toward the heights is enough to fill a man's heart. One must imagine Sisyphus happy.

1955

QUESTIONS FOR DISCUSSION

Content

a. Who exactly was Sisyphus, and what does Camus mean when he calls him an "absurd hero"?

b. How do the various explanations behind his condemnation contribute to his portrayal as an "absurd hero"? In what way does the nature of Sisyphus' punishment help define that term?

c. What does Camus mean by the "underworld"? Why are Sisyphus' efforts in this place "measured by skyless space and time without depth" (paragraph 4)?

d. What is Camus driving at when he tells us that "There is no fate that cannot be surmounted by scorn" (paragraph 6) and that we "must imagine Sisyphus happy" (paragraph 10)?

e. Does Camus succeed in comparing Sisyphus with a modern human being? Discuss this analogy, and explain in what way a modern human might also be called absurd.

f. In order for Sisyphus to qualify as a "tragic hero," the author tells us, he must know the "whole extent of his wretched condition." In what way does this "lucidity" ennoble Sisyphus?

g. In what works do the famous literary characters Oedipus and Kirilov appear? How do their stories help illustrate "the recipe for the absurd victory"? What is "Gethsemane," which Camus mentions in paragraph 7?

h. What, for Camus, is "sacred" about Oedipus' conclusion that " 'all is well' "? In what way does this remark make "of fate a human matter, which must be settled among men" (paragraph 8)?

i. Discuss the "higher fidelity that negates the gods and raises rocks" (paragraph 10).

Strategy and Style

j. Camus uses the pronouns "you," "I," "one," and "he." To whom does each of these pronouns refer? In what ways do they create a persona for Camus?

k. What does Camus, or at least the persona of the essay, think of Sisyphus?

SUGGESTIONS FOR SHORT WRITING

a. Write a job description for what Sisyphus does.

b. What image does this essay call to mind? Try drawing that image and then writing a short description of it.

SUGGESTIONS FOR SUSTAINED WRITING

a. Through a skillful use of analogy, Camus reveals the relevance of a classical myth to the modern world. Recall an ancient myth, parable from the Bible, folktale, or children's story that has special significance for you. Why is it still meaningful, and what does it tell us about life and people today? In short, what lesson(s) does it offer the modern reader?

b. In paragraph 6, Camus tells us that "The workman of today works every day in his life at the same tasks, and this fate is no less absurd [than that of Sisyphus]." Do you agree? If so, develop your own analogy of the fate of Sisyphus with that of a modern factory worker, storekeeper, or civil servant. In what way is the latter's "fate" similar to that of Camus's mythical hero? Would it be accurate to describe this person as a "tragic hero"? In what way is she or he "tragic"? In what way a "hero"?

Canadians: What Do They Want?

Margaret Atwood

Born in 1939, Margaret Atwood has become arguably Canada's most recognized and important writer. She has achieved success with her poetry, her novels, and her literary criticism. Significant works include Surfacing, Survival: A Thematic Guide to Canadian Literature, The Handmaid's Tale, *and* Alias Grace. *Variety and diversity are her trademarks: her essays range from the quite conventional to the quite unusual. What runs through all her essays is a sharp tongue and an ever-caustic wit.*

Last month, during a poetry reading, I tried out a short prose poem called "How 1 to Like Men." It began by suggesting that one start with the feet. Unfortunately, the question of jackboots soon arose, and things went on from there. After the reading I had a conversation with a young man who thought I had been unfair to men. He wanted men to be liked totally, not just from the heels to the knees, and not just as individuals but as a group; and he thought it negative and inegalitarian of me to have alluded to war and rape. I pointed out that as far as any of us knew these were two activities not widely engaged in by women, but he was still upset. "We're both in this together," he protested. I admitted that this was so; but could he, maybe, see that our relative positions might be a little different.

This is the conversation one has with Americans, even, uh, *good* Americans, 2 when the dinner-table conversation veers round to Canadian-American relations. "We're in this together," they like to say, especially when it comes to continental energy reserves. How do you *explain* to them, as delicately as possible, why they are not categorically beloved? It gets like the old Lifebuoy ads: even their best friends won't tell them. And Canadians are supposed to be their best friends, right? Members of the family?

Well, sort of. Across the river from Michigan, so near and yet so far, there I 3 was at the age of eight, reading *their* Donald Duck comic books (originated, however, by one of *ours;* yes, Walt Disney's parents were Canadian) and coming at the end to Popsicle Pete, who promised me the earth if only I would save wrappers, but took it all away from me again with a single asterisk: Offer Good Only in the United States. Some cynical members of the world community may be forgiven for thinking that the same asterisk is there, in invisible ink, on the Constitution and the Bill of Rights.

But quibbles like that aside, and good will assumed, how does one go about 4 liking Americans? Where does one begin? Or, to put it another way, why did the Canadian women lock themselves in the john during a '70s "international" feminist conference being held in Toronto? Because the American sisters were being "imperialist," that's why.

But then, it's always a little naive of Canadians to expect that Americans, of 5 whatever political stamp, should stop being imperious. How can they? The fact is that the United States is an empire and Canada is to it as Gaul was to Rome.

It's hard to explain to Americans what it feels like to be a Canadian. Pessimists 6 among us would say that one has to translate the experience into their own terms and that this is necessary because Americans are incapable of thinking in any other terms—and this in itself is part of the problem. (Witness all those draft dodgers who went into culture shock when they discovered to their horror that Toronto was not Syracuse.)

Here is a translation: Picture a Mexico with a population ten times larger than 7 that of the United States. That would put it at about two billion. Now suppose that the official American language is Spanish, that 75 percent of the books Americans buy and 90 percent of the movies they see are Mexican, and that the profits flow across the border to Mexico. If an American does scrape it together to make a movie, the Mexicans won't let him show it in the States, because they own the distribution outlets. If anyone tries to change this ratio, not only the Mexicans but many fellow Americans cry "National chauvinism," or, even more effectively, "National social-ism." After all, the American public prefers the Mexican product. It's what they're used to.

Retranslate and you have the current American-Canadian picture. It's changed 8 a little recently, not only on the cultural front. For instance, Canada, some think a trifle late, is attempting to regain control of its own petroleum industry. Americans are predictably angry. They think of Canadian oil as *theirs*.

"What's mine is yours," they have said for years, meaning exports; "What's 9 yours is mine" meaning ownership and profits. Canadians are supposed to do retail buying, not controlling, or what's an empire for? One could always refer Americans to history, particularly that of their own revolution. They objected to the colonial situation when they themselves were a colony; but then, revolution is con-sidered one of a very few home-grown American products that definitely are not for export.

Objectively, one cannot become too self-righteous about this state of affairs. 10 Canadians owned lots of things, including their souls, before World War II. After that they sold, some say because they had put too much into financing the war, which created a capital vacuum (a position they would not have been forced into if the Americans hadn't kept out of the fighting for so long, say the sore losers). But for whatever reason, capital flowed across the border in the '50s, and Canadians, tra-ditionally sock-under-the-mattress hoarders, were reluctant to invest in their own country. Americans did it for them and ended up with a large part of it, which they retain to this day. In every sellout there's a seller as well as a buyer, and the Canadians did a thorough job of trading their birthright for a mess.

That's on the capitalist end, but when you turn to the trade union side of 11 things you find much the same story, except that the sellout happened in the '30s under the banner of the United Front. Now Canadian workers are finding that in any empire the colonial branch plants are the first to close, and what could be a truly progressive labor movement has been weakened by compromised bargains made in international union headquarters south of the border.

Canadians are sometimes snippy to Americans at cocktail parties. They don't 12
like to feel owned and they don't like having been sold. But what really bothers
them—and it's at this point that the United States and Rome part company—is the
wide-eyed innocence with which their snippiness is greeted.

Innocence becomes ignorance when seen in the light of international affairs, 13
and though ignorance is one of the spoils of conquest—the Gauls always knew more
about the Romans than the Romans knew about them—the world can no longer
afford America's ignorance. Its ignorance of Canada, though it makes Canadians
bristle, is a minor and relatively harmless example. More dangerous is the fact that
individual Americans seem not to know that the United States is an imperial power
and is behaving like one. They don't want to admit that empires dominate, invade
and subjugate—and live on the proceeds—or, if they do admit it, they believe in
their divine right to do so. The export of divine right is much more harmful than the
export of Coca-Cola, though they may turn out to be much the same thing in the end.

Other empires have behaved similarly (the British somewhat better, Genghis 14
Khan decidedly worse); but they have not expected to be *liked* for it. It's the final
Americanism, this passion for being liked. Alas, many Americans are indeed likable;
they are often more generous, more welcoming, more enthusiastic, less picky and sar-
donic than Canadians, and it's not enough to say it's only because they can afford it.
Some of that revolutionary spirit still remains: the optimism, the 18th-century belief in
the fixability of almost anything, the conviction of the possibility of change. However,
at cocktail parties and elsewhere one must be able to tell the difference between an individual and a foreign policy. Canadians can no longer afford to think of Americans as
only a spectator sport. If Reagan blows up the world, we will unfortunately be doing
more than watching it on television. "No annihilation without representation" sounds
good as a slogan, but if we run it up the flagpole, who's going to salute?

We *are* all in this together. For Canadians, the question is how to survive it. 15
For Americans there is no question, because there does not have to be. Canada is just
that vague, cold place where their uncle used to go fishing, before the lakes went
dead from acid rain.

How do you like Americans? Individually, it's easier. Your average American 16
is no more responsible for the state of affairs than your average man is for war and
rape. Any Canadian who is so narrow-minded as to dislike Americans merely on
principle is missing out on one of the good things in life. The same might be said, to
women, of men. As a group, as a foreign policy, it's harder. But if you like men, you
can like Americans. Cautiously. Selectively. Beginning with the feet. One at a time.

1982

QUESTIONS FOR DISCUSSION

Content

a. Why does Atwood begin with the anecdote about the young man who attended
   her reading?

b. In what way are Americans "imperialist"? What does Atwood mean by this term?
c. Why does Atwood create a fictitious analogy with Mexico?
d. What is Atwood implying about "international" trade unions?
e. Why does Atwood bring in labour unions into the discussion?
f. This essay was originally written with an American audience in mind. What does Atwood expect from her audience?
g. What is Atwood's thesis?

Strategy and Style

h. Atwood opens and closes her essay by comparing the relationship between men and women with the relationship between the U.S. and Canada. How effective is this analogy?
i. When Atwood comments that war and rape are "two activities not widely engaged in by women," is she making a comment, through her analogy, about the U.S.?
j. How effective is Atwood's "translation" featuring Mexico? Why does she create this fictitious comparison? Why doesn't she find a real example or comparison?
k. Atwood compares Canada's relationship with the U.S. with Gaul's relationship with the Roman Empire. Is this comparison fair? How does she justify the comparison?
l. Do Atwood's comments about men alienate you as a reader?
m. How does Atwood use humour to carry her argument?

SUGGESTIONS FOR SHORT WRITING

a. Create an analogy that helps to explain this relationship: the corner grocery competing against Superstore, Safeway, or Loblaws.
b. Have your friends ever used analogy to explain something to you in an argument? How did you respond to the analogy? Why did they resort to analogy?
c. Write about your province's relationship with the rest of the country.

SUGGESTIONS FOR SUSTAINED WRITING

a. Research the U.S.'s attitudes towards Canada at the time of the American Revolution. Discuss the nature of these attitudes and see if these attitudes are still present in Canada–U.S. relations.
b. Write an argument either for or against extending free trade internationally.
c. Examine the media and try to discern how Americans portray themselves. What characteristics do they use to define themselves? Discuss the accuracy of this portrayal using current affairs to support your argument.

The Cosmic Prison

Loren Eiseley

An anthropologist, educator, and poet, Loren Eiseley (1907–1977) was one of the most highly respected and prolific scientific writers of the twentieth century. Born in Lincoln, Nebraska, Eiseley was educated at the University of Pennsylvania, where he later became professor of anthropology and of the history of science. His other teaching assignments included appointments to the faculties of the University of Kansas and of Oberlin College. The recipient of numerous honours and awards for public service, Eiseley is also known for his work as a conservationist and nature lover. He contributed scores of scientific studies and articles to scholarly journals but has also authored two books of poetry, a genre he found difficult to escape even when writing highly "technical" prose. Eiseley will probably be best remembered for the unique, eloquent, and sometimes verselike style with which he treats subject matter that would otherwise seem cold, abstract, and esoteric. In short, his work represents the best of both the worlds of poetry and of science: perceptiveness, accuracy, insight, and, above all, an ability to make profound contact with the reader. Eiseley's major works include The Immense Journey *(1957),* Darwin's Century *(1959),* The Firmament of Time *(1960),* The Unexpected Universe *(1969), and* The Invisible Pyramid *(1970), from which this selection is taken.*

"A name is a prison, God is free," once observed the Greek poet Nikos Kazantza- 1
kis. He meant, I think, that valuable though language is to man, it is by very necessity limiting, and creates for man an invisible prison. Language implies boundaries. A word spoken creates a dog, a rabbit, a man. It fixes their nature before our eyes; henceforth their shapes are, in a sense, our own creation. They are no longer part of the unnamed shifting architecture of the universe. They have been transfixed as if by sorcery, frozen into a concept, a word. Powerful though the spell of human language has proven itself to be, it has laid boundaries upon the cosmos.

No matter how far-ranging some of the mental probes that man has philo- 2
sophically devised, by his own created nature he is forced to hold the specious and emerging present and transform it into words. The words are startling in their immediate effectiveness, but at the same time they are always finally imprisoning because man has constituted himself a prison keeper. He does so out of no conscious intention, but because for immediate purposes he has created an unnatural world of his own, which he calls the cultural world, and in which he feels at home. It defines his needs and allows him to lay a small immobilizing spell upon the nearer portions of his universe. Nevertheless, it transforms that universe into a cosmic prison house which is no sooner mapped than man feels its inadequacy and his own.

He seeks then to escape, and the theory of escape involves bodily flight. 3
Scarcely had the first moon landing been achieved before one U.S. senator boldly announced: "We are the masters of the universe. We can go anywhere we choose." This statement was widely and editorially acclaimed. It is a striking example of the comfort of words, also of the covert substitutions and mental projections to which they are subject. The cosmic prison is not made less so by a successful journey of some two hundred and forty thousand miles in a cramped and primitive vehicle.

360

To escape the cosmic prison man is poorly equipped. He has to drag portions 4 of his environment with him, and his life span is that of a mayfly in terms of the distances he seeks to penetrate. There is no possible way to master such a universe by flight alone. Indeed such a dream is a dangerous illusion. This may seem a heretical statement, but its truth is self-evident if we try seriously to comprehend the nature of time and space that I sought to grasp when held up to view the fiery messenger that flared across the zenith in 1910. "Seventy-five years," my father had whispered in my ear, "seventy-five years and it will be racing homeward. Perhaps you will live to see it again. Try to remember."

And so I remembered. I had gained a faint glimpse of the size of our prison 5 house. Somewhere out there beyond a billion miles in space, an entity known as a comet had rounded on its track in the black darkness of the void. It was surging homeward toward the sun because it was an eccentric satellite of this solar system. If I lived to see it it would be but barely, and with the dimmed eyes of age. Yet it, too, in its long traverse, was but a flitting mayfly in terms of the universe the night sky revealed.

So relative is the cosmos we inhabit that, as we gaze upon the outer galax- 6 ies available to the reach of our telescopes, we are placed in about the position that a single white blood cell in our bodies would occupy, if it were intelligently capable of seeking to understand the nature of its own universe, the body it inhabits. The cell would encounter rivers ramifying into miles of distance seemingly leading nowhere. It would pass through gigantic structures whose meaning it could never grasp—the brain, for example. It could never know there was an outside, a vast being on a scale it could not conceive of and of which it formed an infinitesimal part. It would know only the pouring tumult of the creation it inhabited, but of the nature of that great beast, or even indeed that it was a beast, it could have no conception whatever. It might examine the liquid in which it floated and decide, as in the case of the fall of Lucretius's atoms, that the pouring of obscure torrents had created its world.

It might discover that creatures other than itself swam in the torrent. But that 7 its universe was alive, had been born and was destined to perish, its own ephemeral existence would never allow it to perceive. It would never know the sun; it would explore only through dim tactile sensations and react to chemical stimuli that were borne to it along the mysterious conduits of the arteries and veins. Its universe would be centered upon a great arborescent tree of spouting blood. This, at best, generations of white blood cells by enormous labor and continuity might succeed, like astronomers, in charting.

They could never, by any conceivable stretch of the imagination, be aware 8 that their so-called universe was, in actuality, the prowling body of a cat or the more time-enduring body of a philosopher, himself engaged upon the same quest in a more gigantic world and perhaps deceived proportionately by greater vistas. What if, for example, the far galaxies man observes make up, across void spaces of which even we are atomically composed, some kind of enormous creature or cosmic snowflake whose exterior we will never see? We will know more than the phagocyte in our bodies, but no more than that limited creature can we climb out of our universe, or successfully enhance our size or longevity sufficiently to thrust our heads through the confines of the universe that terminates our vision.

Some further "outside" will hover elusively in our thought, but upon its na- 9 ture, or even its reality, we can do no more than speculate. The phagocyte might observe the salty turbulence of an eternal river system, Lucretius the fall of atoms creating momentary living shapes. We suspiciously sense, in the concept of the expanding universe derived from the primordial atom—the monobloc—some kind of oscillating universal heart. At the instant of its contraction we will vanish. It is not given us, nor can our science recapture, the state beyond the monobloc, nor whether we exist in the diastole of some inconceivable being. We know only a little more extended reality than the hypothetical creature below us. Above us may lie realms it is beyond our power to grasp.

1970

QUESTIONS FOR DISCUSSION

Content

a. What is Eiseley saying in the last two sentences of this essay, and how do they relate to the analogy he has created? Would it be accurate to say that these ideas comprise his thesis?

b. What is the "fiery messenger" to which Eiseley alludes in paragraph 4? How does it and the analogy of the human life span to that of a mayfly help him convey the immensity of time and space?

c. How would you explain the analogy between humans and the white blood cell that forms the basis of this essay? What makes the analogy logical and consistent?

d. Who was Lucretius, and what was his "atomic theory"? How does mentioning this theory help Eiseley develop the central analogy of his essay?

e. What does Eiseley mean when he says that "some further 'outside' will hover elusively in our thought" (paragraph 9)? Why can we only "speculate" on "its nature, or even its reality"?

f. In paragraph 4, the author tells us that the dream of escaping from the "cosmic prison" is a "dangerous illusion." What does he mean by this curious statement, and why would someone like the U.S. senator quoted in paragraph 3 find it "heretical"?

g. What is "the oscillating universal heart" (paragraph 9) that we can only "suspiciously sense"? How would you define a "monobloc"?

h. How do the quote from Nikos Kazantzakis and the explanation that proceeds from it serve as an appropriate introduction to this selection?

Strategy and Style

i. Define "the cosmic prison" that Eiseley describes in this selection. Why does he call it a prison? How does his use of the term *prison* relate to Plato's use of the word in "prison-house"?

j. How would you characterize Eiseley's tone in this piece? What image of Eiseley himself does the tone project?

SUGGESTIONS FOR SHORT WRITING

a. Find a passage (a sentence or a paragraph) that has meaning for your own life, and write about the connections you see between Eiseley's words and your life.

b. Eiseley writes of humankind's condition from an earthbound position; writing from a position outside the Earth, describe what you see as humankind's relation to the rest of the cosmos. You might try writing from the point of view of Halley's Comet.

SUGGESTIONS FOR SUSTAINED WRITING

a. Write a short essay in which you make clear what Eiseley means by "the cosmic prison." Use analogies of your own making to get your point across.

b. Eiseley has created a startling comparison between the existence of a human being in the universe with the life of a white blood cell in the human body. Create your own analogy by comparing yourself or someone you know well to a fictional character, to a famous historical figure, or even, for that matter, to an animal whose habits would be easily recognized by your audience. Incidentally, the analogy you develop need not be complimentary.

Tabula Asiae*

Michael Ondaatje

Michael Ondaatje was born in Colombo, Sri Lanka, in 1943. He immigrated to Canada in 1962 and has since become one of Canada's major literary figures both at home and internationally. He has twice won Governor General's Awards for his poetry: The Collected Works of Billy the Kid *(1970) and* There's a Trick with a Knife I'm Learning to Do *(1979). Of his novels,* The English Patient *(1992) is his most famous, partially because it was turned into an Oscar-winning film. The novel also co-won the prestigious Booker Prize. Ondaatje is also a filmmaker, and his writing has often been noted for its cinematic qualities.*

On my brother's wall in Toronto are the false maps. Old portraits of Ceylon. The result of sightings, glances from trading vessels, the theories of sextant. The shapes differ so much they seem to be translations—by Ptolemy, Mercator, François Valentyn, Mortier, and Heydt—growing from mythic shapes into eventual accuracy. Amoeba, then stout rectangle, and then the island as we know it now, a pendant off the ear of India. Around it, a blue-combed ocean busy with dolphin and sea-horse, cherub and compass. Ceylon floats on the Indian Ocean and holds its naive mountains, drawings of cassowary and boar who leap without perspective across imagined 'desertum' and plain. 1

At the edge of the maps the scrolled mantling depicts ferocious slipper-footed elephants, a white queen offering a necklace to natives who carry tusks and a conch, a Moorish king who stands amidst the power of books and armour. On the southwest corner of some charts are satyrs, hoof deep in foam, listening to the sound of the island, their tails writhing in the waves. 2

The maps reveal rumours of topography, the routes for invasion and trade, and the dark mad mind of travellers' tales appears throughout Arab and Chinese and medieval records. The island seduced all of Europe. The Portuguese. The Dutch. The English. And so its name changed, as well as its shape,—Serendip, Ratnapida ("island of gems"), Taprobane, Zeloan, Zeilan, Seyllan, Ceilon, and Ceylon—the wife of many marriages, courted by invaders who stepped ashore and claimed everything with the power of their sword or bible or language. 3

This pendant, once its shape stood still, became a mirror. It pretended to reflect each European power till newer ships arrived and spilled their nationalities, some of whom stayed and intermarried—my own ancestor arriving in 1600, a doctor who cured the residing governor's daughter with a strange herb and was rewarded with land, a foreign wife, and a new name which was a Dutch spelling of his own. Ondaatje. A parody of the ruling language. And when his Dutch wife died, marrying a Sinhalese woman, having nine children, and remaining. Here. At the centre of the rumour. At this point on the map. 4

1982

Tabula Asiae: Map of Asia (in Latin; apparently the words Ondaatje sees on his brother's old maps of Ceylon.)

QUESTIONS FOR DISCUSSION

Content

a. Why are the maps on Ondaatje's brother's wall "false"?
b. Why does Ondaatje draw attention to the other things on the maps?
c. Why does Ondaatje discuss the "edge of the maps"?
d. What is the point of the third paragraph? What has been the relationship between the world and Sri Lanka?
e. What is Ondaatje's connection to this island?

Strategy and Style

f. Ondaatje's essay uses a number of sentence fragments (for example, "Old portraits of Ceylon"). Why doesn't he write in complete sentences?
g. Ondaatje, in a very short essay, uses the word "pendant" a number of times. What is a pendant and what is the effect of the word?
h. Why does Ondaatje approach Sri Lanka strictly through old maps, "false maps"?
i. What kind of a "mirror" is Sri Lanka?
j. Ondaatje writes that Sri Lanka was "courted by invaders who stepped ashore and claimed everything with the power of their sword or bible or language." By connecting the bible and language with the sword, how does Ondaatje want us to see religion and language?
k. Sri Lanka has been "the wife of many marriages." Has she been "courted" or conquered? Why does Ondaatje use the analogy of a bride?

SUGGESTIONS FOR SHORT WRITING

a. Develop either of these analogies: My college is a tapestry, or my college is white bread and butter.
b. Discuss how you feel when you look at an old, out-of-date map.
c. How can a map or a picture reflect or mirror an understanding of the place being mapped or illustrated? Which comes first, the place or the understanding?
d. Think of a magical place in our culture (Hawaii, Disneyland, New York City, Hollywood). What makes it magic?

SUGGESTIONS FOR SUSTAINED WRITING

a. Find old maps of your country or province or city. Compare and contrast the old maps with a current map. How do the old maps differ in their understanding of the place?
b. Write an essay describing your family's "point of origin." How long do your ties to that place extend?
c. Architecture can tell us much of the values current in a society. Find the oldest picture available of the skyline of your city or town. Compare it with the current skyline. Have the function of the dominant buildings changed? Discuss the shift in values and their connection with the shift in architecture.

Am I Blue?

Alice Walker

Born in Eatontown, Georgia, Alice Walker (b. 1944) attended Spelman College and took her BA at Sarah Lawrence. She has taught and been a writer-in-residence at several prestigious American colleges and universities, but she has also worked for the New York City Department of Welfare, for a Head Start program in Mississippi, and for voter registration drives in Georgia. Among her many literary awards are a Pulitzer Prize and an American Book Award for The Color Purple *(1982), which was turned into a major film. Walker's other fiction includes* In Love and Trouble: Stories of Black Women *(1973) and* The Temple of My Familiar *(1989). She is also a well-known activist, literary critic, biographer, and essayist. She has recently written the memoirs* The Same River Twice *(1996) and* Anything We Love Can Be Saved: A Writer's Activism. *"Am I Blue?" first appeared in* Ms. *magazine in 1986.*

For about three years my companion and I rented a small house in the country that stood on the edge of a large meadow that appeared to run from the end of our deck straight into the mountains. The mountains, however, were quite far away, and between us and them there was, in fact, a town. It was one of the many pleasant aspects of the house that you never really were aware of this. 1

It was a house of many windows, low, wide, nearly floor to ceiling in the living room, which faced the meadow, and it was from one of these that I first saw our closest neighbor, a large white horse, cropping grass, flipping its mane, and ambling about—not over the entire meadow, which stretched well out of sight of the house, but over the five or so fenced-in acres that were next to the twenty-odd that we had rented. I soon learned that the horse, whose name was Blue, belonged to a man who lived in another town, but was boarded by our neighbors next door. Occasionally, one of the children, usually a stocky teenager, but sometimes a much younger girl or boy, could be seen riding Blue. They would appear in the meadow, climb up on his back, ride furiously for ten or fifteen minutes, then get off, slap Blue on the flanks, and not be seen again for a month or more. 2

There were many apple trees in our yard, and one by the fence that Blue could almost reach. We were soon in the habit of feeding him apples, which he relished, especially because by the middle of summer the meadow grasses—so green and succulent since January—had dried out from lack of rain, and Blue stumbled about munching the dried stalks half-heartedly. Sometimes he would stand very still just by the apple tree, and when one of us came out he would whinny, snort loudly, or stamp the ground. This meant, of course: I want an apple. 3

It was quite wonderful to pick a few apples, or collect those that had fallen to the ground overnight, and patiently hold them, one by one, up to his large, toothy mouth. I remained as thrilled as a child by his flexible dark lips, huge, cube-like teeth that crunched the apples, core and all, with such finality, and his high, broad-breasted *enormity;* beside which, I felt small indeed. When I was a child, I used to ride horses, and was especially friendly with one named Nan until the day 4

366

I was riding and my brother deliberately spooked her and I was thrown, head first, against the trunk of a tree. When I came to, I was in bed and my mother was bending worriedly over me; we silently agreed that perhaps horseback riding was not the safest sport for me. Since then I have walked, and prefer walking to horseback riding—but I had forgotten the depth of feeling one could see in horses' eyes.

I was therefore unprepared for the expression in Blue's. Blue was lonely. 5
Blue was horribly lonely and bored. I was not shocked that this should be the case; five acres to tramp by yourself, endlessly, even in the most beautiful of meadows— and his was—cannot provide many interesting events, and once rainy season turned to dry that was about it. No, I was shocked that I had forgotten that human animals and nonhuman animals can communicate quite well; if we are brought up around animals as children we take this for granted. By the time we are adults we no longer remember. However, the animals have not changed. They are in fact *completed* creations (at least they seem to be, so much more than we) who are not likely to change; it is their nature to express themselves. What else are they going to express? And they do. And, generally speaking, they are ignored.

After giving Blue the apples, I would wander back to the house, aware that he 6
was observing me. Were more apples not forthcoming then? Was that to be his sole entertainment for the day? My partner's small son had decided he wanted to learn how to piece a quilt; we worked in silence on our respective squares as I thought . . .

Well, about slavery: About white children, who were raised by black peo- 7
ple, who knew their first all-accepting love from black women, and then, when they were twelve or so, were told they must "forget" the deep levels of communication between themselves and "mammy" that they knew. Later they would be able to relate quite calmly, "My old mammy was sold to another good family." "My old mammy was ——— ———." Fill in the blank. Many more years later a white woman would say: "I can't understand these Negroes, these blacks. What do they want? They're so different from us."

And about the Indians, considered to be "like animals" by the "settlers" (a 8
very benign euphemism for what they actually were), who did not understand their description as a compliment.

And about the thousands of American men who marry Japanese, Korean, 9
Filipina, and other non-English-speaking women and of how happy they report they are, *"blissfully,"* until their brides learn to speak English, at which point the marriages tend to fall apart. What then did the men see, when they looked into the eyes of the women they married, before they could speak English? Apparently only their own reflections.

I thought of society's impatience with the young. "Why are they playing the 10
music so loud?" Perhaps the children have listened to much of the music of oppressed people their parents danced to before they were born, with its passionate but soft cries for acceptance and love, and they have wondered why their parents failed to hear.

I do not know how long Blue had inhabited his five beautiful, boring acres 11
before we moved into our house; a year after we had arrived—and had also traveled to other valleys, other cities, other worlds—he was still there.

But then, in our second year at the house, something happened in Blue's life.   12
One morning, looking out the window at the fog that lay like a ribbon over the
meadow, I saw another horse, a brown one, at the other end of Blue's field. Blue
appeared to be afraid of it, and for several days made no attempt to go near. We
went away for a week. When we returned, Blue had decided to make friends and
the two horses ambled or galloped along together, and Blue did not come nearly
as often to the fence underneath the apple tree.

When he did, bringing his new friend with him, there was a different look in   13
his eyes. A look of independence, of self-possession, of inalienable *horse*ness. His
friend eventually became pregnant. For months and months there was, it seemed
to me, a mutual feeling between me and the horses of justice, of peace. I fed apples to them both. The look in Blue's eyes was one of unabashed "this is *it*ness."

It did not, however, last forever. One day, after a visit to the city, I went out   14
to give Blue some apples. He stood waiting, or so I thought, though not beneath
the tree. When I shook the tree and jumped back from the shower of apples, he
made no move. I carried some over to him. He managed to half-crunch one. The
rest he let fall to the ground. I dreaded looking into his eyes—because I had of
course noticed that Brown, his partner, had gone—but I did look. If I had been born
into slavery, and my partner had been sold or killed, my eyes would have looked
like that. The children next door explained that Blue's partner had been "put with
him" (the same expression that old people used, I had noticed, when speaking of
an ancestor during slavery who had been impregnated by her owner) so that they
could mate and she conceive. Since that was accomplished, she had been taken
back by her owner, who lived somewhere else.

Will she be back? I asked.   15

They didn't know.   16

Blue was like a crazed person. Blue *was*, to me, a crazed person. He galloped   17
furiously, as if he were being ridden, around and around his five beautiful acres.
He whinnied until he couldn't. He tore at the ground with his hooves. He butted
himself against his single shade tree. He looked always and always toward the road
down which his partner had gone. And then, occasionally, when he came up for
apples, or I took apples to him, he looked at me. It was a look so piercing, so full
of grief, a look so *human*, I almost laughed (I felt too sad to cry) to think there are
people who do not know that animals suffer. People like me who have forgotten,
and daily forget, all that animals try to tell us. "Everything you do to us will happen to you; we are your teachers, as you are ours. We are one lesson" is essentially
it, I think. There are those who never once have even considered animals' rights:
Those who have been taught that animals actually want to be used and abused by
us, as small children "love" to be frightened, or women "love" to be mutilated and
raped. . . . They are the great-grandchildren of those who honestly thought, because someone taught them this: "Women can't think," and "niggers can't faint."
But most disturbing of all, in Blue's large brown eyes was a new look more painful
than the look of despair: The look of disgust with human beings, with life; the look
of hatred. And it was odd what the look of hatred did. It gave him, for the first time,

the look of a beast. And what that meant was that he had put up a barrier within to protect himself from further violence; all the apples in the world wouldn't change that fact.

And so Blue remained, a beautiful part of our landscape, very peaceful to look 18 at from the window, white against the grass. Once a friend came to visit and said, looking out on the soothing view: "And it *would* have to be a *white* horse; the very image of freedom." And I thought, yes, the animals are forced to become for us merely "images" of what they once so beautifully expressed. And we are used to drinking milk from containers showing "contented" cows, whose real lives we want to hear nothing about, eating eggs and drumsticks from "happy" hens, and munching hamburgers advertised by bulls of integrity who seem to command their fate.

As we talked of freedom and justice one day for all, we sat down to steaks. 19 I am eating misery, I thought, as I took the first bite. And spit it out.

1986

QUESTIONS FOR DISCUSSION

Content

a. To what is Blue analogous?

b. In paragraph 5 Walker writes that animals are "completed creations." What does she mean by this? Is she saying that humans are incomplete?

c. According to Walker, what is the usual relationship between animals and humans? What is the relationship that ought to exist?

d. What connections does Walker make between the treatment of animals and slavery?

e. What does Walker assume we will see if we really look into an animal's eyes? What would we see if we really looked into a person's eyes?

f. What is it that animals are trying to tell us?

Strategy and Style

g. Though this essay primarily uses the strategy of analogy, it is also an argument. What is Walker arguing for or against? Is she making more than one argument?

h. The author projects human feelings onto Blue. What mood or tone does this create for the essay? How does it affect the argumentative nature of the essay? Does it make the essay seem less or more convincing?

i. The essay gets increasingly emotional as it progresses. How effective is this strategy?

j. At what point does Walker explicitly mention cruelty to animals? At what point does she mention cruelty to people?

k. Why is the childhood memory described in paragraph 4 necessary? What does it tell us that is essential to understanding the entire essay?

SUGGESTIONS FOR SHORT WRITING

a. What is this essay mainly about? Slavery? Animal rights? Vegetarianism? Another subject? Decide what the main subject of the essay is and write a brief explanation of your choice. Cite examples from the text to illustrate your explanation.

b. Describe the enclosed pasture, from Blue's point of view. What does he think about his life? What does he think of Walker?

SUGGESTIONS FOR SUSTAINED WRITING

a. Use analogy to write an argument. Begin by listing several possible analogies. In Walker's essay, for example, the life of Blue is analogous to the lives of slaves, Native Americans, and women, and to those of other animals. In creating your analogy, think of things that are microcosms, i.e., miniature versions, of a larger world or of an important issue. Consider what you could argue by using such analogies.

Use Walker's essay as a model for organization and as a guide for generating the kinds of examples to include. Draw on your own experiences and observations for such examples.

b. Write an extended response to Walker's essay. Analyze her use of childhood memories, description, personification, and emotional appeals to create a unified argument. Include your own reactions as you read her essay, both what you felt and what you thought as you read. Finally, explain whether you find her use of memories, description, and so on, effective. In other words, do her strategies help her to persuade you?

Selling Illusions: The Cult of Multiculturalism in Canada

Neil Bissoondath

Neil Bissoondath, an important novelist, short story writer, and essayist, was born in Arima, Trinidad, in 1955. He emigrated to Canada in 1973 to attend York University. After graduating, he taught English as a second language and French in Toronto. His short stories, particularly those from his second collection, On the Eve of Uncertain Tomorrows, *have brought many accolades. His best-known work is* Selling Illusions: The Cult of Multiculturalism in Canada *(1994), which criticizes Canada's multiculturalism policies for emphasizing differences rather than similarities. The following essay is from that book.*

If the York University campus was a safe haven from which to discover the pleasures of Canada, though, it was also the place where I first encountered reasons for unease. 1

York operates on a college system. New students choose, or are assigned to, one of the various colleges on the campus. Unfamiliar with the system, ignorant of the purposes behind the individual colleges, I allowed myself to be assigned to Bethune College. 2

Familiarity with the college brought a certain dismay. Bethune College, named in honour of Dr. Norman Bethune, is an institution devoted to Third World studies; it had a certain reputation for left-wing radicalism. The reason for my dismay was simple: my major was to be French language and literature. The bilingual Glendon College, my logical "home," was never mentioned. I can only assume that I was enrolled at Bethune in part because I had come from a Third World country and in part because my adviser assumed that I would be most comfortable in an environment where a high percentage of students were, like me, non-white. It was an assuredly benign assumption, one made with the best of intentions, but also with no regard to my personal beliefs or intellectual interests. My adviser, then, had looked at me through the lens of her own stereotype and guided me according to the presumed comforts of "sticking with your own." 3

Although I was not at first aware of it, the concept of "sticking with your own" was just then in vogue at York. This became clear the moment you entered the main cafeteria at Central Square in the massive concrete bunker of the Ross Building. It was large and brashly lit, institutional in character, a place for feeding oneself rather than enjoying a meal. I remember it as a loud and busy place, brash with the sounds of trays and cutlery roughly handled, of a multitude of voices blended into a steady roar. 4

And yet, it seemed a benign atmosphere, friendly in an impersonal way. The controlled chaos offered an anonymity that would ease the task of inserting oneself, of fitting in. Or so it seemed at first. 5

Chaos is always subtly ordered, and it did not require a very discerning eye to decode the chaos of the Central Square cafeteria. Indeed, a map could be drawn, various sections coloured in to denote defined areas. To highlight, for instance, the 6 table at which Chinese students congregated behind a wall of Cantonese; or the tables over in the corner protected by the raucous enthusiasm of West Indian accents; or the table more subtly framed by yarmulkes and Star of David pendants.

To approach any of these tables was to intrude on a clannish exclusivity. It was **7** to challenge the unofficially designated territory of tables parcelled out so that each group, whether racially, culturally or religiously defined, could enjoy its little enclave, its own little "homeland," so to speak, protected by unspoken prerogatives.

The idea of "sticking with your own" was reinforced by various student or- **8** ganizations, many of which were financially assisted by the university. Controversy arose at one point when an application for membership in the Black Students' Federation was received from a student—a writer for the campus newspaper, as it turned out—whose skin colour seemed to disqualify him. Questions arose: Was being black a prerequisite for belonging to the Black Students' Federation? Or was a commitment to the issues raised by the association sufficient justification for belonging? Just how relevant was skin colour, how relevant cultural background, how relevant political belief?

A hint of the complexity of the question may be discerned in a story once **9** told to me by a friend. One afternoon, he stopped in at his favourite coffee house in Toronto's Kensington Market, a small place brightly decorated in the tropical style. It featured reggae music and the rich Blue Mountain coffee from Jamaica. As he sipped his coffee, he eavesdropped on a conversation at the table behind him, three young men, evidently musicians, discussing their next gig. My friend understood little of what was said—their thick Jamaican accents made their words undecipherable—but he enjoyed listening to their speech in the same way that he enjoyed the sounds of reggae. Cup empty, he rose to leave. On his way out he glanced at the men and with delight saw, as he put it, "one black guy with dreadlocks and two white guys with blond hair and blue eyes." An encounter, then, with the wickedness of history. He left the coffee house thrilled at abandoning the wreckage of a stereotype.

The issue at York was eventually settled by the decision to admit the white **10** student to the Federation—not on the grounds that race was irrelevant but that, as an organization financially assisted by the university, it had to respect the university's regulations prohibiting discrimination on the grounds of race and colour. I did not belong to the Federation, but the resolution was pleasing anyway, even though there was a tincture of discomfort at the way in which it had come about: through technicality, and not through the application of principle. None of the real questions had been grappled with, none answered.

Questions of segregation and exclusivity kept raising their heads. One day a **11** Jewish friend invited me to join him for coffee in the Jewish Students' Federation lounge. I was reluctant—the lounge seemed to me governed by even stronger pro- scriptions than the table in the cafeteria—but he insisted. As he fixed us each a cof- fee, he said in a voice clearly intended for others in the room that I should feel free to help myself from the coffee-machine at any time. And then he added in strained tones that the lounge, provided by the university, was open to all: I was to ignore anyone who tried to stop me. It was in this way that he sought to make me part of unsuspected internecine tensions, while publicly declaring his own position.

The issues made me wary: I neither joined the Black Students' Federation 12 nor revisited the Jewish Students' Federation lounge. I learned instead to keep my distance from the tables that would have welcomed me not as an individual but as an individual of a certain skin colour, with a certain accent, with a certain assumed cultural outlook—the tables that would have welcomed me not for *who* I was and for what I could do but for *what* I was and for what they presumed I represented. I had not come here, I decided, in order to join a ghetto.

Alone in a new land, I faced inevitable questions. Questions about my past 13 and my present, about the land left behind and the land newly found, about the nature of this society and my place in it. At eighteen, about to embark on a new life, I felt these to be weighty issues.

For many people at those cafeteria tables, though, these were questions of 14 no great importance. They were almost aggressive in dismissing any discomfort they might have experienced by flaunting the only government policy that seemed to arouse no resentment: Canada as a multicultural land. Officially. Legally. Here, they insisted, you did not have to change. Here you could—indeed, it was your duty to—remain what you were. None of this American melting-pot nonsense, none of this remaking yourself to fit your new circumstances: you did not have to adjust to the society, the society was obligated to accommodate itself to you.

An attractive proposal, then, a policy that excused much and required little 15 effort. And yet I found myself not easily seduced.

The problem was that I had come in search of a new life and a new way of 16 looking at the world, "to expand my horizons" (to use a cliché) from the narrow perspectives of my youth in Trinidad. I had no desire to transport here life as I had known it: this seemed to me particularly onerous baggage with which to burden one's shoulders. Beyond this, though, the very act of emigration had already changed me. I was no longer the same person who had boarded the aircraft in Trinidad bound for Toronto: I had brought with me not the attitudes of the tourist but those of someone embarking on an adventure that would forever change his life. This alone was a kind of psychological revolution.

Multiculturalism, as perceived by those at whom it was most explicitly aimed, 17 left me with a certain measure of discomfort.

At the end of my first university year, I returned to Trinidad to visit my parents. 18 It wasn't long before I was impatient to get back to Toronto. This had to do in part with the realization that, even after so short a time, old friends had become new strangers, and that old places had remained simply old places. More importantly, though, the desire to return had to do with me and with the life I had begun con- structing in my adopted city. I relished the freedom this life offered, the liberation of the anonymity of the big city. I had made new friends—some of them from among "my own kind," some not—and had found all the books, magazines and films denied me in Trinidad. I had, for the first time in my life, found a place other than my parents' house that I wished to call home: a place where I could be myself.

Sharing this with those who wished me to bolster their ethnic bastion in **19** Toronto made me distinctly unpopular. I was seen as a kind of traitor, unwilling to play the game by indulging in a life best described as "Caribbean North." If there was any alienation, it came not from the society at large but from those who saw themselves as the front-line practitioners of multiculturalism. By establishing cultural and racial exclusivity, they were doing their bit to preserve the multicultural character of the country, while I, seeking to go beyond the confines of my cultural heritage, was seen as acting counter to those interests.

To put it succinctly, they coveted the segregated tables of the cafeteria, while **20** I sought a place at tables that would accommodate a greater variety.

1994

QUESTIONS FOR DISCUSSION

Content

a. Why does Bissoondath begin his essay with a discussion of a cafeteria?
b. What does Bissoondath mean by "controlled chaos"?
c. What is the point of the story about the white reggae musicians?
d. Why doesn't Bissoondath return to the Jewish Students' Federation lounge?
e. Why doesn't Bissoondath join the Black Students' Federation?
f. Why does Bissoondath object to multiculturalism?

Strategy and Style

g. The essay begins and ends with the cafeteria. What does this cafeteria represent?
h. What is the effect of the phrase "I had not come here, I decided, in order to join a ghetto"? What impact does the word "ghetto" have on you as a reader?
i. What is the impact of the words "segregated" and "cultural and racial exclusivity"?
j. What does Kensington Market represent in the context of the essay? How is the market different from the university?

SUGGESTIONS FOR SHORT WRITING

a. Write about a time when you were disillusioned. What caused the disillusionment?
b. What are your attitudes towards multiculturalism?
c. How do you feel when someone identifies or labels you for what, rather than who, you are (for example, white male, black, Native, Indian, Asian, feminist, gay, and so on)? Do we sometimes embrace or encourage these connections?

SUGGESTIONS FOR SUSTAINED WRITING

a. Research the idea of cultural rights vs. individual rights. Where and when did the notion of cultural or collective rights originate? Argue for or against cultural or group rights.

b. Our society argues that we are individuals first and foremost. Does multiculturalism threaten our individuality by categorizing us into groups? Be specific in your use of examples to support your argument.

c. How does the media portray minorities (for example, the sitcom *Will and Grace*)? Discuss the media portrayal of a certain minority group. The media portrayal can be serious (news) or fictional (comedies, advertising, movies, dramas, and so on).

10

Argument and Persuasion

Strictly speaking, argument is a rhetorical technique used to support or deny a proposition by offering detailed evidence for or against it in a logically connected fashion. Classical argument relies on deductive and inductive thinking; it appeals to reason and reason alone. Deduction proceeds from a general truth or principle to a more specific instance based on that principle. You would be using deduction if you argued:

All full-time students are permitted to use the college weight room free of charge;
I am a full-time student;
I am permitted to use the weight room free of charge.

Inductive reasoning, on the other hand, proceeds from several specific occurrences to one general truth. Let's say you come down with a bad case of food poisoning—fever, cramps, vomiting, the works! When you feel better, you call up the five people with whom you had dinner; each of them claims to have suffered the same symptoms. It is probably safe to infer that all six of you ate contaminated food.

Sometimes, of course, one's purpose may go beyond simply proving a point. The writer may feel a need to *persuade,* that is, to convert the audience, or even to convey a sense of urgency that will convince readers to act and to act quickly. In such cases, pure logic may not suffice. Thus, while grounding the paper in logic and well-developed evidence, a writer may also wish to appeal to the emotions.

Both methods are legitimate forms studied under the general category of argumentation, and both are represented, to varying degrees, in the essays that follow. Indeed, it is often hard to draw a line. Jonathan Swift's "A Modest Proposal," a model of deductive reasoning expressed in language that is cool, clear, and eminently logical, is couched in a bitter irony that expresses the author's rage over Britain's treatment of the Irish.

Argument lends itself naturally to debate on matters scientific, social, and political. Note the selections by Barbara Ehrenreich, Garrett Hardin, and Stephen

Jay Gould. In an essay that recalls a campus incident involving freedom of speech, Nat Hentoff condemns the university's handling of the case. His essay is followed by two letters that attempt to refute his logic. It is important to note that, as reasoned and clear as these selections are, each remains unique, varying in tone and urgency according to the proximity from which its author views the subject.

The five persuasive selections illustrate techniques you might use when trying to move your readers or convince them to act. Make sure to read "I Have a Dream" by Martin Luther King, Jr.; it is a classic. However, Armstrong's "Veiled Threat: The Women of Afghanistan" and Cameron's "Our Daughters, Ourselves" also offer excellent insight into the workings of persuasion, and they are sure to interest and even move you. Finally, the essay by Ann N. Martin will surely get you to consider the issue of animal rights and, perhaps, write a response agreeing with or attacking her point of view.

In fact, that is true of every piece in this chapter. Even though these essays are examples of well-written arguments, you might wish to take issue with the positions they advocate and write a rebuttal to one or two of them. Keep in mind, however, that the essential ingredient in building an effective argument is a thorough knowledge of your subject. Without it, your readers will remain unconvinced despite your ability to stir their emotions. Think of yourself as an attorney. You will have difficulty defending your client unless you know all the facts. Anything less will jeopardize your credibility with the jury. This idea also applies to your role as a writer. Good readers will approach your thesis with a healthy skepticism. They may be open to persuasion—some may even want to be convinced—but most will insist that you provide reasonable, well-developed, and convincing evidence before they give you their trust!

ARGUMENT

Should This Student Have Been Expelled?
Nat Hentoff

Nat Hentoff writes a regular column for The Village Voice, *the New York City weekly, and he contributes frequently to the* Washington Post, *the* New Yorker, *and other major magazines, journals, and newspapers. Born in Boston, he took his BA at Northeastern University and attended Harvard University for postgraduate study. He also studied at the Sorbonne in Paris as a Fulbright fellow. Hentoff describes himself as an "advocacy writer," and his interests range from jazz to educational reform, subjects on which he has written several books and articles. He has also written several novels and biographies. However, Hentoff's reputation rests chiefly on his writings on the First Amendment to the U.S. Constitution. Indeed, he is among America's staunchest defenders of free speech and its most outspoken opponents of censorship. One of his books on this subject is* The First Freedom: The Tumultuous History of Free Speech in America *(1989). "Should This Student Have Been Expelled?," which first appeared in* The Village Voice *in 1991, responds to a letter to the* New York Times *by Vartan Gregorian, president of Brown University, and to a* Times *editorial supporting Brown's expulsion of Douglas Hann. Both the letter and the editorial appear after Hentoff's essay.*

The day that Brown denies any student freedom of speech is the day I give up my presidency of the university.

—Vartan Gregorian, president of Brown University,
February 20, 1991

Doug Hann, a varsity football player at Brown, was also concentrating on orga- 1
nizational behavior and management and business economics. On the night of
October 18, 1990, Hann, a junior, was celebrating his twenty-first birthday, and
in the process had imbibed a considerable amount of spirits.

At one point, Hann shouted into the air, "Fuck you, niggers!" It was aimed 2
at no one in particular but apparently at all black students at Brown. Or in the
world. A freshman leaned out a dormitory window and asked him to stop being so
loud and offensive.

Hann, according to reporters on the *Brown Daily Herald,* looked up and 3
yelled, "What are you, a faggot?" Hann then noticed an Israeli flag in the dorm.
"What are you, a Jew?" he shouted. "Fucking Jew!"

Hann had achieved the hat trick of bigotry. (In hockey, the hat trick is scor- 4
ing three goals in a game.) In less than a minute, Hann had engaged in racist, anti-
Semitic, and homophobic insults.

He wasn't through. As reported by Smita Nerula in the *Brown Daily Herald,* 5
the freshman who had asked Hann to cool it recruited a few people from his dorm
"and followed Hann and his friends."

378

"This resulted in a verbal confrontation outside of Wayland Arch. At this 6 time, [Hann] was said to have turned to one of the freshman's friends, a black woman, and shouted, 'My parents own your people.' "

To the Jewish student, or the student he thought was Jewish, Hann said, 7 "Happy Hanukkah."

There are reports that at this juncture Hann tried to fight some of the students 8 who had been following him. But, the *Brown Daily Herald* reports, he "was held back by one of his friends, while [another] friend stretched his arm across the Wayland Gates to keep the students from following Hann."

John Howard Crouch—a student and Brown chapter secretary of the Ameri- 9 can Civil Liberties Union there—tells me that because Hann had friends restraining him, "nobody seriously expected fighting, regardless of anyone's words."

Anyway, there was no physical combat. Just words. Awful words, but noth- 10 ing more than speech. (Nor were there any threats.)

This was not the first time Hann's disgraceful drunken language had sur- 11 faced at Brown. Two years before, in an argument with a black student at a fraternity bar, Hann had called the student a "nigger." Thereupon he had been ordered to attend a race relations workshop and to get counseling for possible alcohol abuse. Obviously, he has not been rehabilitated.

Months went by after Hann's notorious birthday celebration as Brown's 12 internal disciplinary procedures cranked away. (To steal a phrase from Robert Sherrill, Brown's way of reaching decisions in these matters is to due process as military music is to music. But that's true of any college or university I know anything about.)

At last, the Undergraduate Disciplinary Council (five faculty or administra- 13 tion members and five students) ruled that Doug Hann was to leave the university forevermore. Until two years ago, it was possible for a Brown student to be dismissed, which meant that he or she could reapply after a decent period of penance. But now, Brown has enshrined the sentence of expulsion. You may go on to assist Mother Teresa in caring for the dying or you may teach a course in feminism to 2 Live Crew, but no accomplishments, no matter how noble, will get you back into Brown once you have been expelled.

Doug Hann will wander the earth without a Brown degree for the rest of 14 his days.

The president of Brown, Vartan Gregorian—formerly the genial head of the 15 New York Public Library—had the power to commute or even reverse the sentence. But the speech code under which Hann was thrown out had been proposed by Gregorian himself shortly after he was inaugurated in 1989, so he was hardly a detached magistrate.

On January 25, 1991, Vartan Gregorian affirmed, with vigor, the expulsion 16 decision by the Undergraduate Disciplinary Council.

Hann became a historic figure. Under all the "hate speech" codes enacted 17 around the country in recent years, he is the first student to actually be expelled for violating one of the codes.

The *New York Times* (February 12) reported that "Howard Ehrlich, the re- 18
search director of the National Institute Against Prejudice and Violence, said that
he did not know of any other such expulsions, but that he was familiar with cases
in which students who had harassed others were moved to other dormitories or
ordered to undergo counseling."

But that takes place in *educational* institutions, whose presidents recognize 19
that there are students who need help, not exile.

At first, there didn't seem to be much protest among the student body at 20
Brown on free speech grounds—except for members of the Brown chapter of the
ACLU and some free thinkers on the student paper, as well as some unaffiliated
objectors to expelling students for what they say, not for what they do. The number of these dissenters is increasing, as we shall see.

At the student paper, however, the official tone has changed from the liber- 21
tarian approach of Vernon Silver, who was editor-in-chief last semester. A February 13 *Brown Daily Herald* editorial was headed: *"Good Riddance."*

It began: "Doug Hann is gone, and the university is well to be rid of him." 22

But President Gregorian has been getting a certain amount of flack and so, 23
smiting his critics hip and thigh, he wrote a letter to the *New York Times*. Well, that
letter (printed on February 21) was actually a press release, distributed by the
Brown University News Bureau to all sorts of people, including me, on February
12. There were a few changes—and that *Brown Daily Herald* editorial was attached
to it—but Gregorian's declaration was clearly not written exclusively for the *Times*.

Is this a new policy at the *Times*—taking public relations handouts for the 24
letters page?

Next week I shall include a relentlessly accurate analysis of President Gre- 25
gorian's letter by the executive director of the Rhode Island ACLU. But first, an
account of what Gregorian said in that letter to the *Times*.

President Gregorian indignantly denies that Brown has ever expelled "any- 26
one for the exercise of free speech, nor will it ever do so." Cross his heart.

He then goes into self-celebration: "My commitment to free speech and 27
condemnation of racism and homophobia are well known. . . ."

"The university's code of conduct does not prohibit speech; it prohibits 28
actions."

Now watch this pitiable curve ball: 29

"Offense III [of the Brown code]—which deals with harassment—prohibits 30
inappropriate, abusive, threatening, or demeaning actions based on race, religion,
gender, handicap, ethnicity, national origin, or sexual orientation."

In the original press release, Gregorian underlined the word *actions*. There, 31
and in the letter to the *Times*—lest a dozing reader miss the point—Gregorian emphasizes that "The rules do not proscribe words, epithets, or slanders, they proscribe behavior." Behavior that "shows flagrant disrespect for the well-being of
others or is unreasonably disruptive of the University community."

Consider the overbreadth and vagueness of these penalty-bearing provi- 32
sions. What are the definitions of "harassment," "inappropriate," "demeaning,"
"flagrant," "disrespect," "well-being," "unreasonably"?

Furthermore, with regard to Brown's termination of Doug Hann with ex- 33
treme prejudice, Gregorian is engaging in the crudest form of Orwellian
newspeak. Hann was kicked out for *speech,* and only speech—not for *actions,* as
Gregorian huffily insists. As for behavior, the prickly folks whose burning of the
American flag was upheld by the Supreme Court were indeed engaged in behavior, but that behavior was based entirely on symbolic speech. So was Hann's. He
didn't punch anybody or vandalize any property. He brayed.

Art Spitzer, legal director of the ACLU's National Capital Area affiliate, 34
wrote a personal letter to Gregorian:

"There is a very simple test for determining whether a person is being pun- 35
ished for his actions or his speech. You just ask whether he would have received
the same punishment if he had spoken different words while engaging in the same
conduct."

"Thus, would your student have been expelled if he had gotten drunk and 36
stood in the same courtyard at the same hour of the night, shouting at the same
decibel level, 'Black is Beautiful!' 'Gay is Good!' or 'Go Brown! Beat Yale!' or
even 'Nuke Baghdad! Kill Saddam!'?

"I am confident," Spitzer said, that "he would not have been expelled for 37
such 'actions.' If that is correct, it follows that *he was expelled for the unsavory
content of his speech,* and not for his actions. I have no doubt that you can understand this distinction. (Emphasis added.)

"Now, you are certainly entitled to believe that it is appropriate to expel a 38
student for the content of his speech when that content is sufficiently offensive to
the 'university community.' . . .

"If that is your position, why can't you deliver it forthrightly? Then the uni- 39
versity community can have an open debate about which opinions it finds offensive, and ban them. Perhaps this can be done once a year, so that the university's
rules can keep pace with the tenor of the times—after all, it wouldn't do to have
outmoded rules banning procommunist or blasphemous speech still on the books,
now that it's 1991. Then students and teachers applying for admission or employment at Brown will know what they are getting into.

"Your recent statements, denying the obvious, are just hypocritical. . . ."   40

And what did the *New York Times*—in a stunningly fatuous February 21 ed- 41
itorial—say of Vartan Gregorian's sending Doug Hann into permanent exile? "A
noble attempt both to govern and teach."

The *Times* editorials should really be signed, so that the rest of the editorial 42
board isn't blamed for such embarrassments.

1991

How Much Hate to Tolerate

New York Times editorial, (February 21, 1991)

Free speech and human relations seemed to collide last month at Brown Univer- 1
sity when it expelled a student for racial and religious harassment. In fact, however, to judge by all that is publicly known, the school walked a fine line with
sensitivity toward its complex mission.

One mission of a university is to send into the world graduates who are tol- 2
erant of many races, faiths and cultures. Another mission is to teach the value of
free expression and tolerance even for hateful ideas. But should such tolerance
cover racist, sexist or homophobic speech that makes the learning environment intolerable for racial and religious minorities, women and other targets of abuse?
Brown found a reasonable basis for saying, clearly, no.

Douglas Hann, white, a junior and a varsity football player, had previously 3
been disciplined for alcohol abuse and for racial insults against a black fellow student. Then, one evening last fall, he shouted racial insults in a university courtyard.
A Jewish student who opened a dormitory window and called for quiet was answered with a religious insult. Later that evening Mr. Hann directed a racial insult
at a black undergraduate.

The student-faculty discipline committee found him guilty of three viola- 4
tions of student rules, including another count of alcohol abuse. Vartan Gregorian,
the university's president, upheld the student's expulsion last month. He had a
sound basis for doing so. If the facts are reported correctly, Mr. Hann crossed the
line between merely hateful speech and hateful speech that directly confronted and
insulted other undergraduates.

Some courts have found that public universities are bound by the First 5
Amendment's ban on state censorship and thus may not punish students for expressing politically incorrect or socially distasteful ideas. Brown, like other private
schools, is less directly bound by the Constitution but committed to its precepts. It
is trying to avoid censorship but draws a line between strong language and what
the courts often call "fighting words."

In the adjacent Letters column today, Mr. Gregorian insists that Brown does 6
not punish unruly speech as such but will decide case-by-case whether a student has
passed "the point at which speech becomes behavior" that flagrantly disregards the
well-being of others or "subjects someone to abusive or demeaning actions."

That formula is a noble attempt both to govern and teach. It offers a princi- 7
pled basis for disciplinary action against Mr. Hann for his direct, confrontational
conduct.

The lines may not be so clearly drawn in other cases. There may also be 8
more of them in the present climate of evidently increasing student intolerance.
But when bigots attack other students with ugly invective, universities, whether
public or private, need not remain silent. Their presidents, like Mr. Gregorian, may
denounce indecency and, in so doing, protect tolerance.

Brown Expulsion Not About Free Speech

New York Times letter to the editor, (February 21, 1991)

To the Editor:

"Student at Brown Is Expelled Under a Rule Barring 'Hate Speech'" (news article, 1 Feb. 12) suggests I have instituted "hate-speech" prohibitions at Brown University and that the expulsion of a student who shouted racial and homophobic epithets on campus last October is the first such in the nation based on restrictions of free speech. Brown University has never expelled anyone for free speech, nor will it ever do so.

My commitment to free speech and condemnation of racism and homopho- 2 bia are well known. In April 1989, several students were subjected to a cowardly attack of racial and homophobic graffiti. The words and slogans scrawled anonymously on doors in one of our dormitories were vicious attacks threatening the well-being and security of Brown students.

I condemned that anonymous poisoning of our community and said I would 3 prosecute vigorously and seek the expulsion of those who incite hatred or perpetuate such acts of vandalism. Nothing I said then or have done since should be construed as limiting anyone's freedom of speech, nor have I revised the university's code of conduct to that effect.

The university's code of conduct does not prohibit speech; it prohibits 4 actions, and these include behavior that "shows flagrant disrespect for the well-being of others or is unreasonably disruptive of the university community."

Offense III, which deals with harassment, prohibits inappropriate, abusive, 5 threatening or demeaning actions based on race, religion, gender, handicap, ethnicity, national origin or sexual orientation.

"The Tenets of Community Behavior," which outline community standards 6 for acceptable behavior at Brown, have been read for more than 10 years by entering students, who agree in writing to abide by them.

The rules do not proscribe words, epithets or slanders; they proscribe be- 7 havior. The point at which speech becomes behavior and the degree to which that behavior shows flagrant disrespect for the well-being of others (Offense II), subjects someone to abusive or demeaning actions (Offense III) or is related to drug or alcohol use (Offense IV) is determined by a hearing to consider the circumstances of each case. The student is entitled to an appeal, which includes review by a senior officer and a decision by the president.

I cannot and will not comment about any specific case. I regret the release 8 of any student's name in connection with a disciplinary hearing and the exposure any case may receive in *The Brown Herald.*

Freedom-of-speech questions lie at the heart of any academic community. 9 The very nature of the academic enterprise necessitates that universities remain partisans of heterodoxy, of a rich and full range of opinions, ideas and expression.

383

Imposed orthodoxies of all sorts, including what is called "politically correct" speech, are anathema to our enterprise.

The university's most compelling challenge is to achieve a balance between 10 the right of its individual members to operate and speak freely, and fostering respect for and adherence to community values and standards of conduct.

VARTAN GREGORIAN
President, Brown University
Providence, R.I., Feb. 21, 1991

QUESTIONS FOR DISCUSSION

Content

a. In a sentence or two, summarize Hentoff's argument against Hann's expulsion.
b. Explain the analogy the author uses in paragraph 12.
c. Why, according to Hentoff, wouldn't Vartan Gregorian "commute or even reverse" Hann's sentence (paragraph 15)?
d. What does Hentoff imply about Brown's president in paragraph 19?
e. What is "Orwellian newspeak" (paragraph 33)? According to Hentoff, in what way is Gregorian engaging in "newspeak"?
f. Explain the test "for determining whether a person is being punished for his actions or his speech" as articulated by Art Spitzer in paragraphs 35–37.
g. Explain the advice Spitzer gave Gregorian as quoted from his letter in paragraph 39.
h. What purpose does Hentoff's conclusion serve? What is his point in the essay's very last paragraph?

Strategy and Style

i. Why does Hentoff include paragraph 10? Is it really necessary?
j. Why does he characterize Gregorian's letter to the *Times* as a "public relations" handout (paragraph 24)? How would you describe Hentoff's attitude toward the newspaper's editorial board?
k. Analyze the structure of the essay. If necessary, write a brief outline that includes its key points and reveals its organization.
l. Where in this selection does Hentoff appeal to authority by quoting expert testimony? Who are those experts? Is their testimony convincing?
m. What advantage does Hentoff achieve by quoting directly from Gregorian's letter to the *Times?* Other than directly attacking the letter's contents, how does he refute Gregorian?

SUGGESTIONS FOR SHORT WRITING

a. Summarize the arguments made by the writer of the *New York Times* editorial "How Much Hate to Tolerate." Then, do the same for Vartan Gregorian's letter to the editor.

b. Are you in favour of unlimited freedom of expression? If so, explain why. In an attempt to anticipate opposing arguments, explain how you would defend the right of others to express themselves in ways you consider immoral, abhorrent, or even dangerous.

c. Do you believe we should limit freedom of expression in certain instances? If so, provide one or two examples.

SUGGESTIONS FOR SUSTAINED WRITING

a. In your own letter to the editor, attack or defend Hentoff's position on the expulsion of Doug Hann and on its implications vis-à-vis the exercise of free speech on college campuses. Whichever position you take, make reference to or quote from Hentoff's essay, the *New York Times* editorial, and/or Gregorian's letter. On the other hand, remember that this is your letter, so rely heavily on your own arguments and insights.

b. A university or college is a place where open and free debate should be encouraged. You probably know of several important issues—academic, political, cultural, scientific, theological, economic, and so on—being discussed by students and faculty at your college. Take a clear position on an issue that affects you as a student, that you have studied or read about, or that you have debated with others at your school. You need not choose an issue of universal significance. Interesting and effective arguments can be written on increasing scholarship aid, providing more parking spaces for college commuters, keeping the library open late at night and on Sundays, or giving students access to computer labs free of charge.

A Step Back to the Workhouse?

Barbara Ehrenreich

Barbara Ehrenreich (b. 1941) earned her BA from Reed College in 1963 and her PhD from Rockefeller University in 1968. A noted feminist and socialist, she is a contributing editor for Ms. *but frequently writes for other magazines such as* The Nation, Utne Reader, New Republic, *and* Time. *One of her central concerns is women's status in social institutions such as the health-care system, politics, and, as in this article reprinted from* Ms., *the welfare system. The many books she has authored or coauthored deal with these and related concerns; they include* Complaints and Disorders: The Sexual Politics of Sickness *(1973),* Remaking Love: The Feminization of Sex *(1986), and* Fear of Falling: The Inner Life of the Middle Class *(1990). She has been the recipient of several awards, including a National Magazine Award in 1980, a Ford Foundation Award for Humanistic Perspectives on Contemporary Issues in 1981, and a Guggenheim Fellowship in 1987.*

1 The commentators are calling it a "remarkable consensus." Workfare, as programs to force welfare recipients to work are known, was once abhorred by liberals as a step back toward the 17th-century workhouse or—worse—slavery. But today no political candidate dares step outdoors without some plan for curing "welfare dependency" by putting its hapless victims to work—if necessary, at the nearest Burger King. It is as if the men who run things, or who aspire to run things (and we are, unfortunately, talking mostly about men when we talk about candidates), had gone off and caucused for a while and decided on the one constituency that could be safely sacrificed in the name of political expediency and "new ideas," and that constituency is poor women.

2 Most of the arguments for workfare are simply the same indestructible stereotypes that have been around, in one form or another, since the first public relief program in England 400 years ago: That the poor are poor because they are lazy and dissolute, and that they are lazy and dissolute because they are suffering from "welfare dependency." Add a touch of modern race and gender stereotypes and you have the image that haunts the workfare advocates: A slovenly, over-weight, black woman who produces a baby a year in order to augment her welfare checks.

3 But there is a new twist to this season's spurt of welfare-bashing: Workfare is being presented as a kind of *feminist* alternative to welfare. As Senator Daniel Patrick Moynihan (D.–N.Y.) has put it, "A program that was designed to pay mothers to stay at home with their children [i.e., welfare, or Aid to Families with Dependent Children] cannot succeed when we now observe most mothers going out to work." Never mind the startling illogic of this argument, which is on a par with saying that no woman should stay home with her children because other women do not, or that a laid-off male worker should not receive unemployment compensation because most men have been observed holding jobs. We are being asked to believe that pushing destitute mothers into the work force (in some versions of workfare, for no other compensation than the welfare payments they would have received anyway) is consistent with women's strivings toward self-determination.

386

Now I will acknowledge that most women on welfare—like most unem- 4
ployed women in general—would rather have jobs. And I will further acknowledge
that many of the proponents of workfare, possibly including Senator Moynihan and
the Democratic Presidential candidates, have mounted the bandwagon with the best
of intentions. Welfare surely needs reform. But workfare is not the solution, because "dependency"—with all its implications of laziness and depravity—is not the
problem. The problem is poverty, which most women enter in a uniquely devastating way—with their children in tow.

Let me introduce a real person, if only because real people, as opposed to 5
imaginative stereotypes, never seem to make an appearance in the current rhetoric
on welfare. "Lynn," as I will call her, is a friend and onetime neighbor who has
been on welfare for two years. She is also about as unlike the stereotypical "welfare mother" as one can get—which is to say that she is a fairly typical welfare recipient. She has only one child, which puts her among the 74 percent of welfare
recipients who have only one or two children. She is white (not that that should
matter), as are almost half of welfare recipients. Like most welfare recipients, she
is not herself the daughter of a welfare recipient, and hence not part of anything
that could be called an "intergenerational cycle of dependency." And like every
woman on welfare I have ever talked to, she resents the bureaucratic hassles that
are the psychic price of welfare. But, for now, there are no alternatives.

When I first met Lynn, she seemed withdrawn and disoriented. She had just 6
taken the biggest step of her 25 years; she had left an abusive husband and she was
scared: Scared about whether she could survive on her own and scared of her estranged husband. He owned a small restaurant; she was a high school dropout who
had been a waitress when she met him. During their three years of marriage he had
beaten her repeatedly. Only after he threw her down a flight of stairs had she realized that her life was in danger and moved out. I don't think I fully grasped the terror she had lived in until one summer day when he chased Lynn to the door of my
house with a drawn gun.

Gradually Lynn began to put her life together. She got a divorce and went on 7
welfare; she found a pediatrician who would accept Medicaid and a supermarket
that would take food stamps. She fixed up her apartment with second-hand furniture and flea market curtains. She was, by my admittedly low standards, a compulsive housekeeper and an overprotective mother; and when she wasn't waxing
her floors or ironing her two-year-old's playsuits, she was studying the help-
wanted ads. She spent a lot of her time struggling with details that most of us
barely notice—the price of cigarettes, mittens, or of a bus ticket to the welfare office—yet, somehow, she regained her sense of humor. In fact, most of the time we
spent together was probably spent laughing—over the foibles of the neighbors, the
conceits of men, and the snares of welfare and the rest of "the system."

Yet for all its inadequacies, Lynn was grateful for welfare. Maybe if she had 8
been more intellectually inclined she would have found out that she was suffering
from "welfare dependency," a condition that is supposed to sap the will and
demolish the work ethic. But "dependency" is not an issue when it is a choice

between an abusive husband and an impersonal government. Welfare had given Lynn a brief shelter in a hostile world, and as far as she was concerned, it was her ticket to *independence.*

Suppose there had been no welfare at the time when Lynn finally summoned 9
the courage to leave her husband. Suppose she had gone for help and been told she would have to "work off" her benefits in some menial government job (restocking the toilet paper in rest rooms is one such "job" assigned to New York women in a current workfare program). Or suppose, as in some versions of workfare, she had been told she would have to take the first available private sector job, which (for a non-high school graduate like Lynn) would have paid near the minimum wage, or $3.35 an hour. How would she have been able to afford child care? What would she have done for health insurance (as a welfare recipient she had Medicaid, but most low-paying jobs offer little or no coverage)? Would she have ever made the decision to leave her husband in the first place?

As Ruth Sidel points out in *Women and Children Last* (Viking), most women 10
who are or have been on welfare have stories like Lynn's. They go onto welfare in response to a crisis—divorce, illness, loss of a job, the birth of an additional child to feed—and they remain on welfare for two years or less. They are not victims of any "welfare culture," but of a society that increasingly expects women to both raise and support children—and often on wages that would barely support a woman alone. In fact, even some of the most vociferous advocates of replacing welfare with workfare admit that, in their own estimation, only about 15 percent of welfare recipients fit the stereotype associated with "welfare dependency": Demoralization, long-term welfare use, lack of drive, and so on. rely on welfare rather than getting a job

But workfare will not help anyone, not even the presumed 15 percent of "bad 11
apples" for whose sake the majority will be penalized. First, it will not help because it does not solve the problem that drives most women into poverty in the first place: How to hold a job *and* care for children. Child care in a licensed, professionally run center can easily cost as much as $100 a week per child—more than most states now pay in welfare benefits (for two children) and more than most welfare recipients could expect to earn in the work force. Any serious effort to get welfare recipients into the work force would require childcare provisions at a price that would probably end up higher than the current budget for AFDC. But none of the workfare advocates are proposing that sort of massive public commitment to child care.

Then there is the problem of jobs. So far, studies show that existing state work- 12
fare programs have had virtually no success in improving their participants' incomes or employment rates. Small wonder: Nearly half the new jobs generated in recent years pay poverty-level wages; and most welfare recipients will enter jobs that pay near the minimum wage, which is $6,900 a year—26 percent less than the poverty level for a family of three. A menial, low-wage job may be character-building (from a middle-class vantage point), but it will not lift anyone out of poverty.

Some of my feminist activist friends argue that it is too late to stop the work- 13
fare juggernaut. The best we can do, they say, is to try to defeat the more pernicious proposals: those that are over-coercive, that do not offer funds for child care,

or that would relegate work clients to a "subemployee" status unprotected by federal labor and civil rights legislation. Our goal, the pragmatists argue, should be to harness the current enthusiasm for workfare to push for services welfare recipients genuinely need, such as child care and job training and counseling.

I wish the pragmatists well, but for me, it would be a betrayal of women like   14
Lynn to encourage the workfare bandwagon in any way. Most women, like Lynn, do not take up welfare as a career, but as an emergency measure in a time of personal trauma and dire need. At such times, the last thing they need is to be hustled into a low-wage job, and left to piece together child care, health insurance, transportation, and all the other ingredients of survival. In fact, the main effect of workfare may be to discourage needy women from seeking any help at all—a disastrous result in a nation already suffering from a child poverty rate of nearly 25 percent. Public policy should be aimed at giving impoverished mothers (and, I would add, fathers) the help they so urgently need—not only in the form of job opportunities, but sufficient income support to live on until a job worth taking comes along.

Besides, there is an ancient feminist principle at stake. The premise of all the   15
workfare proposals—the more humane as well as the nasty—is that single mothers on welfare are not *working*. But, to quote the old feminist bumper sticker, EVERY MOTHER IS A WORKING MOTHER. And those who labor to raise their children in poverty—to feed and clothe them on meager budgets and to nurture them in an uncaring world—are working the hardest. The feminist position has never been that all women must pack off their children and enter the work force, but that all women's work—in the home or on the job—should be valued and respected.

Barbara Ehrenreich's essay stimulated a lively response from Ms. *readers. The following letters were published in the February 1988 issue.*

I was absolutely thrilled when I read Barbara Ehrenreich's article on work-   16
fare ("A Step Back to the Workhouse?" November 1987). As a single mother who received welfare for several years (with no child support) I'm against everything that workfare stands for. I belong to an organization called Women, Work, and Welfare, a group of current and former welfare recipients trying to empower ourselves and become a part of the decisions that affect our lives as poor women. It seems as if everybody but the welfare recipient herself has a hand in the decisions that are made.

CHERI HONKALA
Minneapolis, Minn.

I arrived in Chicago in 1952 with a husband and two children from a camp   17
in Europe. I had another child in 1953, lost a newborn in 1954, had a miscarriage, a hysterectomy, and a divorce in 1955. I never received child support. My ex-husband was remarried within two months.

I *never* received welfare. I worked in another culture, while in very bad   18
health. I found a two-room flat, had no furniture and slept for years on the floor. I

even went back to school at night and had to contend with companies like Gulf Oil Corp., which did not believe in promoting women. But I just slugged on.

By the end of the sixties, I had two daughters in college, and I had bought a 19 house. My total earnings for 1970 from three jobs came to a whopping $8,000.

A full-time minimum wage job *can* support one adult and one child. One just 20 has to learn how to do it.

URRSULA SCHRAMM
Hurley, Wis.

I found myself agreeing with the problems that Barbara Ehrenreich outlines 21 in the present workfare program.

Yet deep inside a protesting rumbling exploded when I read that impover- 22 ished mothers should receive sufficient income support to live on "until a job worth taking comes along." *Bullshit!* Sure, we all should have the right to only work a job we love, but how many of us can afford to wait for it? That we are often forced to work at jobs that are not fulfilling says a lot about our society in which more needs to be changed than just the welfare system!

My mother was forced to go to work when I was nine years old. Our family 23 was in dire financial straits and at the age of 50 she took a job in a factory. Was that job "worth taking"? Did it utilize her unique talents? *No!* Did it bring her personal fulfillment? *No!* Did it prevent the bank from foreclosing on our home? *Yes!* Did it give my mother the power to overcome our financial crisis and maintain her autonomy? *Yes!* You tell me if it was "worth taking." That depends on what your self-respect is worth to you.

GAIL FREI
Newtown Square, Pa.

Barbara Ehrenreich omitted a major element in her discussion of the vic- 24 timization of welfare families: The inability or unwillingness of the legal system to award *and enforce* realistic child support. Until it stops being easier to abandon your children than to default on that car loan, women and those who depend on them will be welfare/workfare victims.

SUSAN MARTIN RYNARD
Durham, N.C.

I went on welfare when my daughter was three, when I left my husband. I 25 had a high school education, but had always wanted to go to college. I was 25.

So, with the help of the government, I got my B.S. in nursing. I worked for 26 several years as an R.N. and then returned to school for my master's degree. For graduate school, I lived on savings, loans, and grants. The loans ($19,000 for undergrad and graduate in all) will be paid off in less than a year, in time for my daughter to begin college!

KATHRYN REID
Silverado, Calif.

A Step Back to the Workhouse?   Barbara Ehrenreich

391

Although I share Barbara Ehrenreich's concerns about workfare and the plight of her friend Lynn, the conclusions she draws strike me as misguided. We live in a society where the myths of the work ethic and self-help are deeply embedded in the popular culture; where resort to the dole is frowned upon unless the need is temporary or arises from disability; where the middle-class majority feels inequitably taxed, as compared to the wealthy, to support a system that directly benefits few of its members. 27

Feminists and other liberals should acknowledge the swelling demand for welfare reform. Our support should be conditional upon the incorporation in any welfare reform plan of provision for *quality* childcare facilities; upon the minimization of coercion; and upon further efforts to compel ex-spouses to pay their fair share of support. Nothing in this approach rules out our going ahead simultaneously with other, parallel efforts to question the mystique of work or to expose the links between welfare and poverty, on the one hand, and capitalism and the subordination of women, on the other. 28

DAVID G. BECKER 29
Hanover, N.H.

California is serious about workfare, but we call it GAIN (Greater Avenues for Independence). It offers welfare recipients vocational counseling, up to two years of vocational training, and workshops in how to get and hold a job.

GAIN also pays for child care and transportation. No job need be accepted by the recipient unless she/he will *net* at least as much as their AFDC grant, *including* child care, transportation, and medical insurance. And even then, they will receive funds to cover these costs for three months after they begin working to help them make the transition to the work force. 30

JANE KIRCHMAN
Guerneville, Calif.

QUESTIONS FOR DISCUSSION

Content

a. What does Ehrenreich mean when she writes: "We are being asked to believe that pushing destitute mothers into the work force . . . is consistent with women's strivings toward self-determination" (paragraph 3)? How is *self-determination* used in this context?

b. Where is Ehrenreich's thesis, her argument in a nutshell? What are the two main points she uses to support this argument? Evaluate these points. Do you agree with the argument?

c. Discuss the stereotype of "welfare dependency" she tries to dispel in this essay.

d. What do the "pragmatists" she mentions in paragraph 13 want? Why won't she oblige them?

e. What, according to the author, are the benefits of the welfare system?

Strategy and Style

f. Why does she begin by attacking opposing arguments? Is her strategy effective? In what other essays in this chapter is this strategy used?

g. In paragraph 5, Ehrenreich tells the story of a woman she knows. Why is narration a particularly effective strategy at this point in the essay?

h. Besides telling Lynn's story, the author uses many statistics. Which is more effective in convincing you? Why?

i. In what parts of this essay does the author use the opinions of authorities on the welfare system to support her arguments?

j. Why does she begin an essay on so serious a subject with sarcasm ("putting its hapless victims to work—if necessary, at the nearest Burger King," paragraph 1)? Does doing so make her argument more effective? If so, in what ways?

k. Point to other uses of irony and sarcasm. How would you characterize the overall tone of this essay?

SUGGESTIONS FOR SHORT WRITING

a. Use freewriting to address Ehrenreich's point in paragraph 3. Do you agree with the author, with Senator Moynihan, or with neither? Explain your position.

b. Reread paragraph 15. Respond negatively or positively to Ehrenreich's premise that "every mother is a working mother."

SUGGESTIONS FOR SUSTAINED WRITING

a. Write an argument for or against workfare in which you take into account the arguments cited in Ehrenreich's essay.

b. Write a letter in response to a recent newspaper or magazine article with which you find yourself strongly agreeing or disagreeing. Submit it as a letter to the editor of that newspaper or magazine.

Lifeboat Ethics: The Case Against Helping the Poor

Garrett Hardin

Garrett Hardin (b. 1915) is a human ecologist who writes, lectures, and teaches about this subject. Though his formal scientific training has been extensive (he was educated at the University of Chicago and at Stanford University, where he received a PhD in biology) and he has written many academic articles, he has always been most interested in making the connections between science and society clear to a wide, nonacademic audience. His desire is to "explain science to the public" and his many books written for lay readers show this. Among his publications are several books on population growth, including Population, Evolution and Birth Control *(1964),* The Limits of Altruism *(1977), and* Living Within Limits: Ecology, Economics, and Population Taboos *(1993). Some of his essays are collected in* Naked Emperors: Essays of a Taboo-Stalker *(1982).*

1 Environmentalists use the metaphor of the earth as a "spaceship" in trying to persuade countries, industries and people to stop wasting and polluting our natural resources. Since we all share life on this planet, they argue, no single person or institution has the right to destroy, waste, or use more than a fair share of its resources.

2 But does everyone on earth have an equal right to an equal share of its resources? The spaceship metaphor can be dangerous when used by misguided idealists to justify suicidal policies for sharing our resources through uncontrolled immigration and foreign aid. In their enthusiastic but unrealistic generosity, they confuse the ethics of a spaceship with those of a lifeboat.

3 A true spaceship would have to be under the control of a captain, since no ship could possibly survive if its course were determined by committee. Spaceship Earth certainly has no captain; the United Nations is merely a toothless tiger, with little power to enforce any policy upon its bickering members.

4 If we divide the world crudely into rich nations and poor nations, two thirds of them are desperately poor, and only one third comparatively rich, with the United States the wealthiest of all. Metaphorically each rich nation can be seen as a lifeboat full of comparatively rich people. In the ocean outside each lifeboat swim the poor of the world, who would like to get in, or at least to share some of the wealth. What should the lifeboat passengers do?

5 First, we must recognize the limited capacity of any lifeboat. For example, a nation's land has a limited capacity to support a population and as the current energy crisis has shown us, in some ways we have already exceeded the carrying capacity of our land. So here we sit, say 50 people in our lifeboat. To be generous, let us assume it has room for 10 more, making a total capacity of 60. Suppose the 50 of us in the lifeboat see 100 others swimming in the water outside, begging for admission to our boat or for handouts. We have several options: We may be tempted to try to live by the Christian ideal of being "our brother's keeper," or by the Marxist ideal of "to each according to his needs." Since the needs of all in the

water are the same, and since they can all be seen as our "brothers," we could take them all into our boat, making a total of 150 in a boat designed for 60. The boat swamps; everyone drowns. Complete justice, complete catastrophe.

Since the boat has an unused excess capacity of 10 more passengers, we 6 could admit just 10 more to it. But which 10 do we let in? How do we choose? Do we pick the best 10, the neediest 10, "first come, first served"? And what do we say to the 90 we exclude? If we do let an extra 10 into our lifeboat, we will have lost our "safety factor," an engineering principle of critical importance. For example, if we don't leave room for excess capacity as a safety factor in our country's agriculture, a new plant disease or a bad change in the weather could have disastrous consequences.

Suppose we decide to preserve our small safety factor and admit no more to 7 the lifeboat. Our survival is then possible, although we shall have to be constantly on guard against boarding parties.

While this last solution clearly offers the only means of our survival, it is 8 morally abhorrent to many people. Some say they feel guilty about their good luck. My reply is simple: "Get out and yield your place to others." This may solve the problem of the guilt-ridden person's conscience, but it does not change the ethics of the lifeboat. The needy person to whom the guilt-ridden person yields his place will not himself feel guilty about his good luck. If he did, he would not climb aboard. The net result of conscience-stricken people giving up their unjustly held seats is the elimination of that sort of conscience from the lifeboat.

This is the basic metaphor within which we must work out our solutions. Let 9 us now enrich the image, step by step, with substantive additions from the real world, a world that must solve real and pressing problems of overpopulation and hunger.

The harsh ethics of the lifeboat become even harsher when we consider the 10 reproductive differences between the rich nations and the poor nations. The people inside the lifeboats are doubling in numbers every 87 years; those swimming around outside are doubling, on the average, every 35 years, more than twice as fast as the rich. And since the world's resources are dwindling, the difference in prosperity between the rich and the poor can only increase.

As of 1973, the United States had a population of 210 million people, who 11 were increasing by 0.8 percent per year. Outside our lifeboat, let us imagine another 210 million people (say the combined populations of Colombia, Ecuador, Venezuela, Morocco, Pakistan, Thailand, and the Philippines), increasing at a rate of 3.3 percent per year. Put differently, the doubling time for this aggregate population was 21 years, compared to 87 years for the United States.

Now suppose the United States agreed to pool its resources with those seven 12 countries, with everyone receiving an equal share. Initially the ratio of Americans to non-Americans in this model would be one-to-one. But consider what the ratio would be after 87 years, by which time the Americans would have doubled to a population of 420 million. By then, doubling every 21 years, the other group would have swollen to 3.54 billion. Each American would have to share the available resources with more than eight people.

But, one could argue, this discussion assumes that current population trends 13 will continue, and they may not. Quite so. Most likely the rate of population increase will decline much faster in the United States than it will in the other countries, and there does not seem to be much we can do about it. In sharing with "each according to his needs," we must recognize that needs are determined by population size, which is determined by the rate of reproduction, which at present is regarded as a sovereign right of every nation, poor or not. This being so, the philanthropic load created by the sharing ethic of the spaceship can only increase.

The fundamental error of spaceship ethics, and the sharing it requires, is that 14 it leads to what I call "the tragedy of the commons." Under a system of private property, people who own property recognize their responsibility to care for it, for if they don't they will eventually suffer. A farmer, for instance, will allow no more cattle in a pasture than its carrying capacity justifies. If he overloads it, erosion sets in, weeds take over, and he loses the use of the pasture.

If a pasture becomes a commons open to all, the right of each to use it may 15 not be matched by a corresponding responsibility to protect it. Asking everyone to use it with discretion will hardly do, for the considerate herdsman who refrains from overloading the commons suffers more than a selfish one who says his needs are greater. If everyone would restrain himself, all would be well; but it takes only one less than everyone to ruin a system of voluntary restraint. In a crowded world of less than perfect human beings, mutual ruin is inevitable if there are no controls. This is the tragedy of the commons.

One of the major tasks of education today should be the creation of such an 16 acute awareness of the dangers of the commons that people will recognize its many varieties. For example, the air and water have become polluted because they are treated as commons. Further growth in the population or per-capita conversion of natural resources into pollutants will only make the problem worse. The same holds true for the fish of the oceans. Fishing fleets have nearly disappeared in many parts of the world; technological improvements in the art of fishing are hastening the day of complete ruin. Only the replacement of the system of the commons with a responsible system of control will save the land, air, water and oceanic fisheries.

In recent years there has been a push to create a new commons called a 17 World Food Bank, an international depository of food reserves to which nations would contribute according to their abilities and from which they would draw according to their needs. This humanitarian proposal received support from many liberal international groups, and from such prominent citizens as Margaret Mead, the U.N. Secretary General, and Senator Edward Kennedy.

A world food bank appeals powerfully to our humanitarian impulses. But 18 before we rush ahead with such a plan, let us ask if such a program would actually do more good than harm, not only momentarily but also in the long run. Those who propose a food bank usually refer to a current "emergency" or "crisis" in terms of world food supply. But what is an emergency? Although they may be infrequent and sudden, everyone knows that emergencies will occur from time to time. A well-run family, company, organization or country prepares for the likelihood of accidents and emergencies. It expects them, it budgets for them, it saves for them.

What happens if some organizations or countries budget for accidents and 19 others do not? If each country is solely responsible for its own well-being, poorly managed ones will suffer. But they can learn from experience. They may mend their ways, and learn to budget for infrequent but certain emergencies. For example, the weather varies from year to year, and periodic crop failures are certain. A wise and competent government saves out of the production of the good years in anticipation of bad years to come. Joseph taught this policy to Pharaoh in Egypt more than 2,000 years ago. Yet the great majority of the governments in the world today do not follow such a policy. They lack either the wisdom or the competence, or both. Should those nations that do manage to put something aside be forced to come to the rescue each time an emergency occurs among the poor nations?

"But it isn't their fault!" some kind-hearted liberals argue. "How can we 20 blame the poor people who are caught in an emergency? Why must they suffer for the sins of their governments?" The concept of blame is simply not relevant here. The real question is, what are the operational consequences of establishing a world food bank? If it is open to every country every time a need develops, slovenly rulers will not be motivated to take Joseph's advice. Someone will always come to their aid. Some countries will deposit food in the world food bank, and others will withdraw it. There will be almost no overlap. As a result of such solutions to food shortage emergencies, the poor countries will not learn to mend their ways, and will suffer progressively greater emergencies as their populations grow.

On the average, poor countries undergo a 2.5 percent increase in population 21 each year; rich countries, about 0.6 percent. Only rich countries have anything in the way of food reserves set aside, and even they do not have as much as they should. Poor countries have none. If poor countries received no food from the outside, the rate of their population growth would be periodically checked by crop failures and famines. But if they can always draw on a world food bank in time of need, their population can continue to grow unchecked, and so will their "need" for aid. In the short run, a world food bank may diminish that need, but in the long run it actually increases the need without limit.

Without some system of worldwide food sharing, the proportion of people 22 in the rich and poor nations might eventually stabilize. The overpopulated poor countries would decrease in numbers while the rich countries that had room for more people would increase. But with a well-meaning system of sharing, such as a world food bank, the growth differential between the rich and the poor countries will not only persist, it will increase. Because of the higher rate of population growth in the poor countries of the world, 88 percent of today's children are born poor, and only 12 percent rich. Year by year the ratio becomes worse as the fast-reproducing poor outnumber the slow-reproducing rich.

A world food bank is thus a commons in disguise. People will have more 23 motivation to draw from it than to add to any common store. The less provident and less able will multiply at the expense of the abler and more provident, bringing eventual ruin upon all who share in the commons. Besides, any system of "sharing" that amounts to foreign aid from the rich nations to the poor nations will carry the taint of charity, which will contribute little to the world peace so devoutly desired by those who support the idea of a world food bank.

As past U.S. foreign-aid programs have amply and depressingly demon- 24 strated, international charity frequently inspires mistrust and antagonism rather than gratitude on the part of the recipient nation.

The modern approach to foreign aid stresses the export of technology and 25 advice, rather than money and food. As an ancient Chinese proverb goes: "Give a man a fish and he will eat for a day; teach him how to fish and he will eat for the rest of his days." Acting on this advice, the Rockefeller and Ford Foundations have financed a number of programs for improving agriculture in the hungry nations. Known as the "Green Revolution," these programs have led to the development of "miracle rice" and "miracle wheat," new strains that offer bigger harvests and greater resistance to crop damage.

Whether or not the Green Revolution can increase food production as much 26 as its champions claim is a debatable but possibly irrelevant point. Those who support this well-intended humanitarian effort should first consider some of the fundamentals of human ecology. Ironically, one man who did was the late Alan Gregg, a vice president of the Rockefeller Foundation. Two decades ago he expressed strong doubts about the wisdom of such attempts to increase food production. He likened the growth and spread of humanity over the surface of the earth to the spread of cancer in the human body, remarking that "cancerous growths demand food, but, as far as I know, they have never been cured by getting it."

Every human born constitutes a draft on all aspects of the environment: 27 Food, air, water, forests, beaches, wildlife, scenery and solitude. Food can, perhaps, be significantly increased to meet a growing demand. But what about clean beaches, unspoiled forests, and solitude? If we satisfy a growing population's need for food, we necessarily decrease its per capita supply of the other resources needed by people.

India, for example, now has a population of 600 million, which increases 28 by 15 million each year. This population already puts a huge load on a relatively impoverished environment. The country's forests are now only a small fraction of what they were three centuries ago, and floods and erosion continually destroy the insufficient farmland that remains. Every one of the 15 million new lives added to India's population puts an additional burden on the environment, and increases the economic and social costs of crowding. However humanitarian our intent, every Indian life saved through medical or nutritional assistance from abroad diminishes the quality of life for those who remain, and for subsequent generations. If rich countries make it possible, through foreign aid, for 600 million Indians to swell to 1.2 billion in a mere 28 years, as their current growth rate threatens, will future generations of Indians thank us for hastening the destruction of their environment? Will our good intentions be sufficient excuse for the consequences of our actions?

Without a true world government to control reproduction and the use of 29
available resources, the sharing ethic of the spaceship is impossible. For the foreseeable future, our survival demands that we govern our actions by the ethics of a
lifeboat, harsh though they may be. Posterity will be satisfied with nothing less.

1974

QUESTIONS FOR DISCUSSION

Content

a. What are ethics? How does Hardin use the term in the context of his essay?
b. Summarize Hardin's argument. What is his main point?
c. Hardin uses the lifeboat as the primary metaphor to create a lasting image in
    his readers' minds. Describe this lifeboat as you see it.
d. The other key metaphor is the spaceship. What is the difference between think-
    ing of Earth as a lifeboat and of Earth as a spaceship?
e. What other metaphors does Hardin use?
f. Who are the people Hardin positions himself against? What is the main fault he
    finds with their thinking?

Strategy and Style

g. Hardin asks questions occasionally as a way to guide our thinking (see para-
    graphs 2 and 6 for examples). What other questions could be asked that Hardin
    would not have easy answers to?
h. Does the lifeboat metaphor stand up under close scrutiny? If not, where do you
    think the metaphor is weak?
i. Where and how does Hardin use statistics? What kind of a writer's "voice" do
    these statistics create?
j. Hardin continually refers to "we." Who is "we"? Is Hardin necessarily included
    in this pronoun?
k. In paragraph 19 Hardin backs up his point with an allusion to the Bible:
    "Joseph taught this policy to Pharaoh in Egypt more than 2,000 years ago." In
    the next paragraph, he says that "slovenly rulers will not be motivated to take
    Joseph's advice." What does the biblical reference add to his argument? Who
    might be the slovenly rulers he is referring to?

SUGGESTIONS FOR SHORT WRITING

a. Reread the essay and mark passages that grab your interest because they puz-
    zle, please, or irritate you, or because they connect with things you are learn-
    ing in another class. Choose one such passage and write a brief response to it,

explaining why it puzzles, pleases, or irritates you, or showing the connections between Hardin's essay and ideas discussed in your other classes.

b. Summarize the essay. Since the essay is complex, you may wish to do this summary in a creative way, perhaps in the form of a letter to someone outside the class.

SUGGESTIONS FOR SUSTAINED WRITING

a. Write a counterargument to this selection. Present an alternative solution (or at least a first step in the solution) to the problems of overpopulation and hunger. Do library research to find statistics that will argue with Hardin's statistics. You may want to take a creative approach and write this paper as a letter to Hardin.

b. Find another metaphor that could be used to describe the Earth's current situation. Frame an argument around that metaphor. Some examples of metaphors: race car, leaky barge, tapestry, pond, house.

Sex, Drugs, Disasters, and the Extinction of Dinosaurs

Stephen Jay Gould

Stephen Jay Gould (b. 1941) is a professor of biology, geology, and the history of science at Harvard University, where he has taught since 1967. He was born in New York City, attended Antioch College, and took his PhD at Columbia University. A prolific writer, he publishes a monthly column in Natural History *magazine and has contributed well over a hundred articles to scientific journals across the United States. Among his full-length works are several collections of essays first published in* Natural History. *They include* Ever Since Darwin *(1978),* The Panda's Thumb *(1980),* Hens' Teeth and Horses' Toes *(1983),* The Flamingo's Smile *(1985), and* Bully for Brontosaurus *(1991). He is also the author of* The Mismeasure of Man *(1980) and* Wonderful Life *(1990), which argue against the theory of biological determinism and explain the notion of chance in evolution. Gould makes scientific fact and theory appetizing even to the reader with no scientific training. John Noble Wilford, science editor of the* New York Times, *has called him "one of the most spirited essayists of our time." Indeed, his common sense and delightful wit make it seem as if we are reading an article in a popular magazine rather than a reasoned and thoroughly researched scientific study.*

1 Science, in its most fundamental definition, is a fruitful mode of inquiry, not a list of enticing conclusions. The conclusions are the consequence, not the essence.

2 My greatest unhappiness with most popular presentations of science concerns their failure to separate fascinating claims from the methods that scientists use to establish the facts of nature. Journalists, and the public, thrive on controversial and stunning statements. But science is, basically, a way of knowing—in P. B. Medawar's apt words, "the art of the soluble." If the growing corps of popular science writers would focus on *how* scientists develop and defend those fascinating claims, they would make their greatest possible contribution to public understanding.

3 Consider three ideas, proposed in perfect seriousness to explain that greatest of all titillating puzzles—the extinction of dinosaurs. Since these three notions invoke the primally fascinating themes of our culture—sex, drugs, and violence—they surely reside in the category of fascinating claims. I want to show why two of them rank as silly speculation, while the other represents science at its grandest and most useful.

4 Science works with testable proposals. If, after much compilation and scrutiny of data, new information continues to affirm a hypothesis, we may accept it provisionally and gain confidence as further evidence mounts. We can never be completely sure that a hypothesis is right, though we may be able to show with confidence that it is wrong. The best scientific hypotheses are also generous and expansive: They suggest extensions and implications that enlighten related, and even far distant, subjects. Simply consider how the idea of evolution has influenced virtually every intellectual field.

400

Useless speculation, on the other hand, is restrictive. It generates no testable 5
hypothesis, and offers no way to obtain potentially refuting evidence. Please note
that I am not speaking of truth or falsity. The speculation may well be true; still, if
it provides, in principle, no material for affirmation or rejection, we can make
nothing of it. It must simply stand forever as an intriguing idea. Useless speculation turns in on itself and leads nowhere; good science, containing both seeds for
its potential refutation and implications for more and different testable knowledge,
reaches out. But, enough preaching. Let's move on to dinosaurs, and the three proposals for their extinction.

1. *Sex:* Testes function only in a narrow range of temperature (those of mammals
   hang externally in a scrotal sac because internal body temperatures are too high
   for their proper function). A worldwide rise in temperature at the close of the
   Cretaceous period caused the testes of dinosaurs to stop functioning and led to
   their extinction by sterilization of males.
2. *Drugs:* Angiosperms (flowering plants) first evolved toward the end of the dinosaurs' reign. Many of these plants contain psychoactive agents, avoided by
   mammals today as a result of their bitter taste. Dinosaurs had neither means to
   taste the bitterness nor livers effective enough to detoxify the substances. They
   died of massive overdoses.
3. *Disasters:* A large comet or asteroid struck the earth some 65 million years
   ago, lofting a cloud of dust into the sky and blocking sunlight, thereby sup-
   pressing photosynthesis and so drastically lowering world temperatures that
   dinosaurs and hosts of other creatures became extinct.

Before analyzing these three tantalizing statements, we must establish a 6
basic ground rule often violated in proposals for the dinosaurs' demise. *There is
no separate problem of the extinction of dinosaurs.* Too often we divorce specific
events from their wider contexts and systems of cause and effect. The fundamental fact of dinosaur extinction is its synchrony with the demise of so many other
groups across a wide range of habitats, from terrestrial to marine.

The history of life has been punctuated by brief episodes of mass ex- 7
tinction. A recent analysis by University of Chicago paleontologists Jack
Sepkoski and Dave Raup, based on the best and most exhaustive tabulation of
data ever assembled, shows clearly that five episodes of mass dying stand well
above the "background" extinctions of normal times (when we consider all
mass extinctions, large and small, they seem to fall in a regular 26-million-
year cycle). The Cretaceous debacle, occurring 65 million years ago and separating the Mesozoic and Cenozoic eras of our geological time scale, ranks
prominently among the five. Nearly all the marine plankton (single-celled
floating creatures) died with geological suddenness; among marine inverte-
brates, nearly 15 percent of all families perished, including many previously
dominant groups, especially the ammonites (relatives of squids in coiled

shells). On land, the dinosaurs disappeared after more than 100 million years of unchallenged domination.

In this context, speculations limited to dinosaurs alone ignore the larger phe- 8 nomenon. We need a coordinated explanation for a system of events that includes the extinction of dinosaurs as one component. Thus it makes little sense, though it may fuel our desire to view mammals as inevitable inheritors of the earth, to guess that dinosaurs died because small mammals ate their eggs (a perennial favorite among untestable speculations). It seems most unlikely that some disaster peculiar to dinosaurs befell these massive beasts—and that the debacle happened to strike just when one of history's five great dyings had enveloped the earth for completely different reasons.

The testicular theory, an old favorite from the 1940s, had its root in an in- 9 teresting and thoroughly respectable study of temperature tolerances in the American alligator, published in the staid *Bulletin of the American Museum of Natural History* in 1946 by three experts on living and fossil reptiles—E. H. Colbert, my own first teacher in paleontology; R. B. Cowles; and C. M. Bogert.

The first sentence of their summary reveals a purpose beyond alligators: 10 "This report describes an attempt to infer the reactions of extinct reptiles, especially the dinosaurs, to high temperatures as based upon reactions observed in the modern alligator." They studied, by rectal thermometry, the body temperatures of alligators under changing conditions of heating and cooling. (Well, let's face it, you wouldn't want to try sticking a thermometer under a 'gator's tongue.) The predictions under test go way back to an old theory first stated by Galileo in the 1630s—the unequal scaling of surfaces and volumes. As an animal, or any object, grows (provided its shape doesn't change), surface areas must increase more slowly than volumes—since surfaces get larger as length squared, while volumes increase much more rapidly, as length cubed. Therefore, small animals have high ratios of surface to volume, while large animals cover themselves with relatively little surface.

Among cold-blooded animals lacking any physiological mechanism for 11 keeping their temperatures constant, small creatures have a hell of a time keeping warm—because they lose so much heat through their relatively large surfaces. On the other hand, large animals, with their relatively small surfaces, may lose heat so slowly that, once warm, they may maintain effectively constant temperatures against ordinary fluctuations of climate. (In fact, the resolution of the "hot-blooded dinosaur" controversy that burned so brightly a few years back may simply be that, while large dinosaurs possessed no physiological mechanism for constant temperature, and were not therefore warm-blooded in the technical sense, their large size and relatively small surface area kept them warm.)

Colbert, Cowles, and Bogert compared the warming rates of small and large 12 alligators. As predicted, the small fellows heated up (and cooled down) more quickly. When exposed to a warm sun, a tiny 50-gram (1.76-ounce) alligator heated up one degree Celsius every minute and a half, while a large alligator, 260 times bigger at 13,000 grams (28.7 pounds), took seven and a half minutes to gain a degree. Extrapolating up to an adult 10-ton dinosaur, they concluded that a one-degree rise in body temperature would take eighty-six hours. If large animals absorb heat so slowly (through their relatively small surfaces), they will also be unable to shed any excess heat gained when temperatures rise above a favorable level.

The authors then guessed that large dinosaurs lived at or near their optimum 13 temperatures; Cowles suggested that a rise in global temperatures just before the Cretaceous extinction caused the dinosaurs to heat up beyond their optimal tolerance—and, being so large, they couldn't shed the unwanted heat. (In a most unusual statement within a scientific paper, Colbert and Bogert then explicitly disavowed this speculative extension of their empirical work on alligators.) Cowles conceded that this excess heat probably wasn't enough to kill or even to enervate the great beasts, but since testes often function only within a narrow range of temperature, he proposed that this global rise might have sterilized all the males, causing extinction by natural contraception.

The overdose theory has recently been supported by UCLA psychiatrist 14 Ronald K. Siegel. Siegel has gathered, he claims, more than 2,000 records of animals who, when given access, administer various drugs to themselves—from a mere swig of alcohol to massive doses of the big H. Elephants will swill the equivalent of twenty beers at a time, but do not like alcohol in concentrations greater than 7 percent. In a silly bit of anthropocentric speculation, Siegel states that "elephants drink, perhaps, to forget . . . the anxiety produced by shrinking rangeland and the competition for food."

Since fertile imaginations can apply almost any hot idea to the extinction of 15 dinosaurs, Siegel found a way. Flowering plants did not evolve until late in the dinosaurs' reign. These plants also produced an array of aromatic, amino-acid-based alkaloids—the major group of psychoactive agents. Most mammals are "smart" enough to avoid these potential poisons. The alkaloids simply don't taste good (they are bitter); in any case, we mammals have livers happily supplied with the capacity to detoxify them. But, Siegel speculates, perhaps dinosaurs could neither taste the bitterness nor detoxify the substances once ingested. He recently told members of the American Psychological Association: "I'm not suggesting that all dinosaurs OD'd on plant drugs, but it certainly was a factor." He also argued that death by overdose may help explain why so many dinosaur fossils are found in contorted positions. (Do not go gentle into that good night.)

Extraterrestrial catastrophes have long pedigrees in the popular literature of 16 extinction, but the subject exploded again in 1979, after a long lull, when the father-son, physicist-geologist team of Luis and Walter Alvarez proposed that an asteroid, some 10 km in diameter, struck the earth 65 million years ago (comets, rather than asteroids, have since gained favor. Good science is self-corrective).

The force of such a collision would be immense, greater by far than the 17 megatonnage of all the world's nuclear weapons. In trying to reconstruct a scenario that would explain the simultaneous dying of dinosaurs on land and so many creatures in the sea, the Alvarezes proposed that a gigantic dust cloud, generated by particles blown aloft in the impact, would so darken the earth that photosynthesis would cease and temperatures drop precipitously. (Rage, rage against the dying of the light.) The single-celled photosynthetic oceanic plankton, with life cycles measured in weeks, would perish outright, but land plants might survive through the dormancy of their seeds (land plants were not much affected by the Cretaceous extinction, and any adequate theory must account for the curious pattern of differential survival). Dinosaurs would die by starvation and freezing; small, warm-blooded mammals, with more modest requirements for food and better regulation of body temperature, would squeak through. "Let the bastards freeze in the dark," as bumper stickers of our chauvinistic neighbors in sunbelt states proclaimed several years ago during the Northeast's winter oil crisis.

All three theories, testicular malfunction, psychoactive overdosing, and asteroidal zapping, grab our attention mightily. As pure phenomenology, they rank about equally high on any hit parade of primal fascination. Yet one represents expansive science, the others restrictive and untestable speculation. The proper criterion lies in evidence and methodology; we must probe behind the superficial fascination of particular claims. **18**

How could we possibly decide whether the hypothesis of testicular frying is right or wrong? We would have to know things that the fossil record cannot provide. What temperatures were optimal for dinosaurs? Could they avoid the absorption of excess heat by staying in the shade, or in caves? At what temperatures did their testicles cease to function? Were late Cretaceous climates ever warm enough to drive the internal temperatures of dinosaurs close to this ceiling? Testicles simply don't fossilize, and how could we infer their temperature tolerances even if they did? In short, Cowles's hypothesis is only an intriguing speculation leading nowhere. The most damning statement against it appeared right in the conclusion of Colbert, Cowles, and Bogert's paper, when they admitted: "It is difficult to advance any definite arguments against the hypothesis." My statement may seem paradoxical—isn't a hypothesis really good if you can't devise any arguments against it? Quite the contrary. It is simply untestable and unusable. **19**

Siegel's overdosing has even less going for it. At least Cowles extrapolated his conclusion from some good data on alligators. And he didn't completely violate the primary guideline of siting dinosaur extinction in the context of a general mass dying—for rise in temperature could be the root cause of a general catastrophe, zapping dinosaurs by testicular malfunction and different groups for other reasons. But Siegel's speculation cannot touch the extinction of ammonites or oceanic plankton (diatoms make their own food with good sweet sunlight; they don't OD on the chemicals of terrestrial plants). It is simply a gratuitous, attention-grabbing guess. It cannot be tested, for how can we know what dinosaurs tasted and what their livers could do? Livers don't fossilize any better than testicles. **20**

The hypothesis doesn't even make any sense in its own context. Angiosperms were in full flower ten million years before dinosaurs went the way of all flesh. Why did it take so long? As for the pains of a chemical death recorded in contortions of fossils, I regret to say (or rather I'm pleased to note for the dinosaurs' sake) that **21**

Siegel's knowledge of geology must be a bit deficient: Muscles contract after death and geological strata rise and fall with motions of the earth's crust after burial—more than enough reason to distort a fossil's pristine appearance.

The impact story, on the other hand, has a sound basis in evidence. It 22 can be tested, extended, refined, and, if wrong, disproved. The Alvarezes did not just construct an arresting guess for public consumption. They proposed their hypothesis after laborious geochemical studies with Frank Asaro and Helen Michael had revealed a massive increase of iridium in rocks deposited right at the time of extinction. Iridium, a rare metal of the platinum group, is virtually absent from indigenous rocks of the earth's crust; most of our iridium arrives on extraterrestrial objects that strike the earth.

The Alvarez hypothesis bore immediate fruit. Based originally on evidence 23 from two European localities, it led geochemists throughout the world to examine other sediments of the same age. They found abnormally high amounts of iridium everywhere—from continental rocks of the western United States to deep sea cores from the South Atlantic.

Cowles proposed his testicular hypothesis in the mid-1940s. Where has it 24 gone since then? Absolutely nowhere, because scientists can do nothing with it. The hypothesis must stand as a curious appendage to a solid study of alligators. Siegel's overdose scenario will also win a few press notices and fade into oblivion. The Alvarezes' asteroid falls into a different category altogether, and much of the popular commentary has missed this essential distinction by focusing on the impact and its attendant results, and forgetting what really matters to a scientist—the iridium. If you talk just about asteroids, dust, and darkness, you tell stories no better and no more entertaining than fried testicles or terminal trips. It is the iridium—the source of testable evidence—that counts and forges the crucial distinction between speculation and science.

The proof, to twist a phrase, lies in the doing. Cowles's hypothesis has gen- 25 erated nothing in thirty-five years. Since its proposal in 1979, the Alvarez hypothesis has spawned hundreds of studies, a major conference, and attendant publications. Geologists are fired up. They are looking for iridium at all other extinction boundaries. Every week exposes a new wrinkle in the scientific press. Further evidence that the Cretaceous iridium represents extraterrestrial impact and not indigenous volcanism continues to accumulate. As I revise this essay in November 1984 (this paragraph will be out of date when the book is published), new data include chemical "signatures" of other isotopes indicating unearthly provenance, glass spherules of a size and sort produced by impact and not by volcanic eruptions, and high-pressure varieties of silica formed (so far as we know) only under the tremendous shock of impact.

My point is simply this: Whatever the eventual outcome (I suspect it will be 26 positive), the Alvarez hypothesis is exciting, fruitful science because it generates tests, provides us with things to do, and expands outward. We are having fun, battling back and forth, moving toward a resolution, and extending the hypothesis beyond its original scope.

As just one example of the unexpected, distant cross-fertilization that good   27
science engenders, the Alvarez hypothesis made a major contribution to a theme
that has riveted public attention in the past few months—so-called nuclear winter.
In a speech delivered in April 1982, Luis Alvarez calculated the energy that a ten-
kilometer asteroid would release on impact. He compared such an explosion with
a full nuclear exchange and implied that all-out atomic war might unleash similar
consequences.

This theme of impact leading to massive dust clouds and falling tempera-   28
tures formed an important input to the decision of Carl Sagan and a group of colleagues to model the climatic consequences of nuclear holocaust. Full nuclear exchange would probably generate the same kind of dust cloud and darkening that
may have wiped out the dinosaurs. Temperatures would drop precipitously and
agriculture might become impossible. Avoidance of nuclear war is fundamentally
an ethical and political imperative, but we must know the factual consequences to
make firm judgments. I am heartened by a final link across disciplines and deep
concerns—another criterion, by the way, of science at its best. A recognition of the
very phenomenon that made our evolution possible by exterminating the previously dominant dinosaurs and clearing a way for the evolution of large mammals,
including us, might actually help to save us from joining those magnificent beasts
in contorted poses among the strata of the earth.

1984

QUESTIONS FOR DISCUSSION

Content

a. In paragraph 1, Gould claims that science is a "fruitful mode of inquiry," not a
   set of "conclusions." What does he mean, and how does this assertion help explain his argument? Where is this assertion illustrated in his essay?
b. Why can we "never be completely sure" that a hypothesis is correct (paragraph 4)?
c. Summarize the three hypotheses on the extinction of dinosaurs. What is the
   main element in each that makes it testable or untestable?
d. What distinctions does the author make between scientific hypothesis and
   speculation? Explain his assertion that the "proper criterion lies in evidence and
   methodology" (paragraph 18).
e. Why, according to Gould, is a hypothesis suspect if one cannot mount arguments against it?
f. What does he mean when he implies that science should be fun (paragraph 26)?
   In what way does the Alvarezes' hypothesis meet this criterion? Why are the
   other two theories not fun?

Strategy and Style

g. In paragraph 9, Gould reports that the "testicular theory" had its origins in a respectable scientific study. Why does he say this if he wishes to discredit that theory?

h. What are his views of the various scientists whose studies he cites? Compare his opinions of the team of Colbert, Cowles, and Bogert (paragraphs 9–13); of Siegel (paragraphs 14 and 15); and of the Alvarezes (paragraphs 16 and 17). What words does he use to describe each? How do these words provide foreshadowing?

i. In paragraph 6, Gould writes, "Too often we divorce specific events. . . ." Who is "we"?

j. Is Gould's intended audience limited to scientists or people interested in science? How do you know?

k. What is the effect of quoting poet Dylan Thomas in paragraph 17 ("Rage, rage against the dying of the light")?

SUGGESTIONS FOR SHORT WRITING

a. In paragraphs 15 and 17, Gould quotes from "Do Not Go Gentle into That Good Night" by Dylan Thomas. Find a copy of the poem in your library and read it. Then, briefly explain the significance of the lines that Gould takes from it.

b. Read through the essay once more, writing questions in the margins that you would ask the author if you had the chance to meet with him. For example, you might inquire why he thinks it's "silly" to think that elephants might experience anxiety (paragraph 14).

c. Look around your town or college. Briefly "speculate" about what it or the land it sits on might have looked like 50, 100, or even 1,000 years ago.

SUGGESTIONS FOR SUSTAINED WRITING

a. When he brings in the idea of nuclear war in his concluding paragraphs, Gould suggests that the Alvarezes' theory has implications beyond the scope of paleontology. What other implications might their theory have? Write an essay in which you speculate on these implications.

b. Relying on the basic method of analysis that Gould uses and taking as your subject a current problem of national importance, brainstorm a list of hypotheses to account for the problem's cause. Then, write an essay in which you take three of the hypotheses from your list and discuss how each one could be proved or disproved. Which of the hypotheses is most probable?

Rebels with Sponsors

Andrew Cash

Andrew Cash was born in Toronto in 1962 and is a professional musician. His first group was the punk group L'Etranger, which disbanded in 1986. He worked as a solo artist for a number of years and recorded two albums: Boomtown *and* Time and Place. *Cash recently joined his brother Peter in the studio to record* Raceway *as the Cash Brothers. The following article appeared in 1995, and in 1997 Cash appeared before a Senate committee on tobacco use to explain the Export A program discussed in the essay.*

It is 1987. The singer is standing offstage on the grounds of the University of Toronto, waiting. Beyond the stage is a throng of university students. They are drunk. It's their first week of post-secondary education. The band is announced over the p.a. system. As the singer begins to climb the stairs to the stage, a strange man turns to him and says, "I'd like to change your mind about corporate sponsorship." 1

That singer was me. The man backstage was the rep for the brewery sponsoring the show. But wait a minute: If the show was already sponsored by a brewery, what did the singer need to be convinced of? 2

This is how it happens. Band books a show. Band and promoter make an agreement—in this case, the promoter is the University of Toronto. But when the band arrives at the show, it discovers that there has been a third party involved in the deal. The telltale signs being the huge beer banners across the stage, the inflatable beer cans on the stage, and other beer-promotion material scattered about including baseball hats, tote bags and plastic cups. The only beer available is the sponsor's beer. And perhaps worst of all, the band is constantly being pestered by the evangelical beer rep. 3

If the band had any ethical questions about corporate sponsorship, the journey up to the stage is not the time to hammer them out. It's too late to cancel the show or to rip down the signs. Instead, the band goes on and it looks like they have given the brewery permission to advertise at their show. In an instant, what is for virtually all musicians the most precious of things—the making and performing of music for others—has become a vehicle for the promotion of beer. 4

That event at U of T crystallized the vague feeling I was having about a phenomenon which, like the emergence of rock videos, took most young Canadian bands by surprise. At that time, musicians like me were finding more and more that at the end of the night, our gigs were paid for, either wholly or in part, by a brewery. 5

Today, corporate sponsorship has permeated the music business on all fronts, through live music, radio and television. Given this reality and the seeming indifference of music fans to it, why are we still wringing our hands? 6

It all started back in the mid-eighties. 7

That's when Molson and Labatt discovered that rock promotion was a unique marketing tool—not to mention a cash cow. One of the first big, sponsored Canadian 8

408

rock tours was Labatt's promotion of Platinum Blonde. Remember them? The Blondes were on their way to becoming a Canadian phenomenon, eventually selling half-a-million albums in this country. While there was some concern in the music business over the ethics of pushing beer to young rock audiences, the success of that tour set the stage for a war between Molson and Labatt for the rock dollar.

What ensued was a spending spree. Between 1985 and 1990 there was virtually 9 no summer outdoor music or community event that did not have some financial support and advertising presence from one of the two big breweries. Whenever young people gathered around rock music, they were chaperoned by a beer company. Over the years, the constant use of promotions like the Molson Rocks campaign has helped entrench the idea that beer is what rock music is all about.

Today, many mega-rock acts and medium concert draws are paid directly by 10 a brewery. Take the recent Rolling Stones tour. Canadian rock promotion company CPI promoted the entire *Voodoo Lounge* tour and CPI is owned by Labatt. CPI's rival MCA Concerts is owned by Molson. And wherever these two promoters are— and they are everywhere—you'll find their parent companies.

A new corporate player has recently entered the rock and roll sponsorship 11 sweepstakes. Export A cigarettes began funding a program last year called the Export A Inc. Plugged New Music Series. According to John Donnelly, its creator and producer, the program works as a trust fund. Unlike the sponsorship programs of the past where the sponsor would approach bands or promoters, individual bands are encouraged to apply to Export A themselves. For a club show, the band will receive $500 and free print and radio ads which promote the show and mention the sponsor. If the venue's capacity is over 1,000 people, the band gets $1,000.

In real terms, this is what the deal means: a fledgling band is doing a 15-date 12 tour from Montreal to Vancouver. At $200 a night, the tour will inevitably lose money. The math is simple: $200 will just barely cover the gas costs to travel this vast country in a van. Add to that the cost of van rental, meals on the road, agent costs, long-distance phone bills and someone is out a couple of grand.

If, on the other hand, the band applies to Export A, it receives an extra $500 13 a night. A tour that is only netting $3,000 is now getting an extra $7,500. And that's not the end of it. Export A may also throw in the agent's 15 per cent fee. What would have been a money-losing tour is now netting the agent an extra $1,125.

In return for the cash, the band has to hang a few innocuous banners on the 14 walls of the venue (you have to look very hard to see the Export A Inc. Plugged logo). This is definitely not the hard sell of the Molson Rocks blow-up beer bottle variety. That's because Donnelly, himself a 25-year veteran musician of the Canadian club scene, has been careful to allow the bands to remain the focal point.

But despite Donnelly's sympathies, for Export A, this deal isn't about musi- 15 cians—it's about getting their product's name into the bars and on the radio. That's why anyone who can book a club can get sponsored; to date Export A Inc. hasn't turned anyone down. Forty-five bands and $400,000 later, Export A has just announced that it will be extending its program for 1995. Its rumoured budget is $1-million, which will include two fully-loaded tour buses.

As I write these words, I am tempted to call up Export A and jump on board.   16
This truly seems like a great deal for a band. The only problem is that both my
parents died from cancer, linked to smoking cigarettes. Both of them grew up in
an era where the health risks of tobacco use were unknown. In fact, cigarettes back
then were sometimes marketed as having health benefits.

It isn't the purpose of this article to go into the costs of our culture's addic-   17
tion to tobacco, but it does need to be mentioned. After all, can any real discussion
of sponsorship take place without considering the nature of the products with which
we are involved and the impact they may have on our fans?

While Export A has limited its sponsorship to shows with audiences 19 years   18
and older, the print and radio ads will reach a much larger market. This market
includes teenagers—the people most likely to take up smoking, particularly if it is
associated with something as important to them as music.

There is every reason to expect that other cigarette companies will jump into   19
the fray. In fact, Belvedere has its own regional sponsorship program for bands in
eastern Canada. In an industry that has such limited avenues to market its product,
John Donnelly's brainchild may ignite a new spending spree similar to the one by
the breweries in the eighties.

I am aware that my career as a musician and songwriter has been buoyed by   20
corporate involvement in rock. Once you have been written up in a magazine, been
on MuchMusic or had any radio play, you have achieved wider exposure through
an advertising vehicle. So if you are offered more money and more exposure by
becoming more directly involved with a sponsor—especially if the promotional
idea isn't tacky—then why not take it? Is there really a difference between taking
money from Warner Music or Sony Music and taking it from Labatt?

I think there is. Involving your art with a corporate sponsor is not the same as   21
doing the work involved in trying to sell your art. Nor is it the same as accepting
public money in the form of arts grants. Public arts funding gives the work a sense
of public ownership and public service. Ultimately, that should mean public
accountability.

If the existence of rock and roll relied upon the largesse of the corporate   22
culture, sponsorships would be easier to justify. But it doesn't. The Canadian music
business is a $900-million industry—we are not talking about modern dance or
avant garde music, arts which need financial assistance from both the public and
private sectors to survive. Rock and roll would exist without the involvement of a
corporate sponsor. It would exist in a somewhat different form, but it would still
have a large audience.

Advertisers, particularly cigarette companies, need music more than music   23
needs sponsors. But corporate reps like Export A's John Donnelly say that we need
to piggyback on their steam in order to get our message (i.e. music) out. "Hey look,
you are in the music business," he says. "Remember that there is a second word in
the title of our industry. You want to reach millions of people. Here are these giant
corporations that do reach millions, that have the clout to run ads in newspapers
simultaneously in every market in the country. They do have the clout to buy radio.
But they need something to put in the spot."

But the truth is that it is the sponsor that needs to reach the rock audience. 24
Music is one of the few media that has the attention and fidelity of young people;
the relationship could be described as sacred. To be able to tap into, even mediate,
between this reverential bond is any advertising executive's dream. The presence and
influence of pop music is the envy of anyone—like beer and cigarette companies—
who wants to sell to the 15- to 40-year-old rock demographic. While legislation
prevents cigarette manufacturers from advertising directly (and curtails beer companies, albeit to a lesser degree), rock music has free-flowing access to this fertile
consumer group.

Desperate to "fill their spots" with rock, advertisers will throw money at 25
bands notorious for being broke. Helping the band, however, is really incidental to
the process, but if a band does well, the sponsor is quick to grab the credit.
Donnelly claims that without Export A's involvement, for example, west-coast
singer/songwriter Art Bergman's recent tour would never have made it to Toronto.

While the corporate sponsor loves to paint itself as a patron of the arts, the 26
truth is that there have been many more failures than successes in the rocky world
of corporate sponsorship. Ethics aside, it could be argued that it isn't a wise business
move to be sponsored directly by a beer or tobacco company if one of your career
goals is longevity. Where is Platinum Blonde today? Or Chalk Circle? How is
Allanah Myles' career going? What happened to the Spoons, whose career seemed
to nose-dive around the time they did a clothing commercial? The problems of some
of these acts can't necessarily be blamed on sponsorships, but there is no denying
that, time and again, the famed naïveté of rock musicians has turned us into
corporate dupes.

This happens in part because, just as the products the sponsors sell are 27
addictive, so is their sponsorship money. There was a time when a band was booked
into a venue when there was demand for the band. If no one wanted to see the band
or didn't know of their existence, you did what you could to create a buzz. You
played a Monday, Tuesday and Wednesday for free until you started drawing an
audience. This protocol for rising up through the ranks tested a band's mettle and
resolve. Quickly the weak cut out. Soon the poseurs did too because they discovered that the myth of the rock and roll lifestyle is a lie—it is bloody hard work and
humbling. The bands that were left were the ones with an over-riding passion and
gift and a pretty intense work ethic.

Corporate sponsorship works on very different principles. It plays on the 28
bands' short-sighted desperation for overnight success. It is drummed into a
band's head from day one that if they don't "make it" now they will be replaced.
And it is very hard to go back—once a band has a little taste of sponsorship money,
it will be difficult to imagine life without it. Small wonder the average career of a
recording artist is about two years.

There is one obstacle faced by sponsors wishing to use rock as an advertising 29
vehicle—part of the allure of rock is its rebellious image, its alternative views and
counter-cultural lifestyle. This is part of the attraction for people who become
musicians and part of the reason music is so important to its fans. Today, many bands
become well known through word-of-mouth and grass-roots support. The hard sell

and the over-hype make the discerning fan suspicious. The advertising world, however, has taken note of this shift in the public's taste and like Export A's low-key push—adjusted its own strategies accordingly.

Take last summer's Labatt ad campaign. Four bands appeared in very stylized, 30 grainy black-and-white commercials. None of the bands were hyping the beer. In fact, the spots I saw looked no different than a good rock video. In one commercial, the lead singer for Toronto band The Headstones appeared and simply said, "Who cares."

In exchange for the appearance, cases of Labatt's beer contained a free CD 31 single from one of the four bands. From the musician's standpoint, they weren't selling beer—they were selling themselves. And it worked. Both Hugh Dillon of the Headstones and Tom Wilson of Junkhouse have said that their records sold much better during the length of the campaign.

For Wilson the issue is simple. Labatt included 125,000 copies of Junkhouse's 32 single "Praying for Rain" in cases of beer, and Wilson, who is a respected 20-year veteran of the Canadian music scene, is finally enjoying some success. "We have an obligation to ourselves as artists but we also have an obligation to our kids who are looking for their next meal," Wilson says. "I put all my integrity into my music. My responsibility after I finish creating music is to sell it so I can continue doing this. If I have to put an Export A banner up that doesn't bother me at all. It has nothing to do with me, with creating music or the next song I am going to write."

Wilson's bottom line is that the promo must be tasteful. If the band appears 33 simply as an addition to a corporate promotional event, then no thanks. As he puts it, "If you want to be involved in my show then fine, but I don't feel like being involved in yours."

But whose show is it really? Part of the unwritten terms of any agreement 34 with a sponsor is a certain measure of self-censorship—even if the restriction simply means not badmouthing the sponsor. Toronto Celtic stomp band the Grievous Angels found out the hard way that their involvement with the Mariposa folk festival a few years ago had some strings attached. Mariposa had swung a deal with Molson, who underwrote the cost of the festival at Molson Park in exchange for a promotional presence at the event. Since the band had been hired by Mariposa, not Molson, they decided to speak out against the level of beer advertising at the legendary folk festival. The remark offended the brewery reps and Mariposa threatened to withhold the band's pay and cancel the Grievous Angels' remaining shows at the festival.

Chalk Circle had a similar experience when the late-eighties pop band was 35 booked to play a show in Ottawa. The Labatt promotion was so intense (there was an inflatable beer can right in the middle of the room, blocking some of the sight lines) that lead singer Chris Tait thought it would be funny to thank rival company Molson for putting on the show. Unbeknownst to Tait, Labatt was having a convention in Ottawa that weekend and all of the regional reps and the president of Labatt were on hand. They didn't see the humour in Tait's joke. One week later, the band was notified that the brewery would like a written apology. Tait refused and what followed, according to him, was that the band's entire summer festival tour mysteriously "fell through." Tait estimates that the band lost between $15,000 and $20,000 worth of work.

What lingers from all of this is an after-taste of control. Far from being the [36] independent purveyors of alternative culture—let alone the last line of defense against conformity and excessive consumption—the music community ends up beholden to corporate sponsors. Maybe rock and roll doesn't really matter that much anymore. One of its fundamental components, after all, is its disposability. Still, it's undeniable that in a culture that has virtually no credible institutional role models, rock and roll has become what John Lennon hinted it was over 25 years ago: more important than religion, politics or school.

The bottom line is that bands don't want to be seen as vehicles for advertisers. [37] Those of us who long for a place free from the incessant noise of the great North American selling machine have come to expect music and, more specifically, rock and roll, to be that place. Music turns all the rules around. It communicates in so many ways at the same time. There is no substitute for it. It is inclusive of all people and gives voice to our fears, longing and happiness. Advertising in music is about something very different.

If, as musicians, we don't wish to dwell on the ramifications of our affiliations, [38] that is one thing, but it is highly doubtful that at some level the corporate sponsor hasn't weighed its affiliation with the band. Advertising has its own agenda. It excludes those who can't afford their products and it defines the way the product is consumed for those who do consume it.

The great danger for all musicians is that we lose the most important power [39] we have: to set the terms for what we do. We lose ownership of it. We think we are still free to say what we want but we generally don't test the boundaries of that freedom. Those who do, whether by accident, stupidity or sheer audacity, discover that there is a price.

What is the effect, then, of the sponsor's mediation between band and audi- [40] ence? In among the vague nuances of what is cool and what isn't in pop culture, the question is hard to answer. This isn't the first time and it won't be the last that the corporate world has raided the innovations of youth culture and attempted to harness it to sell beer, burgers, blue jeans and now cigarettes. What is clear, however, is that this intervention definitely puts the band-audience relationship at risk. On a fundamental level, the nature of corporate sponsorship seeks to define what is acceptable rock and roll, just as it seeks to define who is acceptable as a consumer. It would suit corporate sponsors very well if rock and roll only meant partying, but at its best, rock has never been just about that.

If rock and roll was never to mean anything other than those inane beer [41] commercials, all those band sponsors would be delighted. The irony is that if rock and roll were only that, it would never have attracted the corporate community in the first place.

1995

QUESTIONS FOR DISCUSSION

Content

a. What idea does the anecdote that opens the essay introduce into the essay?
b. When does the connection between corporate sponsorship and rock music come to the fore, according to Cash?
c. What products have tried to connect themselves with rock music? Why does Cash single these companies out?
d. Why, according to Cash, do products want to associate themselves with rock music?
e. Has corporate sponsorship ever backfired for a band?
f. Do beer companies ask bands to endorse their products? What examples does Cash provide that this is not the case?
g. How do bands justify these connections with products?
h. What, for Cash, are the dangers of corporate sponsorship?

Strategy and Style

i. How does Cash establish his own credibility, his own expertise?
j. Why does Cash state, "I am aware that my career as a musician and songwriter has been buoyed by corporate involvement"?
k. Why does Cash write that "I am tempted to call up Export A and jump on board"?
l. Does Cash condemn bands that have attached themselves to corporations?
m. Does Cash condemn corporate sponsors?

SUGGESTIONS FOR SHORT WRITING

a. What does it mean for a music group to "sell out"?
b. In Australia, there is talk of limiting the access of children to movies where the protagonists smoke. Is this concern justifiable or is it censorship?
c. Are rock musicians more important than religion, politics, or school?

SUGGESTIONS FOR SUSTAINED WRITING

a. Artists have had a long tradition of sponsorship or patronage. Finding specific historical examples of a tension between a patron and an artist (a basic art history book would be a good starting point), discuss the impact such sponsorship has on the art itself.
b. Absolut Vodka hires top artists to produce their ads. Are these ads "art"? This question raises the larger question: Can advertising be art?
c. What would be a *healthy* relationship between the arts and corporate sponsors? Provide examples of healthy and unhealthy relationships to flesh out your argument.

A Modest Proposal

Jonathan Swift

Jonathan Swift (1667–1745) was born in Dublin, Ireland; studied at Trinity College, Dublin; and took an MA at Oxford. Ordained an Anglican priest, eventually he was made Dean of St. Patrick's Cathedral in Dublin. He is remembered chiefly for his satires, the most famous of which are A Tale of a Tub *(1704), a vicious satire on government abuses in education and religion, and* Gulliver's Travels *(1726). After the death of Queen Anne in 1714, Swift remained almost the rest of his life in Ireland. There he wrote many essays defending the Irish against English oppression. "A Modest Proposal" is one of a series of satirical essays that exposed English cruelties in Ireland. It demonstrates Swift's keen sensitivity to the problems of the poor in his native country as well as his ability to create satire that is both ironic and incisive.*

It is a melancholy object to those who walk through this great town or travel in the country, when they see the streets, the roads, and cabin doors, crowded with beggars of the female sex, followed by three, four, or six children, all in rags and importuning every passenger for an alms. These mothers, instead of being able to work for their honest livelihood, are forced to employ all their time in strolling to beg sustenance for their helpless infants: Who as they grow up either turn thieves for want of work, or leave their dear native country to fight for the Pretender in Spain, or sell themselves to the Barbadoes. 1

I think it is agreed by all parties that this prodigious number of children in the arms, or on the backs, or at the heels of their mothers, and frequently of their fathers, is in the present deplorable state of the kingdom a very great additional grievance; and, therefore, whoever could find out a fair, cheap, and easy method of making these children sound, useful members of the commonwealth, would deserve so well of the public as to have his statue set up for a preserver of the nation. 2

But my intention is very far from being confined to provide only for the children of professed beggars; it is of a much greater extent, and shall take in the whole number of infants at a certain age who are born of parents in effect as little able to support them as those who demand our charity in the streets. 3

As to my own part, having turned my thoughts for many years upon this important subject, and maturely weighed the several schemes of our projectors, I have always found them grossly mistaken in their computation. It is true, a child just dropped from its dam may be supported by her milk for a solar year, with little other nourishment; at most not above the value of 2s., which the mother may certainly get, or the value in scraps, by her lawful occupation of begging; and it is exactly at one year old that I propose to provide for them in such a manner as instead of being a charge upon their parents or the parish, or wanting food and raiment for the rest of their lives, they shall on the contrary contribute to the feeding, and partly to the clothing, of many thousands. 4

There is likewise another great advantage in my scheme, that it will prevent those voluntary abortions, and that horrid practice of women murdering 5

415

their bastard children, alas! too frequent among us! sacrificing the poor innocent babes I doubt more to avoid the expense than the shame, which would move tears and pity in the most savage and inhuman breast.

The number of souls in this kingdom being usually reckoned one million and 6 a half, of these I calculate there may be about 200,000 couples whose wives are breeders; from which number I subtract 30,000 couples who are able to maintain their own children (although I apprehend there cannot be so many, under the present distress of the kingdom); but this being granted, there will remain 170,000 breeders. I again subtract 50,000 for those women who miscarry, or whose children die by accident or disease within the year. There only remain 120,000 children of poor parents annually born. The question therefore is, how this number shall be reared and provided for? which, as I have already said, under the present situation of affairs, is utterly impossible by all the methods hitherto proposed. For we can neither employ them in handicraft or agriculture; we neither build houses (I mean live in the country) nor cultivate land; they can very seldom pick up a livelihood by stealing, till they arrive at six years old, except where they are of towardly parts; although I confess they learn the rudiments much earlier; during which time they can, however, be properly looked upon only as probationers; as I have been informed by a principal gentleman in the county of Cavan, who protested to me that he never knew above one or two instances under the age of six, even in a part of the kingdom so renowned for the quickest proficiency in that art.

I am assured by our merchants, that a boy or a girl before twelve years old 7 is no saleable commodity; and even when they come to this age they will not yield above 3l. or 3l.2s. 6d. at most on the exchange; which cannot turn to account either to the parents or kingdom, the charge of nutriment and rags having been at least four times that value.

I shall now therefore humbly propose my own thoughts, which I hope will 8 not be liable to the least objection.

I have been assured by a very knowing American of my acquaintance in 9 London, that a young healthy child well nursed is at a year old a most delicious, nourishing, and wholesome food, whether stewed, roasted, baked, or broiled; and I make no doubt that it will equally serve in a fricassee or a ragout.

I do therefore humbly offer it to public consideration that of the 120,000 10 children already computed, 20,000 may be reserved for breed, whereof only one-fourth part to be males; which is more than we allow to sheep, black cattle, or swine; and my reason is, that these children are seldom the fruits of marriage, a circumstance not much regarded by our savages; therefore one male will be sufficient to serve four females. That the remaining 100,000 may, at a year old, be offered in sale to the persons of quality and fortune through the kingdom; always advising the mother to let them suck plentifully in the last month, so as to render them plump and fat for a good table. A child will make two dishes at an entertainment for friends; and when the family dines alone, the fore or hind quarter will make a reasonable dish, and seasoned with a little pepper or salt will be very good boiled on the fourth day, especially in winter.

I have reckoned upon a medium that a child just born will weigh 12 pounds, 11 and in a solar year, if tolerably nursed, will increase to 28 pounds.

I grant this food will be somewhat dear, and therefore very proper for land- 12 lords, who, as they have already devoured most of the parents, seem to have the best title to the children.

Infant's flesh will be in season throughout the year, but more plentiful in 13 March, and a little before and after; for we are told by a grave author, an eminent French physician, that fish being a prolific diet, there are more children born in Roman Catholic countries about nine months after Lent than at any other season; therefore, reckoning a year after Lent, the markets will be more glutted than usual, because the number of popish infants is at least three to one in this kingdom; and therefore it will have one other collateral advantage, by lessening the number of papists among us.

I have already computed the charge of nursing a beggar's child (in which list 14 I reckon all cottagers, laborers, and four-fifths of the farmers) to be about 2s. per annum, rags included; and I believe no gentleman would repine to give 10s. for the carcass of a good fat child, which, as I have said, will make four dishes of excel- lent nutritive meat, when he has only some particular friend or his own family to dine with him. Thus the squire will learn to be a good landlord, and grow popular among the tenants; the mother will have 8s. net profit, and be fit for work till she produces another child.

Those who are more thrifty (as I must confess the times require) may flay 15 the carcass; the skin of which artificially dressed will make admirable gloves for ladies, and summer boots for fine gentlemen.

As to our city of Dublin, shambles may be appointed for this purpose in the 16 most convenient parts of it, and butchers we may be assured will not be wanting; although I rather recommend buying the children alive, and dressing them hot from the knife as we do roasting pigs.

A very worthy person, a true lover of his country, and whose virtues I highly 17 esteem, was lately pleased in discoursing on this matter to offer a refinement upon my scheme. He said that many gentlemen of this kingdom, having of late de- stroyed their deer, he conceived that the want of venison might be well supplied by the bodies of young lads and maidens, not exceeding fourteen years of age nor under twelve; so great a number of both sexes in every country being now ready to starve for want of work and service; and these to be disposed of by their par- ents, if alive, or otherwise by their nearest relations. But with due deference to so excellent a friend and so deserving a patriot, I cannot be altogether in his senti- ments; for as to the males, my American acquaintance assured me from frequent experience that their flesh was generally tough and lean, like that of our school- boys by continual exercise, and their taste disagreeable; and to fatten them would not answer the charge. Then as to the females, it would, I think, with humble sub- mission be a loss to the public, because they soon would become breeders them- selves; and besides, it is not improbable that some scrupulous people might be apt to censure such a practice (although indeed very unjustly), as a little bordering upon cruelty; which, I confess, has always been with me the strongest objection against any project, how well so-ever intended.

But in order to justify my friend, he confessed that this expedient was put 18 into his head by the famous Psalmanazar, a native of the island Formosa, who came from thence to London about twenty years ago: And in conversation told my friend, that in his country when any young person happened to be put to death, the executioner sold the carcass to persons of quality as a prime dainty; and that in his time the body of a plump girl of fifteen, who was crucified for an attempt to poison the emperor, was sold to his imperial majesty's prime minister of state, and other great mandarins of the court, in joints from the gibbet, at 400 crowns. Neither indeed can I deny, that if the same use were made of several plump young girls in this town, who without one single groat to their fortunes cannot stir without a chair, and appear at the playhouse and assemblies in foreign fineries which they never will pay for, the kingdom would not be the worse.

Some persons of a desponding spirit are in great concern about that vast 19 number of poor people, who are aged, diseased, or maimed, and I have been desired to employ my thoughts what course may be taken to ease the nation of so grievous an encumbrance. But I am not in the least pain upon that matter, because it is very well known that they are every day dying and rotting by cold and famine, and filth and vermin, as fast as can be reasonably expected. And as to the young laborers, they are now in as hopeful a condition: they cannot get work, and consequently pine away for want of nourishment, to a degree that if at any time they are accidentally hired to common labor, they have not strength to perform it; and thus the country and themselves are happily delivered from the evils to come.

I have too long digressed, and therefore shall return to my subject. I think 20 the advantages by the proposal which I have made are obvious and many, as well as of the highest importance.

For first, as I have already observed, it would greatly lessen the number of 21 papists, with whom we are yearly overrun, being the principal breeders of the nation as well as our most dangerous enemies; and who stay at home on purpose to deliver the kingdom to the Pretender, hoping to take their advantage by the absence of so many good Protestants, who have chosen rather to leave their country than stay at home and pay tithes against their conscience to an Episcopal curate.

Secondly, the poor tenants will have something valuable of their own, which 22 by law may be made liable to distress and help to pay their landlord's rent, their corn and cattle being already seized, and money a thing unknown.

Thirdly, whereas the maintenance of 100,000 children from two years old 23 and upward, cannot be computed at less than 10s. apiece per annum, the nation's stock will be thereby increased £50,000 per annum, beside the profit of a new dish introduced to the tables of all gentlemen of fortune in the kingdom who have any refinement in taste. And the money will circulate among ourselves, the goods being entirely of our own growth and manufacture.

Fourthly, the constant breeders beside the gain of 8s. sterling per annum by the 24 sale of their children, will be rid of the charge of maintaining them after the first year.

Fifthly, this food would likewise bring great custom to taverns, where the 25 vintners will certainly be so prudent as to procure the best receipts for dressing it to perfection, and consequently have their houses frequented by all the fine gentlemen, who justly value themselves upon their knowledge in good eating; and a skilful cook who understands how to oblige his guests, will contrive to make it as expensive as they please.

Sixthly, this would be a great inducement to marriage, which all wise nations 26 have either encouraged by rewards or enforced by laws and penalties. It would increase the care and tenderness of mothers toward their children, when they were sure of a settlement for life to the poor babes, provided in some sort by the public, to their annual profit instead of expense. We should see an honest emulation among the married women, which of them would bring the fattest child to the market. Men would become as fond of their wives during the time of their pregnancy as they are now of their mares in foal, their cows in calf, their sows when they are ready to farrow; nor offer to beat or kick them (as is too frequent a practice) for fear of a miscarriage.

Many other advantages might be enumerated. For instance, the addition of 27 some thousand carcasses in our exportation of barreled beef, the propagation of swine's flesh, and improvement in the art of making good bacon, so much wanted among us by the great destruction of pigs, too frequent at our table; which are no way comparable in taste or magnificence to a well-grown, fat, yearling child, which roasted whole will make a considerable figure at a lord mayor's feast or any other public entertainment. But this and many others I omit, being studious of brevity.

Supposing that 1,000 families in this city would be constant customers for 28 infants' flesh, besides others who might have it at merry-meetings, particularly at weddings and christenings, I compute that Dublin would take off annually about 20,000 carcasses; and the rest of the kingdom (where probably they will be sold somewhat cheaper) the remaining 80,000.

I can think of no one objection that will possibly be raised against this pro- 29 posal, unless it should be urged that the number of people will be thereby much lessened in the kingdom. This I freely own, and it was indeed one principal design in offering it to the world. I desire the reader will observe, that I calculate my remedy for this one individual kingdom of Ireland and for no other that ever was, is, or I think ever can be upon earth. Therefore let no man talk to me of other expedients: Of taxing our absentees at 5s. a pound: Of using neither clothes nor household furniture except what is of our own growth and manufacture: Of utterly rejecting the materials and instruments that promote foreign luxury: Of curing the expensiveness of pride, vanity, idleness, and gaming in our women: Of introducing a vein of parsimony, prudence, and temperance: Of learning to love our country, in the want of which we differ even from Laplander and the inhabitants of Topinamboo: Of quitting our animosities and factions, nor acting any longer like the Jews, who were murdering one another at the very moment their city was taken: Of being a little cautious not to sell our country and conscience for nothing: Of teaching landlords to have at least one degree of mercy toward their tenants: Lastly, of putting a spirit of honesty, industry, and skill into our shop-keepers; who, if a resolution could now be taken to buy only our native goods, would immediately unite to cheat and exact upon us in the price, the measure, and the goodness, nor could ever yet be brought to make one fair proposal of just dealing, though often and earnestly invited to it.

Therefore I repeat, let no man talk to me of these and the like expedients, till   30
he has at least some glimpse of hope that there will be ever some hearty and sincere attempt to put them in practice.

But as to myself, having been wearied out for many years with offering vain,   31
idle, visionary thoughts, and at length utterly despairing of success, I fortunately fell upon this proposal; which, as it is wholly new, so it has something solid and real, of no expense and little trouble, full in our own power, and whereby we can incur no danger in disobliging England. For this kind of commodity will not bear exportation, the flesh being of too tender a consistence to admit a long continuance in salt, although perhaps I could name a country which would be glad to eat up our whole nation without it.

After all, I am not so violently bent upon my own opinion as to reject any   32
offer proposed by wise men, which shall be found equally innocent, cheap, easy, and effectual. But before something of that kind shall be advanced in contradiction to my scheme, and offering a better, I desire the author or authors will be pleased maturely to consider two points. First, as things now stand, how they will be able to find food and raiment for 100,000 useless mouths and backs. And secondly, there being a round million of creatures in human figure throughout this kingdom, whose subsistence put into a common stock would leave them in debt 2,000,000*l.* sterling, adding those who are beggars by profession to the bulk of farmers, cottagers, and laborers, with the wives and children who are beggars in effect; I desire those politicians who dislike my overture, and may perhaps be so bold as to attempt an answer, that they will first ask the parents of these mortals, whether they would not at this day think it a great happiness to have been sold for food at a year old in the manner I prescribe, and thereby have avoided such a perpetual scene of misfortunes as they have since gone through by the oppression of landlords, the impossibility of paying rent without money or trade, the want of common sustenance, with neither house nor clothes to cover them from the inclemencies of the weather, and the most inevitable prospect of entailing the like or greater miseries upon their breed for ever.

I profess, in the sincerity of my heart, that I have not the least personal in-   33
terest in endeavoring to promote this necessary work, having no other motive than the public good of my country, by advancing our trade, providing for infants, relieving the poor, and giving some pleasure to the rich. I have no children by which I can propose to get a single penny; the youngest being nine years old, and my wife past childbearing.

QUESTIONS FOR DISCUSSION

Content

a. Just what is Swift proposing? What is his purpose in making this absurd proposal?

b. At which point in the essay do you begin to suspect that Swift is being satirical?

c. Indirectly, "A Modest Proposal" provides a clear indication of Swift's attitudes toward the poor and the ruling classes. Recalling information from the text, explain his attitude toward each of these segments of society.

d. Swift makes a number of allusions to the politics and history of his time. Consult an encyclopedia or other appropriate reference work in your college library to learn a bit about the history of Ireland during the early 1700s. In particular, make sure you understand the following:

The Pretender	Episcopal curate
Papists	Psalmanazar, a native of the island of Formosa
Roman Catholic countries	Mandarins
Cottagers	

e. Near the end of the essay, we come upon a list of "expedients." Although the speaker claims otherwise, they represent the kinds of solutions to Ireland's problems that Swift actually believes in. What are these solutions? Why does Swift wait until late in his essay to mention them? Why does he mention them at all?

Strategy and Style

f. Swift, the speaker in "A Modest Proposal," is quite different from Swift the author. Describe the speaker. What function does Swift's use of a persona serve?

g. Swift's mention of Psalmanazar serves a particularly ironic purpose. What is it?

h. Swift's solutions to Ireland's problems, though ironic, are explained in a nononsense, businesslike tone. Point to specific passages in which this tone is most apparent.

i. Swift's irony is especially biting when he says: "I grant this food will be somewhat dear, and therefore very proper for landlords, who, as they have already devoured most of the parents, seem to have the best title to the children" (paragraph 12). What other passages reveal his anger toward the ruling class?

SUGGESTIONS FOR SHORT WRITING

a. How did you respond on an emotional level when you read this essay? Write a response in which you describe your "gut reaction" to "A Modest Proposal."

b. Write a paragraph response to this essay from the point of view of one of the poor of Ireland; then write a paragraph from the point of view of a member of the ruling class. Compare the two responses.

SUGGESTIONS FOR SUSTAINED WRITING

a. Like Swift, approach a serious subject in tongue-in-cheek fashion and write your own "modest proposal." For instance, discuss a controversial government policy and, while pretending to defend it, describe those aspects of it that you find most offensive. Or, you might simply try to convince your classmates that there really are "advantages" to becoming a chain smoker, to walking into class unprepared day after day, or to cramming for exams rather than studying for them systematically.

b. One of Swift's real solutions to Ireland's problems is that its inhabitants use "neither clothes nor household furniture except what is of [their] own growth and manufacture." This seems to be the same idea behind the "Buy American" movement. Do you believe that buying only goods manufactured at home will improve the economy? Explain.

c. One aspect of Swift's proposal focuses on the relationship between tenants and landlords. This is still an important issue. Using your own experiences as sources of information, write an essay that argues for the enactment of:

- Laws that keep rents at reasonable levels and protect tenants from unscrupulous landlords.
- Laws that help landlords make a fair profit and protect their properties from irresponsible tenants.

PERSUASION

I Have a Dream
Martin Luther King, Jr.

Martin Luther King, Jr., (1929–1968) had at first planned to become a doctor or a lawyer, but when he graduated from Morehouse College in Atlanta at the age of nineteen, he abandoned these ambitions and went into the seminary. After seminary, he went to Boston University, where he received his PhD in 1955. He was ordained as a Baptist minister in his father's church, the Ebenezer Baptist Church in Atlanta, which he copastored with his father from 1960 to 1968. He was also founder and director of the Southern Christian Leadership Conference from 1957 to 1968, and a member of the Montgomery Improvement Association, an activist group protesting racial segregation. Inspired by Mahatma Gandhi's principles of nonviolent protest, King led this group in several demonstrations. In May of 1963, he was arrested and imprisoned in Birmingham for demonstrating against segregation in hotels and restaurants. It was while in jail that he wrote his famous "Letter from Birmingham Jail," a work that was published in 1963 and expanded and republished in 1968. It was also in 1963 that King made the speech entitled "I Have a Dream" to over 200,000 people at the March on Washington. King received numerous awards for his work for human rights, including the Nobel Prize for Peace in 1964. On April 4, 1968, while talking with other human rights activists on a motel balcony in Memphis, King was assassinated.

Five score years ago, a great American, in whose symbolic shadow we stand, signed the Emancipation Proclamation. This momentous decree came as a great beacon light of hope to millions of Negro slaves who had been seared in the flames of withering injustice. It came as a joyous daybreak to end the long night of captivity. 1

But one hundred years later, we must face the tragic fact that the Negro is still not free. One hundred years later, the life of the Negro is still sadly crippled by the manacles of segregation and the chains of discrimination. One hundred years later, the Negro lives on a lonely island of poverty in the midst of a vast ocean of material prosperity. One hundred years later, the Negro is still languishing in the corners of American society and finds himself an exile in his own land. So we have come here today to dramatize an appalling condition. 2

In a sense we have come to our nation's capital to cash a check. When the architects of our republic wrote the magnificent words of the Constitution and the Declaration of Independence, they were signing a promissory note to which every American was to fall heir. This note was a promise that all men would be guaranteed the unalienable rights of life, liberty, and the pursuit of happiness. 3

It is obvious today that America has defaulted on this promissory note insofar as her citizens of color are concerned. Instead of honoring this sacred obligation, America has given the Negro people a bad check; a check which has come back marked "insufficient funds." But we refuse to believe that the bank of justice is bankrupt. We refuse to believe that there are insufficient funds in the great vaults 4

423

of opportunity of this nation. So we have come to cash this check—a check that will give us upon demand the riches of freedom and the security of justice. We have also come to this hallowed spot to remind America of the fierce urgency of *now.* This is no time to engage in the luxury of cooling off or to take the tranquilizing drugs of gradualism. *Now* is the time to make real the promises of Democracy. *Now* is the time to rise from the dark and desolate valley of segregation to the sunlit path of racial justice. *Now* is the time to open the doors of opportunity to all of God's children. *Now* is the time to lift our nation from the quicksands of racial injustice to the solid rock of brotherhood.

It would be fatal for the nation to overlook the urgency of the moment and   5 to underestimate the determination of the Negro. This sweltering summer of the Negro's legitimate discontent will not pass until there is an invigorating autumn of freedom and equality. 1963 is not an end, but a beginning. Those who hope that the Negro needed to blow off steam and will now be content will have a rude awakening if the nation returns to business as usual. There will be neither rest nor tranquillity in America until the Negro is granted his citizenship rights. The whirlwinds of revolt will continue to shake the foundations of our nation until the bright day of justice emerges.

But there is something that I must say to my people who stand on the warm   6 threshold which leads into the palace of justice. In the process of gaining our rightful place we must not be guilty of wrongful deeds. Let us not seek to satisfy our thirst for freedom by drinking from the cup of bitterness and hatred. We must forever conduct our struggle on the high plane of dignity and discipline. We must not allow our creative protest to degenerate into physical violence. Again and again we must rise to the majestic heights of meeting physical force with soul force. The marvelous new militancy which has engulfed the Negro community must not lead us to a distrust of all white people, for many of our white brothers, as evidenced by their presence here today, have come to realize that their destiny is tied up with our destiny and their freedom is inextricably bound to our freedom. We cannot walk alone.

And as we walk, we must make the pledge that we shall march ahead. We can-   7 not turn back. There are those who are asking the devotees of civil rights, "When will you be satisfied?" We can never be satisfied as long as the Negro is the victim of the unspeakable horrors of police brutality. We can never be satisfied as long as our bodies, heavy with the fatigue of travel, cannot gain lodging in the motels of the highways and the hotels of the cities. We cannot be satisfied as long as the Negro's basic mobility is from a smaller ghetto to a larger one. We can never be satisfied as long as a Negro in Mississippi cannot vote and a Negro in New York believes he has nothing for which to vote. No, no, we are not satisfied, and we will not be satisfied until justice rolls down like waters and righteousness like a mighty stream.

I am not unmindful that some of you have come here out of great trials and   8 tribulations. Some of you have come fresh from narrow jail cells. Some of you have come from areas where your quest for freedom left you battered by the storms of persecution and staggered by the winds of police brutality. You have been the veterans of creative suffering. Continue to work with the faith that unearned suffering is redemptive.

Go back to Mississippi, go back to Alabama, go back to South Carolina, go 9
back to Georgia, go back to Louisiana, go back to the slums and ghettos of our
northern cities, knowing that somehow this situation can and will be changed. Let
us not wallow in the valley of despair.

I say to you today, my friends, that in spite of the difficulties and frustrations 10
of the moment I still have a dream. It is a dream deeply rooted in the American
dream.

I have a dream that one day this nation will rise up and live out the true 11
meaning of its creed: "We hold these truths to be self-evident; that all men are created equal."

I have a dream that one day on the red hills of Georgia the sons of former 12
slaves and the sons of former slaveowners will be able to sit down together at the
table of brotherhood.

I have a dream that one day even the state of Mississippi, a desert state swel- 13
tering with the heat of injustice and oppression, will be transformed into an oasis
of freedom and justice.

I have a dream that my four little children will one day live in a nation 14
where they will not be judged by the color of their skin but by the content of their
character.

I have a dream today.
                                                                              15
I have a dream that one day the state of Alabama, whose governor's lips are 16
presently dripping with the words of interposition and nullification, will be transformed into a situation where little black boys and black girls will be able to join
hands with little white boys and white girls and walk together as sisters and brothers.

I have a dream today.
                                                                              17
I have a dream that one day every valley shall be exalted, every hill and 18
mountain shall be made low, the rough places will be made plain, and the crooked
places will be made straight, and the glory of the Lord shall be revealed, and all
flesh shall see it together.

This is our hope. This is the faith with which I return to the South. With this 19
faith we will be able to hew out of the mountain of despair a stone of hope. With
this faith we will be able to transform the jangling discords of our nation into a
beautiful symphony of brotherhood. With this faith we will be able to work together, to pray together, to struggle together, to go to jail together, to stand up for
freedom together, knowing that we will be free one day.

This will be the day when all of God's children will be able to sing with new 20
meaning

My country, 'tis of thee,
Sweet land of liberty,
    Of thee I sing:
Land where my fathers died,
Land of the pilgrims' pride,
From every mountain-side
    Let freedom ring.

And if America is to be a great nation this must become true. So let freedom 21
ring from the prodigious hilltops of New Hampshire. Let freedom ring from the
mighty mountains of New York. Let freedom ring from the heightening Alleghe-
nies of Pennsylvania!

Let freedom ring from the snowcapped Rockies of Colorado!   22

Let freedom ring from the curvaceous peaks of California!   23

But not only that; let freedom ring from Stone Mountain of Georgia!   24

Let freedom ring from Lookout Mountain of Tennessee!   25

Let freedom ring from every hill and molehill of Mississippi. From every 26
mountainside, let freedom ring.

When we let freedom ring, when we let it ring from every village and every 27
hamlet, from every state and every city, we will be able to speed up that day when
all of God's children, black men and white men, Jews and Gentiles, Protestants
and Catholics, will be able to join hands and sing in the words of the old Negro
spiritual, "Free at last! free at last! thank God almighty, we are free at last!"

1963

QUESTIONS FOR DISCUSSION

Content

a. What does King hope to evoke in his audience by mentioning various historical documents (the Emancipation Proclamation, the Declaration of Independence, the Constitution)?

b. King makes it a point to address issues that are of particular interest to white
   listeners and readers. What might have been his reasons for doing this?

c. Why might King have decided to quote all of the first seven lines of "My Country 'Tis of Thee"? Why did he not stop at "Of thee I sing"?

d. What effect does King create when he makes reference to specific places,
   events, and public figures?

e. King makes reference to the Bible and to the faith that has sustained him
   throughout his struggle for civil rights. What effect is created with such
   references?

Strategy and Style

f. King's speech is especially moving because he succeeds in creating emphasis
   through parallelism. Find a few examples of this technique.

g. What does King mean when he says: "America has given the Negro people a
   bad check" (paragraph 4)? Identify other metaphors that he uses, and explain
   why they are effective.

h. Why does King use the term *marvelous* to describe the "new militancy which
   has engulfed the Negro community"?

i. How would you describe King's tone? Controlled? Angry? Impassioned?

SUGGESTIONS FOR SHORT WRITING

a. In your opinion, has the situation of black Americans changed, or not changed, since King gave this speech?
b. Briefly describe your own dream for a better world.

SUGGESTIONS FOR SUSTAINED WRITING

a. Do some research in your college library by reading several newspaper or magazine articles that chronicle the events leading up to King's address at the Lincoln Memorial. Summarize these events and try to comment on their significance to the civil rights movement of the 1960s. Be certain to footnote or in some way cite the authorship of material you quote or paraphrase.
b. Do you have a "dream" that in the future some social or political injustice will be eliminated, that a cure will be found for a disease, that war and famine will cease? Describe your "dream" and propose ways in which to make it a reality.
c. Has King's dream of equality and opportunity for African-Americans been fulfilled in the decades since he spoke at the Lincoln Memorial? Explain by using as much specific detail as possible.

Veiled Threat: The Women of Afghanistan

Sally Armstrong

Sally Armstrong, born in 1943, started her writing career with Canadian Living *before becoming editor-in-chief of* Homemaker's *magazine (1988–1999). She is currently editor-at-large for* Chatelaine *magazine. Armstrong has also written for the* Globe and Mail *and the* Toronto Star. *The honesty of her writing has earned her the Order of Canada and an honorary degree from Royal Roads University.*

It's hot in here. Shrouded in this body bag, I feel claustrophobic. It's smelly too. The 1 *cloth in front of my mouth is damp from my breathing. Dust from the filthy street swirls up under the billowing* burqa *and sticks to the moisture from my covered mouth. I feel like I'm suffocating in stale air.*

It also feels like I'm invisible. No one can see me. No one knows whether I'm 2 *smiling or crying. My view isn't much better. The mesh opening in front of my eyes isn't enough to see where I'm going. It's like wearing horse blinders. I can see only straight in front of me. Not above or below or on either side of the path I take. Suddenly the road changes. I step on the front of the hideous bag that covers my body and tumble to the ground. No one helps me. It feels like no one in the world wants to help.*

—Fatana, 28

Who "in the name of Allah" has decreed this wretched fate on the women of 3 Afghanistan? A ragtag band of bandits called the Taliban, who are mostly illiterate and mostly in their 20s, thundered into the capital city of Kabul on September 27 of last year, and overnight the lives of women and girls were catapulted back to the dark ages. After hanging the government leaders in the public square, the Taliban announced their draconian decrees on the radio: schools for girls were immediately closed. Women could no longer work. They had to be completely covered by the head-to-foot wrap called a burqa and kept in purdah (secluded from the public) because, according to the Taliban's leader, Mullah Mohammad Omar, "A woman's face corrupts men." Afghanistan has become a place where mothers and wives, sisters and daughters, are seen as a holy threat. Today, a woman can only leave her home in the company of her husband, brother or son, and only if she is shrouded in the hated burqa and carries a permit that gives her reason to be outside.

To disobey is to die. Soon after the takeover, a group of women in the city 4 of Herat marched in protest. According to eyewitnesses, the Taliban surrounded the women, seized their leader, doused her in kerosene and burned her alive. Women have been sprayed with acid, beaten with twisted wires and shot for crimes such as showing their ankles, letting a hand slip out from under the burqa while paying for food, allowing their children to play with toys. For being outside with anyone who is not a male relative, the sentence is death by stoning. The hooligans in power dig a pit and bury the woman to her shoulders. Then they form a circle around her and throw rocks at her head until she is dead.

428

They say they do it for Islam. But Muslim scholars all over the world say 5 this has nothing to do with Islam. It's a grab for power and control in a country that's been struggling with unrest for 18 years. It is also misogyny, a contempt for women that goes hand in hand with the disturbing rise in extremism in Muslim countries. In Bangladesh, a woman can receive 50 lashes for speaking her mind. In Pakistan, a rape victim can be jailed for fornication. In Saudi Arabia, women are forced to cloak themselves in black chadors that absorb the stifling heat while men walk about in white robes that deflect it. Afghanistan is a human rights catastrophe.

Astonishingly, this throwback to a medieval era has created a strange wall of 6 silence. The United Nations is wringing its hands. Government leaders are looking the other way and the women of Afghanistan are asking what in the world is going to become of them.

I met Fatana, 28, a psychiatrist, Farahnaz, 26, a civil engineer, and Mina, 28, 7 a pharmacist, six months after the beginning of the darkest days this country has ever known. [We agreed that their last names, the towns where they have found shelter and their former employers would not be named to protect them from the terrible retribution of the Taliban.] For them, life under the Taliban is nature thrown into reverse. They're like spring blossoms that were forced to fold their beautiful petals back into their casings. With downcast eyes and sagging shoulders these young women describe their grievances in words that make me think of a line from the poem *In Flanders Fields.* "Short days ago we lived." They went to university in Kabul, wore jeans, short skirts, met at the restaurants on Da Afghanan street and went to discos on Froshga. Like other young people, they walked along the river and through Pul bagh Vuumi park with their boyfriends. Their lives were full, their futures hopeful.

But the convulsions that shook the country out of communism in 1992 threw 8 the formerly cosmopolitan city of Kabul into utter calamity. Extremist factions fought each other for control for four deadly years. Last autumn, the ultra-extremist Taliban won the spoils of war. And women like Fatana, Farahnaz and Mina became invisible. Their jobs, social lives and self-esteem disappeared overnight.

"On September 26, we were at work," says Fatana. "Everyone was anxious. 9 The Taliban were near the city. We were waiting for something bad. At noon most people went home because we could hear the shelling. We'd heard about Taliban policies and we were afraid for our futures."

The next morning they heard about the fate of the government leaders on the 10 radio. And they heard the Taliban's misogynist manifesto for women. "I'd never owned a burqa in my life," says Fatana. "Most women in Kabul had never even worn a scarf over their heads." When I ask her what effect this will have on the mental health of the women, Farahnaz speaks up. "I can answer that question for you. I've lost my mental health. I don't want to leave my house. I start to laugh or cry and I don't know why I feel sad all the time. And I cannot concentrate. The other day I was helping someone with accounting and I realized I'd entered the same number over and over again. I have no hope for my future and, what's worse, I have no hope for the future of my two children."

Today the streets they walked on as students are like a moonscape. The shops   11
are closed. So are the restaurants. Sixty per cent of the city has been destroyed. The
roads are full of holes. There's garbage all over the place, there's no electricity in
most parts of the city and few people have running water. The university has
reopened for boys only. Women doctors have been allowed to return to work but
only to treat women patients. And if women and girls can't find a woman doctor,
tough luck. "Let them die," say the Taliban.

In the absence of any real protest from the international community, a litany   12
of new regulations is visited upon the people on an almost daily basis. Radio and
television are forbidden. So is music, clapping, singing and dancing. Photographs,
even at weddings, are considered unIslamic. So are sports for women. Makeup,
nail polish, high-heeled shoes and white socks—the only item of clothing that shows
beneath the burqa—are also forbidden (white is the color of the Taliban flag). There's
to be no noise made by women's feet when they struggle to the bazaar to find food
and water for their families. Windows must be painted black to prevent anyone
from seeing a woman inside the house. New houses can have no windows on the
second floor. In a stupefying rationale, Omar explains the Taliban's actions against
women by saying, "Otherwise, they'll be like Princess Diana."

There are 30,000 widows in Kabul who are virtually destitute. When asked   13
how they should cope, the Taliban reply again, "Let them die." In a particularly
hateful response to the handicapped, some men have told their disabled wives that
they'll no longer require prostheses as they no longer need to be seen outside.

Afghanistan is a country about the size of Manitoba. It has five major tribes   14
that have warred endlessly throughout the centuries. It was a monarchy until 1972
and a republic until 1978 when the Soviets invaded. Then it became one of the last
violent crucibles of the Cold War. The detested boot camp rule of the Soviets spawned
the Mujahideen (Freedom Fighter) camps across the border in Northern Pakistan.
Funded by the United States, Saudi Arabia and Pakistan itself, the Mujahideen were
like folk heroes who represented a spiritual return to pre-communist Afghanistan.
But within the camps, several factions jockeyed for power, each pretending to be
more religious than the next to win the support of the people. In the process they
planted the seeds for a fratricidal bloodbath that began with the defeat of the
Communists. Life under the victorious Mujahideen proved to be as violent as it had
been under the Communists and more religiously strict than the people had ever
imagined. Enter the Taliban, young hoodlums who had never been to school and
never known anything but war. Presently they control two-thirds of the country.

While the world has clearly grown weary of Afghanistan and its 18 years of   15
war, the people trapped in that country and the 500,000 refugees who escaped to
border towns in Northern Pakistan are hoping someone will "take up our quarrel
with the foe." Although the Taliban have no official role in the Islamic Republic of
Pakistan, their presence throughout the north is threatening. The steady rise in fun-
damentalism in Pakistan leaves many Afghan refugees and native Pakistanis in this
northern region wary. Many women continue to wear burqas out of fear. Others are
careful to cover up just to avoid attention from the extremists. There's an uneasy
calm. It's like waiting for an intruder.

At the northwest corner of a Pakistan border town called Quetta, the Afghan 16 diaspora is burgeoning. The dusty, rock-strewn landscape that unfolds from the huge mountains here at the west end of the Himalayas is similar to the refugees' native land. The miniature yellow wildflowers that push defiantly out of the scrubby soil grow like symbols of their struggle. The diorama of contrasts—mud houses and rented two-story homes, the delicious scent of fresh-baked naan bread from the bakeries and the putrid stench from the latrines in the street, the fear and longing of the people—is the quintessence of life in a refugee centre. It was here in Quetta that the Mujahideen assassinated the leader of the Afghan women's movement a decade ago. It is here that I meet Dr. Sima Samar, a precious bead on the world's scanty string of humanitarians.

"I have three strikes against me," she says by way of introduction. "I'm a 17 woman, I speak out for women and I'm a Hazara, one of the minority tribes." The road she travelled from Helmand, the Afghan province where she grew up, to this refugee centre in Quetta, is strewn with the history and customs of her beloved Afghanistan. Her father had two wives (a usual practice for many Islamic men and one she doesn't approve of). She won a scholarship to go to medical school but her father told her she couldn't leave the family because she wasn't married. So a marriage was arranged (another usual custom) and she went to Kabul University. But during the upheaval that finally rousted the Communists, and soon after she'd given birth to their son, her husband was arrested, never to be seen again. Samar managed to finish medical school and wound up practising medicine in a rural district. Her experiences there brutally demonstrated that the lives of women were nearly unbearable and that lack of education was a direct cause of the turmoil her country was in. She decided to do something about both conditions.

Today she runs medical clinics in Quetta as well as Kabul. And she has clan- 18 destine schools in rural Afghanistan for more than 4,500 girls, as well as a school for refugee girls here in Quetta. Her steadfast refusal to observe purdah and the stand she takes on equality for women have made her anathema to the fundamentalists and a hero to the women she serves.

When asked how she gets around the paralysing rules of the extremists' in- 19 terpretation of the Koran, she shakes her head in astonishment at her own audacity. "Let me tell you a story," she begins. "A 16-year-old girl came with her parents to my clinic. A quick urine test and cursory examination told me what I suspected. She was six months pregnant and terrified. She had been raped. The law according to the extremists is that a woman who is raped must have four male witnesses to prove that she didn't cause the rape. Naturally no such witnesses are ever available. Without them the family is obliged to kill the girl to protect the family honor. This kid had kept her terrible secret until she could hide it no longer. I had to decide what to do. I don't approve of abortions unless there is absolutely no other way. But if I didn't do something for this girl, she would be killed. I chose life.

"Remember, most people here don't have any education, so I can get away 20 with saying things they may not question. I told them their daughter had a tumor and needed surgery. I said she was too sick to have it now and she would have to stay at my clinic. I kept that girl for three months. When the baby was due, I did a Caesarean section. The family waited outside the operating room because it is the custom here to show them what was found in the surgery. I put the placenta in the surgical basin, showed them the so-called tumor and told them their daughter would be fine. Then I gave the baby to a woman who was also in trouble because she is married and infertile."

Dr. Samar can't change the law by herself but she's part of a group that hopes 21 it can. It's an international network called Women Living Under Muslim Laws and it presently has links to 40 countries and an increasingly powerful voice at the United Nations. Farida Shaheed, the Asian coordinator of the association in Lahore, Pakistan, won't even use the word fundamentalist. "It suggests a return to cherished fundamentals of Islam, which it certainly is not," she says. "Extremists aren't religious at all. This is political opportunism. Their strength is in disrupting the political process and using that to blackmail those in political power."

It worries her that such groups are gaining momentum because of what she 22 calls "a refusal of mainstream political parties in Muslim countries to produce democratic rule. But women are gaining as well. There's an unprecedented number of women coming into the workforce [in Pakistan] at the same time that the extremist groups are saying, 'Stay home.'"

They fight back at their peril. Members of the association have been harassed 23 on the street and had firebombs thrown at their houses. And Sima Samar receives so many death threats from the Taliban, she simply replies, "You know where I am. I won't stop what I'm doing."

The rhythms of life rock uncomfortably at Samar's clinic. Her patients, who 24 pay about 30 rupees ($1 Canadian) per visit, come with their full wombs and fears of infertility. They suffer all the ills that refugee camps are heir to: malnutrition, anemia, typhoid fever, malaria. In the lineups at the door, they whisper news of the latest atrocities and decrees of the Taliban. Today, there's a terrible message from Jalalabad, a city across the border in Afghanistan. Yesterday a woman tried to leave. She was wearing her burqa but walking with a man who was not a relative. She was arrested by the Taliban and stoned to death. The man she was with was sentenced to seven years in prison. There's still a hush in the clinic, when suddenly the curtain is pushed aside and a woman appears with her Taliban husband. He tells Samar that his wife bleeds from her nose whenever she works hard in the fields. Samar raises her voice: "She's full-term pregnant, she shouldn't be working so hard." The man replies, "She has to work. Fix her nose." Another young woman has been menstruating for 11 months. Her blood pressure is dangerously low. She's as weak as a sparrow. The doctor says she needs a simple D and C (dilatation and curettage) but culture interferes again. She's a virgin. The simple operation would destroy her virginity, which in turn would destroy her life. So abdominal surgery is scheduled.

As the war against women rages on, a new and menacing problem is turning 25 up at the clinic. "Almost every woman I see has osteomalacia," Samar says. "Their bones are softening due to a lack of vitamin D. They survive on a diet of tea and naan because they can't afford eggs and milk and, to complicate matters, their burqas and veils deprive them of sunshine. On top of that, depression is endemic here because the future is so dark."

Samar is angry with what she sees as all talk and no action on the part of world 26 organizations that claim to be pressing ahead with issues for women. "Recently the UN held a meeting in Quetta for all the various factions to discuss Afghanistan," she says. "They met at a hotel for three days. Can you imagine what that cost? Well, the meeting was for men only. The women were invited to meet for one hour on a different day." There's more. She was invited to attend a meeting in Washington, also held to discuss the situation in Afghanistan. Each delegate was allowed six minutes to speak. Samar was the only woman. She told the gathering, "I represent more than half the people in Afghanistan. How come I only get the same six minutes as all these men?"

When the phone rings in her small office she speaks English to the caller, 27 wanting to know, "Where's my wheat?" The caller explains that her wheat is in Kabul but the priority delivery is to women and girls. "My wheat is going to a school for girls in Ghazni. It's the only school still operating for girls. Why aren't my girls part of that priority?"

Amid the international sound of silence, a lone voice in London is sounding a 28 clarion call for the women. Fatima Gailani, who holds a master's degree in Islamic jurisprudence, is the daughter of Pir Sayyid Ahmad Gailani, the spiritual leader of the Sunni Afghans. He is also a descendant of the prophet Mohammed, which means they both carry a lot of clout. Gailani is outraged with the Taliban's interpretation of Islam. "A woman with a covered head is not more honorable than a woman without a covered head. I can prove that any action of the prophet has nothing to do with this. It goes against the Koran, in fact. The Taliban are against Afghan tradition, against Islam. They only continue because presently there is no alternative." With that in mind, she and her father recently travelled to Rome to meet with the exiled monarch. "My hope is that an Afghan element—the king, the leaders of the tribes, my father—can do something. The Taliban need aid of every description. They need money. They'd respond to pressure." So far there hasn't been any.

Meanwhile, the lineup at Dr. Samar's clinic grows longer. Her schools for 29 girls are working in shifts, since she doesn't have the money to rent more space. The women in Kabul have given up a resistance movement. And some international agencies are caving in to the classic consequences of gender abuse and saying, "At least there's peace under the Taliban." For the women, living in prison isn't peace. The threat of being stoned to death isn't peace. Painting your windows black isn't peace. Being without music isn't peace. And so they wait, for peace.

1997

QUESTIONS FOR DISCUSSION

Content

a. Who are the Taliban?
b. What is a burqa?

c. How have women been treated by the Taliban? What examples does Armstrong use to illustrate their treatment?

d. What type of activities has the Taliban banned?

e. What are the "three strikes" against Dr. Sima Samar?

f. What physical problem is now affecting women?

g. Who is Fatima Gailani? Why does Armstrong introduce her into the essay?

Strategy and Style

h. What type of words does Armstrong use when describing the Taliban?

i. Why does Armstrong talk about women in Pakistan and Bangladesh when the essay is supposed to be about women in Afghanistan?

j. Why does Armstrong describe the streets of Kabul as "a moonscape"?

k. Why does Armstrong spend so much time establishing the credentials and genealogy of Fatima Gailani? Does it make Gailani's position more credible or reliable?

l. How does Armstrong betray her feelings about the situation right from the opening?

m. This essay was written for *Homemaker's Magazine*. What does Armstrong expect of her readers? How does she make you aware of this expectation throughout this essay?

SUGGESTIONS FOR SHORT WRITING

a. Write about your own feelings about the Taliban after reading this essay.

b. Once a group has been labelled as "bad" or "undesirable" (for example, biker gangs or "terrorists"), they are generally portrayed as such in the media. Is this fair? When should the media alter this portrayal?

c. Armstrong uses many terms and names that are emotionally charged and cause us to see the Taliban a certain way. When is it legitimate to use an emotionally charged term (for example, Communist, Fascist, pampered, lazy, and so on)?

SUGGESTIONS FOR SUSTAINED WRITING

a. Examine stories in the media where the terms "Islam" and "Moslem" are used. How are these people or groups portrayed by the media? Discuss how the media reflects our society's attitudes towards these groups.

b. Examine the history of human rights. Where did the idea originate? How has the idea developed over time?

c. Does Canada have the moral authority to tell other countries (for example, China, Indonesia, Afghanistan, Saudi Arabia) how they should behave? If so, what gives us this authority? If not, why not?

Our Daughters, Ourselves

Stevie Cameron

Stevie Cameron, born in 1943 in Belleville, Ontario, is either lauded or condemned for her investigative reporting: it is hard to remain indifferent to her writing. Her book On the Take: Crime, Corruption and Greed in the Mulroney Years, *about the corruption of Mulroney and his government, was either praised as superb investigative reporting or deplored by others as "trash." The following essay is a response to the Marc Lepine tragedy. In 1989, Marc Lepine gunned down 27 students of Montreal's Ecole Polytechnique, killing 14 women. The tragedy was particularly disturbing as it was directed specifically against women. Cameron's essay originally appeared in the* Globe and Mail *and produced an incredible reader response. It was later named by the Canadian Research Institute for the Advancement of Women as the best feminist article of the year.*

They are so precious to us, our daughters. When they are born we see their futures 1 as unlimited, and as they grow and learn we try so hard to protect them: This is how we cross the street, hold my hand, wear your boots, don't talk to strangers, run to the neighbors if a man tries to get you in his car.

We tell our bright, shining girls that they can be anything: firefighters, doctors, 2 policewomen, lawyers, scientists, soldiers, athletes, artists. What we don't tell them, yet, is how hard it will be. Maybe, we say to ourselves, by the time they're older it will be easier for them than it was for us.

But as they grow and learn, with aching hearts we have to start dealing with 3 their bewilderment about injustice. Why do the boys get the best gyms, the best equipment and the best times on the field? Most of the school sports budget? Why does football matter more than gymnastics? Why are most of the teachers women and most of the principals men? Why do the boys make more money at their part-time jobs than we do?

And as they grow and learn we have to go on trying to protect them: We'll 4 pick you up at the subway, we'll fetch you from the movie, stay with the group, make sure the parents drive you home from babysitting, don't walk across the park alone, lock the house if we're not there.

It's not fair, they say. Boys can walk where they want, come in when they 5 want, work where they want. Not really, we say; boys get attacked too. But boys are not targets for men the way girls are, so girls have to be more careful.

Sometimes our girls don't make it. Sometimes, despite our best efforts and 6 all our love, they go on drugs, drop out, screw up. On the whole, however, our daughters turn into interesting, delightful people. They plan for college and university, and with wonder and pride we see them competing with the boys for spaces in engineering schools, medical schools, law schools, business schools. For them we dream of Rhodes scholarships, Harvard graduate school, gold medals; sometimes, we even dare to say these words out loud and our daughters reward us with indulgent hugs. Our message is that anything is possible.

We bite back the cautions that we feel we should give them; maybe by the ⁊
time they've graduated, things will have changed, we say to ourselves. Probably
by the time they're out, they will make partner when the men do, be asked to join
the same clubs, run for political office. Perhaps they'll even be able to tee off at
the same time men do at the golf club.

But we still warn them: park close to the movie, get a deadbolt for your apart- 8
ment, check your windows, tell your roommates where you are. Call me. Call me.

And then with aching hearts we take our precious daughters to lunch and 9
listen to them talk about their friends: the one who was beaten by her boy friend
and then shunned by his friends when she asked for help from the dean; the one
who was attacked in the parking lot; the one who gets obscene and threatening calls
from a boy in her residence; the one who gets raped on a date; the one who was
mocked by the male students in the public meeting.

They tell us about the sexism they're discovering in the adult world at university. 10
Women professors who can't get jobs, who can't get tenure. Male professors who
cannot comprehend women's stony silence after sexist jokes. An administration
that only pays lip service to women's issues and refuses to accept the reality of
physical danger to women on campus.

They tell us they're talking among themselves about how men are demand- 11
ing rights over unborn children; it's not old dinosaurs who go to court to prevent
a woman's abortion, it's young men. It's young men, they say with disbelief, their
own generation, their own buddies with good education, from "nice" families, who
are abusive.

What can we say to our bright and shining daughters? How can we tell them 12
how much we hurt to see them developing the same scars we've carried? How
much we wanted it to be different for them? It's all about power, we say to them.
Sharing power is not easy for anyone and men do not find it easy to share among
themselves, much less with a group of equally talented, able women. So men make
all those stupid cracks about needing a sex-change operation to get a job or a
promotion and they wind up believing it.

Now our daughters have been shocked to the core, as we all have, by the 13
violence in Montreal. They hear the women were separated from the men and
meticulously slaughtered by a man who blamed feminists for his troubles. They
ask themselves why nobody was able to help the terrified women, to somehow stop
the hunter as he roamed the engineering building.

So now our daughters are truly frightened and it makes their mothers furious 14
that they are frightened. They survived all the childhood dangers, they were careful
as we trained them to be, they worked hard. Anything was possible and our daughters
proved it. And now they are more scared than they were when they were little girls.

Fourteen of our bright and shining daughters won places in engineering 15
schools, doing things we, their mothers, only dreamed of. That we lost them has
broken our hearts; what is worse is that we are not surprised.

1989

QUESTIONS FOR DISCUSSION

Content

a. What is the point of Cameron's essay?
b. What kinds of dangers are identified in the very first paragraph?
c. Identify paragraphs where Cameron cites dangers for women. How many different dangers does she identify through this short essay?
d. Find paragraphs where Cameron cites dreams for daughters. What happens immediately after Cameron lists these dreams?
e. How does the last paragraph of the first section anticipate the last paragraph of the essay?

Strategy and Style

f. Why is the essay divided into two parts? What is the relationship between the two halves?
g. The opening of a number of paragraphs verbally echo each other ("But as they grow and learn," "They tell us," "Now our daughters"). Why does Cameron use this technique?
h. How does Cameron's idea that "things will have changed, we say to ourselves" tie in with the end: "what is worse is that we are not surprised"?
i. What is the relationship between paragraph 2, which lists possibilities for young women, and paragraph 3, which lists questions about preferential treatment for boys?

SUGGESTIONS FOR SHORT WRITING

a. Write your own response to the Marc Lepine tragedy. You may wish to imagine the final moments of the victims or you may wish to consider what attitudes contribute to violence towards women.
b. Interview women and men old enough to remember the tragedy to recall their own memories and responses.
c. What are your own feelings when you hear about violence towards women, date rape, and so on?

SUGGESTIONS FOR SUSTAINED WRITING

a. Discuss the relationship, if any, between the media and violence within society.
b. What images of women surround us in advertising and TV? Do these images create a certain attitude about women? How do we perceive women and their role in society?
c. Students killing students has become alarmingly common in North America over the last decade. Are these random events perpetrated by aberrant members of society or are they indicative of a larger problem of violence?

Food Pets Die For

Ann N. Martin

Ann N. Martin (b. 1944) is an animal rights activist who lives in London, Ontario. She also researches and reports on pet foods, and her findings can be found in her recently published book Food Pets Die For: Shocking Facts About Pet Food *(1997), from which this essay is exerpted.*

Pets in pet food? No, you say? Be assured that this is happening. Rendered companion animals are just another source of protein used in both pet foods and livestock feeds. 1

Rendering is a cheap, viable means of disposal. Pets are mixed with other 2 material from slaughterhouse facilities that has been condemned for human consumption—rotten meat from supermarket shelves, restaurant grease and garbage, "4-D" (dead, diseased, dying and disabled) animals, roadkill and even zoo animals [Summer '96 *EIJ*].

In 1990, *San Francisco Chronicle,* reporter John Eckhouse wrote a two-part 3 exposé on the rendering of companion animals in California. While the pet food companies vehemently denied that this was happening, a rendering plant employee told Eckhouse that "it was common practice for his company to process dead pets into products sold to pet food manufacturers."

Eckhouse's informant, upset that some of the most disturbing information 4 was left out of the *Chronicle* article, subsequently brought his story to *Earth Island Journal.* (After the *Journal* published this insider's extensive report ["The Dark Side of Recycling," Fall 1990], the author placed a frantic call to the *Journal* to say that he was "going underground" because he feared for his safety.)

A SEARCH FOR THE TRUTH

I had always assumed that deceased pets were either buried or cremated. I had 5 never heard of rendering. In early 1992, I decided to find out what was happening to the euthanized pets in London, Ontario.

Veterinary clinics advised me that dead pets were incinerated by a local dis- 6 posal company. After hearing U.S. horror stories, I was skeptical. I obtained the name of the company that was picking up the pets, a dead-stock removal operation. Classified as "recollectors," these companies—along with "receiving plants," "brokers," and "rendering plants"—are licensed by Canada's Ministry of Agriculture.

I asked the ministry how the recollector disposed of the dogs and cats that it 7 picked up. Two months later, I received a letter along with a document from the dead-stock removal company. This document, addressed to the investigator, was stamped with the warning that the information in the document was "not to be made known to any other agency or person without the written permission of the Chief Investigator."

438

Small wonder. The document confirmed that dead pets were, in fact, dis- 8
posed of by rendering (unless cremation was "specially requested" and "paid [for]
. . . by their owners or by the veterinary clinic").

The dead animals were shipped to a broker located about 300 miles away 9
who sold the bodies to a rendering plant in Quebec. When I contacted the rendering plant, the owner admitted that cats and dogs were rendered along with livestock and roadkill." Do pet food companies purchase this rendered material?" I
asked. Again, his reply was, "Yes."

I was numb. How had this barbaric practice gone undetected all these years? 10

When I advised the veterinarians in my city about what was happening, most 11
of them immediately ceased using the deadstock company and began using the
local humane society where the animals are cremated.

In the United States and Canada, the rendering of companion animals is not 12
illegal. Millions of pets are disposed of by rendering each year. According to the
Eckhouse article, an employee and ex-employee of Sacramento Rendering, a plant
in California, stated that their company "rendered somewhere between 10,000 and
30,000 pounds of dogs and cats a day out of a total of 250,000 to 500,000 pounds
of cattle, poultry, butcher shop scraps and other material." The rendering plant in
Quebec was rendering 11 tons of dogs and cats per week—from one province alone.

THE SITUATION IN THE U.S.

If this was the case in Canada, I wondered if the U.S. government was aware of 13
what was happening?

The Food and Drug Administration's Center for Veterinary Medicine 14
(CVM) responded to my query regarding the disposal of pets, stating: "In recognizing the need for disposal of a large number of unwanted pets in this country,
CVM has not acted to specifically prohibit the rendering of pets. However, that is
not to say that the practice of using this material in pet food is condoned by CVM."

The U.S. Department of Agriculture's (USDA) Food Safety and Inspection 15
Services (FSIS) informed me that dog and cat cadavers are excluded as an ingredient in pet foods under FSIS regulations. But, when I asked the USDA if it could
provide me with a list of the companies that were using this inspection service, I
was told that only two small facilities were licensed for this service and neither
had subscribed to the service for four years.

Pet food companies advertise that only quality meats are being used in their 16
products. As of 1996, however, not one of the major pet food companies was using the USDA's inspection service.

WHAT'S IN THE CAN?

Television commercials and magazine advertisements for pet food would have us 17
believe that the meats, grains, and fats used in these foods could grace our dining

tables. Over seven long years, I have been able to unearth information about what actually is contained in most commercial pet food. My initial shock has turned to anger as I've realized how little consumers are told about the actual contents of pet food.

Animal slaughterhouses strip the flesh and send the remains—heads, feet, 18 skin, toenails, hair, feathers, carpal and tarsal joints, and mammary glands—to rendering plants. Also judged suitable for rendering: Animals who have died on their way to slaughter; cancerous tissue or tumors and worm-infested organs; injection sites, blood clots, bone splinters or extraneous matter; contaminated blood; stomach and bowels.

At the rendering plant, slaughterhouse material, restaurant and supermarket 19 refuse (including Styrofoam trays and Shrink-wrap), dead-stock, roadkill, and euthanized companion animals are dumped into huge containers. A grinding machine slowly pulverizes the entire mess. After it is chipped or shredded, it is cooked at temperatures between 220 F and 270 F (104.4 to 132.2 C) for 20 minutes to one hour. The grease or tallow that rises to the top is used as a source of animal fat in pet foods. The remaining material is put into a press where the moisture is squeezed out to produce meat and bone meal.

The Association of American Feed Control Officials describes "meat meal" 20 as the rendered product from mammal tissue exclusive of blood, hair, hoof, hide, trimmings, manure, stomach, and rumen (the first stomach of a cud-chewing animal) contents—except in such amounts as may occur unavoidably in "good processing" practices. In his article, "Animal Disposal: Fact and Fiction," David C. Cooke asks, "Can you imagine trying to remove the hair and stomach contents from 600,000 tons of dogs and cats prior to cooking them?"

DRUGS, METAL, PESTICIDES

Pet food labels only provide half the story. Labels do not indicate the hidden haz- 21 ards that lurk in most pet food. Hormones, pesticides, pathogens, heavy metals, and drugs are just a few of the hidden contaminants.

Sodium pentobarbital and Fatal Plus™ are barbiturates used to euthanize 22 companion animals. When animals eat pet food that has gone through the rendering process, it is likely that they are ingesting one of these euthanizing drugs.

Almost 50 percent of the antibiotics manufactured in the United States are 23 dumped into animal feed, according to the 1996 Consumer Alert brochure, "The Dangers of Factory Farming." Pigs, cows, veal calves, turkeys, and chickens are continually fed antibiotics (primarily penicillin and tetracycline) in an attempt to eradicate the many ills that befall factory-farmed animals—pneumonia, intestinal disease, stress, rhinitis, e-coli infections and mastitis.

While this high-level application of antibiotics means millions of dollars for 24 the pharmaceutical companies, the U.S. Centers for Disease Control, National Resources Defense Council and the U.S. Food and Drug Administration (FDA) all warn that these "levels of antibiotics and other contaminants in commercially raised meat constitute a serious threat to the health of the consumer."

Zinc, copper, and iron are listed on most pet food labels. But the metals in 25 pet foods that do *not* need to be listed on the label include: Silver, beryllium, cadmium, bismuth, cobalt, manganese, barium, molybdenum, nickel, lead, strontium, vanadium, phosphorus, titanium, chromium, aluminum, selenium, and tungsten.

The U.S. FDA and Health and Welfare Canada would be very concerned if 26 the level of lead found in pet food were found in the human food chain. For the dog food I had tested, for example, a dog ingesting 15 ounces would receive .43 to 2.4 mg of lead per day. Three mg per day is considered hazardous for a child. But when it comes to pet food, no testing is undertaken by state officials for heavy metals, pathogens, pesticides or drugs.

Although the pet food industry is not regulated in the United States and 27 Canada, we as consumers have been lulled into believing that government and voluntary organizations are overseeing every ingredient stuffed into a container of pet food. What is required is government-enforced regulation of the industry. Only state legislatures can turn the tide, but it will be a long and difficult battle to persuade our representatives to take up the fight.

In the meantime, let the buyer beware!   28

1997

QUESTIONS FOR DISCUSSION

Content

a. What is Martin's answer to the question she asks to open her essay?
b. What is the process of rendering? Why is it done?
c. According to Martin, why should pet owners be concerned about the ingredients in pet food?
d. Summarize Martin's research. What were her first questions, and how did she go about getting the answers to them? Where did each stage of the research lead her? How long did it take her to find the answers?
e. What obstacles did Martin encounter in her research? Why were they obstacles? How did she deal with them?
f. What questions does Martin still have?
g. What points does Martin make that she supports with statistics or evidence?
h. What points does Martin make that she does *not* support with statistics or evidence?
i. How might a pet food company respond to Martin's claims?

Strategy and Style

j. What images does Martin create to instill in readers a negative image of rendering companies?

k. What is the effect of phrases such as "rendered companion animals" (paragraph 1), "euthanized pets" (paragraph 5), "horror stories" (paragraph 6), and other emotionally laden phrases?

l. What is Martin's tone? How might her background as an animal rights activist influence both her tone and what information she chose to include in the essay?

SUGGESTIONS FOR SHORT WRITING

a. Describe your first, "gut" reactions to this essay. How did it affect you as you read it?

b. Write down the list of ingredients on a can of pet food. Look up ingredients you don't know to find out what they are.

SUGGESTIONS FOR SUSTAINED WRITING

a. Analyze Martin's essay, pointing out the flaws in its argument. For example, where are claims made that are not supported with evidence? Where does she use persuasive techniques unfairly?

b. Using Martin's essay as a starting point and reference, do further research about either the practice of rendering animals or about pet food ingredients. Report on your findings to your classmates.

Why Must a Negro Writer Always Be Political?

Dany Laferrière
Translated by Paul Savoie

Dany Laferrière, born in 1953, once worked as a journalist in Port-au-Prince, Haiti, under the repressive regime of Duvalier. After a close friend was murdered, Laferrière made his way to Montreal, Quebec. His first book, and the one that brought him critical and popular fame, was Comment faire l'amour un negre sans se fatiguer *(How to Make Love to a Negro Without Getting Tired). Other works include the novel* Eroshima *and the essay collection* Cette grenade dans la main du jeune Negre est-elle arme ou un fruit? (Why Must a Black Writer Write about Sex?). *The title of his first and most famous book is particularly relevant to understanding the following essay. His work has been frequently translated from the original French.*

First of all, is it essential for a writer to be identified by colour? I have to deal with 1
this kind of question all the time. In the subway, in a restaurant (the bastard eats!),
during a match at the stadium, in a taxi.

The cab driver presents himself as Nigerian. That's how he begins the con- 2
versation. Of course he hasn't visited his homeland in twenty years. To be more
specific, he's African. He wants to make that perfectly clear. If Africa is now made
up of disparate pieces, it's because of the colonialists. They're the ones who divided
up the land. Needless to say, he's against this division. If he introduces himself as
Nigerian, it's because people are always asking him where he comes from exactly.
At first he held his ground. He explained that Africa was made up of a single people. The expression *Black Africa* was not only redundant, he would insist; it was
politically stupid, a dirty trick, something the Western mind concocted to confuse
Africans. In Africa, colour does not exist. When everyone has the same colour,
colour disappears. Differences cease. And South Africa? He'd rather not discuss
South Africa. This topic makes his blood boil. Each time the subject comes up, he
flies into a white rage (*colère noire*). This play on words makes him chuckle. He
recalls a client who spoke out in favour of apartheid. He turned without warning,
gave the fellow a swift blow in the mouth. The jerk complained, which resulted in
a month's lay-off. But he's glad he did it. The judge told him that, in America, we
live in a democracy. Everyone has a right to his opinion. He told the judge it wasn't
an opinion, the creep's just a bloody racist bastard. He began to scream blue murder.
He was tossed out of court. He got a month off, a severe warning. The next time
he would lose his licence. If he hadn't created such a ruckus, his lawyer told him, he
would have gotten off with a week. He can live with it. He has no regrets. He's got to
be careful, though, not to engage in any sensitive conversations with his clients (I
rather doubt he tries very hard. I don't say a word). However, if some jerk comes
into his cab and makes racist remarks, he can't be expected to keep quiet. He can't
let things like that pass. Anyway, if you lose your job you can always find another
one. But if you lose your dignity, you've lost everything. It's not because you're

443

forced to work like a slave that you become less human. I am a Negro. I'm proud to
be one. He spoke without practically ever turning his head. I'm under the impression
he tells this story all the time. It doesn't matter who his passenger is. He eventually
turns in my direction. He looks me over. He seems surprised when he sees me.

—I read your book.   3

He spoke dryly. Expect the worst when a cab driver turns to you and wants 4
to discuss your book. More than likely, he's read it while at the wheel. If this is the
case, books with short chapters, lots of dialogue, are advisable. The kind of book
I also like to read.

—I'd like to ask you a question.   5

—Go ahead.   6

—Why did you write the book?   7

The question shot out, a projectile dangerously aimed at my forehead. I 8
wasn't expecting it. Normally, when a book's out, it's out. You either like it or you
don't. I remain calm. He pretends to look straight ahead. His ears are outrageously
cocked. He is obviously listening.

—You don't want to answer. I know how you feel.   9

He knows bugger-all! Every single Negro in this bloody town thinks each one 10
of his questions strikes like a bomb and will wreak destruction on all of America.

—I wrote the book I was in the mood to write.   11

His look implies, That was a cute answer; now say what's really on your mind. 12
Instead I ask him a question.

—What's wrong with my book?   13

My question throws him off. I notice a slight quiver in his neck. He turns 14
towards me. The cab nearly climbs onto the sidewalk.

—It's a traitor's book.   15

He rams his palms against the steering wheel. He pumps the accelerator pedal. 16
The panel clock shows 2:49 a.m. He remains silent for a while.

—Sometimes I think I know why you wrote that shit. For the money. It's 17
tough out there. I know. Real tough. You get nothing for free, unless you're willing
to sell your soul. There'll always be a buyer for that.

—In my case, no need for a buyer . . . I did it willingly.   18

—That's it. You've learned the ropes. So no one can tell you what to do.   19

—There's another way of looking at it.   20

He looks at me threateningly. He's not the kind of guy you like to contradict. 21
That's quite clear.

—What do you mean?   22

—All writers are traitors, on some level.   23

—That's bullshit.   24

—I mean it's tough for everybody (I hate to use those words). Competition 25
is fierce. When you can't woo them with your know-how, a good striptease will
sometimes do the trick.

—Does that mean you have to sell your race?   26

—Yes.   27

He eyes me while stepping on the accelerator. He wants to scare me. Where 28 are the cops when you need them?

—I write to gain power. Just like what you're doing right now. You're driving 29 like a madman to scare the shit out of me. It's the same for me. It's a matter of who gets leverage. I'll do anything to gain the advantage.

He's a bit puzzled. I've used his own words against him. He's a violent man. 30 Violence is the only language he understands. He changes his tune a little. I notice something softer in him, almost invisible to the naked eye.

—Why not work in tandem with the reader? 31

—I don't consider the reader a friend. It's all an illusion. The reader would 32 ask for nothing better than to tell his life story. He's got a story to tell, one he'd like to shout from every rooftop. So, if you want to glue him to a seat for hours while you tell your tale, you'd better come up with a good line. Nothing fancy. It doesn't even have to be very good.

—That's where I disagree. 33

—I'm listening. 34

I was in fact listening. 35

—Why not use all that energy for the benefit of your race? 36

—That goes against everything that literature stands for. 37

Talk about hyperbole! 38

—How's that? 39

—You don't write to do someone a favour. You must have something to say, 40 you have to want to say it, you have to find ways to say it. In other words, style.

—You mean you don't feel like defending your people, humiliated for 41 centuries!

—Of course I do. It's obvious. But you have to use the right tool. And it won't 42 be literature. At least it won't be good literature.

—Africa has a rich history. Negro writers have a responsibility. They have 43 to convey this knowledge.

—Exactly. I'm a writer in the present tense. I search for traces of the past in 44 the present. Maybe you're right. There are surely Negroes out there quite suited to the task. Let them talk of the beauty that's part of our race. Not me. I don't have the qualifications. I'm only interested in man's fall, his decrepitude, his frustration, the bitterness that keeps men alive.

—Why don't you just admit you're out to make a buck? 45

—Like everyone else. For me, writing is just something I do to earn a living. 46 Like everyone else. Why aren't engineers, doctors, lawyers ever asked to justify their choice? I'm telling you: I write because I want to make a name for myself, with all the benefits that go along with it. I also write to get laid by luscious young girls. Before, they wouldn't even give me the time of day.

Now he's on the same wavelength. A vein puffs up in his neck. His blood is 47 obviously pumped up.

—But why not meld the two . . . I mean, make money and pay homage—I 48 know you hate this word—to your people.

—These are irreconcilable opposites. Commercial sense versus good intentions.   49

—Some people do it.   50

—You mean Soyinka and his Nobel prize?   51

—Yes.   52

—I don't have his talent. That guy'll wind up in all the school books. I'd rather   53
be read by those who despise me. If you beat a horse, I'm not convinced he'll like
you; but anytime you're within striking distance, he'll be aware of your presence.
Do you know what I mean?

—Yes, but why do you continually fall back on clichés about Negroes?   54

—It's an open mine. Everyone has a right to work the soil.   55

—You exploit . . .   56

—Just like anybody else. Don't you think all writers do the same thing? A   57
writer is usually a cannibal. He eats people up, digests them, spews them out in
words. White, black, yellow or red.

—What a cynical view of things!   58

—Not really. An ordinary view of things.   59

—Does that mean you would have preferred being a white writer?   60

—Not at all, and this has nothing to do with politics. Practically speaking,   61
it's quite interesting being a Negro right now. People are ready to listen to us. It's
a new voice. People have had it up to here with the love triangle (you know: the
husband, the wife, the lover). They're so hungry for new stories, they'll beg for
them. Even the old machine "adultery" needs oiling. Look at the job Spike Lee did
in *Jungle Fever.* The same love triangle, except in different colours. The married
couple is black, the mistress white. Any change is welcome. We beg you: change
something.

—Yeah, but there's a difference. Spike Lee makes films for blacks. You give   62
the impression you're writing for the whites.

—I write for readers rich enough to have the luxury to read. It's easy to forget: 63
reading is a luxury. Three-quarters of humanity has no clue this pastime exists.
When Spike Lee says he's making films for blacks, that's bullshit. How can we
know in advance who will be interested in our books, our films? There's no way of
knowing. It's likely Spike Lee's film touched more whites than blacks.

—Why do you talk about him so much? Jealous?   64

—I envy his success, not his talent.   65

—Why, then?   66

—I've told you. He interests me. His energy. We're different, though; we don't   67
share the same enemy. For him, it's the white race. For me, it's all of America.

—Paranoid?   68

—Not enough.   69

He laughs for the first time. Rich laughter, tight at first, then reaching a   70
strident pitch before following a joyful descent, grave, vibrant. Laughter from the
pit of the stomach.

—It's quite simple. Why should I love you? You don't love me. It's not because   71
you're black that I should love you. You, the blacks, are the first to scream for my hide.

He turns. He has a serious look, as if he's just understood something.   72

—I understand. You're going through a bad patch. You'll see. It'll come back.   73

—What'll come back?   74

—Well . . . (he looks a bit embarrassed) . . . humanist feelings . . . fraternal . . .   75
we blacks don't know how to truly hate. . . . We're deficient in hate chromosomes. . . .

That's the best he can do. The cab stops on the side of the road. I pay, get   76
off. Someone else gets in. The cab jerks forward, speeds away. I watch. The driver
starts up a conversation.

—I'm African. More specifically, I'm from Nigeria. If you want my opinion,   77
all blacks are African, we all come from the first Negro, from the first Negress.
Bullshit.
   78

1992

QUESTIONS FOR DISCUSSION

Content

a. What is Dany Laferrière's attitude towards race in this essay? How do you know?

b. What is the Nigerian cab driver's attitude towards race in this essay?

c. How does Laferrière portray the cab driver?

d. What is Dany Laferrière's point in contrasting the two views?

e. To what position is Laferrière trying to persuade the cab driver (and the reader)?

f. How does Laferrière respond to the charge that he has written "a traitor's book"?
Does his response surprise you?

Strategy and Style

g. Laferrière will frequently contrast what he says (dialogue) with what he is
thinking. Why does he do this? What is the effect on the reader?

h. Find elements of humour in the essay. What is the effect of the humour on the
reader? Whom are we laughing at?

i. What is the point of the discussion about filmmaker Spike Lee?

j. In the second paragraph, Laferrière points out, "Of course he hasn't visited his
homeland in twenty years." Why does he say this? Is this a fair comment?

k. Why does Laferrière *tell* us about this first portion of the conversation when
he later *quotes* the majority of the conversation with the cab driver? In other
words, why does the essay shift from narration to dialogue?

l. Laferrière writes, "He's a violent man. Violence is the only language he understands." Does Laferrière use violent language in order to get the cab driver to
say, "I understand"?

m. What assumption about writers does the cab driver possess? Do you, as a reader,
share some of these assumptions?

n. Sketch out Laferrière's "argument." Is it coherent and logical?

SUGGESTIONS FOR SHORT WRITING

a. If Laferrière were white, how would your response to the essay change?

b. Imagine yourself as the *next* passenger of the cab driver. Write down your reactions and your conversation.

c. Write a response from the perspective of the cab driver.

SUGGESTIONS FOR SUSTAINED WRITING

a. How are writers responsible to the communities about which they write? Does this responsibility change if the community consists of a minority within the society?

b. Should the works of writers who portray certain minority groups negatively or stereotypically (even if they are part of that group) be banned from school and public libraries?

c. How are blacks portrayed on TV? How do they interact with each other? Is there more concern about the relationship between white and black on TV than about black and black or white and white?

Permissions
Acknowledgements

Didion, Joan, "The Metropolitan Cathedral in San Salvador" from *Salvador* by Joan Didion. Copyright © 1983 by Joan Didion. Reprinted by permission of the author.

Dillard, Annie, From *Pilgrim at Tinker Creek* by Annie Dillard. Copyright © 1974 by Annie Dillard. Reprinted by permission of HarperCollins Publishers, Inc.

Dowling, Claudia Glenn, "Fire in the Sky" by Claudia Glenn Dowling *Life* magazine, December 1994. © 1994 Time Inc. Reprinted with permission.

Ehrenreich, Barbara, "A Step Back to The Workhouse?" by Barbara Ehrenreich. Reprinted by permission of the author.

Eiseley, Loren, "The Cosmic Prison" reprinted with the permission of Scribner, a Division of Simon & Schuster from *The Invisible Pyramid* by Loren Eiseley. Copyright © 1970 by Loren Eiseley.

Farb, Peter, and George Armelagos, "The Patterns of Eating" from *Consuming Passions* by Peter Farb and George Armelagos. Copyright © 1980 by The Estate of Peter Farb. Reprinted by permission of Houghton Mifflin Company. All rights reserved.

Fiorito, Joe, "Breakfast in Bed" from *Comfort Me With Apples* by Joe Fiorito. Used by permission, McClelland & Stewart, Ltd. The Canadian Publishers.

Foot, David and Daniel Stoffman, "Boomers and Other Cohorts" from *Boom, Bust and Echo*, copyright © 1998 by David K. Foot and Words on Paper Inc. Reprinted by permission of Stoddart Publishing Co. Limited.

Foster, Cecil, "Black and Blue" from *A Place Called Heaven: The Meaning of Being Black in Canada* by Cecil Foster. Toronto: HarperCollings Publishing, 1996.

Frye, Northrop, "The Double Mirror" from *Myth and Metaphor: Selected Essays 1974–1988* Ed. Robert D. Derham. Charlottesville: University of Virginia Press, 1990. 229–37.

Gibbons, Euell, "How to Cook a Carp" from *Stalking the Wild Asparagus* by Euell Gibbons. Copyright © 1962, used by permission of Alan C. Hood & Company, Inc.

Goodheart, Adam, "How to Paint a Fresco" by Adam Goodheart from *Civilization,* July/August 1995. Copyright © 1995 by Adam Goodheart. Reprinted by permission of the author.

Goodman, Ellen, From "Watching the Grasshopper Get the Goodies" reprinted by permission of Simon & Schuster from *At Large* by Ellen Goodman. Copyright © 1981 by The Washington Post Company.

Gould, Stephen Jay, "Sex, Drugs, Disasters, and the Extinction of Dinosaurs" Copyright © 1984 by Stephen Jay Gould, from *The Flamingo's Smile: Reflections in Natural History* by Stephen Jay Gould. Reprinted by permission of W. W. Norton & Company, Inc.

Greenfield, Meg, "Why Nothing Is 'Wrong' Anymore" by Meg Greenfield from *Newsweek,* July 28, 1986. Copyright © 1986 by Meg Greenfield. All rights reserved. Reprinted by permission of the author.

Gregorian, Vartan, Letter to the Editor by Vartan Gregorian from *The New York Times,* February 21, 1991. Reprinted by permission of the author.

Hall, Donald, "Four Kinds of Reading" by Donald Hall from *To Keep Moving: Essays 1959–1969.* Geneva, NY: Hobart & William Smith Colleges Press, 1980. Reprinted by permission.

Hall, Edward T., "The Anthropology of Manners" by Edward T. Hall, *Scientific American,* April 1955. Reprinted with permission. Copyright © 1955 by Scientific American, Inc. All rights reserved.

Hardin, Garrett, "Lifeboat Ethics: The Case Against Helping the Poor" by Garrett Hardin, *Psychology Today,* September 1974. Reprinted with permission from Psychology Today Magazine, Copyright © 1974 by Sussex Publishers, Inc.

Moir, Rita, "Leave Taking" by Rita Moir. Reprinted by permission of the author.

Ondaatje, Michael, "Tabula Asiae" from *Running in the Family* by Michael Ondaatje. Toronto: McClelland & Stewart, 1993.

Orwell, George, "A Hanging" from *Shooting an Elephant and Other Essays* by George Orwell. Copyright 1950 by Sonia Brownell Orwell and renewed 1978 by Sonia Pitt-Rivers, reprinted by permission of Harcourt Brace & Company. Copyright © George Orwell 1931. Reprinted with the permission of Mark Hamilton as the Literary Executor of the Estate of the Late Sonia Brownell Orwell and Martin Secker & Warburg Ltd.

Parker, Jo Goodwin, "What Is Poverty?" by Jo Goodwin Parker from *America's Other Children: Public Schools Outside Suburbia* edited by George Henderson. © 1971 by the University of Oklahoma Press. Reprinted by permission.

Petrunkevitch, Alexander, "The Spider and the Wasp" by Alexander Petrunkevitch, *Scientific American,* August 1952. Reprinted with permission. Copyright © 1952 by Scientific American, Inc. All rights reserved.

Philip, M. NourbeSe, "The Absence of Writing of How I Almost Became a Spy" by M. NourbeSe Philip. Reprinted by permission of the author.

Seesequasis, Paul, "The Republic of Tricksterism" by Paul Seesequasis. Reprinted by permission of the author.

Sheehy, Gail, "Predictable Crises of Adulthood" from *Passages* by Gail Sheehy. Copyright © 1974, 1976 by Gail Sheehy. Used by permission of Dutton, a division of Penguin Putnam Inc.

Simeti, Mary Taylor, from *On Persephone's Island* by Mary Taylor Simeti. Copyright © 1986 by Mary Taylor Simeti. Reprinted by permission of Alfred A. Knopf, Inc.

Sontag, Susan, "Beauty" by Susan Sontag. Copyright © 1975 by Susan Sontag. Reprinted by permission of Farrar, Straus & Giroux, Inc.

Steele, Shelby, "White Guilt," by Shelby Steele, first published in *The American Scholar,* Autumn 1990. Copyright © 1990 by Shelby Steele. Reprinted by permission of Carol Mann Agency.

Steinem, Gloria, "Erotica and Pornography" by Gloria Steinem, *Ms.* magazine, November 1978. © 1978 by Gloria Steinem. Reprinted by permission of the author.

Suzuki, David, "Repeating History at Our Peril" from "Science Matters" 06/15/01 by David Suzuki. Reprinted by permission of the author and the David Suzuki Foundation.

Taylor, Charles, "The Sources of Authenticity". Excerpt from *Malaise of Modernity* copyright © 1991 by Charles Taylor and the Canadian Broadcasting Corporation. Reproduced by permission of House of Anansi Press, Toronto.

Toth, Susan Allen, "Cinematypes" by Susan Allen Toth. Reprinted by permission of the author.

Urquhart, Jane, "Returning to the Village" by Jane Urquhart. Reprinted by permission of the author.

Viorst, Judith, "The Truth About Lying" by Judith Viorst originally appeared in *Redbook.* Copyright © 1981 by Judith Viorst. Reprinted by permission of Lescher & Lescher, Ltd.

Walker, Alice, "Am I Blue?" from *Living by the Word: Selected Writings 1973–1987,* copyright © 1986 by Alice Walker, reprinted by permission of Harcourt Brace & Company.

Whitehead, Barbara Defoe, "Where Have All the Parents Gone" by Barbara Defoe Whitehead from *New Perspectives Quarterly,* Vol. 7, Winter 1990. © by The Center for the Study of Democratic Institutions. Reprinted by permission of The Center and Blackwell Publishers, Inc.

Wolfe, Alexander, "The Last Grass Dance" by Alexander Wolfe. Reprinted with permission from *Earth Elder Stories* (Fifth House Publishers, 1988).

Woodcock, George, "The Tyranny of the Clock" from *The Rejection of Politics and other essays on Canada, Canadians, anarchism and the world.* Toronto: New Press, 1972.

Woolf, Virginia, "The Death of the Moth" from *The Death of the Moth and Other Essays* by Virginia Woolf. Copyright 1942 by Harcourt Brace & Company and renewed 1970 by Marjorie T. Parsons, Executrix, reprinted by permission of the publisher.

Index of Authors and Titles